D1001341

Towards a Transcultural Future

Literature and Society
in a 'Post'-Colonial World

C | r o s s
u l t u r e s

Readings in the Post / Colonial
Literatures in English

79

ASNEL Papers 9.2

Series Editors

| Gordon Collier | Hena Maes–Jelinek | Geoffrey Davis |
| (Giessen) | (Liège) | (Aachen) |

ASNEL Papers appear under the auspices of the

Gesellschaft für die Neuen Englischsprachigen Literaturen e.V. (GNEL)
Association for the Study of the New Literatures in English (ASNEL)

Heinz Antor, President
(English Seminar, University of Cologne,
Albertus-Magnus-Platz, D-50923 Cologne)

Formatting and layout: Gordon Collier

FRONT COVER IMAGE: *Spiritual Song* by Matseluca (1989; acrylic on paper)
BACK COVER IMAGE: *African Alps* by Matseluca (1989; acrylic on canvas)

Towards a Transcultural Future

Literature and Society
in a 'Post'-Colonial World

ASNEL Papers 9.2

Edited by

Geoffrey V. Davis, Peter H. Marsden,
Bénédicte Ledent and Marc Delrez

Amsterdam - New York, NY 2005

The paper on which this book is printed meets the requirements of
"ISO 9706:1994, Information and documentation - Paper for documents -
Requirements for permanence".

ISBN: 90-420-1736-8 (Bound)
©Editions Rodopi B.V., Amsterdam - New York, NY 2005
Printed in The Netherlands

FLORIDA GULF COAST
UNIVERSITY LIBRARY

IN MEMORIAM
Edward W. Said
* Jerusalem (British Mandate of Palestine), 1 November 1935
† New York, NY, 25 September 2003

Table of Contents

ABORIGINAL LITERATURE

MULTICULTURALISM AND ETHNICITY

THE BLACK EXPERIENCE IN BRITAIN

Acknowledgements

In our dual role as organizers of the XXIII Annual Conference of the Association for the Study of the New Literatures in English (ASNEL) for the year 2000 and editors of the present proceedings we should like to express our thanks to all those who contributed to making both projects possible through their academic input and/or their financial support. Without their active cooperation these complex cross-border undertakings would never have come to fruition.

The list is long and comprehensive – we hope we have not overlooked anyone. For all the massive collective effort, however, there are two individuals who we do feel deserve to be singled out for special mention, namely Professor Hena Maes–Jelinek and Professor Peter Wenzel, both of whom, representing with appropriate symbolism English Studies at Liège and Aachen respectively, enthusiastically identified with the enterprise from the start and gave us much valuable and invaluable solidarity, sympathy and support before, during and after its implementation.

We are indebted to the following:

The Vice-Chancellor of Aachen University, Professor Burkhard Rauhut (Rektor der RWTH Aachen)

The Vice-Chancellor of the University of Liège, Professor Willy Legros (Recteur de l'Université de Liège)

The Dean of the Philosophical Faculty of Aachen University, Professor Christian Stetter (Dekan der Philosophischen Fakultät der RWTH Aachen)

Professor Peter Wenzel, Department of English, Aachen University

Professor Lilo Moessner, Department of English, Aachen University

Professor Wolfgang Butzkamm, Department of English, Aachen University

Professor Paul Georg Meyer, Department of English, Aachen University

Professor Rudolf Beier, Department of German, Aachen University

The English Department of the University of Liège

Professor Hena Maes–Jelinek, Liège

The Lord Mayor of the City of Aachen (Oberbürgermeister der Stadt Aachen), Dr Jürgen Linden

Mayor of the City of Aachen (Bürgermeisterin der Stadt Aachen), Sabine Verheyen

Mayor of the City of Aachen (Bürgermeisterin der Stadt Aachen), Meike Thüllen

FNRS, Belgium

CECODEL, Belgium

La Fondation universitaire, Belgium

The Minister of Culture of the Flemish Community in Belgium (Minister van Cultuur, Ministerie v/o Vlaamse Gemeenschap), de Heer Bert Anciaux
The Nieuwe Realisaties Theatre Group of Antwerp, Belgium and its director, Ivan Pecnik
Rick Takvorian of the International Ludwig Forum, Aachen
The Cultural Office of the City of Aachen (Ms Silvi Tyla)
L'Institut Culturel Franco-Allemand d'Aix-la-Chapelle and its director, Dr Michael Jansen
The Windmüller–Zeiss Party Service, Aachen
Indien-Restaurant Ganges, Aachen (Rohit Nayar)
Dr Thomas Brückner, Leipzig
Dr James Gibbs, University of the West of England, Bristol
Reiner A. Müller, Leichlingen
The British Council (Brussels)
The British Council (Cologne)
The Commonwealth Foundation, London
The Board for Development-Related Education and Media of the Protestant Church in Germany (der Ausschuß für Entwicklungsbezogene Bildung und Publizistik, ABP) Stuttgart
The Society for the Promotion of African, Asian and Latin American Literature (Die Gesellschaft zur Förderung der Literatur aus Afrika, Asien und Lateinamerika e.V.), its director Peter Ripken, and his colleague Cory van Mayenburg
Tina Jerman, Exile-Kulturkoordination, Essen
Kultursekretariat Nordrhein–Westfalen and its director, Dr Dietmar N. Schmidt
The Association for the Study of the New Literatures in English (ASNEL)
The Gesellschaft für Kanada-Studien
The New Zealand Embassy, Berlin
The Canadian Embassy, Berlin
Walter Larink, Canadian Embassy, Berlin
Carfax Publishers, UK
Continuum International (Cassell)
Heinemann Publishers, Oxford
Taylor & Francis Publishers, UK
MISEREOR Medien
– and, last but not least –
Editions Rodopi B.V, Amsterdam and its director, Fred van der Zee.

Through the joint generosity and support of the above we were able to invite the following writers to the conference:

Erna Brodber (Jamaica)
Tone Brulin (Antwerp)
Bernard Cohen (Australia)
Lindsey Collen (Mauritius)

Robert Fraser (GB)
Katherine Gallagher (Australia)
Peter Goldsworthy (Australia)
Geoff Goodfellow (Australia)
Wilson Harris (Guyana/GB)
Aritha van Herk (Canada)
†Amryl Johnson (Trinidad/GB)
Jan Kemp (Aotearoa–New Zealand)
Karen King-Aribisala (Nigeria)
Sindiwe Magona (South Africa)
Jack Mapanje (Malawi/GB)
Lee Maracle (Canada)
Don Mattera (South Africa)
Babila Mutia (Cameroon)
Mike Nicol (South Africa)
Lewis Nkosi (South Africa)
Vincent O'Sullivan (Aotearoa–New Zealand)
Malcolm Purkey (South Africa)
Mike Philips (Trinidad)
Caryl Phillips (St. Kitts/GB)
Lesego Rampolokeng (South Africa)
Andrew Sant (Australia)
Laurence Scott (Trinidad/GB)
Sujay Sood (India/USA)
Robert Sullivan (Aotearoa–New Zealand)
Patrick Womba (Martinique).

And keeping the whole infrastructure going were our tireless and dedicated staff at the two universities:

Ingrid Schiro [Davis]
Annette Welker
Ben Basell (also University of Western Australia)
Thorsten de Jong
Nicole Deller
Eva Dikow
Elvira Djurič
Sabine Düllmann
Elena Gross
Birgit Haupt
Gesine Herhaus
Börje Hörn
Gavin Hopps
Susanne Jünger
Melanie Kaltwasser

Miriam Kirk
Sonja Kremer
Jean–Michel Lejeune
Monique Lemoine
Timo Lothmann
Silke Mills
Andrew Norris
Arno Özgen
Beate Premper
Silvia Pschierer
Ute Quinkertz
Laura Reece (also University of Western Australia)
Nina Stücke
Bettina Tiburzy
Lorraine Turner
Annette Welker

⟨⟨•⟩⟩

Permissions

The Ibis Tapestry first published by Alfred A. Knopf, 1998; by permission of the author.

"Jet Lag," first published in *Poetry Review* (1999); "My Mother's Garden," first published in *Stand* (1999); "Reckoning," first published in *Tigers on the Silk Road* (Arc Publications, 2000); by permission of the author.

"Evil Eye" and "Bed"; by permission of the author.

"What do you see when you watch that hillside above the lake?"; "A Lover's Anguish in King William St."; "No Title"; and "Aroma Therapy"; by permission of the author.

"A Change in the Weather," first printed in *The New Zealand Author*, No. 213 (February–March issue, 2000); by permission of the author.

Permission to quote from the following works of Lauris Edmond kindly given by Frances Edmond and Ms Bridget Williams, Literary Executors for the Estate of Lauris Edmond:

"In the Chemin Fleuri," "Directions," "The Written Word," "Sober Truth," "Before a Funeral," "Road Works," "The Outside Room" appear in *Selected Poems 1975–2000*, edited by Ken Arvidson and published by Bridget Williams Books in 2001.

"Pancakes for Breakfast" and "Rhineland" appear in *Selected Poems 1975–1994*, edited by Anne French and published by Bridget Williams Books in 1994.

"I name this place" appears in *Scenes from a Small City*, published by Daphne Brasell Associates Press in 1994.

《●》

In Memoriam
Lauris Edmond
(1924–2000)
A Tribute

KEN ARVIDSON, GORDON COLLIER, CLAUDIA DUPPÉ,
KONRAD GROSS, VINCENT O'SULLIVAN, JUDITH
DELL PANNY, NORBERT PLATZ (Chair), JOSEPH
SWANN, JANET WILSON

[GNEL/ASNEL Conference
Aachen/Liège, 3 June 2000]

NORBERT PLATZ: The idea of having this memorial meeting was born immediately after Joe Swann had rung me to tell me that Lauris Edmond had died. This was a couple of months ago. Following this phone call, I was trying to get in contact with Pete and Geoff asking them whether we could have a brief memorial in Aachen because Lauris Edmond did have so many German friends, some of whom would be attending the ASNEL conference. But it was an essential part of the original plan that we should open this memorial session to Lauris's both European and New Zealand friends as well, so that we could all share our recollection of this outstanding poet across physical and cultural distances. I am very pleased that so many people have followed Joe Swann's and my own invitation – both as contributors and as listeners. There is no agenda for this meeting. But we have agreed to commemorate Lauris Edmond by telling personal memories. Also, we are going to read a poem or two that may have gained a special meaning for each of us.

The first of Lauris's friends whom I am inviting to speak to us now is Joe Swann.

JOSEPH SWANN: Lauris's first visit to Germany was in 1986 for the Salzburg Conference held in Laufen and that's where we first met her, that's where we first met you as well, Janet, and Syd Harrex and one or two other friends from "Down Under." After the Laufen Conference I started reading Lauris's poetry a bit, got into it a bit, I was very much taken by its direct personal tone, by the ordinary speech that she used and by its concentration on a world that we have in common.

What Lauris, I think – I *think*, anyway – did supremely well was to put the unique quality of each moment into language. Listen to this, for example, written while she was on the Katherine Mansfield Fellowship at Menton in 1981:

In the Chemin Fleuri

I will remember today
I know it by its tingling –
the print on the skin of my back
of the iron fleur-de-lis of the fence,
the touch of the crabbed loquat branch
with its marbles of fruit,
against the white wall
the date palm's green tongues
whispering as usual and the grey dove
that comes every day strutting over the stones . . .

The very breath of the moment is flickering
here where I lean on the warm whorls
noting the first passionfruit flower
on the vine –
while all the time hearing
far off
the howl of the wind in the mountains
ice-black behind, if I look . . .

knowing that nothing is mine.

It's a spring morning,
it's a life, it's a shred I draw into the light
from that dark space where
nothing and no one belongs.
this is a day I'll remember.

Everything is movement, everything is movement over darkness. Lauris became a close personal friend, a friend who came several times to Wuppertal. She always enjoyed Germany. She was very generous; she gave herself to this country as well. My acquaintance with her developed into one of the major friendships of my life. Also, I think, for my young daughter. Lauris talked to her, read her poem hanging up there on the fridge and took her very seriously. It was the only poem Jane, as far as I know, has ever written.

Lauris was a very strong person, I felt, to meet. She was a very wise person, she was a person who was willing to get involved in the darkness of individual lives – and I think a lot of you know very much more than I do quite how much darkness that was; but it was there in my life, too. She saw personal lives, she saw people she knew, people she loved, she saw this as the vibrancy of being. Listen again to this:

Pancakes for Breakfast

It is simply the mist
standing light and quiet
on the morning water

and I, too, am suddenly clear
having for weeks been embedded
in days as though
they had all set hard and I stuck
like an old turd in the clay path
where the children trample

but the mist is perfect
it has the shape and sheen of the harbour
in the sunlight
yet rests unafraid beside
the bright colonising sea

and I see how each thing
gathers into its separate self
– the thin grass tufted on bog-coloured clay
a raw egg someone has dropped
rolling its small yellow wave
(absorbed as the hen herself, squatting)

yes, the egg is complete
– whether broken or whole –
as I am
walking with a slow jog over the hill
to be whipped in the kitchen
and eaten with Barry's pancakes.

I'm not going to say anything about Lauris's late poems. These were the poems written at a time when her life and her poetry seemed to become one – a single continuum – and, indeed, her death as well. Her voice for me is still, I think, one of the most intimately real. We rejoice that she has lived and that we have known her.

NORBERT PLATZ: Yes, "we rejoice that she has lived and that we have known her". Thank you, Joe, for this comforting statement. Claudia Duppé is our next speaker. Claudia was the person who saw Lauris two days before she died. Let's listen to what she remembers, and to which of Lauris's poems she is lending her voice.

CLAUDIA DUPPÉ: I wrote my MA thesis on Lauris's analysing her conception of home. 'Home' is a concept Lauris struggled with a great deal. It encompasses not only her own story, but also that of her place, her people, and her culture. Reading Lauris's poems we often saw ourselves, our hopes, our fears. So, far from being ordinary or "domestic," as some critics depicted her work, her poems reveal a unique sense of wisdom and knowledge about the everyday 'art of living'. I believe that Lauris touches the heart of things in her poetry. Having stressed this, I would like to quote her own words. In an interview, Lauris said: "It is never a poem we want, never this plausible mask of smoke; it is the burning substance."

I became friends with Lauris through her poetry long before I met her in person. Her poetry was the initial connection, and it started a relationship that turned into friendship. Through her poetry, I feel I have entered her world, a feeling Lauris once again confirms in one of the numerous interviews. She said:

> My work is coming quite particularly out of a sense of close relationship with my world –
> the physical world. I don't just mean the conventional kind of relationship, I mean a strong
> sense of belonging, of being close to the heart of what's happening.

That is why I believe that phrases like "I felt at home" do not refer to a house, but to her relationships with people – her family and friends.

I first met Lauris in '98 at her house in 22 Grass Street, a place which Lauris had an almost symbiotic relationship with. Initially, I was so nervous about meeting her that I kept staring at her letter-box. Well, I think this letter-box would encourage anyone to go in and knock at her door and have a chat with her.

Lauris relished one-on-one conversations, conversations that where triggered by two words. She kept saying "Tell me!" I think a lot of people remember such 'Lauris conversations'. She made you talk about yourself, but you felt slightly embarrassed leaving her and yet happy at heart. When I went back to New Zealand at the beginning of this year, meeting Lauris for lunch was similar and yet very strange. We had a conversation so rich and lively and Lauris was so full of plans that the news of her death three days later just didn't want to sink in.

The grief during the days before and after her funeral was paramount and yet, as always with Lauris, there was this constant sense of celebration. She wanted to celebrate and she helped us do it. It was Bob Marley's song played at her reception, for instance, or the champagne at her place that made me smile despite my sadness. Of course this was Lauris! Only she could have celebrated life in between the lines of grief and death.

I want to read you the poem "I name this place," because to me it encapsulates the home in Lauris's writing. The place she seeks in the poem is home, a home she could never sufficiently define and yet she always knew it was there. It precedes her autobiography:

> I name this place
> to find it.
>
> by looking truly
> I can hear and speak my dream
>
> this is where I stand,
> also my journey
> for nothing rests
> except within its timeless motion.

the names of things are sleeping
in the way they've come

this is my waking up, my camp,
my resting place along the never-ending

lines that cross the world. My song
waits here – I sing it.

In these few lines, Lauris manages to establish a consonance between the song of life
and the song of the poet. I believe that this is her place, or – to put it in other words –
this is her songline. I'm very sad to say it is now up to others to continue singing it.

NORBERT PLATZ: Yes, thank you very much, Claudia. Moving words, and so, then
others are called upon to sing Lauris's words. Now, Konnie, would you like to be next?"

KONRAD GROSS: I wouldn't mind, not at all. I think I met Lauris twice or three
times, for the first time in 1986 when she came to Kiel and gave a wonderful reading.
Fortunately no one has picked the poem that I'm going to read. I want to read it because
it has to do with Germany and with Europe. She came back to Kiel in 1997. I remember
that reading very well and what I remember is something that you have just mentioned.
She was not interested in talking about herself, she would glean information from
people she was conversing with. I hope the only thing that I can do is to read out the
poem that I think is perhaps suitable for this situation. It's called "Directions" and it's
taken from her second book of poems entitled *The Pear Tree and Other Poems*:

Directions

Strange, that there should be so much tumult
at your going – you who so gently
moved among us, the cool wind
that cleared our confusion; whose standing
still could steady us.

But for you perhaps it was something else
– an uncertainty so vast you had
no choice but standing still, seeing
no way home – did you not know
the quiet place was always there
with you, *was* you, and only you
could ever find it?

We came often to its cool shadow,
a green dark that held us after the long
climb, the struggle with hard clay, roots
and rocks – ah I am broken now
by more than weariness; I look
back and I am there resting
not noticing until too late
that you had gone to search the tangle

of tracks, and again could find
no way to go.

'There is no home for me on earth'.
In the quick walk you suddenly took
into the silence did you not pause at all,
even for a moment wish to stay?
Free at last of our confusing claims
did your feet hurry and a strong wind
lift you into the no-place
beyond hills and skies where there are
no roads to take, no difficult
directions?

I lean on the old earth-smelling tree
breathe the same air, see
in the leafed light your hand still
pointing through the shadows; the difference
is that now I also cannot
recognise the way to go.

I only know that this – no more
than this – in time and out of it
unites us now.

NORBERT PLATZ: May I ask you now to listen to a New Zealand friend who would like to honour Lauris Edmond. Janet, would you mind addressing us, offering us some New Zealand reactions to Lauris's death, reactions of which we haven't been aware in this part of the world?

JANET WILSON: Well, this is a poignant time for me, because as Joe Swann pointed out, this recalls the conference in Laufen in 1986. The first time that Lauris herself came to a conference in Germany was in fact the first time that I too came to a conference in Germany. In fact, I came to Laufen to give a paper on her work, and it was my very first foray into the world of New Zealand literature, in a formal sense. Lauris had the year before in London won the inaugural British Airways Commonwealth Poetry Prize for her *Selected Poems* (1984). That was in 1985 and I was there on that night, as it happened, when the announcement as made. She won against quite stiff competition. We were absolutely jubilant and it was a wonderful evening. This was also the first time I met Lauris properly. I'd spent a long time trying to understand her poetry before writing about it and had great difficulty grappling with some of the poems in *Wellington Letter* about the death of her daughter. I think that such themes that she engaged with in her poetry are very difficult to do justice to in any kind of critical discourse as they are so emotional, so from the heart.

I returned to New Zealand a few years later and we had the opportunity to develop a closer friendship. For the next ten years our lives criss-crossed. We met when she came to Dunedin or I went to Wellington. We came together on all kinds of issues in many different ways. We talked about our lives, of course, and celebrated the good bits when

we were together. We met each other's friends. And when I visited I was always heart-
ened to see the colourful letter-box because Lauris lived on a perilously high hill and I
used to stagger up with my bags and greet the letter-box with a sigh of relief, but also
with a feeling of uplift that I had finally made it to this hilltop area where she lived; it
was rather like entering a different world, where she held her own court, as it were, of
friends, with all sorts of literary activities, a whole circle that was quite unique to her.

So how did we connect with each other? It happened on a public as well as a personal
level. She wrote her autobiography in three volumes just after I returned to New Zealand in 1988 – the first one, called *Hot October*, was published by Bridget Williams in
1989 and I gave a little talk at her and Bridget's invitation when it was launched in
Dunedin. I'd never done anything like that in public before. Another point of overlap
was when *New Zealand Books* was founded in 1991: Lauris was a co-founder with John
Thomson. And again because I was living in Dunedin and Lauris could not be there, I
made a speech at the launch at the New Zealand Writers' Week held in Dunedin.

And so this continued even after I returned to the UK to live in 1998. This year, at the
beginning of the year, I went back to New Zealand – I've been back and forth between
New Zealand and England in the last few years –, and she understood, more clearly than
I did, I think, a different side of my life which belonged to another part of the world.

I rang her, of course, having no idea until the next day that this was, in fact, the last
conversation she had with anyone. She said, among other things, how pleased she was
that I was now living in Oxford and I was startled at this, that she thought it was the
right place for me, but, perhaps that's right – I didn't think I ever would end up living in
Oxford, but I do now – and I said to her: "I'm always glad to know that you are here in
Wellington, that it has always seemed the right place for you." She said: "Yes, it
absolutely does, I couldn't think of ever leaving." She said: "The years we moved
around the country because Trevor (her ex-husband) had jobs in little country schools, it
seemed as if I would never get there and I always wanted to. It was something I strived
for." And that was the end of the conversation, possibly the last words she ever said, I
don't know for sure, but she ended on an emphatic note, that this was absolutely the
right place for her, and that she never really could think of living anywhere else or even
of leaving.

The tributes to Lauris were very full and I thought that I would read some of them to
you. What I've chosen are some poems that were inspired by Lauris's life and death.
One of these, published in *The Listener*, was written by a student of ours at Otago University who I visited once with Lauris; it made me aware of how much she inspired
younger women, how much she was a role model for them, because of the ways in
which she'd broken out of the mould that was expected for women of her own generation. Sandra Smith has not only been a student, as I said; she has raised children of her
own. She wrote:

Dear Lauris, it was you who taught us more
about afterlives before the afterlife
and I was to see all that we could be
and shall in deed and in word
that there's no wall which has no door
and no door that has no key.

And another poem, by Riemke Ensing, the Dutch poet – well, she lives in New Zealand but she's from the Netherlands – which she sent to me saying "Please publish this or read it, I would be very happy." It's called

A Change in the Weather
For Lauris Edmond

Last night the sky turned red. It seemed
to bleed. The wind got up and the storm blew
itself through the surf, breaking on the beach.
Trees keened and clamoured in angst.
I thought of earthquakes, some terrible destruction,
a national calamity, and turned on the teletext.
It read you'd died just then. For a moment
everything seemed very still
then tempest raged again.
All night I worried on mortality, but drifted
off to wake to rain and clouds in mourning.
Further south, floods are closing roads.
A deepening depression is expected
across the country.[1]

And one final piece, by Fiona Kidman, who was a very close friend of Lauris's:

Lauris, dear friend, in these last days we have gathered around you at Grass Street, greeted one another, wept, shared memories, laughed, talked on the phone – of course – fazed by your unfamiliarly silent presence, now when it comes to the final day and the parting as we lay your body in the earth may your spirits soar in this beautiful peaceful place. Your great understanding in matters small and large, your exquisite sense of the world around you, nourished and enriched us and that is your legacy. Know that we will hold in our hearts your wisdom, your humanity, your laughter and your love always. Dearest friend. Farewell.

So, the influence of Lauris, already strong in life, has grown deeper in memory as these responses suggest. For me, the friendship with her coincided with a shift in my own

---

[1] Riemke Ensing's poem was first printed in *The New Zealand Author* 213 (February–March issue): 5 and again in *KITE* 18 (May 2000): 1; it also appears in her *Selected Poems: Talking Pictures* (Wellington: Headworx, 2000): 138.

career towards New Zealand writing as the subject for research; becoming involved in her public life made this seem more credible. Riemke's poem describes a real shock at her death and a sense of bereavement which reverberates throughout the natural world while Fiona brings home the fact that the shared appreciation of Lauris was the response of a community and, in being so, became more than the sum of its individual parts.[2]

Finally, Syd Harrex, who is not here, asked me to mention that he will be reading a poem that he wrote for Lauris at the reading at 6 o'clock tomorrow.

NORBERT PLATZ: Thank you very much, Janet, for sharing your personal memories and some of the poetic obituaries with us. Now I would like to ask Ken Arvidson to speak to us. Ken must have known Lauris much longer than any of us. In the *Listener* he once praised her poetry by stating that it "abounds in wonder, awe, delight, transience, tranquillity, mystery ...."

KEN ARVIDSON: Thanks. Just a few words. I had the good fortune to know Lauris for twenty-two years. I first met her in 1978, when I had reviewed her second volume of poetry and she came to see me at the University of Waikato, where I work. That was the university where ten years before she had graduated, taken her first degree, her BA, and so a nice place to meet her in. And I always remember the very strong impression that her personality made on me then and on everyone, I think, that she met. The personality which was partly formed by her appearance and her voice, which has been remarked on, and a particular quality of vivaciousness and a wide-ranging interest in everything that was going on. That kind of impression endured over the remaining twenty-two years of her life, I became friendly with her as people do, with frequent meetings over a rela- tively long period. It was certainly a great pleasure in my own life. Claudia Duppé has already commented on the gift that Lauris possessed to make you the centre of her inter- est whenever you were with her. It was a very remarkable gift, I think, the kind of genius she had for friendship; it was quite apart from her genius for poetry, but it did manifest itself in her poetry too, because human relationships are the chief material of her poetry. She was a really remarkable personality; so after an hour or two in her com- pany you would come away feeling yourself very much raised two or three notches in your own estimation. It was always great to talk with her. That's probably the most important thing that I want to say about her, I think, her enduring presence. That's hardly as much as could be said, of course, for anyone so vivacious as she was so interested in life and all the rest. But it's worth emphasizing that aspect of her, because it's quite striking that so many of her poems are actually concerned with death, and the nature of death and its implications and so on. – An enormous number, I'll just read one of them, from *Summer Near the Arctic Circle*, the little poem called "The Written Word." She imagines leaving her house to somebody else for a while, a typically auto- biographical sort of scene, as in so much of her poetry. The scene quickly becomes a metaphor for death, and the potentially meaningful vestiges of her life that are left

---

[2] Tributes to Lauris, including these poems and an interview with Fleur Adcock about their friendship, will be printed in the next issue of *KITE*, a newsletter that goes out from Otago Uni- versity and in the next issue of *CRNLE*, the journal of the Centre for Research into the New Literatures in English published from Flinders University.

behind are all verbal, in the image of the cards that are left lying around. But the messages on the cards are personal and private, and of no interest to the newcomer. The poet's life is language, a "violent 'I'," which in death dissolves in "a froth of words". The loss of life, the loss of personality, is total, leaving behind only "the litter of our correspondences," to be cleared away. The poem gives a good sense of the strange darkness that underlay Lauris's bright personality:

The Written Word

Leaving's a little death. Packing,
I see already its wake of signs
and messages, to be witnessed
by another woman who will draw
my long red curtains, take books from
my shelves, sleep in my bed.

Cards left on the window sill
are leaning, a bit drunk, very knowing,
ripe with love and friendship's
intimate knowledge of me
which they won't bother to conceal
or care if they distort, for her.

So it must surely be
with a whole existence's accumulations;
the pronoun that begins our breath,
the violent 'I', becomes at last
a dissolving froth of words
that follows us away.

and others will of right come in
and occupy our days and nights
and breathe our air and walk about
the great rooms of the world
when they have cleared away
the litter of our correspondences.

NORBERT PLATZ: Thank you, Ken. Now, the next speaker is Dell Panny.

DELL PANNY: Lauris has been a wonderful friend, to many people, she always found time, and you knew that you could phone her without interrupting, because the answerphone would be on and very shortly she'd phone you back. She was always willing to support friends, and writers and those who were attempting to write. Often involved in writers' *hui* (gatherings or meetings), or in running poetry workshops and creative writing courses, she shared her experience and expertise as a writer with others. This was an inspiration to young people, and to older people, like myself, I felt that women in their fifties, their sixties, their seventies could do anything that they set out to do, given a degree of confidence and belief in themselves. Somehow, Lauris inspired that confidence.

Lauris possessed the special capacity to value her friends and to understand them in a profound way. I would like to read "Sober Truth," a poem written for Hone Tuwhare. It shows a wonderfully warm appreciation for Hone's individuality:

Sober Truth

It's a sharp morning, sea and city
tipped to acutest angles; bare roots of the ngaio
tie the clay bank in knots,
the stark edge of building cranes
slices the distance – nothing gives,
except perhaps in my head where last night's
celebration slides like a heavy sack
over the floor when I bend.

I'll sit here
on the cracked asphalt margin of the bush path,
feet in the crumbly dirt, wind and shadow
setting quietly down beside me
to write you a letter
settling quietly down beside me
to write you a letter, old mate, rascally charmer,
your bumble-bee voice still brushing my ear
with the whirring
of incorrigible whisperings.

Each of us lives in the body differently.
Yours is a total occupation, Full House
to the last crease and capillary, the quick
of the smallest toe-nail, each follicle and fibre,
to the fingers that tingle with mischief
and magic as they move the pen
over your own page, your poems.

You're yourself all the way through,
the breathing radiator I've often stood near
in a spell of hard weather of the heart,
warmed by some great buzz
of laughter and love at the centre.
This, old friend, is to tell you
I got safely home last night
after the party.

NORBERT PLATZ: Thank you very much, Dell, for reminding us of this accomplished piece of "Sober Truth." You have also given us, to quote your own words, "a wonderfully warm appreciation" for Lauris Edmond's individuality. This has put us in a pensive mood.

I would now like to call on Vincent O'Sullivan for his tribute.

VINCENT O'SULLIVAN: In one of Alexander Pope's letters he says something that rather surprises one for such a cool man. He says that when we lose a dear friend, we lose the best part of ourselves. I was very aware of that a week ago last Monday, when Lauris's family carried out a request of hers that her close friends be invited to take a book from her library as a memento, and that the choice be accompanied with champagne. A grief party, you might say, and typical of Lauris's wry irony. As I came down the long path from her home in Grass Street, it was as though her absence was now sealed, and Pope's words rang true. I was thinking too of an early poem of hers which it seems appropriate to read now, called "Before a Funeral," etc. It seems to equate very much with this occasion *after* the funeral:

Before a Funeral

The great bright leaves have fallen
outside your window
they lie about
torn by the season from
the beggared cherry trees.
In your room, alone,
I fold and hide away
absurd, unnecessary things –
your books, still ready and alert,
it seems, for understanding,
clothes, dry and cold,
surprised in holding still
to hairs upon the collars,
handkerchiefs in pockets,
socks, awry, not ready for
the queer neglect of death.

Mechanically useful, I make
preparations for some possible
impossible journey no one
will ever take; work will help
they tell me, and indeed
your room is now nothing
but things, and tidy.
I have put away your life.

Out in the autumn garden
a sharp rapacious wind
snatches the brilliant booty
of the leaves. The blackened branches
Groan. They knot, and hold.
And yet the cold will come.

NORBERT PLATZ: Thank you, Vincent. We very much appreciate your very personal reminiscences. Another friend's voice deserves to be listened to: Gordon Collier, a New Zealander who met Lauris in Germany.

GORDON COLLIER: Joe talked about Lauris's coming to Germany. We all had our own university obligations, our own university contacts and our own interest in literature and living authors, and that always starts a kind of ball rolling. Consequently, Lauris was part of the daisy chain of writers who came to our universities. It wasn't really so much a case of me welcoming her but, right away, the peculiar feeling that Lauris was making me feel at home.

One of the things that have been mentioned or intimated was that Lauris was coming as a 'mature' writer, and this impressed me as well – the kind of quiet maturity that she would bring with her was something new in the classroom. For my students, grappling with her poems, this was something that came out of the experience that the poem is always a whole thing; they never seemed to have to ask what it was about when Lauris read something. It was always a total experience, and then there was always the segue over to Lauris's enfolding the class and maybe getting them to extend themselves. The boundary between art and life kept getting dissolved.

Most of you have had a long-lasting personal contact with Lauris, whereas I have been sitting in this place, not marooned and not exiled, but somehow removed. And being 'removed' can create a kind of absence inside, also, one of the things I brought with me from New Zealand was a disease called a desire for High Modernist Complexity, and something more personal – a tendency, which has not gone away, to self-protective irony. Lauris was a hell of a challenge on both these scores, because she *can* be ironical, but you would have to find another word for that quality of accepting wryness that gets through now and again. Her poems were always a delight; they would warm the cockles of my heart, but they were something I could just accept; they usually didn't worry me. They were for me a kind of self-evident thing; nothing, or almost nothing, she wrote would nourish my cynicism or my sense of scepticism, because her world was so whole, so complete. She had for me a high blue clarity. But I'm going to read a poem which still contains a mystery for me, where she is expecting a different kind of generosity in life. It is called "Road Works," from *Summer Near the Arctic Circle*:

> Road Works
>
> In this street that has ignored so many
> poignant or desperate encounters
> I may meet my angry daughter. Will she smile,
> Speak? Would she brush past?
>
> I blush at my imagined confusion; I who
> am too old to be awkward, too long tried
> to be shy, become clumsy before
> the urgent legitimate rage of the young.
>
> Today the whole world has not allowable space
> For us both. I loiter, hesitate, one of those

seen peering through street barricades
trying to make out the movements

of workers inside. Does she lean, press,
straighten and bend as, back turned, fired
by a furious assurance, she piles up
the fragile sandbags of the future?

Nobert Platz: Thank you so much, Gordon.
"Death is the signal, the summoning – all those / scattered ones now to come back to
the house," Lauris Edmond wrote in her poem "The Task." So her death has sum-
moned us too, in remembrance of her, to this unsophisticated lecture hall at the
University of Aachen. But all of us who have assembled here have generously provided plenty of "allowable [imaginative] space" for remembering and honouring a
superb poet, and a human being with whom we were privileged to have happy encounters when she was still alive.

As far as I personally am concerned, I met Lauris about three or four times. On one
occasion, she was a guest in my home in Trier. It so happened that Dell Panny and
Rolf, her husband, were my guests at the same time. We had an exciting evening
together. On the following morning, Lauris gave a reading to my students. We recorded her reading; I have still got the cassette. There is another aspect I'd like to
mention. I felt greatly honoured when I was invited to write a brief article on Lauris
Edmond in the German *Kindlers Neues Literaturlexikon* where the alphabetical order
of authors means that she follows Umberto Eco. In regard to her poetry, a couple of
lines from "The Outside Room" have produced a lasting impression on me:

> ... the stars beyond –
> all whispering, explaining, declaring
> that the persecuted earth has not yet
> resigned its ancient romance with seasons
> and creatures

There is another poem which I began to like soon after Lauris had written it during one
of her visits to Germany. As someone who has had a personal attachment to the River
Rhine since early childhood, I am intrigued by Lauris Edmond's poetic salute to "the
Old Survivor". By way of concluding this session, and paying my personal tribute to
Lauris, let me read this poem to you:

Rhineland

> I walked in the early morning
> down the path by the water, and there
> I could smell the old river smell
>
> of the brimming Rhine, hear
> its purposeful lapping, see the long barges
> linked together GEFO TANK 2GEFO ROTTERDAM

out already, plugging steadily on,
and brown-stained, long abused as it is,
the capable waterway taking on yet another

of its numberless days for shouldering
Europe's cargoes, bearing poisons
on that wide and glistening back;

and it was as though it turned and looked up
from its liquid trudging, to remind me
that a continent's dying still richly harbours

the knowledge of ancient endurance – which
I acknowledged, nodding to the Old Survivor,
though all around me the elderberry flowers

narrowed, going down with their season
and the faintly acrid-scented may sprigs,
dying too in their own stiff arms

《•》

LITERATURE OF THE SETTLER COLONIES

An Anatomy of Violence
A Conversation with Mike Nicol[1]

Thomas Brückner

*T*HE FIRST QUESTION *I should like to ask you is where you see the difference between a poet and a prose writer? I mean, you started your writing career as a poet.*

*W*ELL, THIS IS DIFFICULT TO SAY. At least, where my so-called career is concerned. Definitely, in poetry there is a different rhythm needed. However, I think, that one is well taught by going through poetry because one learns an appreciation of words, rhythm, how words fit together and so on, and even to this day I tend to favour writers who have been poets or still write poetry – Faulkner comes to mind as an immediate example – rather than prose writers.

Do you think that a prose writer is distinguishable from one who has been through poetry?
I think they are distinguishable.

And where does this distinction lie?
Probably in the use of dialogue, just to come down to a technicality. I think, for the more prosaic writers there will be a tendency towards more dialogue. For the poetic writers – these terms are not judgmental, they are just descriptive – there seems to be a tendency to give greater attention to landscape, to description, to placing an individual within a landscape. There is an awareness of the individual within an environmental context. The focus is on that interaction rather than on the psychological dimension. When one looks at Faulkner it is the way his characters respond historically and geographically that is of primary importance, and it is this that drives the narrative.

If we now come to your writing I should like to ask you if my impression is right that violence has been your major subject so far. Is it correct to say that you are, somehow, 'obsessed' with the causes and effects of violence?

---

[1] This interview was conducted in Leipzig, June 2001.

[smiles] It is difficult in South Africa not to be obsessed with violence. I think in my poetry there is an obsession, if you like, with the tension between the state and the individual. The early work, I hope, deals with the injustices of the apartheid years and the system that encouraged state violence. Out of this growing awareness of the extent of institutionalized violence came a fascination with the nature of power and how the state uses violence to enforce and retain power. On top of this it was clear that the violence was a part of our history, it wasn't just a factor of apartheid. It had its roots in the country's colonial history. From the arrival of the Dutch the history is made up of a series of conflicts. What I have tried to do in the novels is show how that violence works in us today.

So, is it your objective to display the anatomy of violence? I mean, in your novels from This Day and Age *through* Horseman *down to* The Powers That Be[2] *you focus on different aspects of violence. Is it your objective to produce a sequence of novels through which all aspects of violence are covered?*
I did not set out with this in mind.

So, it came up in the course of writing?
Yes, but now it is starting to become a conscious exploration. I mean, it was an aspect of *The Powers That Be*, just as it was an aspect of *This Day and Age*. But it started to become clear to me in *Horseman* that this was a central concern for me. There is a critic in Cape Town who reviewed *This Day and Age* badly and then wrote me a letter to apologize for the review – which was quite strange – and to wish me well in my project. I thought that "project" was a strange word, but that was when I began to see the books as a project. Obviously, they are individually conceived, they are individually written. There is no master plan but the themes continue and the exploration of these themes from different aspects continues so, in many aspects that reviewer was actually right to call it a project. It is part of the fiction, and in *The Waiting Country*[3] I was able to deal with it in non-fiction.

So, in a way, it has developed into a project?
Definitely, it has. It is now more conscious. And it continues. For example, in my current work I look at it from the perspectives of the victims. *Horseman* presented another way of handling it. But it would have been self-destructive and limiting to continue along that track.

Well, for me, This Day and Age *already dealt with violence to a large degree. Violence as some kind of superior force hovering above society.*
Yes, I think you are right. While I was writing that book the deeper violence in South Africa began to manifest itself. I mean, *The Powers That Be* was written during the mid-1980s. Hit squads were operating but they were not yet public knowledge. By the end of the 1980s and by the early 1990s hit squads were an established fact, a common

---

[2] Mike Nicol, *This Day and Age* (Cape Town: David Philip, 1992); *Horseman* (London: Bloomsbury, 1994); *The Powers That Be* (London: Bloomsbury, 1999).
[3] Mike Nicol, *The Waiting Country: A South African Witness* (London: Gollancz, 1995).

thing, there were private armies loose on the landscape. Violence was more visible, more tangible. The effects of the "Third Force" were quite obvious. I think, these constant acts of violence shaped my fiction to a large extent because the shift had been made from an abstract historical tendency to a hard physical reality. And, I think, that influenced *This Day and Age* and, of course, went straight into *Horseman*, because *Horseman* is, in many ways, about a nineteenth-century hit-squad.

And how did Horseman *come into being?*
The novel actually had its origins in Europe. In 1991 I was travelling by car in what was then still Czechoslovakia when I saw a figure emerge from a forest and walk off across a snow-covered field. That image haunted me. In my mind this figure from the forest was heading out of the North towards the South. To me he became one of the underclass of people who went from the North to the South during the nineteenth century. This was something I wanted to write about: the movement of people from a shattered Europe to the mining camps of South Africa that seemed to promise so much yet destroyed so many lives through prostitution, drink, hard living. And also about the rag-tag bunch of desperate men who ended up in the private armies that were so much a part of imperialism, of a structure that was merely reinforced by their political masters.

You mean, the political masters simply took over this violent sub-structure that had been laid down by these outcasts?
Partly. Take the discovery of diamonds and gold in South Africa. A mass of people flocked there from Europe in the hopes of instant wealth. There was a dream. They came and created a city out of nothing and then the manipulators – men like Cecil Rhodes, [Abe] Bailey – used this seething mass for their own ends, both political and financial. For example, in *Horseman* there is a character called Podumo who wears a turban. He was part of the *amaWashi*, Zulu men who went to Johannesburg to earn a living by doing the town's laundry. Over time they were deprived of this means of earning a living as "big business" established large laundry operations. So, the *amaWashi* lost their means of employment and some of them drifted into crime. Such was the process of industrialization.

Would you, therefore, see Horseman *as a highly moralistic work? On the surface, you seem to be rather hesitant in judging the violence you depict. Do you see yourself as a rather uninvolved social commentator?*
The third-person narrator was a deliberate choice. I did not want to prescribe at all. I wanted to describe something.

Without interfering?
Without interfering. I wanted to put the reader in a position – an almost voyeuristic position – in which he would have to judge. In other words, present the violence in a way that would make the reader complicit in it. And then the reader has to make a judgement. I was not going to do that. But I feel that obviously the book as a whole carries an intention which is to condemn the violence that is destroying society. It is an issue which we have to address, but as yet there is not the political and social will to

really stop it. You hear some black and coloured academics and politicians rather smugly saying that now violence is at least ubiquitous, as prevalent in the white areas as the black. I'm sorry: you can't let a country plunge into criminal violence and say it's one of the unfortunate spin-offs of democracy. That's not good enough. And when I hear people – like the rector of a university – mouth such platitudes I know that we have not yet got the political will to face our history. So if there is any scheme in which books work then I think it must be to point up these issues.

What struck me in Horseman *is the statement by this mythological figure, the dark man, the Satan, in the catacombs of the monastery, who says: "Man is evil." Is this your general opinion of man, of mankind?*
This, of course, is a reference to Genesis, where God despairs of what he has created. I decided to work from that point of view. People, of course, are both, good and evil. I do not necessarily think that we are inherently evil, although history shows that we have an extraordinary capacity for evil. I do believe that there is a quality that can be called evil that can take possession of people at certain times and is all consuming when it does. It happened here in Germany and it happened in South Africa during the apartheid years. Of course, the people running the system did not think of themselves as being evil. In fact, quite the opposite. They prayed in their churches every Sunday, and they ran what they thought was a highly Christian society. The great paradox is that these God-fearing Christians were blind to the evil they perpetrated.

If one follows your train of thought, the next question has to be: Where would you see hope? Is there any? Or is man simply a self-destructing animal doomed to failure and, finally, to disappear?
Hope is an interesting word. We use it all the time: I hope that tomorrow the sun will shine; I hope that this and that may happen ...

What I mean is a different quality of hope, though ...
Well, what I wanted to say is that I really do not know what hope is. That is why this word is so interesting to me. Additionally, what strikes me is that the question of hope is frequently put to people living in the South: What hopes do you have for the future? I would like to suggest that the question is more valid in the North than it is in the South. To me, at least. In the South, despite the violence, I feel attempts are being made to re-create society. Here, one senses decay, whereas in South Africa in the last couple of years there has been the feeling of social reinvention. Of course, it's imperfect, and there are a hell of a lot of troubles, and it may still collapse completely but there is at least this feeling, this sense of re-imagining, of creating.

But is this feeling not due to euphoria, to the euphoria of having successfully over-thrown the hated apartheid system?
Not entirely. I think, the euphoria was quite short-lived. What I found more instructive was witnessing the constitution-writing process where people from different political perspectives had to come and hammer out a document that is supposed to reflect our social intentions. Of course, this document is an ideal – let's face it – because what happens in the streets – the violence, for example – is completely at odds with the con-

stitution. But, at least, the constitution means that there is a group of people, political leaders, who have some kind of vision about the society they want. And what they produced is the most progressive constitution and Bill of Rights in the world. I think, this is a significant achievement. I am pleased to belong to a society that is able to do this. The fact that it has not yet been realized is another issue. But, at least, people who came out of a society that had been permeated with evil were able to sit down and compromise and produce a document like this constitution. And this comes back to your question about hope. The constitution I see as a beacon of hope. On the other hand, hope is also bumbling along. And this is, to me, what mankind is doing: just bumbling along. At some times we do things better than at other times. If one looked at the course of human history over, say, the last two centuries would one say that things have progressed? I am not sure that one would. For a sector of the world's population things got really good but I would hazard that more people are worse off than was the case in some regions two hundred years ago. Africa being a case in point: two hundred years ago people may have been unhappy, they may have been fighting with one another, but the kinds of poverty, the kinds of devastation that one sees today did not exist.

Nevertheless, when I go through Horseman *I get the impression that there is no single positive force. The most evil character of the book – Daupus – walks away at the end into nowhere, unharmed, and it is quite clear that one day or the other he will start anew. Is this due to some state of disillusionment? Also with regard to the actual South African situation?*

If one sees the book as a moral tract, then it is a warning. And warnings – by their nature – tend to say that things have to be changed, they are positive critiques. So, I would rather say I'm distressed, not disillusioned. The other way I tried to show this was by creating a tension between the content and the form. I hoped that the form was of a sufficiently aesthetic quality to contain the content and produce a tension between the two, that language – which is, to me, the most important thing that mankind has produced – can contain this violence and can, by describing the horror rise above this violence. And that again is where our hope lies.

So it was not some kind of despair, of disillusionment, you were writing from?

No, absolutely not. It was not out of a sense of absolute hopelessness but out of a conviction that we can contain this thing and that language is one way to do it. Because, as I have just said, this is the most sophisticated thing that we have produced. It is the one thing that we do that no other species does. And it is this that allows us and has allowed us to shape our reality. And which will allow us to bumble along. Of course, I agree that the content of the novel is unrelenting. But it is my belief that we have to face the dark. We have to come to acknowledge the dark side of our nature, we have to admit that it exists.

Still, in the catacombs of the monastery we have the image of the bones lying there and the task of working them into some kind of new order the youth has set upon. Is this task – in your eyes – some kind of initiation into violence for him, some rite of passage? Do you think that a new order can be built out of the bones of an old one?

Yes, it was a rite of passage. Also, the youth, in this passage, is contracted against his wishes. He does not like what he is contracted to do and he tries to flee by jumping out of the window, but the essential thing is that he is not happy with what he has been contracted to or forced into. So, it does become a rite of passage through his involvement with the gypsies and finding out that, perhaps, there is a meaning to his life even if the meaning is not clear to him. And later on the passage south becomes a real rite of passage, the scene in the catacombs some kind of prelude to it. By the time he is seen as the horseman he has clearly come to accept his fate.

Again, would you tend to think that a new society can be build upon the bones of an old one or would you rather say that all old structures have to be brought to the ground?

The thing about the bones in the book is, first of all, that the bones are there in the catacombs because of the people who had died during the Black Plague and the youth is asked to pattern these bones into some kind of new order. But, the monk explains, you cannot identify any longer whether the bones belonged to males or females; everything is mixed up. The skeleton is our essential architecture: when you take away the flesh we are all the same *[smiles]*. When the youth gets to Southern Africa there is a passage where he and his men are crossing the veld and come across a place where bones are lying around. Daupus gets off his horse to examine them and the missionary says that people had been massacred there. Now, that was a reference to a commonly accepted historical fact that the Zulu *mfecane* had led to the decimation of many people in the interior, and that it was not uncommon to come upon bones lying about the veld. However, recent historiography suggests that there may be another interpretation to the accounts of bones on the veld. In the book, Daupus points out that from the way the bones are distributed and their condition it doesn't look as if a massacre had been enacted. He suggests they were quietly murdered. What I was trying to suggest here was that these were possibly the remains of slaves: perhaps they had been slaughtered because the slave drivers decided, for whatever reason, maybe the slaves were too emaciated, that it was no longer worth driving their captives to the coast. What is important to me is that the bones that are our history have a tendency to resurface. And unless we actually deal with them and know what they are when they are scratched up they tend to cause disruption. I think one is witnessing this to a certain extent here in Europe now, fifty years after the Second World War. Bones come up that were not dealt with in the course of these fifty years and this is causing – what seems to me from people I have been speaking to – anxiety in people's lives because they now have to confront issues they had tried to forget about. There is an interesting quote in the play *The White Devil* to the effect that the wolves are always around and will scratch the bones up again if they are not properly buried. Burying in this sense is not a matter of covering up. This is a matter of official ritual, acknowledging that they are there and that this piece of history can now be laid to rest.

Later on in your book, Daupus becomes the reincarnation or impersonation of the dark figure in the catacombs. This is a hint that he finally had taken on the contract. You say in the book that the contract had been sealed in the catacombs. Yet, the youth did not agree but tried to run away from it. It was more like a burden, a damnation,

rather, to him. Somehow, the horseman – Daupus – seems to be an intertextual refer-
ence to the myth of Ahasver, the wandering Jew. Would you please elaborate on this?
Sure. The youth has a friendship with Madach both before and after the contract scene
in the catacombs. Madach is clearly fond of him. They travel south together. They
share hardships together. During the course of a battle Madach is wounded. The youth
looks after him and arranges for him to be treated by a ship's doctor. Unfortunately,
Madach dies while his hand is being amputated and his death changes the youth. In the
very next chapter he has become Daupus and has, apparently, taken on the contract to
revenge because his first act is to hire men – outcasts – for that purpose.

But the revenge theme is the overall image even at a time already when Madach and
the youth meet for the first time with Madach capturing the youth and telling him his
life's story which is a story of revenge. So, although there has been the bond of friend-
ship between the two of them there has always been the revenge as something larger
than even their friendship?
Agreed. Although the youth initially resists Madach's ideas on revenge, it's only
Madach's death that propels him into accepting them. When he does take on the
revenge contract it is deliberately left unclear whether the contract comes from God or
the Devil. …. However, I can't really comment on the role of the wandering Jew, as
it's not a myth with which I am all that familiar.

What about Joe Silver, then, whose name may sound familiar to all who have read
Treasure Island?
That's the fictional reference. The other is to a real person who made a name for himself as a pimp in New York in the latter part of the nineteenth century, and was literally
run out of town. Early Johannesburg was ready-made for him.

We were just talking about the biblical references and there is another in which you
alter a saying from the Bible: "In the beginning was the word and the word was
KILL!" So, are all historical players devils in a way?
[laughs] It was an attempt to subvert language. Language is one of the book's themes.
As you know a whole range of languages are spoken in the book and a lot of them
have to be translated. Sometimes the translations are inaccurate, or inaccurate because
they are cryptic. In the same way the sentence "In the beginning was the word and the
word was kill!" has to be translated, although the emphasis remains one word. As
Clarence points out when he says "You quote incorrectly!" things are obviously not
quite what they seem, they are open to manipulation, which is an issue I wished to
explore in the novel. So we can go back to the theme of violence and argue that it is
being used not gratuitously, but to point up moral issues. In other words, it argues that
violence is not an answer to social upheaval.

Since you mentioned his name: what is the role of Clarence in the book?
He is quite a significant figure because he talks to the landscape, he tries to recite the
Greek classics to the landscape and the landscape is completely unresponsive. This,
once again, returns to the issue of language and how a colonial language is literally laid
onto a country. I mean, South Africa already has a myriad of languages and then, sud-

denly, there are new languages superimposed onto it and they become the dominant languages, they constitute the master-narrative. The question then is, how does one handle this?

I am glad that we have come to the issue of language again. Going through your novels I always got the impression of a very refined language being used. In this novel, Horseman, *it is almost biblical. In* This Day and Age *you utilized parts of the oral tradition of African peoples. How come?*
Well, it came about ...

Sorry. Were you, perhaps, brought up with it?
No. *[smiles]* Perhaps it is almost osmosis to a certain extent. Something in the air that one becomes aware of it. I suspect one of the luckiest things that happened to me, and something that definitely shaped my approach to *This Day and Age* was a commission to write a book on *Drum* magazine which eventually came to be called *A Good-Looking Corpse*.[4] At that time, I was completely disillusioned with journalism. I thought that it had reached a dead end, particularly in South Africa. It seemed a spent force that really could not explain – or help explain – the world and its meaning to us. Then, suddenly I was given the task of writing about a bunch of journalists who worked on a magazine in the 1950s. It was rather like discovering a lost century, because various apartheid acts had caused them and their magazine to disappear. With the easing of censorship in the late 1980s their books were re-published and as I read them and began the interviewing suddenly there was this country that I had known nothing about. What I wanted to do with that book was to try and trace as many of the *Drum* people – or their relatives – as I could and get them to tell me what it had been like during that time. I concentrated on the major themes that the *Drum* journalists had dealt with and then got those few who were still alive, their wives and people who had something to do with *Drum*, to talk about their experiences. My intention was to put their voices into the book. Without sounding arrogant, what I was trying to do was let these people speak their history. Obviously, I had to provide a framing narrative which is the journalist's function. This task made me realize the importance of journalism. Now, journalism is dear to my heart. It has been my profession since the early 1970s. And I felt, this was something journalism could do: provide the context in which others could talk. One has to accept that without the journalistic overview these voices would not necessarily have been heard. While I was putting this book together I was writing *This Day And Age* which, I think, reflects the same kind of technique in that there is no dominant point of view. There are a number of voices, which finally, is what South Africa is about. South Africa is not one story or one history, it is a whole lot of stories. And the task of the writer/journalist is to provide some framework for all these voices. This is where *A Good-Looking Corpse* fed directly into *This Day and Age*. During the writing of those books I became fascinated, and still am, with people telling their stories and oneself, as the journalist, not interfering, just recording. I used the same technique in *The Waiting Country* where I asked some of the victims of the Heidelberg

---

[4] Mike Nicol, *A Good-Looking Corpse* (London: Secker & Warburg, 1991)

Tavern massacre where some P A C terrorists shot up a pub in 1993 to tell their stories because I wanted their suffering to be remembered. So, that is where my fascination with what could possibly be described as an oral tradition lies. It certainly has nothing to do with the question of African orality which so fascinates academics these days.

But it is taking up the old and creating something new out of it. And it struck me that here there was – and I apologize for the racist term – white writer taking up forms of expression that were based in a sector of society he had been separated from for several hundred years.

Well, and this separation will remain to a certain degree for the rest of my life. But I do not think that that excludes me from using ways of telling stories ...

No, that is not what I am driving at. I mean, this is a rare thing. So far Gordimer has not done that, Coetzee has not, Brink certainly has not, although he has tried ... So, it is still an unusual thing to think of. Of course, I tend to think that this lies in the natural course of things, but it has remained a rare thing.

That may be. The way I would like to see it is that of a mutual exchange between people, of learning from one another. When I wrote both the *Drum* book and *This Day and Age* it simply felt the right thing to do, to try and utilize parts of the oral tradition. So, I did it. One has also to remember, that in a certain sense, I suppose, a certain political and historical sense, I was lucky in that – although I believe that the material has always been available – it simply was the right time to write such books. With the collapse of the walls – both the one in Europe and "ours" in South Africa – one was suddenly in a completely different political arena and suddenly there was a great freedom. But that freedom demands a re-imagining.

Has this got something to do with your "involvement" in, say, "magical realism"?

Perhaps it played an important part because it showed me a way, a way into the society. It offered, I think, an opportunity to get in. However, when I got in, I then found it was not the right thing, that it did not quite fit. It works fine in South America, Günter Grass has his own version of it for Germany, but it was not something that you could take from South America and implant willy-nilly on the South African situation. So, what has resulted is a gradual working away from magical realism into something else. What this "something else" is I simply do not know. I just know that it cannot be termed 'magical realism' any longer.

Well, that is what quite a lot of African writers have been doing throughout the years: adopting something from elsewhere to their own reality, to their literary environment and – by doing so – creating something new.

Look, what also struck me is that – when I thought about literature in South Africa – I had an image of a small black box. And all the writers were huddled inside the small black box, writing about the inside of this small black box. And one just had to break out of this thing. My perception was that a lot of writers would have to do a lot of kicking to break a hole in this black box. To push one fist through it and let the light in, for themselves and for writers yet to come. This, I think, is what the transition in literary terms is going to be all about.

And what do you tend to see as "magical" and "realist" in this process of cutting a whole and letting the light in?
Well, I do not like the term "magic." I would rather call it "fantasy."

But then, fantasy is a different category, and I do not think that your novels fit into that.
Maybe not entirely. But then, I would re-phrase it as 'realistic fantasy', because one was working in a system which was 'fabulous'. I mean, apartheid as a system was 'fantastic', very inventive – in a completely evil sense. But it was 'fantastic' or 'fabulous' nonetheless, in the sense of being a grim fable. And so, one grows up with and has this sense of reality which is ... crazy. And one has to work some kind of decent compassionate humanity into it.

All right. But, on the other hand, if we come back to Horseman *once more, you have all these references based on reality: the massacre, the African queen, the character of the missionary who is – as I have learned – based on Reverend Moffat, the father-in-law of David Livingstone ...*
Yes, of course, there are real events recounted. If you read Moffat's diary on the massacre – it is fantastic, it is surrealistic. Moffat is Thorne in the book. So, I chose to render the fictional telling in completely fantastic language. It had to seem imaginary, as if it had not happened. This seemed appropriate because the way the massacre was recorded historically – and Moffat was the only witness to record it – was so completely and utterly fantastic. Thus, when I came to re-tell it I wanted to have it rendered more or less as Moffat had recorded it: a choreographed massacre, comparable to a game of chess. It was completely surrealistic.

Could you tell me more about Moffat, please, because people here may not be very familiar with this part of South African history?
He worked for the London Missionary Society and had a mission station in what is now the Northern Cape. In the 1820s a drought in Botswana caused people to move south in search of pasture for their cattle, and water. This, obviously, put pressure on Moffat and his converts. Moffat asked the colonial authorities to protect him but when they declined he decided, literally, to raise a private army of his own. He contracted a group of bandits living on the Orange River islands, gave them weapons, and effectively planned a massacre so that he could ease the economic pressure around the mission. His private army – a hit-squad if you like – slaughtered, in the course of eight hours, some five hundred men. Moffat then took the women and children captive. The majority he gave to the bandits, who, it is speculated, may have taken them off to Maputo to be sold as slaves. He took five women for himself as slaves and the rest went to a government agent who was with him, one Melville, whose name I didn't change in the novel. Melville took his slaves down to Graaf Reinet and sold them there. Clearly, the whole exercise was, firstly, to protect Moffat's natural resources and, secondly, to make some money by selling the captives. It is not a well-known scene in South African history, it is one of these things in our society that is not supposed to be there. I'm sure there is plenty of this hidden history. But as the historians start to dig it out, I think it will be up to writers to fictionalize these events so that they can be re-told and re-lived.

When you write about events like that do you have a particular audience in mind?
No, apart from the feeling that I write for people living in something which one could call a geographical entity I do not have any particular audience in mind. One of the ironies is that one's books are read more widely in the North, but well ...

Thank you for the interview.

《•》

from *The Ibis Tapestry*

MIKE NICOL

Part I: Reconstruction

1

This – once I'd shut out predatory professors, banshees, lawyers, meths-besotted itinerants – is how I imagined it: when Christo Mercer dreams of the death of the four girls for the second time he is filled with such apprehension that he becomes obsessed with them. He sits in his study looking out over the early morning gardens where spring has brought back the blossom and the leaves, but he doesn't see the lushness: he sees the girls' bodies lying on the sand. There is no blood. They don't even seem to be wounded yet still the automatic fire echoes in his head.

I see him mournfully unlock a drawer in his desk where he keeps – with his passports, cheque book, credit cards and bank statements – the old exercise book in which he made a note of all his alarming or recurring dreams. He opens it and writes the date: Thursday 6 October 1994. Then, I see Christo Mercer put down his pen because he doesn't want to relive the dream. He looks across the tops of the trees into the air that is endless and blue. Blue over the whole continent: a single sky of blue without any clouds just the awful anxious blue stretched tightly from horizon to horizon. 'Alas, poor fools', he sighs eventually (a literary quote: he was given to literary quotes), and, taking up the pen, begins hurriedly to write down what he's dreamt. When he's finished his anxiety hasn't lessened. There's a taste of onions in his mouth, a taste that won't go away all day.

As he drives to work, Christo Mercer wonders if the angels are walking on the walls of heaven as sentinels to warn his immortal soul. (Another quote.)

Let me explain: to Christo Mercer dreams were important. They were the diary of his life, a diary he'd first started on the morning of Friday 21 November 1975. The previous night he'd dreamt of eating lobster: sucking the meat out of the legs, cracking open the tail to reveal the white flesh. When he was finished eating a face appeared in the plate and told him the lobster was poisoned with toxic red tide.

And so the book of dreams was begun. And kept up – secretly – through his seventeen-year marriage to Wilma nee Mostert (which occasioned a dream of drowning among yellow fish on the wedding night), the birth of their first daughter, Olive, now aged eleven, (a dream of freezing in snow) and then, Emily, now aged seven, (a dream of falling from a high building). Dreams not only of his death but of the deaths of others. Dreams that weren't necessarily portents or foretellings or prophecies, dreams that were often simply visions of horror. Dreams that disconcerted him; that caused his chest to constrict with anxiety. As did the dream of the death of the four girls. For one thing it raised an abject memory. For another it presaged a threat. Both caused fear in Christo Mercer. By the night of Thursday 6 October 1994 he had became obsessed with the girls to the point of neurosis.

To him they were teenagers wearing jeans and T-shirts with their hair covered in the Muslim way. He pictured them walking out of an old walled town and being gunned down. He could see the town, a mud town of mosques and casbah, alleys, lanes, wells, date palms, the houses rising against one another cool and shuttered, the stench of camel dung on the streets, a town anywhere in Saharan Africa: Mali, Libya, Chad, Morocco. Towns he'd got to know well: the town of Malitia where he had an office, the town of Djano where he sometimes stayed with the old warlord, Ibn el-Tamaru, or Bilo, Misana, Taghazi, Murzuk where he'd met with an array of men wanting to buy arms and ammunition. For some of these places he had recurring dreams: dreams of burning, desiccation, garrotting, and those places he tried not to revisit. He went by the old adage:

> dream a dream thrice
> cockatrice.

Which was the other reason Christo Mercer felt the angels were warning his immortal soul and made him anxious not to dream of the deaths a third time.

Moreover, it was with the second dream of the death of the four girls that he realized the town was Djano. As he had closed the exercise book and locked it away in the drawer he considered delaying his trip there. But in the end he decided merely to be cautious. That afternoon he sent a fax to his people in the northern office asking them to get word to the customers that he would be in Malitia later in the month but unable to journey to outlying towns, like Djano. He hoped Ibn el-Tamaru would consider it worth making the journey to see him. He was confident he would. About the others, particularly the Englishman, he was less confident. He would not be as accommodating. He would...

What?

Christo Mercer went back to wondering about the girls. He gave them names. Names he took from a file of foreign newspaper clippings about the wars in his territory. His territory – his empire – was extensive, it covered most of the Sahara. So the girls became Farida, Dirie, Gali, Salma.

When he got home that evening, the evening of Thursday 6 October 1994, there was an e-mail message from the Englishman waiting for him.

Go away Justine, you bitch, I'm not opening the door. For Christ's sake I'm trying to write a serious book!

2

The gardens that Christo Mercer's study overlooked belong to the suburb of Waterkloof, Pretoria. I have stood in that study (Sunday 1 October 1995) and noted the view:
it's the sort of detail that every writer needs as he begins the process of reimagining a
life.

The house itself is a double storey of mock-Tudor design with leaded windows.
Shortly after he became a director of International Ventures, in other words sometime
early in 1986, he bought the house. He was captivated by anything that hinted at old
England. He thought of this house with its six bedrooms, three bathrooms, study, two
lounges, family room, large kitchen including a breakfast nook, dining room, pantry
and laundry as 'his cottage'. When he arrived home at the end of the day and the automatic gates locked across the driveway he considered himself safe.

Like so many in the suburbs, Christo Mercer believed he was living in a state of
siege. I suppose the statistics supported his belief. For instance, in late 1994 a survey
reported that in each hour of each day some ninety nine violent crimes were committed, including the rape of three women and the murder of two people.

So it is hardly surprising that as the country became increasingly prone to suburban
violence Christo Mercer took precautions. In 1988 he had a high wall fringed with
barbed metal spikes built around the property. He had burglar bars fastened to the
windows and security grilles bolted at the doors. Even the double doors which opened
from the lounge onto the patio and swimming pool were protected in this way. At the
top of the staircase another metal grille secured the bedrooms at night. He had two
Alsatians called Chaka and Dingaan. His house was wired to an armed response unit.
Locked in a safe in his study were a magnum .35 pistol, an R1 automatic rifle, an AK-
47, and a side by side Smith and Wesson shotgun. He was also storing five hundred
rounds of ammunition.

To me this speaks of a siege mentality.

Waterkloof is a suburb of large houses set in large grounds – not unlike the Cape
Town suburb from which I was evicted three months ago. A suburb of swimming
pools and tennis courts. A suburb of lawns, gardeners, beds of rhododendrons. The
streets are lined with jacaranda trees which in September blossom into purple and in
October lay this purple on the pavements.

The people of Waterkloof do not walk, they drive. They drive to their offices in the
city, they drive to the shopping malls, they drive their children to school. The cars they
drive are usually made by Mercedes Benz or BMW. Christo Mercer drove a BMW.
The people who live in Waterkloof are ambassadors, consuls, military attaches,
bankers, corporate executives, senior civil servants. As a director of International Ventures, Christo Mercer was not out of place.

Before the Mercer house was sold in October 1995 the estate agent opened it as a
show house for two consecutive Sundays. On those two days it was like a museum to
Christo Mercer so I went there to wander among the furniture (Sanderson floral sofas)
he had sat on when he entertained or read the Sunday papers. I stared at the prints of
English race horses hung in wide gold-leafed frames. I felt the weight of the silver
candlesticks placed at the end of the mantelpiece. I couldn't resist smelling the richness

of the sherry he kept in crystal decanters on a sideboard. I marvelled at how well-stocked his liquor cabinet was.

In the family room I tried out the Morris chair he lounged in to watch television or listen to music. There is something peculiar about sitting in a dead man's chair. It's like sitting on someone's lap: intimate, uncomfortable.

Among Christo Mercer's CDs I noted a propensity for masses and requiems (four different versions of Mozart's Requiem), some jazz (mostly Keith Jarrett), a full collection of Crosby Stills and Nash, and a curious assortment of musicians from western Africa: Ali Farka Toure, Salif Keita, the sound of Wassoulou, Youssou n'Dour, Ismael Lo.

In the dining room I sat down at the yellowwood table where he had sat to eat. (Fortunately the estate agent was busy with prospective buyers so I was unsupervised.)

Upstairs I stood in his daughters' bedrooms (immaculate neat pink rooms); in the main bedroom I wondered on which side of the king-sized bed he had slept. I smelt the pillows for a trace of his scent but I could detect only fabric softener. I felt the mattress for its spring. I would have ignored the dressing table with its jars of cream, its glass ornaments, had I not stooped to glance at myself in the mirror and seen instead, stuck in the mirror's frame, a colour photograph of Christo Mercer. I pulled it loose.

What struck me first was the size of his head. It didn't belong to his body. It was too big, too heavy, too old. He had jowls. His hair was thin, the dome of his forehead gleamed in the sun. His lips were closed, he didn't smile, his eyes had no light.

'How do you do, Christo Mercer', I said aloud, for a moment forgetting where I was.

He stood on a beach wearing a costume and an unbuttoned shirt. A blue towel was bunched in his right hand, sunglasses dangled from the other. His body was in no worse condition than mine: ordinary, neither fat nor thin, no bones showing, no obvious muscles, a slight swelling at the gut, hairy legs and arms. It was just the head that didn't match it. With a head like that he should have been thick set: a dictator. At his shoulders the azure of the sky met the cyan of the sea: it seemed to disembody him, to let his head float free.

I pocketed the photograph and continued my explorations.

I looked in the wardrobe at the neat line of suits, at the collection of ties, at the white ironed shirts, at the rows of shoes. There were fifteen pairs.

In the bathroom I found three bottles of men's aftershave: Dolce & Gabbana, Armani, Paco Rabanne. Wilkinson's shaving foam. Prep shaving cream. Razor blades for a Gillette contour. Safari-for-Men deodorant. An old black comb with dirt at the start of the teeth and dirt caked between them. I noted that what was missing was a toothbrush, razor, nailclippers, brush: the items he would take on a business trip.

In his study I listed the books: Marlowe, Shakespeare, Kyd, Tourneur, Webster, all the Elizabethans great and small. Nothing else, just the Elizabethans.

On his desk were photographs of his wife and daughters. The background to the pictures didn't locate them anywhere.

I opened the desk drawer – the key was in the lock – and riffled through his bank statements (healthy credit balances), details of his mortgage repayments (the loan was almost paid off), credit card slips (mostly for restaurants), bond certificates (numerous), the portfolio of his stock exchange investments (impressive), and a ten-page essay typed on a manual typewriter and dated 1985. But then I heard the estate agent climbing the stairs. I slid the drawer closed and sat at Christo Mercer's desk looking out over the trees and roofs of Waterkloof as he had done almost exactly a year previously.

I imagined him writing down his second dream of the death of the four girls on the morning of Thursday 6 October 1994. The trees then, as now, would have been full-leafed, fresh. Here and there would have shown the purple of a late-flowering jacaranda. The brown and the dust of the winter was gone. The lawns were green again. The brunsfelsia was in mauve and white flower. Its scent and that of a jasmine were the perfume of the night. It was the time of year Christo Mercer called the 'English days'.

'It's a fine property, don't you think', said the agent.

She was one of those women for whom the short thigh-length skirt was fashioned. All my women wear such skirts: it's how they ensnare men. Before them spies, mercenaries, arms dealers, drug barons, diamond magnates, stock brokers are stricken, paralyzed, their eyes compelled to slide up those long shapely legs that strut from the tight material where all promise is moulded yet aggressively withheld. My eyes were similarly enraptured.

'Don't you think?' she repeated.

I agreed it was, and left.

On the next Sunday (8 October 1995) I revisited the house because I needed to verify a few details.

'Weren't you here last week?' asked the agent, her legs this time sheer in navy tights.

I nodded.

'There've been a few offers. But nothing's signed and sealed yet', she said.

'I'd need my wife to see it before we can commit ourselves', I said.

My wife! That's a joke.

'Do you mind if I look round again?'

'Help yourself', she smiled.

I noticed details I hadn't seen before: the ivory handled sword leaning against the wall in the second lounge, an old kelim hanging on the staircase wall. But most importantly, in the study a small crucifix on a chain was pinned to the bookshelf above the desk.

3

This on my answering machine (Friday 17 November 1995):

'Hello Robert, it is Richard here. You must surely be back from your travels by now. Nobody could possibly stay in Malitia longer than ten days, it sounds a perfectly sordid place. How did things go? Did you find out why your mysterious Christo Mercer was killed? Or should I say did you get to the bottom of the matter? – if you'll excuse the pun. [Jolly ho ho laughter.] Do give me a call so that we can arrange to meet for that elusive drink, I'm curious to hear all your news. Ciao for now!'

'Robert, I know you're back and when I come knocking at your door I expect you to open it. I also expect you to pick up the receiver and talk to me. Me. Justine. You can't just ignore me. I know you're listening. Come on pick it up. Robert! Robert, damn you, pick it up, you can't hide behind that machine forever. Robert! For God's sake be your age, stop acting like a teenager. You've got obligations you know. You've got obligations to Matthew and Luke. They're your sons. This is screwing Luke up. You can't just pretend they don't exist. Jesus, Robert you can be an arsehole. It's no wonder I felt you were driving me out of my mind'.

'Good morning, Mr Poley, this is Ursula, Mr Melnick's secretary. He wonders if it would be possible to arrange a meeting for 3pm on the 21st. Apparently there are some new matters which have to be discussed before a final divorce settlement can be drawn up. Also he says to let you know he doesn't see this going to court until sometime in January'.

'Hullo dear, it's your mother. If you can, please call round over the weekend. Bye'.

This is what I have to work against! How am I expected to concentrate?

However.

4

The e-mail message from the Englishman to Christo Mercer read: Christo, whatever you're up to don't renege. Let's just say it wouldn't be in the interests of your livelihood. We'll see you in Malitia.

The message was signed with the initials NS.

5

To reconstruct: that is the researcher's – my – task. To find the life among the few scattered details and put together some motive for why what happened, happened. Also to imagine: to make the leap from the fact to the emotion it elicited. Which is hardly scientific but then what is scientific these days? Stephen Hawking wants a Theory of Everything. Don't we all! But to get from here to Everything is going to take educated guess work, most probably it will never go beyond that. My reconstruction follows the same principle. Start from facts, reality, what is known. When the gaps come, jump, but only if there's something out there to land on. I'm not making anything up. I'm reporting.

So.

To begin: I can think of no better moment than the night of Thursday 6 October 1994 when Christo Mercer sat in his study looking out over the dark gardens of Waterkloof. The taste of onions was still in his mouth and it raised a memory he thought he'd long forgotten. Or rather a memory he'd learnt not to remember. One which even now he kept hidden from himself.

On his desk was a flask of coffee; next to it a plastic pill bottle of amphetamines he'd bought at the Avalon Pharmacy in Beatrix Street. He was using both stimulants in a desperate bid to stay awake. To borrow from the immortal bard – although I shouldn't because, as I shall show, Christo Mercer's idee fixe was that other Elizabethan giant, Christopher Marlowe – to sleep would be perchance to dream and that was the last thing my subject wanted.

The first thing my subject wanted – I'm assuming this, of course, but on good authority – was to see if his fax to Malitia had caused any 'ripples in the universe' – which is the way I would normally phrase such things.

So, pumping with uppers and caffeine, he plugged in his laptop and track-balled his way to his cyberspace postbox where awaited the foreboding e-mail from NS. A message of electronic impulses, a virtual message, a troubling reality. One that he could not ignore.

Here I have to jump from fact – he downloaded the message to his harddrive and stored it in a file named, somewhat (in Christo Mercer's case) amusingly therefore somewhat surprisingly, 'e-pisodes' – to imaginative reconstruction. I don't know what reaction he had to the warning from NS. I don't know if he got up and stared out into the darkness as if it contained all danger and all evil. I don't know if the fascination of the words made him read them again and again and again until they accelerated his heart rate to alarming levels. I don't know if he checked his guns, if he went round the house locking all the doors and windows, if he made telephone calls. I just don't know how he responded.

Except.

Except that he must have got up from his desk and gone to his bookshelf and selected a book – haphazardly? for distraction? on purpose? because he remembered something? – and became preoccupied with it. He entered its world. Nothing strange here people do it all the time: it's called reading. Escapism. Swapping realities. The thing about Christo Mercer is that he went one step further: he wanted his own fantasy, so he started writing it.

How do I know?

I know this because sometime on that (fateful) Thursday night Christo Mercer opened a file in his word processor called 'virgins.txt'. He then typed a large segment from this – accidentally? deliberately? – selected book, followed by, one below the other, the four names he'd found by scanning through the newspaper clippings. He ignored the real lives of Farida, Dirie, Gali, Salma. Instead he fictionalized them.

To him, Farida was the most beautiful of them all. Her skin was as glossy as molasses, unblemished. She had almond eyes, a delicate nose, high cheekbones, soft velvet lips. Her father was a musician and her mother was dead. Her father was famous: he'd played in Paris, Berlin, London, New York, Tokyo. They called him Le Popstar. From his travels he'd brought her back sunglasses, transistor radios, the just released records of the dreadlocked Bob Marley, jeans, a poster of Muammar Qaddafi, another of Haile Selassie, French copies of *VOGUE*. She could read and write French. She hadn't been circumcised. She wanted to be a model. She was the best dressed among the four as they walked towards the gunmen on a day at the end of the 1960s.

She hated living in Djano. She wanted to live in New York. She'd never been out of Djano but she could imagine New York. She wanted to live where there was rain and snow and the lakes froze. But more than that she wanted electricity. And she wanted the colours green, black, grey. She couldn't stand the browns and ochres of Djano. It was a town of dry mud. To her it was a place of the crippled and the malformed and the crazy with drool on their chins. It was a town of camels and donkeys. She wanted a city of cars. She wanted a city of pavements where people were dressed in the fashions of *VOGUE* or *ELLE* or *PARIS MATCH*. She wanted water and muted light and an air the colour of tarnished silver. She wanted a sun that was distant: not a heat but a glow that would touch her skin gently. She wanted a great city built of concrete and glass. She wanted a river, a harbour, highways. She wanted a city of light. A city that dimmed the stars. She wanted New York.

Farida was fourteen years old.

Gali was fifteen.

She was the exact opposite of Farida. Not that she was ugly but her face was flatter and her skin was sallow. She probably ate too much fat. She wasn't wearing jeans. She was the only one wearing a dress, a brownish dress from which the colour had long been washed. She was barefoot. She came from a poor family. She was tagging behind the other three girls as they walked out of the town.

Her parents were both alive although her father was little better than a living dead man who hadn't spoken a word or cured a hide since the death of his mother. Once he'd been famous for the skins he'd tanned. People had called him the finest tanner between Djano and Timbuktu, and his racks had always been full of salted pelts. But now her mother did the tanning and he sat on a stool in the yard, unmoving, even when flies crawled on his face.

Gali, being the eldest, helped her mother with the skins. She salted and limed and worked in fat to soften the hair on the pelts. Or she checked on her father to make sure he hadn't died and fed him the food he wouldn't eat himself.

Yet Gali sang as she worked. She sang the songs her mother sang about love and death and good times and bad times and the birth of fat babies but the words meant nothing to her. Gali didn't expect anything of life. She couldn't imagine another way of being. She didn't know her hands were hard and cracked. She didn't know what it meant to read and write. At five she had been raped by an uncle; at nine she'd been circumcised. She didn't know that her mother was going to sell her to a man as old as her father. As she walked towards the gunmen she was the one least terrified.

Dirie?

Dirie was circumcised but she'd not been raped. As the four of them walked across the sand she was the one just slightly behind Farida, who, predictably, was in front. Dirie wore plastic thongs on her feet, her jeans were patched, her T-shirt had a ban the bomb sign on the chest. It'd been given to her in exchange for a bagful of dates by a young Swiss motorbiker passing through some months before. Under her scarf Dirie had hair that would spill about her shoulders like silk when she let it loose. It was black, it was rich, it could be admired only in the mirrors of her room. When Dirie smiled she showed teeth so white they were almost translucent.

Dirie's father worked on distant oil wells and was only at Djano for a month each
year. Dirie's mother was a typist for the *Gouverneur*. She'd been to Marseilles and
Paris when she was Dirie's age. Dirie had photographs of her standing at the Eiffel
Tower. In one of them she was with Dirie's grandfather who had once been the *sous-
préfet* at Djano. All she could remember of him was a smell of aniseed. She couldn't
remember him dying.

At the age of eight Dirie went to M. Vincent's school. She learnt to read and write in
French. She began to wonder at the world that lay beyond the sand. She listened to
Farida's Bob Marley records. She coveted the poster of Muammar Qaddafi. She had her
own pair of sunglasses, her own transistor radio. She read Farida's magazines. She'd
written letters to Warren Beatty and Sasha Distel. She wanted to live in Paris. But she
didn't want to be a model. She wanted to be the newly-married Jackie Onassis and walk
beside the Seine.

Dirie was fourteen years old.

Salma, the last and the youngest, was thirteen.

Salma was the one Christo Mercer saw most clearly. He could see the fineness of
her eyelashes when she closed her eyes. Then, without those sad Kalamata eyes to
distract him, he could picture the sharp lift of her cheeks, the oval line of her jaw, the
lips slightly parted and the hint of teeth behind them. He imagined the faint warmth of
breath coming from her nostrils. He gave her the fine nose of an Arabian princess.

Salma was a refugee. She'd not been born in Djano. She'd been there only three years
when she was chosen to face the gunmen. Her mother and father had gone to Djano
because they'd thought it was a place so out of the way that they'd be safe there. They
wanted a town that knew nothing of bloodletting, of corpses in the street, or of fear: the
hourly terror of dying. A town for their daughter. They wanted this because they'd been
forced to flee from so many places carrying what they could: the elderly, the children,
food. Too often they'd looked back at villages that had become pillars of flame, or
they'd walked through fields of burnt crops, the air still black, falling with ash. Too
often they'd had to bury their kin along the road as they'd had to bury Salma's younger
sister and brother. Too often they'd been raped and beaten. And so for them Djano was
a sanctuary beyond the reach of warring men. It was protected by the desert. It was un-
touchable.

Salma's father was a candlemaker, a good occupation in a town where the generator
powered only the fans and the lights in the *Gouverneur*'s office and home. Her mother
grew herbs in the garden beside the well. Salma helped them both. M. Vincent tried to
persuade them to let Salma attend his school but they argued that they needed her help.
According to custom Salma had been circumsized when she was ten years old and
although the wound had turned sceptic her mother's herbs had kept her alive. When
she reached the age of fifteen her parents expected to sell her to a marriageable man.
They anticipated a good price for such a beauty.

Salma knew about Bob Marley. She knew about transistor radios. Djano was not
such a big town that she could live without knowing of these things. Like most of the
other young people in Djano – even Gali – she would rush to stand outside Farida's
house whenever Le Popstar was practising with his band.

But Salma didn't know about *VOGUE* or *ELLE* or *PARIS MATCH*. She didn't know about New York or Jackie Onassis. She couldn't imagine electricity. She could imagine a husband and children. She could imagine her life as the Qur'an said it would be.

On the morning Salma walked out of the town gates with Farida and Dirie and Gali she was dressed in old jeans and a T-shirt supplied by USAID. She wore leather sandals, her head-scarf was pale blue and embroidered. She looked back once at the people gathered on the wall and clustered at the gate, and moments after that the shooting started.

⟨⟨•⟩⟩

Coetzee's *Disgrace*
A Linguistic Analysis of the Opening Chapter

JOHN DOUTHWAITE

Introduction

T HE ASPECT OF THIS NOVEL that struck me most when I first read it was the sense of void it expressed. This void created a feeling of sadness. A second reaction gradually developed as I read on: that of frustration and anger against a void that seemed to condemn life wholesale.[1]

This essay is in three parts. The first discusses briefly the concept of void. The second and main part analyses the opening four paragraphs in some depth in order to show by what linguistic means this sense of void is created. The deployment of these linguistic mechanisms will help delineate the personality and ideological stance of the protagonist, David Lurie. These constitute the cornerstone of the deeper levels of significance in the novel. The final section projects the theme into the whole novel.

1. Void

Void has been identified as central to Coetzee's work. As Stephen Watson argues,

> both Coetzee's Jacobus Coetzee and Schreiner's Bonaparte Blenkins occupy a world that knows no social restraint [...] both characters have the opportunity to indulge that sadism

---

[1] I wish to thank John Gamgee, Brian Worsfold, and all those who participated in the lively and enlightening debate on Coetzee that formed part of the original occasion for this essay. That discussion helped to crystallize my ideas as well as to make new points emerge. I have, of course, integrated suggestions into the article. Unfortunately, the only participants who contributed ideas that I have incorporated and whom I know personally are Bernard Cohen, Johan Jacobs and André Viola. The others receive grateful, albeit anonymous, thanks. I am particularly indebted to Johan for the discussion we had together afterwards. There was one woman participant who found my stress on negativity particularly upsetting. My objectives here do not allow me to develop this aspect more fully; my thanks go to her nevertheless, for her views lead me to stress that I am deliberately emphasizing one aspect of the novel that I consider fundamental. Other readings are, of course, possible. Thanks also to Antonella Emina, who tracked down Baudelaire.

[...] through which they assert the reality of their own egos against a wilderness whose very emptiness would seem to mock all human endeavour. Coetzee [...] makes use of a conception of Africa which was first elaborated by Conrad in *Heart of Darkness*. The notion that the colonial experiences at the heart of Africa, a void which would seem to penetrate every level of existence, from biological to the metaphysical, is hardly foreign to him.[2]

The void that lies at the centre of man (and I use the term in both its gendered and generic senses) is the novel's point of departure. It is the source of pain and hopelessness. It expresses not angst but defeat. The impossibility of communication, hence of meaningful human relationships, which David Lurie both embodies and theorizes, is indirectly described as well as explicitly stated from the outset.

It is almost explicitly stated when Lurie defines his life through the metaphor "the desert of the week" (S13)[3] and when he identifies the origin of communication in song, "and the origins of song in the need to fill out with sound the overlarge and rather empty human soul" (4). For the indirect description, I turn to part two of the essay, the linguistic analysis of the opening paragraphs.

2. The opening paragraphs

[1] For a man of his age, fifty-two, divorced, he has, to his mind, solved the problem of sex rather well. [2] On Thursday afternoons he drives to Green Point. [3] Punctually at two p.m. he presses the buzzer at the entrance to Windsor Mansions, speaks his name, and enters. [4] Waiting for him at the door of No. 113 is Soraya. [5] He goes straight through to the bedroom, which is pleasant-smelling and softly lit, and undresses. [6] Soraya emerges from the bathroom, drops her robe, slides into bed beside him. [7] 'Have you missed me?' she asks. [8] 'I miss you all the time', he replies. [9] He strokes her honey-brown body, unmarked by the sun; he stretches her out, kisses her breasts; they make love.

[10] Soraya is tall and slim, with long black hair and dark, liquid eyes. [11] Technically he is old enough to be her father; but then, technically, one can be a father at twelve. [12] He has been on her books for over a year; he finds her entirely satisfactory. [13] In the desert of the week Thursday has become an oasis of *luxe et volupté*.

[14] In bed Soraya is not effusive. [15] Her temperament is in fact rather quiet, quiet and docile. [16] In her general opinions she is surprisingly moralistic. [17] She is offended by tourists who bare their breasts ('udders', she calls them) on public beaches; she thinks vagabonds should be rounded up and put to work sweeping the streets. [18] How she reconciles her opinions with her line of business he does not ask.

[19] Because he takes pleasure in her, because his pleasure is unfailing, an affection has grown up in him for her. [20] To some degree, he believes, this affection is reciprocated. [21] Affection may not be love, but it is at least its cousin. [22] Given their unpromising

---

[2] "Colonialism and the Novels of J.M. Coetzee," in *Critical Perspectives on J.M. Coetzee*, ed. Graham Huggan & Stephen Watson (Basingstoke: Macmillan, 1996): 14–15.

[3] The reference is to "Sentence 13" of the opening paragraphs; see below. J.M. Coetzee, *Disgrace* (London: Secker & Warburg, 1999): 1. Further page references to the novel are in the main text.

beginnings, they have been lucky, the two of them: he to have found her, she to have found him.

The first sentence of the novel is clearly a topical sentence.[4] The topic is announced as being that of sex. The lexical choice immediately highlights a physical aspect of life, a basic drive that must be satisfied to ensure the functional integrity of the system. The way the topic is expressed throws light over a major number of central themes and linguistic techniques in the novel.

First of all, sex is defined as a "problem." This in itself conveys many messages. To begin with, it (covertly) emits the first of an interminable number of value judgements. Like the majority of the value judgements expressed in the novel, the opinion that is manifested is negative. Negativity characterizes the climate of human relationships throughout the novel where Lurie is concerned.

Second, classifying this particular topic as a "problem" implies treating it as a functional phenomenon: namely, a negative situation that needs to be transformed into positivity – an ironic metonym for the entire novel, since Lurie's "solution" is about to fail. Lurie's life is dysfunctional.

Third, the semantic field evoked by the lexeme "problem" is thus that of problem-solving behaviour, with its connotations of a cold, rational evaluation of the situation, a cool appraisal of the means available or devisable to solve the problem, and the adoption of the most efficient and effective solution that can be envisaged in the circumstances. The other (overt) evaluative term employed in the sentence, "rather well," confirms this interpretation as constituting an evaluative noun and not a value-free, objective description.

Fourth, couching the topic in terms of a logico-scientific problem also establishes a matter-of-fact, detached tone, reflecting the narrator's ostentatious attitude to his topic. There is no passion in his behaviour – physical or emotional. This will be a constant feature of his conduct, a feature that is underlined by the coldness and formality of the language employed.

Fifth, coldness and matter-of-factness also have a distancing effect, a point we shall return to at the end of this section.

A sixth aspect of sex is that it may refer to two crucial domains of human behaviour, physical pleasure and the solution to the problem of survival of the human race. The conceptual content of the sentence is one of the features that eliminates the second domain. Hence the interpretation to be placed on sex is that of the satisfaction of a strong drive to obtain bodily comfort.

Sex as survival symbolizes life. Eliminating this sphere of life is thus an ironic comment on Lurie's own life. In this sense, it is closely linked to a third crucial domain pertaining to sex in human behaviour. This third domain is activated by the exploitation of the Gricean maxim of quantity.[5] Characteristic features of the sentence such as evoking the problem-solving schema, the matter-of-fact tone and attitude, and regard-

---

[4] Teun van Dijk, *Text and Context: Explorations in the Semantics and Pragmatics of Discourse* (Burnt Mill, Harlow: Longman, 1977).

[5] Paul Grice, *Studies in the Way of Words* (Cambridge MA: Harvard UP, 1989).

ing sex as the satisfaction of bodily comfort logically exclude the involvement of the emotional or psychological spheres at the personal and interpersonal levels in the sexual act. Yet normal sexual relationships involve two people in an act of exchange. To put it in Gricean terms, if a phenomenon is important, it is mentioned. If it is not mentioned, then it either does not exist or it is not important. In conclusion, the fact that emotional and psychological spheres are not talked about means that interpersonal relationships are excluded from Lurie's vision of sex.

This individualistic, egoistic and hedonistic stance is confirmed by grammatical structure. "He has solved" indicates individual, independent agency through the third-person singular, and through an active, transitive verb. Lurie implies he has found the solution all by himself without requiring any other human aid or intervention in order to achieve the solution, thus making the other person involved in the physical act a mere instrument by means of which the solution is implemented. Such an implicature constitutes another apt and ironic comment on the nature of the solution Lurie has opted for, on this metaphor of life.

The smugness and self-satisfaction Lurie expresses, though infringing the politeness principle[6] by uttering self-praise, thereby flaunting anti-social behaviour, further under-score his individualistic attitude.

Sex is thus presented as the central topic of the novel. And presenting it in this way is fully appropriate, for sex conveys a variety of crucial messages, as we have begun to note. We may now turn to more exquisitely linguistic matters in order to qualify the broad statement that the topic of the novel is sex, by examining the thematic structure of the first sentence.[7]

The thematic structure of the opening sentence of the novel is of vital significance. Thematic position is occupied by a prepositional phrase: "For a man of his age." This is in itself a marked choice, for the standard, or unmarked, element, the element that normally occupies thematic position, is the noun phrase acting as subject.

In addition, the prepositional phrase has been upgraded to the status of clause. Hence, technically speaking, the phrase has been 'foregrounded',[8] for the operation of upshifting increases the value of the information conveyed by the unit in question.

---

[6] Geoffrey Leech, *Principles of Pragmatics* (Burnt Mill, Harlow: Longman, 1983).

[7] By 'thematic structure' I am referring to the bipartite division of the sentence into 'theme' and 'rheme' in Prague Circle and Hallidayan terms (M.A.K. Halliday, *Functional Grammar*, [London, Arnold, 1985]). I am no longer dealing with 'topic' as a 'macrostructure' in van Dijk's terms (*Text and Context*), as the principal ideational content of a text or of a significant section of a text, as that with which the text is concerned. I am dealing, instead with what is the concern of each individual sentence. For an account of the application of functional-systemic grammar to stylistics, as well as for an account of the other theoretical frameworks employed in this article, see John Douthwaite, *Towards a Linguistic Theory of Foregrounding* (Alessandria: Edizioni dell'Orso, 2000). For a more 'traditional' account of systemic-functional grammar, see Halliday, *Functional Grammar*, and Thomas Bloor, *The Functional Analysis of English* (London, Arnold, 1997).

[8] John Douthwaite, *Towards a Linguistic Theory of Foregrounding* (Alessandria: Edizioni dell' Orso, 2000).

Now, this upshifted clause conveys a central proposition – gender. Significantly, the terrain is immediately restricted to that of the male, thereby establishing a specific point of view. In technical terms, a modalized[9] expression has been thematized to foreground focalization.

This point of view is then specified even further through two additional, hence subordinate, appositions. These appositions limit point of view to that of a male who is middle-aged and divorced. That these two facts are also important is underscored by two further instances of foregrounding: first, both appositions are phrases upshifted to the level of clause, as is the first phrase; second, the infringement of the Gricean maxim of quantity, for Coetzee could have written more simply, "For a divorced man of 52." This would have avoided promoting the phrases to clause status, and would consequently have attributed far less importance to the information conveyed by these units.

Specification through thematization, through upgrading and through apposition, has a triple function here. First it warns the reader that the text is modalized; it is positioned. This is, in fact, a covert way of undermining the character's authority, as well as of signalling the implied author's critical voice. Second, Lurie's stance will be compared and contrasted with that of other situated roles in the course of the novel – males and females of the same and of other ages and other ethnic groups. This technique, too, works to undermine Lurie's authority, his world-view. Third, it also constitutes a means of exploring the social situation at a given point in time in the society described.

The previous point brings to light one of the most important linguistic features characterizing the opening of this novel: the high number of modalizing expressions employed. Modality is one major method of conveying point of view in language. The first two-and-a-half pages of the novel contain seventy modalizing expressions (see Appendices 1–3). Only one expresses deontic modality: namely, the expression of duty, of the degree of obligation inherent in action. All the other sixty-nine modals belong to the epistemic and perception categories of modality – categories that express attitude and opinion, and the degree of confidence the speaker expresses with regard to the truth of the ideational content he is conveying.

Significantly, the first sentence contains five modal or modalizing[10] expressions: i) "for a man of his age"; ii) "fifty-two"; iii) "divorced"; iv) "problem"; v) "to his mind"; vi) "rather well." All of these items obviously fall squarely into the class of epistemic modality. (Stated differently: almost the entire sentence is modalized!)

---

[9] On modalization and its use as a means of conveying/revealing point of view, especially ideological point of view, or mind-style, see Paul Simpson, *Language, Ideology and Point of View*, (London, Routledge, 1993).

[10] It should be noted that "fifty-two" is not a modal expression as defined by the code. At a literal level, it is simply an assertion, a statement of fact. Simpson, *Language, Ideology and Point of View*, provides a comprehensive survey of codified modality. However, as Austin, Searle, Grice and others have observed, linguistic expressions may be used non-literally to produce implicatures. In this particular novel, constatives and other unmodalized linguistic items are frequently employed to modalize: that is, they imply a value-judgement, a point of view. This is the case with informing the reader of Lurie's age and marital status. Such information also helps the reader to activate schemata relating to Lurie's possible mind-set.

What effect does epistemic modality have in this sentence? Lurie's objective in employing these expressions is to exhibit confidence in his opinion. To the reader, however, they signal Lurie's smugness. More importantly, the very fact that Lurie should include epistemic modal expressions such as "for a man of his age" and "to his mind" conveys the locutionary force that he is actually only expressing an opinion. Opinions are not the same as facts. Consequently, Lurie is ironically undermining his assertion of confidence by unwittingly drawing attention to the fact that he is indeed only expressing a personal opinion, a very particular opinion at that. This, in turn, automatically makes the reader question the validity of Lurie's assertion. Again it is the infringement of the Gricean maxim of quantity that helps set up this implicature. If Lurie is certain, why should he feel the need to include phrases which necessarily decrease the degree of commitment attached to the assertion made and which puts the reader on the alert? The immediate answer is that the novel is a questioning of the whole of Lurie's stance: hence, of his past.

Stated differently, Lurie is unintentionally subverting his own discourse through the selection of content. This subversive activity concurrently unveils the implied author's stance.

Modalization and redundancy are not the only means employed to dispute Lurie's surface assertions. A third device is employed – graphological and syntactic fragmentation. The first sentence consists of six graphological units:

> // For a man of his age // fifty-two // divorced // he has // to his mind // solved the problem of sex rather well //

This is a high number of units in such a short sentence. Fragmentation is achieved through a variety of devices. First and foremost, expansion – increasing the number of lower-level units in the higher-level unit: in this case, the number of clauses in the sentence. (Here I am referring to the first three phrases which are upshifted, as the two points which follow will immediately clarify. The second synthetic alternative below furnishes further illustration of the concept I am driving at.) Second, rankshift working together with ellipsis. The first three phrases are all rankshifted up to the level of clause. Two of the rankshifted phrases appear as phrases only because of the operation of ellipsis. The second phrase eliminates the premodifier and head of the phrase, while the third phrase is, in fact, a reduced relative clause. In other words, ellipsis giving rise to rankshift, to graphologically short phrases is a deliberate operation of foregrounding. Third, redundancy means concepts are duplicated ("age" equals "fifty-two"). Fourth, two 'deviant', or non-canonical, syntactic devices have been employed concurrently. The prepositional phrase "to his mind" has been dislocated right, and out of its normal sentence-initial position. In addition, it has been placed in an unusual position along the syntagmatic axis, between the auxiliary and the lexical verb, a place which may be standardly occupied only by negators and frequency adverbs.

The sense of fragmentation – created by graphological and phonological fragmentation: note especially the deceleration and change in intonation pattern caused by the insertion of "to his mind" – and the devices employed to create this sensation may be illustrated by comparing the sentence to the two more 'normal', or 'unmarked', synthetic alternatives:

To his mind, for a man of his age, for a man of fifty-two, for a man who is divorced, he has solved the problem of sex rather well.

To his mind, for a man of fifty-two who is divorced, he has solved the problem of sex rather well.

Comparing the original with the alternatives, we find that the latter flows smoothly. Fragmentation, instead, creates a sense of interruption, a *coitus interruptus* almost, a lack of harmony which denies the easy and well-adapted existence supposedly vouchsafed by the stable solution Lurie claims, at the locutionary level, that he has achieved. In conclusion, form negates content.

Summing up, the first sentence performs three high-level operations which construct the setting of the entire novel. First, sex is announced as the main topic. Sex is, as we have seen, symbolic, for it brings out a plethora of problems, ideas, attitudes and personality-traits concerning the protagonist which will be central to the development of the entire novel.

Second, it establishes that the novel is focalized through Lurie (though confirmation of this point naturally requires a knowledge of the entire novel). Hence, the surface values and attitudes that are conveyed are Lurie's.

Third, Lurie's values and attitudes are challenged while they are being conveyed. This happens in three ways. First, and crucially in this chapter, through modalization, which leads to Lurie's producing the opposite effect of what he wishes to achieve. Second, through a variety of other linguistic devices, such as fragmentation. Third, through a contextual implicature related to Lurie's role, or professional status. Lurie is a professor of literature and communication. He is thus a master of the language. The sophisticated writing technique proves this. Yet Lurie fails to control his writing (and therefore himself) fully, and in so doing inadvertently questions his own existence.

The ultimate, and ironic, consequence of all three techniques is that Lurie unwittingly undermines his own standpoint. At the same time, the critical voice of the implied author seeps through. Finally, these techniques also uncover the voice of the author himself, for Coetzee, too, is an accomplished linguist, as the well-wrought writing demonstrates. Whether Coetzee is being critical or is self-reflexively directing irony against himself can only be considered in the light of the entire novel. What the present analysis does reveal, though, is the polyphonic nature of the text.

In conclusion, the novel sets out with a theme, a point of view, a challenge to that point of view, and with an ironic comment on a supposedly cultured and highly articulate person who in actual fact does not know what is happening to him and around him, or does not want to know.

Sentences two and three exhibit a set of 'parallel' features.

First, time occupies thematic position, but why this concept should occupy a position of importance in the two sentences is not transparent. More specifically, one asks oneself the relevance of informing the reader of why Lurie should always arrive "On Thursday afternoons" and "Punctually." Routine seems to imply the cold and mechanical, the inhuman, or non-human, nature of Lurie.

Secondly, the two sentences minutely describe mundane, almost child-like propositional content. Of what interest is it to inform the reader that Lurie presses the buzzer, unless one's normal mode of entering an apartment is by breaking down the door? Similarly, what do you usually do when someone answers your ring at the door? Make a rude noise? And when the door is opened, do you turn round and go home? As with the information supplied regarding time, the Gricean maxim of relevance seems to have been infringed. Stated differently, the information furnished is redundant. Our schemata in long-term memory would normally ensure that such information does not need to be conveyed.

Thirdly, what detail is provided is an external description of actions. No internal mental or emotional state is described.

The effect of precision of detail, of external description reinforcing the effects of third-person narration, is to imply cold, mechanical regularity. Again, the implicature is that the solution lacks emotional and psychological components.

Two further points should be noted. Only Lurie has been given voice so far. Second, sentence three has a fragmented character similar to sentence one, albeit not so extreme, for the first part of the sentence is fragmented phonologically ("punctually / at two p.m. / he") but not graphologically. Note also the less usual choice of the lexical verb "speaks" in place of the more normal "says," to draw the reader's attention to the fact that the entire sentence is foregrounded.

Sentence four is foregrounded by three mechanisms. First, its graphological brevity compared to the sentences that immediately precede and succeed it. Second, and crucially, there is the use of inversion. Thirdly, we have the connotations of servitude, of "waiting on a person."

Inversion serves two purposes. First, it bestows upon the lexical verb the status of marked theme (or 'front focus'[11]), thereby underlining the importance of the proposition it conveys (Soraya's functional subservience). Second, it concurrently places Soraya in end-focus, underlining her importance, an importance she would not be accorded were the unmarked version of the structure employed: namely, "Soraya is waiting for him at the door." Instead, what is created is a sense of expectancy, and at the 'climax' of the sentence is servile Soraya – Lurie's solution to the problem of existence.

Thus the significant symbolic propositional content (service) is placed in the two pragmatically and structurally important positions in the English sentence by deploying an emphatic construction. Coetzee could hardly do more to signal the implicature of the master–slave relationship between Lurie and Soraya.

Sentence five exploits the Gricean maxims of quantity and relevance. The main point to note is what information is included and what information is withheld. The topic is sex. This is highlighted by the two pieces of information provided about the bedroom. "Pleasant smelling" and "softly lit" make the room attractive and conducive to sex. Nothing, however, is said about the contents of the room which would indicate, for instance, Soraya's personality. The description, hence the place by logical extension, is functional to the use to which it is put. Such a use is impersonal, anonymous, as well as socially frowned-upon. This helps account for the absence of details indicating personal identity. Alliteration using the letter *s* draws attention to the functionally conducive nature of the environment:

---

[11] See Douthwaite, *Towards a Linguistic Theory of Foregrounding*.

> Punctually at two p.m. he presses the buzzer at the entrance to Windsor Mansions, speaks his name, and enters. He goes straight through to the bedroom, which is pleasant smelling and softly-lit, and undresses. Soraya emerges from the bathroom, drops her robe, slides into bed beside him. 'Have you missed me?' she asks.

Even more surprisingly, nothing is said about Soraya herself in this paragraph, either about her character or about her physical aspect (is she attractive?) – bar the colour of her skin (subtly implicated by the expression "unmarked by the sun" qualifying "her honey-brown body," S9, another unusual collocation), which makes Soraya a 'native', a 'subaltern', symbolizing another dimension of exploitation: colonial exploitation in addition to gender exploitation.

Lurie is theme and agent of S5. The lexical verbs are intransitive – no patient is required. The two actions described lead to one goal. The inclusion of the intensifying adverb "straight" underlines the single function realized by and in the room. The speed connoted by "straight," the lack of attention paid by Lurie to any other detail, the lack of any intervening episode (there is no pre-move such as a social chat and a whiskey in the living room), and the silence in which the affair is conducted, all underscore the purely functional, one-sided nature of the event.

Sentence six finally sees Soraya acting as theme – theoretically, a pragmatic status theoretically signalling importance. However, the propositional content ("emerges," "drops," "slides") instantly cancels out such importance by restricting her relevance and agency exclusively to her functional role as acted out, to boot, in classic, almost theatrical, satirical terms. Note that the alliterative *s* connoting sex continues to be adopted in the sentence, a function which is paralleled by alliterative *b* strategically underscoring location: "bathroom," "bedroom," "beside."

Sentence seven finally breaks the astonishing silence that has reigned so far – astonishing, since Lurie has been availing himself of Soraya's services for "over a year" (S12) and even claims he feels "affection" (S19) for her, though the text offers no evidence to support his claim. Surprisingly, talk is initiated by the subordinate 'partner', Soraya.

Breaking the silence deviates from the preceding co-text. In addition, successful topic initiation is one possible signal of power.[12] Hence, we might expect that some sort of change is about to take place. But no. First of all, the topic introduced remains sexual. Second, although the lexical verb "to miss" generally connotes emotion, given the lack of any human intercourse so far, Soraya's utterance may be taken as relating to the customer service-provider role. She is maintaining a façade of a purportedly intimate relationship. Third, this also explains why it is she who starts the conversation. It merely underscores her subordinate status. She is simply doing her job in order to keep her customer. Fourth, the utterance remains in tune with the short clauses characterizing most of the sentences. Fifth, the sentence is stark and isolated – stark, because it conveys only one proposition and includes no terms of endearment or reference to the participants' 'outside lives'; isolated, because it does not signal the beginning of a conversation.

---

[12] Pamela Fishman, "Interaction: the work women do," *Social Problems* 25.4: 397-406.

A final point regards layout. When a character starts talking, a new paragraph is normally begun. This generally indicates a new turn at talk or a new topic or a development of the topic introduced by the previous speaker. In this case, no new paragraph is begun, thus confirming that no change in topic has taken place. The words uttered have nothing to do with interpersonal relationships between human beings, as the verb *miss* might initially mislead one into thinking.

Lurie's reply in sentence eight is specularly formulaic. It adds nothing new, propositionally or socially. Lurie's *addendum* "all the time" ironically confirms the formulaic, hence surface nature of the words exchanged. Again, no new paragraph is begun, thereby confirming topic continuity.

The final sentence in the paragraph completes the movement initiated by the opening topic sentence with a concluding topic clause: "they make love." This topic clause is foregrounded by being 'end-focused', by having been rendered perceptually salient through the use of a semi-colon preceding it, by its brevity contrasting with the preceding two sections of the sentence (also signalled by a semi-colon), and by having third-person plural as subject in contrast to the preceding third-person singular of the three preceding clauses (two instances of parallelism ending with deviation). One might also hazard that the three sections are of decreasing length, ending in the brief climax.

"He" is in thematic position in this final sentence. "He" is also the subject of three main clauses which describe material processes in which Lurie, the master, acts upon Soraya's body. The first main clause also contains evaluative expressions denoting appreciation of Soraya's body. In this connection it is pertinent to refer to the symbolic value of Lurie's surname – "lurid."

In this connection, one might also care to note the euphemistic value of "stretches," which devalues actions such as "stroke" and "kiss," which generally have positive connotations. Indeed, one can again note the particular care taken in lexical choice – "stroke" in place of "caress," with "stroke" having connotations of violence (beating), and its collocation with animals (servants of man), extra meanings which "caress" does not possess. Such lexical choice might also be related to alliteration, with "s" and "b" again being prominent, and contrasting with the final clause.

It is perhaps significant that the most vulgar indicator of male dominance and will ("stretches her out") is 'hidden' between two clauses containing verbs with generally positive associations. This, together with the euphemistic value of the verb "stretches," shows that Lurie is trying to cover his tracks; he is playing down the starkness of reality, and his responsibility in that reality.

Significantly, the cold, detached tone of the external description rules out passion. Not even during the sexual act itself does Lurie seem to take on human characteristics. The act remains mechanical, calculated – the satisfaction of a physical need.

The final material process has both participants realizing the subject-function. Although, on a formal level, this makes them both appear as agents, equally involved, this interpretation may be countered by observing that the utterance constitutes a fixed expression in English. This deprives it of its formal syntactic value. The alternative expression "He made love" would be highly abnormal, and another alternative, "he made love to her," would change the meaning. Thus, in this final sentence, Lurie is the initiator and agent, either explicitly or implicitly, in every clause. He is the actor, the agent, the person with power. He decides what happens.

《•》

The second paragraph finally introduces Soraya, the woman. However, the description in S10 is exclusively physical. Hence, given the topic of the novel and on the basis of the Gricean maxim of relevance, yet again the information furnished is exclusively functional to Soraya's sexual role.

Now it might be objected that, bar the adjective "slim," which generally has positive connotations, and perhaps the adjective "liquid," which often has positive connotations when collocated with "eyes," all the other adjectives employed could be taken not as sexual, but quite simply as providing an objective, neutral description of Soraya, since such lexemes are not defined as evaluators by the code. However, this would leave us with the problem of the relevance of the inclusion of the description. In order to satisfy the maxim of relevance, we must therefore infer that the qualities Lurie lists signify that he finds Soraya physically attractive. In other words, these adjectives are covert modalizers conveying Lurie's positive evaluation of the woman as a physical object. Note that Lurie refrains from employing other overt evaluators, such as degree adverbs. Again, Lurie is covering his tracks.

Here, too, there is not the slightest glimmering of passion. This is confirmed by the following sentence, S11, which opens with a stark, cold, bureaucratic lexeme, "technically," unexpectedly so in the context of a 'love scene'.

The rest of sentence eleven is equally shocking. The first clause creates several implicatures. First of all, Lurie implies that Soraya is young. Second, Lurie appears to be conveying strict, conventional moral values – old men should not lie with young women – the implicature being that he is expressing a criticism of his own behaviour.

His holding a critical view of his own behaviour seems quite unwarranted by previous co-text, however, which maintains the contrary: namely, that he has solved "the problem of sex rather well."

This apparent contradiction is resolved by the second clause in S11. In terms of speech-act theory, this sentence constitutes a rebuttal of the criticism implied by the wide age-gap between the two people. Lurie is defending himself against accusations levelled against him.

One can thus discern dialogism here: Lurie is carrying on a conversation with the addressee; taken one step further, this argument indicates that we have the makings of a confessional novel, one in which Lurie does not, however, beat his breast and admit his guilt. This foreshadows the 'impeachment' scene reminiscent of the Stalinist trials and, more directly referential, of the Truth and Reconciliation Commission, where Lurie could have retained his post at the university if only he had been willing to recite the *mea culpa*. Note, again, the cold, dispassionate rationality of Lurie's rebuttal.

Sentence twelve is even more startling. At the locutionary level, the sentence merely informs the addressee that the 'relationship' is a long-standing one, especially in view of its nature. At the illocutionary level, the expression "on her books" is a quasi-bureaucratic expression creating a purely business setting. This points up the economic and exploitative aspects – sex and money as goods of exchange in a market situation. This negates the existence of any personal rapport between himself and Soraya. The relationship is a business one. The explicit, low, crude style confirms this interpretation, as does the detached evaluation of the second clause in the sentence: "he finds her entirely satisfactory." Since he pays the piper, Lurie calls the tune. Had her tune been not to his liking, Lurie would have changed musician. Soraya's subaltern status is brutally underscored.

In linguistic terms, information-sequencing juxtaposes money with physical aspect and physical performance. Juxtaposition created by information-sequencing is bolstered by information-distribution By distributing the information over the two clauses in the same sentence, but separated by a semicolon instead of rendering each independent clause as a sentence, the narrator is inviting the reader to take the two clauses as somehow conceptually related rather than independent. The narrator is thus inviting the reader to think hard about the implicature of juxtaposing money with physical aspect and physical performance. There is no hint whatsoever of any deeper personal level to the relationship. Had there been, such a deeply insulting comment would have killed this aspect dead. This will force the reader to question the assertion Lurie will make in S12 that he feels affection for Soraya.

Sentence thirteen exhibits topic-continuity. It confirms that sex is the main – indeed, the only – topic. The metaphors (the "oasis of *luxe et volupté*" in the "desert of the week") also underscore the adequacy of the solution found by Lurie, as did the comment "entirely satisfactory" in the previous sentence. The use of the metaphors, of intertextuality, and of a foreign language constitute an important rhetorical strategy here. What the sentence is in fact saying, conceptually, is that Lurie lives solely and exclusively for sexual intercourse, an act which he carries out mechanically, once a week, with a prostitute. The sadness and nihilism behind this reality are masked by the linguistic devices employed, which create indirectness and give the sentence a flavour of exoticism and high style covering the lowliness of the concept.

The most interesting aspect about S13, however, is that it is a quotation taken from Baudelaire's "L'invitation au voyage."[13] Two major points emerge from this quotation.

First, as the title of the poem suggests, whereas Lurie thinks his solution has permanently solved his problem, he is actually about to undertake a 'voyage' at Soraya's behest, for when he discovers her name and address and contacts her, violating the rules of the service offered, she immediately drops him, sending his life into an even deeper crisis than the one he fails to realize he is traversing.

Second, Baudelaire's original line reads *luxe, calme et volupté*. Symbolically, Coetzee has omitted the word *calme*. This omission performs two functions. First, it emphasizes the purely sexual nature of the relationship, with 'luxury' recalling the older meaning of 'lust', as does the adjective 'voluptuous'. Second, omitting the word "*calme*" is ironic, for the attitude conveyed by the content and style of the language is intended to represent a state of calmness which Lurie's supposedly optimal solution has created for him. But this vaunted state of tranquillity is about to be shattered and

---

[13] Baudelaire, "L'invitation au voyage," *Les Fleurs du Mal*, LIII.

Lurie's life about to be tossed and turned on the high seas of a changing (South African) environment.

In conclusion, the second paragraph started out with a description of Soraya, creating the expectation that perhaps the spotlight would be turned on her. Instead, the discourse remained fixedly in the hands of and about Lurie himself.

⟨⟨•⟩⟩

Like the second, the third paragraph also opens with Soraya. Unlike the second paragraph, promises appear to be kept this time, for all five sentences are indeed about Soraya. Furthermore, she is considered not simply from a sexual angle, but from a more personal angle, since the moral opinions she expresses are an indication of her character, as is the quality of being "docile." Or so it would seem, at first reading.

To begin with, the theme of S14 (in the Hallidayan sense of the term) is "in bed." As soon as things appear to be changing, back we go to the old, well-trodden ways. Furthermore, a character trait – "effusiveness" – is limited to the sexual sphere by the theme of the sentence.

We might also be led into believing that Lurie is angry or displeased at her lack of passion, or that he is understanding with her because of this 'fault' of hers, forgiving her lack of passion, given that 'passion'[14] is what Lurie presumably pays for.

S15 confirms the character-trait asserted in S14. Indeed, S15 is redundant, inasmuch as a 'quiet temperament' is externalized in 'non-effusive' behaviour. Furthermore, the quality "quiet" is repeated in the sentence. Soraya really is quiet, we conclude.

Yes, at a literal level. But we must not forget that the entire novel is focalized through Lurie. The repetition of the adjective "quiet" and the deployment of the expression "in fact" are indicators of a conversational, or dialogic, text. Thus, if we now take the unusual repetition of "quiet" together with the adjective it appears with – "docile" – then another hypothesis may be formed: Soraya is "quiet" and, above all, "docile" (above all, for the term occupies end-focus), and, remembering that Lurie is divorced and is paying for Soraya's special subaltern services and enjoys them, then it may be hypothesized that Soraya's not being effusive is a result of Lurie's own behavioural demands – recalling the concept that he who pays the piper calls the tune. An alternative explanation would not change the basic situation: Lurie has gone through several women, and he finally finds the one who fits his needs. The key point, one that all the preceding utterances lead the reader to expect, is that Lurie is the dominant party. His will be done.

S16 criticizes Soraya's 'moralistic' attitude through the deployment of one of the most important explicit modalizing expressions in the passage – "surprisingly." The next two sentences furnish concrete exemplifications of Soraya's moralizing. The paragraph ends with a repetition of Lurie's critical attitude. The sarcasm of his stance in

---

[14] It is interesting to note that the novel has a close intertextual relationship with the Bible, to which it almost 'writes back', in one sense, for the novel may be said to recount the 'passion of Lurie', who, though not an antichrist, is nevertheless an anti-hero. Intertextuality, in this instance, is thus ironic. Johan Jacobs pointed out to me that *Disgrace*, the title itself, is to be intended in its biblical sense, over and above its literal meaning.

S18, conveyed by the foregrounding operation of fronting the direct object realized by the finite clause ("How she reconciles her opinions with her line of business"), ironically turns against him.

Lying below the surface of Lurie's attack on Soraya is the attitude that Soraya's being a prostitute disqualifies her from the right to hold moral opinions.

In this way, Lurie quite clearly, if indirectly, reveals his superior, white, male stance, for Soraya is a female and non-white ("her honey-brown body, unmarked by the sun" – S9). Inferiors (prostitutes, females, coloured people), he implies, have no human rights.

Not "surprisingly," what Lurie fails to consider is how a person who avails himself of the services of a prostitute should be judged. By his omission, Lurie is implying that no iniquity is ascribable to the client. Apart from Lurie's tainted logic, his stance seems, ironically, most unfair when we consider that Lurie uses prostitution as a means of escaping the world, while Soraya is compelled to engage in immoral activity by historico-socio-economic circumstances (feeding her children). Lurie's implied virtuosity is self-contradictory. Once more he gives himself away.

The final observation about this paragraph is that it conveys Lurie's state of mental unbalance. My employing the blasphemous expression 'His will be done' earlier was a deliberate reference to Lurie's madness. For Lurie does dispose of Soraya just as he wishes. The entire analysis so far aims at establishing precisely this point. He is judge and jury, he is God on earth, or in South Africa.

The final sentences I quote, constituting the beginning of the fourth paragraph, confirms this point. The point of view is Lurie's. The stance is that of an absolute monarch. The logic is insane.

《•》

S19 expresses a value-judgement, inasmuch as "affection" growing in a person is a positive reaction to a real-life experience. The real pity is that what Lurie has grown fond of is not Soraya, the person, or woman even, but Soraya the identity-less prostitute who serves her master well. For not once does he acknowledge her as a person. Note that the logic of the sentence implies that the second his pleasure fails, he will drop Soraya, for there is nothing else in their relationship.

S20 contains two modalizing expressions – "to some degree" and "he believes." The operation here is exactly the same as that described for S1.

Where Lurie thinks he is being cautious, non-committal[15] and realistic (for, after all, Soraya is a prostitute and she herself will not wish to enter into a close relationship with her clients), the expression "to some degree" backfires by downgrading the value-judgement.

Similarly, "he believes" is ironic, for it underlines the fact that it is only Lurie that believes, not Soraya. He is deluding himself. Stated differently, his reality-principle is gravely unreal.

---

[15] Since the manner maxim is flouted by the vagueness of the quantifier.

S21 continues in Lurie's perverse logic. Given the low aspirations he has set himself, as a consequence of the limits expressed in the opening sentence of the novel, affection is the most he hopes for. What he fails to realize, of course, is that what he gets from Soraya is not affection at all. And not simply because he pays for sex, but, crucially, because he does not give her anything, bar money. There is not one sentence in the opening chapter where Lurie actually 'gives' something to Soraya, in the humanist or Christian sense of the word. His failure to realize this is tragic, especially so, given his high level of education – a university professor, at the personal level, and as a colonizing white, at the level of postcolonial analysis.

This is underscored by the total madness of the final sentence quoted. Their "beginnings" are not "unpromising" – for him – the white, male professor in South Africa. They are for Soraya, the coloured, female native. He has been "lucky," because she has solved his problems for him by making no demands on his psyche and on his emotions. She does what he wants. He can act out his male, colonial fantasies. It is difficult to understand where her luck lies, unless, of course, it lies in the money she gets for giving away her body and repressing her personality in order to be able to look after her children.

One final, general linguistic comment will serve to take the discussion to a more general level.

The third-person narrative could be written as first-person narration without having to make many or radical changes to the text. Thus, what is superficially heterodiegetic narration is, in deep structure, homodiegetic.

The effect of transferring to third person what it would be natural to recount in the first person is to achieve a sense of distance. David distances himself from his story.

David's distancing himself from the story has four consequences. First, it helps create the impression of cold calculation, of rationality, of a lack of emotion, of an absence of human values. The only value expressed is smug self-satisfaction and the narrator's personal desires. Second, the previous operation helps David absolve himself of any guilt he might secretly feel. It helps him to avoid facing facts and thinking about change. Third, it helps to create the sense of void, that sense of void that lies at the core of his existence and that is aptly and succinctly symbolized by his having selected a purely depersonalized, merchandized physical act, one where there is no human exchange, but merely one-sided taking, as the topic to convey his world-view.

Fourthly, in so doing, however, David also distances the reader from him. The reader feels the void. This alienates him and influences his interpretation, his judgement of David.

3. Projections

My analysis of the opening chapter has concentrated on the linguistic devices Coetzee employs to achieve his objectives. What, on the surface, appears to be simple writing masks a highly sophisticated and self-conscious technique conveying complex, indirect, and sometimes ambiguous messages.

However, the linguistic approach serves a second, indirect, objective, that of identifying some of the major themes of the novel.

From the preceding analysis, I believe the novel may be read on at least four levels. First, it is the story of an individual, David Lurie. Second, a gendered interpretation may be offered – David is the typical male chauvinist, a breed that is moving slowly towards extinction, perhaps. Third, the novel conveys the condition of modern or postmodern man (in the generic rather than gendered sense of the word). Finally, a postcolonial reading may be placed on the novel – Lurie as the symbol of the white colonialist, or, more narrowly, the white colonialist in South Africa, another dying breed, perhaps.

Clearly, such themes are both broad and profound. Furthermore, the complexity, as well as constituting part of the greatness of the novel, lies in the important fact that the four levels are not distinct, but merge into one another. The most cogent instantiation is that the theme of gender relations is intimately connected with that of colonialism, almost to the point of being indistinguishable from it.

The overlap, however, is not perfect. Not all of the 'facts' fit on all four planes. This, I would argue, is one source of the (limited degree of) ambiguity that characterizes the novel, an ambiguity which is significant because it is in part deliberate.

The breadth and complexity of the novel do not allow me to work out my interpretations. My objective, therefore, is to relate some of my previous comments to these four readings in a schematic fashion to show how the opening chapter foreshadows the rest of the novel.

The first level of reading is that of Lurie as a person. The key feature here is Lurie's incapacity to develop any stable relationships – superficial or profound, intellectual or emotional – with other people in any role whatsoever, whether it be as husband, as father, as friend, as acquaintance, as teacher, or as citizen. At the centre of this incapacity lies void, the central aspect of the novel.

Void characterizes all four levels of interpretation. The fact that Lurie's aspirations as expressed in the first sentence are low shows he is only exploiting others in an attempt to fill the void of his own existence. Stated differently, the cost of colonization is alienation and isolation, the Conradian void Watson talks about. For Lurie does not give, he only takes.

Void is symbolically conveyed, in the first instance, by sex. Sex is life for Lurie. However, as we have seen, Lurie's engagement in sex merely externalizes his alienated and isolated existence, for sex is a purely physical and individualistic experience for Lurie. His sexual relationships with Melanie and with his first wife bear this out. Here is Lurie's comment on his 'deep' relationship with his ex-wife:

> His best memories are still of their first months together: steamy nights in Durban, sheets damp with perspiration, Rosalind's long, pale body thrashing this way and that in the throes of a pleasure that was hard to tell from pain. Two sensualists: that was what held them together, while it lasted. (187)[16]

---

[16] For a brief commentary on this passage, see Douthwaite, *Towards a Linguistic Theory of Foregrounding*, 213–15.

Such a state of alienation takes us to interpretation three, Lurie as the symbol of the modern condition of man.[17]

Secondly, modalization highlights void from the very first sentence of the novel by subverting the face Lurie presents to the world and to himself. Such subversion is powerful because it is inadvertent on Lurie's part. Furthermore, it introduces the dissenting voice of the (implied) author. Indeed, the questioning set up in the very first sentence suggests universality rather than particularism.

Thirdly, even the single details such as living on a farm and rape indicate universality, for details such as these have Southern Africa as the real-world referential framework. And the university inquiry committee calls up both Stalinist purge trials and the Truth and Reconciliation Commission.

Finally, the first chapter ends with a crisis. This crisis, though specific in the novel, clearly signals the postcolonial level of interpretation, for post-apartheid South Africa with its new social relationships is clearly the referent.

In this sphere, it is significant that it is Soraya the prostitute who rebels against Lurie, the white male colonizer. We thus enter the second level of interpretation, that of gender relations. That the question of gender is broached is shown by the fact that all of Lurie's relationships with all (unrelated) females save one are of the same nature, as the quotation above demonstrates.

However, gender is inseparable from colonialism in this novel, because both are products of white male hegemony. The trope of sexual penetration and domination as economic penetration and domination in non-colonial as well as colonial contexts is as old as man. It is no coincidence that the first two relationships with women described in the novel may be assimilated to rape – the rape of Africa.

Lurie's relationship with Soraya is inhuman, unfeeling, despite his (ironic) love of the Romantic poets. It is pure male, white exploitation – exploitation of colony, not just of woman. This is why the first chapter is crucial. It marks the end of the old dispensation.

However, Soraya rebels only when Lurie tries to make his possession of her complete – her affection and personality as well as her body. Lurie's exploitation of his wife, described later, widens the framework to include the dual subaltern status of women – slaves to men as well as to whites.

It is also significant that Soraya never speaks in the initial scene, except to utter (untrue) role-related formulaic expressions. She is given voice only *after* her rebellion – an action – a clear signal that she was allowed no voice before that, despite Lurie's assurances to the contrary.

It is another irony of the book that it is the subaltern female who produces the greatest flame of hope in the novel, a flame that flickers rather than blazing.

One final observation returns us to what is apparently an individual detail – the opening phrase: "For a man of his age, fifty-two, divorced." Such an expression would appear to fit squarely into the category of the particularistic. However, it situates the novel historically, as the end of apartheid.

---

[17] 'Good' relationships in the novel are virtually non-existent, and what good there is, is highly circumscribed. However, this level of interpretation merges into the fourth level of interpretation.

The way the crisis is met (how men and women will react, though the emphasis is on the symbolic protagonist) is the subject of the novel. The first chapter sets the scene – personal, social and historical – that will then be worked out on the various levels.

There is one final point I need to at least touch on – the negativity stemming from the void, and the ambiguity connected with this negativity. Such ambiguity has even led to interpretations of non-referentiality and of a postmodernist reflexivity which, in the act of giving voice to the subaltern, actually deprives the subaltern of all opportunity to really reclaiming identity and rights.[18] While it is true that Coetzee works his novels out through indirectness, it is not true, at least of *Disgrace*, that referentiality is a myth and that the disempowerment of the subjected is the result of Coetzee's strategy of silence.

I would see alienation and disempowerment more as a general phenomenon, affecting both subjugator and subjugated. Ambiguity is a result of a series of factors. First, life is a complex business. Second, it is not the task of literature to simplify, or to provide ready-made solutions. Third, South Africa is one of the many countries in which the political situation is particularly turbulent, and where the future appears bleak to many. Finally, no one can know what the future holds. Factors of this type, together with the madness and cruelty that man is capable of, as Coetzee has documented in previous novels, lead to Coetzee's leaving the ending an open one. There is no victory in *Disgrace*, despite its apparently hopeful ending, for the future remains unknown, to be constructed, in a difficult situation; so difficult that the chances of success are not especially high. Lucy's stance perhaps best embodies this message, rather than that of Lurie's apparent abandoning of his old self. She has decided to accept, whatever happens, a stance one feels Lurie has not offered sufficient evidence of being capable of.[19]

---

[18] Benita Parry, "Speech and Silence in the Fictions of J.M. Coetzee," in *Critical Perspectives on J.M. Coetzee*, 37–65.

[19] Since submitting this essay, John Douthwaite has published a further development of his ideas entitled "Melanie: Voice and its Suppression in J.M. Coetzee's *Disgrace*," in *Current Writing* 13.1 (2001): 130–62 (Eds.).

WORKS CITED

Baudelaire, Charles. "L'invitation au voyage" *Les Fleurs du Mal*, LIII, in *Œuvres complètes* (Bibliothèque de la Pléiade; Paris: Gallimard, 1961): 51–52.

Coetzee, J.M. *Disgrace* (London: Secker & Warburg, 1999).

Douthwaite, John. *Towards a Linguistic Theory of Foregrounding* (Alessandria: Edizioni dell'Orso, 2000).

Fishman, Pamela. "Interaction: the work women do," *Social Problems* 25.4 (): 397–406.

Grice, H.P. *Studies in the Way of Words* (Cambridge MA: Harvard UP, 1989).

Halliday, M.A.K. *Functional Grammar* (London: Arnold, 1985).

Leech, Geoffrey. *Principles of Pragmatics* (Burnt Mill, Harlow: Longman, 1983).

Parry, Benita. "Speech and Silence in the Fictions of J.M. Coetzee," in *Critical Perspectives on J.M. Coetzee* ed. Graham Huggan & Stephen Watson (Basingstoke: Macmillan, 1996): 37–65.

Simpson, Paul. *Language, Ideology and Point of View* (London: Routledge, 1993).

van Dijk, Teun. *Text and Context. Explorations in the Semantics and Pragmatics of Discourse* (Burnt Mill, Harlow: Longman, 1977).

《●》

APPENDIX 1
Markers of Modality[20]

	MARKER	EXAMPLES
1	modal auxiliaries (i.e. confidence or caution, obligation or commitment)	might, could, must, should
2	modal adverbs (or sentence adverbs)	certainly, probably, perhaps, surely, arguably, it is certain that …
3	evaluative adjectives and adverbs	lucky, luckily, regrettably, excellent, miserable, clear, obvious, uncertain
4	verbs of knowledge, prediction and seem, believe, guess, foresee, approve, evaluation (*verba sentiendi*)	like, dislike, assume, suppose, understand, feel
5	generic sentences	generalized propositions claiming universal truth and usually cast in a syntax reminiscent of proverbs or scientific laws: e.g. 1) At sixteen, the mind that has the strongest affinity for fact cannot escape the illusion and self-flattery (*The Mill on the Floss*) 2) It is a truth universally acknowledged, that a single man in possession of a good fortune, must be in want of a wife (*Pride and Prejudice*)
6	categorical assertions	you are right

---

[20] Adapted from Paul Simpson, *Language, Ideology and Point of View.*

APPENDIX 2
Modal Systems in English (adapted from Simpson 1993)

deontic	duty – the speaker's attitude to the degree of obligation attaching to the performance of an action; ranges from requirement to obligation; e.g., *you may leave; you should leave; you must leave*
boulomaic	desire; e.g., *I hope you will leave; I wish you'd leave; I regret that you are leaving*
epistemic	the speaker's confidence or lack of confidence in the truth of a proposition expressed; opinion, attitude to "fact" or "reality", belief; e.g., *you could be right, you may be right, you must be right, [you are right]*
perception	degree of commitment to the truth of a proposition is predicated on some reference to human perception; e.g., *It's clear you are right; it appears you are right; I feel you are right*

APPENDIX 3
Modality Markers in the Opening Section of *Disgrace*

1. *For a man of his age, fifty-two, divorced,* he has, *to his mind,* solved the *problem* of sex *rather well.*
2. The bedroom, which is *pleasant smelling* and *softly-lit*
3. He *strokes* her *honey-brown* body, *unmarked* by the sun
4. Soraya is *tall* and *slim,* with *long black hair* and *dark, liquid eyes.*
5. *Technically* he is old *enough* to be her father. He *finds* her *entirely satisfactory*
6. In bed, Soraya is *not effusive*
7. Her temperament is *in fact rather quiet, quiet* and *docile*
8. She is *surprisingly moralistic*
9. His *pleasure* is *unfailing*
10. An *affection* has grown up in him for her.
11. *To some degree,* he *believes,* this *affection* is reciprocated.
12. *Affection may not* be *love,* but it is *at least* its cousin
13. Given their *uncompromising* beginnings, they have been *lucky,* the two of them
14. His sentiments are, he is *aware, complacent, even uxorious*
15. It *seems a pity* that Discreet Escorts *should* get *so much.*
16. He *would like* to spend an evening with her, *perhaps* even a whole night. But not the morning after.
17. Is he *happy?* By *most* measurements, yes, he *believes* he is.
18. Intercourse between Soraya and himself *must be,* he *imagines,* rather like the copulation of snakes.
19. Yet at the level of temperament her *affinity* with him *can surely not* be *feigned*
20. She *knows* the facts of his life. She has heard the stories of his two marriages, *knows* about his daughter and his daughter's ups and downs. She *knows* many of his opinions.
21. It *may be* that she is not a professional *at all.* She *may work* for the agency *only* one or two afternoons a week ...
22. That would be unusual for a Muslim, but all things are possible these days (2 generic sentences).

《•》

Unruly Subjects in Southern African Writing

DOROTHY DRIVER

ONTEMPORARY ENGLISH SOUTHERN AFRICAN writers are faced with the task of writing a new literature in a language inherited from an oppressive colonial and patriarchal past.

Bessie Head's second published novel, *Maru*, strove in the 1970s to evade the hierarchies and exclusions of the racism and sexism which made up contemporary notions of individual and national identity. The novel used artwork to create a consciousness, which we can perhaps call feminine, beyond such hegemonic control. The "language of national belonging comes laden with atavistic apologues," says Homi Bhabha[1]; the language of "identity" is similarly laden. Head's writing had to wriggle itself loose from a novelistic tradition obsessively concerned with romantic love not just as the true destiny for women but also as the site of women's proper representation. It had also to deal with a more localized tradition of colonial racist writing and its response in protest writing, both of which saw race in exclusionary terms and often deployed women as mediators between different racial groups. In *Maru*, Head produced an intricate, ironic juxtapositioning of romantic and political plotting which not only addresses the ways in which nationalism has used women and marginalized their aspirations (so that sexual liberation is always said to have to come after national liberation), but also shows how the conventional dependence of the novelistic tradition on conceptualizations of romantic love is fundamentally hostile to the kind of creativity that can simultaneously subvert and transcend the combined subjectifications demanded by racism and sexism. In that deceptively simple sentence, "I am a Masarwa," the female protagonist breaks the Tswana taboo on Masarwa speaking and – given her figurative associations with South African "coloureds", immigrant Chinese, and Indian "untouchables" – re-names Masarwa-ness, including in it "a little bit of everything." Head's novel does not discard ethnic identity but deftly negotiates it, making nonsense of the exclusionary practice of contemporary nationalisms, yet simultaneously asserting a complex ethnic basis from which subjectivity might be claimed.

The novel offers other re-conceptualizations. A dislodgement of the binarisms of "animal" and "human," and "human" and "divine," manifests itself in various of Mar-

---

[1] Homi K. Bhabha, *The Location of Culture* (London: Routledge, 1994): 141.

garet's paintings – most notably, those of the Masarwa villagers and of the protagonist's royal Tswana friend, Dikeledi – as well as in the verbal and visual representations of the goats, totemic creatures for the Masarwa. The antics of the kid-goat which
watches while she paints, and whose "windscreen-wiper" of a tail recalls Margaret's
feverish paintbrush, also represent this dislodgement. However, on her entry into the
romantic plot, Margaret herself becomes "woman," first compelled by the onrush of a
possessive love she has not hitherto experienced, and then drawn into marriage. With
this romantic representation, Margaret's creative energy is snapped. At the story's end,
which Head gives as the novel's prolepsis, Margaret is the victim of her husband's
moods; she lacks her own will, and loses all access to her dreams. Earlier, the novel
names her as Maru's "experiment" in racial reform, much as she had been with her
white missionary foster-mother, who enacted through the foster-daughter her own
missionary zeal. Once again, Margaret is subjected to another's plans and desires.

Even Margaret's unconscious is now figured as a site of male domination. She lives,
as the text puts it, in one room inhabited by her husband, but dreams of another room
inhabited by the man she truly loves. Not even this second room – her unconscious –
can signify escape from male domination, since it is jealously watched over by her
husband, seems to be his rather than her construction, and, in any case, it also issues
from the kind of possessive and exclusionary love that the text was elsewhere quietly
and unlawfully refusing. Unlike the Masarwa, then, who are freed from their dark, airless room by Margaret's representations of them in her paintings and through her marriage into Tswana royalty, Margaret cannot get out of her dark, airless room – not, at
least, at the level of plot. However, the point of the novel is the freedom offered in the
act of writing.

Are metaphors of re-birth appropriate for our new century? If so, it is less the birth
of a new mode of identity we should celebrate – new in the sense of a heterogeneous
subject position liberated from the totalizing categories of the past – than the opening
up of strategies of writing. Breaking free of the demands of gendered, ethnic and
national 'identity', disrupting the binaries not just of 'animal' and 'human', and
'human' and 'divine', but also of 'individual' and 'nation', and of 'female' and 'male',
Margaret's painting celebrates the indefinable or unfixed. Flouting the practices of
exclusion and repression, her novel likewise gestures towards reconstructing a world
infused both by a patriarchal ancestral past and modernity's various dominations. Her
texts turn aside from the numbing focus on character, role model and stereotype in-
cumbent on the South African 'protest' tradition, and inaugurate a trend taken up, in
South African writing, by Zoë Wicomb's fiction most notably. Since connections between Head and Wicomb have been discussed elsewhere,[2] it is now worth looking at
another fictional pairing for their literariness; that is, for their interest in fiction as writing rather than simply as social document, and for their engagement with writing
(rather than event) as an escape from hegemonic control.

As the title indicates, Tsitsi Dangarembga's novel *Nervous Conditions* examines
(after Frantz Fanon) the effects of colonialist conceptualizations of the 'native', but it

---

[2] See my essay "Transformation Through Art: Writing, Representation and Subjectivity in Recent South African Fiction," *World Literature Today* 70.1 (1996): 45–52.

expands the discussion to include the impact of both Shona patriarchy and Christian colonial patriarchy on Shona women and men living in what was then Rhodesia. Calling its characters "reflections," the novel makes a difference between some characters' entrapment in local and imported patriarchal formations, and others' escape. Even as it charts 'escape', the text subtly preserves in this notion the cultural anxiety, ambivalence, contradiction and political complicity that a Fanonesque rebellion would wish to expunge. The novel's pragmatic postcolonial solution depends explicitly on what it calls an "encompassing expansion," which we might think of as a local version of (and precursor to) Bhabha's "hybridity," and – at least in part – as an articulation of what so interested Head as well: the creative combination of African and European symbolic traditions. Like Bhabha, Dangarembga sees hybridity not as an achieved state so much as an ongoing process; this she represents through a creative use of the novelistic convention of the *doppelgänger* or 'double', where the relation between self and other, or the self and its double, is chiastic rather than oppositional. Her two major characters, Nyasha and Tambudzai, are sometimes opposed, but intimately connected nonetheless in an unstable relation which explicitly grounds the success of Tambudzai's escape in Nyasha's failure. This suggests the continuing co-implication of escape and entrapment, escape leading inevitably into new entrapments from which must be forged another escape. For Dangarembga, then, the Zimbabwean human subject, poised at the point of Zimbabwean independence, remains invested in 'nervous conditions'. One positive aspect of this investment is a canny marginality, a kind of double vision, offered through the protagonist's recognition of her marginal class, race and gender positions, which allows her to question all she aspires to, and all that has made her what she is.

《●》

Head's novel proposes artwork as the space where new forms of identification and new angles of vision might emerge. At the level of plot, however, a struggle for freedom is (once again) just beginning. Dangarembga's novel foregrounds writing, through its use of a self-conscious first-person narrator who later writes the book, and also through the chiastic connection between the two characters, so that any "illusion of reality" they impart is superseded by their being signs on a page. The novel's lack of closure emphasizes the unstable relation between the character who escapes and the one who does not, and points determinedly to the intervening and constitutive act of writing not simply as triumph (in that education is achieved, and a book is written) but also as the means whereby any stability or maturity of perspective achieved by the narrator-protagonist must remain troubled. Tambudzai continues to be haunted by her cousin's total slide into a hysteria she herself somehow managed to maintain at the level of strategy, and by her mother's recriminations about cultural aphasia. These constitute important moments of self-interrogation, worked into the novel on the level of event.

However, as if not quite content with Dangarembga's production of a cultural hybridity which remains 'nervous', and which (self-interrogation notwithstanding) speaks very much from the position of the missionary educated woman reaching back to a precolonial culture fairly remote from her, Yvonne Vera's *Under the Tongue* is

altogether more assertive. Offering a powerful critique of current notions of the libera-
tory event, while at the same time deftly defining writing and speaking as both source
and product of an altogether more enduring liberation, Vera's novel moves away from
Dangarembga's dualistic patternings of character and plot into the 'third space' of
writing (Bhabha), a space which Dangarembga has indeed started to offer but which
she does not explore. For Vera, writing itself becomes event, especially insofar as it
emerges from a consciousness corrective of the Shona mythological system. *Under the
Tongue* focuses much more positively than does *Nervous Conditions* on the connections between grandmother, mother and (grand)daughter, thus shifting the binarisms of
'past' versus 'present', 'tradition' versus 'modernity', and 'orality' versus 'writing'.
Taking these three figures to signify a national past, present and future, I argue that
they are so intertwined and mutually constitutive that readers are invited to see in the
interactions between them a newly articulated and previously un-authorized subject-
position readily conceptualized as an act of speech in which both orality and writing
are present. By means of this act of speech/writing, the novel retrieves a memory of the
past which has been suppressed through male domination, and expunged moreover
from the male imagination.

The word that lies under the tongue is a word not used by the text but everywhere
alluded to: the rape of a young girl by her father. The rape's cosmological figuration
suggests that this rape is symptomatic of an ancestral violence against women. When
Muroyiwa rapes his daughter, he steals "the light of the moon and its promises of
birth."[3] The now muted daughter thinks to herself, "I search for the moon which has
left the sky. Memory has left the sky" (4). "Africa," says Vera, "has erred in its memory."[4] The Shona symbolic system, she suggests, has been hijacked by men. Here *Under
the Tongue* echoes a recent account of the religious thinking behind the liberation war,
which claims that male understanding of the relations between the ancestors, the
people and the land ruptures women's relations to the ancestors and the land.[5] In Shona
cosmology this male/female power struggle presents itself through the gendered symbolism of lightning, the moon, and rain, all of which are central to *Under the Tongue*.

Shona spokespeople have it that female sexual power is associated not with descent
or generation but with affinity, or the expansion of kinship, brought about when men
marry women from other family lines. Male sexual power, in contrast, is associated
with patrilineal descent. Lightning is a symbol for this descent. The Shona word
kupenya covers both moon and lightning, and lightning's masculine association thus
stands as an effective denial of the female power of the moon. The moon's potential as
symbol of biological reproduction has been stolen, says Lan (98). Hence, then, the
novel's statement, Father has stolen "the light of the moon" (31), or – in the first
description of the rape – Father whispers an embrace of lightning. [...] Lightning finds

---

[3] Yvonne Vera, *Under the Tongue* (Harare: Baobab, 1996): 31. Further page references are in
the main text.

[4] "Preface" to *Opening Spaces: An Anthology of African Women's Writing* (Harare: Baobab &
Oxford: Heinemann, 1999): 3.

[5] See David Lan, *Guns and Rain: Guerrillas and Spirit Mediums in Zimbabwe* (London: James
Currey; Berkeley: U of California P, 1985).

me, embraces the moon, finds me fallen from the sky" (3). It is the task of this novel to give back to women the symbol of the moon.

In Shona mythology, the absence or marginality of women "implies that each royal lineage is able to produce its own rain with no help from wives" or those connected only through marriage.[6] The question "who owns the land?" has always meant those whose ancestors bring the rain and hence control its fertility.[7] Remembering the power of the moon, the grandmother and granddaughter remember also the river; to remember the river is to remember that rain, claimed by men to symbolize male sexual power in generation or descent, comes as much from the earth as from the sky (as in rituals of possession where men connect with the ancestors who bring the rain). Thus women re-enter the spiritual world.

Through its retrieval of memory, *Under the Tongue* reaches for a way to bring to writing a re-mythicized relation between women and the land, women and the ancestors, women and spirituality, so that consciousness itself is reformed. Retrieving the memory of the river is to retrieve the memory of the rape, and vice versa. "A memory is a mouth with which to begin" (42); "My hands touch the river which grows from inside my mouth" (41).

In other ways, too, Vera's novel addresses the corruption of Zimbabwean consciousness. Land-ownership, for instance, is a European conception, but it was – says Vera – the basis on which the second Chimurenga was fought: "those who were fighting in the bush were fighting to enter the white man's world, not to preserve their own."[8] Through a set of echoes and incremental repetitions in its figurative language, the novel brilliantly connects land ownership, warfare, retributive murder, mining, and rape, and then also associates with such activities a certain kind of writing, which the novel opposes through its own kind, carried forward in the memory of women.

In reincorporating women's voices and women's history into a patriarchal Shona ancestral religion, the novel foregrounds the importance of remembering repressed loss, sorrow and pain. Crucially, however, these are not just the provenance of women, for Vera courageously includes among the wounded even the father-rapist whose narrative fragments deploy the same metaphors of vulnerability as those relating to the raped daughter. Vera's figurative language recognizes the Zimbabwean mine-worker as not now rapist but raped, so that the gender binarisms used elsewhere in the novel are here overturned, and the psychic and social identifications that make up human subjectivities are freed from the crudities of gender constraints. Solidarity with men returning from the war depends not on women's capacity to forget male crimes against women but on their remembering pain, some caused by – and some shared with – their men. For Vera, men have the habit of repressing pain (burning it up is one of her metaphors here) and their compensation is violence, often against women. Pain needs to be spoken if memory is to be restored. Restoring women to speech is to restore speech itself, and by extension, writing.

---

[6] Lan, *Guns and Rain*, 98.

[7] Lan, *Guns and Rain*, 98.

[8] Vera, "Ancestral Links," in *Why Don't You Carve Other Animals?* (Harare: Baobab, 1994): 79–87.

As in the case of the two other novels discussed, it is writing, and not speaking, which affords what Vera calls "a moment of intervention" for women. In the real world, says Vera, women's speech is often blocked by "interruption" and "shocked reaction," and speaking is "still difficult to negotiate."[9] The book, in contrast, "retains its autonomy."[10] Vera's book offers a blend of writing and orality, a writing that restores the magic of embodied speech, and of the letter's physicality. Thus Zhizha experiences the presence and the mystery of the Singer sewing machine:

> Across the bottom of the large black handle, in gold: S i n g e r. Sometimes I remove the cover very cautiously, my heart beating rapidly: S i n g e r. I run outside.[11]

When Zhizha's mother teaches her to spell, "[t]he letters flow from me to mother." Her words flow to the reader too, who slowly develops (as in the reading of poetry) an understanding of the specific symbolic order being offered through its combination of symbolisms from a Shona oral ancestral culture and a European tradition, each one feeding into the other, as in *Maru* and *Nervous Conditions*, yet with the added emphasis, here, on the ethical contribution made by the indigenous world – once it has been reconstructed by women. Head hints at such a feminist intervention in her cosmological patterning, in that Margaret breaks up the primary homoerotic relation between the two royal men. Dangarembga, very differently, hints at it too, in the strategies of survival her women deploy. Yet it is Vera's novel that brings to fruition these hints about women's tongues and women's writing as regenerative acts, as acts which turn a male-dominated symbolic system into a world where memory, speech, and pain are shared, and where the old race and gender divisions no longer reign.

Note

My thanks to the National Research Foundation for providing some of the funding that made it possible for me to deliver the paper on which this essay is based. My thanks also to Meg Samuelson for alerting me to David Lan's book *Guns and Rain*, and also for her invaluable close reading of *Under the Tongue*.

---

[9] Vera's refusal to romanticize orality runs contrary to some recent critical essays, e.g., one on African women's writing by Cynthia Ward: "Bound to Matter: The Father's Pen and Mother Tongues," in *The Politics of (M)Othering: Womanhood, Identity, and Resistance in African Literature*, ed. Obioma Nnaemeka (London: Routledge, 1997): 114–29. Instead, for Vera, it is writing that offers reciprocity and democracy.

[10] Vera, "Preface," 3.

[11] Vera, *Under the Tongue* (Harare: Baobab, 1996): 25.

WORKS CITED

Bhabha, Homi K. *The Location of Culture* (London: Routledge, 1994).

Head, Bessie. *Maru* (London: Heinemann, 1971).

Dangarembga, Tsitsi. *Nervous Conditions* (London: The Women's Press, 1988).

Driver, Dorothy. "Transformation through Art: Writing, Representation, and Subjectivity in Recent South African Fiction," *World Literature Today* 70.1 (1996): 45–52.

Hunter, Eva. "'Shaping the Truth of the Struggle': An Interview with Yvonne Vera," *Current Writing* 10.1 (1998): 75–86.

Lan, David. *Guns and Rain: Guerrillas and Spirit Mediums in Zimbabwe* (London: James Currey; Berkeley: U of California P, 1985).

Samuelson, Meg. "Grandmother Says We Choose Words, Not Silence: Trauma, Memory and Voice in the Writings of Yvonne Vera" (unpublished MA thesis. University of Leeds, May 1999).

Vera, Yvonne. "Ancestral Links," in Vera, *Why Don't You Carve Other Animals* (Harare: Baobab, 1994): 79–87.

——. "Preface" to *Opening Spaces: An Anthology of African Women's Writing* (Harare: Baobab / Oxford: Heinemann, 1999): 1–5.

——. *Under the Tongue* (Harare: Baobab, 1996).

Ward, Cynthia. "Bound to Matter: The Father's Pen and Mother Tongues," in *The Politics of (M)Othering: Womanhood, Identity, and Resistance in African Literature*, ed. Obioma Nnaemeka (London: Routledge, 1997): 114–29.

《●》

The White Tribe
The Afrikaner in the Novels of J.M. Coetzee

JOHN GAMGEE

A LTHOUGH J.M. COETZEE'S FICTION cannot be reduced to works about South Africa, most of his stories are set in that country.[1] In addition, although one must be careful not to pigeon-hole Coetzee as a "South African writer" (with all the political overtones that can carry), he is South African and he is, among other things, a writer. Apart from some time spent in Britain and the United States in the 1960s and 1970s, he has always lived in the country of his birth.[2] Coetzee was eight years old when the Afrikaners won the white man's election of 1948 that made apartheid official government policy. His family on his father's side is Afrikaans. But, one may ask, to what extent does he consider himself an Afrikaner?

Coetzee has always been sceptical of, suspicious of, or downright hostile to, belonging to a group, with the inevitable compromises on individual freedom that such a notion involves. In *Doubling the Point*, a collection of essays with accompanying interviews, Coetzee says to David Attwell:

> No Afrikaner would consider me an Afrikaner. That, it seems to me, is the acid test for group membership, and I don't pass it. Why not? In the first place, because English is my first language, and has been since childhood. [...] In the second place, because I am not embedded in the culture of the Afrikaner [...] and have been shaped by that culture only in a perverse way.[3]

The phrase "not embedded" expresses rather well a certain reluctance to "embrace" the Afrikaner culture, yet what is most interesting for my present purposes is the expression "only in a perverse way." One is naturally led to ask what this "perversion" may

---

[1] While it is true that *Waiting for the Barbarians* takes place in a purely invented space, it can easily be seen to represent South Africa allegorically, even though one must be careful not to reduce it to this. *Foe* can also be seen to represent certain aspects of the South African situation, although not, of course, geographically.

[2] He now lives in Australia. [Ed.]

[3] J.M. Coetzee, *Doubling the Point*, ed. David Attwell (Cambridge MA & London: Harvard UP, 1992): 341–42.

be, whether the shaping of which he speaks would be in resistance to, rather than in accordance with, such a culture. Concerning the Afrikaners' role in history, Coetzee faces the question of individual and collective responsibility:

> Is it in my power to withdraw from the gang? I think not. […] More important, is it my heart's desire to be counted apart? Not really. Furthermore […] I would regard it as morally questionable to write something like the second part of *Dusklands* […] from a position that is not historically complicit.[4]

This, surely, is good faith. Spoken in the early 1990s, when people were trying to distance themselves from a régime and a doctrine that, to put it mildly, was losing credibility, Coetzee refuses all self-righteousness. Although the answer remains somewhat ambivalent ("Not really" rather than "No"), it is neither ambiguous nor contradictory. This is a position which will be clarified in *Boyhood*, published twenty-four years after *Dusklands*, his first novel.

For Afrikaners who identify with the concept of Afrikanerdom, the criteria are those of shared blood, earth, culture, traditions and beliefs. Their strength lies in their common historical heritage.

In 1986, in the middle of the State of Emergency, Coetzee wrote an article for *Vogue* entitled "The White Tribe."[5] He explains how the isolation within a literal and metaphorical *laager* increased the solidarity of Afrikaners, rendering each individual subservient to the group in the process. In fact, therefore, apartheid was used not for the furtherance of the country as a whole but for the survival of one particular group:

> The first priority remains the preservation of the tribe. The ultimate disaster, as they see it, is *extinction*. […] The end of the tribe – loss of power followed by the loss of the hold of tribal culture over its members, followed by mingling and/or diaspora – would be just as bad.[6]

For Coetzee, the individual must at all costs preserve his freedom of action and speech; belonging to a group inevitably compromises this freedom. Remaining faithful to his own *Weltanschauung*, Coetzee necessarily rejects the tribal aspect of the Afrikaner community, but, as we have seen, would see it as bad faith to reject all that Afrikaners represent.

《●》

"The Narrative of Jacobus Coetzee" is the second half of his first novel, *Dusklands*, published in 1974. Based on a genuine eighteenth-century *burgher*, it is in the form of fictionalized history within a complex metatextual frame. At the beginning of the eighteenth century, certain Boers undertook exploratory expeditions into the hinterland. By about 1760, they had difficulty progressing into the extremely arid Namaqualand. John Coetzee's narrative is an imagined account of a real expedition into this area, and it is

---

[4] Coetzee, *Doubling the Point*, 343.

[5] "The White Tribe: An Acclaimed South African Novelist Explains Why the Afrikaners Will Never Give In)," *Vogue* (March 1986): 490–91 & 543–44.

[6] Coetzee, "The White Tribe," 544.

this date, 1760, that is to be found on the deposition of Jacobus Coetzee, included as an annexe within the novel's metatext. Another annexe puts the expedition into its supposed historical perspective: a highly parodic fictional "Afterword." Its author, a certain S.J. Coetzee, professor from 1934 to 1948 at that most Afrikaner of universities, Stellenbosch, is speaking to fellow-Afrikaners:

> The present work ventures to present a more complete and therefore more just view of Jacobus Coetzee. It is a work of piety toward an ancestor and one of the founders of our people, a work which offers the evidence of history to correct certain of the anti-heroic distortions that have been creeping into our conception of the great age of exploration when the White man first made contact with the native peoples of our interior.[7]

This fictional annexe was supposedly 'published' in 1951, three years after the National Party came to power. The first sentence can therefore be seen as a type of corrective to supposed errors of interpretation before 1948 – in fact, a rewriting of history.

Yet Jacobus Coetzee (factual and fictional) had no intention at all of settling in the interior. His expedition, primarily to hunt elephants for their ivory, was under the auspices of the Dutch East India Company, and he duly returned – not laden with ivory, however, but empty-handed, on foot and as naked as a new-born babe, after a humiliating encounter with the Namaqua. In his "Afterword," however, Professor Coetzee chooses to ignore the more ignominious aspects of Jacobus's expedition, preferring to see it in the broader context of heroic colonial expansion:

> The generations of the Coetzees illustrate well the gradual dispersal into the hinterland which has constituted the outward story, the fable, of the White man in South Africa, trekking ever northwards in anger or disgust at the restrictiveness of government, Dutch or British.[8]

These Boers were convinced that they belonged to a privileged group within society – that of the free man over the slave, the Christian over the atheist, the white man over the black, the *burgher* over the functionary of the Dutch East India Company. S.J. Coetzee wants to prolong the romantic myth of the free, courageous adventurer:

> Coetzee was part of a gathering tide of people turning their backs on the south. For farmers of the interior, the monthly struggle to meet the demands of a voracious Company [...] had become too much. Such men turned their eyes to the naked plains of the interior, seeing themselves as lords of their own lives.[9]

---

[7] J.M. Coetzee, *Dusklands* (Harmondsworth: Penguin, 1983): 108. The last words – "our interior" – represent, as Sarah Christie et al. put it, "a brilliant stroke of John Coetzee's bitter irony. He is, after all, trying to offer us 'the evidence of history' to damn the entire colonial mythology." See Sarah Christie, Geoffrey Hutchings & Don Maclennan, "Conclusion: the Landscapes of Paradise," in *Perspectives on South African Fiction* (Johannesburg: Ad. Donker, 1980): 187.

[8] Coetzee, *Dusklands*, 108–109. Expressions such as "outward story" and "fable" in this parodic context call, of course, for a historiographical analysis which is unfortunately beyond the scope of the present study.

[9] *Dusklands*, 109.

Jacobus Coetzee is presented as docile *burgher* before his departure for the north. Since the reader of John Coetzee's novel has read the "Narrative" before reading the "Afterword," the irony is all the more caustic. He has read of the organized, cold-blooded slaughter of indigenous men, women and children (including his own former servants) on Jacobus's second journey, as a means of revenge for his humiliation during the first. Now he reads the following description of Jacobus as a hard-working, peaceful, hospitable, Christian family-man:

> We picture him in his rough year-round working clothes and lionskin shoes, with his round-brimmed hat on his head and his whip sleeping in the crook of his arm, standing with watchful eye beside his wagon or on his stoep ready to welcome the traveller with hospitality [...]. Or we picture him [...] seated of an evening with his family about a water-basin having the sweat of a day's toil washed from his feet preparatory to evening prayers and connubium.[10]

This tableau is clearly based on the romantic image of the Boer in the paintings of the period. By juxtaposing such a description with the narrative of a sadistic megalomaniac, John Coetzee exposes the mythical façade of the Boer as hero. Although the fictional professor does later show an awareness of the violent nature of Jacobus's second journey, he chooses to allude to it only obliquely within the mass of other such missions, in order to exonerate his ancestral hero from any guilt: "The commando missions were [...] in no sense genocidal. Even some adult males survived in captivity."[11]

But is J.M. Coetzee's intention in describing in some detail the gruesome annihilation of Namaqua and other Khoi purely one of exposing the heroic myth? It is clear that this is only one of his purposes. Coetzee is also investigating the psychology of sadism, the unconscious motives behind the desire to commit atrocities. At the end of his narrative, Jacobus writes:

> Through their deaths I [...] again asserted my reality. No more than any other man do I enjoy killing; but I have taken it upon myself to be the one to pull the trigger, performing this sacrifice for myself and my countrymen, who exist, and committing upon the dark folk the murders we have all wished. All are guilty, without exception. [...] I am a tool in the hands of history.[12]

This argument for exoneration of the individual in the face of collective guilt, the impotence of the individual in the face of a superior power (be it history, God, destiny, or whatever), is, of course, all too familiar.

---

[10] Coetzee, *Dusklands*, 109–10.

[11] *Dusklands*, 114. The assertion is clearly ridiculed, the second sentence implicitly contradicting the first.

[12] *Dusklands*, 106. Rosemary Gray quotes this passage as an example of what Rowland Smith calls "a key to the mythology of white violence." See Rosemary Gray, "J.M. Coetzee's *Dusklands*: Of War and War's Alarms," *Commonwealth: Essays and Studies* 9.1 (1986): 32; and Rowland Smith, "The Seventies and After: The Inner View in White English-Language Fiction," in *Olive Schreiner and After*, ed. Malvern van Wyk Smith & Don Maclennan (Cape Town: David Philip, 1983): 200.

So where is the authorial voice in all this? Is he suggesting, as Tony Morphet maintains he may be, that "the drive of the positivist mind into the wilderness is inevitable given the culture which forms it,"[13] that it is the natural state of man to seek to subjugate others? As so often with Coetzee, it is (I would suggest) futile to attempt to grasp an authorial voice within the many discursive layers of this text. He poses questions, yet is too self-questioning, too sceptical or, quite simply, too honest to propose answers to problems that have kept philosophers busy since philosophizing began.

《•》

Coetzee's second novel, *In the Heart of the Country*, is in the form of an interior monologue written in 266 numbered sections over (in the Penguin edition) 139 pages. The intradiegetic author of what she calls her "locked diary"[14] is Magda, an ageless[15] Afrikaner spinster living alone with her father and the servants on an isolated farm in the Karoo. Not long after the beginning of the novel, Magda kills (or imagines she kills) her father and his young second wife, recently arrived on the farm. Although certain elements would tend to situate the novel towards the end of the nineteenth century, references to period are deliberately vague or contradictory; it would go counter to the spirit of the work to attempt to fix it in time. It is perhaps preferable, therefore, to see the portraits of the Boer farmer and his daughter as not only atemporal but also, in a way, ahistorical or archetypal, representing the spirit of the eternal Afrikaner.

The farmer is presented[16] as the patriarchal Boer, father of all Fathers: severe, intransigent, often cruel, but also, in the eyes of the daughter, a lost soul who refuses to let himself be loved. Magda herself is portrayed as a scrawny, bitter, frustrated virgin, thwarted in her desires to live a fulfilled life both by the authority of her father and by the tradition of generations which keeps her imprisoned on the farm. Unable to live other lives, she can only imagine them.

In attempting to understand who she is in the *hic et nunc* in which destiny has cast her, Magda often makes highly lyrical imaginative forays into colonial history:

> One day fences began to go up – I speculate of course – men on horseback rode up and from shadowed faces issued invitations to stop and settle that might also have been orders and might have been threats, one does not know, and so one became a herdsman, and one's children after one, and one's women took in washing. […] There is another great moment in colonial history: the first merino is lifted from shipboard, […] bleating with terror, unaware that this is the promised land where it will browse generation after generation on the nutritious scrub and provide the economic base for the presence of my father and myself in the lonely house where we kick our heels waiting for the wool to grow and gather about ourselves the remnants of the lost tribes of the Hottentots to be

---

[13] Tony Morphet, "J.M. Coetzee's *Dusklands*," *Bolt* 11 (December 1974): 61.

[14] J.M. Coetzee, *In the Heart of the Country* (Harmondsworth: Penguin, 1982): 3.

[15] If she indeed seems ageless, for one can never put an age on her, she is nonetheless ageing, as she appears to be relatively young at the beginning of the novel and relatively old at the end.

[16] In this analysis of the portraits of farmer and daughter, it must be remembered that the narrative voice is that of the daughter herself, and that any authorial voice must be sought at one remove at least.

hewers of wood and drawers of water and shepherds and body-servants in perpetuity and where we are devoured by boredom and pull wings off flies.[17]

The inexorable rhythm of these two long sentences (the second of which has even been slightly reduced) translates well the historical process which, for Magda, has a dynamics of its own, sweeping the individual up in its passage. Magda has here a somewhat ironic, self-mocking vision of herself as a passive individual in this process, doomed to live out a life of monotony that destiny has reserved for her. She generally sees herself as a monstrous being who does not fit in; nevertheless, she also occasionally sees herself not as an exception but as one of those she calls "the daughters of the colonies."[18] In being subjected to the will of her father (and of the Fathers), to the great "No!" Magda is one of many lonely women throughout the generations, growing old on the farm in a patriarchal society:

> The land is full of melancholy spinsters like me, lost to history, blue as roaches in our ancestral homes, keeping a high shine on the copperware and laying in jam. Wooed when we were little by our masterful fathers, we are bitter vestals, spoiled for life.[19]

Leaving aside the seductive expression "wooed," which begs the Father of psychoanalysis himself to intervene in this most Freudian of texts, let us consider the word "masterful," for if the fathers are the masters, the daughters (and not only the servants) are the slaves:

> When he came in hot and dusty after a day's work my father expected that his bath should be ready for him. It was my childhood duty to light the fire an hour before sunset so that the hot water could be poured into the enamelled hipbath the moment he stamped through the front door. Then I would retire to the dark side of the floral screen to receive his clothes and lay out the clean underlinen.[20]

This clearly reveals the paternal authority which, in microcosm, can be seen to represent the patriarchal society as a whole, a society which continued for generation upon generation and for which Magda chooses (or imagines) the most radical of solutions: patricide.

《●》

In the elections of 26 May 1948, the National Party under Daniel Francis Malan unexpectedly defeated Smuts's United Party, and everything was set for the implementation of apartheid. It was in the years leading up to and following these elections that John Coetzee grew up. It is also during these years that the protagonist of the text *Boyhood* (also, strangely, called John) grows up, passing from the age of eight to the

---

[17] Coetzee, *In the Heart of the Country*, 18–19. The "hewers of wood and drawers of water" is a reference to the infamous speech by Hendrik Verwoerd, who referred to the blacks of South Africa as filling such roles for the white man, thereby rendering their education unnecessary.

[18] Coetzee, *In the Heart of the Country*, 3.

[19] *In the Heart of the Country*, 3. The final phrase, "spoiled for life," has a dual meaning, of course: she has been damaged forever, rendered incapable of living a fulfilled life.

[20] *In the Heart of the Country*, 9.

age of fourteen. Published in 1997 and carrying the ironic subtitle borrowed from Balzac, "Scenes from Provincial Life," the text is written in the present tense (which suggests immediacy) and the third person (which suggests distance); the tension between the two is one of the chief stylistic devices of the narrative.

In *Boyhood*, the boy John is split between, on the one hand, the British, the English language and his mother, and on the other, the Afrikaners, Afrikaans, and his father.[21] His loyalty goes naturally towards the first, but he develops an untainted love for the farm which belongs to an uncle on his father's side and where he spends his holidays. John tries to find his identity within this split world, but refuses a Manichean view of the British/Afrikaner divide that would make his life easier. Despite his natural preference, he neither can nor wants to reject the Afrikaners in their entirety, for, on the farm, he senses certain qualities in them that the English lack.

The farm is central to the history of Afrikaners.[22] They settled on the infertile lands of the Karoo, passed on their farms from generation to generation, believing they (unlike the British) had a natural right to the land. This continuity, the inner strength of this filiation through the earth, the tacit solidarity of the Afrikaans family – such are the elements that so appeal to John.

The boy is particularly sensitive to the physical traits of Afrikaners. On the farm he meets and falls in love[23] with his Afrikaner cousin Agnes (barefoot, beautiful, slender, graceful), with whom he feels perfectly free and natural, despite being so different. On the other hand, in Worcester, where he goes to school, there are only boys with whom he has nothing in common: "He loathes and fears the hulking, barefoot Afrikaans boys."[24] He, the over-protected mother's boy who never goes barefoot, looks down on them, thinking with some satisfaction that he could never pass for an Afrikaner: "(he thinks of them as rhinoceroses, huge, lumbering, strong-sinewed, thudding against each other as they pass)."[25]

In John's mind, the Afrikaners' physique and character go together: if they are ugly, this is because they are angry. He feels imprisoned within this hard, insensitive world: "What he hates most about Worcester, what most makes him want to escape, is the rage and resentment that he senses crackling through the Afrikaans boys."[26] He has heard about the violations these boys inflict on others and is terrified at the thought of being transferred to an Afrikaans class. He feels that Afrikaners are ignorant, insensitive, pitiless, in the image of their leader: "An image of Dr Malan is engraved in his

---

[21] Although of Afrikaans stock, his father uses his second language, English, to John and is fond of crossword puzzles and English poetry, owning books by Shakespeare, Keats and Wordsworth. John is dubious about the value of his father's apparent appreciation of literature.

[22] See Coetzee's analysis of the novelist Van den Heever in Chapter 4 of his collection of essays *White Writing: On the Culture of Letters in South Africa* (New Haven CT & London: Yale UP, 1988): 82–114.

[23] He is not quite sure what love is, but he thinks this must be it: "Is this love – this easy generosity, this sense of being understood at last, of not having to pretend?" (*Boyhood*, 95).

[24] Coetzee, *Boyhood*, 69.

[25] *Boyhood*, 124.

[26] *Boyhood*, 69.

mind. Dr Malan's round, bald face is without understanding or mercy. His gullet pulses like a frog's. His lips are pursed."[27] They seem just like the Afrikaner heroes as they are presented in the textbooks: "angry, obdurate and full of menaces and talk about God."[28] Indeed, religion seems to be just one more weapon. When asked about his religion, he maintains he is a Catholic simply because he likes Romans; he thereby escapes having to be with the Christians (as the Protestants call themselves): that is, with the Afrikaners. But it is with the Jews, the outcasts, the boys most hated and bullied by the Afrikaners, that he feels best.

John's mother tells him what her own mother told her about the Anglo-Boer war: "When the Boers arrived on their farm [...] they demanded food and money and expected to be waited on. When the British soldiers came, they slept in the stable, stole nothing, and before leaving courteously thanked their hosts."[29] He realizes that this is no doubt rather simplistic, yet he is pleased, because his choice of sides seems justified. He refuses to be taken in by National-Party propaganda in school textbooks:

> In stories of the War one is supposed to side with the Boers, fighting for their freedom against the might of the British Empire. However, he prefers to dislike the Boers, not only for their long beards and ugly clothes, but for hiding behind rocks and shooting from ambush, and to like the British for marching to their death to the skirl of bagpipes.[30]

The "however" is evocative both of the pride of the child who seems to take a perverse pleasure in going against the tide, despite the resultant exclusion, and of the inner strength of the boy who refuses to be told what to think.

Yet, once again, things are not so clear-cut. He and two friends discover a cave on an Afrikaner's land. They are discovered by the farmer's son, who warns them that his father will come with whip and cane. When the father does come, he has neither whip nor cane; he simply tells them they are lucky and must be off. John is ashamed; his pride has been hurt: "There is nothing they can say to redeem the experience. The Afrikaners have not even behaved badly."[31] In his search for an identity in his split world, this episode confuses him even further.

《●》

The Soweto massacre of 16 June 1976 led to a crisis the like of which South Africa had not known since Sharpeville in 1960. It was the beginning of a long series of riots; the instinctive Afrikaner reaction of retreating into their protective *laager* proved inefficient. Repression came, followed by a period of relative calm, but riots again erupted in the townships in September 1983. Even greater repression ensued, and the period of Total Onslaught began. On 20 July 1985, Prime Minister Botha declared a State of Emergency in certain regions, extending it to the country as a whole on 12 June 1986.

---

[27] Coetzee, *Boyhood*, 70.
[28] *Boyhood*, 66.
[29] *Boyhood*, 66.
[30] *Boyhood*, 66–67.
[31] *Boyhood*, 71.

It was during the State of Emergency that Coetzee began writing *Age of Iron*, a novel in which there are scenes of rioting and repression in the Western Cape township of Guguletu, portrayed as a modern Inferno. The novel is in the form of a letter from an English-speaking mother in Cape Town to her daughter in the United States. Elizabeth Curren, a retired teacher of Classics, is dying of cancer, burning within as the country burns without. She is, one could say, a 'liberal humanist' who has lived through the whole period of apartheid and attempts to express the repugnance she feels towards its leaders. When one of the tribe (as she herself calls them) pontificates on television, she stands up in order not to debase herself before them:

> The slow, truculent Afrikaans rhythms with their deadening closes, like a hammer beating a post into the ground. [...] The disgrace of the life one lives under them: to open a newspaper, to switch on the television, like kneeling and being urinated on. Under them: under their meaty bellies, their full bladders.[32]

The word "disgrace" prefigures the title of Coetzee's later novel, published in 1999. The word as it is used here (and in the later novel, in fact) must be understood not merely in the customary sense of shame or dishonour, but also in the more literal sense of being without grace, devoid of elegance and beauty. This is the world of Afrikaners that will become that of all who suffer their authority without resistance. The images (which, as we have seen, will recur in mitigated form in *Boyhood*, published seven years later) are those of animality, heaviness, slowness and death, an absence of all sense of nuance or reflection. The victim is passive, defenceless, humiliated. Mrs Curren, in her impoverished position of a dying old lady, whom nobody understands or even listens to, resists as best she can in the name not only of her own honour but also of ideas in which she has believed all her life. These people (or, metaphorically, beasts) ruling the country are, in fact, the same schoolboys of *Boyhood* forty years on. The same images recur in the description:

> The bullies in the last row of school-desks, raw-boned, lumpish boys, grown up now and promoted to rule the land. [...] a locust horde, a plague of black locusts infesting the country, munching without cease, devouring lives. [...] Reason they have shrugged off. What absorbs them is power and the stupor of power. Eating and talking, munching lives, belching. Slow, heavy-bellied talk. Sitting in a circle, debating ponderously, issuing decrees like hammer-blows: death, death, death. [...] Heavy eyelids, piggish eyes, shrewd with the shrewdness of generations of peasants. [...] Pressing downward: their power in their weight. Huge bull-testicles bearing down on their wives, their children, pressing the spark out of them. In their own hearts no spark of fire left. Sluggish hearts, heavy as blood-pudding.[33]

The essence of humanity has been lost or has never been there; of humanism, too, there is no trace.

---

[32] J.M. Coetzee, *Age of Iron* (London: Secker & Warburg, 1990): 9.

[33] Coetzee, *Age of Iron*, 25–26.

Even though they realize, during this period of *interregnum*,[34] that their time is
coming to an end, they carry on, mechanically, devoid of all reason, all feeling, all sensitivity, until their victims themselves become equally insensitive. The benumbed
viewers are rendered incapable of any resistance:

> A ritual manifestation, like the processions of hooded bishops during Franco's war. A
> thanatophany: showing us our death. *Viva le muerte!* their death cry, their threat. Death
> to the young. Death to life. Boars that devour their offspring. The Boar War.[35]

It is a system for the propagation of mental, spiritual and often physical death. Such is
the sad inheritance of the South African populations, bequeathed by these Fathers, to
whom one owes a blind, absolute devotion: Fathers who, like Chronos, devour their
own children. This is why one must resist. Yet, facing imminent death herself, Elizabeth no longer has the consolation of seeing the end of the régime she so loathes:
"'Your days are numbered', I used to whisper once upon a time, to them who will now
outlast me."[36]

《•》

If one were foolhardy enough to search for an authorial voice in this depiction of the
Afrikaner, one would be tempted to say that it is *Boyhood*, the autobiographical text (if
I may venture this *parti pris*), that best reveals Coetzee's complex view of the ethnic
group which he is both within and without, which he rejects in part yet understands,
which he loathes but at the same time has an affection for. Jean Sévry has described
Coetzee as a "reluctant Afrikaner,"[37] a phrase that implies internal opposition. There is,
indeed, such an opposition, yet Coetzee does not shy away from assuming his heritage,
even if somewhat regretfully. As an individual who, like all of us, had no say in his
own birth, he cannot feel directly responsible for the excesses of Afrikanerdom. That it
is a heritage with which he has quite naturally struggled is evident from his work. Yet
does he come to any conclusion? Perhaps, for in his novels the Afrikaner undoubtedly
comes out badly, and this, quite simply, should be sufficient testimony to the place
that, albeit tentatively and sceptically, Coetzee assigns to the White Tribe.

WORKS CITED

Christie, Sarah, Geoffrey Hutchings & Don Maclennan. "Conclusion: The Landscapes of Paradise," in Christie, Hutchings & Maclennan, *Perspectives on South African Fiction* (Johannesburg: Ad. Donker, 1980): 184–89.
Coetzee, J.M. *Age of Iron* (London: Secker & Warburg, 1990).

---

[34] The expression in the South African context comes from Nadine Gordimer, following
Gramsci.
[35] Coetzee, *Age of Iron*, 26.
[36] *Age of Iron*, 9.
[37] Jean Sévry, "Afrique du Sud: Le dernier écrit de Coetzee: *Les confessions d'un enfant*,"
Commonwealth: Essays and Studies 21.1 (Autumn 1998): 94.

——. *Boyhood* (London: Secker & Warburg, 1997).

——. *Doubling the Point*, ed. David Attwell (Cambridge MA & London: Harvard UP, 1992).

——. *Dusklands* (Harmondsworth: Penguin, 1983).

——. *Foe* (London: Secker & Warburg, 1986).

——. *In the Heart of the Country* (Harmondsworth: Penguin, 1982).

——. *Waiting for the Barbarians* (London: Secker & Warburg, 1980).

——."The White Tribe: An Acclaimed South African Novelist Explains Why the Afrikaners Will Never Give In," *Vogue* (March 1986): 490–91 & 543–44.

——. *White Writing: On the Culture of Letters in South Africa* (New Haven CT & London: Yale UP, 1988).

Gray, Rosemary. "J.M. Coetzee's *Dusklands*: Of War and War's Alarms," *Commonwealth: Essays and Studies* 9.1 (1986): 32–43.

Morphet, Tony. "J.M. Coetzee's *Dusklands*," *Bolt* 11 (December 1974): 58–61.

Sévry, Jean. "Afrique du Sud: Le dernier écrit de Coetzee: *Les confessions d'un enfant*," *Commonwealth: Essays and Studies* 21.1 (Autumn 1998): 93–96.

Smith, Rowland. "The Seventies and After: The Inner View in White, English-language Fiction," in *Olive Schreiner and After*, ed. Malvern van Wyk Smith & Don MacLennan (Cape Town: David Philip, 1983): 196–204.

⟨⟨●⟩⟩

Wholeness or Fragmentation?
The New Challenges of South African Literary Studies

RICHARD SAMIN

S OUTH AFRICA'S POLITICAL TRANSITION to democracy in the 1990s has created objective conditions which have fostered the emergence of new discourses and new knowledge. Within this renewed epistemological field, cultural and literary theories and practices have focussed on issues and themes linked to the new historical environment. The rhetoric of memory, the writing of history, generic hybridity have become topics which are currently debated along with the concept of literature whose content is re-examined given the wide range of practices it subsumes. Likewise, the connections between literature and politics, written and oral traditions and the social disparity of audiences must be redefined in the light of the formal and linguistic heterogeneity of a multi-cultural field. The emphasis, as Kelwyn Sole remarks, can no longer be laid on "who should speak?" but on "who will listen?"[1] After a brief survey of how recent critical approaches have tried to theorize the changing conditions of literary and cultural production, this essay will examine how some fictional writings have tried to evade the framing of conventional critical approaches and what kind of reading such fiction posits by examining two of the most outstanding novels of the period Zakes Mda's *Ways of Dying* and Marlene van Niekerk's *Triomf*.[2]

Literature and history

South Africa's liberation has opened up an arena which offers many possibilities for the development of individual creation now freed from the necessity of having to make a choice between the dichotomies which the struggle against apartheid had imposed.

In a controversial paper delivered to an African National Congress in-house seminar in October 1989, Albie Sachs advocated a dissociation of culture from struggle: "our members should be banned from saying that culture is a weapon of struggle. I suggest

---

[1] Kelwyn Sole, "Democratising Culture and Literature in a 'New South Africa': Organisation and Theory," *Current Writing* 6. 2 (1994): 29.

[2] Zakes Mda, *Ways of Dying* (Cape Town: Oxford UP, 1993); Marlene van Niekerk, *Triomf*, tr. Leon de Kock (*Triomf*; Cape Town: Queillerie, 1994; tr. Johannesburg: Jonathan Ball, 1999).

a period of say, five years,"[3] on the grounds that it is a cause of impoverishment and strongly encourages the writer to widen his range of themes and deal with the more complex and ambivalent issues of ordinary life.

If Nadine Gordimer dismisses Sachs' statement as "poking fun at his own previous rigidity"[4] it nevertheless raises a more fundamental question on whether, for the sake of writing good literature, one should be allowed to dictate the conditions which are supposedly conducive to it. Sachs's stance brings to mind an article written by Lewis Nkosi in 1966 in which he recommended a suspension of black literary production for the sake of quality: "It may even be wondered whether it might not be more prudent to 'renounce literature temporarily' [...] and solve the political problem first rather than continue to grind out hackneyed third-rate novels."[5]

Sachs also gives the impression of introducing a form of teleology whereby this anticipated excellence will necessarily accrue to a homogenizing cultural discourse. While he acknowledges the linguistic and cultural diversity of the country and the equality of all South African cultures stating that "there is no culture that is worth more than any other"[6] his paper is nevertheless underpinned by the assumption that culture must serve a social agenda and further national aims.

In much critical writings published after 1994, such as the essays of *Rethinking South African Literary History* and of *Negotiating the Past*,[7] many cautionary voices sounded warnings against the temptation of teleology, closure and homogeneity in the construction of truth and history. As Peter Horn suggests in an article published in 1997, "sometimes one has to take one's distance and has to allow his readers to distance themselves."[8] Others, like Ampie Coetzee, have clearly evinced some uneasiness about a national discourse on account of its positivity, arguing that "colonialism is a positivity of the past [...] that can still have influence on the conditions of possibility of discursive practices today."[9] Peter Horn, again,[10] points to the limits inherent to an official history: "Fiction deals with the possibilities which are excluded from official documents. What is possible excludes all the possibilities which have been officially judged impossible."

[3] Albie Sachs, "Preparing Ourselves for Freedom," repr. in *Exchanges: South African Writing in Transition*, ed. Duncan Brown & Bruno van Dyk (Pietermaritzburg: U of Natal P, 1991): 117.

[4] Interview with Nadine Gordimer in *Exchanges: South African Writing in Transition*, ed. Brown & van Dyk, 26.

[5] Lewis Nkosi, "Fiction by Black South African Writers," *Black Orpheus* (19 March 1966): 49.

[6] Albie Sachs, "Preparing Ourselves for Freedom," 121–122.

[7] *Rethinking South African Literary History*, ed. Johannes A. Smit, Johan Van Wyk & Jean–Philippe Wade (Durban: Y Press, 1996); *Negotiating the Past*, ed. Sarah Nuttall & Carli Coetzee (Cape Town: Oxford UP, 1998).

[8] Peter Horn, "Parallels and Contrasts: *Wendezeit* in South African and German Literatures," *Literator* 18.3 (November 1997): 29.

[9] Ampie Coetzee, "Rethinking South African National History: South Africa? History? Literary History?" in *Rethinking South African Literary History*, ed. Smit et al., 13.

[10] Peter Horn, "Parallels and Contrasts," 3.

In the wake of political liberation, certain conceptual patterns in the cultural field are no longer applicable. There has been a shift from the concept of binary opposition to that of the fragmented continuum of non-hierarchized differences no longer based on racial criteria. Cultural practices such as fiction, poetry and drama turned to new themes such as redefining personal or communal identities or urgent social problems. More generally, the abandonment of former binary antagonisms allowed writers to reconsider the social implications of literary patterns and norms and probe into the question of how to shape the meanings of the momentous times they were witnessing. Thus recent literary texts have tried to register through such categories as intertextuality, hybridity, magical realism and the carnivalesque the elusive, contradictory and ambivalent post-apartheid meanings of the period.

One must note, however, that this concern with issues outside the usual political dichotomies is not new. It was already manifest in Njabulo Ndebele's short stories from the early 1980s and in his seminal collection of essays *Rediscovery of the Ordinary*[11] and, earlier still, in Es'kia Mphahlele's Lesane Stories,[12] in which, by depicting ordinary people's lives, he indirectly sought to re-create the oppressive presence of apartheid. Both writers felt the need to move away from the dramatic, the heroic or the sensational to deal with ambiguities and contradictions in order to explore issues which an aesthetics based on starkly contrasted opposites had necessarily left aside.

Hence the current diffidence of critics and writers alike towards any discourse which seeks to impose homogeneous shaping patterns on cultural practices with the aim of endowing them with a meaning they do not intrinsically possess or, as Jean-Philippe Wade puts it, with "an essential unity grounded in some transcendental signified"[13] such as a national or an ethnic culture. The publication of Michael Chapman's *Southern African Literatures* in 1996 brought this controversy to the forefront. It was debated in a spate of articles and conference papers and, more especially, at a conference held at the University of South Africa on 21 February 1997 on the theme of literary studies. Chapman's book was criticized for applying a predetermined epistemic structure and an ethical teleology to a field which is varied, complex and discontinuous. The poet Leon de Kock pointed out, in his critique of Chapman's book, that "the South African literary-cultural archives are too vast, and too discontinuous to be configured within a singular narrative of political-ethical accountability."[14]

The roots of this controversy lie in fact in the contradiction that opposes the conventional meaning of literature and the wide range of cultural practices the term is supposed to subsume in South Africa. To apply the concept of literature to such diverse

---

[11] Njabulo Ndebele, *Fools and Other Stories* (Johannesburg: Ravan, 1983), and *Rediscovery of the Ordinary: Essays on South African Literature and Culture* (Johannesburg: C O S A W, 1991).

[12] Es'kia Mphahlele, "Lesane," *Drum* (December 1956): 41–43, 45, 47, 49; "Lesane," *Drum* (January 1957): 60–61, 63, 65, 67; "Lesane," *Drum* (February 1957): 53–57; "Lesane," *Drum* (March 1957): 45–46, 49; "Lesane," *Drum* (April 1957): 42–43, 45, 47.

[13] Jean–Philippe Wade, "Genealogies of Desire," in *Rethinking South African Literary History*, ed. Smit et al., 239.

[14] Leon de Kock, "Becoming Different from Ourselves." *Journal of Literary Studies/Tydskrif vir Literatuurwetenskap* 13.1 (June 1997): 226.

cultural practices as performance poetry, theatre for development, workshopped plays or fiction carries with it a conceptual framework which partly distorts or conceals the social import of these practices in terms of production and reception.

For instance, the concept of literature is too narrowly centred on the written word, on the single author and on a particular mode of communication to explain the theatrical work currently being done by the FUBA School of Dramatic Art or the Organisation of African Writers to sensitize people in the townships or in the rural areas to the AIDS pandemic. Yet in the interviews which the director of both organizations gave me there is no doubt in their minds that what is being done is genuine creative work, combining a variety of artistic media – words, songs, dances – and taking into account the capacity of their audiences to respond to specific cultural patterns or languages so as to appeal to them more efficiently. The plays produced in this context are impro- vised, work-shopped around issues discussed collectively by the playwright, the actors and members of the community so as to meet their specific needs.

Some critics have accordingly suggested that the concept of literature should more appropriately be replaced by that of cultural studies. Rory Ryan, for instance, suggests that "perhaps the only way of breaking the cycle of a series of ideologies of 'literari- ness' is to reinvent the notion of literary studies as cultural study, whereby texts are studied as cultural objects and not as capitalized objects."[15]

So as to circumvent the discursive stranglehold which the concept of literature im- plies, Rory Ryan has even claimed that all critical activities should be historicized: "different historical circumstances require different intellectual strategies."[16] In other words, his idea is to wrench the concepts and evaluative procedures of literary studies from transhistoricism.

I would, rather, be inclined to see in this claim a move to relocate cultural produc- tions, including literature, within a dialogical context – whether the listeners are pres- ent or absent does not fundamentally change the situation – so as to interpret them in terms of the pragmatics of cultural communication. As a case in point, the young poet and playwright Sipho ka Ngwenya, a member of COSAW, explained to me in an interview that in his praise-poetry he "needs to use the language people are most com- fortable with and introduce traditional performing modes,"[17] adding, you can even add things as you communicate with them by alluding to particular persons or topical events."[18] He encapsulated his remarks on the performing arts by saying that "they need to be audience-oriented."[19]

《•》

[15] Rory Ryan, "Some Processes and Functions of Literary Knowledge Production," *AUETSA Conference Papers* (Fort Hare & Potchefstroom, AUETSA 1991): 585.

[16] Rory Ryan, "Some Processes and Functions of Literary Knowledge Production," 592.

[17] Siphiwe ka Ngwenya, personal interview (Johannesburg, Newtown, 26 August 1999.

[18] Ka Ngwenya, interview, 1999.

[19] Ka Ngwenya, interview, 1999.

Ways of Dying and *Triomf*

It is this dialogic tension which implicitly sustains the rhetoric of two outstanding novels published in the mid 1990s: *Ways of Dying* by Zakes Mda, published in 1995, and *Triomf* by Marlene van Niekerk, published in Afrikaans in 1994 and in English in 1999. Both novels cleverly explore the extent to which the past shapes the present. Through frequent reminiscences and flashbacks, their narratives are fragmented by repeated allusions to past historical episodes which have personal or communal bearings.

Until the early 1990s, South African literature could be roughly and unequally divided into two trends: one following the tenets of critical realism or naturalism and the other to the uncertainties and free-floating meanings of post-modernism. Since then writers like Zakes Mda, Martene van Niekerk, Chris van Wyk and Ivan Vladislavic[20] have mapped out new imaginary terrains, forged new languages and strategies to address the changes brought about by political developments and shaped new meanings. While seemingly rejecting both the strictures of critical realism and the a-historicism of postmodern literary self-reflexivitiy, they created imaginary loci more responsive to the rich and complex varieties of discourses which criss-crossed the cultural space immediately before and after the demise of apartheid.

Ways of Dying relates the adventures of two picaresque heroes – a man, Toloki, and a woman, Noria – hailing from the same village. They try to survive, after being rejected either by their community or their family, as they follow their respective paths to the same anonymous harbour city.

Noria, who reportedly possesses mysterious powers, was expelled from the village for her too easy-going ways with men. She later married a man who turned out to be a drunkard, beat her, and abducted their son, Vutha. One day, sunk in a drunken stupor, the father left his son unattended, tied in chains, while dogs attacked and half-devoured him. After her son's death Noria further drifted to the informal settlement of the anonymous harbour city where the story is set, a few months before the elections of 1994.

Toloki, who had likewise found his way to the same city doing all sorts of jobs to survive had finally landed as a self-styled professional mourner in the garb of a magician. It is in this attire that he accidentally met Noria while attending the funeral of her second son, also named Vutha (meaning burning fire), after he had died a tragic death, necklaced by the young militants of a self-defence unit whose duty it was to protect the inhabitants of the settlement against the attacks of neighbouring hostel dwellers.

In Mda's novel, the past is not simply re-created through the evocation of life under apartheid, the transition to democracy and the turmoil in the townships, it is also inscribed in the literary discourses and themes which are fused in the text. Part of the discourses originate in the realism and naturalism of the 1960s, as exemplified in the novels and short stories of Alex La Guma and Es'kia Mphahlele, especially his Lesane stories. Others are rooted in the traditional African lore of religious beliefs, tales and proverbs. Mda thus brings together within the compass of his novel African cultural practices and discourses, which for ideological reasons had been kept apart and even

---

[20] See, in particular, Chris van Wyk, *The Year of the Tapeworm* (Johannesburg: Ravan, 1996), and Ivan Vladislavic, *The Folly* (Johannesburg: David Philip, 1993).

opposed. By juxtaposing urban and rural traditions, or written and oral discourses, without attempting to rationalize and fuse their contradictions, Mda creates a space of indeterminacy and ambivalence where the rational and the irrational co-exist but where neither one nor the other are prioritized. By resorting thus to a form of magical realism at a crucial historical moment, Mda problematizes the reader's relation to the present and pre-empts the temptation of a non-contradictory reconstruction of history.

This discursive stance is further reinforced by his use of the carnivalesque. The Bakhtinian reading of the term implies a temporary questioning and reversal of power, hierarchy and official culture by popular culture. Accordingly, Mda uses two marginal characters living on the fringes of a city to expose the hypocrisy and selfish consumerist aspirations of an emerging black middle-class represented in the novel by Nefolohodwe who, with his invention of the collapsible coffin, shamelessly trades on the sudden deaths which occurred during the period of transition. Likewise, Mda deflates the seriousness, sincerity and reliability of would-be politicians whose ostensible commitment to the cause of the most destitute victims of the former political order pales into insignificance when compared with the selfless dedication of Toloki, Noria and others to the welfare of the orphans of the informal settlement where they live. However, the main target of Mda's scathing satire is violence and more precisely the arbitrariness of revolutionary violence culminating in the necklacing of a five-year-old child after he was declared a traitor to the cause in a mockery of a trial.

Unlike the traditional carnivalesque, however, Mda's version obviously precludes the possibility of a return to a previous order. It rather serves to articulate in the novel an internal dialogics between the desire to integrate the totality of cultural differences within a new national framework and the diffidence towards an order which might be tempted to create a new divisions and exclusions for the sake of political unity. The uncertainties which the literary codes of magical realism and the carnivalesque create in the novel thus condition the reading of the social reality in which it is set.

At the other end of the racial and political spectrum, van Niekerk's novel is a satirical debunking of the Afrikaner myth. As in *Ways of Dying*, the action is situated a few months before the elections of 1994 in a white Johannesburg neighbourhood that used to be an African freehold location, Sophiatown, razed to the ground in the mid-50s after its inhabitants had been forcefully removed, and renamed Triomf.

The central characters belong to a family of poor whites, the Benades, made up of two brothers, Pop and Treppie, their sister Mol, and their incestuous son Lambert, a half-wit and epileptic, feared by the others on account of his unusual physical strength and sudden outbursts of violence. They symbolically represent the grotesque, monstrous legacy of the Afrikaner myth of group and racial solidarity and particularly of the founding myth of Afrikaner nationalism, the Great Trek. At the beginning of the novel, as the inevitability of the political transition to democracy is dawning upon them, they get ready to set off on their own trek by making preparations for a journey to the north of the country when "the shit hits the fan," as Lambert keeps repeating.

Van Niekerk's novel is jubilantly subversive in the sense that her characters happily and deliberately transgress all norms: the political norms of Afrikanerdom (whose representatives are turned into ridicule), the religious norms of the Dutch Reformed Church (whose creeds and texts are parodied), sexual norms (since all the male characters freely indulge in incestuous intercourse with their sister or mother whenever they feel like it). Finally, the novel transgresses against the norms of political correctness by serving the reader with liberal doses of racist abuse and "K" words – "K" for kaffir, which is today an actionable offence.

The carnivalesque in *Triomf* re-appropriates the past by savagely turning the tenets of Afrikaner supremacy upside down. The butt of Van Niekerk's satire is the literary tradition of the 'farm novel' or '*plaasroman*' which formerly idealized the white farm on the veld as a pastoral haven. In *Triomf*, this idyllic world has been reduced to the size of a dilapidated estate house with its ubiquitous car-port and lawn built on land stolen from its original occupiers. It is ironical that the more these characters claim their 'natural' superiority the more these claims belie their pretensions, since everything they say and do betrays their mediocrity and self-serving short-term morality. Instead of giving the image of a united community, living in peace among themselves and with others, the Benades lash into each other savagely and keep antagonizing their Afrikaner neighbours. What is, in fact, laid bare in this parody is precisely how Afrikanerdom shaped their subjectivity as free individuals and how they misused their freedom and squandered the many advantages accruing from the single criterion of race.

Besides the carnivalesque, ambivalence constitutes another dominant feature. The narrative strategy, which essentially makes ample use of scenes and dialogues, sometimes combined with indirect free speech or thought, ensures that the reader always directly receives the full blast of the characters' racist rantings. It is up to the reader, therefore, to produce his own moral shield to deflect the characters' paranoid outbursts and simultaneously tune in to the irony of the text. Moreover, the system of multiple focalization that structures the novel inevitably brings the reader to endorse, however briefly, the validity and values of each character's point of view in spite of the moral repulsion they otherwise inspire. As a result, the characters eventually interest us more for what they are than for what they socially represent, and there are moments in the narrative when they become genuinely moving as they unexpectedly and awkwardly reveal that they are still endowed with human feelings – when, for instance, they occasionally evince compassion for others or sentimentally evoke the hardships of their past life. As in *Ways of Dying*, ambivalence and the carnivalesque are here the two major discursive modes which characteristically shape the perception of the uncertainties and complexities of the period.

<((•))>

The controversies briefly alluded to in this essay show the extent to which some sectors of the South African cultural field are responsive to the changing patterns of history. Critics, cultural workers and writers alike feel the need to rethink their creative and analytical tools in order to account for the complexities and contradictions of the social context. In this respect, the novels of Mda and van Niekerk are exemplary. Through a renewal of novelistic techniques they induce new forms of reading. The paradox of today's fiction lies in the fact that its predominantly dialogical mode questions the fallacy of a direct, univocal access to truth precisely at a time when the construction of the truth is the order of the day. This, however, does not mean that fiction and culture deny the possibility of arriving at some truth. It simply means that in coming to grips with the ambivalence and complexity of today's changing reality, contemporary fiction is trying to create new modes of representation which provide discursive room for contradictory voices to exist. It also shows the extent to which the interpretation of texts, and of cultural productions in general, is context-dependent, and that the time has come to abandon an aesthetic of conviction for one which is prepared to cope with the indeterminacy and elusiveness of new meanings.

WORKS CITED

Brown, Duncan, & Bruno Van Dyk, ed. *Exchanges. South African Writing in Transition* (Pieter-maritzburg: U of Natal P, 1991).

Chapman, Michael. *Southern African Literatures* (London: Longman, 1996).

Coetzee, Ampie. "Rethinking South African National History.South Africa? History? Literary History?" in *Rethinking South African Literary History*, ed. Smit et al., 10–19.

De Kock, Leon. "Becoming Different from Ourselves." *Journal of Literary Studies/Tydskrif vir Literatuurwetenskap* 13.1 (June 1997): 223–26.

Gordimer, Nadine "Interview," in *Exchanges. South African Writing in Transition*, ed. Duncan Brown & Bruno van Dyk (Pietermaritzburg: U of Natal P, 1991): 26—28.

Horn, Peter. "Parallels and Contrasts: *Wendezeit* in South African and German Literatures," *Literator* 18.3 (November 1997): 25–40.

Ka Ngwenya, Siphiwe. Personal interview, Johannesburg, Newtown, 26 August 1999.

Mda, Zakes. *Ways of Dying* (Cape Town: Oxford UP, 1993).

Mphahlele, Es'kia. "Lesane," *Drum* (December 1956): 41–43, 45, 47, 49; "Lesane," *Drum* (January 1957): 60–61, 63, 65, 67; "Lesane," *Drum* (February 1957): 53–57; "Lesane," *Drum* (March 1957): 45–46, 49; "Lesane," *Drum* (April 1957): 42–43, 45, 47.0

Ndebele, Njabulo. *Fools and Other Stories* (Johannesburg: Ravan, 1983).

——. *Rediscovery of the Ordinary. Essays on South African Literature and Culture* (Johannes-burg: C O S A W, 1991).

Nkosi, Lewis. "Fiction by Black South African Writers," *Black Orpheus* (19 March 1966): 48–54.

Nuttall, Sarah, & Carli Coetzee, ed. *Negotiating the Past* (Cape Town: Oxford UP, 1998).

Ryan, Rory. "Some Processes and Functions of Literary Knowledge Production," *AUETSA Conference Papers* (Fort Hare/Potchefstroom, A U E T S A, 1991).

Sachs, Albie. "Preparing Ourselves for Freedom.," repr. in *Exchanges*, ed. Brown & van Dyk.

Smit, Johannes A., Johan Van Wyk & Jean–Philippe Wade, ed. *Rethinking South African Literary History* (Durban: Y Press, 1996).

Sole, Kelwyn. "Democratising Culture and Literature in a 'New South Africa': Organisation and Theory," *Current Writing* 6.2 (1994): 1–37.

Van Niekerk, Marlene. *Triomf*, tr. Leon de Kock (*Triomf*; Cape Town: Queillerie, 1994; tr. Johan-nesburg: Jonathan Ball, 1999).

Van Wyk, Chris. *The Year of the Tapeworm* (Johannesburg: Ravan, 1996).

Vladislavic, Ivan. *The Folly* (Africasouth New Writing; Johannesburg: David Philip, 1993).

Wade, Jean–Philippe. "Genealogies of Desire," in *Rethinking South African Literary History*, ed. Smit et al., 236–46.

《●》》

Post-Apartheid Transculturalism
in Sipho Sepamla's *Rainbow Journey*
and J.M. Coetzee's *Disgrace*

BRIAN WORSFOLD

A COMPARISON of Sipho Sepamla's *Rainbow Journey*, which was first published in 1996, with J.M. Coetzee's *Disgrace*, first published in 1999, is appropriate because they are very recent novels by two well-known contributors to what have been perceived as the black South African and white South African literary discourses respectively. Furthermore, the narrative line of both works is framed within a journey which takes the central character from one cultural environment to another. In *Rainbow Journey*, Beauty Radebe transculturalizes from the Ciskei village of Ditapoleng to the Soweto townships while, in *Disgrace*, Professor David Lurie escapes the city life of Cape Town to go to live with his daughter, Lucy, on her small farm in Eastern Cape. In sociological terms, Beauty moves from rural village to urban sprawl, while David Lurie moves from Cape Town suburbia to the rural Eastern Cape; in political terms, Beauty moves from the apartheid-engendered poverty of the homelands towards black empowerment in the post-apartheid cities of South Africa, while David Lurie abandons white privilege in the city and resigns himself to total dis-empowerment in the countryside. In short, while the physical directions of the journeys are diametrically opposed, that is, rural-urban and urban–rural, the political backdrop is the same: namely, decreasing white empowerment giving way to increasing black empowerment in an all-race democratic South Africa.

Were it not for the last two chapters, Sipho Sepamla's *Rainbow Journey* would be unremarkable. Although published at the outset of the post-apartheid period, *Rainbow Journey* is set in apartheid South Africa and, as the backcover note warns, "revisits the popular theme of a country girl escaping the debility of rural life to seek happiness in the bright lights of city life."[1] To be fair to Sepamla, the story-line is not quite that bland. However, Beauty's journey from her rural Ciskei home to the Soweto townships is a well-trodden path in South African literature and even her link with the murder of Thapelo Konopi, her wealthy and influential sugar-daddy, and the mystery and sus-

---

[1] Sipho Sepamla, *Rainbow Journey* (Florida Hills, S.A.: Vivlia, 1996): back cover.

90   BRIAN WORSFOLD

pense surrounding motive and assassin-identification, do not relieve the unrelenting
gloom or raise the novel much above the category of 'pulp fiction'. However, what
gives *Rainbow Journey* its discursive significance is the strong dynamic, positive,
entrepreneurial spirit which imbues its last two chapters. It is as if the novel had been
conceived and written for the most part during apartheid and completed during the
early months of the post-apartheid period. In this sense, it is a novel that straddles two
radically opposed eras, and the transition shows through the text.

    Sepamla dedicates *Rainbow Journey* "to all women, especially those who have had
to overcome abject adversity."[2] There is no doubt that the original authorial intention is
to narrate how a young black South African countrywoman moves to an urban
environment and survives a whole catalogue of iniquities and setbacks. In general, the
women in *Rainbow Journey* come off well, much better than the men, who are either
killed or end up besotted in the local shebeen. By the end of the novel, Beauty is
reconciled with MaMoeketsi, her mother-in-law, even though the latter lays some of
the blame for her son's murder while in police detention at the feet of her daughter-in-
law; and even Sis Eunice, Konopi's wife, who paid for her husband's assassination in
order to avenge herself of her husband's philandering with Beauty, is acquitted, to the
collective approval of the Soweto townswomen. Again, as the backcover coyly points
out, "The story raises a number of questions related to women's lib." Yet the narrative
drive of the last two chapters appears to stem not from any defence of feminism, but
from a new-found freedom; from Sepamla's own realization that the recent turn of
events in South Africa – the advent of the new all-race democracy – enables Beauty to
cast off the shackles of her recent past, which she had allowed her sexuality to place on
her, to make a clean break, and to reinvent herself in such a way that she does not need
to depend on her sexuality for survival.

    Beauty's change of fortune is extreme, her trajectory meteoric. She moves from the
poverty of her Ciskei home to become the well-known manufacturer of the "Afro-
dress." To Beauty, "It seemed she had walked the whole trip: from the rugged mountains of the Eastern Cape to the tall glassy buildings of Jo'burg. The rainbow journey
had been worthwhile."[3] Sepamla describes Beauty's transculturalization:

> Gone was the young girl who wore petticoats made of cotton bags of mealie-meal. She
> spoke eloquent English, never mind the heavy accent here and there. Her Afro-dresses
> became progressively outrageous; she wore earrings, bangles, rings, outlandish neck-
> laces; sometimes her waistbelts looked more like prison chains than ornaments for the
> body and her bead-brimmed hats were stylish [...] she drove top of the range cars usually
> associated with wealthy businessmen. (164–65)

Moreover, the young countrywoman who had been raped by Dusty, the co-driver of the
lorry which had brought her from Bloemfontein to Johannesburg, has succeeded in reconstructing her self-esteem:

[2] Sepamla, *Rainbow Journey*, dedication.
[3] *Rainbow Journey*, 164. Further page references are in the main text.

[Beauty] soared like a bird in the sky. She was so successful materially that nothing struck terror in her heart: she could look at her past without flinching from it. She was confident of herself. What she didn't have she would soon get because she had the means to attain anything money could buy. And a home she could call her own was at that moment uppermost in her mind. (171)

And all this is buoyed up by MaJoseph's consumer philosophy:

"The world is like a bottomless pit […]. It takes in everything as if never satisfied with what is offered. There are people out there waiting for new ways, new ideas. They are never saturated with something new: they will take what you offer and ask for more. Prepare to go big in your work, my child." (163)

In this way, Seplama transforms Beauty, the Ciskei countrywoman who created *isish-weshwe* skirts and dresses for Soweto's womenfolk, of "brown cloth spotted with yellow leaves" and of "green with dark blue flowers blooming all over" (162), into a model new South African female entrepreneur.

If changed circumstances in the new South Africa enable Sepamla to empower his female protagonist, the reverse is true for J.M. Coetzee, whose fifty-two-year-old David Lurie is subjected to a post-apartheid trajectory which is in essence an inverted mirror-image of that of Sepamla's heroine. Disgraced by the revelation of his affair with a student, Melanie Isaacs, Lurie descends from holding a professorship at Cape Town's Technical University to burning dead dogs at the Settlers' Hospital incinerator for a Grahamstown animal-welfare clinic. Professor David Lurie's quasi-tragic fall from grace is Coetzee's symbolization of white disempowerment in post-apartheid South Africa. With Lurie's sexuality as catalyst, Coetzee systematically deconstructs his protagonist, leading him from the weekly "oasis of *luxe et volupté*" in Cape Town, with the tall and slim Soraya with her "honey-brown body […] long black hair and dark, liquid eyes,"[4] to wild love-making sessions with Bev Shaw, the married lady who puts the dogs down, on the floor of Grahamstown's animal clinic. Even a brief return visit to Cape Town cannot restore any of Lurie's lost dignity, and he resigns himself to spending the rest of his days incinerating animal corpses in Grahamstown. In short, the trajectories of Sepamla's Beauty and Coetzee's Lurie are diametrically opposed. But for both writers, it is their characters' sexuality that provides the catalyst for their upward and downward mobility respectively.

During the apartheid era, the textualization of sexualities was a feature common to a large number of literary contributions to apartheid discourse by South African writers. White South African writers in particular appeared not to hesitate before focusing on the sexualities of white and black South Africans and, in so doing, provided an unintentional base for the perpetration of white supremacy in South Africa. As Ronald Hyam has said, "Sex is at the very heart of racism. […] Sexual fears are obviously capable of manipulation for political ends, such as the maintenance of white control."[5] Nadine Gordimer, Alan Paton, André Brink and J.M. Coetzee himself, to mention just

---

[4] J.M. Coetzee, *Disgrace* (London: Vintage, 2000): 1.

[5] Ronald Hyam, *Empire and Sexuality: The British Experience* (Manchester: Manchester UP, 1992): 203–04.

a few of the best-known South African writers, have all focused on differentiated and sometimes aberrant sexualities in their novels. It is not surprising, therefore, that J.M. Coetzee should parallel David Lurie's sexuality-linked disempowerment with the simultaneous, contiguous empowerment of the new black South African man. When Lurie goes to stay with his daughter on her farm at Salem in Eastern Cape, Lurie is forced to look on as Petrus, Lucy's black farmhand, takes control not only of her farm but even of her survival. When Petrus proposes to her father that Lucy would be best protected if she were to become another of his wives, Lurie is shocked to hear his daughter accede to the black man's conditions: "How humiliating," Lurie says finally. "Such high hopes, and to end like this" – to which Lucy responds:

> "Yes, I agree, it is humiliating. But perhaps that is a good point to start from again. Perhaps that is what I must learn to accept. To start at ground level. With nothing. Not with nothing but. With nothing. No cards, no weapons, no property, no rights, no dignity."
> "Like a dog."
> "Yes, like a dog."[6]

Lurie's own sexuality has lost all its power, even to be of help to his own daughter. He has been effectively emasculated by the changed circumstances, and the only gleam of light in Coetzee's plunge down the tunnel of white despair is that Lucy, the pragmatist, has understood this fact.

Black South African writers, on the other hand, have generally kept representations of sexuality well out of the spotlight. While the focus on sexuality in Coetzee's novel, therefore, is not unexpected, Sepamla's presentation of Beauty Radabe's sexuality in *Rainbow Journey* constitutes a departure from the conventional. Beauty's sexuality is a catalyst of the narrative. As a trainee nurse at Ditapoleng, she had had a brief relationship with Justice Moeketsi,

> She had not expected much from a boy from Soweto, known for jive and Kwela dances. But he swept her off her feet with his grace and panther-like movements on the floor... Everyone marvelled as they glided across the floor. Ah, Justice.
> She recalled their first night of passion. She had known men before, but Justice opened her eyes to all parts of the body. (111)

Then, later, once married to Justice, Beauty is forced to win the favours of Thapelo Konopi, a wealthy businessman, in order to get a Soweto residence permit and live legally with her husband in Soweto. She prepares herself carefully for her meeting with Konopi:

> If as it was said he had a way with young women, then he was going to meet one he couldn't touch because he would be down, smitten by her voluptuousness.
> That last look in the mirror brought a smile to her face. She looked at herself in the same way a sculptor admired his own work of art. She turned left, pushed a leg forward, turned right, did likewise, stood back, went forward, bit her lower lip, touched it with a light finger and then smiled to herself. She was truly a piece of art. (80–81)

---

[6] Coetzee, *Disgrace*, 205.

As Beauty grows increasingly aware of the power of her sexuality, so Justice is forced to realize his own weakness; as Justice complains bitterly about how he is "treated like a child" and is tired of "being lectured on how to live with [his] wife," Konopi is doing things for Beauty "which she never dreamt would be part of her life" (105).

However, Beauty's relationship with Konopi leads to his murder, carried out on the instructions of Sis Eunice, his wife, and to the death in detention of Justice, Beauty's husband. Beauty regrets the death of Konopi more than that of Justice. Konopi had "looked after her, gave her a confidence in herself [and] had made her dreams come true" (112), whereas Beauty's loss of innocence causes her to realize that "life with Justice had been like a drifter's because they did not have a place of their own to call home" (172). In her widowhood, this realization provides grounds enough for Beauty to turn all her energies and her charms towards "building the house of her dreams [and] modelling hers on Konopi's [which she] had seen on the day of his burial" (171).

Both novels are about the survival of men and women in post-apartheid South Africa. Both Beauty and Lucy are entrepreneurs, both pragmatists, both realists, both capitalists, both consumers, and both resigned to the fact that relationships with men should be based on their usefulness. Beauty has used Konopi and Lucy intends using Petrus. Otherwise, they learn to be entirely self-sufficient and independent. However, by the end of *Rainbow Journey*, Sepamla leaves Beauty in an "Afro-dress she wore for the event [which] was green with rectangular figures in black, yellow and white. It matched her turban-like *doek* resembling a high-roofed hut. Beauty was so smart and elegant no-one could miss her in a crowd" (167). By contrast, Coetzee leaves Lucy in a field "wearing a pale summer dress, boots, and a wide straw hat."[7] As for the men, at his funeral, Justice Moeketsi is revered as a popular hero, an example of the new Soweto man, an icon epitomizing "the youth of Soweto [...] who had led his life with a bang and now his death reverberated throughout the ghetto and the city" (133). Conversely, Coetzee's David Lurie prepares to eke out the rest of his life, incognito, in a Grahamstown boarding-house, in a "dark, stuffy, overfurnished [room], the mattress lumpy."[8] In short, both Coetzee's *Disgrace* and Sepamla's *Rainbow Journey* constitute important contributions to South African literary discourse, and Seplama's focus on female sexuality in his novel signifies a subliminal convergence with what Coetzee has termed "white writing,"[9] hinting at the future shape of all-race discourse parameters in South African literature. The respective transculturalizations of Beauty Radebe and David Lurie have an aesthetic significance and are not simply cultural.

---

[7] Coetzee, *Disgrace*, 217.

[8] Coetzee, *Disgrace*, 211.

[9] See J.M. Coetzee, *White Writing: On the Culture of Letters in South Africa* (New Haven CT: Yale UP, 1988).

WORKS CITED

Coetzee, J.M. *Disgrace* (London: Vintage, 2000).

——. *White Writing: On the Culture of Letters in South Africa* (New Haven CT: Yale UP, 1988).

Hyam, Ronald. *Empire and Sexuality: The British Experience* (Manchester: Manchester UP, 1992).

Sepamla, Sipho. *Rainbow Journey* (Florida Hills, RSA: Vivlia, 1996).

⟨⟨•⟩⟩

Translating Oneself Into the New South Africa
Fiction of the 1990s

ANDRÉ VIOLA

T HIS STUDY examines the fiction of transition – in its white and black components – in the years before and after the 1994 general elections, with an
occasional plunge back into time so as to suggest possible antecedents.
Changes, even in literary matters, are rarely brought about overnight, and this is true
of the white interregnum from the period of the dismantling of apartheid to the dawn of
a more democratic South Africa. The early 1990s were indeed characterized by impos-
sibilities, "impassabilities," people continuing to put up "screens against the sky" – as
intimated by Elleke Boehmer's title of 1990. Similarly, at the beginning of Coetzee's
Age of Iron (1990), the man who fits bars on Mrs Curren's windows declares "Now
you are safe,"[1] completely unaware as he is of the ironical undertones he generates.
With barriers thus erected against any prospect of change – a situation also reflected in
the frequent use of the narrative present – many novels were unable to translate themselves into the future, and not a few still looked back towards the past.

Thus, W.P.B. Botha, a long time exile, published *A Duty of Memory* in 1997, a novel
staging forty years of unabated sound and fury on Afrikaner farms up to the time of the
Truth and Reconciliation Commission. In this involved story, the multiple viewpoints
and distorted chronology no doubt reflect the difficulty of putting the past into perspective, as well as an obscure sense of guilt. The same comments may apply to the two
novels by Jo–Anne Richards, *The Innocence of Roast Chicken* (1996) and *Touching
the Lighthouse* (1997), in which violent or painful past events continue to determine
the present. Geoffrey Haresnape's *Testimony* (1992), a baffling allegorical work,
attempts somewhat unconvincingly to redeem a past of brutality by a final transfiguration. André Brink's novels – either in part or as a whole – also keep returning to the
past. Yet, although violence can be found everywhere, they are at least written with a
gusto that generally precludes any feeling of morbidity. This is far from being the case
with Mike Nicol's *The Powers That Be* (1989), *This Day and Age* (1992), and, above
all, *Horseman* (1994). This novel, with its unrelenting string of cruel scenes, appar-

---

[1] J.M. Coetzee, *Age of Iron* (London: Secker & Warburg, 1990): 25.

ently implies that violence is innate in man, that might is right, so that any oppression seems to be justified, and nobody is guilty – a disturbing position to adopt at the time of the Truth and Reconciliation Commission. Lastly, one might mention *Dance with a Poor Man's Daughter*, in which the author, Pamela Jooste, re-creates the past life of another community, thus reactivating the *Poppie* syndrome – "who has a right to speak for whom?" – that in itself would require a whole discussion.

A few novels, however, do envisage the future, but with a great diversity of approaches. On the one hand, Steve Jacobs' *The Enemy Within* (1995) boils down to an advocacy of exile after the "bloody war" announced on the last page. For her part, Maureen Isaacson, in her title story "Holding Back Midnight" (first published in 1992), projects herself to the eve of the new millennium and brings devastating irony to bear on white people entering the future backwards. Very often, one comes across curiously suspended endings, as in the typical last sentence of Menán du Plessis' *Longlive!*: "What are we supposed to do now?"[2] Nadine Gordimer has, from the start, practised these suspended endings with consummate skill. As if everything had been planned in advance, her novels stop short at a stage that will be taken up again in some later novel, each time with a deeper involvement of the main character in the South African situation. Consequently, when we look back with hindsight, the last words of her first novel, *The Lying Days* (1953), have a somewhat comical ring. The heroine, after having lived a very sheltered youth, has just boarded a ship sailing for England and declares: "I'm not running away [...] I know I'm coming back here,"[3] a fulfilled prophecy that no doubt allowed the author to win the Nobel Prize. The return of the character is effected in the next novel, *A World of Strangers* (1958), in the guise of an Englishman who frantically immerses himself in the night life of the black townships. In *The Late Bourgeois World* (1966), Liz Van Den Sandt will probably – after the end of the novel, that is – facilitate the funding of the black resistance movement, while Rosa, Burger's daughter, actually comes back to help in a concrete way in the aftermath of the Soweto uprising. *July's People* (1981) ends with Maureen's notorious leap into the unknown – friend or foe? – a kind of animal response which will be part of Hillela's attitude to life (*A Sport of Nature*, 1987). This attitude has not been to every critic's taste, but Hillela will carry the baton, tentatively handed on by Maureen, as far as a marriage (a trans-alliance?) with a revolutionary leader.

J.M. Coetzee has also made use of suspended endings or, more accurately perhaps, of ineffectual gestures. Magda utterly fails in getting nearer her two servants who soon desert her, leaving her desperately signalling to extraterrestrial beings. The magistrate attempts to establish contact with the Barbarian girl, but his doings are so riddled with guilt and repressed sadism that he too is left suspended, waiting for Barbarians that may never come. With two other novelists, suitcases come to play the role of an objective correlative for these aborted gestures. The protagonist of Michael Cope's *Spiral of Fire* (1987) agonizes over a suitcase he has accepted to hide for a time at the request of an activist friend, while Elleke Boehmer's heroine in *Screens Against the Sky* is soon persuaded to dump a similarly compromising suitcase on a rubbish heap. In Boehmer's

---

[2] Menán Du Plessis, *Longlive!* (Cape Town: David Philip, 1989): 255.
[3] Nadine Gordimer, *The Lying Days* (London: Virago, 1983): 367.

next novel, *An Immaculate Figure* (1993), Rosandra drives two militants across the border, but this isolated act leaves her completely "immaculate" as regards political consciousness.

There are however more effective translations, in the sense that new issues and new situations come to the foreground, such as homosexuality, which begins to be transcribed into visibility after decades of nearly complete blackout.[4] Only Stephen Gray had begun to tackle the theme openly in his 1988 and 1989 novels, followed by Damon Galgut and Anthony Sher.[5] One could also mention the serial killings of homosexuals in Botha's *A Duty of Memory* (1997), or an overt lesbian episode in Jo-Anne Richards' *Touching the Lighthouse* (1997), but an index of the enlarged currency of the theme is that Gordimer and Coetzee fully take it into account. In *None to Accompany Me* (1994), Vera Stark has great difficulties in accepting that her daughter should declare herself satisfied with her lesbian couple and their adopted child, while the parents in *The House Gun* (1998) discover all of a sudden that their son has been living complex sexual relationships. In Coetzee's *Disgrace*, Lucy's father finds it hard to conceive how she could have lived for a time with another woman, and he often broods over her daughter's sexual preferences.

Another important issue is the question: "which house are the whites going to live in?" – a question that has haunted Gordimer from an early date. Mehring's dream of a house in the country soon becomes a nightmare as he feels his farm is inhabited by the corpse of an unknown African.[6] Lionel Burger, in spite of a comfortable house, chooses to spend his life in prison for his political convictions, whereas his daughter is tempted to spend the rest of her existence in comfortable villas on the French Riviera. The translation of the Smales to a hut in a remote village – when they have become part of July's people – gives rise to unexpected readjustments that completely destabilize Maureen. Even in her 1991 collection of short stories (*Jump and Other Stories*), the metaphor of the house, as shown in a fine analysis by Johan Jacobs, underlies the

---

[4] There are, for instance, inconclusive allusions concerning Mehring's son in Gordimer's *The Conservationist* (1974).

[5] See: Stephen Gray, *Time of our Darkness* (1988), *Born of Man* (1989), and *Accident of Birth: An Autobiography* (1993); Damon Galgut, *Small Circles of Being* (1988) and *The Beautiful Screaming of Pigs* (1991); Anthony Sher, *Middlepost* (1988), *The Indoor Boy* (1991), and *Cheap Lives* (1995); there is also an episode in Isaac Mogotsi's *The Alexandra Tales* (Johannesburg: Ravan, n.d. 1994?; 56–57); Mark Behr's *The Smell of Apples* (1995) caused quite a stir, but it was originally published in Afrikaans. On homosexuality in South Africa, see also: *The Invisible Ghetto: Lesbian and Gay Writing from South Africa*, ed. Matthew Krouse & Kim Berman (Johannesburg: COSAW, 1993); *Defiant Desire: Gay and Lesbian Lives in South Africa*, ed. Mark Gevisser & Edwin Cameron (Johannesburg: Ravan, 1994); Michiel Heyns, "A Man's World: White South African Gay Writing and the State of Emergency," in *Writing South Africa*, ed. Derek Attridge & Rosemary Jolly (Cambridge: Cambridge UP, 1998): 108–22; *Journal of Southern African Studies: Masculinities in South Africa* 24.4 (December 1998).

[6] Conversely, Mehring keeps remembering a taunting remark by his former mistress: "No one'll remember where you're buried"; Gordimer, *The Conservationist* (Harmondsworth: Penguin, 1978): 177; 184; 250.

various situations represented.[7] A significant stage is reached in the 1994 novel *None to Accompany Me*, whose title clearly indicates that Vera will be the only white "tenant"[8] living in an "annexe" of a black friend. To everyone's surprise, she has indeed sold the house that symbolized her former privileged status, "a late bourgeois tomb," as Coetzee's Mrs Curren, apparently well-read in South African fiction, had dubbed her own house in *Age of Iron*.[9]

Coetzee's more recent novel *Disgrace*, published in 1999, takes into account the new conditions for white settlement. As shown in a dialogue between daughter and father, Lucy is no longer romanticizing about the house and the land she bought: "This is not a farm, it's just a piece of land where I grow things."[10] Yet, despite the ordeal she had to undergo and the entreaties of her father, she adds: "But no, I'm not giving it up," and she is actually prepared to accept the "deal" her former African "assistant"[11] is offering her: "I contribute the land, in return for which I am allowed to creep in under his wing. Otherwise, he wants to remind me, I am without protection, I am fair game."[12] The house she will be allowed to retain will also harbour the child of rape she declares she will keep, being – according to other characters – "adaptable," "forward-looking."[13] This is the startling decision she has finally reached and which her father has still to come round to. Lastly, in an entirely different mood, Ivan Vladislavic's *The Folly* (1993) equally centres on a house that is painstakingly erected and then abandoned, a fascinating verbal construction which should probably be read as a parable on the desirability of metafictional writing versus mimetic realism, of migrancy versus fixity, or, in Deleuze and Guattari's terms, of nomadism versus territorialization.[14]

In all these novels, the African characters may generally be said to represent survival in various guises – in other words, the power to endure. Gordimer's characters, for instance, when she works within the terms of the Lukács brand of realism she advocates, stand as representative members of a changing society, like the successfully integrated Zeph Rapulana, who does good business in *None to Accompany Me*, or Hamilton Motsamai, the famous black lawyer who, in a complete reversal of former roles, now assists the bewildered white parents of the accused in *The House Gun*. This is why the earlier Gordimer was perhaps a more creative novelist than in the later novels, not appealing, as Njabulo Ndebele would say, to a mere sense of recognition in readers, but to their imaginative powers also. Thus, in the allusive mode of approach of *The Conservationist*, we observe how the dead African gradually takes possession of Mehring's

---

[7] Johan Jacobs, "Finding a Safe House of Fiction: Nadine Gordimer's *Jump and Other Stories*," in *Telling Stories: Postcolonial Short Fiction in English*, ed. Jacqueline Bardolph (Cross/ Cultures 47; Amsterdam & Atlanta GA: Rodopi, 2001): 197–204.

[8] Nadine Gordimer, *None to Accompany Me* (London: Bloomsbury, 1994): 321.

[9] Coetzee, *Age*, 137.

[10] Coetzee, *Disgrace* (London: Secker & Warburg, 1999): 200.

[11] Coetzee, *Disgrace*, 62.

[12] *Disgrace*, 203.

[13] *Disgrace*, 210 & 136.

[14] See Gilles Deleuze & Félix Guattari, *Anti-Oedipus*, vol. 2, *A Thousand Plateaus*, tr. Brian Massumi (London: Athlone, 1988).

mind, then, after being given a proper burial by the African labourers, how he symbolically repossesses "this earth, theirs,"[15] a land he will regenerate with his own body. In this sense, Gordimer prefigured the novels of J.M. Coetzee, which have often been criticized for their non-mimetic approach to the South African situation. Coetzee's aim was certainly not to try and create life-like Africans, but to conceive strange figures with a marginal status – a Barbarian girl, a hare-lipped dull-witted gardener, a mutilated black slave, an alcoholic tramp – but who are, in the end, more attuned to their surroundings than the confused whites. Thus, the Barbarian girl finds refuge in her community, whereas the magistrate remains a thoroughly lonely man; Michael K has more definite plans for the future than the two white officials, and Vercueil in *Age of Iron* is spared the agonizing uncertainties of Mrs Curren. Since this old lady is locked up in the liberal notions of honour and shame, it takes her a long time to perceive the message of heroism of Bheki and John, the bearers of new values. The two boys, who represent all those who had formerly been outside the frame of the white family photograph,[16] are now placed at the centre of a moment of glory which, in spite of their deaths, becomes meaningful for the people around them. This novel is a meditation on the historical 1986 state of emergency, reinterpreted through ancient myths. Nearly ten years afterwards, *Disgrace* represents a new stage, and Petrus, within a realistic envelope, plays an emblematic if somewhat enigmatic role. He thus passes from the status of "dog-man"[17] to that of new owner of the land, protector and potential husband of the white heroine. Again, Petrus may be said to have two ancestors in Gordimer: first, July, who, from obedient house servant, becomes a potentate in his own village, no longer needing to translate his vernacular to tell Maureen his own version of things; and, further back in time, Mehring's headman Jacobus, 'he who supplants', according to biblical etymology (Genesis 25:26).

The black African writers, having been subjected to particular historical circumstances, have developed an approach to novel-writing which is necessarily different from that of the whites, even though some of them also look towards the past and others try to cope with the new situation. The first group, considering themselves as bearers of memory in the wake of Bessie Head in *Serowe: Village of the Rain Wind* (1981) or Ellen Kuzwayo in *Sit Down and Listen* (1990), aim at restoring experiences long repressed, as can been seen in various texts by Sindiwe Magona or in the flashback sections of Zakes Mda's *Ways of Dying* (1995). A singular approach is that of Chris van Wyk's *The Year of the Tapeworm* (1996), in which he rewrites the past as an absurd farce, no doubt with a view to exorcizing it. Other novels plunge further back into the 1950s and 1960s: Réshard Gool's *Cape Town Coolie* (1990), Ronnie Govender's *At the Edge* (1996; subtitled *Cato Manor Stories*), Johnny Masilela's *Deliver Us from Evil* (1997), a series of interconnected vignettes of life in the country, James Matthews' *The Party is Over* (1997), a novel that shows how an artistic career could be blocked by apartheid. Apart from these texts, which often border on the anecdotal, the

---

[15] Gordimer, *The Conservationist*, 267.

[16] See Coetzee, *Age of Iron*, 102–03 & 138.

[17] Coetzee, *Disgrace*, 64.

concern with the past mainly takes the form of a tribute to the militants against apartheid.

There is, first, an odd novel, *The Innocents* (1994) by Tatamkhulu Afrika – a work that, although the author participated in the struggle, unexpectedly presents armed resistance in a humoristic way.[18] Mbulelo Mzamame in *The Children of the Diaspora* (1996) deals with the everyday difficulties of exile, without the least trace of idealization. Similarly, Mandla Langa's *The Naked Song* (1996) emphasizes the casualties of exile and guerrilla fighting, as well as the role of women in military action. Mongane Serote, in *Gods of our Time* (1999), explores all the consequences of underground resistance on human personality, so that the lack of round characters seems the price to pay for a life of hidden or double identities.[19] These last two novels are of particular interest because they foreground the often neglected role of women in society, a concern shared by Sindiwe Magona. In the latter's denunciation of the conditions imposed on women, in particular various forms of violence done to them mainly in an urban context, she continues what Lauretta Ngcobo had done for village women of the 1950s in *And They Didn't Die* (1990). Magona's first full-length novel (*Mother to Mother*, 1998) echoes the issues of guilt and forgiveness raised by the Truth and Reconciliation Commission as it centres on the grief of two mothers, a white mother whose daughter was murdered, a black mother whose son was one of the murderers. Quite different in tone is Sipho Sepamla's *Rainbow Journey* (1996), which is entirely devoted to a South African Jagua Nana, a township Moll Flanders actuated by remarkable resilience. This is a story which, in spite of all the odds, culminates in a positive ending. Zakes Mda's *Ways of Dying* (1995) strikes a similar note, notwithstanding its grim subject-matter. The main character is a professional mourner, and the horrors of violent deaths and of funerals are either reported with the deadpan voice of the narrator or presented in the unemotional tone of the professional who plays the role of a modern-day gull. Yet, after a succession of harrowing situations, the end is more serene, and a desired marriage can be envisaged for the main character. Conversely, in the years before the 1990s, the possibility of a short-term change for the better was rarely considered by novelists, who tended to situate it in an unspecified future.[20]

On the whole, most of the recent works written by black novelists have one element in common, corresponding to the category of the ordinary as defined by Ndebele. Thus, among the characters, there are fewer exceptional beings exclusively committed to the fight against the regime, and more people entangled in the problems of everyday life, bearing the brunt of apartheid in an oblique fashion, as was already the case in the stories of Joël Matlou, collected in 1991. In that respect, these unexceptional people can be said to represent the majority of the population who resisted oppression through an obscure fight for survival. In addition, a typical marker of the ordinary in the texts is

[18] The book cover mentions a mixed Middle East ancestry.

[19] Gillian Slovo's *Betrayal* (1991) deals with the atmosphere of suspicion that could exist in the underground world of the ANC on account of the potential betrayals.

[20] See examples of what I called "meteorological millenarianism" in André Viola, Jacqueline Bardolph & Denise Coussy, *New Fiction in English from Africa, West, East, and South* (Cross/Cultures 34; Amsterdam & Atlanta GA: Rodopi, 1998): 166–67.

the increasing number of references to the independent African churches and to traditional religions.[21] Previously, apart from satirical portraits or Maseko's "Mamlambo"
(1982) and Ndebele's "The Prophetess" (1983), this strong undercurrent of South African life had been overlooked, no doubt because it was presumed to offend the canons
of Western rationality. And yet, for about a hundred years, the popular appeal of syn-
cretism and of Zionist churches has denoted a strong resistance to the wholesale introduction of foreign ways of apprehending existence, including religious experience.[22] A
return to the ordinary, both by black and white novelists, thus implies a presentation of
South African life in all its quirks and particularities, and paradoxically takes into
account as well what would be defined as non-rational by Western positivist thinkers.
This new attitude in turn affects the mode of writing itself. In the wake of Ivan
Vladislavic and Mike Nicol, fantastic situations have begun to inform some narratives,
as can be observed in those of Zakes Mda and Chris van Wyk, even though magical
realism as it is generally understood has not really penetrated the literary scene. Perhaps Achmat Dangor's novella *Kafka's Curse* (1997) is the best example of what is
gradually taking place. It is a cocktail of South African Muslim life and multiple inter-
marriages, shifting points of view with no authorial reassurance, not even with respect
to the numerous mysterious murders, bewildering happenings and, above all, characters changing names and identities in a constant process of transmutation. This novella,
indeed, can be regarded as representing one of the possible directions South African
literature may take to escape the exclusive predominance of realism in its traditional
acceptation.

WORKS CITED

Afrika, Tatamkhulu. *The Innocents* (Cape Town: David Philip, 1994).
Behr, Mark. *The Smell of Apples* (London: Abacus, 1995).
Boehmer, Elleke. *An Immaculate Figure* (London: Bloomsbury, 1993).
——. *Screens Against the Sky* (London: Bloomsbury, 1990).
Botha, W.P.B. *A Duty of Memory* (London: Heinemann, 1997).
Brink, André. *Devil's Valley* (London: Secker & Warburg, 1998).
——. *The First Life of Adamastor* (London: Secker & Warburg, 1993).
——. *Imaginings of Sand* (London: Secker & Warburg, 1996).
——. *On the Contrary* (London: Secker & Warburg, 1993).
Coetzee, J.M. *Age of Iron* (London: Secker & Warburg, 1990).
——. *Disgrace* (London: Secker & Warburg, 1999).
——. *In the Heart of the Country* (London: Secker & Warburg, 1977).
——. *Life and Times of Michael K* (London: Secker & Warburg, 1983).

---

[21] See, for instance, Isaac Mogotsi, *The Alexandra Tales* (Johannesburg: Ravan, 1994?): 113–
30; Zakes Mda, *Ways of Dying* (Cape Town: Oxford UP, 1995): 96–98; 152; Mandla Langa,
"The Resurrection of the River Artist," in *The Naked Song* (1996); Sindiwe Magona, "A Drowning in Cala," in *Push-Push!* (1996); Chris van Wyk, *The Year of the Tapeworm* (Johannesburg:
Ravan, 1996): 77.

[22] See B.G.M. Sundkler, *Bantu Prophets in South Africa* (London: Oxford UP, 1948; revised
1968); Mike Nicol's *This Day and Age* deals obliquely with the so-called Bulhoek rebellion.

Cope, Michael. *Spiral of Fire* (Cape Town: David Philip, 1987).
Dangor, Achmat. *Kafka's Curse* (Cape Town: Kwela, 1997).
Deleuze, Gilles, & Félix Guattari. *Anti-Oedipus*, vol 2, *A Thousand Plateaus*, tr. Brian Massumi (London: Athlone, 1988).
Du Plessis, Menán. *Longlive!* (Cape Town: David Philip, 1989).
Galgut, Damon. *The Beautiful Screaming of Pigs* (1991; Abacus, 1992).
——. *The Quarry* (Johannesburg: Viking Penguin, 1995).
——. *Small Circle of Beings* (1988; Abacus, 1990).
Gevisser, Mark, & Edwin Cameron, ed. *Defiant Desire: Gay and Lesbian Lives in South Africa* (Johannesburg: Ravan, 1994).
Gool, Réshard. *Cape Town Coolie* (London: Heinemann, 1990).
Gordimer, Nadine. *Burger's Daughter* (London: Jonathan Cape, 1979).
——. *The Conservationist* (1974; Harmondsworth: Penguin, 1978).
——. *The House Gun* (London: Bloomsbury, 1998).
——. *July's People* (London: Jonathan Cape, 1981).
——. *Jump and Other Stories* (London: Bloomsbury, 1991).
——. *The Late Bourgeois World* (London: Victor Gollancz, 1966).
——. *The Lying Days* (1953; Virago, 1983).
——. *None to Accompany Me* (London: Bloomsbury, 1994).
——. *A Sport of Nature* (London: Jonathan Cape, 1987).
——. *A World of Strangers* (London: Victor Gollancz, 1958).
Gool, Réshard. *Cape Town Coolie* (London: Heinemann, 1990).
Govender, Ronnie. *At the Edge and Other Cato Manor Stories* (Pretoria: Manx, 1996).
Gray, Stephen. *Accident of Birth: An Autobiography* (Johannesburg: C O S A W , 1993).
——. *Born of Man* (Rivonia, SA: Justified; London: G.M.P., 1989).
——. *Time of Our Darkness* (London: Century Hutchinson, 1988).
Haresnape, Geoffrey. *Testimony* (Rivonia, S.A.: Justified, 1992).
Head, Bessie. *Serowe: Village of the Rain Wind* (London: Heinemann, 1981).
Heyns, Michiel. "A Man's World: White South African Gay Writing and the State of Emergency," in *Writing South Africa*, ed. Derek Attridge & Rosemary Jolly (Cambridge: Cambridge UP, 1998): 108–22.
Isaacson, Maureen. *Holding Back Midnight* (Johannesburg: COSAW, 1992).
Jacobs, Johan. "Finding a Safe House of Fiction: Nadine Gordimer's *Jump and Other Stories*," in *Telling Stories: Postcolonial Short Fiction in English*, ed. Jacqueline Bardolph (Cross/Cultures 47; Amsterdam & Atlanta GA: Rodopi, 2001): 197–204.
Jacobs, Steve. *The Enemy Within* (London: Heinemann, 1995).
Jooste, Pamela. *Dance with a Poor Man's Daughter* (London: Doubleday, 1998).
Journal of Southern African Studies: Masculinities in South Africa 24.4 (December 1998).
Krouse, Matthew, & Kim Berman, ed. *The Invisible Ghetto: Lesbian and Gay Writing from South Africa* (Johannesburg: COSAW, 1993).
Kuzwayo, Ellen. *Sit Down and Listen* (London: The Women's Press, 1990).
Langa, Mandla. *The Naked Song and Other Stories* (Cape Town: David Philip, 1996).
Magona, Sindiwe. *Forced to Grow* (Cape Town: David Philip, 1992).
——. *Living, Loving, Lying Awake at Night* (Cape Town: David Philip, 1991).
——. *Mother to Mother* (Cape Town: David Philip, 1998).
——. *Push-Push!* (Cape Town: David Philip, 1996).
——. *To My Children's Children* (Cape Town: David Philip, 1990).
Maseko, Bheki. *Mamlambo and Other Stories* (Fordsburg & Johannesburg: COSAW, 1991).
Masilela, Johnny. *Deliver Us from Evil* (Cape Town: Kwela, 1997).

Matlou, Joël. *Life at Home and Other Stories* (Fordsburg & Johannesburg: COSAW, 1991).
Mattera, Don. *The Storyteller* (Johannesburg: Justified Press, 1991).
Matthews, James. *The Party* (Cape Town: Kwela, 1997).
Mda, Zakes. *Ways of Dying* (Cape Town: Oxford UP, 1995).
Mogotsi, Isaac. *The Alexandra Tales* (Johannesburg: Ravan, n.d. 1994?).
Mzamane, Mbulelo. *The Children of the Diaspora and Other Stories of Exile* (Johannesburg: Vivlia, 1996).
Ngcobo, Lauretta. *And They Didn't Die* (London: Virago, 1990).
Nicol, Mike. *Horseman* (London: Bloomsbury, 1994).
——. *The Ibis Tapestry* (New York: Alfred A. Knopf, 1998).
——. *The Powers That Be* (London: Bloomsbury, 1989).
——. *This Day and Age* (Cape Town: David Philip; London: Bloomsbury, 1992).
Richards, Jo Anne. *The Innocence of Roast Chicken* (London: Review, 1996).
——. *Touching the Lighthouse* (London: Review, 1997).
Sepamla, Sipho. *Rainbow Journey* (Johannesburg: Vivlia, 1996).
Serote, Mongane. *Gods of our Time* (Johannesburg: Ravan, 1999).
Sher, Anthony. *Cheap Lives* (London: Little, Brown: 1995; Abacus, 1996).
——. *Middlepost* (London: Little, Brown: 1988).
Slovo, Gillian. *Betrayal* (London: Michael Joseph, 1991).
Sundkler, B.G.M. *Bantu Prophets in South Africa* (London: Oxford UP, 1948; rev. ed. 1968).
Van Wyk, Chris. *The Year of the Tapeworm* (Johannesburg: Ravan, 1996).
Viola, André, Jacqueline Bardolph & Denise Coussy. *New Fiction in English from Africa* (Cross/Cultures 34; Amsterdam & Atlanta GA: Rodopi, 1998).
Vladislavic, Ivan. *The Folly* (Cape Town: David Philip, 1993; London: Serif, 1994).
——. *Propaganda by Monuments* (Cape Town: David Philip, 1996).

《●》

The S(p)ecular 'Convert'
A Response to Gauri Viswanathan's *Outside the Fold*

CLARA JOSEPH

> When your mind is no longer disturbed by the flowery
> language of the *Vedas* and when it remains fixed in the trance
> of self-realization, then you will have attained the divine
> consciousness.
> — *Bhagavad-gītā* 2.56

ITHIN A FRAMEWORK of Marxian and Lacanian theories of representation and language consider the 'convert' as Other through whom the
subject is defined. While conversion remains a suspect activity, the convert is at once the cause and effect of contending religious and political discourses. As
outsider, the convert's position within the representational and the social demands a
second look at subjectivity in the context of which the "s(p)ecular" suggests the
deflective link between the reflective and the worldly where gender roles and gendered
narratives have material effects. This essay offers a reading of Lalithambika Antherjanam's short story "Vidhibalam," translated from Malayalam by Gita Krishnankutty
as "The Power of Fate," as a response to Gauri Viswanathan's arguments on conversion and its role in society. In the preface to her book, Viswanathan argues that Indian
secularism is actually a very Hindu policy, one which encourages Hindu fanaticism at
the expense of minority religions and laws. However, her arguments advance the
nationalist claims of the dominant religion.

Gauri Viswanathan's *Outside the Fold* won the Ananda K. Coomaraswamy Prize,
the James Russell Lowell Prize, and the Harry Levin Prize in 1999. Viswanathan's
main focus in this work is the destabilizing effect of conversion on modern society.
The author defines conversion as not just a spiritual phase but as a political activity.
She relates the issue of the place of belief in subject-formation – what she terms
"worldliness"[1] – to the creation of secular societies both in England and in India.[2] Vis-

---

[1] In *The World, the Text and the Critic*, Edward Said argues against the formalist notion of the
literary text where textuality is isolated from "the circumstances, the events, the physical senses

wanathan establishes several links between religious and political occurrences in England and India in the eighteenth and nineteenth centuries. For example, she notes that Macaulay's "Minute on Indian Education. 2 February 1835" that aimed at producing Indians who were Indian in race but English in everything else was in England paralleled by attempts to "turn Jews into non-Jewish Jews, Catholics into non-Catholic Catholics, Dissenters into non-Dissenters, Non-conformists into non-Nonconformists, and so forth."[3] This, Viswanathan explains, is secularization, the process by which belief is privatized and made subordinate to the reason of the state. She continues: "Secularization in the colonies remains a flawed project, even more than in England, because of the absence of an emancipatory logic that steers *a once monolithic religious culture* into the gradual absorption of pluralized groups into the nation state." She argues that religious differences in England are successfully "subsumed within a national identity," except of course, she admits, for some disturbance along class lines. On the other hand, in India structures of governance were initially "colonial" and after independence "hegemonic," rather than national; minorities never really became citizens.[4]

Here are two of Viswanathan's premises:

1. Conversion is a key element in the definition of modern society. The identity of the state as "supreme legislator and arbitrator" (16) proceeds from the tensions that conversion raises.

2. Whereas the religious culture of England was always diverse, the religious culture of India was once *monolithic*.

The two premises are linked: the premise of A is B. That is to say, conversion in the context of India is politically troublesome because India (a colony), once "a monolithic religious culture," knew no need for conversion until recently. India therefore lacks an indigenous system to survive in the face of this newcomer. Colonization is one major force that often created converts and, even more, attempted an (impossible) assimilation of the various groups into the nation-state. Later on, the (still colonial) hegemony of secularism did no better.

In "Secularism, Hindu Nationalism and the Fear of the People," Ashis Nandy defines secularism as that which replaced "the traditional concepts of inter-religious understandings and tolerance that had allowed thousands [...] of communities living in the subcontinent to co-survive in neighbourliness"; the distinctive feature of this traditional co-survival was that it often involved violence that was not along religious

---

that made it possible and render it intelligible as the result of human work." For him, "texts are worldly, to some degree they are events, and, even when they appear to deny it, they are nevertheless a part of the social world, human life, and of course the historical moments in which they are located and interpreted"; Said, *The World, the Text and the Critic* (Cambridge MA: Harvard UP, 1983): 4. Viswanathan takes off from her *guru*'s stance to recognize Said's "realities of power and authority" in belief and identity; Viswanathan, *Outside the Fold: Conversion, Modernity, and Belief* (Princeton NJ: Princeton UP, 1998): 5.

[2] Viswanathan, *Outside the Fold*, xvi–xvii. Unless otherwise indicated, further page references to this study are in the main text.

[3] Viswanathan, *Outside the Fold*, 5.

[4] *Outside the Fold*, 12–13 (emphasis mine).

lines.[5] Whereas both Viswanathan and Nandy agree that secularism is an unwholesome product of modernity, they differ on an interpretation of tradition: for Viswanathan, pluralism is a modern and secular invasion, for Nandy, pluralism already existed in the non-secular, within traditional faith. The violence inflicted by secularism lies, then, for Nandy, in its disregard for plurality so that only a ripening of modernity could finally bring about the destruction of the Babri Masjid in Ayodhya and that too with the support of not rural locals but urban outsiders.[6]

Viswanathan's insistence on the monolithic nature of Hinduism forces her to downplay, if not deny, divisions of caste and culture in Hinduism. Consequently, religions that have dwelt in India for almost two thousand years remain "foreign" and episodes of caste-based exclusion become a British yarn. Further, it leads her to conclude arbitrarily, based on what Sr. Geraldine writes to Pandita Ramabai, that religious excommunication and the "withholding of citizenship rights" are the same and, moreover, that the sameness is 'naturalized', notwithstanding the fact that the original letter at no point suggests this link beyond the level of metaphor.[7] Viswanathan's claims that Pandita Ramabai's conflict with missionaries was in itself an assertion of national independence on her side and that religious restriction placed by the missionaries was a version of "colonial control" lack supporting evidence in her work.[8] Needless to say, the kingdom–government imagery in the aforementioned quotation is widespread, and certainly not exclusive to St. Geraldine's Church.[9]

Viswanathan's choice of topic – conversion – and period – the colonial – flags colonialism as a religious and not economic mission. While it is obvious that Christian missionaries were at work in the different colonies, precolonial religious missions, too, are not unheard of. In the case of India, the period 7 B C –7 A D was marked by Brahmin, Jewish, Buddhist, Christian, Jain, and Muslim migrations to certain parts of the land.[10]

---

[5] Ashis Nandy, "Secularism, Hindu Nationalism and the Fear of the People," in *Religion and Nationalism: Concilium,* ed. John Coleman & Miklós Tomka (London: S C M, 1995): 99.

[6] Nandy, "Secularism, Hindu Nationalism and the Fear of the People," 98.

[7] "Secularism, Hindu Nationalism and the Fear of the People," 89, 153, 124. Using the imagery of the kingdom in religious discourse can suggest a militant agenda, even if unintended.

[8] "Secularism, Hindu Nationalism and the Fear of the People," 135. Christianity and colonialism have often been described as essentially one by both colonizers and the colonized. While colonizers find justification in defining colonialism as a missionary and hence redemptive enterprise, the colonized consider Christianity to be colonialism's unkindest cut, in that it undermined indigenous religions and cultures. At least one result of this obsession with the religious effect and role of colonialism is that both the colonizers and the colonized unwittingly join to marginalize precolonial Christians and, eventually, those of other minority religions.

[9] And this is precisely why, in "The Power of Fate," lying in the lap of a Brahmin son is equivalent to being in the ancestral home, the holy land. Land and religion become inextricably bound and often border on the militant.

[10] K.P. Padmanabha Menon refers to various theories suggesting the arrival of the Namboodiris on the south-west coast between the 7th century B C and the 7th century A D. While several historians (including William Logan) argue for A D, Padmanabha Menon insists that the period of Arya Brahman advent was 700 BC (42–76) Similarly, Jews are recorded as having arrived in the west coast either during the conquest of Jerusalem by King Cyrus of Persia in the 6th century or during

The link between trade and religion cannot be ignored. Hermann Kulke and Dietmar Rothermund note that the increased trade of the first century AD, following Hippalos' discovery of a monsoon that could take ships across the Arabian Sea in just two weeks, was paralleled later only by European trade by the end of the fifteenth century.[11] The spread of Christianity and Islam to Kerala immediately after their inception doubtless owes much to this trade. However, it is dangerous to subordinate the economic factor in discussions of modern India. One of the major errors repeated in the nineteenth and early twentieth centuries by native and colonial administrators was to misinterpret rebellions as expressions of religious aggression rather than as economic distress. Thus, in Kerala, the Muslim peasants' agitation against landlords and British imperialists was termed the "Moplah Rebellion," with the focus on the rebels' being *Moplah (Mapilla)* or Muslim rather than on their status as oppressed agricultural tenants.

Replacing class or gender with religious identity locates national discourse within that of 'race'. The insistence on a monolithic religious cultural past unwittingly abets the votaries of Dalitsthan and Dravidasthan, as it does those of the Rashtriya Seva Sangh (RSS), whose anthem conflates land and religion: "Forever I bow to thee, O loving Motherland! O Motherland of us Hindus...."[12] Ashis Nandy argues that it is not only secularism that has its origins in 'modernity' but fundamentalism as well. Thus, for him, the khaki uniforms of the RSS recall the colonial police force.[13] "Us Hindus" conjures up a religious identity that is 'racial', not national, so that a fundamentalist nationalism depends more on what Sumit Sarkar calls "a permanent majority" of census-based Hindus than on

the first century AD soon after the arrival of the Syrian Christians; Padmanabha Menon, *History of Kerala*, ed. T.K. Krishna Menon, 4 vols. (1924–36; New Delhi: Asian Educational Services, 1982–86), vol 2: 504. Buddhism spread to Kerala under the patronage of King Ashoka in the 3rd century BC; during the time of the visit of the Chinese traveller Hiuen Tsiang, Buddhism was the state religion of Kerala, while Jainism is said to have spread into the south by the 5th century AD; Padmanabha Menon, *History of Kerala*, vol 2: 47, 461. According to tradition, the last ruler of the Perumāl dynasty of Kerala, Cheramān Perumāl, influenced by pilgrims from Arabia who were on their way to Adam's peak in Ceylon, joined them in their return journey to Arabia. There the Peramāl met Prophet Muhammad and accepted Islam. He planned to return to Kerala but took ill and died in Arabia. However, before his death he was able to write letters to his governors in Kerala asking them to support the spread of the faith there. This tradition has been highly debated. However, the *Tarisāppalli* copperplate grant of 849 AD that was made to a Christian group bears the names of several Muslim merchants who were residents; Asghar Ali Engineer, ed. *Kerala Muslims* (New Delhi: Ajanta, 1995): 17–20. Also see K.N. Panikkar, *Against Lord and State: Religion and Peasant Uprisings in Malabar, 1836–1921* (Delhi: Oxford UP, 1989): 50. Trade with the various countries predated the encounter with the various religions.

[11] Kulke & Rothermund, *A History of India* (New York: Routledge, 1986): 105.

[12] K. Jayaprasad, *RSS and Hindu Nationalism: Inroads in a Leftist Stronghold* (New Delhi: Deep & Deep Publications, 1991): 363.

[13] Ashis Nandy, "The Politics of Secularism and the Recovery of Religious Tolerance," in *Mirrors of Violence: Communities, Riots and Survivors in South Asia*, ed. Veena Das (Delhi: Oxford UP, 1990): 83.

a democratic government.[14] Unfortunately, attempts are then made to recover indigenous origins as well as to imagine possibilities of 'racial erasure' through conversion.

Religious ideology does not constitute conversion where ideology, as Althusser defines it, is "lived life" – that is, where ideology represents the imaginary relation of the individual to the system of real relations.[15] An Althusserian definition cannot separate the private from the public so that life as lived equates with social effect rather than being any fictional or essentialist approximation to reality or realism.[16] In "The Politics of Secularism and the Recovery of Religious Tolerance," Nandy differentiates between religion as a plural tradition (religion-as-faith) and religion as a monolithic political tool (religion-as-ideology). For him, these "specific private meanings" are necessary, for example, to understand the creation of religious states by persons who are privately far from the representative faith.[17] "The people who today provoke or participate in communal frenzy guided by secular political cost calculations do have an ideology apparently based on faith," Nandy notes, "but on closer scrutiny it turns out to be only secularized, arbitrarily chosen elements of faith."[18] Nevertheless, as Viswanathan points out, this compartmentalizing of the two concepts is suspect, for the political impact of private faith is always a possibility.[19] It is also likely, then, that 'religion-as-ideology' can in turn be permeated by religion-as-faith, so that ideology as a political tool is, in the last instance, revealed to be not monolithic. The often resistant element of faith brings to ideology that which is unthinkable. As an examination of Lalithambika Antherjanam's short story "The Power of Fate" reveals, what is unthinkable within a patriarchal ideology is the fact that the name of God is equally accessible to 'the fallen woman'. Thinking this unthinkable within literary and religious discourse pronounces conversion an impossibility. Where the Lacanian symbolic order, of language, does not foreclose on the signifier God, the salient presence of the phallic within both the specular and the secular renders the female convert nonexistent.

In their essay "Literature as an Ideological Form," Balibar and Macherey begin their discussion of the reflective function of literature with the following quotation from Mao Tse-tung: "Works of literature and art, as ideological forms, are the product of the reflection in the human brain of the life of a given society." Literature as such does not "fall from heaven" but is part of "a material process" in which form and content are not

---

[14] Sumit Sarkar, *Writing Social History* (Delhi: Oxford UP, 1997): 361.

[15] Louis Althusser, *Lenin and Philosophy and Other Essays*, tr. Ben Brewster (New York: Monthly Review Press, 1971): 155.

[16] In *Representation: Cultural Representations and Signifying Practices*, Stuart Hall categorizes three approaches to theories of representation: the reflective, the intentional, and the constructionist. According to Hall and the school of cultural studies, the constructionist approach is particularly useful because it suggests that meaning can be produced by the representation beyond the worldly existence of what is represented or the intentions of the producer of the representation.

[17] Nandy, "The Politics of Secularism and the Recovery of Religious Tolerance," in *Mirrors of Violence: Communities, Riots and Survivors in South Asia* ed. Veena Das (Delhi: Oxford UP, 1990): 70.

[18] Nandy, "Secularism, Hindu Nationalism and the Fear of the People," 99.

[19] Viswanathan, *Outside the Fold*, 173.

opposing categories and reflection is constituted in material reality.[20] Literary language is produced as linguistic conflicts that are historically determined. Balibar and Macherey reject the metaphor of the mirror in their explanation of reflection in terms of dialectical materialism. The specular, they argue, denies the empiricism of ideology, for the image in the mirror is reversible. Within the Marxist paradigm, reflection is related, not to realism: i.e. literature as "a fictive image of the real," but to materialism: i.e. literature as "a material reality [...] a certain social effect." Literature is not without what the authors refer to as its "reality-effect" and "fiction-effect," both of which indicate the 'real' to be an effect of literary discourse rather than an external presence that can be understood in terms of "straight mirroring" (287).

In *Speculum of the Other Woman*, Luce Irigaray introduces the not straight mirror, the concave mirror of the speculum that produces a real, not virtual, image. This is the mirror about which Plato in *Timaeus* (46a-c) explains: "right appears right and the left left, when the position of one of the two concurring lights is reversed."[21] This instrument of gynaecological diagnosis exposes woman in terms of Otherness, not as lack. Irigaray's examination of woman as Other derives from Lacanian theories of the Imaginary and language.

As Other and not lack, Irigaray's Woman *becomes* the speculum in and from which the male subject draws his identity. "'She' must be only the path, the method, the theory, the *mirror*, which leads back, by a process of repetition, to the recognition of (his) origin for the 'subject'."[22] The subject needs the Other and the Other reflects subjectivity – as in the case of any visual image that demands scanning at least forty times per second to be believable – by 'repetition'.

Woman as specular is penetrated by the stubborn presence of the phallus, (p), the subject of opacity through which light cannot pass. Thus, the subject persists as "desire of the Other."[23] The desire or need is represented "by means of a subjective opacity."[24] The subject's opacity functions literally at two levels – in its visible presence at the specular as in its imperviousnes to light, and in its apparent absence, at the secular, in a certain unintelligibleness that must inevitably accompany the deferential nature of the symbolic order. The s(p)ecular hence remains as the site of phallic intervention, in which self-identity assumes Viswanathan's "worldliness," of being belief-based and political. The mirror initiates the entrance of the subject into the symbolic order, "the deflection of the specular I into the social I," and announces the omni-potence/ presence of "cultural mediation."[25]

[20] Étienne Balibar & Pierre Macherey, "Literature as an Ideological Form: Some Marxist Propositions," in *Marxist Literary Theory*, ed. Terry Eagleton & Drew Milne (Oxford: Blackwell, 1996): 278. Theories of the material reality of ideology and language are aligned with constructionist approaches that see meaning as produced in language.

[21] Quoted in Irigaray, *Speculum of the Other Woman*, tr. Gillian C. Gill (Ithaca NY: Cornell UP, 1985): 147.

[22] Irigaray, *Speculum of the Other Woman*, 239.

[23] Jacques Lacan, *Écrits: A Selection*. tr. Alan Sheridan (London: Tavistock, 1977): 312.

[24] Lacan, *Écrits*, 311.

[25] Irigaray, *Speculum of the Other Woman*, 5–6.

The textual/sexual reflection attributes to the reflector, the speculum of the other woman, the place of signifier in its capacity to represent the subject "for another signifier."[26] That is, reflected in the Other, the subject sees himself as not as he is. The signifying Other 'controls' the subject; the signifier governs the signified and the signified derives its meaning from the signifier. As Lacan says, "it is from the Other that the subject receives even the message that he emits."[27]

Understanding the s(p)ecularity of the Other is crucial to a symptomatic reading of feminist narratives. If a child's ability to grasp *his* own mirror image is "an essential stage of the act of intelligence,"[28] one can deduce that, within a patriarchal system, the s(p)ecular woman is desired and rendered appropriate, in that she 'permits' the comprehension of distinct gender roles. The homologous structure of the specular and the secular suggests that gender roles are not from heaven but are embedded in the social. Raymond Williams says that it "puts the origin of determination in men's own activities."[29]

Lalithambika Antherjanam's short story "The Power of Fate," written when the author was twenty-three years old, opens onto a scene of poverty, a hut, from which a dying woman in a Muslim household makes a strange wish – she wants to see Namboodiripad, the senior Brahmin (*namboodiri*), one last time. The woman's daughter seeks the help of the senior Brahmin's steward, and together they manage to get Namboodiripad to check out the land near the hut. As expected, cries soon bring the *namboodiri* into the hut, and the dying woman gets her wish. However, this moment of wish-fulfilment is also one of multiple shocks and surprises: the woman recognizes in the senior Brahmin her very own son – he had last seen his mother in his childhood, when she was publicly and ritually cast out of the household and her community; for the reader, this moment of *agnorisis* is both the climax and the conclusion of the story, along with the significance of "Narayana," the name of God, which is the last word that the dying woman utters.

Viswanathan's quarrel with the colonial census of 1872–1901 is grounded in the fact that excommunication is defined in this census as the cause of conversion rather than as a side-effect of it.[30] The Hindu and feminist narrative of "The Power of Fate" constructs, once again, a scenario of excommunication as originator. As a feminist portrayal, though, choice plays a decisive role in this narrative. The mother has choices, foremost among which is suicide. While her choice of re-marriage and life proceeds from the excommunication, a patriarchal society determines the various choices, so that what is once again practical, hence desirable, is the survival of woman as wife and mother.

---

[26] *Speculum of the Other Woman*, 316.

[27] Lacan, *Écrits*, 305.

[28] *Écrits*, 1.

[29] Williams, "Base and Superstructure in Marxist Cultural Theory," in *Debating Texts: Reading in Twentieth Century Literary Theory and Method*, ed. Rick Rylance (Toronto: U of Toronto P, 1987): 204.

[30] Viswanathan, *Outside the Fold*, 168.

In writing this story of exclusion, Antherjanam, as a female member of the *namboo-diri* caste, is responding to centuries of injustice to her sex. Antherjanam's stories and poems are again and again about the plight of the *antherjanam*, the secluded Brahmin women, who, if unlucky in a husband, often faced conditions of bitter isolation and suffering, proving that religious bulwarks of protection are sometimes as oppressive as the secular. If the woman became the object of an accusation, the situation worsened, especially because trials were lopsided. The most fearful punishment, meted out to a woman accused of having an affair, involved incarceration followed by excommunica-tion and the terrible labelling of the woman as 'a thing' (*sadhanam*) for whom even the rites of the dead (*shraddha*) were performed.

The story goes to show that feudalism is the link between the dead and the living. The terms on which Namboodiripad and his mother meet are unmistakenly economic and feudal. Pathumma, the Muslim daughter, is only too aware of the economic struc-ture that manages many other relationships and therefore introduces the complaint against an infiltrating Muslim neighbour as a viable reason for a visit from Namboo-diripad. Namboodiripad is not the only one motivated by the prevalent economic sys-tem; the mother, too, wishes to see her son for purposes beyond her immediate and personal gratification. She desires him as a landlord (*jenmi*), to take care of his Muslim tenants ([*verum*]*pattakar*), especially her daughter. Religious difference is subordinate to the economic within this narrative of life and death.

A tale of Muslim or Mapilla tenants for a *namboodiri* landlord harbours multiple im-plications. Apart from suggesting the economic struggle between the tenants, who are described as "emaciated," "all bones,"[31] and the landlord, who is depicted as over-weight and carefree, the plot also indicates the silent, hence acquiescent, presence of the colonizers. K.N. Panikkar notes that when Malabar (part of present Kerala) came under British rule in 1792 following the defeat of Tippu Sultan, the colonizers viewed the Muslim inhabitants as natural supporters of the Mysore sultan by dint of their reli-gion and therefore as enemies; the castes that stood to gain from the British presence were the *namboodiris* and the Nayars, with regard to land settlements as well as gov-ernment employment.[32] However, under British rule, there was considerable change in the feudal structure – landlords were transformed from a ruling class to "a class of rent-receiver-parasites."[33]

Within this explicitly economic realm, caste and religion are not neutral grounds. Exclusion and denigration define the other castes and religions. Thus, just as the native rarely appears in the settler stories of Canada, the lower castes of *ezhava* and *shudra* disappear from Antherjanam's story, and non-Hindus continue as 'mlecchas'. In her translation of Antherjanam's short stories, Gita Krishnankutty explains *mleccha* as a term that upper-caste Hindus use to designate non-Hindus.[34] The explanation skirts

---

[31] Lalithambika Antherjanam, "The Power of Fate," in Antherjanam, *Cast Me Out If You Will: Stories and Memoir*, tr., ed. & intro. Gita Krishnankutty (New York: The Feminist Press, 1997): 3.

[32] Panikkar, *Against Lord and State*, 55, 23, 29.

[33] E.M.S. Namboodiripad, *Kerala Society and Politics: An Historical Survey* (New Delhi: National Book Centre, 1984): 74.

[34] Gita Krishnankutty, ed. Antherjanam, *Cast Me Out If You Will*, 185.

loaded implications. Romila Thapar points out that the word *mleccha*, which first appeared in the *Rig Veda*, referred to 'tribals' (Non-Aryans) in north and central India.[35]
It was either that the term was then used outside a religious context or that the tribals
were considered as being outside the dominant religious culture. In *Interpreting Early
India*, Thapar explains that *mleccha* also means 'impure' and as such applied to non-
Sanskrit speaking people. Even high-ranking people could be called *mleccha*.[36] Later
on, what Viswanathan refers to as Hindu nationalism's language of 'foreignness' and
'otherness' to refer to Muslims may not have depended entirely on the lessons of the
British census.[37] *Mleccha*, then, appears to have been a term signifying those outside
the dominant community, religion being but one definer of that community. The land
occupied by these others would be called *mleccha desa*, i.e., impure lands.[38]

What allows for the entrée of the upper caste into the *mleccha desa* in "The Power
of Fate" is partly the economic system. Partly. Even if it is feudal business that brings
Namboodiripad into the vicinity of the Muslim hut, what takes him further, right into
the hut, is the sound of a woman. The "groan," a female voice of helplessness that
propels Namboodiripad into the forbidden Muslim hut, interprets feudal relationships
in terms of victim–protector. That the "groan," the cry for help, of suffering, should
emanate from a woman indicates the common cause of patriarchy within both religious
and economic structures. Rather sarcastically, yet not without some sense of truth, the
narrator of "The Power of Fate" insists that it is profitable for women (of all castes and
creeds) to cry and plead whenever they want something from the senior *namboodiri* or
his officers. Antherjanam's "groan" of the "something"[39] recalls "the Freudian thing"
about which Lacan writes: "*it speaks* [...] where it is least expected, namely, where
there is pain."[40] Just as Freud's suffering speaker, as the subject of psychoanalysis,
signifies for the analyst (Freud) his own authority, the groaning woman is the signifier
for and of the authority vested in the *namboodiri* and the landlord. As such, the signification occurs not within religious differences but within similarities between religious and economic structures that are at bottom patriarchal.

The social effect of the narrative, the subjectivity of the patriarch, reflects repeatedly
from and in the speculum of the woman as (m)other.[41] Like the child in the mirror
stage who exits the Imaginary and enters the Symbolic order, Namboodiripad in the
hut bids farewell to the illusory unity of the ancestral home where the family ought to

---

[35] Romila Thapar, Harbans Mukhia & Bipin Chandra, *Communalism and the Writing of Indian History* (Delhi: People's Publishing House, 1969): 8.

[36] Thapar, *Interpreting Early India* (Delhi: Oxford UP, 1992): 78.

[37] Viswanathan, *Outside the Fold*, 163. What Viswanathan sees as a purely colonial insistence on the common origins of the Hindus and the Muslims is paralleled throughout the book by her own proclivity to see Christianity and the English originating from the same source.

[38] *Outside the Fold*, 134.

[39] Antherjanam, "The Power of Fate," 3.

[40] Lacan, *Écrits*, 125.

[41] As Lacan puts it, "the subject who is actually led to occupy the place of the Other, namely, the Mother" (*Écrits* 311).

stay united but does not. As in the movement into the Symbolic order, the *namboodiri*'s encounter with the (m)other-woman is characterized by confusion.

> Namboodiripad thought confusedly of many things. However mistakenly she had been condemned, he felt that he could not touch a woman who had been cast out, who had lived with a *mleccha* for years and had two children by him. It would be a terrible sin! A namboodiri woman who had changed her religion was no better than a mleccha. It was a crime even to have looked at her![42]

The crime at this (mirror-)stage is the crime of looking, where vision is linked to power and identity. It is in looking that the speculum signifies the 'desire of the Other' in the subject. The resultant patriarchal image is marked by the tension between roles of mother and wife, and adherent and renegade. The initial confusion arises from the imaginary past, the 'mother' that Namboodiripad last saw at the age of ten, and this woman before him, a sexual being who 'lived with' a *mleccha* and "had two children by him." Confusion marks the relationship between Self and Other, and the vision of the fragmented (m)other resolves itself temporarily into two equally patriarchal and interchangeable signifieds: the sin of sex, and the sin of conversion. Irreligion, the condition of being 'godless' (*asura*), is also to belong to another religion *and* another family, so that the direct result feared in 'conversion' is, as the *Bhagavad-gītā* declares, "unwanted progeny"[43] Within the *namboodiri* caste, suspicion of a woman's infidelity was called *adukkaladosham*, 'pollution of the kitchen', because, as Krishnankutty explains, "since the ritual purity of the kitchen, crucial for maintaining the household's caste status, was in the hands of the women, it was called into question the moment a woman of the household was suspected of an illicit relationship."[44] Thus sex and conversion, 'race' and religion, within this explicitly patriarchal system of power and discourse, are essentialized and made interchangeable in a definition of the Other, so that 'a fallen woman' was in essence 'a convert', also resulting in the argument that conversion "erases racial identity."[45]

In "The Power of Fate," Namboodiripad, entering the hut, feels threatened by what he sees, for the possibility of pollution, if not excommunication (like oedipal castration), is too real to be ignored. But even as he decides to go, he, as it were, (mis)recognizes the image for what it is – an image: "I've seen her now and I'll have to do the purificatory rituals anyway. After all, she is my mother." Both religious signifiers ("purificatory rituals") and familial signifiers ("my mother") can be safely invoked to (en)counter each other. As Viswanathan notes, the "transgressive act" of conversion disturbs convention,[46] yet the 'act' invokes those very traditions within changing con-

---

[42] Antherjanam, "The Power of Fate," 10.

[43] A.C. Bhaktivedanta Swami Prabhupāda, *Bhagavad-Gītā As It Is* (New York: Bhaktivedanta Book Trust, abridged ed. 1968): 1.40.

[44] Krishnankutty, ed. Antherjanam, *Cast Me Out If You Will*, xxii.

[45] Viswanathan, *Outside the Fold*, 164.

[46] *Outside the Fold*, 86.

texts. Culture's rootedness in language,[47] in meaning and power, makes inculturation the destiny of all religions.[48] Consequently, separating 'land' from "habits and customs"[49] defines 'land' as the property of the dominant culture, suggests that other religions elsewhere are somehow 'authentic', claims that dominant domestic practices are monolithic, and dumps the rest as counter-cultural, if not antagonistic. The chasm between religion "as the source of cultural and national identity" and "as universal moral values"[50] becomes unbridgeable only when inculturation is denied. If Namboodiripad's initial impulse is to run away from the otherness of the familiar one, it is because he sees the Other as fragmented. The 'unwholesomeness' of the other is frightening because it is specular and indicates the subject's painful disillusion of the self, the revelation that he is always already 'polluted' in the (m)other. Namboodiripad learns to recognize himself through the mother, himself as bound by filial duty to actually commit the crime of looking and touching, thus symbolically bringing her back to the ancestral home. The interaction and consequent influences are unavoidable, welcome. Becoming the subject means moving from the specular I into the social I, where the (m)other initiates the subject's entrance.

The 'transformation' of the Muslim hut into the ancestral home cannot be interpreted as what Viswanathan calls "a crossing over."[51] Viswanathan defines conversion as a movement *from* one national and racial space *to* another. Antherjanam's story functions outside this paradigm of uni-directional travel, and alternatively represents the inclusionary nature of faith in God. Within this representation, "country, culture, religion, and identity" are not, as Viswanathan counts, "one,"[52] but *always* complex and multiple. The *mleccha desa* is the holy land. That is, no change or travel or transformation or reconversion either occurs or is necessary.

However, patriarchal and class ideologies attempt to undermine the inclusiveness of faith. In the story, the acknowledgement that "the body that had suffered infinite sorrow and pain dissolved into the essence of truth" is unambiguously designated as "at least that is what Namboodiripad, immersed in the intensity of prayer, believed"[53] Namboodiripad's belief is marked off as just one of several conclusions, so that the only privileges recognized as such in Namboodiripad are those of gender and class. As son and landlord, Namboodiripad will do his duty by his mother and his tenants.

---

[47] Meaning as a construction suggests that a culture relies on a system of representation or, what Stuart Hall refers to as "code"; Hall, in *Representation: Cultural Representations and Signifying Practices*, ed. Stuart Hall (Thousand Oaks CA & London: Sage / Open University, 1997): 21. Shared ways of interpreting a language define a culture. The study of culture partakes of Saussurean semiotics and Foucauldian discourse analysis.

[48] Matteo Ricci's inculturation efforts in China and De Nobili's in India, even if suppressed by the church at the time, are being emulated more recently.

[49] Viswanathan, *Outside the Fold*, 116.

[50] *Outside the Fold*, 121.

[51] V.S. Naipaul's *Beyond Belief* runs along similar lines in explaining Islam away as an 'Arab' religion.

[52] Viswanathan, *Outside the Fold*, 244.

[53] Antherjanam, "The Power of Fate," 11.

The irony is that what Namboodiripad does – from his entry into the Muslim's land and hut to his prayerful attendance at the deathbed of his mother – is controlled by the mother. The mother reflects the subjectivity of the character as son and landlord. But the mother as specular woman, the site of patriarchal intervention, is also the space of divine consciousness. Irigaray contemplates this consciousness from within a Christian theological framework: "How could 'God' reveal himself in all his magnificence and waste his substance on/in so weak and vile a creature as woman?"[54] Interestingly, this event of God's recognizing a female human being is classified within patriarchal ideologies as a miracle. As 'miracle', then, the word of God enters the vacant (m)other and 'it speaks from the place of pain'.

The speech of the suffering thing indicates also the power of silence. The mother is "authorized to remain silent"[55] as her son pours *tulasi* water into her mouth and chants the thousand names of Vishnu. She breaks the silence with the name of God: "Allah! No, … Narayana!"[56] Where Narayana is a name for Vishnu, this utterance might suggest the patriarchal authority of the *namboodiri* that can re-convert the convert. However, neither scripture nor ritual offers any such opportunity of reconversion and return for 'the fallen woman'. She is dead, the 'thing'. Even if the son might desire this return/reconversion of the mother, the *namboodiri* world accommodates no pertinent signifiers. The only name that can function is "Narayana."

Within religious discourse, the name "Narayana" is denied to the fallen woman, who is now a *mleccha*, so that "Narayana" fails to stand as a religious ideological signifier. The name is available only as a signifier of faith, as a slip of the tongue, even before the *namboodiri* enters. The slip-of-the-tongue or unsuccessfully suppressed utterance suggests faith's position simultaneously outside and inside, or in the margins, of ideology. "Allah" and "Narayana," words *virtually* reflected as opposite and exclusionary, are now turned right side up in the s(p)ecular and posited as different-yet-same in the realm of faith: i.e. as a material reality.

The name "Narayana" *is* redemptive, as the story of Saint Ajamila testifies. According to the *Bhāgavata Purāna*, the Brahmin Ajamila, after leading a life of depravity, gambling and thieving, and keeping a concubine of a low caste, at the time of his death called out "Narayana," the name of his youngest son by the concubine, and automatically gained Vishnu's heaven. The mother in the "Power of Fate" defies caste and custom through the name of God: through what she *always* knew, Vishnu.

"Narayana" is a signifier that cannot be excluded from the "the Name-of-the-Father," essentialized in the thousand names of Vishnu held tantalizingly close to one whose subjectivity is in the works and to whom it is denied.[57] The signifier may be

[54] Irigaray, *Speculum of the Other Woman*, 199.

[55] *Speculum of the Other Woman*, 200.

[56] Antherjanam, "The Power of Fate," 11.

[57] In *Totem and Taboo*, Freud discusses how laws against murder and incest were formulated in the name of the father, supreme authority, so as to bring about civilization. Lacan interprets Freud to explain subject-formation. According to Lacan, it is the interference of the father in the child–mother relationship that at once causes a lack in, and catapults the child into, the Symbolic order. Accordingly, subjectivity entails subjection to the Name-of-the-Father.

denied, but not excluded. Had this essential signifier been excluded from the symbolic order (of 'worldliness') there would have been a condition of psychosis, like the disruptive conversion that Viswanathan fears. A chaotic attempt to make meaning through delusional metaphors of conversion might then have followed.

And yet, the Name-of-Narayana is not subordinate to the Name-of-the-Father, the Symbolic order. The moment that follows the uttering of the name of God, the name of the Real, Narayana, is the end of the Symbolic order – death. In this latter phase of redemption, of the absence of all phallic-marked representations of her, comes the Lacanian statement that proclaims the basic unavailability of the essentialized woman – "Woman does not exist."[58]

This, again, is the stage that Irigaray describes: "she has left the others behind, disconcerted, unable to follow her that far. Unable to go and see"[59]

"Narayana," a name that marks 'the death of the Father', of patriarchal systems of signification (*namboodiri*, Muslim, the whole lot), breaks the speculum of the otherness of the woman. From *within* the Symbolic order, even as a slip of the tongue, conversion is declared impossible. The mother cannot re-convert, because she was never converted. For her, the name of Narayana was never lost, never forsaken – hence, never to be recovered. Pathumma (the daughter), too, was never a convert; she was always a Muslim. A monolithic culture is nowhere on the horizon; never was. If what disrupts society is conversion, then there is no fear of disruption of the feudal society in "The Power of Fate" – Namboodiripad will continue to 'protect' his tenants, Muslim or not.

WORKS CITED

Althusser, Louis. *Lenin and Philosophy and Other Essays*, tr. Ben Brewster (New York: Monthly Review Press, 1971).

Antherjanam, Lalithambika. *Cast Me Out If You Will: Stories and Memoir*, tr., ed. & intro. Gita Krishnankutty (New York: The Feminist Press, 1997).

Balibar, Étienne, & Pierre Macherey. "Literature as an Ideological Form: Some Marxist Propositions," in *Marxist Literary Theory*, ed. Terry Eagleton & Drew Milne (Oxford: Blackwell, 1996).

Engineer, Asghar Ali, ed. *Kerala Muslims: A Historical Perspective* (New Delhi: Ajanta, 1995).

Freud, Sigmund. *Totem and Taboo: Some Points of Agreement Between the Mental Lives of Savages and Neurotics* (London: Routledge & Kegan Paul, 1961).

Hall, Stuart, ed. *Representation: Cultural Representations and Signifying Practices* (Thousand Oaks CA & London: Sage / Open University, 1997).

Irigaray, Luce. *Speculum of the Other Woman*, tr. Gillian C. Gill (Ithaca NY: Cornell UP, 1985).

Jayaprasad, K. *RSS and Hindu Nationalism: Inroads in a Leftist Stronghold* (New Delhi: Deep & Deep Publications, 1991).

Kulke, Hermann, & Dietmar Rothermund. *A History of India* (New York: Routledge, 1986).

Lacan, Jacques. *Écrits: A Selection*. tr. Alan Sheridan (London: Tavistock, 1977).

---

[58] See Lacan, *The Seminar Book XX*, "Woman does not exist" (7), and *Écrits*, "the Other does not exist" (317).

[59] Irigaray, *Speculum of the Other Woman*, 199.

——. *The Ego in Freud's Theory and in the Technique of Psychoanalysis 1954–1955: The Seminar Book II*, ed. Jacques–Alain Miller; tr. Sylvana Tomaselli (Cambridge: Cambridge UP, 1988).

——. *On Feminine Sexuality: The Limits of Love and Knowledge: The Seminar Book XX*, tr. Bruce Fink (New York: W.W. Norton, 1998).

——. *The Psychoses 1955–56: The Seminar Book III*, ed. J.A. Miller, tr. R. Grigg (New York: W.W. Norton, 1993)

Namboodiripad, E.M.S. *Kerala Society and Politics: An Historical Survey* (New Delhi: National Book Centre, 1984).

Naipaul, V.S. *Beyond Belief: Islamic Excursions among the Converted Peoples* (New York: Random House, 1998).

Nandy, Ashis. "The Politics of Secularism and the Recovery of Religious Tolerance," in *Mirrors of Violence: Communities, Riots and Survivors in South Asia* ed. Veena Das (Delhi: Oxford UP, 1990).

——. "Secularism, Hindu Nationalism and the Fear of the People," in *Religion and Nationalism: Concilium*, ed. John Coleman & Miklós Tomka (London: SCM, 1995).

Padmanabha Menon, K.P. *History of Kerala*, ed. T.K. Krishna Menon, 4 vols. (1924–36; New Delhi: Asian Educational Services, 1982–86).

Panikkar, K.N. *Against Lord and State: Religion and Peasant Uprisings in Malabar, 1836–1921* (Delhi: Oxford UP, 1989).

Prabhupāda, A.C. Bhaktivedanta Swami. *Bhagavad-Gītā As It Is* (New York: Bhaktivedanta Book Trust, abridged ed. 1968).

Said, Edward. *The World, the Text and the Critic* (Cambridge MA: Harvard UP, 1983).

Sarkar, Sumit. *Writing Social History* (Delhi: Oxford UP, 1997).

Thapar, Romila, Harbans Mukhia & Bipin Chandra. *Communalism and the Writing of Indian History* (Delhi: People's Publishing House, 1969).

——. *Interpreting Early India* (Delhi: Oxford UP, 1992).

Viswanathan, Gauri. *Outside the Fold: Conversion, Modernity, and Belief* (Princeton NJ: Princeton UP, 1998).

Williams, Raymond. "Base and Superstructure in Marxist Cultural Theory," in *Debating Texts: Reading in Twentieth Century Literary Theory and Method*, ed. Rick Rylance (Toronto: U of Toronto P, 1987).

⟨⟨•⟩⟩

Submerging Pasts
Lee Kok Liang's *London Does Not Belong To Me*

BERNARD WILSON

> London, the lost city of Atlantis, under an ocean of fog; and I
> am one of its denizens, groping, and groping towards the pin-
> point punctures of the lamps opposite. Out from the misty
> closeness swam the dark ghouls in overcoats and hats – the
> limbs moving stiffly as if fighting their way against some
> treacherous currents.
> (Lee Kok Liang, *Sketches, Brushstrokes and Vignettes*)

L EE KOK LIANG'S LITERARY CAREER parallels Malaysia's own
traumatic transition from British colony to emergent nation. Along with other
noted resident writers, including K.S. Maniam and Lloyd Fernando, and ex-
patriate authors such as Shirley Lim, Lee's writing redresses previous rigid eurocentric
notions of power to create more protean senses of individual, cultural and national
identity(ies). As such, his first novel, the semi-autobiographical *London Does Not
Belong To Me*, not only affords valuable insights into the fledgling writer honing his
skills of description and thematic development, but also provides a vivid portrait of
postcolonial angst through its young protagonist. Set in London and Paris in the early
1950s, *London Does Not Belong To Me* deals with the disillusion and isolation of marginalized people as shown through a disparate collection of expatriates from the far-
flung reaches of a crumbling empire, who seek to establish identity, purpose and a
sense of belonging in an alien environment. The action of the text takes place through
the complex and almost symbiotic relationships of the main characters. Narrating in
the first person, the protagonist is a Straits-Chinese Malaysian who, in his search for
identity(ies), is compelled to negotiate a spatial existence between the European city-
scapes which dominate his physical and intellectual existence and the conflicting
memories of a Malayan homeland. Further, he endeavours to come to terms with his
own sexuality and the ambivalent sexualities of those (mostly expatriates) with whom
he interacts.

What Lee is attempting, in part, in this novel is an exploration of self in the context of an environment that is both familiar to the author/narrator, given the eurocentric epistemology of his colonial education, and, at the same time, hostile and alienating. In the novel, and in his unpublished journal *Sketches, Brushstrokes and Vignettes*, upon which much of the action in the novel is based, the young (25-year-old) Lee charts a psychological map for his personal identity and artistic integrity – against the backdrop of a London and Paris themselves being reinvented after the devastations of World War II.

Collectively, and individually, the novel and diary constitute a powerful, subversive counter-colonial discourse, pre-dating the publication of Sam Selvon's *Lonely Londoners* in 1956 and occupying some of the same chronological and geographical space as V.S. Naipaul's recently published epistolary collection, *Between Father and Son*. In terms of Malaysian literature written in English, the novel and diary offer a unique and historical perspective on the fading imperial axis of power, as perceived by a colonial subject whose nation is moving rapidly towards independence (1957).

Lee's writing and thematic thrust, though, are broader than a redressing of the colonizer/colonized polemic. His quest is more personal and more universal: at the heart of the novel is the search for individual identity through the ordinary, everyday betrayals and triumphs of isolated, ostracized individuals. Beyond this, the young writer's goals are to put in place guidelines through which artistic integrity may be achieved and through which the fraught condition of cultural and sexual marginalization may be articulated.

Unlike *London Does Not Belong To Me*, Lee's previously published collections of short stories and his novel *Flowers in the Sky* (1981) are set in the territory of his youth and working life: the north-western states of Malaya/Malaysia against the backdrop of the Chinese-Malaysian community. But thematically, there are many similarities. His early stories are particularly concerned with isolation, repression and the mutilation (psychological and physical) of self; with, as Syd Harrex termed it many years ago,

> the outsider's fascination with the repulsive, as well as the exciting characteristics of human society [which] complements his psychological dissection of human fallibility and the frailty of love as these are revealed in individual characters.[1]

The external claustrophobic landscapes of much of Lee's fiction – and this is evident time and again in *London Does Not Belong To Me* – reflect what Lee perceives to be the vulnerabilities and blighted potential of many of his characters.

In terms of structure, the novel is very much a first effort, betraying the difficulties of marrying a myriad of characters into a workable plot, and at times these characters are drawn in such a way as to become Huxley-like representations of various ideological viewpoints. The confused identities of the main characters are, however, mirrored in their eclectic conversations, their (often forlorn) attempts at self-parody and mimicry of others, and their self-loathing, brought about in some cases by sexual experimenta-

---

[1] Syd Harrex, "Mutes and Mutilators in the Fiction of Lee Kok Liang," in *Individual and Community in Commonwealth Literature*, ed. Daniel Massa (Malta: The University Press, 1978): 142.

tion or sexual frustration coupled with the constant (invariably justified) fear of rejection. Reflecting Lee's own tentative and self-conscious steps towards artistic fulfilment, the overall framework of *London Does Not Belong To Me* is, at first glance at least, seemingly of less merit than the series of pastiches and characterizations it contains. The young author's primary concerns reside in the following areas: transcultural and sexual identity, communication, and the aesthetics of writing, all of which are evident in the prologue, which provides valuable evidence of Lee's powers of clinical observation, coupled with a recognition of his paradoxical existence, through a suffocating – yet in many ways alluring – vision of London in the 1950s:

> Two milk bottles stood on the table – one full, the other three quarters full – and spreading out beneath them *The Times* lay prostrate, its columns dirtied with the spilt contents of chilli sauces and mashed pickled prawns that dripped from the abandoned bottles and vials. At one corner, a small bowl balanced on the edge, its leafy green surface tarnished with gluey remains. This was my dining table, a littered no-man's land. The opened can, quarter full, its bright purple wrapper torn, gave out a rich smell. What was it she had said, as she scooped out the lychee, balancing the fruit on the tip of her forefinger? "Flesh pink" with a laugh, as she rested her hand against her bare throat.
>
> London was full of rooms. I went from one to the other. Slowly I adjusted myself and lived the life of a troglodyte, learning the tribal customs of feints and apologies. And sitting with my back to the brown wall-paper, on the narrow bed, I looked across the small room, through the pale patch of the window, dreaming of mynah birds shooting like beads along branches of casuarinas, and of pale spidery crabs on warm sands and the dark button-sized shells buried just above the tides. With my mouth opened against the crumpled pillow, after she left, I listened to the hollow breathing that filled my lungs and the two cords of muscles along my spine tensed with regrets, watching heavy-lidded, how my forefinger twitched forlornly. And a few phrases came to my mind. Once she had written "Understand – and your heart can be mother to all things – I have found a big red tomato this afternoon – soft and full of silky dreams."
>
> Solitary like a spider, weaving a web, I had written to her. Not of love, because we did not speak of love. But of what I had dreamt, awkwardly framing the words, with the concentration of a child filling in his first notebook, intent to please, and words became my courage and her tribute. Not about the past either; for in this city, men and women submerged their past. I swam along with them, flipping my fins.

The tone of the novel is immediately established through these images of isolation, desperate need, regret and self-recrimination, and the passage is strongly counter-colonial in implication. The narrator's description of his confined living quarters – and the surrounding city – articulates his sense of alienation, displacement and negativity. His table is "a littered no-man's land." London is described in primitive and subterranean terms: he "live[s] the life of a troglodyte," moving from room to room, taking on the "tribal customs of feints and apologies." Superficiality, in this world, is the norm; indeed, it is the key to survival. Juxtaposed against this is the world of his memory, a space described in fecund and vibrant terms: the natural warmth and light of the past contrasting with the superficial suffocating bleakness of the present. He dreams of the mynah birds of his home country, but in London can only survive as a cave-dweller, a spider, a submerged sea-creature. Lee postulates the necessity of metamorphosis for survival in such an environment, but, more than this, there is a mutation – almost a regression – of humanity indicated in the final two lines, which portray civilization in retreat towards the "primordial swamp," distinctly in contrast to perceptions of the centre of Empire as light, learning and civilization, the "distant lodestar of good for all of us" as Edward Said ironically terms it.[2] The narrator depicts himself through foetal imagery – as submerged in the amniotic fluid of a 'maternal' London – an inversion of the city as nurturer of and provider to her colonial subjects. In this setting, individual and national histories are obfuscated and buried; in this Eliotesque wasteland, individual identity and individual history are unimportant – indeed, they are perceived as debilitating weaknesses. Rather, subterfuge and suppression, "submerg[ing] [one's] past," constitute the natural state of things.

This, then, sets the scene for a narrative of displacement and betrayal. The opening action in the novel relies heavily on the interaction between the narrator and the two women Cordelia and Beatrice. The narrator's description of his initial encounter with Cordelia reveals several of the methods that Lee would refine in later writing:

> I saw the girl first. Nothing much at first – a large head, massive I thought at that time, and bright golden hair like a huge tight cap, gleaming against the light from the fireplace. I remained standing in the doorway, running my tongue over the jagged upper molar, that smelled even to me. Silence. Concentrated study from me of her outline against the glass of flames.

The introduction to Cordelia is noteworthy, in that some of the descriptive devices later used by Lee in the short-story collections *The Mutes in the Sun* and *Death is a Ceremony* can be seen to take shape. Perceived purity and innocence are juxtaposed against corruption in this chiaroscuro, providing clear indications of the tragedy about to be played out. Shades of dark and light are implied; the profile of the girl's head (curiously described as massive, emphasizing the narrator's fascination with imperfection and vulnerability) is silhouetted against the flames while the watching narrator, worrying a decayed tooth, is only too aware of his own – in this case, less visible – imperfections. Lee's choice of name for the narrator's obsession is also important in the context of the plot: the intrinsic goodness of *Lear*'s Cordelia is gradually inverted as this Cordelia proves to be temptress and betrayer to the narrator's needs, in a subtle rewriting of canonical British literature.

Secondly, one may observe the seeds of the voyeuristic style that governs much of Lee's later prose. As an observer, his descriptions are often clinical and precise – at times almost microscopic – and his tone emphasizes the furtiveness and insecurity common to the outsider, a style that finds greater maturity in his description of the alienated characters of his own tropical landscape in his published writing. His central characters are rarely active protagonists but are, rather, individuals who are swept along in a swirling current of complex, muted desires and deceptions. The narrator of *London Does Not Belong To Me* is the first of Lee's crippled observers, emotionally and verbally debilitated by his sense of cultural and physical 'otherness':

[2] Edward Said, *Out of Place* (New York: Alfred A. Knopf, 1999): 82.

> The easy casual manner in which strangers picked me up frightened me, as if I were a bargain find or a trinket.

In this society, the narrator often depicts himself as a kind of oriental curio – passed, as interest wanes, from one individual to another. Accentuating the image of the timid but clinical observer, the prose style of the initial description of Cordelia is simple and spare, creating a sense of immediacy in its staccato recording of a scene as a series of loosely connected slides.

In his references to Malaysia, Lee combines idyllic descriptions with harsh social observations. Flagging thematic preoccupations in his short-story collections, his first specific reference to his homeland, in a conversation with Cordelia in Chapter 2, is poetic but brutally frank:

> I came from a world where fathers were adulterous and mothers vicious and a river of lies poured itself between them, separating.

The young Lee is already acknowledging the reality of isolation and divisiveness evident in his country of birth, despite the often idyllic images he uses to portray Malaya. When the narrator takes Beatrice to a Chinese restaurant in a symbolic gesture of closure to their relationship, he finds it acceptable – indeed, appropriate – that Beatrice remember him in a stereotypically occidental view of the East: "A memory of golds and reds and dragons." This is the preferable image or 'truth' of the East for both the narrator and Beatrice (who, as an Australian, is a partial representative of the West). But, as the narrator muses, such images are only ever half-truths, concealing far more than they can reveal:

> Should I also tell her about the dirt and the flies and the diseases? But what's the point anyway? Everyone of us must preserve a certain romantic viewpoint about far distant places to which the mind could return in the midst of our grimy surroundings or when life pressed too harshly upon our individual existence. She would, I had hoped, always associate the glitter and the shadow with me and when I had gone, perhaps on some wintry morning when she looked out from her window at the dull soft-drizzling sky and the dark street, she would think of me walking slowly, my long shadow falling before me, carefully dressed in white, along a dry street that burned like a salt mine. And I on my part would recapture the glitter in her eyes sitting in the dark of a cinema hall, her coat unbuttoned, breathing gently by my side with the tips of her fingers resting coldly on my palm. I was conscious that I was a craftsman, weaving on the loom of memory, sending out a rhythm that would enfold our lives like the caresses of waves on a sandy beach.

These decidedly romantic sentiments reveal the narrator's perceived sense of duality: in his relationship with Beatrice, in his cultural displacement, and possibly in his more covert questionings of his own sexual nature. Woven into these lines are the eclectic questionings of the apprentice postcolonial writer: the exploration of cultural representation, the function of memory, the nature of art. The narrator is only too aware that he functions, in part, as willing cliché, embracing the role of exotic Other as he narrates his existence.

As I mentioned earlier, the basis of Lee's writing, both in *London Does Not Belong To Me* and his later collections of short stories, is that of (often deliberate) miscommunication and obfuscation. Such miscommunications stem from cultural, political, racial and gender differences and, in common with the writing of K.S. Maniam and Lloyd Fernando, depict language as a sociopolitical tool – occasionally liberating, but, more often than not, imprisoning the individual from within and without. The narrator experiences the practical difficulties and misapprehensions of a Straits-Chinese communicating in British English – "Marbles in my mouth: I spewed them out" – and his resultant sense of inadequacy. He is, in his own description, "a human sponge absorbing [...] words, now and then giving out a squirt in reply." And through this linguistic osmosis, as it were, he often provides the reader with glimpses of the poetic description and whimsical humour that were to reach full maturity in *The Mutes in the Sun* and *Flowers in the Sky*, such as in this excerpt:

> "I'm sorry I must go now. Got to catch the tube." I nearly said, "Got to tube a catch."
> Language was a loose string of beads to me. I got tired easily trying to express it in a
> logical way. Even in my native language.

What is also clear here is that the narrator's (and Lee's) underlying mistrust of words is not limited to the lingua franca of the colonizer; *all* language proves inadequate as the narrator attempts to communicate the "thoughts which [are] locked in behind a barrier in [his] mind, leaping like shoals of caged fish."

Language, either oral or written, is described in various passages of the first five chapters alone as: "a web"; "my [the narrator's] courage and her [Cordelia's] tribute"; "a bottle of strange wine"; "a river of lies"; "marbles in [the narrator's] mouth"; "a loose string of beads"; "ping pong balls"; "the posings of self and non-self"; "a castle"; "a silly badminton game"; "shadows that moved and changed with the sun"; and "an ocean full of ice-floes." The majority of these images are negative, conveying the frustration of the marginalized when faced with the limitations and ambiguity of the basic tool of communication or, as Lee perhaps sees it, *mis*communication. Conversation is depicted as battle; a conversation between Beatrice and the narrator is described as "a preliminary bout"; the narrator temporarily sees himself "on safe ground [...] a vantage point"; and Beatrice is seen as "not avoid[ing] the quarry" and "behaving like a well-trained pointer." Conversation as pursuit; conversation as entrapment; conversation as paradox, as in this simile: "I skipped from topic to topic, testing each one, trying like a passenger thrown into the ocean to locate a lifebelt."

Although the narrator dreams in "words and colours," these are bitter dreams. Language in these images signifies isolation and disillusion. The narrator's pronunciation, even of the name of the woman he believes he loves, serves only to increase his awareness of his otherness and alienation:

> Cordelia, that's how she should be pronounced. I did it the wrong way every time. To
> Beatrice she was not a strange word in a foreign language.

Significant in the text is the fact that the narrator's name is never revealed. Moreover, Lee goes to some lengths to keep the narrator's name hidden from the reader, revealing the trauma of the outsider and serving to emphasize the discomfort that the narrator may feel at his Chinese-Malaysian name (indeed, in jest, he at one stage gives himself a deliberately false Anglo name) in such eurocentric and often hostile surroundings. Such concealment is also symptomatic of the sense of fracturing self that the narrator is experiencing, both in his relationship with his physical surroundings – the geographical and cultural antithesis of his birthplace – and in his relationship with the other characters in the novel, very few of whom have any solid sense of cultural, or sexual, identity (with the possible exception of Beatrice).

Steve, on the other hand, seeks to establish a sense of identity through verbal attacks on the colonial centre, describing it as "a long-teated bitch":

> Everything here is so bloody faded. No push. No guts. Loss of nerve. A great unending diarrhoea. Old England squatting over an effluence of words, words, words.

But, in a way, Steve is – intentionally or otherwise – mocking his own sexual and cultural dissipation. Like Tristam, his utterances are often glib and contrived, revealing through their mimicry and posturing an overwhelming sense of personal displacement. Regardless of such theatrical harangues, these expatriates are still drawn to London, though their reasons for remaining are obscured by the author and are seemingly secondary to the plot function. Despite nebulous references to employment or studies, they drift aimlessly through the city, lured by its reputation yet despising it – and themselves – for their own alienation. Steve, who alludes vaguely to employment in the fledgling television industry, is the most overtly derisive in his comments on empire, yet his motivations seem shallow: his desire to be accepted and belong manifests itself in verbal banter and aggressive witticisms – what the narrator dismisses as the tiresome "posings of self and non-self." With the possible exception of Beatrice, identity, for these people, is a parasitic process and rests in feeding on the insecurities of others to affirm one's own sense of self. As such, they are a desolate and emotionally retarded group, though their physical circumstances and cultural marginalization are at the base of their actions. Need – rather than desire – is their motivation.

Isolation and sexual frustration provide Lee's characters with a pathos that is reinforced by his use of naturalistic descriptions. Sexual relations are more about a desperate need to reclaim space – to re-establish one's humanity – than about romance or simple physical desire, such as may be seen in the forlorn, almost despairing, image of connection between lonely individuals in this description of the narrator's first sexual advance to Cordelia:

> Slowly she relaxed and I touched her again on the thighs and pushed her down on the carpet. A seagull was like this I thought, on the wing preparing to swoop down over the flotsam on the quay.

Rarely are Lee's descriptions of physical and emotional connection portrayed positively. Characters such as Cordelia, Steve, Tristam and the narrator himself are often described as, at best, scavengers – and, at worst, as predators. Loneliness, as the narrator muses when he sees a child reading out loud to herself, "[makes] humans out of walls," and indeed, in *London Does Not Belong To Me*, the reverse may also be said to be true:

the external pressure of marginalization and the consequent isolation this engenders cause the characters to construct emotional and psychological barriers in order to survive in this alien and unwelcoming environment. Relationships are transient and devoid of physical and emotional fulfilment. Contact between individuals is invariably overshadowed by cultural or sexual incompatibility. Paradoxically, to reaffirm one's existence in such surroundings, and as a reflection of their own self-loathing, Lee's characters form emotional and physical links that are inherently destructive and negative though not, it must be said, necessarily shallow. His descriptions of such moments seek to encapsulate the desperation and bitter-sweet futility that mark his later short stories, and act as a catharsis for a young would-be author longing to make sense of self and surroundings. And it is this search for self that fuels the narrator's futile pursuit of Cordelia – despite his knowledge of certain failure:

> There was in me a fear, a secret doubt, that she in her loneliness had used me as perhaps I might have been using her. Did she too have such a thought? Were people like this, using each other in order to achieve a momentary fruition? A release, perhaps, from the *rigor mortis* of the heart? What better choice than to search among those who had no common past or future – a chance encounter of the sea fish and the river fish at the estuary?

Tristam's constant and empty justifications of his sexual identity evoke a similar sense of pathos. He is, in essence, parasitic, living vicariously through – and feeding on – others. Despite his unremarkable appearance and borrowed philosophies, Tristam views himself (and homosexuality) as exotic; he considers himself (falsely) a combination of oriental insight and mysticism and continental sophistication, more at ease with the universal wisdom of Gandhi or the liberated views of Proust than with the mainstream English (read: heterosexual) male. Validating his own sexuality with references to the duality of Shakespeare, Donne and Proust, Tristam refers to the hermaphroditism of the earthworm, reducing heterosexuality to a "chemical reaction" while elevating homosexuality to a "flowering of self." But despite the purple prose and ostentatious allusions chosen by Tristam – "when one looks around, one sees a host of others, brilliant rainbow fishes among the dull worms" – his defence of his nature rings hollow; he is surface without substance.

Such descriptions, evoking a (flawed) sense of belonging and identity, do carry an aesthetic appeal for the narrator, but they are effectively offset in the text by his knowledge that Tristam's sense of difference is little more than a physical desire for 'otherness', a lust for the erotica of the exotic. As he and the narrator sit beneath an idyllic Indian pastoral in a restaurant, Tristam's initial rejection of his countrymen is based purely on physicality:

> Without warning, his voice took on a bitterness. "You know, I don't like the English. They're so pallid. So shrunken."

Tristam's real desire is for that of *physical* difference. He equates non-Anglo races with innocence and sexual allure, analysing in collectives, reducing and essentializing nations and races through false allusion. Under the guise of free-thinker and libertarian, he seeks to quell his increasing self-loathing. His fascination with 'otherness' and his supposed championing of all things non-British are still distinctly colonial and occidental in implication, clearly exhibiting the traits that Said would expound two decades later, when analysing Western attitudes to the Orient in the late nineteenth century onwards:

> Orientals were rarely seen or looked at; they were seen through, analysed not as citizens, or even people [...] the very designation of something as Oriental involved an already pronounced evaluative judgement.[3]

Likewise, the narrator and other Asian characters in the novel are not individuals but collective representations for Tristam. In his terms, of course, these evaluative judgements have everything to do with things of the Orient as representations of sexual fantasy, forbidden desire, and as a (false) source of self-justification. Tristam and Steve – sexually marginalized themselves – resort to these same dismissive tactics in their relationships with the narrator. In essence, they are sexual colonizers, as in this extract in which the narrator repositions Tristam's role from parasite to predator, while reinforcing his own role as innocent victim:

> On first noticing him, I remained very still in my bed and focussed my gaze on the top of his head; my hands became tensed under the sheets. My expression must have been blank; I had the same feeling that I experienced as a child when I lay in bed looking at an eight-legged spider moving across the ceiling.

The narrator perceives Tristam's and Steve's sexual advances as threatening but is nevertheless drawn to the alienation they experience: a common thread because of the narrator's own physical alienation and experiences of hostility.

Constantly underscoring these colonizer/colonized polemics, and continuing the allusions introduced in the prologue, are postmodernist preoccupations with fragmented humanity and meaningless repetition, as in this extract, set in a cafe outside the Albert Hall:

> The room was crowded with duffle-coated denizens, pale alert sunless faces, moving slowly among themselves, and from where I sat, sliding past one another, like those tortoises in a well which I remembered seeing as a young boy, flippers scraping over shells, crawling and heaving towards me for the vegetables falling from my outstretched hand [...] I held up my hand, freezing the gesture, low above the counter as though I was afraid that she might notice me too soon. It had to be done quietly without any fuss. Two cups pushed across the counter, silver coins in pincer-like grip exchanging from my hand to hers. After three more persons were served, my turn came. A bored expression on her face, thin lines seaming her neck, the waitress dealt with me with the expertise of a card sharp.
> Returning, and ad-libbing excuse-mes through the crustaceans of gabbing humanity, I managed to reach her without spilling a drop.

---

[3] Edward Said, *Orientalism* (New York: Pantheon, 1978): 207.

This description reduces the crowd to a bland urban mass, blending tropical imagery with its binary opposite – a London cafe. These are people whose individuality has been crushed by meaningless repetition and social mores, rendering them as subservient as any colonial subject. As a group, they are a "gabbing humanity" whose connections are tenuous at best, providing a portrait of uniformity and individuality extinguished, causing the narrator to associate these pallid, pinched features with images from his homeland. In both instances, the allusions are to shelled creatures, an indication of the protective masks of social conduct and appearance. Cultural penetration, for the narrator it seems, remains unattainable.

The final extracts I wish to examine have to do with the narrator's (and Lee's) attempts at personal resolution. Lee seeks a sense of postcolonial spatial existence through a form of personal arrival – to become, as the narrator terms it upon his return from Paris to London, "a first person instead of a third person." To do this, one must acknowledge the inherent paradox – perhaps even falsity – of the concepts of home and homecoming, especially from colonial/postcolonial perspectives. Transition and acceptance, the narrator perceives, stem not from seeking liberation but from the acknowledgement that entrapment is the natural state for the individual:

> A sudden vision came to me; that of a snake sloughing off his old skin. But human beings, like whale sharks which kept on adding layers of skin until their bodies were armour-plated, retained their experiences and fed on them.

As the time for the author's return to Malaya fast approaches, the narrator wrestles with the disillusionment of his European experience. Cordelia – and London – in terms of what each represents, are already dead to him – the memories of both now incompatible with the memories of his homeland. In many ways, Cordelia, although Australian, is interchangeable as a symbol of the narrator's conflicting responses to London – he must accept the betrayal of both of these false maternal figures and reform his identity through his tenuous links to Malaya. If one accepts Cordelia's only partly explained but seemingly mesmeric hold on the narrator as symbolic of the colonizer/colonized dynamic, the symbolism of the following extract becomes a clear recognition of the problematic colonial experience and, ultimately, a tentative validation of self:

> And I lay quietly for the ache to return, fearfully but with gladness, like a sick person counting the hours when the next attack would come so that his lying in wait would not prove abortive. And therefore I immured myself in my room, putting order into everything I could lay my hands on, as I patiently awaited the return of the terrible feeling that struck me when she left me. In order to meet her again I had to revive that feeling. Without it, everything would be such a waste. I might as well be a puppet, manipulated by her hands, if I did not repossess my feelings.

But the effect of Cordelia's sudden re-appearance is to shock the narrator into transcultural confusion:

> The room suddenly felt warm and beads of sweat frosted my temples. It took me more than three seconds to recognise Cordelia. And for three more seconds, so it seemed, I was whisked away from this bright, glaring room and those hideous Christmas cards,

into the still centre of my whirlpool, and strangely, an old tune from "The Opium War"
cranked up in my mind, as though I was back home, lying on the camp-bed listening to
the arabesque immobility of its melody, something that was plaintive, something far-off.
"Ta ya Ta. Ni Nsin, hsin pa." Like a translating machine, my mind rendered it into the
English version. "Tak oh Tak. Wake, wake up." It sounded most ludicrous in my translation; the beauty and the call to the heart were lost. And yet in my own language the song
spoke convincingly. Give up, it had said, the opium pipe, your beauty, your love, your
strength-absorber, your spirit-demolisher. Tak oh Tak. Garish, oh so very garish. The
stillness of my centre was muddied by an automatic translation machine.

Resolution and resurrection lie in finally recognizing the opium pipe for what it is.
Through his rejection at the hands of Cordelia – and London – the narrator takes the
first tentative steps towards, in his own words, "disinterring" the "great ghost of [his]
past." In this way, then, *London Does Not Belong To Me* may be read in one sense as a
triumphant exorcism. Only in confronting the centre and burying the imperial ghosts of
the past can the narrator move into a liberated future. In the brief concluding chapter,
the narrator receives a parting gift from Tristam as he boards the train on the first leg of
his return to Malaya. The gift Tristam brings (a Norman Collins novel entitled *London
Belongs to Me*) provides the ironic inversion of Lee's title. The sense of disillusionment that pervades this novel can, then, from a Malaysian perspective, be seen as
liberation and illumination. Lee's realization that London does not belong to him is a
painful but salutary acknowledgment of the deception of Empire, but a necessary stage
in the re-invention of his identity in transcultural terms. If, in essence, *London Does
Not Belong To Me* is an articulation of postcolonial grief and the betrayal of memory, it
also charts an ultimately enriching journey, representing, as it does, the narrator's/
author's first tentative and ambivalent steps towards a repositioning of identity in the
call and response of transcultural space.

WORKS CITED

Harrex, Syd. "Mutes and Mutilators in the Fiction of Lee Kok Liang," in *Individual and Commu-
nity in Commonwealth Literature* (Malta: The University Press, 1978): 140–46.
Liang, Lee Kok. *London Does Not Belong To Me* (Kuala Lumpur: Maya Press, 2003).
——. "Sketches, Brushstrokes and Vignettes" (manuscript held at the Centre for New Literatures
in English, Flinders University, South Australia).
Said, Edward. *Orientalism* (New York: Pantheon, 1978).
——. *Out of Place* (New York: Alfred A. Knopf, 1999).

《•》

Bicultural Identities in Discourse

The Case of Yvonne du Fresne

ANNE HOLDEN RØNNING

C AN WE SPEAK OF BICULTURAL IDENTITIES in our globalized world, or has this very concept outdated itself? This is a timely question as we enter a new millennium. Contemporary postcolonial literary discourse, in its concern with the hyphenated culture of the individual, has been paralleled in other times and places. Conflicts of cultures and the imposing of one on another are far from being a new phenomenon – we have only to think of the ancient and still extant cultures of the Middle Eastern region, of Egypt, and of the lost glory of the Greek and Roman Empires. History has often failed to illuminate the hybridity of these imperial powers.

In the twentieth century, countries settled either by imperial colonizers or by settler immigrants have frequently overlooked the diverse backgrounds of the immigrants and colonizers in their theoretical analyses of postcolonial discourses. Settlers cannot be assimilated any more than indigenous peoples, but instead represent a mosaic of cultures. Contemporary ethnic studies in America reflect this diversity.

As Henry Louis Gates, Jr., Tzvetan Todorov and Homi Bhabha have indicated, there is no such thing as racial homogeneity, hence the abandonment of the search for a national identity and the replacement of it with a discourse of cultural identities. This discourse negotiates between cultures, crossing cultural boundaries which are ever-changing. Traditionally these boundaries have been associated with colour and indigeneity, but I do not agree with Joel Kahn that postcolonialism is "a language of culture, alterity and identity that [...] also tends to draw a firm boundary between 'indigenous' and 'Western' cultural representations" for Westerners have colonized other Westerners down through the ages as the history of Europe illustrates, imposing their own cultural criteria.[1] Although Kahn talks of this as "part of an earlier expressivist discourse on culture and difference," he fails to account adequately for the cultural diversity within the various settler/immigrant backgrounds of white peoples, not least from the European continent, whose experiences are far from homogeneous in language or traditions.

---

[1] Joel Kahn, *Culture, Multiculture, Postculture* (London: Sage, 1995): 14. Further page references are in the main text.

Discourses of bicultural identities can be contributive to "postcolonial social restitution and reconstruction," as Helen Tiffin suggests, if they increase social understanding.[2] They can be reconstructive and identity-building, expressing a collective experience shared by some few, trying to appease a sense of estrangement at the same time as attempting to portray a communal memory: what could be termed a creolization of cultures. The description of cultural creolization would seem a hopeless task and is undoubtedly a balancing act, but the concept, if we may call it that, does open up a way of regarding literary texts as an expression of cultural identity or identities, a means by which minority groups can express their own particular sense of belonging and subvert and adapt canonical approaches to literature to the needs of different environments.

The use of the term 'creolization' has undergone a change from denoting the intermixing of races and cultural change, seen specifically in language, to "a more comprehensive sense of cultural process interaction," as Kamau Braithwaite has suggested.[3] Looked at in this way it can be seen as closely linked to contemporary views of cultural identity, a result of the cross-fertilization of cultures and its textual expression. As our cultural identities are formed socially by the environment in which we live, what we read and how we view ourselves and others are crucial elements in our understanding of our own identities.[4] I agree with Stuart Hall that "actually identities are about questions of using the resources of history, language and culture in the process of becoming rather than being: not 'who we are' or 'where we came from', so much as what we might become, how we have been represented and how that bears on how we might represent ourselves."[5] This approach to reading stresses the manner in which the interpretation of texts changes according to the life experience and increased knowledge of the individual reader.

In a recent article, Tiffin argues that literary texts have "culturally and racially interpellative effects on [the] attitude and self-conceptions"[6] of colonized peoples, as well as providing information about other cultures which help to counterbalance discriminatory attitudes. Tiffin expresses the problems facing anyone writing about a marginal group or minority in a colonized country where the colonizers of one national or ethnic

---

[2] Helen Tiffin, "Colonial Pretexts and Rites of Reply," *Yearbook of English Studies* 27 (1997): 219.

[3] Quoted by Bill Ashcroft, Gareth Griffiths & Helen Tiffin, *The Empire Writes Back: Theory and Practice in Post-Colonial Literatures* (London & New York: Routledge, 1989): 147.

[4] Cultural identity can be defined as the result of a process wher"eby the individual or group evaluate consciously or subconsciously their own situation in society, and attempt to establish a sense of self-esteem and self-confidence which enables them to accept their own place in life. It involves an acceptance of difference from others whilst forming a new belonging. It answers the questions "Who am I?"/"What am I?" and the answer is learnt in a process of interaction, of dialogue between the text and the reader in the case of literature. See Anne Holden Rønning, "Patricia Grace and Keri Hulme in the Discourse of New Zealand Cultural Identity," in *Identities and Masks: Colonial and Postcolonial Studies*, ed. Jakob Lothe, Anne Holden Rønning & Peter Young (Kristiansand: Høyskoleforlaget, 2001): 109–24.

[5] Stuart Hall & Paul du Gay, in *Questions of Cultural Identity*, ed. Hall & du Gay (London: Sage, 1996): 4.

[6] Helen Tiffin, "Colonial Pretexts and Rites of Reply," 220.

origin form the dominant peoples. In this respect, New Zealand is a particularly interesting area for discussion, as it has its base in a very strong canonical British literary tradition which forms the backdrop for the work of both minority (Māori) and immigrant writers.

As a starting-point for reflecting on the biculturality of identities, I have chosen a novel, *Frédérique*, by the New Zealand writer Yvonne du Fresne. A third-generation descendant of Danish-Huguenot immigrants to New Zealand, she expresses in this book the multiplicity of identities that characterizes the people of many nations today. The fictional autobiographical element is often strong in such texts, the narrator portrayed as torn between belonging to the new society and country aand being haunted by past history and his/her ancestral roots and traditions. As du Fresne told me when I met her in Wellington in 1996, this is her way of expressing her own cultural identity and biculturality, a point underscored by a 1987 review of *Frédérique* entitled "The ethnic author of Makara."[7]

Du Fresne's work confronts New Zealand with its own heterogeneity, as she depicts the problem of belonging to a minority group of European descent in a country dominated by British thought and culture, described by Leonard Wilcox as "the rawness of a postcolonial society and the ill-fitting and superficial overlay of British culture".[8] William Broughton, too, has pointed out that du Fresne's themes show "a concern for Scandinavian cultural identification [...] and a sense of alienation from the dominant local culture."[9] By her insistence on cultural difference, yet herself within a dominant group, the Pakeha or New Zealanders of European stock, her texts could be seen as examples of what Vijay Mishra and Bob Hodge call "complicit post-colonialism" – an implicit aspect of colonization itself.[10] This is an example, then, of how a writer acknowledges the power-structure inherent in the colonial situation and attempts to counteract it, but at the same time subconsciously confirms the very existence of that structure. Her texts may be said to be postcolonial in the New Zealand context, as they deal with the need for a sense of belonging and positioning of the 'self' which many immigrants from countries other than Britain try to establish – processes which are similar though not necessarily the same. They are discourses of cultural identities, or a search for present identity through a reliving of the past.

Among several narratological devices employed by du Fresne, I shall comment on her play with language and its implications, and her use of historical and mythological references to communicate a sense of alienation and difference. One strategy used to represent cultural ethnicity is language – what may be called the creolization of the text. We can ask whether mixed-language writing in English is determined by the cultural

---

[7] Iona McNaughton, "The Ethnic Author of Makara," *Dominion Sunday Times* (3 May 1987): 16.

[8] Leonard Wilcox, "Postmodern or Anti-Modernism?" *Landfall* 155 (September 1985): 359.

[9] W.S. Broughton, "Short Fiction 1985 to 1987," *Journal of New Zealand Literature* 6 (1988): 86.

[10] Vijay Mishra & Bob Hodge, "What is Post[-]colonialism?" (1991), in *Colonial Discourse and Post-Colonial Theory: A Reader*, ed. Patrick Williams & Laura Chrisman (New York: Columbia UP, 1994): 284.

background of those writing, or whether this is just a moment in time when it is important to express difference as a part of defining identities in our "imagined communities," or as part of a discourse of sociopolitical critique. The basic concerns of this debate can be summed up in Ngugi's words:

> Over a time, a particular system of verbal signposts comes to reflect a given people's historical consciousness of their twin struggles with nature and with one another. [...] Such a language comes to embody both continuity and change in their historical consciousness.[11]

For, as Ngugi pointed out in the Sir Douglas Robb lectures at the University of Auckland: "The choice of language and the use to which language is put is central to a people's definition of themselves in relation to their natural and social environment, indeed in relation to the entire universe."[12]

A frequent literary strategy for the subversion of the established and the representation of biculturality in postcolonial texts is the use of non-English words and phrases in a text otherwise in English, thus making the reader the 'Other'. Such discourse highlights the difference between intelligibility and meaningfulness as pointed out by, among others, Reed Dasenbrock and Witi Ihimaera.[13] This strategy is common in Māori literature in English. Du Fresne's work uses the same strategy, only with Danish as the foreign element. Those with knowledge of both languages and cultures are in a privileged position in relation to those who only know the one. This does not change the meaning of the text, but by putting it into a wider context opens up a variety of interpretations, providing overt and covert readings.

Frédérique opens dramatically with the protagonist sitting dreaming on the shore, suddenly finding herself giving a speech in seventeenth-century French:

> All the Reformed here, and about to come, whatever condition they may be, whether ecclesiastical or secular, shall be obliged to swear an oath of fidelity either by mouth or written in front of the Magistrate, of the place where they have settled, or shall settle.[14]

In the opening sequences of the novel, du Fresne deliberately informs the reader of the mixed cultural identities of the protagonist and her family: "The man from the seventeenth century spoke slowly and carefully, but the rr's were swallowed, the phrases too

[11] Ngugi wa Thiong'o, *Writers in Politics. A Re-Engagement with Issues of Literature and Society* (Oxford: James Currey, 1997): 57.

[12] Quoted by Michael Neill, "Coming Home: Teaching the Post-Colonial Novel," *Islands* 2.1 (April 1985): 50.

[13] Reed Way Dasenbrock. "Intelligibility and Meaningfulness in Multicultural Literature in English," *PMLA* 102 (1987): 10–19. Witi Ihimaera et al., "Kaupapa," in *Te Ao Marama*, vol. 1: *Contemporary Maori Writing*, ed. Witi Ihimaera (Auckland: Reed, 1992): 14–18, and interview with Witi Ihimaera (June 1994, February 1995), in *Spiritcarvers: Interviews with eighteen writers from New Zealand*, ed. Antonella Sarti (Cross/Cultures 31; Amsterdam & Atlanta GA: Rodopi, 1998): 71–79.

[14] Yvonne du Fresne, *Frédérique* (Auckland: Penguin, 1987): 3. Further page references are in the main text.

suavely rapid" (26). Frédérique's foreignness is underlined throughout the text, either by herself through strategies of fictional autobiography or through other characters. On first meeting her on the shore, William Cooper, an Englishman and catechist, comments on the fact that she speaks in broken English, her voice "very deep and full of threatening rr'rs" (9). The discussion of linguistic difference is further developed in the situation when William Cooper comes to the d'Albrets' house in a state of delirium – rescued from the shore by Frédérique. He hears this strange tongue being spoken – old-fashioned French and Danish – and he feels "cut off, shut out by their torrents of alien language" (29). Their voices are described as hoarse, hard and guttural – probably a reference to the Danish language, rather than the French – and his own sense of alienation is heightened by frequently hearing the d'Albrets "speaking only in their own languages, very fast" (84). Cooper describes them as almost mythical beings with "goblin hands and pour[ing] out those liquid streams of words which left him baffled, offended and exhausted" (85). Du Fresne's choice of words to describe these scenes underscores Cooper's inability to come to terms with what is strange and unknown. Like the Danes, he too is lost in this foreign land; he thus heaves a sigh of relief when he meets Eleanor Acton-Avery, for at last he has met "An Englishwoman. [...] He felt he had been a lifetime away from all he knew, and now at last he glimpsed his home again" (51). The equation of a person with a country is played on throughout the text. Du Fresne refers here to the role played by language and linguistic compatibility in asserting any individual's identity in a strange place, a way not always comprehended by those who live in a linguistically homogeneous environment, and a feature of postcolonial discussion.

Du Fresne has exactly mimicked not only some of the typical Scandinavian errors in speaking English but also French-derived linguistic problems that Frédérique's parents experience. The phrases are almost satirical in their precision. Several examples in the text underline du Fresne's emphasis on the implications of the way we speak and understand language. We are presented with a creolized mix of French-Danish English (Jacob and Olympe d'Albret) and Danish-English (Frédérique, Axel), as the following examples show:

"You have had the good sleep," [...] "Come," he said. "Regard the work!"
"Behold the cauliflower," said Jacob. "The potato. The cabbage!" (45)

"I proceed backward, [...] from my existence as an estate owner, to the small task of vegetable growth." (29)

Here first-language interference is visible, for instance, in the use of the imperatives "regard," "behold" – typical of French but seldom used thus in the English language. There are also elements of Scandinavian sentence-structure in statements such as

"Watch horse – I must do little work." (10)

"It is a habit of French [...] that in time of danger, to tell stories, for the amusement." (35)

"We work 'ard [...] to – solve – new words for all our new countries." (99)

At the same time, there is frequently a note of irony, and we can ask whether in reality du Fresne is making fun of her characters, a point overlooked by most reviewers of her work. For instance, in the following incident she balances her comments on Danish-English with a critique of the way some English people speak. Reminiscing, Frédérique describes an occasion when she and Axel Søndergaard, her fiancé, made fun of their English teacher in Denmark, Miss Chester, and her pronunciation. Frédérique "purse[s] her lips, [...] and recite[s] in a high remote voice, 'At home [...] Papa *excels* himself at carving the saddle of beef. The roast beef of Old England!'" (74). She concludes: "'But it must tire them so speaking in those high voices'" (74).

Du Fresne also includes examples of different English dialects, such as that used by the Robinsons from Lincolnshire (91), William Cooper's nanny, and the Blacks from Yorkshire (93), but all these incidents are accompanied by some parallel to her own linguistic ancestry. For example, Mrs Black says: "Please to coom in t'hoose!" to which Frédérique replies "'Hus' [...] It is Danish words" (93). Du Fresne's own experience as a teacher has no doubt played a significant role in developing this strategy of critiquing language often in a humorous way, but as several reviewers, not least of her short stories, have indicated, du Fresne is walking a tightrope in her didactic insistence on comparing languages in this manner. She risks defeating her own purpose.

The search for roots is a central theme in all of du Fresne's work, and is conducted by looking at and reliving history, and by drawing on folklore symbolism. The protagonist, in a search for an understanding of her roots, weaves in and out of her family's past history, in particular the Schleswig–Holstein crisis of 1860s Denmark as remembered through the minds of the first Danish immigrants to the Manawatu region in New Zealand. They recall incidents which are sources of pride in the family ancestry, as well as episodes of racial discrimination. As du Fresne remarks in her preface to *The Book of Ester*,

There were two kinds of stories told me in my beginnings. On one side were the stories of the Danish families. The legends. Gods and heroes illuminating the landscape; giant, half-misty figures, well suited to inhabiting the moors of Jutland, the waters of the Baltic and the North Sea–the plains of Manawatu.

And on the other side of my life – there were stories of the French Huguenots. They were still trying to fit in with the Danes, let alone the New Zealanders! Quick-tempered, then suddenly noble, patient. Like the Huguenot gentlemen of the French novels – guarding doors, utterly faithful to causes and friends. Quickly moved by words, by music. But underneath a terrible constancy of purpose. [...] The Huguenot women sat in their large Manawatu houses and surveyed their lands and their history. Just as they had surveyed their lands and their history in seventeenth century France, Pfalz, Brandenburg and Prussia. Their eyes absorbed centuries. [...] Both men and women held secrets, in their heads, in their hands.[15]

These are the people Philippe describes as "practised émigrés in the most alien, the most distant country they could find" (111). But as Frédérique explains to him, "the d'Albrets have learned one lesson [...] as did many émigrés. We dig in."

---

[15] Yvonne du Fresne, *The Book of Ester* (Auckland: Longman Paul, 1982): v–vi. Further page references are in the main text.

We plant the corn, the potato. We feed the animals and at the same time we exercise the singing voice, keep up the art of conversation, learn how to teach and how to handle cattle [...] I watch this land – or any land [...] and learn its patterns, its changes of light and sounds. I fit myself into its rhythm. I am like my Danish mor [...] I am a woman of the land. (113–14)

Intercultural differences dominate many of the incidents in a text where the protagonist's parents are of different cultural backgrounds, Danish and Huguenot. By making Frédérique's stepmother a Huguenot, du Fresne is able to centralize the intercultural conflict in many conversations. For example, questions of inheritance are raised, as the Danish Huguenots married within their own people to avoid Danish laws where their property would have been inherited by the Danish member of the family, regardless of gender (134). Frédérique's family is torn between allegiance to their French heritage – of Protestant, culturally superior, and very strict townspeople – and their Danish ancestors, who are portrayed as more open, and culturally a more rural, people who have a wealth of pagan legends and mythology. On one occasion, Frédérique gets a letter telling her that Axel, her Danish fiancé, is leaving the army and coming to New Zealand. This worries the d'Albrets, as they fear that "The French will not like it. Those politicals, those intriguers!" Whereupon Frédérique reminds her father that his first wife was a Dane – to which he replies: "I outwitted the plotters." And so the two plan to break down family resistance by the combination of "Huguenot tactics, Danish stubbornness" (129), both characteristics inherited by Frédérique.

Throughout the text Frédérique is described as a hybrid: she is like "the alien child with the French father who had come as the others of his kind in 1711 as spies from Germany" (44). She is someone "coming out of her northern silence into the French colony, [with] eyes the remote blue of winter" (18). Physiognomic features are commented on at various stages of the book. Frédérique's blond Danish hair, and ice-blue eyes (25), her "hair of spun sugar" (30), her "wheat-yellow hair, the long pale eyes of Axel Søndergaard. Of Kong Sven of Jutland" (34), are contrasted with the dark black hair and brown eyes of her parents. William Cooper, fascinated by Frédérique but unsure of his choice of her as a wife, sees her as "a witch of the north." In his dreams he sees that this "girl with hair like kelp and eyes of blue ice leaned over him and spoke in a voice that swarmed with the languorous hum of bees" (164). Philippe, too, is aware of her difference from other Danes, for he "could not stop himself from glancing at [Frédérique's] delicate wrists, her long slender hands; the hooded clever eyes of Jeanne d'Albret" (114). He sees in her "a scion of a noble and ancient family in France" (109), "the mother of the old Protestant king" (113).

Du Fresne also uses other narrative literary strategies reminiscent of Victorian literature, which emphasized dress and even ways of walking as a comment on, as well as a manner of creating and asserting, identity and of positioning a character in relation to others. Whenever Madame d'Albret appears, she is described as immaculately dressed, usually in black, in contrast to the less formal dress of the other characters. Her foreignness is indicated by language and appearance, as on the occasion when she meets Victoria and Evangeline: "'Bonjour, mes enfants,' said Madame d'Albret and enfolded the girls in a hiss of silk. They gazed wide-eyed at the feathers in her hat that turned her into a black swan luring them into her dangerous waters" (102).

Frédérique is well aware that her biculturality is evident even in the way she walks. She remembers being told by her mother to "Walk heel and toe like a Dane" (30), very different from the demands of her stepmother, who, as in a Jane Austen novel, did not think it suitable for young ladies to go for long walks: "I put on my Jutland boots. I turned myself into my other half: that Danish countrywoman, capable of walking a long way in one afternoon. And [Maman] was silent then, as she always is when she is reminded of my Danish blood" (5).

However, Frédérique is not the only character whom du Fresne portrays as criticising colonialism in New Zealand. Philippe, her cousin visiting New Zealand, longs even more for Nordhavn in Denmark, to get away from "his hated farm work, and go back to his Sunday night soirées in Nordhavn, the gratifying response to his small but promising compositions for the flute. The delightful acclamation of the young ladies, black ringlets bobbing, brown eyes sparkling" (18). Throughout, Philippe is used to contrasting Danish/Huguenot reactions to New Zealand and those of the English – the cultivated, culturally minded, town-bred French Danes and the rougher country-bred, cattle-farming Brits. But even the Brits are dissatisfied with their new country. The sense of belonging, or lack of such, is expressed in the Acton–Averys' reaction to being in New Zealand. The mother has constant migraine and hates the country, whereas her daughter, Eleanor, is better-adjusted, though even she can feel homesick. Frédérique notices that Eleanor hides "behind her spectacles when she is homesick. She shuts out this land and insists that Ramsgate and Margate are here. And I think of Jutland sunflowers" (139).

Topographical features are often found in New Zealand literature as symbolic of identities and biculturality. Dreaming on the shore among the dunes, Frédérique carries on an imaginary conversation in her head with Axel:

> Here, the salt, the desert takes over our world. The air flashes with diamonds of light. When the wind blows in from the sea the salt rises in a glitter of crystals and slowly billows in over the land. It is like the snowclouds that rise over the moors of Jutland. That mouthless fog that gnaws at every thorn bush, every patch of lyng. (5)

One might say that the geological faultlines which traverse New Zealand are echoed in the text by the cultural faultlines which exist between the Danish Huguenots and the Danes: for example, the story of Axel and Frédérique's visit to the old Jutland couple, (44), and the fear expressed by Olympe and Jacob when the Reverend Bull tells them that some stranger has been seen around the area. Immediately they assume that it is someone, even in this faraway place, looking for them as French spies. The cultural balancing-act is fragile. To some readers this may seem rather far-fetched, but psychological research on refugees and immigrants has shown only too clearly that for many the phobia of pursuit never disappears, and can be passed on from one generation to another. Du Fresne is thus here touching on a known phenomenon which, though fictionalized, has deep roots in the reality of contemporary society.

Folklore symbolism is another narrative pattern used by du Fresne to express the bicultural conflict in its many facets. Underlying the text, surfacing from time to time, is the Danish myth of the Swanneskind: i.e. swanskin feathers (36–40), a legend considered a "crude Danish story" by Jacob's wife (35). It is said to be associated with a part of Denmark known as the region of the swans: "Some people call us the swan folk. They are saying that at certain times we turn into swans" (35). The story follows a traditional folklore pattern of a young girl imprisoned by a wicked stepmother on an island, separated from her lover, whom the stepmother tries to poison when he flies in with his swan wings to rescue the girl. Her only chance of escape is to make a pair of swan wings which will give her freedom and happiness. Like most legends, it ends happily.

In this text, the legend is symbolic of how the protagonist is entrapped between, and imprisoned by; conflicting cultures, and of how it is only by coming to terms with the relation between these cultures that she can be free. The swan feathers, or swan-cloak as some versions have it, is a magic sign which will keep a person safe from harm, and the recurrence of this image leads up to the moment when Frédérique has found out how to make her "swan skin" and can feel free to choose for herself where and how she will live.

All of du Fresne's novels to date can be read as examples of autobiographical storytelling, memory and dreams being used as devices for investigating cultural identity. The first-person narrator relates her story as if she were experiencing it herself and using it to tell the history of her people and family, expressing their triple cultural bind. The narrator is homodiegetic, closely observing and also closely involved in the events described. An analysis of 'difference', of being the 'Other', can be seen as part of the autobiographical search for the self, the 'I-persona' investigating his/her own life through the use of contrast. The autobiographical nature of the text is underscored in the last section, which is written partly in the form of a diary (Chapter 17), then as letters, and finally as part of a journal. These are some of the oldest forms of autobiography, and by using them du Fresne endeavours to persuade the reader to accept the veracity of her story. The novel ends with a strong critique of postcolonialism, as well as an attempt to come to terms with identities at a point where Frédérique attempts to tell her husband about the family history but meets with incomprehension:

> I tried to tell him about us, the Huguenots, and our tireless followers, our shadows. And he backed away from me, his face full of horror. He shouted, "I am an Englishman, and Englishmen abhor these dreadful things you have been telling me. Foreign things." (204)

And she retorts:

> "But I am the invader of Maori territory [...] the Pakeha parents are also invaders. Should we all go back? We are so far from the world here. We have come with ploughs, seed, language and hunger. And greed. And guns. [...] Then I thought, it is too late. The world has come to New Zealand as the Maori came here." (205–206)

Du Fresne's tendency to identify the situation of the Danes in New Zealand with that of the Māori has been much criticized, and not without reason. It is symptomatic of a lack of critical balance in her work which is conveyed most clearly in her extreme negativism towards the English, in this novel especially in her characterization of

William Cooper. His unfortunate marriage to Frédérique, who neither can nor will conform to his conservative ideas of a woman's place, and his revulsion at her foreignness
define him as a stereotypical colonizer. On the other hand, I think that through texts
such as *Frédérique* du Fresne is primarily concerned with issues of negotiating between cultures, and emphasizing the hybridity of the New Zealand people at the cost of
objectivity. We can ask, therefore, how successful she is in portraying bicultural identities. Her discourse can be seen as a key to a future based on shared memory, but at
the same time as a key that can lock the door by keeping the cultural groups apart. The
frequent references to a superior, ancient Scandinavian culture, in particular the Kings
of Jutland, often seem exaggerated, as several reviews of her work indicate.

Put into a postcolonial and colonial context, however, this book brings to the fore a
dominant feature of our globalized world: Where do we really belong with our multiple cultural backgrounds? The ending of *Frédérique* posits a solution at the personal
level. The only one who understands Frédérique is her lost lover, Axel, killed in the
war. Thus she closes:

> Beloved Axel. We live at the end of the world here. This is a land that lies on the other
> side of the moon. I live in one of its deserts, made of crystals, salt grains, rocks splintered
> from meteors ribbed with silver quartz, hoar frost older than time. You may not wish to
> travel so far to this country. You may not want to enter its silence, its great gales, its
> empty distances. [...] But I cannot leave my dead daughter. I cannot leave our school or
> the people here. We are all we have in the world .
> Here I have sewn my new swanskin. [...] I am starting to make my own flights again.
> [...] For I am learning to live with grief, and this land, and myself. (214–15)

The folklore myth of the swanskin is complete. Frédérique's story as a struggle to
come to terms with her opposing cultural heritages and identities has reached its end.

WORKS CITED

Ashcroft, Bill, Gareth Griffiths & Helen Tiffin. *The Empire Writes Back: Theory and Practice in
    Post-Colonial Literatures* (London & New York: Routledge, 1989).
Broughton, W.S. "Short Fiction 1985 to 1987," *Journal of New Zealand Literature* 6 (1988):
    81–95.
Chilwell, Jan. Review of *Frédérique*, in *The Listener* 117 (2476; 1 August 1987): 68–69.
Dasenbrock, Reed Way. "Intelligibility and Meaningfulness in Multicultural Literature in Eng-
    lish," *PMLA* 102 (1987): 10–19.
du Fresne, Yvonne. *The Book of Ester* (Auckland: Longman Paul, 1982).
——. *Frédérique* (Auckland: Penguin, 1987).
Hall, Stuart, and Paul du Gay, ed. *Questions of Cultural Identity* (London: Sage 1996).
Kahn, Joel. *Culture, Multiculture, Postculture* (London: Sage, 1995).
Ihimaera, Witi. Interview (June 1994, February 1995), in *Spiritcarvers: Interviews with eighteen
    writers from New Zealand*, ed. Antonella Sarti (Cross/Cultures 31; Amsterdam & Atlanta GA:
    Rodopi, 1998): 71–79.
——, et al. "Kaupapa," in *Te Ao Marama*, vol. 1: *Contemporary Maori Writing*, ed. Witi Ihi-
    maera (Auckland: Reed, 1992): 14–18.
McNaughton, Iona. "The Ethnic Author of Makara," *Dominion Sunday Times* (3 May 1987).

Mishra, Vijay, & Bob Hodge. "What is post[-]colonialism?" (1991), in *Colonial Discourse and Post-Colonial Theory: A Reader*, ed. Patrick Williams & Laura Chrisman (New York: Columbia UP, 1994).

Neill, Michael. "Coming Home: Teaching the Post-Colonial Novel," *Islands* 2.1 (April 1985): 38–53.

Ngugi wa Thiong'o. *Writers in Politics. A Re-Engagement with Issues of Literature and Society* (Oxford: James Currey, 1997).

Rønning, Anne Holden. "Patricia Grace and Keri Hulme in the Discourse of New Zealand Cultural Identity," in *Identities and Masks: Colonial and Postcolonial Studies*, ed. Jakob Lothe, Anne Holden Rønning & Peter Young (Kristiansand: Høyskoleforlaget, 2001): 109–24.

Tiffin, Helen. "Colonial Pretexts and Rites of Reply," *Yearbook of English Studies* 27 (1997): 219–33.

Wilcox, Leonard. "Postmodern or Anti-modernism?" *Landfall* 155 (September 1985): 344–64.

《●》

The (Un)Fortunate Traveller and the Text
Bill Manhire and *The Brain of Katherine Mansfield*

BERND HERZOGENRATH

B ILL MANHIRE'S SELECTION OF POEMS *Zoetropes* was published in 1984.[1] A zoetrope, the OED informs us, is "a cylinder with a series of images on the inner surface; when observed through slits in the wall of the rotating cylinder, these images produced the illusion of movement." Much like the twenty-four frames per second of your ordinary movie, the illusion of movement, or, to be more precise, the illusion of *linear movement*, of *linearity*, is achieved through a series of discrete, successive elements – a strategy closely resembling our 'inherited' Western way of reading or writing: from left to right, from top to bottom, the linear sequence of words makes for the effect of meaning, of the coherence of the printed text.

However, the first part of the title poem of Manhire's selection tells a different story:

> Zoetropes
>
> A starting. Words which begin
> with Z alarm the heart:
> the eye cuts down at once
>
> then drifts across the page
> to other disappointments.

Manhire is here suggesting an alternative to the standard linear way of reading: a non-linear, zig-zagging way of reading. And it is this notion that I want to analyse and follow in Manhire's text *The Brain of Katherine Mansfield* (and I use the term 'text' advisedly, in preference to the term 'book'). Thus, I will not be going into the problematics of the 'New Zealand-ness' of the text, or the difficulties a non-New-Zealand reader has to face when confronted by a text that addresses its reader as "an ordinary New Zealander," even if s/he happens to be an exceptional Irish/wo/man. My essay can thus be seen as a 'complementary reading' to Gordon Collier's essay on Manhire's

---

[1] Bill Manhire, *Zoetropes: Poems 1972–82* (Sydney: Allen & Unwin, 1984).

text, in which he presents both the New Zealand background to this small book and Manhire's indebtedness to American Popular (and Official) Culture.[2] It was, in fact, Collier's essay that led me to buy Manhire's book in the first place. Now, ten years later, I will try and tackle this text from a different perspective, presenting not so much a reading of its content as a kind of 'structural reading', trying to focus on yet another instance of being situated *in between* two cultures.

I am going to read this text as a *zoetrope* – that is, as a kind of machine that *both* creates a kind of illusion of linearity through discrete cuts *and* introduces a non-linear, zig-zagging course to get there. I see Manhire's text as symptomatic of the (post) modern break with the conventions of traditional modes of narrative. Being mainly concerned with textual structures and strategies, my reading will draw on poststructuralist theories and the concept of hypertext.[3]

For those not familiar with Manhire's slim volume, a brief summary might be appropriate, though providing a summary might be the hardest part of the enterprise. To put it as simply as possible: what we have here are the grotesque adventures of an "ordinary New Zealander." The first thing that strikes us as readers is not only that this New Zealander is nameless, but also that from the word 'go', the adventures are not merely *presented to us*, but *enacted by us* as readers. Manhire's book is one of the quite rare instances of a second-person narrative, addressing the reader as 'you' in order to facilitate an immediate identification. There is thus a collapse of reader address and character reference, one falling into the other. Let us have a look at how *The Brain of Katherine Mansfield* starts:

1.

You are just an ordinary New Zealander. You have strength, intelligence and luck, though you are not particularly good at languages. Your family and friends like you, and there is one special friend who really thinks you're swell. Yours is a well-rounded personality; your horoscope is usually good; your school report says "satisfactory." But somehow you are restless. Your life is missing challenge and excitement. You want to make things happen. Go to 2.

2.

On your way home from school one day, you find an old man waiting outside your house. He is holding a leather-bound book. He looks as if he has been expecting you.

---

[2] Gordon Collier, "Gebrauchsanweisungen sorgfältig lesen: Erzähltechnik in der zeitgenössischen Prosa Neuseelands, am Beispiel von Bill Manhires *The Brain of Katherine Mansfield*," in *Neuseeland im Pazifischen Raum*, ed. W. Kreisel, P.H. Marsden, G.V. Davis & J. Jansen, (Aachen: Verlag der Augustinus Buchhandlung, 1992): 261–78.

[3] Collier himself suggests that Manhire's text might owe something to computer games and cybernetic simulation; "Gebrauchsanweisungen sorgfältig lesen," 271.

"I have been reading your story," he says. "But it seems to have stopped. Something seems to happen when you enter the house. "

He goes on to explain that he is eager to know how your life will continue. In fact, he says, your life is essentially an unwritten story. You yourself are the hero of the story.

"Many are the choices you must face, but the outcome of the tale will depend on you alone. "

You stare at the stranger speechless, but your heart is beating with excitement. Dimly, as at a distance, you hear him say that you will need more than human help on the adventures which await you: you must choose one of three magic weapons to take with you on your journey. But you will have to come with him to his house. It lies in a distant suburb of the city.

It is getting late. The dark clouds of a winter afternoon swoop down over the familiar hills and houses. You shiver. The time of your first decision is upon you. Do you dare to turn the pages of adventure?

If you decide to accompany the old man, go to 5. If you decide to go home and think it over, go to 11.[4]

In 2, then, we are faced with our first 'real' decision, having to decide between two options for two different storylines, that might lead to two different results and further bifurcations.

As the attentive reader will have already noticed, *The Brain of Katherine Mansfield* follows the structure of the choose-your-own-adventure story, or that of computer games, for that matter. Each of its fifty 'chapters' presents a 'fragment' of a storyline to be chosen by the reader – the reader has to find his/her pathway through the alternatives offered by the chapters, and your choices, reader, are crucial: life or death, it's in your hands. In Paul Auster's novel *Moon Palace*, one of its characters voices the postmodern contention that life is a text written by a subject: "Every man is the author of his own life."[5] *The Brain of Katherine Mansfield* stages this notion in all its clarity and with all its consequences. Like Foucault's Don Quixote, the protagonist of Manhire's book – which is *you*, the reader – is a 'you', a linguistic category, a "thin graphism, a letter [...] he is writing itself, wandering through the world among the resemblances of things."[6] The options of the reader/adventurer decide whether the life-text will be lethal or not, whether the text will produce a fortunate or an unfortunate traveller. Mind you, the options themselves – however strategic, rational or ethical they may

[4] Bill Manhire, *The Brain of Katherine Mansfield* (Auckland: Auckland UP, 1988). There is no pagination in the book; the only numbering is that of the fifty 'chapters'.

[5] Paul Auster, *Moon Palace* (London & Boston MA: Faber & Faber, 1990): 7. For a more detailed analysis of this idea, see Bernd Herzogenrath, *An Art of Desire: Reading Paul Auster* (Amsterdam & Atlanta GA: Rodopi, 1999): ch. 5–6.

[6] Michel Foucault, *The Order of Things: An Archaeology of the Human Sciences*, tr. Alan Sheridan (*Les Mots et les choses: Une archéologie des sciences humaines*, 1966; tr. New York: Vintage, 1970): 46.

appear – are ultimately reduced to pure chance, to the bifurcating logic of the text itself, which somehow closely resembles the Feigenbaum set in chaos physics, iterating into chaos or a higher order.

To bring in some dry facts: in *The Brain of Katherine Mansfield* the reader is faced with twelve different pathways/'lifetexts' altogether. Eight pathways lead to doom, terror, destruction, death, four lifetexts somehow present a 'good ending', even though only one of those seems to provide what one would call a 'happy ending' ('Chapter' 48); one ending, for example, the last chapter of the book, presumably the 'real end', presents the reader/protagonist – although still alive – as having mutated into a kind of fascist. In addition, several derivations are presented, which in one way or another lead back to one 'main route'. Manhire's book thus seems to be based on the structure of computer adventure games in which the player (or: reader) assumes the role of an avatar and has to explore a mythical world. In the case of *The Brain of Katherine Mansfield*, we are faced with the paradox that the mythical country to be explored is the Southern Part of New Zealand, which in fact happens to be the home country of the explorer. Here is Manhire 'in his own words' on the 'birth' of this book while on a sabbatical in London in 1987:

> I must have arrived in London just before Christmas in 1986. [...] For some reason, I went to New Zealand House [...] and it was in the middle of some kind of promotional exercise where there were lots of brochures about New Zealand, which were all very sunny and colourful and presented a stupid fantasy-land in stupid tourist language. I think I was feeling rather homesick at the time but the only evidence of home I could find was this nonsense.[7]

The 'alienating experience' thus seems to be an integral part of the enterprise.

The Brain of Katherine Mansfield belongs to what Jay David Bolter terms "interactive fiction," a kind of "non-linear fiction, which invites the reader to conduct a dialogue with the text,"[8] a category that Bolter ultimately links to the realm of electronic publishing, of hypertext. As a 'printed text', however, despite its hypertextual structure, it is still inscribed into the realm of the book, and thus shares its peculiar status with 'border-line cases' such as Julio Cortázar's *Hopscotch*, with its 156 episodes which can be read in many combinations: the author proposes only two possibilities. However, a closer look at the defining structure of a hypertext might be fruitful.

When Gutenberg printed the first book in 1448, he unleashed a revolution in the realm of 'Western literature', replacing the hitherto oral culture with the written word, turning something variable, something fluctuating, into something stable, fixed, some-

---

[7] Iain Sharp, "Bill Manhire," in *In the Same Room: Conversations with New Zealand Writers*, ed. Elizabeth Alley & Mark Williams (Auckland: Auckland UP, 1992): 30. See http://www. nzepc. auckland.ac.nz/authors/manhire/sharp.ptml

[8] Jay David Bolter, *Writing Space: The Computer, Hypertext and the History of Writing* (Hillsdale NJ: Lawrence Erlbaum Associates, 1990): 121. For a reading of hypertext within the context of poststructuralist theory, see George P. Landow, *Hypertext: The Convergence of Contemporary Critical Theory and Technology* (Baltimore MD: Johns Hopkins UP, 1992). Landow particularly draws on Derridean deconstruction and its notion of 'de-centering'.

thing that could be reproduced identically. Half a millennium later, a new paradigm shift is about to replace or at least change the medium of literature once again. The computer, and the digitalization of literature it enables, is again opening up pathways leading to vistas we are barely glimpsing at the moment, reconfiguring the traditional concept of authorship and text as fixed, 'originating' entities, returning us once again to a more oral, tribal tradition, where the text is handed on and over, is modified and extended by simultaneous users and succeeding generations. When electronic hypertext is compared to the traditional notion of a 'text', the main features that are stressed are its non-linearity and its interactivity.

Yet, in a certain sense, fiction is always interactive; the reader is an active agent in the reading process, and every text is *always already* imbedded in a larger textual framework: text/language can be regarded as *metaphor as such*. However, the reader's active participation in the forming of the structure of a real hypertext is more radical, to say the least. Hypertext, or hyperfiction, can be essentially of two basic types, either *exploratory* or *constructive*. Exploratory hyperfiction "allows readers to navigate through fixed bodies of material, while constructive texts represent 'structures for what does not yet exist'."[9] The exploratory hyperfiction does not, after all, differ very much from the printed fiction, the difference being more quantitative than qualitative: in electronic text you may have many more possible story lines than in a printed book. So, in exploratory hyperfiction the control over the narratives is (almost) as strongly in the hands of the author as in printed fiction, only the swapping from story line to story line is made easier for the reader. Constructive hypertexts, on the other hand, offer more opportunities for controlling the *unfolding* of the story, as well as of the *realization* of the plot. Thus, hypertext fiction can take on a multitude of manifestations: the simple 'up-loading' of conventional texts into the Internet or on CD-ROM (which is the most elementary form, yet, I think, the most widespread to date) and multifaceted, polyvocal, fragmented hypertexts such as Shelley Jackson's *Patchwork Girl*. On its most basic, but also most important, level, a *hypertext* radically differs from the traditional rhetorical structures of the book with its linear, indivisible, beginning-to-end flow of print: a hypertext is a fluid, non-linear network *composed of* nodes (Manhire's 'chapters') and *connected by* links (the alternative options offered at the end of each chapter). Each node is independent of what came before and of what comes after, since each node is a document in itself.

Of course, just to drive the point home once again, Manhire's text is still inscribed into the realm of the book, it thus does not present a hypertext in all its radical consequences. For example, in a 'true' hypertext – at least theoretically – each node should be connected with all the other existing nodes. Any 'true hypertext' should allow its readers to opt for themselves where to begin, where to end, and the order in which its nodes are read, its links are followed. Thus, reader-function and author-function are indeed collapsed, creating each reader's individual version of the text, maybe even putting the text beyond its original bounds. In *The Brain of Katherine Mansfield*, there are at least three instances in which the text does not necessarily go

---

[9] Stuart Moulthrop, "Travelling in the Breakdown Lane: A Principle of Resistance for Hypertext," www.ubalt.edu/ygcla/sam/essays/breakdown.html

beyond its original bounds, but in which the plot folds in on itself. In 'Chapter' 49, 'you' are actually "being ingested by your own story, swallowed whole." 'Chapter' 29, another dead-end of the story, in a meta-fictional gesture presents the paradoxical loop that "For you, the story is over. But maybe your brain will live on in some future adventurer" – which, more likely than not, will be 'You' personally again, dear reader, giving it another try, and hopefully using the knowledge of your 'first life' to make it through the text to a more happy ending – exactly what happens if 'you' make it to 47. In another instance, the story ingests itself as well: another grim ending takes place in 9, where, if you are an unlucky textual traveller, somewhere between Milton and Balclutha, you are "about to be run down and killed by a passing sheep-truck as you hobble along the median strip." If you have been luckier and opted for another pathway, you have made it close to Milton and you are getting a lift on a large sheep-truck – presumably that same sheep-truck that has run over an unluckier version of yourself. In Manhire's book – as well as in other Internet/computer hypertexts, frankly – this claim for an absolute openness and open-endedness of the text is still realized only insufficiently. Manhire's book thus has to be situated at the margin, *in between* two cultures indeed: the culture of the book, and the culture of the hypertext.

Deleuze and Guattari's *A Thousand Plateaus*, a book published in 1987, the year that Manhire conceived his book, though not dealing with the phenomenon of electronic writing, uncannily probes and describes the philosophical implications of a hypertext in comparison with the traditional, linear text. Their idea of the *rhizome* shows an elective affinity with the idea of hypertext. In contrast to the hierarchical structure of the tree (the basic model for 'the book'), the "characteristics of the rhizome"[10] are the "principles of connection and heterogeneity: any point of a rhizome can be connected to anything other, and must be. This is very different from the tree or root, which plots a point, fixes an order."[11] Because a rhizome does not have an hierarchical structure, it has no real beginning, no real end. The reader can actually start whereever s/he pleases. This idea of a hypothetically unrestricted number of entrances into the rhizomatic text prevents the intrusion of 'the one interpretation', of 'the *meaning*' of the text: a rhizomatic text has to be *experienced*, not de-coded. That's why, in *The Brain of Katherine Mansfield*, the Pounamu Decoder is ultimately of no use – it makes no sense, because it wants to make sense.

One result of the hypothetically unrestricted number of entrances into the rhizomatic text is the equally unrestricted 'freedom' of the reader. Freedom here signifies an endless 'becoming' of the subject in its interplay with any text whatsoever (hypertext, lifetext, etc). The endlessly-becoming subject is the nomadic Anti-Oedipus. Thus, on yet another level, Manhire's *zig-zag course* in *Zoetropes* can be read with respect to the 'becoming-subject' as well: the '*Z*' on the page is just 'established' as a 'specular axis', the same specular axis as the one Jacques Lacan 'draws' in his so-called *Schema L* (Fig. 1), which illustrates the relation of the symbolic and imaginary registers, as well

[10] Gilles Deleuze & Félix Guattari, *A Thousand Plateaus: Capitalism and Schizophrenia,* tr. Brian Massumi (*Mille Plateaux*; Paris: Minuit, 1980; tr. Minneapolis: U of Minnesota P, 1987): 7.
[11] Deleuze & Guattari, *A Thousand Plateaus,* 7.

as the decentring of the subject, always becoming, never in one place, "stretched over the four corners of the schema."[12]

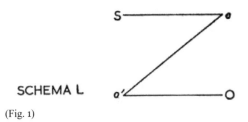

SCHEMA L

(Fig. 1)

In their discussion of rhizomatic structures, Deleuze and Guattari ask the following question, which is quite paradigmatic for the shift from linear to non-linear writing: "a book composed of chapters has culmination and termination points. What takes place in a book composed instead of plateaus that communicate with one another across microfissures, as in a brain?"[13] The connection with Manhire's book becomes clearer when we ask: where is the brain (of Katherine Mansfield or whoever) in *The Brain of Katherine Mansfield*? A strictly materialistic reading would identify the brain as one of the numerous brains bottled and labelled in 41:

> "The Brain of Captain Cook." "The Brain of Te Rauparaha." "The Brain of Samuel Marsden." There are row upon row of them [...] Sitting by itself on the top shelf is a jar whose label reads "The Brain of Katherine Mansfield." But this jar differs from its fellows. It seems to be full of black jelly beans.

A structural reading, however, would identify the brain as the text itself, more explicitly the hypertextual quality of the text. In 1945, Vannemar Bush, one of the pioneers of the conception of a hypertextual system, conceived of a new electronic indexing device called 'memex', "an enlarged intimate supplement to [an individual's] memory."[14] Bush discussed the fact that the human mind does not work in a linear way: "It operates by association [...] in accordance with some intricate web of trails carried by the cells of the brain." The brain, the mind, and the idea of hypertext thus collide in the notion of a structure composed of nodes and links. A comparison of a 'structural map' of Manhire's text (Fig. 2) with both a structural map of a hypertext (Fig. 3) and Freud's diagrammatic representation of the nerve apparatus, the "synapse model" (Fig. 4) of his 'Project for a Scientific Psychology', makes the connection clear. Thus it also comes as no surprise that the central 'brain-chapter' in Manhire's text takes place "in an artificial cavern [...] An elaborate system of conduits and corri-

---

[12] Jacques Lacan, "On a Question Preliminary to any Possible Treatment of Psychosis," in Lacan, *Écrits: A Selection*, tr. Alan Sheridan (*Écrits*; Paris: Seuil, 1966, tr. New York & London: W.W. Norton, 1977): 194. The *Schema L* is to be found on page 193.

[13] Deleuze & Guattari, *A Thousand Plateaus*, 22.

[14] Vannemar Bush, "As We May Think," *Atlantic Monthly* 176 (July 1945): 101–108. See www.theatlantic.com/unbound/flashbks/computer/bushf.htm. Subsequently quoted as (Bush).

dors connects it to the control centre of the hydro-electric power project at Mana-
pouri's West Arm" (41). The control centre of the text, the brain behind it all, *is* exactly
this elaborate system of conduits and corridors.

A Structural Map of *The Brain of Katherine Mansfield*

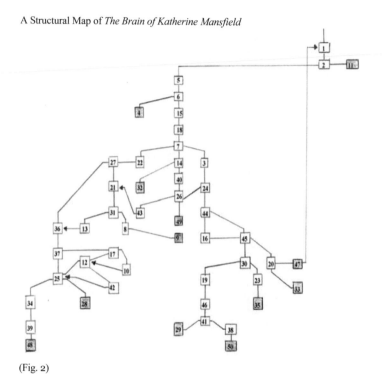

(Fig. 2)

Hypertext-Map created with "*Storyspace*" (Hypertext System)

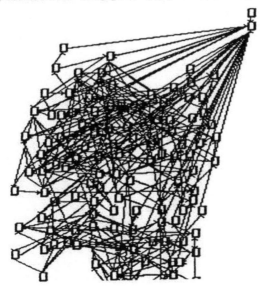

(Fig. 3)

**Freud's structural map of the 'nerve apparatus'
in
Project for a Scientific Psychology (1895)**

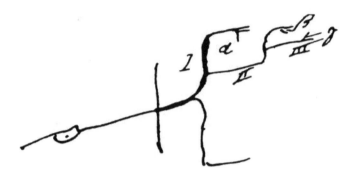

(Fig. 4)

The Brain of Katherine Mansfield is as much inscribed in the strategies of hypertext – or: text as dissemination – as it is in a personal poetics of Manhire the poet, which he revealed both in a book on his Creative Writing Courses[15] and in an essay with the revealing title "Breaking the Line."[16] To break the line – in its prosodic meaning in poetry, and also in its reference to the ability to split linearity – seems to be a seminal feature of Manhire's writing. In this essay, Manhire states that he is most attracted by the idea of the artist as *"bricoleur* – the figure who lurks around the edges of the human settlement, scavenging all the bits of tribal junk and discards, constructing something new from them." The *assemblage* or montage of the *bricoleur* once again is paralleled by the nodes-&-links structure of hypertext.

Manhire sees this strategy as closely linked to his life: he explicitly connects the "tonal drifts and lurches" of his writing with "the diversities, disjunctions, juxtapositions and incongruities which constitute [his] experience."[17] However, even this connection between poetry and experience is paralleled in *The Brain of Katherine Mansfield* as 'just another hyper-link', a link trying to connect 'real life' and 'text'. The first

---

[15] Bill Manhire et al., *Mutes & Earthquakes: Bill Manhire's Creative Writing Workshop at Victoria* (Wellington: Victoria UP, 1997).

[16] Bill Manhire, "Breaking the Line: A View of American and New Zealand Poetry," in *The American Connection*, ed. Malcolm McKinnon (Sydney: Allen & Unwin, 1988): 106.

[17] Manhire, "Breaking the Line," 106.

link in Manhire's book does in fact occur, not *within* the text itself, but on the back cover of the book:

> You are just an ordinary New Zealander. One day, with nothing better to do, you enter a bookshop; your eye is caught by a book in a large display case. Interesting title: *The Brain of Katherine Mansfield*. And it's attractively designed and illustrated, too.
> [...]
> This is the moment of choice. It is up to you. [...] And yes! you were born to turn the pages of adventure! Your grip tightens on *The Brain of Katherine Mansfield*. Your heart thunders with anticipation . . .

There is thus no escape from *The Brain* – even the presumably 'first link' *always already* belongs to the system, can in fact only be inferred from *within* the system – there is no outside of the (hyper)text: in the beginning was the link . . .

Thus, the *Zig-Zag-Zoetrope* has come full circle: the word is etymologically derived from the Greek words *zoe* = life, and *tropos* = turning ... so, *life* as a (hyper)text changes at every *turning*, at every link, until it comes to its paradoxical, incongruous (happy) ending: "So it was all true! It really happened! Close the book" (48). Since, still, seeing is believing, let me add a final note, which somehow summarizes *and* stages most of what I have said in this essay: the very title of Manhire's 1984 selection of poems, the very name of that curious machine, has become the brand name for an on-line institution – *Zoetropes* is a home on the web for New Zealand literature. As a part of this project, its creators – all of them ordinary New Zealanders stranded in North American academe – included *The Brain of Katherine Mansfield*, bringing to the fore the potential of that text by publishing it on-line as a hypertext-novel. Thus, this essay could have been abridged to the following:

http://www.het.brown.edu/people/easther/brain/index.html

simply giving you, the attentive reader, 'the first link' . . .

WORKS CITED

Auster, Paul. *Moon Palace* (London & Boston MA: Faber & Faber, 1990).

Bush, Vannemar. "As We May Think," *Atlantic Monthly* 176 (July 1945): 101–108. See also: www .theatlantic.com/unbound/flashbks/computer/bushf.htm.

Bolter, Jay David. *Writing Space: The Computer, Hypertext and the History of Writing* (Hillsdale NJ: Lawrence Erlbaum Associates, 1990).

Collier, Gordon. "Gebrauchsanweisungen sorgfältig lesen: Erzähltechnik in der zeitgenössischen Prosa Neuseelands, am Beispiel von Bill Manhires *The Brain of Katherine Mansfield*," in *Neuseeland im Pazifischen Raum*, ed. W. Kreisel, P.H. Marsden, G.V. Davis & J. Jansen (Aachen: Verlag der Augustinus Buchhandlung, 1992): 261–78.

Cortázar, Julio. *Hopscotch*, tr. Gregory Rabassa (*Rayuela*; Barcelona: Planeta-Agostini, 1963; tr. New York: Avon, 1966).

Deleuze, Gilles & Félix Guattari. *A Thousand Plateaus: Capitalism and Schizophrenia*, tr. Brian Massumi (*Mille Plateaux*; Paris: Minuit, 1980; tr. Minneapolis: U of Minnesota P, 1987).

Foucault, Michael. *The Order of Things: An Archaeology of the Human Sciences*, tr. Alan Sheridan (*Les Mots et les choses: Une archéologie des sciences humaines*; Paris: Gallimard, 1966; tr. New York: Vintage, 1970).

Herzogenrath, Bernd. *An Art of Desire: Reading Paul Auster* (Amsterdam & Atlanta GA: Rodopi, 1999).

Jackson, Shelley. *Patchwork Girl* (Hypertext for Windows; Watertown: Eastgate Systems, 1995).

Lacan, Jacques. "On a Question Preliminary to any Possible Treatment of Psychosis," in Lacan, *Écrits: A Selection*, tr. Alan Sheridan (*Écrits*; Paris: Seuil, 1966, tr. New York & London: W.W. Norton, 1977): 179–225.

Landow, George P. *Hypertext: The Convergence of Contemporary Critical Theory and Technology* (Baltimore MD: Johns Hopkins UP, 1992).

Manhire, Bill. *The Brain of Katherine Mansfield* (Auckland: Auckland UP, 1988).

——. "Breaking the Line: A View of American and New Zealand Poetry," in *The American Connection*, ed. Malcolm McKinnon (Sydney: Allen & Unwin, 1988): 94–108.

—— et al. *Mutes & Earthquakes: Bill Manhire's Creative Writing Workshop at Victoria* (Wellington: Victoria UP, 1997).

——. *Zoetropes: Poems 1972–82* (Sydney: Allen & Unwin, 1984).

Moulthrop, Stuart. "Travelling in the Breakdown Lane: A Principle of Resistance for Hypertext," www.ubalt.edu/ygcla/sam/essays/ breakdown. html.

Sharp, Iain. "Bill Manhire," in *In the Same Room: Conversations with New Zealand Writers*, ed. Elizabeth Alley & Mark Williams (Auckland: Auckland UP, 1992): 15–36. http://www.nzepc.auckland.ac.nz/authors/manhire/sharp.ptml

《●》

Multiculturalism in Helen Darville's
The Hand That Signed The Paper?

JAROSLAV KUŠNÍR

H ELEN DARVILLE'S NOVEL *The Hand That Signed The Paper* (1994) has a specific position in Australian imaginative writing. It is not only because it has provoked both an 'affair' and a heated discussion on plagiarism, on authorial morality and the nature and purpose of art, but also because, in the view of literary critics, the thematic aspects of her novel, especially after the revelation of her true identity, problematize her position both as an Australian and as an immigrant, migrant or ethnic writer. Were she the descendant of the immigrant parents she had claimed to be, her novel could be understood and classified as a novel about the migrant, Ukrainian, past (the Holocaust, war crimes) and about its consequences for both the present in general, and present migrant experience in particular. Taking into account Marko Pavlyshyn's definition and understanding of Ukrainian literature in Australia, this novel might formally and thematically be considered closest to the mood of Ukrainian writing in Australia that he calls "elegiac."[1] In Darville's novel the features of this kind of writing manifest themselves formally in the combination of fiction and memoirs and in the theme, which is related to Ukrainian history. It must be added, however, that in her novel Darville neither expresses "sorrow for the loss of things past" (74) nor does she present heroic episodes from Ukrainian history, as should the elegiac genre in Pavlyshyn's definition (75).

Darville's position as an Australian author is even more problematic. Her novel deals mostly with historical Ukrainian events, and the Australian setting serves only as a seemingly unimportant background to both the immigrants' story and history. Thus the question arises of whether this novel is a work of migrant, ethnic, immigrant, Australian or national literature, since the author's emphasis is neither on the immigrant experience in Australia nor on the treatment of traditional Australian themes. The other question, when speaking about Darville's novel, is: what, then, can be understood as

---

[1] Marko Pavlyshyn, "Aspects of Ukrainian Literature in Australia," in *Writing in Multicultural Australia*, ed. Jacques Delaruelle, Alexandra Karakostas–Šedá & Anna Ward (North Sydney: Australia Council, 1985): 74–75.

Australian (national) literature? According to Sneja Gunew, "literature is the way in which human subjects transmute their own physical implausibility into metaphysical terms. The mere fact of physical presence carries little substance until it has been re-created in storytelling."[2] Referring to Australia and its literature, Gunew further observes that

> A national literature is the way in which, collectively, we re-build this continent inside our own heads. It does not have a recognisable reality until it has been named, and, having done this we are then able to recreate it for others. (17)

Gunew's undermining of the notion of national literature underlines, at the same time, the importance of the notion of ethnic, immigrant literature as well as almost any classification as such. Her definition of national literature evokes both biblical allusions (the naming of the world with words) and the universality each national literature is marked by in the process of mythological re/creation of meaning. That is why I think no single classification of Darville's novel really helps us to recognize its aesthetic/ artistic qualities as well as its moral and spiritual message. Her novel is historical and political, Australian as well as Ukrainian, both immigrant and national at the same time. Perhaps I can paraphrase something Valdemar Vilder has said in a different context in order to state what my essay is *not* about. It is not concerned with "ethnic writing" – or "multicultural writing" in the sense of the definition that regards it as a special category of Australian English literature: i.e. "writings in English by authors whose first language is not English." And it is not concerned with "migrants" or "migrant literature."[3]

The main focus of my essay is on the way Darville uses and re-creates the historical past and contrasts different settings representing different cultural backgrounds to question human nature and to present moral issues and different cultural experiences in a challenging way. Dominant settings in Darville's novel such as the Ukraine, Australia and Poland represent a metaphoric connection of past and present, guilt and innocence, danger and safety. In Darville's depiction, Australia is presented mostly as a modern, technologically advanced and safe country, as the country of the present. This idea is emphasized by her use, for example, of imagery which evokes an almost harmonious link between education (Fiona, one of the narrators, is a university student), technology (cars, comfort) and nature:

> The sunlight slants more precipitously, behind me an angry driver honks his horn. He wants the pump. I sit in the sun-warmed car briefly before starting it and driving along the access road onto the highway. I turn on the radio [...].[4]

---

[2] Sneja Gunew, "Multicultural Writers: Where we are writing from and who we are writing for?" in *Writing in Multicultural Australia*, ed. Delaruelle, Karakostas–Šedá & Ward, 17. Further page references are in the main text.

[3] Valdemar Vilder, "The Invisible Quarter," in *Writing in Multicultural Australia*, ed. Delaruelle, Karakostas–Šedá & Ward, 87.

[4] Helen Darville, *The Hand That Signed The Paper* (St. Leonards, N.S.W.: Allen & Unwin, 1994): 5. Further page references are in the main text.

Such harmony is undermined from the very beginning of the novel by the allusions to political events in the world in both past and present. In Fiona's mind, the past evokes the feelings of remorse and guilt. These feelings are juxtaposed with the imagery of safety and the relative innocence of the present represented by the protagonists' contemporary position in Australia. Fiona Kovalenko, the daughter of a Ukrainian father involved in the Holocaust in the Ukraine and an Irish Protestant mother, begins her narrative as follows:

> As I drive down the Pacific Highway, the French are busy dropping bombs into the waters in which my nieces swim, the Americans and Iraqis are engaged in a bizarre competition to see who can destroy the world many times over most, and my uncle will soon be on trial for war crimes and crimes against humanity. (1)

Showing an outer world that evokes the feelings of indifference (the French, Iraqis, the Americans, the waters of the Pacific) and a shifting of responsibility to the others, Darville establishes the link between the ambiguous Other and the personal 'I'. She shows how the seemingly 'Other', 'the 'impersonal', must needs become personal in order to emphasize the internalization of responsibility for personal and political decisions, for things that do not seem to be of personal concern. It is the French who drop the bombs, but they drop them into the waters "in which her nieces swim," and it is someone of Ukrainian origin, namely Fiona's uncle, who will soon be tried for war crimes. Thus, from the very beginning, this novel has not only a political, but also especially a moral dimension.

Not only the contemporary but also past, historico-political events are looked upon as something other, different, dark, and unknown. As the omniscient narrator observes: "THE PAST, someone has said, is another country, foreign, strangely inviting, beautiful. Other people live there, not us, so we are safe from it" (7). The allusions to indifference and a lack of political and moral consciousness and responsibility are balanced by the protagonist's contemporary political activities: her mother is a member of the right-wing National Party of Australia; her father is a supporter of the DLP; her cousin Siobhan is a radical feminist; and the narrator supports the Labor Party. Referring to her own family, Fiona claims that "We were a typical enough family, although more political than most" (4).

In addition, both the political activities and the hard work of the Kovalenko family in the new country make Australia the symbolic territory of a new beginning, new hope, in a promised land, either as a compensation for past evil (Vitaly's and Evheny's crimes) or as a vision of a new prosperity in the multicultural society (Kateryna's Scottish husband Cliff MacDermott; Evheny's wife and Fiona's mother, a British emigrée). To underline his belonging to a new country, his new identity, Evheny Kovalenko proudly declares: "I'm all Australian now. I've worked so hard to be Australian [...]." (3); Kateryna lives quite a happy and secure life with other (Scottish) immigrants and their children; and Evheny Kovalenko's family story is reminiscent of the typical multicultural success story: "Maggie had five children, and they sent these five children to a good school and made sure that they matriculated at the top of their classes. The school academic honour board had five Kovalenkos on it" (35). Not only marital bonds but also the symbolic links between the guilt represented by Evheny and Kate-

ryna Kovalenko and the innocence of Evheny's wife and Kateryna's husband stand for
a new beginning that is to neutralize and help them to forget the sinful past.

Economic security and multicultural 'happy families' in a new country, however,
cannot, in Darville's presentation, either replace or compensate for the dark past and
history. The image of Australia turns from a Promised Land, a *multicultural paradise*
(with the ethnic diversity of the protagonists and their economic, social, and personal/
emotional success) into a symbolic site of contemplation of the issues of guilt and
moral values. It represents a symbolic link between the guilty past and the seemingly
innocent present. Juxtaposing German racism and fascism with Ukrainian, Polish and
Australian racism (towards Aborigines), World War II and the Vietnam war (Fiona's
brother's involvement in it), barbarism and culture, the present and the past, Darville
explores not only the horrors of war, but also the nature of evil. As I suggested earlier,
through the depiction of her protagonists Darville interiorizes the indifference of the
outer, distant, seemingly other experience of formerly foreign people in order to emphasize the moral aspects of her story.

The seemingly distant, ambiguous, unclear and tabooed past influences the current
relationships and raises doubts about the historical truth and its emotional impact on
the contemporary generation. The grandmother of Fiona's best friend died in Au-
schwitz and, as a child, Fiona could not understand that her father was fighting for the
Germans: that is, actually, against her maternal grandfather. Thus the past influences
the present and history becomes an ultimate and inescapable reality. Darville suggests
that not only history but also moral consciousness cannot be escaped. Moral failure
and the evil of the past should not be forgotten, whatever their cause or motivation
might have been. In presenting Kateryna's, Vitaly's and Evheny's stories, Darville
tries to find the reasons for their support of the Nazis. This does not mean that she
justifies their cruel deeds and behaviour. In a chaotic historical and political situation,
the oppression of the Ukrainians, for which they blame both Russian Bolsheviks and
Jews, evokes their hope that prosperity and the end of their suffering might possibly be
brought about by the Nazis – not, of course, that anything can excuse the Ukrainians'
cruelty to the Jews and Russians. But racism is always a negative force, no matter who
it is perpetrated by. Fiona Kovalenko, a narrator and a descendant of the people who
have committed crimes, cannot escape the moral consequences of the past deeds of her
family. She is presented as a moral conscience of the family. For her, crimes from the
past should not be forgotten. That is also why she adopts a critical stance towards her
own family. She comments on them: "Vitaly did unspeakable things [...] my father and
my uncle became part of the machinery of the Holocaust" (5). Her critique of her own
family and the evil deeds committed by Vitaly and Evheny in the past is even more
intensive when she contrasts her brother's response to his involvement in the Vietnam
war and the Kovalenko brothers' response to their crimes during the Holocaust. While
her brother suffers from nightmares and the war experience almost drives him mad, the
Kovalenkos' response to their past deeds is confusing, and they rather tend to justify
their deeds. Fiona comments:

> My brother Bret went to Vietnam, and came back nearly mad from what he did, with
> dreams about little gook children pocked with bullets and Vietnamese girls raped by both

Americans and Vietcong. My father is sane. So are Vitaly and aunt Kateryna. None of them mad. Not now. Not one. (5)

Unlike Bret, Fiona's father, when asked about his past, only "shrugs his shoulders" and says: "'You don't know what it was like. It was a crazy time. People did things, and you...you can't explain them now'" (3). Kateryna unconvincingly tries to explain her marriage with a SS officer by his physical attraction; and Vitaly tries to justify his deeds in a similar way to his brother Evheny: "In those days, people didn't say no, or start protesting. We were too scared. Both Germans and Russians, they were very ... strong" (41).

In Darville's depiction, the past can be neither justified nor forgotten. A new beginning separating the past from the present is impossible. That is also why neither Evheny, Vitaly, nor Kateryna can become the prototypes of the multicultural success story in the "lucky country." The idea of Australian (or any other) multiculturalism can never be justified unless young Fiona Kovalenko, and not the Kovalenkos of the older generation, as an objective and sensitive observer of the past and present as well as a representative of a moral consciousness, is seen as both a model and a hope. Moreover, Darville suggests that neither a sophisticated culture and religion nor education and technological progress can guarantee morality and humanity. In this novel, German Nazis are educated and 'civilized' people, they listen to Liszt, read literature and philosophy (Eberl, one of the SS officers, reads Shakespeare, Goethe and Heidegger) and worship God. But that, on the other hand, does not prevent them from exhibiting profoundly uncivilized behaviour – not to mention committing brutal, inhuman crimes and atrocities. Despite their ostensible Christianity, the Nazis' brutal barbarism in their relationship to Jews and Russians is morally the same as that of the Ukrainians or Russians. Darville does not present war as an impersonal and indifferent force which causes irrational behaviour, but as a liminal situation, a situation of crisis, in which individuals bear personal responsibility for their own deeds.

Thus war unmasks human hypocrisy in crucial situations – the Ukrainian priests drink vodka and breach the celibacy rules; the Polish priests are willing to accept toys and clothes taken from the dead people from the concentration camps and to excuse their sins by their religion; the businessmen can abuse the war situation for profit; the Germans read literature and listen to classical music and, at the same time, murder both adults and children; Vitaly is ready to play sensitively and emotionally with his son and, at the same time, brutally to kill other children. Australia and Europe (the Ukraine, Poland) represent both concrete and symbolic settings through which Darville questions both particular and more universal issues. They are the issues of human dignity, responsibility for oneself and for others, sincerity. These are mostly represented by the position and behaviour of the Kovalenko family in the past (during the war) and in the present, as well as by the Holocaust as the author depicts it. On the other hand, Darville's depiction of Australia as a contemporary country challenges the very notion of a multicultural society. In her understanding, neither multiculturalism nor any multicultural society can be successful unless governed by moral, rather than political, correctness. As Jacques Delaruelle argues, "the core of multicultural literary expression seems to be more concerned with the reflection of personal dilemmas or biographical experiences than with the creation of fictional worlds or the questioning of the cultural frame within which it takes place."[5]

Helen Darville's book *The Hand That Signed The Paper* both confirms and undermines the author's status as a multicultural author and shows the unreliability of any classification. Playing with her identity, mixing fact and fantasy, journalistic and poetic style, Darville both uses *biographical experience* and at the same time creates a *fictional world*, questioning all the while the cultural frameworks of both fictional and real worlds. The perspective she is writing from is not only Australian – national, nationalist, racist – but also migrant, multicultural and cosmopolitan. Her novel is concerned at once with historical fact and symbolic significance, and it emphasizes the role of morality in human life. As Andrew Riemer argues, "Within its secular framework *The Hand That Signed The Paper* does reveal a moral or ethical bias, one that could well have been passionately held by its author, whatever her name or national antecedents."[6] Thus Darville's novel can be seen as making a definite contribution to the enrichment of both multicultural, ethnic, migrant and national Australian writing.

WORKS CITED

Darville, Helen. *The Hand That Signed The Paper* (St. Leonards, N.S.W.: Allen & Unwin, 1994).

Delaruelle, Jacques, Alexandra Karakostas–Šedá & Anna Ward, ed. *Writing in Multicultural Australia* (North Sydney: Australia Council, 1985).

Delaruelle, Jacques. "Multiculturalism: 'A Walk in The Garden of the I Don't Know What'," in *Writing in Multicultural Australia*, ed. Delaruelle et al., 50–53.

Gunew, Sneja. "Multicultural Writers: Where we are writing from and who we are writing for?," in *Writing in Multicultural Australia*, ed. Delaruelle et al., 15–23.

Pavlyshyn, Marko. "Aspects of Ukrainian Literature in Australia," in *Writing in Multicultural Australia*, ed. Delaruelle et al., 70–77.

Riemer, Andrew. *The Demidenko Debate* (St. Leonards, N.S.W.: Allen & Unwin, 1996).

Vilder, Valdemar."The Invisible Quarter," in *Writing in Multicultural Australia*, ed. Delaruelle et al., 87–89.

《●》

---

[5] Jacques Delaruelle, "Multiculturalism: 'A Walk in The Garden of the I Don't Know What'," in *Writing in Multicultural Australia*, ed. Delaruelle, Karakostas–Šedá & Ward, 52.

[6] Andrew Riemer, *The Demidenko Debate* (St. Leonards, N.S.W.: Allen & Unwin, 1996): 51.

Mad 'Mad' Women
Anger, Madness, and Suffering
in Recent White Australian Fiction

CHANTAL KWAST–GREFF

A SIGNIFICANT NUMBER of white Australian women have been writing about 'mad' women in the last twenty years. This does not really come as a surprise as there is a definite tradition of the 'mad' woman in literature. What is interesting is that what can be read as 'madness' is clearly linked to the physical and mental manifestations of absolute misery and helplessness, and deep anger in the female characters – they suffer in their souls and act on their own bodies. What is interpreted, in social terms, as 'madness' actually appears to be the expression of devastating anger. I am not discussing here the relation between madness and anger in female characters. I am exploring what these 'mad' women do when they are angry – or, to put it in other words, how they enact their anger on their own bodies, and how their anger can eventually be deciphered and interpreted.

Angry women in Australian novels and short stories are in no way passive. They shout and break things, and act out their rage in cold anger or tempestuous fury. They become Other when they are under the influence of their anger.[1] They are 'other' than what is expected of them and therefore become "unacceptable."

One example is the mother, in a short story by Olga Masters entitled "On the Train." The mother and two little girls get on the train. There is one other passenger, a woman, who attempts to make conversation. The mother is extremely distant, does not answer, does not even look at her children. The passenger thinks that the mother is "worthy" and above the common ruck, because she is "handsome," and that the children are common, and "might look like their father," "putting them into a category unworthy of the handsome mother."[2] She does not realize that the mother is angry and mad. The mother's anger is of the silent type. Her murderous fury makes itself clear when she simply states that she will kill the two little girls.

---

[1] How far their anger is influenced by external factors will not be discussed here.

[2] Olga Masters, "On the Train," in Masters, *The Home Girls* (St Lucia: U of Queensland P, 1984): 21.

The Other into which the angry/mad woman is metamorphosed when the drama unfolds is, as described in *The Gripping Beast* by Joan Dugdale, "utterly unapproachable [...], translated beyond ordinary human congress by something profoundly other which has sprung up from the depths of herself."[3] The title of the novel itself is transparent in that respect. As a "gripping beast" herself, or as being possessed by a "gripping beast," the angry woman is potentially dangerous, both to herself and to those around her. Her anger is power. She can strike out in anger. She has the power to do real harm, to herself and to others: an angry woman is a threat. Like all power, anger is uncontrollable and potentially dangerous. An angry woman could kill. The question is, does she?

The mother in Masters' "On the Train" is one of the rare angry/mad woman who actually makes a decision to kill in cold anger. But the field of speculation is open as we are not told whether she kills her two little daughters or not. The short story ends, abruptly, on the words " I am going to kill them', the mother said" (23).

Unlike her, most angry women fear being overcome by their murderous rage – and they often fight against it. One example is Erica in *Dance for the Ducks* by Penelope Rowe. Erica is merely defined by the personal pronoun "she" at the beginning of the novel, as if she were emblematic of all young mothers of small children who "did not need the rebellion at her side."[4] She tries hard to keep her exasperation/anger/fury under control:

> It was an obstacle course of loose gravel, sand and, even on this hot day, the stubborn muddy puddles that refused to dry out. Exasperation with these obstacles had grown to anger and now a wild fury was welling up inside her. Enough that she had that to contend with. Why did the children have to add to it? She fought the fury knowing that if she allowed her control to waver she was capable of delivering a hail of blows upon the child, or worse still, blocking the mouth to shut out the shrieks.[5] (1)

Here, too, the reader is left in ignorance of whether the mother hits the children or stifles them. She actually appears to be the victim of her own anger, more so than her children.

In Janet Shaw's "Blood and Milk" there is less doubt about the child's fate. The entire short story is woven around the baby's screams and the mother's attempts to stifle these screams. She is angry at him because he screams and never stops. And she is utterly helpless. The baby is back from hospital, and "the bruises had faded." (There is, of course, a strong suspicion the baby had been mistreated). The mother is pushed to extremes by poverty, unhappiness and loneliness. The "man" – not otherwise defined than by this word – refuses to come and have a look at the baby, and to give the mother any more money. She is alone and desperate, and, arguably, crazy or driven crazy by circumstances. Her attempts at silencing the baby are quite inadequate and ineffective – she first puts him under the bed in the bedroom and shuts the door, so that she won't hear him any more. When this does not work, she puts him in the wardrobe and shuts it,

---

[3] Joan Dugdale, *The Gripping Beast* (St Lucia: U of Queensland P, 1993): 3.

[4] Penelope Rowe, *Dance for the Ducks* (Sydney: Methuen of Australia/Hicks Smith & Sons, 1976): 1.

[5] Rowe, *Dance for the Ducks*, 1.

then shuts the bedroom door, and the kitchen door again, switches on the radio loud, and the washing-machine too. But she can still hear him. So she locks him in the outside toilet. The reader does not really *see* the baby die, but what else can have happened once the mother had "knocked the toilet lid down," "put him on the lid and saw him arching as she slammed shut the door"?[6] But even here, the mother is a victim, maybe just as much as the baby. He is the target of her anger because he stridently voices his despair, and she cannot deal either with him or with that "voice," which is also *her* voice. So she disposes of him.

Children are, in some sense, clearly 'ideal' victims. They are (or are supposed to be) weak; their mother has power over them, physically and otherwise, and they can hardly defend themselves. But a small child can also be seen as another Self for the mother. If we consider this, we will see that if the woman actually crosses the line and harms the child, she will not only reject the role traditionally devoted to her – that of protecting and raising the children – but may also harm her own Self.[7] Therefore, angry women can be seen here as victims more than executioners. They hardly ever harm anybody stronger than themselves. They sometimes hit their husbands a little, as does Erica, in *Dance for the Ducks*, who "flailed out, kicking [her husband] hard in the back, pulling his hair, hating him" (93). The hitting is not meant to do any real hurt or harm and certainly not to kill, at first. It is more of a scream for attention and existence. Ambrose had refused to listen to Erica when she had cried out for help, and he had acted as if he was sleeping, deliberately.[8] Later, things are different:

> Without tempering the force she smashed her fist into his face, and again and again. [...] But Erica had lost all sanity. She didn't see Ambrose. She saw only a hated thing she was going to annihilate and an anger in herself that could only be quenched with total release. (143)

Because she is not heard, listened to, and heeded, Erica becomes *really* mad.

A murderous anger like hers is no frequent occurrence in the fiction considered here. And, anyway, Erica does *not* kill Ambrose. There are very few occurrences of murder, committed by "mad" women, in Australian fiction. Writings like Jennifer Maiden's *Play with Knives*[9] or Leone Sperling's "Thanatos" are atypical, in the sense that they feature actual murder. In both books, the "mad" woman kills with a knife. In "Thanatos", Ruth, the daughter, kills Eve, the mother (who is also her lover, and her boyfriend's lover), in a particularly atrocious way. Eve is pregnant – she "knows that labour

---

[6] Janet Shaw, "Blood and Milk," *In This House* (Port Melbourne: Heinemann, 1990): 70.

[7] That a child may be hurt deliberately in an act of vengeance, to get at the 'other' parent, will not be considered here, as there is no occurrence of this in my reference corpus.

[8] In this Erica behaves very much like Henny Pollitt, the mother in Christina Stead's *The Man Who Loved Children* (1940; Harmondsworth: Penguin, 1970). Here too, the woman is a victim, before she even becomes angry, and later, when she is truly angry. But I am not discussing here the various ways in which women are made victims, and how their systematic oppression leads to their becoming angry and/or "mad".

[9] Jennifer Maiden, *Play With Knives* (Sydney: Allen & Unwin, 1990). This novel features a psychopathic killer. Dealing with this work would be beyond the scope of the present study.

will begin soon and decides to have a bath." Ruth is angry, maddened, and jealous. She stabs her mother with a carving knife while she lies in her bath, with her eyes closed, breathing sharply because she is in the pains of childbirth:

> [Ruth] plunges the knife into Eve's throat. She withdraws the knife and stabs Eve again and again, into her face, into her breasts, into her heart. [...] Then she slits Eve's belly open and cuts away the sack that surrounds the baby. She lays down the knife and puts in her hands and pulls the baby out. She lifts it up and looks at it. She notes that it would have been a boy. She puts the baby back into the bathtub.[10]

This is a rare case of a (mad) daughter killing her mother. Most fictional narratives are less extreme and more 'credible', in that they describe characters and situations with which readers can easily identify – what I would call "ordinary deranged" women, in realistic life situations.

As a matter of fact, female characters are more often depicted – in novels and short stories written by white Australian women over the last twenty-five years – as harming themselves and suffering in their bodies and minds than as harming others (except for the children, as mentioned previously). Many are described as violently, "madly" acting out their anger on their own bodies, causing themselves physical pain, depriving them-selves of food or over-eating, and maiming their bodies. Some women in fiction develop self-destructive eating disorders which seem to be related more to anger than to madness. If, among other female characters, Kate Grenville's Lilian develops bulimia, and Margaret Coombs' Helen Ayling[11] develops anorexia – disorders which are con-sidered by some to be "the extreme end point of normal feminine development"[12] – it is because they are angry at what is being done to their female Self. Anorexia and bulimia are nowadays generally accepted as "mental" disorders (as in "anorexia mentosa"). In both anorexia and bulimia, the spirit dominates the body. The female body is clearly the battlefield where a drama is enacted by an angry spirit. The line between victim and executioner, between wilful acting and mere submissiveness, is as tenuous here as it is in madness.

Angry women not only act on their bodies by the intake or refusal of food, they also mutilate themselves. This is another circumstance in which angry women lash out at the wrong culprit, and "madly" victimize their own bodies. This is what Penelope Rowe writes about in *Tiger Country*. Matti, who is a teenager at the time, is angry at her father, whom she cannot please, no matter what she does. "She is angry and critical and full of hate. [...] So she must look for victims." Matti's first victim is a 'weaker'

---

[10] Leone Sperling, "Thanatos," in Sperling, *Mother's Day* (Glebe, N.S.W.: Wild & Woolley, 1984): 86–87.

[11] Kate Grenville, *Lilian's Story* (1985; Harmondsworth: King Penguin, 1987); Margaret Coombs, *The Best Man For This Sort of Thing* (Moorebank, Aus.: Black Swan, 1990).

[12] Ellyn Kaschak, *Engendered Lives: A New Psychology of Women's Experience* (New York: Basic Books, 1992): 190, quoted by Judy Crump, "Related Emotions," *Literature Review on Women's Anger and Other Emotions* [http://www.csc-scc.gc.ca/crd/fsw/fsw22e.htm]. online 24.08.99 : 6.

classmate, described as "this short-sighted, uncoordinated girl who cannot read," but later her victim 'of choice' will be herSelf. Matti hurts herself viciously:

> In the darkness she feels for the pins. Her fingers brush the blunt darning needle. She presses the pad of her finger on the sharp points of the scissors. No. Not that! Then she catches it on the pins. She withdraws one. [...] Now, dreamily, slowly, deliberately, she positions the pin-point against the soft inner arm flesh. She takes her bottom lip between her teeth and rakes the pin harshly across her skin.[13]

And later: "she reaches into her cupboard and draws out a small bottle of liniment that she keeps there. She dips her finger into the greasy mass and, standing very still, carefully touches the finger to both eyeballs" (161). In this instance, obviously, the line between anger and madness is narrower than ever. Matti is not mad, in the sense of "crazy". She is mad at her father, at his rejection of her, at his sadism and spitefulness. She finds relief, however briefly, in torturing her own body.

This is so for the central character in Fiona Place's *Cardboard*, too. *Cardboard* is the life-story of Lucy, a young anorexic woman who occasionally binges and habitually engages in self-mutilation. It is a strange first-person narrative laced with third-person poetry:

> lasers of anger pierced through her body the captain of anger careering in anger.[14] (2)

"But I was polite. I kept the anger pointed inside," the narrator declares (133). Therefore, by way of consequence,

> her wrist burned was burnt. (122)

Never does Place actually say that Lucy mutilates herself. The words are discreet, as is the (interesting) mention that Lucy's mother also does painful things to her body:

> her mother had arm tweezer picked at her own scabs (64)

and:

> My mother never held me [...]. It never wanted me, let me hold it, [...] She'd arm tweezer pick at the long bedded afternoons, pick at her flesh. at the scabs of her own childhood. (202–203)

The use of the pronoun "it," of course, deserves attention and comment here, as does the mother–daughter relation that is hinted at. Not only does the mother ("it") not love/ like/touch her daughter, thus (not surprisingly) maiming her for life, but both women also display the same (painful) symptoms of internalized suffering and, arguably, despair and anger.[15] Lucy is in and out of the psychiatric ward at hospital, where she is treated for anorexia. She explains what she does to herself – "I just go to any toilet and

---

[13] Penelope Rowe, *Tiger Country* (London: The Women's Press, 1992): 143.

[14] Fiona Place, *Cardboard: The Strength Thereof and Other Related Matters* (Sydney: Local Consumption, 1989): 2.

[15] This is clearly too vast a subject to be studied in the present context.

quiet hole into my arm with the stub of an old cigarette picked up from the cheap
waiting room ashtray" (203) – and what she tries to do:

> To kill the desire to burn my arm, to binge, or engage in any of the other charming
> activities that suggested themselves to me. I tried to resist their pleas for pain and impose
> a different focus. A more manageable focus.
> One not related to my body.
> I knew that burning my arm was cheating. Deflecting the Focus. (321)

But "Anger would chase me, until it could kill. Kill kill kill. Me," she says (88). Nevertheless, she does not in fact kill herself.

Suicide – which may be seen as the ultimate form of self-inflicted injury – is common among angry women in 'real' life, though not all suicide attempts are successful,
of course. But, interestingly, there are very few female characters in recent Australian
literature who actually commit suicide, with the notable exception of Margaret, the
mother in Sperling's "Narcissus"[16] – Margaret cannot relate to her children at all. Her
husband beats her up, shouting: "They're your children! Look at them! Look at them!"
(99). So she silently picks up her baby boy, briefly hugs her daughter, and walks out
onto the lawn, where she pours petrol over herself and the baby. The husband burns to
death, too, trying to save them, while the daughter watches from the living-room
window.

Most female characters in the novels and stories I am referring to do not commit
suicide, but many do physical harm to themselves. They often suffer in their souls
before suffering in their bodies.

Clearly, the waves of anger build up on emotions, not only on actual external facts.
Not all pain and suffering is physical, obviously. An example of this can be found in a
short story by Penelope Rowe entitled "Rosebud." Rose, the angry wife, decides to
withstand the sexual obsession her husband has with the growth she has on her lip. He
calls this growth "Rosebud" and is "rather fond of it," he says. She, on the other hand,
sees it as "a soggy Rice Bubble [...] with a dark coarse hair growing out of her."[17] Her
husband is a doctor and forbids her to touch it. She "gagged in revulsion" while "Rosebud became the focus of his erotic attentions" (63). (The parallel with "Rosebud" in
Citizen Kane is clearly not unintentional.) It is plain to see that Rose is emotionally –
not physically – in pain, because "it was Rosebud he murmured to, Rosebud he rubbed
with his cheek, Rosebud he flicked with his reptilian tongue prior to ejaculation. She
had become defined by her disfigurement" (63).

In her anger and her shame at being thus dispossessed of her Self, Rose has the wart
removed while her husband is away (at a conference). This makes her feel guilty (a
reaction which women seem prone to when their anger has petered out), all the more
so as her husband then "recoiled from her and turned away." The short story ends on
the words "'Emasculating bitch', he snarled and buried his head in his pillow" (67).

---

[16] In Sperling, *Mother's Day*.

[17] Rowe, "Rosebud," in Rowe, *Unacceptable Behaviour* (North Sydney: Allen & Unwin,
1992): 62.

Here, too, the woman acts on her own body to relieve her anger and emotional pain, and evidently to regain her own identity. But the originality lies in the fact that the acting on the body itself, namely the removal of "Rosebud," is not physically painful. The character who is (or thinks he is) mutilated is the husband, not the wife. This short story is interesting because it is the sole occurrence of a woman acting on her body in a non-painful way, in a way that is not associated with her own madness or mad behaviour. Whether it is socially more or less acceptable is not the point.

What clearly is socially acceptable now is *writing* about "madly" angry women who harm their own bodies. This is extremely meaningful in the sense that "angry" women, along with "mad" women, seem to be a literary product and the trademark of cultures (not only Western) where there is a conjuncture of two elements. On the one hand, the women (in real life) are oppressed in various ways in the male-dominated society in which they live. On the other, the writers, male or female,[18] decide – and are permitted – to give a voice to these women. The fact that Australian women born in the 1950s[19] should be 'ready' to write about angry mad women in the 1980s and 1990s, when one would have thought that the sort of oppression mentioned above was truly dead and gone, is intriguing.

I will conclude with a personal – and possibly controversial – comment. It seems to me that a society mainly produces writers who will deal with a specific issue when it can '*afford to*'. There are two aspects to this. One is that a society *cannot* 'afford' to deal with issues that are not central and immediate to its survival as a society, at a given time in its history. This is, I think, the reason why there is so little (if any) material related to angry and mad women in Aboriginal Australian fiction, for instance. The other aspect is that writers will write about a specific issue when that issue is starting to be recognized as unacceptable – hence interesting and controversial.[20] White Australia seems to be at this stage now, when dealing with mad and angry women and with the patriarchal oppression of women.

WORKS CITED

Coombs, Margaret. *The Best Man For This Sort of Thing* (Moorebank, W.A.: Black Swan, 1990).
Dugdale, Joan. *The Gripping Beast* (St Lucia: U of Queensland P, 1993).
Grenville, Kate. *Lilian's Story* (1985; St Leonards, N.S.W.: Allen & Unwin & Harmondsworth: King Penguin, 1987).
Kaschak, Ellyn. *Engendered Lives: A New Psychology of Women's Experience* (New York: Basic Books, 1992), quoted by Judy Crump, "Related Emotions," *Literature Review on Women's Anger and Other Emotions* [http://www.csc-scc.gc.ca/crd/fsw/fsw22e.htm]. online 24.08.99 : 6.
Maiden, Jennifer. *Play With Knives* (Sydney: Allen & Unwin, 1990).
Masters, Olga. *The Home Girls* (St Lucia: U of Queensland P, 1984).

---

[18] Apparently more often male than female in the Australian context.

[19] With the notable exception of Christina Stead, who was born in 1902 and wrote *The Man Who Loved Children* (which is set outside Australia) in 1940.

[20] At this stage, it is, in terms of societal evolution, not vitally topical any more but, rather, anachronous, an issue of the past.

Place, Fiona. *Cardboard. The Strength Thereof and Other Related Matters* (Sydney: Local Consumption Publications, 1989).

Rowe, Penelope. *Dance for the Ducks* (Sydney: Methuen of Australia/Hicks Smith & Sons, 1976).

——. *Tiger Country* (London: The Women's Press, 1992).

——. *Unacceptable Behaviour* (North Sydney: Allen & Unwin, 1992).

Shaw, Janet. *In This House* (Port Melbourne: William Heinemann, 1990).

Sperling, Leone. *Mother's Day* (Glebe, N.S.W.: Wild & Woolley, 1984).

Stead, Christina. *The Man Who Loved Children* (1940; Harmondsworth: Penguin, 1970).

⟨⟨•⟩⟩

Myopic Visions
Rodney Hall's *The Second Bridegroom*

SIGRUN MEINIG

*T*HE *SECOND BRIDEGROOM*, the novel opening Rodney Hall's *Yandilli Trilogy*, takes Georges Bataille's demand seriously: "It is time to abandon the world of the civilized and its light."[1] Bataille's use of "light" to figure forth reason or rationality evokes the rich metaphoric realm of visuality which, with its cultural and philosophical ramifications, represents a fundamental field of reference for Hall's novel. Indeed, *The Second Bridegroom* directs the reader's attention to interconnections between the physical and the cultural aspects of visuality through its use of tropes such as the narrator's short-sightedness or the Aborigines' capacity for invisibility. This essay traces the implications of the visual in this novel, the most explicitly concerned with epistemology and transculturation[2] in Hall's historical trilogy, by discussing the significance of myopia in the context of the perceptual and ideological frameworks which cultures offer. This will lead me to focus on the term 'vision' and to discuss two of its meanings. Indeed an analysis of the status which sight – or 'vision' – acquires in the novel as one of the physical senses begs the question of 'visions' as guiding patterns or ideals, a function which is particularly relevant for the ideology underlying the colonial project. The essay will then examine how the alternative vision sketched in *The Second Bridegroom*, with its abandonment of the world of the civilized, may form the basis for a critical depiction of colonialism and its history.

Early on in the first letter he writes to Mrs Atholl, the wife of his "Master," the narrator explains: "I am near-sighted. [...] I see a blurred world of large simple shapes."[3]

---

[1] Quoted in Martin Jay, *Downcast Eyes: The Denigration of Vision in Twentieth-Century French Thought* (Berkeley: U of California P, 1993): 211.

[2] Transculturation is defined by Mary Louise Pratt as a "phenomenon of the contact zone" and refers to the "reciprocal influences" of cultures when they meet, especially during colonialism. See Bill Ashcroft, Gareth Griffiths & Helen Tiffin, *Key Concepts in Post-Colonial Studies* (London: Routledge, 1998): 233.

[3] Rodney Hall, *The Yandilli Trilogy* (London: Faber & Faber, 1994): 3. Further page references are in the main text.

In the narrator's letters, penned in 1838, to this woman he does not know, intended to explain himself and his love for her, references to his short-sightedness recur frequently. A transported convict, the narrator had escaped into the bush on arrival in the Yandilli area, where the Atholls' newly-bought property lies, for fear of being punished for the killing of a fellow convict – though, as he later finds out, the victim was actually left alive. The narrator consequently spends time in the bush travelling with an Aboriginal tribe. On his return he is regarded as a wild man and is incarcerated in a shed stocked with provisions, where he finds pen and paper. Beginning his account with their first sight of the Yandilli area, the narrator describes how he detected a sunken ship not far from where their own ship was anchored. Reading this as a premonition of the failure of their settlement plans and of their future, the narrator wonders whether he alone is able to see this ship: "Surely those with long sight could not fail to notice?" (3). The deviance of short-sightedness from normal or "long" sight is emphasized even more strongly in a passage where the narrator explains the particularities of a myopic's perceptions:

> He can see such fine points as others may detect only with a magnifying glass. His hearing is acuter, his sense of smell more delicate. Agreed, the universe beyond the reach of his hand loses its detail and fine lines [...]. The near-sighted person moves in a bubble of complications through his simplified world, more aware of being private than others and less brash in what he claims to know. (130–31)

The inclusion of not only the sensory but also the psychological and behavioural effects of short-sightedness here indicates, as does the narrator's view of the sunken ship, that the physical impairment of sight has wider, non-physical repercussions for the narrator's outlook as well as for the novel as a whole.

The physical factor of myopia develops its full figurative potential when the narrator describes the offence occasioning his transportation. His short-sightedness and the accompanying love of detail qualify him for the trade of printing[4] and also facilitate his development from printer's apprentice to forger, since forgery demands great meticulousness to reproduce even faults. Because he forged a manuscript by William Caxton found in his native Isle of Man, he is convicted of the theft of a national – English – treasure, which makes the narrator realize that he is regarded as a foreigner, though one subject to English law. Only when he can prove his forgery by revealing that his initials, FJ (standing for Felim John Stanley), were planted in the manuscript is the death sentence changed to transportation to Australia. The narrator's short-sightedness thus finds a parallel in his colonial 'double vision', which is based in his Celtic 'foreignness', since Felim's wish to integrate elements of his Celtic culture, like its myths and stories, is interpreted from an English perspective as a form of stubborn insistence on

---

[4] Interestingly, both Marshall McLuhan and Walter Ong comment on the link between the invention of the printing press and the ascendancy of sight as the dominant sense in Western culture. Ong identifies the decisive change thus: "[Man] began to link visual perception to verbalization to a degree previously unknown." In consequence, "with the shift in the sensorium by print [...] the large-scale campaign for the 'clear and distinct' soon began, led by Ramus and focused by Descartes." See Jay, *Downcast Eyes*, 67.

irrelevant details. The context in which myopia is placed indicates that its metaphoric relevance pertains to the field of culture. Indeed, the way in which short-sightedness forces the narrator to question conventional knowledge in the above passage reminds one of the effect of colonial double vision, as defined in *The Empire Writes Back*: "The 'double vision' imposed by the historical distinction between metropolis and colony ensures that in all post-colonial cultures, monolithic perceptions are less likely."[5] While the short-sighted person experiences his or her myopia with reference to the dominant mode of long sight, the colonized can only experience their own culture by taking the colonizing culture into consideration. In both cases the 'long' view is regarded as superior and consequently cannot be ignored, in view notably of the power it possesses. Thus, short-sightedness and long-sightedness in *The Second Bridegroom* can be read as, respectively, metaphors for deviant and dominant perspectives, and for the power which these possess.

The narrator realizes that the dominant perspective and its power demand uniformity: "I am putting the sublime and simple largeness of the whole at risk by focussing on yet more complications – supposing we mortals are capable of taking in the whole in the first place" (72). The doubt expressed here about the possibility of a perspective encompassing the whole runs against long-held beliefs in Western philosophy. After all, Martin Jay identifies "Cartesian perspectivalism" as "the dominant scopic regime of the modern era."[6] Descartes's argument is based on the assumption that "it is the mind, not the eye, that really 'sees'."[7] Furthermore, in Jay's words, "Descartes assumed that the clear and distinct ideas available to anyone's mental gaze would be exactly the same [...]. Individual perspectives did not, therefore, matter."[8] Such an assumption of the universality of one perspective[9] is denied in *The Second Bridegroom* with its emphasis on the relativity of a variety of perspectives. The central instrument for this denial is the narrator's encounter with the radical alterity which Aboriginal culture and the Australian bush present for the British point of view. Felim's distance from the colonizer's perspective, which is due both to his short-sightedness and to his Celtic 'double vision', allows for his joining the Aboriginal tribe: "When the British cast me out to the remotest strand on earth, the natives of this place – part man, part

---

[5] Bill Ashcroft, Gareth Griffiths & Helen Tiffin, *The Empire Writes Back: Theory and Practice in Post-Colonial Literatures* (London: Routledge, 1989): 37.

[6] Jay, *Downcast Eyes*, 70.

[7] Descartes invokes religion to explain this uniformity, which he believes to rest on "the divinely ensured congruence between such ideas and the world of extended matter." Jay, *Downcast Eyes*, 76.

[8] Jay, *Downcast Eyes*, 189.

[9] A similar impetus is attributed to the discovery or invention of perspective in Renaissance painting, which helped to fix the moving bodily eyes into a uniform, directed gaze. See Thomas Kleinspehn, *Der flüchtige Blick: Sehen und Identität in der Kultur der Neuzeit* (Reinbek bei Hamburg: Rowohlt, 1989): 45. Similarly John Berger writes that "the convention of perspective [...] centres everything in the eye of the beholder. It is like the beam from a lighthouse – only instead of light travelling outwards, appearances travel in"; Berger, *Ways of Seeing* (Harmondsworth: Penguin, 1972): 16.

plant, part bird – recognized me" (53). Not surprisingly, a description of the narrator's relationship with the Aborigines can be organized around aspects of visuality, in particular visibility.

At first, the narrator is unable to identify his future companions as human beings: "The black tree stumps ahead of me were not trees at all. [...] They had eyes and the eyes watched me from under shadowy brows, but they did not have proper faces or torsos; theirs were face-shaped clumps of feathers, and torsos of leaves" (23). Felim's Western outlook at this point produces the fragmentation of the Aborigines' bodies as those of the Other, which is characteristic of the colonial encounter. Equally, his earlier inability to perceive the Other at all follows the familiar pattern described by Homi Bhabha: "These repeated negations of identity dramatize [...] the impossibility of claiming an origin for the Self (or Other) within the tradition of representation that conceives of identity as the satisfaction of a totalizing, plenitudinous object of vision."[10] The notion of subjectivity that is inextricably linked to the unifying European perspective and its perceptual frame determines who is visible and who is not. After a number of months of travelling with the Aborigines, the narrator has adapted to the bush and to Aboriginal life, and ranks for some time among those who cannot be seen by the British: "They were looking right at me but I was invisible to them" (39).[11] Similarly, he is able to adopt the Aborigines' perspective when assessing the progress of the settlement and its farming grounds: "I also saw, with the sight of Men, the horror of it, the plunder, the final emptiness" (32). Felim feels so distant from the English culture in which he grew up that he can make little sense of the English language, as in the encounter with the man he believes he has killed: "He uttered cries in a language I no longer knew" (101). Yet the novel leaves no doubt as to the impossibility of completely joining another culture. After all, Felim longs for the culture he knows and is tormented by "an unbearable ache to reclaim my right to belong in the hateful familiarity of meanings" (36). He recognizes the shaping power of a culture's language: "The idea of a house was my inheritance," one which "whispered an irresistible call to my loyalty" (83). Furthermore, the inescapability of the culture in which the individual grows up manifests itself in a 'politics of the gaze'[12] that governs the narrator's relationship with the tribe: "What I did, they observed. What they did, I observed. That is

[10] Homi K. Bhabha, *The Location of Culture* (London: Routledge, 1994): 46. As Bhabha explains earlier, "From within the metaphor of vision complicit with a Western metaphysic of Man emerges the displacement of the colonial relation" (42).

[11] Myopia participates in the narrator's invisibility in the shape of a snake. While his body has adapted to the bush environment and is thus less recognizable as a (white) man's to the white settlers, the coiling of a snake around his body during his encounter with the settlers helps to perfect his invisibility. The narrator remembers that snakes are known for their short-sightedness, which, together with the Biblical symbolism of the snake, seems to point to a community of those who are excluded from the dominant view and thus possess additional knowledge.

[12] The 'colonial gaze' presents a relevant foil for this visual exchange. After all, the latter conforms to the typical "commanding perspective assumed by the European in the text" only in a very limited way, since the Aborigines are presented not only as objects but also as subjects of the gaze. For a discussion of the typical forms of the colonial gaze and the behaviour connected to it, see Elleke Boehmer, *Colonial and Postcolonial Literature* (Oxford: Oxford UP, 1995): 71.

how we were" (61). During his travels with the tribe, the Aborigines avoid his eyes and he theirs.[13] This visual wariness on both sides can be explained by the mutual inability to come to any final understanding of the other's cultural background.

Present-day readers with some knowledge of traditional indigenous cultures in Australia can speculatively fill the gaps left by the narrator, who recognizes the special status he possesses with the Aborigines but does not interpret it correctly when he describes himself as the "King of Men" (39, 54). They assume that the Aborigines' treatment of Felim – and the terror in their eyes when they first see him – represents one of the colonial encounters where the indigenous population took the white skin of the newly arrived as indicating a returned spirit. While the narrator is eventually convinced that what he, too, first thought of as "spirit beings" (28) are actually human, he nevertheless interprets their behaviour according to the categories he knows. Thus, he regards the constant movement of their nomadic life as a "quest" (29) and finds that their behaviour speaks of "good manners" (60). This distanced perspective of an integrated outsider tempts the narrator to idealize "the Men" (30), as he refers to them, and to regard their community as his ideal of a "brotherhood of man" (52). In such instances, the reader realizes that, although the Aborigines in *The Second Bridegroom* are not only objects but also subjects of the gaze, as when they see the narrator in the bush while he can only feel their presence, they are nevertheless the objects of his narrative, and their perspective is circumscribed by it. Thus, even the narrative situation shows that the bias – and the familiarity – of the individual perspective, with its specific cultural roots and its personal history, can never be finally overcome. In this sense, the fences, which serve as the novel's central metaphor for cultural separation, remain in place. Furthermore, the variety of outlooks in the narrative – Celtic, Aboriginal, or that of those with power, like Mr Atholl or Gabriel Dean – produces a web of perspectives in which each world-view reveals its limited scope. Short-sightedness with its vista of 'large, simple shapes' consequently emerges as a condition of culture in the novel.

Instead of the uniformity of Cartesian perspectivalism, Hall's novel consequently seems to adopt the perspectivism of Nietzsche, who pointed out in *The Genealogy of Morals* that "all seeing is essentially perspective, and so is all knowing." Nietzsche showed great disdain for the doctrine of "immaculate perception"[14] and insisted instead on the validity and value of the individual point of view as the origin of perception and knowledge, denying the assumption of a Cartesian 'mental gaze'. Owing to his myopia and colonial double vision, Felim possesses a similar awareness of the plurality and relativity of possible perspectives. Even if he cannot fully comprehend the Aborigines on their own terms, he nevertheless refrains from succumbing to the dominant view held by the other settlers, who regard the indigenous people as "a childlike race" or as "simpletons" in a "primitive land." Felim feels no need to "rescue them from the doomed calm of their backward ways" (74).

By tracing the protagonist's sensitivity back to the linkage of colonial double vision and myopia, *The Second Bridegroom* insists that the individual point of view is shaped

---

[13] Such 'politics of the gaze' are presented in *The Second Bridegroom* as also informing the social hierarchy of the convicts and their masters.

[14] Quotations from Jay, *Downcast Eyes*, 188, 191.

not only by culture[15] but also by the body and its experience. As a consequence, the
novel avoids the traditional "duality of visuality,"[16] a term which refers to the two
dominant, mutually exclusive attitudes – denigration or elevation – that philosophy has
adopted towards sight.[17] In Hall's novel, the movement to elevate a metaphorical (i.e.
non-physical) faculty of sight in the idealist sense is avoided, since the narrator is not
blind – blindness being a traditional image for depicting the seer with a mental eye.[18]
Instead, Felim is myopic, which forces him to reflect on the impact of vision and, thus,
to combine mental and physical activities. In the confrontation with the Australian environment, myopia thus eventually enables Felim to give eyesight a new place among
the senses. Since the typical denigrating move of simply privileging the other senses is
equally avoided, his sight adapts, and the narrator sees with "forest eyes used to the
gentle forest light." The narrator continues: "Indeed, I wondered whether my eyes
might not have strengthened" (31). This new strength lies in the avoidance of the stasis
and the limitations of what has been called the "disincarnated gaze," which disregards
the waywardness of the body and its sensory messages because of a focus on either the
mental and universal or on the empirical and measurable.[19] In the Australian bush,
Felim manages, at least occasionally, to leave behind the epistemology he is used to
and to adopt the mobility and openness of the "incarnated glance" which is based on
physical experience:[20]

---

[15] George Berkeley influenced his successors by exposing the conventional nature of vision in
his elaboration on the analogies between language and seeing. See Ralf Konersmann, "Die Augen
des Philosophen: Zur historischen Semantik und Kritik des Sehens," in Kritik des Sehens, ed. Ralf
Konersmann (Leipzig: Reclam, 1997): 15.

[16] My translation from Konersmann, "Die Augen des Philosophen," 14.

[17] The opposition is roughly the equivalent of that between the idealist and the materialist position. The elevation of sight is most prominent in the philosophical position of empiricism, which
relies on visual verification, either by the eye on its own or with the help of technical appliances
like microscopes or telescopes. See Jay, Downcast Eyes, 70; Konersmann, "Die Augen des Philosophen," 28. The denigration of sight is evidenced in the insistence on a mental gaze, found, for
example, in Descartes, German idealism, or famously in Plato's myth of the cave; see Jay, Downcast Eyes, 187; Konersmann, "Die Augen des Philosophen," 18. The denigration of sight, however, can also result from an insistence on sensual perception or on the privileging of hearing, as
in German hermeneutics and phenomenology (Jay, Downcast Eyes, 265). For a historical novel
involved in 'rewriting history', the distinction between visual perception in history and in philosophy is of interest. While philosophy engages in abstraction and employs the 'mental eye', history privileges experience and bodily seeing in its focusing on past events and details, as exemplified by its reliance on the eye-witness; see Konersmann, "Die Augen des Philosophen," 23.

[18] See Konersmann, "Die Augen des Philosophen," 17. The most famous example of a blind
seer is Tiresias in Greek mythology.

[19] Jay, Downcast Eyes, 29.

[20] Jay, Downcast Eyes, 134; 195. This shift also permits the narrator to leave behind the restricting notions of identity connected to vision, in its limiting, Western sense, to explore himself
and his development in the letters he writes. He thus fulfils Homi Bhabha's ideal of "shifting the
frame of identity from the field of vision to the space of writing" (The Location of Culture, 48).
See Hall, Trilogy, 59; 138; and especially 125, where the narrator explains how he has achieved
the freedom to take captivity captive through writing.

When I could, I made a beginning: I promised not to try reading the messages I heard
and smelled and touched, tasted and saw. I would respect them as having no use. None of
them would be the same tomorrow. Nor were they the same yesterday. Each moment is
the present: it sounds and smells and tastes only of itself. (15–16)

This sort of sensory experience, in which all the senses are on a par with each other,
radically changes the nature of experience and foregrounds the dimension of time. By
trying to participate in the "experiential nature of landscape"[21] and its presentness,
Felim's view of the Australian continent becomes incompatible with the typical colonial enterprise of charting, mapping and eventually taking possession of a territory. Indeed, the colonial explorer, as a "discoverer of ignorance," disregards time in favour of
space and "takes up his pen [...] and prints BOTANY BAY – so many degrees so many
minutes south, by so many degrees so many minutes east" (134–35). Such spatializing
impulses underpin a colonial project with a fixed perceptual frame, which affects the
experience of time – as the narrator points out:

> My dreams of the past [...] had skies of torn paper [...]. The present was something hap-
> hazard. We lived for the future. Any piracy, any theft, any evil would be made right by
> the future: isn't this the truth of our colonial philosophy? [...] we became Australians, a
> race with one foot in the air, caught stepping forward. (12)

With the assistance of its prop universal history, the inexorable colonial vision of space
and power takes over the perception of time by privileging the future. The individual
sensory experience – in the sense of Bergsonian *durée*[22] – which finds its place in the
presentness of the Australian bush and Aboriginal life, is eclipsed by the familiar
linearity which teleologically connects the spaces of 'past' and 'present' into a perspective that opens out onto the vista of a glorious 'future'. *The Second Bridegroom*
unveils the exclusivity and power of the colonial project by identifying it as "the vision
[beyond which] nothing matters a damn" (56).[23]
    The narrator's experience of the Australian bush and of life with the Aboriginal tribe
renders this colonial vision unacceptable to him. Having come a long way since the
forgery occasioned by his myopia, he decides to "take part on the savage side of the
question" (135): he escapes from the shed for a life in the bush as a wild man. The
novel, however, puts into perspective the alternative vision of a colonial encounter
offered in Felim's narrative, with its sensitivity to plurality and to the limitations of
cultural perspectives, and with its exploration of a new experience of perception in

---

[21] Gillian Tyas, "Transformations: Landscape in Recent Australian Fiction" (doctoral dissertation, Deakin University, Victoria, Australia, 1995): 144.

[22] "The internal experience of individually endured time, the private reality of *durée*" (Jay,
Downcast Eyes, 197), is closely related to the individual bodily movement that Bergson posits as
central to human experience and perception. This movement integrates not only all the senses but
also different time spheres, by connecting the presentness of the body with recollection and anticipation; see Jay, *Downcast Eyes*, 193.

[23] Hall, *Trilogy*, 56; see also 32–33 and 72–73 for more expansive considerations on and explorations of colonial vision.

which sight is the equal of the other senses. The success heralded by the narrator's escape is limited. In the second novel of the trilogy, *The Grisly Wife*, the reader learns that the wild man in the bush is shot. In *The Second Bridegroom*, the letters of William Earnshaw and Mrs Atholl reveal that the protagonist's own letters will be employed as a model case to require from the governor greater thoroughness in dealing with convicts and Aborigines in order to prevent other such incidents. With the hindsight of history, the reader knows only too well that this fictional entreaty proved successful. It is appropriate that the alternative experience of the Australian continent sketched in *The Second Bridegroom* is not shown to eclipse other approaches, since the narrator is explicit about the impossibility of creating an entirely new community: "Such a frail ideal as a new life or a new society will remain forever beyond reach" (89). Instead, this alternative vision is offered as a complement to the familiar, colonial perspective. As the narrator recognizes, "nothing was more foreign than this happiness, nothing was less English" (50). Like its myopic narrator, *The Second Bridegroom* attempts to give both Australia and the Aborigines as much space as possible in their own terms, with the result that, like the narrator's short-sightedness, this alternative vision prompts one to rethink and to question the dominant, historically established view. In this way the novel shares its protagonist's expectancy: "How delicious to hope that you will find in my confusion a new country" (124).

WORKS CITED

Ashcroft, Bill, Gareth Griffiths & Helen Tiffin. *The Empire Writes Back: Theory and Practice in Post-Colonial Literatures* (London: Routledge, 1989).
———. *Key Concepts in Post-Colonial Studies* (London: Routledge, 1998).
Berger, John. *Ways of Seeing* (Harmondsworth: Penguin, 1972).
Bhabha, Homi K. *The Location of Culture* (London: Routledge, 1994).
Boehmer, Elleke. *Colonial and Postcolonial Literature* (Oxford: Oxford UP, 1995).
Hall, Rodney. *The Yandilli Trilogy* (London: Faber & Faber, 1995).
Jay, Martin. *Downcast Eyes: The Denigration of Vision in Twentieth-Century French Thought* (Berkeley: U of California P, 1993).
Kleinspehn, Thomas. *Der flüchtige Blick: Sehen und Identität in der Kultur der Neuzeit* (Reinbek bei Hamburg: Rowohlt, 1989).
Konersmann, Ralf. "Die Augen des Philosophen: Zur historischen Semantik und Kritik des Sehens," in *Kritik des Sehens*, ed. Ralf Konersmann (Leipzig: Reclam, 1997).
Tyas, Gillian. "Transformations: Landscape in Recent Australian Fiction" (unpublished doctoral dissertation, Deakin University, Victoria, Australia, 1995).

《•》

KATHERINE GALLAGHER

Jet Lag

I didn't go round the world. It went around me
crossing time zones in my sealed-off balloon,

following inflight-arrows across Europe,
Asia, Australia. Don't ask what day it is –

my body clock ticks in those concertinaed
intervals between borders and continents,

oceans urging them forward.
I can't find sleep. Instead I have birds

crisscrossing the lanes of my head.
They saw my airship slip by and me peering

through a window, setting my watch
by the stars. I'll catch up with this shaky life,

wrap it around me like a quick nap.
Leonardo put such problems on hold

with his *ornithopter*, needing wings
to flap before it could move.

So much for all that sky-gazing,
Wanting to get off the ground.

Now I'll just sleep on possibilities.
I'm still thiry thousand feet up,

Nudging clouds like a sunset, the day
slipping through my fingers.

My Mother's Garden
(*i.m.* C.)

Banksias, lemon gums, golden wattle: fire-prone
native trees she was afraid of planting close
to the house. And she preferred the softer greens
of the Europeans. Long summer evenings she'd walk
among the fragrances – lavender, jasmine, rose.
Leaning into the plants, talking to them,
pulling off dried leaves, dead-heading blooms.
Another snip? More water?
She'd scoop up canna lilies, dahlias, daisies
that cascaded over her freckled, weatherworn arms.
She saw herself forever in her *Park*.

Now I circle the rowan, golden ash,
flowering cherry; follow lines of lavender
and bougainvillea – exploding purple.
My feet don't tire of this walk
I've come back to for her sake and mine.
The current owners of the house left the gate open –
they may come back, tell me to go. I have my alibi,
talk to my mother through the soles of my feet.

Reckoning

Each foot taking us
faster-slow, shadows
before the range
we angled towards it.
Beyond the scattered
settlements, our paths
spanned out.

Soon, we hiked by
waterfalls;
our tracks zigzagged
the mountain's furred skin.
This was like work:
the weight and sweat
of the climb
pulling us back

in our push towards
that line
far away enough
to meet the sky.

Stepping over bramble
we urged each other forward,
leaving everything we knew
behind. The mountain
owned us. Our faces
wore together
like two sides of a coin.

⟨⟨•⟩⟩

PETER GOLDSWORTHY

Evil Eye

If we could talk to the animals
we might ask how they escape
from being bored, having few
hobbies, and two, perhaps three,
things to think. Some sleep
for days between kill, the rest
comfort binge in clover.
Only the young have time
for computer games, running
simulations on their brains
called Chase and Nip and Frisk.
Watching or being watched
is adult business; evil eyes
are everywhere, especially
on the dark side of the head,
though even in the deepest
jungle there are opportunities
for introspection which remain
untapped, as if the secret
of happiness is to lower
the mind's eye below the mirror-sill,
and keep it politely downcast.

Bed

With age you learn to love it
for itself and not the company
it keeps. The hint of coffin
in the clean cool sheets becomes
a plus, the tugging up of quilt
is suddenly a jokey nailing down
of lid. Even when the eyes slide
shut, this too, becomes a wish:
the little daily death of sleep
beaming us forward in time,
if not, this time, that far.

⟨⟨•⟩⟩

SYD HARREX

What do you see when you watch that hillside above the lake?
(for Nihal, Som, Sudesh, Chandani, Faridah)

I would love to emulate
the stealth and silence

with which the circular
shadows under eucalyptus

trees on the parched hillside
(no vagrancies of sheep in sight)

move their sleeping-bag positions
under the rotunda of a sunlit

hour: nudging death, as it were,
in a different direction.

Endlessly adjectival
Deferring the full stop

A Lover's Anguish in King William St.
(for T.G.F.)

A Doctor of Baltic Studies
wondering where his next
overseas grant was coming from,

stopped at the red light
& glancing at the sun-blocking
vehicle in the right-hand line

saw this sign on the truck's
left-indented panel:
HORIZONTAL BORING SPECIALISTS

which even in Adelaide's
Queen Victoria Square
is still capable of exciting

the genitalia of exhausted angels.

No Title

An empty chair
in the silent corridor

there are name-plates
on the polished doors

a door opens and lets
the wet darkness out

a cleaner later removes
all traces of footprints

there's no evidence
the chair was sat upon

the chair collapses
into thin air

the corridor haunted
by the hands of talk

swallows all its tongues;
walls, floors, rooms disappear.

Aroma Therapy

At Pondicherry Bengal jaded seas
counteract a sacred mass of land. Wide
boulevards make for leisurely walks
as if in and out of transparencies
tapestried with cancer tracks, while ashram
renunciation whites out all café
society. I munch croissants and say
to myself the French were no worse a sham
than Clive and Macaulay manufactured,
and what's more they left behind grace and taste
which tart British tea and chota pegs could
not entirely dissipate. Room Service
is still a bouquet of tissue language:
"bonjour," "merci," aromas void of rage.

Screen Images

The craft, the calligraphy, the magic
Of original manuscripts, written
by hand, uncomputerised, fingerprints
intact: how can they be re-dehydrated
or the saliva impetus of words
unpredictable, music of a phrase
no visceral autopsy of language
can explain away like a summer's day?
Unless we script the voice of our own tongue
in oneself's hand. Every poet's style
has its special hunger sign, so do we
know we are whom we claim to be? One bee
in the hive's complexity, your lost face
in the mirror smoke-screeing lake-deep grace.

《●》

ABORIGINAL LITERATURE

Narrative and Moral Intelligence
in Gordon Henry Jr's *The Light People*

DAVID CALLAHAN

Balance and narrative protocols

G
ORDON HENRY JR'S *THE LIGHT PEOPLE* is a complex work at first
sight. In this Henry can be seen to be continuing enthusiastically with directions signposted by one of his obvious mentors, Gerald Vizenor. After all, as
Vizenor says, "oral cultures have never been without a postmodern condition,"[1] and
Henry's use of multiple trickster figures (including himself) along with frequent recourse to the narrative surprises generated by his interlocking narratives, places what
might have looked like postmodern devices firmly in the domain of Native American
resources. Moreover, Henry radically relocates one of the validating sources of those
stories, in the realm of visions and dreams, and makes the links that need to be followed between them a matter of moral good practice rather than narrative (de)con-
struction.

My desire to write about Henry's book (and to choose it as the one Native American
novel my syllabus allows) arises out of the ways in which the novel deflected my
initial moves, disputed my reading strategies, and then opened up a narrative reality
that was ultimately much more challenging to me than what I had taken to be the
radical challenges of modernist or postmodern fiction. For practised readers of Native
American texts, then, this may serve as an indication of the ground that readers such as
myself (which is probably the situation of most readers) need to cover in our encounter
with the self-conscious, complex and moral universe of Henry's novel.

Henry's book refers, cuttingly and often, to the depredations white people and history have wrought upon the Anishinabe, but delineating threats or developing a paranoid representation of Indian-white relations is not its central thrust. As Louis Owens
says, "A fiction that shows Indian communities in dysfunctional disarray, fragmented
and turned inward in a frenzy of alcoholism and mutual self-destruction [...] is both

---

[1] Gerald Vizenor, "Preface" to *Narrative Chance: Postmodern Discourse on Native American Indian Literatures* (1989; Norman: U of Oklahoma P, 1993): x.

entertaining and comfortable to the non-Native reader."[2] Owens might be reductively
homogenizing the "non-Native reader" here (it's not entertaining or comfortable for
this non-Native reader, at any rate), but one takes his point: "such novels depict Indians
who are non-threatening to a white readership."[3] This seems to suggest that an appropriate fiction for Owens would be one that *was* threatening for a white readership, a
confrontation that I think could be framed more positively perhaps in terms of the
word I have used above: challenging. Owens's "threat" in this case would occur in the
realm of representation: that is, the depiction of Native Americans who are not fading
away, whose culture is surviving and adapting, and who are taking a measure of control over their own fates. *The Light People* does show us this, although not always or
only this. However, the challenges I have in mind relate to the very construction of the
narrative itself: not simply Native American political defiance, but defiance of the very
terms and strategies by which the problems might be dealt with in writing.

For one thing, the book does not proceed by means of linear cause and effect, but,
rather, by means of story units that are intertwined with each other, gaining their coherence through their relationship with other stories. This accords with the general movement of Native American explanatory manoeuvres. This means that the apparent fragmentariness does not correspond to a validation of the fragment and is not even
fragmentariness at all but, rather, a type of inclusiveness which attempts to pay heed to
the many-sidedness and multiply-connected nature of people's lives. Inclusiveness is
the key term here, so that in order for one person's story to be told, many people's
stories need to be told. Indeed, one person's story can never be simply their story, for
we are all so multiply connected that our story is always already other people's stories,
and only in the telling of all of them can our story become clearer.

Beginnings and invisibility

The Light People begins and ends with Oskinaway. At the beginning he is a boy, at the
end a man, but most of the novel between these sections does not focus on him. In
opposition to the individualistic *Bildungsroman*, the contexts that frame Oskinaway's
growing up are communal, as we might expect from Native American writing, and
have to do with the articulation of this communality through a relation to several
things. Instead of grafting the communal onto the narrative of an individual's development, however, instead of even showing the individual in society, what we get is that
communal context *as* most of the novel. And we further see that many of the rituals
and strategies used in this context for dealing with the awesomeness and mysteries of
life as well as its pain and absences, thus many of the events narrated in the novel,
involve the exposure of characters to, their interaction with, what would be thought of
in a Western sense as 'the invisible'. Thus it is that the first chapter of the book is
called "Invisible Trails," a typically doubled reference on Henry's part, in that it suggests both the incorporeality of the trails Oskinaway needs to follow and the difficulty

---

[2] Louis Owens, *Mixedblood Messages: Literature, Film, Family, Place* (Norman: U of Oklahoma P, 1998): 77.
[3] Owens, *Mixedblood Messages*, 76.

he might have in locating them. However, the fact that they are invisible doesn't mean that they don't exist.

In fact, the rest of the book is going to consist of these trails, and what we find is that they are stories. In order to follow the clues that will point towards more grounded ways of thinking of himself, many stories will have to be told, and listened to. These stories take place in two basic modes: stories told by others in the realistic mode, and narratives of dreams or visionary experiences. The stories told by others begin with the second chapter, with Oskinaway listening sleepily to "Arthur Boozhoo on the Nature of Magic," an apparently playful heading, and yet necessarily focused on the seriousness of the Invisible ("Boozhoo" is a greeting in Anishinabe, a friendly "hello," while it can also be seen as an echo of the Anishinabe trickster figure, Nanabooshoo). This chapter, in turn, will give way to Arthur listening to "Rose Meskwaa Geeshik's Monologue on Images." From the invisible to images, we see that to become visible the trails need to be brought into sight partly through the tales of others. The communal sources of the meanings Oskinaway searches for become apparent. The stories within stories are thus not digressions but integral to the enfolded nature of the truths Oskinaway seeks.

The Light People in general, then, can be said to articulate the contending forces of fragmentation/disintegration and those of connection and suturing. So far, this could be said of many books among the astounding upsurge of Native American literature. But Henry, in my view, is unique in his blend of story cycle, the centrality of visions and dreams, intellectual speculation, lyrical intensity, wicked humor, and guarded optimism. These characteristics are spread among several different stories, each of which relates in varying ways to the personal recuperation of meaning and foundation as well as to the larger Anishinabe recuperation. Henry, however, has brilliantly managed to avoid separating them into discrete entities – atomized tales whose structuring might have been mimetic of a fractured and painful separation within and between Indian nations, families and individuals. Instead, as one tale unfolds, it leads to another within it, which in turn leads to another interlocking tale. All of these tales are eventually worked through, returning later in the book, related to the tales within which they began. That is, the characters in one tale are part of, and are implicated in, the tales that spring up within their own tales. This is a world of connection, then, a world in which the fragmentation is real, and in which the disorientation of the reader becomes a part of this; at the same time, the unfolding completion of the stories reminds us that fragments can be brought together, that the stories can be told, and that our tales might only find their completion in other people's tales; that our own stories, in fact, are not only our own. Thus it is that in order to tell Oskinaway's tale, the stories of many people need to be told, for no individual's place in the world is isolate. Indeed, although the book begins and ends with Oskinaway, it may be an error to say it is "his" tale. The book's title refers to a plurality, to "people," and numerous people tell their stories in the course of the narrative.

The form of the book is thus not that of a linear narrative (a hypothetical form, given that no narrative is ever completely linear, no narrative never doubles back, never anticipates or in some way comments on itself). It makes frequent use of poems, chants, and non-prose pieces, which further break up the narrative as plot and refer the reader to more lyrical or sacramental modes of apprehending reality. And the constant deflection of the narrative drive of the stories might be considered mimetic of the connection between all things, an assertion that separation and opposition are illusions, generated by telling the stories wrongly, by installing a narrative morality of teleological intensity and triumphalistic (or, worse, fatalistic) conclusiveness.

The way to enable creativity to be possible links going forward with going backwards, in a twinned manoeuvre typical of Henry. The interpenetrating of realms that might be considered as separate commences when we see that Oskinaway remembers being a child and that his first memories – the first we encounter in the book – concern something he has imagined. This quite definitely does not dilute the import of these memories; rather, it establishes the primacy of an imaginative relation to the world – indeed, of the way in which this is always already the way we relate to the world. In addition, the child does not settle on one or other of these memories. The memories begin (the novel begins) with this positive, lyrical and complex sentence:

> As a child under blinking constellations, in the conversations of old people, he imagined a man descended from the sky, streaming arrays of star life into the deep reflective ocular fires he sometimes saw in the face of his mother, Mary Squandum, as she stroked his hair or shifted his collar.[4]

From the vast perspectives of the constellations to the domestic closeness of adjusting a collar, from the imagined irruption of the heavens to the remembered presence of the mother (whose surname means "door"), this opening sentence joins all in a single memory that energizes the book's strategies of inclusiveness. It also institutes the reconstruction of memories as a central activity. And it inflects these memories with the presence of the awesome and the inexplicable.

By placing the (apparently) inexplicable at the beginning of the novel, the quest becomes one of making sense of it, of integrating it in some meaningful fashion. When Oskinaway tries to reconstruct his father, the latter exists within this imaginative economy, spliced with visions of the magical, and divided among the various versions told to him by others which place him within this or that group or which simply don't remember him at all. Ultimately, "Oskinaway never saw the man outside the workings of his own head. He came to no final conclusion" (3). The rest of the book will resonate with these conclusions to its first paragraph. To what extent can representations exist outside our own head, and to what extent can we come to conclusions?

"Streaming arrays of star life": Visions and dreams

The loss of a father is a recurrent theme in American Indian writing, where it also assumes mythic contours, articulating the loss of guidance, stability and continuity, and Henry's text, in its lyrical beauty, even when dealing with such subjects, testifies to the possibility that they can be dealt with, that they need not be debilitating or crushing to the extent that they might be; that, in fact, writing is a way of healing in a continuum

---

[4] Gordon Henry, Jr., *The Light People: A Novel* (Norman: U of Oklahoma P, 1995): 3. Further page references are in the main text.

with the telling of others. As if the loss of the father were not bad enough, however, Oskinaway's mother leaves him, a double loss that leaves him prey to the need to imagine her, to construct a place for her in the world.

Uncertainties can, in certain texts, become debilitating, defying our yearning for order; however, in Henry's text they become absences to be filled in by the creative intelligence. Rather than surrendering to such things, rather than Modernist despair at being unable to shore fragments against ruins or to piece them together meaningfully, Oskinaway inhabits them creatively and actively, even in the extremities of the loss of both parents. Rather than making his world fall apart, as we see, for example, in the world of the nameless protagonist of James Welch's *Winter in the Blood*,[5] the circumstances exist, in some distant way, as an analogue to the challenges faced by the adolescent boy sent into the wilds on his own to discover things out about himself and his relation to the world and to the community. Not simply to what is called the 'natural' world (a separation from the supposedly 'cultural' world that makes little sense for an inclusive view of our being in the world) in all of its composite richness, but to a world in which all of its realms, which many Westerners would separate into real and imaginary, exist in a dynamic continuum. Indicative of the centrality of *interpretation* in American Indian life, as in this book, is the significance of visions and dreams.

At moments of intensity in Henry's novel, characters are likely to be faced with visions or dreams. Oskinaway, for example, goes out walking to deal with the loss of his mother and Henry's lyrical intensity is mirrored in the mythic event that happens to him when he goes to pick up a stone from the river, "the only thing that did not move in the river's flow" (5), and finds that he cannot remove his hand, that the river has him trapped. After studying this phenomenon all day, rather than fighting against it, looking into the reflections in the water, a boy finally appears on the opposite bank, at which time the reflection disappears and Oskinaway is able to pull his hand out of the water. By studying his reflection, Oskinaway has called up a double in some way, one who advises him, and it seems that this enables a period of stability in his life, as he then remains with his grandparents and learns "their varied ways and beliefs" (6). But despite all of this varied input, "the past never reached him" (7), and he has to reach beyond his immediate family for help in bringing it together.

Arthur Boozhoo then begins to tell his tale, and we move away from Oskinaway. Arthur's father also disappeared – in this case, electrocuted at work: in Henry's corrosive irony, a mini-parable, one might say, for the 'benefits' of technological progress. His mother also abandons the children for another man, so there are clear parallels with Oskinaway's own life. So far we appear to be seeing a succession of broken bonds, against which older people fight a difficult battle. Arthur drifts toward a fascination with magic, in the Western sense of illusion and prestidigitation. Only when he becomes ill does he learn of a different sort of magic, the magic of the reservation, and thence of people who are "'relatives of light people'" (15), the first time they are mentioned.

---

[5] James Welch, *Winter in the Blood* (New York: Harper & Row, 1974).

The light people are people who possess wisdom and the capacity to heal and teach. Given the fact that this is the novel's title, this appears to posit the book as a text that attempts to reassert the presence and the possibility of the gifts of the light people, the possibility of learning and teaching. And Arthur's own story confirms this. He is cured by Jake Seed, and embarks on a programme of learning from Jake that is as long as the university course he had dropped out of in the city. Within this apprenticeship, he has to endure a night buried up to his neck out on a hill. While there he has a vision, one half of which involves communing with a magical ring of animals that come and sit round him and with whom he sings, while the other half involves the appearance of a little man of mythical presence who threatens him and defiles him before singing "a song of sorrow" (18).

The resonances and relevance of the intensity and challenging enigma of the vision need to be faced up to, not simply by Arthur but also by the reader. What Arthur is experiencing is a vision, and this does not relate transparently to the action at all, so that we need to be alert to the conventions of the vision and its representation as well. More, we need to be able to take it seriously.

Familiar to many Western readers through J.G.Neihardt's transmission of *Black Elk Speaks*,[6] American Indian visions fulfil patterns that necessarily challenge not simply the conventions of mimesis but the very disposition of reality as previously perceived by the quester. They challenge the experiencer to recalibrate the way in which reality has hitherto been perceived and categorized. Not so much explanations as they stand, they test the ability of the vision-experiencer to harmonize apparently disparate and non-contiguous planes of existence in such a way that they become not disparate, that their connections are apprehended. Another way of saying this might be that they test one's ability to tell another story. And in so many instances this is what we see in American Indian writing, the search for different ways to tell the story; this is what makes it so absorbing. Although we don't get an exposition of what this vision might signify for Arthur, we see that he has passed a barrier and, significantly, the vision of light in a tree emanated by a woodpecker is the last thing to carry Arthur through his experience and somehow to meld his experience of the disturbing things he has undergone. We don't get an explanation, for various reasons. In the first place, it is in the nature of vision-experience that its meanings for us might not be revealed until some while later. And secondly, as Leonard Peltier points out,

> You never celebrate, or even speak of, the most important things that happen to you, the deepest and most spiritual things [...] To put those into words is to freeze them in space and time, and they should never be frozen in that way because they're continually unfolding, changing with and adapting to each passing moment.[7]

---

[6] Black Elk, *Black Elk Speaks: Being the Life Story of a Holy Man of the Oglala Sioux*, as told through John G.Neihardt (1932; Lincoln: U of Nebraska P, 1995).

[7] Leonard Peltier, *Prison Writings: My Life is my Sun Dance* (New York: St Martin's, 1999): 184.

This does not mean that you cannot recount your visions, as Peltier does this himself, but that their meanings for the individual need to be seen as something personal and fluid. Although the sacramental or secret aspects are not the same, does this not also describe the contract between the reader and the text – something constantly changing, with which we carry on an active, personal and difficult-to-specify relationship?

Dreams have entered Western fiction since the Romantic period, although they have an uncertain status as explanatory or causal devices. In Native American life, however, dreams are not radically severed from waking realities and are considered as something that must be attended to if one is to comprehend the multiple connections and balance of all things. Ignoring these intense mental experiences would seem foolhardy if one desires to relate as fully as possible to the continuum of inner and outer. Treating dreams as adventitious or dispensable, even treating them as something dangerous and mysterious, when sleeping comprises so much of our lives, appears in Native American eyes as one more way in which European culture considers reality in highly reductive fashion. Dreams are clearly a part of who we are and must not be spurned as we construct our view of ourselves and where we fit in. Taking this seriously is one of the hardest things the Western reader has to cope with in his or her encounter with many Native American narratives.

Creating and constructing

And then a new story begins, "Rose Meskwaa Geeshik's Monologue on Images." For the non-Indian reader of this book, this chapter is a pointed reminder of the complexity of how we represent peoples that we identify as different – specifically, American Indian peoples. Rose ventilates her suspicion of the ways in which whites claim to know Indian peoples, "and for a long time I swallowed it all and grew sick with anger, knowing the images inside can kill you and put faces on you that you can't get off" (25). Her devotion to Jake includes her gratefulness for his having taught her "greater things about images, about the imagination, and growing toward healing" (25). Creativity and constructiveness are at the heart of this book's project, in which its own structure challenges us and our ability to imagine, to bring disjunctive parts together and to shape.

For Rose, this creative act is carried out by means of creating counter images, of painting. She loses her creative impulse, significantly, on experiencing another of the losses the book has shown thus far – the loss of her husband to the draft and Vietnam. It seems as if the USA enunciates itself through an ideology of destruction and aggression that ends up consuming itself as much as its supposed enemies. In Rose's case, the loss of Leon signifies the loss of her ability to paint, a suggestion that the creative activity the book returns to as an opposing act to the forces of destruction is intimately connected with the possibilities of connection and not simply as the expression of self in the Western Romantic tradition.

Only when Rose has her self metaphorically decomposed is she able to begin again. This occurs when the large window she has been accustomed to sitting in front of is broken by a stone, throwing shards all over her and her desk. As Rose looks around,

[she] realized [her] own image in the glass was gone. The person I had been seeing there through the seasons, without realizing it, had torn out into the spring day with the memory of someone barely recognizing an enduring exterior image in the interior inertia. Then I looked back to the paper and saw some of the broken pieces scattered out into the incomplete face of the old woman I was sketching. (29)

Moreover, the stone is no ordinary stone, it has colours and a man and a bird painted on it, but Rose doesn't know who threw the stone, nor what these things mean.

Despite what might appear to be an act of aggression and destruction, Rose has a dream in which the stone is linked to creation, and is said to be "a gift" (30). As the dream points out, "with every gift comes / a shortcoming / You must care / for a stranger / at your door" (30), and, sure enough, when she goes to the door a little man is standing there, recalling the little man who had assaulted and defiled Arthur when he was buried up to the neck in the woods. While he sits, having been fed, in Rose's kitchen, her mind is flooded with images. At white heat, she sketches a series of extraordinary images, all having to do with dismantling the claims to authority of white male power; but suddenly the little man goes berserk, smashing everything, including the stone, and only running off when she stabs him with the sharpened end of her easel. He is finally to be seen on a death platform.

As enigmatic and intense as Arthur's vision, Rose's dream seems to be centred on creation and destruction. Nonetheless, like Oskinaway and Boozhoo, Rose has to go through layers of story before being able to use her vision usefully. Without any idea of what she has made of all this, we read that, four days later, a boy calls by to say he is sorry he broke her window, that the stone has been in the family from time immemorial, and that some believe the "little people" (33) gave it to his family. In any event, the end of Rose's monologue is signalled when Oshawa starts to explain in his story, the fourth short section of the book.

Oshawa's Story in turn leads into "Oshawa's Uncle's Story," which continues with the importance of stories, and speaks of the stone's doubled function, both as a tool by which to remember and as a weapon. The importance of memory is not simply in holding onto the past but in further creation, for "remembrance opens you up to forms of creation" (41). Creation is not so much the wresting of an individual presence out of the materials of art as the symbiotic fact that "your safety will reside in your willingness to understand the story of the stone and use the story in the stone to understand and create your own story as you remember the stories of our family, our people" (41). Indeed, the Western postmodern insistence upon the inescapably intertextual nature of whatever we might produce has exploded the Romantic myth of creativity and returned it, albeit in modern garb, to an earlier understanding of creation as arising out of interaction with tradition. Nonetheless, this postmodern intertextuality is still shot through with discourses of contention, opposition, parody and rejection, so that it is only a distant avatar of the double-facing nature of the stone and of story as articulated by Oshawa's uncle.

At this point we could say that the story that takes up much of the heart of the book 'begins': the story of Four Bears's leg. Four Bears had to have half a leg amputated after lying, dead drunk, in a frozen ditch. He then wants the leg buried properly and asks Oshawa's uncle to do it. Unfortunately, the ground is so frozen that he is unable to dig a hole, so he decides to wedge the leg in the branches of a tree and come back to bury it later. It is so cold that he breaks into a library, and uses the books to both make a fire and to read to keep him going until the "white storm" (48) blows over. After reading, he goes to sleep and doesn't wake up until page 140. In the meantime we see what he reads, the first book, by a Bombarto Rose, being called "Mixed-Blood Musings," followed by the "Autobiographical Profile of Bombarto Rose: An Essay on Personal Origins."

In inventing these varied voices, Henry typically both uses seriously and enjoys humorously the conventions he is relating to. When we get "Franklin Squandum's Death Dream: A Mini-Drama for Native Dancers," for example, instead of the sonorous and ponderous register in which aspects of Native American spirituality have been considered in Western culture, even when being respectfully considered, Henry makes liberal use of humour, although the humour is biting. In this death dream, we have a dancer and "a man in a suit and tie on a white horse (98)," conflating the Lone Ranger with, as we see, a robber of Indian lands.

At Squandum's funeral, in the next section, a section of some beauty in which a syncretistic relation to Squandum's death is uttered through the Catholic rite and Anishinabe keening, a deer breaks into the middle of the ceremony and looks into Squandum's casket. Even the deer has a story, or has a story to be told about it, once a family pet. It bursts into the ceremony again as the flag is being folded (Squandum was a Vietnam vet) and runs away with the flag draped over it, swimming off into the distance with it.

This curious event is one of numerous events in the novel that subvert the intended direction of events, rendering society's conventions less stable and more liable to the disturbances of the uncontrollable, the wild. More than that, however, the presence of animals in Native American cultures is generally of significance, a sign of the irruption of the greater purposes of existence into the limited visions and explanations of merely human interaction. Great importance is given to respecting and interpreting the unexpected presence or behaviour of animals, specifically where there is some chance that this might be less under human control (studying the urban pigeon will offer little in this context). In Bobby Lake–Thom's explanation, "to the traditional Indian, nothing is a coincidence,"[8] so that it is reasonable to assume that "nature can and does communicate to us humans."[9] As this takes place in a language that is necessarily symbolic, it needs to be learnt, both via tradition and from direct experience. Moreover, like any language it exists in interplay with its readers, so that contexts can have a large influence on how it is read. For a deer to appear like this is something readers (both the fictional characters and the readers of the novel) needs to come to terms with according with their own lives, although the fabular humour of the deer running off with the U.S. flag draped over it is not something we are likely to have the good fortune to witness. For Bobby Lake–Thom, "Deer are good powers and can be messengers in different

---

[8] Bobby Lake–Thom, *Spirits of the Earth: A Guide to Native American Nature Symbols, Stories, and Ceremonies* (New York: Plume, 1997): 50.

[9] Lake–Thom, *Spirits of the Earth*, 1.

ways."[10] The trouble is, that the message is as variable as the circumstances of the reader's situation (although much of the deer's symbolic power relates to its connection with myths of potency and the dance of the sexes), and Henry is not one to push us along a certain path. As befits Native American life, in which interpretation is so constant a responsibility, so also *The Light People* is a demanding call to our responsibilities as readers. Not so much a Modernist puzzle to be decoded, it is an experience in which our disorientation becomes part of the self-definition of the interpreting life. And, as I have suggested, it is a self-definition that repeatedly pushes us towards forms of connection, linkage, and interpenetration.

Getting stuck on "We the People"

At the end, we jump forward far into the future; Oskinaway is a man now, and we have the longest section of the book, ironically entitled "We the People." One night, Oskinaway has a vision of a dancing woman, with whom he dances. This woman's arrival is presaged by a dot of blue light entering his trailer, so that she is one of the light people, a person who comes from light and who gives or shows light. Light people show the way to be followed, but they don't show it for passive consumption. In the Indian life, the individual has to interpret, in a thoroughgoing morality of hermeneutical vigor. People have to work out meanings and directions from cryptic texts that they are sensitized to perceiving and receiving through cultural validation of such a channel of knowledge.

The very next day, his life begins to change as he finds a hurt bird and decides to heal it, an activity congruent with the life of his family and his community as he recalls it, in which his grandparents take in a man even older than they are, a man whose identity Oskinaway the child never could work out, but he is remembered as one of the light people, too. That is, he constitutes a link to his people's wisdom, but again he needs to be read by Oskinaway; knowledge is not ladled out on a plate. Light is shed, but we have to decipher by the light of, and in the light of, what we can make out. It may be that the knowledge we gain never comes tidily parcelled all at once but becomes something we return to and construct in differing ways as our lives progress or as we make our way through the text. In this case, at a large level, he has learnt that "helping has meaning, as names have meaning" (188). Lo and behold: when the old man dies Oskinaway learns that his name was Oskinaway as well and that he had been named after him. Connections can take place even beyond the knowledge of words or names. With a desire to connect with the whole bird and not simply to repair an aileron, he goes in for an advertisement claiming to teach your bird to speak.

This programme begins with the preamble to the US Constitution, set out in the Dale Carnegie style of would-be miraculous achievement, and yet its quixotic aims are not despicable: "'Can you imagine speaking to one with the vision of an owl? Can you foresee an interchange of ideas between the architect and the plover?'" (199). Shadowing Native American perceptions of the utility and spiritual necessity according to principles of balance and harmony of being able to communicate with the natural world of

---

[10] Lake–Thom, *Spirits of the Earth*, 87.

which one is a part (and not against which one is opposed), of feeling through it, the tapes suggest a world of greatly expanded inter-species communication, achievable in this case, however, through technology (tapes) and routine.

At first Oskinaway is fired up. The words of the Constitution resonate with an added sense of inclusiveness when they are extended to birds, in that "more perfect union" (200). The ironies, however, must become grating in the context of a listener on a reservation, for, of all the documents of humbug generated in the USA, the Constitution is clearly the most well-known. The hypnotic repetition of this short text and accompanying music sends Oskinaway to sleep, where he encounters another of the many powerful dreams and visions in the novel. This one, notably, commences with extremity, the grotesque, and violence, and if people thought Native American visions only have to do with, or should only have to do with, traditional iconography, then this dream indicates that the significance of the dream persists just as actively into the modern age. The presence of a mission launcher, baseball, cars, cities and photographs reveal that the tokens of modern life are as suitable as any other for the grammar of dreams – in this case, the interpenetration of violence and the life of a young man from the reservation who remains only in photographs reverberate against each other.

The bird progresses satisfactorily to "We the people" but doesn't get beyond that. The "of the United States" stubbornly refuses to come. The bird can only enunciate the inclusive subject – the localizing reference doesn't come; there are no United States for these people. Oskinaway discovers that the tape runs out of music half way through and as he is writing to the tape's deviser, a reservation official comes to ask him to give a speech to commemorate 500 years since Columbus's arrival. Despite Two Birds's injunction, Oskinaway's is a poetic and political remonstration against what Columbus has meant for Native American nations. Among his comments is one that relates to the form of the narrative – he mentions the irony, the cruel irony, that Columbus is traditionally seen as proving that the world was round, by coming to a land where the inhabitants had/have always inhabited values based on "the concept of the circle" (209), Paula Gunn Allen's "Sacred Hoop."[11]

The concept of the circle animates the narrative structure of this book, as can be seen in the tales that come back to those nesting inside them. However, they don't complete themselves in neat and tidy ways, but take surprising directions, and, indeed, don't necessarily complete themselves but merely fill in aspects of what they were talking about, for the concept of the circle can be seen as paradoxically inimical to the notion of completion. A circle does not complete itself (where is the beginning, where the end?) but eternally repeats itself. This brings certain ambiguities with it, for eternal repetition suggests changelessness, the inability to learn, the self-satisfied assumption that all is perfect and need not be reflected upon or improved. On the other hand, it also runs counter to the race toward doom that appears to characterize the Western destruction of the environment, our opening of the Pandora's box of our genetic inheritance. Henry is cognizant of these resonances, and, with his customary humour, after his impassioned speech focusing on the death-dealing ways of modern Americans, a reserva-

---

[11] Paula Gunn Allen, *The Sacred Hoop: Recovering the Feminine in American Indian Traditions* (Boston MA: Beacon, 1992).

tion woman says: "'Shit [...] You wouldn't know a vision if it were standing in front of you, glowing like a star. You sound like the old man, dreaming of days gone, working the mind for a spark against dead stone'" (211). Henry does not let conventional Indian pieties obscure his searching enquiry into the situation of his people.

The book ends with Oskinaway moved by the phrase "We the people" which he hears outside, and which may be the bird calling it in its new life, or even the boy Oskinaway had taken home the night before (one of a series of mysterious boys who appear at moments of crisis to hint at connection and caring beyond any notion of reciprocity, as Oskinaway had done for the bird). In any event, the connection between the bird and Oskinaway can stand for the connection between the visionary experience and the one who experiences the vision, but also between the writer and the reader, a relation of mystery and poignancy even when no guarantee can be made about anything to do with the meaning of the experience for either side of the relationship: "the bird once spoke to him through the limits of understanding of what the bird knew inside and through the limits of what he saw outside in the place that was his home" (226).

As Louis Owens says, "Native American writers are insisting that rather than 'use' Native American literature, the world must enter into dialogue with that literature and make it profoundly a part of our modern existence, just as Native Americans have for centuries made European literature a part of Native America."[12] Gordon Henry's *The Light People* is a novel that cannot be simply visited on tour from that Euro-American literature, to which the reader returns after stocking up on a repertoire of images of the exotic Other. In order to follow it at all, the reader needs to enter into the circular structure as articulating a morality; as, indeed, being mimetic of it. Not only that, the reader needs to be able to respect the presence of vision and dream experience undifferentiated within the narrative from other forms of experience, to be able to read it as a continuum and not as sites of rupture. When the non-Indian reader can do this, or at least when we try hard and honestly to do so, some progress will have been made towards making Native American writing that part of our modern existence Louis Owens desires.

WORKS CITED

Allen, Paula Gunn. *The Sacred Hoop: Recovering the Feminine in American Indian Traditions* (Boston MA: Beacon, 1992).
Black Elk. *Black Elk Speaks: Being the Life Story of a Holy Man of the Oglala Sioux*, as told through John G. Neihardt (1932; Lincoln: U of Nebraska P, 1995).
Henry, Gordon Jr. *The Light People: A Novel* (Norman: U of Oklahoma P, 1995).
Lake–Thom, Bobby. *Spirits of the Earth: A Guide to Native American Nature Symbols, Stories, and Ceremonies* (New York: Plume, 1997).
Owens, Louis. *Mixedblood Messages: Literature, Film, Family, Place* (Norman: U of Oklahoma P, 1998).
Peltier, Leonard, *Prison Writings: My Life is My Sun Dance* (New York: St Martin's, 1999).

[12] Owens, *Mixedblood Messages*, 23–24.

Vizenor, Gerald. "Preface," *Narrative Chance: Postmodern Discourse on Native American Indian Literatures* (1989; Norman: U of Oklahoma P, 1993): ix–xiii.

Welch, James. *Winter in the Blood* (New York: Harper & Row, 1974).

《●》

Transcultural Negotiations of the Self
The Poetry of Wendy Rose and Joy Harjo

NICOLE SCHRÖDER

> The colonizer and the colonized meet in my blood. It is so
> much more complex than just white and just Indian.
> Wendy Rose
>
> I walk in and out of many worlds. I used to see being born of
> this mixed-blood/mixed-vision a curse, and hated myself for
> it. […] I have since decided that being familiar with more
> than one world, more than one vision, is a blessing, and know
> that I make my own choices.
> Joy Harjo

T
HE CONCERN WITH CULTURE AND IDENTITY lies at the heart of a lot
of Native American literature although it is by no means the only one. While
differences between various cultural realms are certainly perceived, culture is
not seen as a stable and delimited phenomenon. Rather, it is understood as emerging,
as being in progress and thus continually changing, which has consequences for the
perception of identity and self. In this essay, I will examine the ways in which cultural
identity is negotiated in the poetry of Wendy Rose and Joy Harjo. I will show that it is
this understanding of culture as emerging that enables the poets (and their respective
lyric voices) to negotiate their identity successfully while facing the difficulty of living
in or in between various cultural realms. Rather than arguing in favour of one or the
other of various cultural backgrounds, the writers approach the question of identity in a
'transcultural' way. Transculturality is, according to Mary Louise Pratt, a phenomenon
of the contact zone; it differs from concepts like acculturation and assimilation in that it
emphasizes activity and creativity in contact situations: "While subordinate peoples do
not usually control what emanates from the dominant culture, they do determine to
varying extents what gets absorbed into their own and what it gets used for."[1] The turn

---

[1] Mary Louise Pratt, "Arts of the Contact Zone," *Profession* (1991): 36.

from passive endurance to active choice is important here. Hence, elements having to do with 'transcultural' identity-making – hybrid characters, border crossings, and in-between spaces that blur the boundaries between different cultural realms – become important. These elements mirror recent approaches to culture, as offered by scholars like Homi Bhabha and James Clifford. Both place the emphasis on an emerging culture: like the writers discussed here, they reject the view that cultures are stable and homogeneous. In connection with Rose and Harjo, three theoretical aspects are especially important: Bhabha's notion of the in-between, Clifford's trope of the traveller, and Pratt's transcultural techniques of the contact zone.[2]

Wendy Rose, a poet of mixed Anglo-American and Hopi–Miwok descent, frequently portrays the (post)colonial situation of Native Americans. Drawing on her mixed cultural background, Rose has written about her own difficult mixed-blood condition as well as about "halfbreedness," as she names it, in general. She was raised in a Catholic context and grew up in an urban area, which led to an estrangement from the native part of her background.[3] Likewise, her training as anthropologist and her academic education have more often than not collided with her identity as Native American. Rose writes: "I am that most schizophrenic of creatures, an American Indian who is both poet and anthropologist. I have, in fact, a little row of buttons up and down my ribs that I can press for the appropriate response."[4] This struggle, linked to the hybrid condition that she experiences, lies at the heart of a lot of her work. Yet her poetry also addresses larger, more universal issues, as she writes in the preface to her poetry collection Bone Dance (1994): "In exploring what it means to be a 'halfbreed', I learned that this is not a condition of genetics and has nothing to do with ancestry or race. Instead, 'halfbreedness' is a condition of history, a result of experience, of dislocations and reunions, and of choices made for better or worse."[5]

Since Rose is a writer who is very much interested in different cultures, she often employs metaphors and images of hybridity, like the "halfbreed," to show the formation of identity by dint of negotiation between clashing cultural realms.[6] Such a negotiation is envisioned in a poem from her collection significantly entitled The Halfbreed Chronicles and Other Poems (1985). The title of one of the poems, "If I Am Too

---

[2] Within the scope of this essay I cannot do justice to, or provide a full-scale discussion of, these theories. I shall only highlight those aspects that are relevant to my argument.

[3] For a fictional but factual account of her background and life, see Rose's remarkable autobiographical essay, "Neon Scars," in Brian Swann's and Arnold Krupat's excellent collection of Native American autobiographical essays, I Tell You Now: Autobiographical Essays by Native American Writers (Lincoln: U of Nebraska P, 1989): 251–61.

[4] Wendy Rose, "Just What's All This Fuss About Whiteshamanism Anyway?" in Coyote Was Here: Essays on Contemporary Native American Literary and Political Mobilization (Aarhus: SEKLOS, 1994): 13.

[5] Wendy Rose, Bone Dance: New and Selected Poems, 1965–1993 (Tucson: U of Arizona P, 1994): xvi.

[6] The fact that 'halfbreed' is normally a derogatory term adds another dimension to the image of hybridity: s/he becomes a twilight figure, a character who deviates from the norm, someone who is dislocated.

Brown or Too White For You," is also its first line.[7] As an address to the implied reader, it provides the frame for the poem and is at the same time an expression of its unfinished condition. It likewise presents the lyric self as "halfbreed," as a character of the in-between. It is useful here to evoke Bhabha's in-between, conceived as the contested realm between different and supposedly distinct cultures. According to Bhabha, the "partial" culture that migrants bring to their new homes is still similar but also surprisingly different from its "parent culture." This partial culture is the "contaminated yet connective tissue between cultures"[8] – it separates and connects at the same time and therefore becomes an "impossible" boundary. It is in this border area that something new emerges: in this sense, the in-between is the "location" of culture. It is exactly this contestation, the paradoxical situation of the neither-nor (and yet the bothness) of Bhabha's in-between, that is conjured up in the poem.

In the opening lines of the poem such a contested space is created. The first line completes the title's "if": "remember I am a garnet woman / whirling into precision / as a crystal arithmetic / or a cluster." The beginning of the poem juxtaposes images of chaos and mixing with those of order. A contradiction between complexity and neat categorization is opened up, emphasizing the intricacy of being. This strategy is used throughout the poem, as subsequent lines show: "you are / at the edge of the river / on one knee // and you are selecting me / from among polished stones / more definitely red or white." The river signifies life itself, whereas the stones are metaphors for identity; the river's fluid movement and constant change contrast the stones' qualities of permanence and immobility. Again, a contradictory space is opened up in which different images grapple with each other. Some stones are "more definitely red or white" – colour in this case refers to cultural background. A hybrid identity is preferred, as the lyric self is selected from among "stones / more definitely red or white." The significance of the stone, a symbol of permanence, is turned around – in the river of change it also becomes a sign for hybridity.

Hybridity is also the main image in the following stanza: "my body is blood / frozen into giving birth / over and over, a single motion." Here, the view of the self's mixed identity turns from a superficial depiction in terms of colour to a more substantial one: images of blood, birth, and motion are foregrounded. The poetic self is portrayed as being in constant motion; she is not fixed but ever-changing, as is expressed in the comparison of her body to the blood cycle. The circular, repetitious movement is interrupted by the act of giving birth. Birth, a new beginning, is contrasted with repetition; "a single motion" links both firmly together. Innovation and interruption, the new and the old, are connected – this paradox proves the lyric self to be an inhabitant of Bhabha's in-between space as the contested realm of seemingly incompatible experiences.

In the following stanzas, repetition and change, sameness and difference are contrasted as well. The "matrix," concept of an ordered self, is destroyed, "shattered in winter," and is then pieced together again. However, "wanting the curl in your palm / to be perfect / and the image less clouded, / less mixed," the implied reader keeps

[7] Wendy Rose, *The Halfbreed Chronicles and Other Poems* (Albuquerque NM: West End P, 1992): 52.
[8] Homi Bhabha, "Culture's In Between," *Artforum* 32.1 (September 1993): 167.

insisting on a homogeneous identity. Yet, "just in time," we see that "there is a small light / in the smoke, a tiny sun / in the blood, so deep / it is there and not there," a suggestion that homogenization is not possible. The dialectical structure of the beginning is taken up. Light – clear vision – and smoke – obstructing, veiling things – are contrasted and, in their contradictory connection, signify the paradox of life itself. Consequently, the sun, the core of life, "is there and not there." The essence of life, of identity, can never be known for sure, and any final decision is always postponed. Still, life is "so pure / it is singing." Identity turns out to be "pure" in the figurative sense of completeness, a completeness which the lyric speaker asserts in "singing," in announcing and presenting it to the world. Thus the hybrid nature of identity, including in cultural terms, is voiced in this poem. Identity is envisaged in terms of participation in a circular yet ever-changing movement, and it is this very heterogeneity that makes the being complete or "pure." Identity is perceived as whole because of the in-between status of the self, not in spite of it.

Another personification of the "halfbreed" condition prevalent in Rose's poetry is the traveller and archaeologist. I borrow the figure of the traveller as a metaphor for cultural identity from James Clifford, who uses it to discuss problematic localizing strategies in anthropological practice. According to Clifford, the informant, a central figure in anthropology, has frequently been seen as a "homebody" with a fixed and stable cultural background. S/he has been assumed to be a "pure" embodiment of a certain culture and its way of life. Instead, Clifford argues, "a great many of these interlocutors, complex individuals routinely made to speak for 'cultural' knowledge, turn out to have their own [...] interesting histories of travel. Insider–outsiders, good translators and explicators, they've been around."[9] Travelling defies the centering of culture and cultural identity around a particular *locus* or core and expresses the problem of negotiating cultural identity, as can be seen in Rose's "Excavation at Santa Barbara Mission."[10] The poem starts with a factual comment in which the setting is given: "When archaeologists excavated Santa Barbara Mission in / California, they discovered human bones in the adobe walls." And indeed, as one goes on to read, one enters Santa Barbara Mission and attends the excavation itself: "My pointed trowel / is the artist's brush / that will stroke and pry, / uncover and expose / the old mission wall." The traveller is embodied in the archaeologist who travels to far and distant worlds, in both a literal and a figurative sense: s/he travels not only in space but also in time. The archaeologist, like the artist, dissects and peels back layers of reality and thus explores new horizons and goes beyond the known. The lyric self, unknowingly exploring her surroundings, feels "in love / with the padres / and the Spanish hymns" and sees herself as a "faithful neophyte." The term "neophyte" seems to be in line with this harmonious atmosphere. It designates, in the most general sense, a "beginner," and in

---

[9] James Clifford, *Routes: Travel and Translation in the Late Twentieth Century* (Cambridge MA: Harvard UP, 1997): 19. It is worth noting that Clifford does not insist on literal travel: "It would be better to stress different modalities of inside–outside connection, recalling that travel or displacement can involve forces that pass powerfully *through* – television, radio, tourists, commodities, armies" (28).

[10] Wendy Rose, *Going to War With All My Relations* (Flagstaff AZ: Entrada, 1993): 6.

the Roman Catholic tradition it is a term for a newly baptized believer. Thus, the lyric speaker celebrates herself as a new "arrival" into the Catholic community. On closer examination, however, this harmony is deceptive, as the semantics of "neophyte" are ambiguous. In biology, it is a term for a plant which is not native to a given area but has nonetheless survived. The image of a welcomed arrival in a community and that of a 'dis-located' plant vie with each other.

This semantic tension is substantiated by the change of atmosphere in the following stanza. The mission building collapses and literally buries the lyric speaker. As the mission falls apart we discover that it was built with human bones: "A feature juts out. Marrow / like lace, piece of skull, / upturned cup, fingerbones / scattered like corn / and ribs interlaced / like cholla." Short sentences, abrupt line endings, and voiceless fricatives at word beginnings and endings mirror the speaker's quick and heavy breathing. The place becomes threatening. Not only does the building start to fall apart, but the lyric self likewise dissolves: "So many bones / mixed with the blood / from my own knuckles / that dig and tug / in the yellow dust." Parts of the mission, human bones, and the lyric speaker herself start to fuse, so that the archaeologist and her "objects" – the dead Indians – become indistinguishable. The speaker's role as archaeologist and her identity as Native American thus enter into conflict. She dissects herself along with the archaeological findings – scientific distance has made way for personal feelings and involvement in the confessional mode: "How helpless I am / for the deeper I go / the more I find / crouching in white dust." The archaeological objects come alive, for they "float and fall," "shiver," and "crouch."

At this point, the lyric self realizes her own destructive role, as her boots trample not only the past but also the future. This culminates in this observation: "Beneath the flags / of three invaders, / I the hungry scientist / sustaining myself / with bones of / men and women asleep in the wall." The military imagery reflects the violent encounter between missionaries and Native Americans. The flags represent the lyric speaker's various identity facets, the archaeologist, the Catholic, and the (Spanish) invader. It becomes clear that the lyric self's identity is not monolithic or homogeneous. Instead, she is a truly hybrid character, struggling with the oftentimes paradoxical facets of her own identity. This becomes most obvious in the contested space that is created between her roles as invader and as invaded, which shows the paradox of her being, since she embodies her own destruction.

The supposedly dead Native American culture, however, is more viable than it first appeared to be: the men and women, their bones, "survived in their own way / Spanish swords, Franciscans / and their rosary whips." Catholic religious imagery, "communion wafers," "rosary," "priests," is countered by words vaguely reminiscent of Native American religious traditions, like "corn" and "cholla." The chant-like ending, with the repetition of a sentence like "They built the mission with dead Indians," can likewise be associated with Native American religion and culture. Thus, another contested space is opened between Native American and Catholic religious traditions, reflecting the lyric speaker's multi-dimensional identity. It is shown that something new and viable has been created, which defies Catholicism's attempt to suppress Native American culture.

Nevertheless, the poem ends with the lyric speaker's expression of horror. Chanting, she repeats her discovery that "they built the mission with dead Indians" as if to make the truth more bearable by stating the deadly facts. Furthermore, the ending takes up the beginning: the chant mirrors the factual statement with which the poem begins, thus forming a frame within which, as I have shown, various spaces are opened up. The poem thus creates an in-between space where different experiences, voices, perceptions, histories and stories are juxtaposed. Opposing views and attitudes echo each other, making a one-dimensional view impossible. Likewise, the lyric self moves, travels between various contradictory but also complementary cultural experiences and identities.

Clearly, Rose's negotiation of identity goes beyond the binary opposition between Native American and Anglo-American culture. She not only shows the in-between state of identity, but also the heterogeneity of the various traditions and cultures themselves. Borders are crossed between perceived contradictions, so that separation and essentialism become impossible. Hybridity is envisaged in the bringing-together of paradoxical elements. To repeat Rose's statement from the beginning: "It is so much more complex than just white and just Indian."

Similarly, the poet Joy Harjo, who is of Muscogee and Anglo-American descent, creates multi-dimensional worlds which are appropriate to her own culturally mixed background. While, as Joseph Bruchac observes, origins are very important in Harjo's work, her poems are also concerned with movement, growth and change, and the bridging of differences and polarities: "The world is not disconnected or separate but whole. All persons are still their own entity but not separate from everything else."[11] Harjo is concerned with culture but also with transculturality, and she frequently portrays the specific circumstances of "urban Indians," Native American women, single mothers, or solitary and desperate people. Hence, the problem of various cultures, of power relations, and inequality is taken beyond the simple portrayal of a "culture clash" with its irreconcilable oppositions.

One of Harjo's most prominent motifs is that of travelling, of people on the move, either between different geographical or spiritual/mythic locations or between various, partly opposed experiences.[12] Especially the figure of Noni Daylight, Harjo's "other self," as Andrew Wiget calls her,[13] is a recurring persona in her poems collected in *What Moon Drove Me to This?* (1979) and *She Had Some Horses* (1983). According to Harjo, Noni Daylight "began quite some time ago, as a name I gave a real-life woman I couldn't name in a poem. Then she evolved into her own person, took on her own

---

[11] Joy Harjo, "All Our Survival," in *Survival This Way: Interviews with American Indian Poets*, ed. Joseph Bruchac (Tucson: Sun Tracks & U of Arizona P, 1987): 92.

[12] Herself a frequent traveller as musician and poet, Harjo sees strong similarities between poetry and physical travel: "I am only now beginning to comprehend what poetry is, and what it can mean. Each time I write I am in a different and wild place, and travel toward something I do not know the name of. " See Joy Harjo, "Ordinary Spirit," in *I Tell You Now: Autobiographical Essays by Native American Writers*, ed. Brian Swann & Arnold Krupat (Lincoln: U of Nebraska P, 1989): 265.

[13] Andrew Wiget, *Native American Literature* (Boston MA: Twayne, 1985): 117.

life."[14] Her most outstanding quality is her capacity for exploration: she is constantly crossing boundaries, refusing to be fixed. Consequently, Noni Daylight is continually moving, thereby exploring the limits not only of her self but also those of the world, although she is not confined to what one could call the "real" world: as Jim Ruppert argues, she "can move easily from the mundane world to the mythic space."[15] She is a travelling figure in Clifford's sense, connecting seemingly separated categories in terms not only of culture but also of gender or race. Moreover, she is an inhabitant of an in-between world, living in the contested space of a "contact zone." She is a defeated, desperate figure and at the same time active and strong, as the opening lines of "Kansas City" show: "Early morning over silver tracks / a cool light, Noni Daylight's / a dishrag wrung out over bones / watching trains come and go."[16] Noni appears to be passive as she watches "trains come and go." The "silver tracks" conjure up a longing for escape. However, the meaning of "tracks" is ambiguous. In the reference to railway tracks, *traces* are echoed, traces of a past movement, a memory of travelling not quite forgotten. Consequently, the next lines tell us that "they are light, motion / of time that she could have / caught / and moved on / but she chose to stay / in Kansas City." Her staying was deliberate, so that the passive image of the "wrung-out dishrag" is opposed by the reality of an active choice. Noni Daylight's strength is underpinned by the fact that she not only chose to stay but also chose to "raise the children / she had by different men, / all colors." This sexual freedom indicates what Kristine Holmes calls Noni Daylight's "role as sexual trickster." Indeed, Holmes argues that "Noni's sexual choices and her refusal to be confined or defined by men simultaneously reveal Harjo's feminism and relate to the trickster's exaggerated sexuality."[17] Like the trickster, Noni incorporates incompatible experiences and characteristics, though this is a source not of problems but of power – a precondition for living in the in-between space of various cultural realms.

Having children by different men, however, signifies more than trickster qualities of (sexual) freedom: it indicates, ather, Noni's view of the world at large: "If she had it to do over / she would still choose: / the light one who taught her / sound, but could not hear his / own voice, the blind one / who saw her bones wrapped / in buckskin and silver, / the one whose eyes tipped up / like swallows wings / [...] all of them, / their stories in the flatland belly / giving birth to children / and to other stories / and to Noni Daylight." The men, different from each other and all in a way "incomplete," are parts of a whole – in their diversity, they complement each other. They "make" Noni Daylight: all of them are important for her life, no matter how diverse their character has been. This image reflects the world at large, which, made out of different parts, is enriched and turned into a whole rather than fragmented.

---

[14] See Laura Coltelli, *Winged Words: American Indian Writers Speak* (Lincoln: U of Nebraska P, 1990): 61.

[15] Jim Ruppert, "Paula Gunn Allen and Joy Harjo: Closing the Distance Between Personal and Mythic Space," *American Indian Quarterly* 7.1 (Spring 1983): 31.

[16] Joy Harjo, *She Had Some Horses* (New York: Thunder's Mouth, 1997): 33.

[17] Kristine Holmes, "'This Woman Can Cross Any Line': Feminist Tricksters in the Works of Nora Naranjo–Morse and Joy Harjo," *SAIL* 7.1 (Spring 1995): 56.

Noni's children likewise reflect this metaphor of parts and whole; having different fathers, they are "half-breed, blue eyes," so that they cannot be categorized. They "would grow up with the sound / of trains etched on the surface / of their bones." Like Noni, they embody, quite literally, travelling. The sound of movement is etched into the very core of their being. As half-breeds, they are "always on the way back home." Being half-breed is connected to being "homeless," restless and on the move. Yet this homelessness is not only meant in the sense of having no roots. To be always on the way back home also means to be at home where one wants to be at home, to make a home "on the road." Home, as Bhabha has it, "may be a mode of living made into a metaphor of survival."[18] The image of being always on the way back home mirrors Noni Daylight's decision to stay in Kansas City. In having her persona choose to stay in the city, Harjo claims the city, the urban space, as another "home" for Native Americans whom clichés otherwise often confine to reservations and rural areas. In this manner, the geographical boundary of the stereotypical Indian is crossed.

In-between spaces are not only constructed through the content and the images of the poem. The structure itself reveals the construction of a complicated, interwoven space. There is a majority of run-on lines, connecting separated images and at the same time separating joined ones. Certain images are constructed in one line, only to be amended or changed by the jump to the next line. Meaning, then, becomes ambiguous, as images add up, complement and change each other, making up a whole from various parts. Similarly, Noni embodies contradictions; in "Kansas City," she is not a traveller in the literal sense, as she chooses to stay in the city. Yet, she travels 'intellectually', because she is receptive to various kinds of experiences and views of the world: her husbands and lovers show her different aspects of life. Loving men "of all colors," Noni crosses racial and cultural boundaries, refusing to remain within fixed categories. The result is a "half-breed" world, meant not only literally as in the half-breed children; it is a general condition. Thus, Noni Daylight is not only a traveller moving between geographical locations – she shows us that moving, changing, being open for 'other' views and stories can also be a condition of the mind. Journeying means changing others as well as oneself; for the persona of Noni Daylight, it not only signifies physical movement but also her own evolving identity. "Home" does not exist as a final destination, only as an urge to go on, to move beyond oneself. Thus, the last image we see of Noni Daylight is "waving / at the last train to leave / Kansas City," looking past the city limits to the space beyond.

In her poem entitled "In the Beautiful Perfume and Stink of the World,"[19] Harjo takes the concern with hybridity and culture one step further, to an even more universal level. Here, the world at large is seen as in-between space, as evolving and in motion. Two alternating voices, marked by different fonts, speak in this poem. Initially they are separate, but in the course of the poem they merge gradually, interweaving and thereby creating a new space. This space echoes the title and its two polarities – perfume and

---

[18] Homi Bhabha, "Halfway House," *Artforum* 35.9 (May 1997): 11.

[19] Joy Harjo, *Map to the Next World: Poetry and Tales* (New York: W.W. Norton, 2000): 133. It is significant that the title of this collection itself points to another world, another level of perceiving and understanding, and thus sums up the essence of Harjo's latest poetic work.

stink. Thus, a superficial reading gives the impression that the voices are isolated from each other, but further examination reveals that they are connected via run-on lines, and the voices can actually be read as talking to each other.

This conversation is the core of the poem. The voices represent two areas of the world, the mundane and the 'mythic' (visionary) realms. Since they echo each other, they open up a third space, dividing and connecting the mundane and the mythic. The two voices take us on a journey. The first voice begins: "In these dark hours of questioning everything matters: / each membrane of lung and how wind travels." The "dark hours" speak of danger and despair and are countered by immediate signs of life: breathing and air. The mood is dark and enigmatic. Breaking up the poem's flow, the next stanza, printed in italics, confuses us even more. Thus the second voice sets in: "*I had been traveling in the dark, through many worlds, / the four corners of my mat carried by guardians in the shape of crows.*" We find ourselves in another time (the past tense is used, instead of the present of the first lines) and in another place as the self is flying on a mat "through many worlds." To Harjo, working with different tenses is extremely significant: "I often change tense within a poem and do so knowing what I am doing. [...] Time doesn't realistically work in a linear fashion."[20] Chronological linearity is dismissed in favour of a structure that highlights the connection of past, present, and future. A circular structure is suggested, underpinned by the interweaving of the two voices (past and present), which cease to be clearly distinguishable.

Moreover, a mythic space is opened up; the mat on which she travels refers to a well-known fairy-tale motif and invokes the far-away and the long ago. Additionally, crows are accompanying the self – Native American tricksters frequently assume the shape of crows and the allusion to a trickster reinforces the impression of a mythic world: ie, of a world beyond.[21] Similar in their enigmatic character, the two stanzas seem to have nothing to do with each other, and yet the break between them is not as abrupt as it seems, since not only is the trope of travelling echoed but so are the allusions to darkness and wind. In these first lines, Harjo creates a new space through the dialectics of different voices that encounter each other. This is continued until the end: each voice is interrupted as well as echoed by the other, so that separation and continuation go hand in hand. Bhabha's concept of the in-between is enacted here: the voices in their difference and their fusion embody the impossible boundary, "the contaminated yet connective tissue" between seemingly different realms.

The alternation and juxtaposition of separation and continuation is carried on in the third stanza, which refers to the first and continues its pending sentence: "the french fry under the table the baby dropped." The reader is taken back to the mundane realm in a

---

[20] Harjo, "Ordinary Spirit," 269.

[21] 'Mythic' does not mean untrue or fictitious. Especially in Native American cultures, the realm of the mythic is as real and significant as what we normally call the 'real' world. Paula Gunn Allen explains: "In the culture and literature of Indian America, the meaning of myth may be discovered, not as a speculation about primitive long-dead ancestral societies but in terms of what is real, actual, and viable in living cultures in America." See Paula Gunn Allen, *The Sacred Hoop: Recovering the Feminine in American Indian Traditions* (Boston MA: Beacon P, 1992): 105.

double sense. Not only does the "french fry" stand in great contrast to the previous lines, it also asserts the importance of everyday things, echoing the first stanza's "everything matters." These lines, with their contrast between the commonplace and the exceptional, are also a comment on life itself with its highs and lows. Subsequently, the seeming gap between mundane and mythic is widened in the voices' dialogue. Whereas one voice tells us about the "*comet, a messenger who flew parallel to my heart,*" evoking understanding and unity with the world beyond and with itself, the other voice says that "loss is measured in tons, not ounces. And what-I-should-have-said / and what-I-should-have-done are creatures of habit." The loss, tangible and overwhelming, stands in complete contrast to the previous and to the following stanzas with the comet-messenger and the "newborn star shimmering." Here, the beauty is so great that it cannot be measured and the lyric self "*stopped counting and began to comprehend the view.*" By contrast, for the other voice comprehension cannot take place: "creatures of habit" are blocking the view of the beyond, the "sleeping moon."

While the voices have so far echoed each other only faintly, from now on they begin to merge slowly. The mythic voice says: "*My son was my dark-eyed baby again, kicking his legs after a bath, / and then he was a man with fire in his hands*" – looking into the past as well as into the future. Likewise, the other voice alludes to the past and counters: "If I get up to pee I'll lessen my chances / of catching the wave of *remembering and forgetting*" (my emphasis). This does not happen, and "so I waver here in the delicate traffic of cast-off ideas and doubt's antennae" – the wave of remembering can continue. Memory for Harjo is a living force that affects not only the past but also the present and future: "I see [memory] as occurring, not just going back, but occurring right now, and also future occurrence so that you can remember things in a way that makes what occurs now beautiful."[22] Consequently, in remembering the second voice mirrors the first, as it is looking into the past and the future.

In the following lines the gradual fusion becomes stronger, since both voices speak about antagonism and destruction. Thus "*children began / killing each other*" is mirrored by "they fought and destroyed each other." Both voices now speak about the "dark side" of the world, concerned as they are with destruction and war. Still, the first voice, which was so despairing at the beginning, can also talk about "the sky bright with a traveler / ... / who drags a starry tail behind him," in obvious sensitivity to "a lyric of beauty" and to the fact that "it is all here. Everything that ever was." Finally, after the darkness and despair of the beginning, the world seems to fall into place for her. Nonetheless, the contrast between the positive and the negative is maintained, since the second voice reports that "*we could not agree among ourselves. / We fought, then destroyed each other.*"

While past and present, memory and future are not only juxtaposed but also connected in the two voices, the end of the poem is linked to the beginning. The poem thus creates a space of seemingly incompatible oppositions. Through the interweaving of voices, however, the poles are linked, the strong opposition is broken up, and in this rupture the opposing poles are reconciled. Harjo's view of the world is enacted here: "We're not separate. [...] Ultimately, when it's all together, there won't be these cate-

---

[22] Harjo, "All Our Survival," 93.

gories. There won't be these categories of male/female and ultimately we will be accepted for what we are and not divided."[23] Thus, in the end both voices can refer back to the beginning, to the "dark" which finally becomes a positive image: *"The cawing, flapping song of the beautiful dark* / In the dark. In the beautiful perfume and stink of the world." This world includes good and bad, high and low at the same time: one cannot be without the other, and the two cannot be separated. This is what hybridity means to Harjo: instead of the either-or of distinct, monolithic categories she emphasizes the enactment of contradicting poles. While a contested space is created, structurally as well as thematically, a dialogue connects the different poles and furthers change and exchange.

Clearly, both Harjo and Rose are concerned with cultural identity in these poems, albeit in different ways and no matter how different their strategies. Rose depicts the at times painful negotiation of (cultural) identity in a very personal way. Harjo frequently takes this same negotiation to a more abstract level and presents it as a characteristic of the world at large. Nevertheless, both poets depict culture and cultural identity as changing and heterogeneous phenomena. They cross categorial borders and see their home in the in-between space, "on the road." Rose's and Harjo's poetry shows us that cultures are always already multicultural, influenced by the 'other', and that it is this influence and change that allows cultures to survive. Likewise, identities are never static, because they are formed in a constant struggling interaction with new influences – hence their transcultural quality.

WORKS CITED

Allen, Paula Gunn. *The Sacred Hoop: Recovering the Feminine in American Indian Traditions* (Boston MA: Beacon P, 1992).

Bhabha, Homi. "Culture's In Between," *Artforum* 32.1 (September 1993): 162; 167–68; 211–12.

——. "Halfway House," *Artforum* 35.9 (May 1997): 11–12; 125.

Clifford, James. "Traveling Cultures," in *Routes: Travel and Translation in the Late Twentieth Century* (Cambridge MA: Harvard UP, 1997): 17–46.

Harjo, Joy. "Interview," in *Winged Words: American Indian Writers Speak*, ed. Laura Coltelli (Lincoln: U of Nebraska P, 1990): 54–68.

——. *Map to the Next World: Poetry and Tales* (New York: W.W. Norton, 2000).

——. "Ordinary Spirit," in *I Tell You Now: Autobiographical Essays by Native American Writers*, ed. Brian Swann & Arnold Krupat (Lincoln: U of Nebraska P, 1989): 263–70.

——. *She Had Some Horses* (New York: Thunder's Mouth, 1997).

——. "The Story of All Our Survival: An Interview with Joy Harjo," in *Survival This Way: Interviews with American Indian Poets*, ed. Joseph Bruchac (Tucson: Sun Tracks & U of Arizona P, 1987): 87–103.

——. *What Moon Drove Me to This?* (New York: Reed, 1979).

Holmes, Kristine. "'This Woman Can Cross Any Line': Feminist Tricksters in the Works of Nora Naranjo–Morse and Joy Harjo," *SAIL* 7.1 (Spring 1995): 45–63.

Pratt, Mary Louise. "Arts of the Contact Zone," *Profession* (1991): 33–40.

---

[23] Harjo, "All Our Survival," 96.

Rose, Wendy. *Bone Dance: New and Selected Poems, 1965–1993* (Tucson: U of Arizona P, 1994).

——. *Going to War With All My Relations* (Flagstaff AZ: Entrada, 1993).

——. *The Halfbreed Chronicles and Other Poems* (Albuquerque NM: West End, 1992).

——. "Just What's All This Fuss About Whiteshamanism Anyway?" in *Coyote Was Here: Essays on Contemporary Native American Literary and Political Mobilization* (Aarhus: SEKLOS, 1994): 13–24.

——. "Neon Scars," in *I Tell You Now: Autobiographical Essays by Native American Writers*, ed. Brian Swann & Arnold Krupat (Lincoln: U of Nebraska P, 1989): 251–61.

Ruppert, Jim. "Paula Gunn Allen and Joy Harjo: Closing the Distance Between Personal and Mythic Space," *American Indian Quarterly* 7.1 (Spring 1983): 27–40.

Wiget, Andrew. *Native American Literature* (Boston MA: Twayne, 1985).

《•》

Inside the Spiral
Māori Writing in English

JUDITH DELL PANNY

T HE NOVELS OF MANY INDIGENOUS AUTHORS reflect mythology and
traditional attitudes which were in place long before colonization. This poses
a problem for the critics who apply postcolonial theory to indigenous writing.
A focus on the colonial process and its legacy may result in neglect of a work's significant and fundamental cultural elements. With specific reference to Patricia Grace's
Potiki and Keri Hulme's *the bone people*, this essay will examine the potential limitation of postcolonial readings and the additional insight that can be offered through a
cultural-historical approach.

In a recent interview, Witi Ihimaera was asked if he was comfortable to have terms
like 'postcolonial' or 'postmodern' applied to his work. "They're international constructs," he said. "They're part of a need to look at a work from the outside. What matters to me is the view from the inside out."[1] It is surely the "view from the inside out"
that readers and critics are seeking. When asked "What, to you, makes a work Maori?"
Ihimaera replied:

> I have to say that Maori ancestry will not make your work Maori. Understanding about
> Maori culture will. And the closer you are to what we call the Aho Tapu or the Sacred
> Thread the more invested with Maoriness your work will be.[2]

The *aho tapu*, literally the sacred thread from which a woven cloak is suspended, also
refers figuratively to the genealogical thread that stretches back to the original parents,
the Sky Father (Rangi) and the Earth Mother (Papa).

At the heart of traditional Māori culture is a genealogical awareness. Families trace
their genealogy to arrivals on the shores of Aotearoa (New Zealand) in the so-called
'great canoes' from Hawaiki, the original homeland, and prior to that, mythologically,
to Rangi and Papa. Consciousness of genealogy permeates all Māori art. However, its

---

[1] Juniper Ellis, "'The Singing Word': Witi Ihimaera interviewed by Juniper Ellis," *Journal
of Commonwealth Literature* 34.1 (1999): 176.
[2] Ellis, "The Singing Word," 176.

significance is likely to be overlooked by those applying postcolonial theory to novels by Māori, since there is nothing quite comparable in Western thought. A critical reading that pays scant attention to cultural components may fail to respond to signs or situations which will have influenced motivation. The significance of belief systems and the observance or failure to observe correct protocol are crucial to indigenous fiction.

The difficulty has been identified by indigenous writers from other cultures. African writers have long complained of "the refusal of a non-local readership to come to terms with the need to understand the work from within its own cultural context."[3] Western literary theory stands accused of being narrow, exclusive, and doggedly eurocentric. The Native American writer Paula Gunn Allen describes the mental set of Westerners: "The study of non-Western literature poses a problem for Western readers, who naturally tend to see alien literature in terms that are familiar to them, however irrelevant those terms may be to the literature under consideration."[4]

Less narrow and exclusive than postcolonial readings, which tend to refer back to the values and attitudes of the 'centre', is the New Historicism. This approach routinely focuses on the relationship between text and context, acknowledging that the context is cultural, ideological, social and historical. The cultural-historical investigation of the New Historicism has most often been applied to works of literature from the past, to Shakespeare's plays and Keats's poems, for example. However, its rigorous literary inquiry could be equally effective in offering a more profound appreciation of indigenous literature.

Specific examples of the limitations of a postcolonial reading and the additional insight possible with a New-Historicist reading can be provided from Patricia Grace's novel *Potiki* (meaning 'youngest child'). Members of a Māori family, living by the sea on a hilly peninsula, are under pressure to sell part of their land to allow road access to the next bay. Two contrasting attitudes to land are clearly stated as part of an ongoing struggle between Māori and Pakeha (European New Zealanders).

A postcolonial reading would invite examination of the contrasting views, but a New-Historicist reading could examine the same issues in the context of New Zealand's history. Some of the young Māori in *Potiki* become activists. They retaliate against the Pakeha developers by sabotaging their equipment. While there is considerable justification for the demolition within the context of the novel, background information is required if readers are to appreciate the attitude of the parents, who are proud of their children's actions. Such information can be provided through revisionist histories.

The Treaty of Waitangi, with its two texts, (Māori and English) is directly relevant. Through the Treaty's Māori text, *kawanatanga* was relinquished to the British Crown, *kawana-tanga* being a transliteration of 'governor-ship'. It was a concept with which the Māori were unfamiliar, but it seemed harmless enough. It is this document that all

---

[3] Bill Ashcroft, Gareth Griffiths & Helen Tiffin, *The Empire Writes Back: Theory and Practice in Post-Colonial Literatures* (London & New York: Routledge, 1989): 127.

[4] Paula Gunn Allen, "The Sacred Hoop: A Contemporary Perspective," in *The Ecocriticism Reader: Landmarks in Literary Ecology* (Athens & London: U of Georgia P, 1996): 241.

but a few Māori signatories signed. The English text is quite different. In Article One, Māori gave over to the Crown, not governorship, but "absolute sovereignty." In return, in Article Two, Māori were guaranteed the "undisturbed possession of their Lands and Estates Forests Fisheries and other properties."[5] The Pakeha have held fast to Article One of the English version, while disregarding Article Two. Māori have frequently failed to receive justice from New Zealand's lawmakers and legal system, a situation which has led, periodically, to individuals and groups taking the law into their own hands, their actions guided by their own concept of what is 'just'.

The New Historicism insists on the consultation of non-literary texts which offer insight into political and social history. In the case of an indigenous work, cultural practices may be fundamental to the very structure of a work. *Potiki* includes a major structuring device, which calls for familiarity with the protocols relating to a baby's *whenua* or placenta. Within minutes of his birth, the *potiki*'s placenta is cast into the sea, where it is lost "to the stomach of a fish."[6] The event foreshadows the danger faced by the child throughout his life, since burial of the *whenua* in the land establishes a contract between the earth and the infant, in which each will succour and protect the other. Without such protection, the *potiki* is at risk, a situation which creates tension. The in-depth probing which a New-Historicist reading encourages would even uncover the link between the placenta (*te whenua* in Māori) and the land (also *te whenua* in Māori).

Hemi, the father in the novel, remarks that the *potiki* "was something special they'd been given, no doubt about it [...]. A taniwha. That's what they'd been given, a taniwha, who somehow gave strength [...] and joy to all of them."[7] While the implications of such a statement would elude many readers and critics, the New Historicist would recognize the need to investigate further. The qualities of mythical monsters named *taniwha* include ancient energies. To describe a person as a *taniwha* is to acknowledge special, mysterious powers. The *potiki* possesses remarkable understanding, as well as an ability to prophesy.

Without background knowledge of Māori culture and history, full appreciation of the novel is not possible. Consider for a moment the example of Latin literature. A critic would not interpret or appraise a Latin literary text without knowledge of Roman values, society and the relevant history and politics. Would any critic presume to understand the subtleties, the allusions or the *irony* of a text by Virgil, without such a background? Equally, the irony of *Potiki*'s conclusion, where the voice and prophecies of the youngest child live beyond his death, will elude those with little knowledge of the culture.

A more problematic work is *the bone people*. Regardless of the critical theory applied, many critics have failed to perceive the Maoriness of this novel. It is not just a failure to decode images and symbols signalling its presence; the symbols have not

---

[5] I.H. Kawharu, *Waitangi: Maori and Pakeha Perspectives of the Treaty of Waitangi* (Auckland: Oxford UP, 1989): 317.

[6] Patricia Grace, *Potiki* (Auckland: Penguin, 1986): 43.

[7] Grace, *Potiki*, 67.

been recognized. Readers have not, for example, perceived the significance of a
treasure chest filled with pounamu or greenstone in the context of this work.

Kerewin, the central female character, expresses a Māori attitude in saying "you
wouldn't keep a named heirloom if it didn't belong in your family."[8] Yet her treasure
chest contains "two meres, patu pounamu, both old and named, still deadly,"[9] and a
hundred or so finely made items. She has no right to any of them. In terms of Māori
values, such hoarding signals a person who is sick in spirit. With the exception of specially gifted pieces, Māori *taonga* or treasures do not belong to individuals, but are the
shared possessions of *iwi* or *hapu*, a tribe or section of a tribe.

Critics have written competently about those aspects of the novel pertaining to
Western culture. Marjorie Fee draws attention to Hulme's rejection through her characters of a whole range of Western fantasies: the happily-ever-after of the lottery win,
the heterosexual liaison, the self-sufficient solitary life-style. Kerewin shows that these
indications of a Pakeha value-system bring her neither happiness nor fulfilment. In
contemplating Western values, it is said that the major concern of most Westerners is
"that which immediately affects our personal economic livelihood."[10] Significant to
New Historicists, who examine economic systems, would be the reasons for Hulme's
choice for her characters of windfall wealth, wasted inheritance and mysterious dis-
inheritance. The author deliberately places characters in *the bone people* outside the
usual Western emphasis on "personal economic livelihood" in order to focus on complex personal relationships and to re-assert particular Māori patterns of thought. While
critics have noted that certain aspects of the Western system have been rejected, their
replacement by traditional Māori values has been ignored.

Loss and physical damage, bringing each of the three main characters close to death,
is followed by hard-won repair, remaking and redemption. This progression by three
characters unifies and structures this novel. It has generally not been noted that the
resolution, finally achieved, can be placed in the context of the traditional Māori
aspiration toward balance and harmony. One may ask if a New-Historicist reading
would be more successful in appraising the work and providing insight into its subtleties. Of immediate interest to a New-Historicist researcher would be the circumstances
surrounding publication, including the reasons for its rejection in the early 1980s by a
succession of publishers. Of even greater interest would be the reasons for its subsequent success, not only as the winner of the Booker Prize, but also as a best-seller. By
August 1998, *the bone people* had sold 1.3 million copies in twenty-three editions in
ten languages. Hulme has turned down over 300 offers to film the novel.[11]

In New-Historicist terms, such success suggests a work of abundant social energy.
Stephen Greenblatt, acknowledged as the originator of the New Historicism, has noted
that the "life" of a literary work depends on the "social energy initially encoded in that

---

[8] Keri Hulme, *the bone people* (1983; Auckland: Hodder & Stoughton, 1985): 253.

[9] Hulme, *the bone people*, 33.

[10] Glen A. Love, "Revaluing Nature: Toward an Ecological Criticism," in *Ecocriticism
Reader: Landmarks in Literary Ecology* (Athens & London: U of Georgia P, 1996): 227.

[11] Warwick Roger, "The Long Silence of Keri Hulme," *North and South* 149 (1998): 66.

work."[12] New Historicists investigate the language responsible for encoding that social energy. In traditional Māori society, an effect would be produced through language that describes situations invoking reciprocation and *tapu*. Reciprocation is obligatory. *Tapu*, in protecting sacred sites and people of high status, as well as signalling that certain conduct is forbidden, exercises a profound effect on motivation and behaviour. Social energy thus 'encoded' could be decoded and re-activated through a New-Historicist reading. An understanding of reciprocation and *tapu* is vital to an appreciation of the powerful interaction and responses of the three main characters in *the bone people*.

Viewed as a whole, *the bone people* should be placed in a timeless, mythological context. A parallel example is Ben Okri's *The Famished Road* (1991), which has been viewed mythologically by Margaret Cezair–Thompson. Having broken free from the constraints of the postcolonial, her essay on *The Famished Road* is entitled "Beyond the Postcolonial Novel." Cezair–Thompson shows Okri to be concerned with "timelessness, cyclical recurrence and transfiguration"[13] rather than "a Eurocentric historical consciousness."[14] The work "proceeds beyond [...] postcolonial issues,"[15] as does *the bone people*. A mythical view of existence is often represented in Māori visual arts by a double spiral. Kerewin observes that "the old people found inspiration for the double spirals they carved so skilfully, in uncurling fernfronds: perhaps. But it was an old symbol of rebirth, and the outward–inward nature of things...."[16] The genealogical emphasis of Māori culture is reiterated in the spiral, which reaches back to the original parents and forward to the people to come. In traditional Māori thought, there is a perpetual awareness of a person's place in time, where the present moment is never divorced from the past or the future.

A "timelessness, cyclical recurrence and transfiguration" is implied by "E nga iwi o nga iwi."[17] Joe, one of Hulme's three main characters, gives expression to this Māori proverb, which means 'O the people of the bones' and 'O the bones of the people'. (The word *iwi* means both people and bones.) The paradoxical statement refers to a traditional Māori view of time, death and birth. Each individual has been shaped by the ancestors, who, in the meantime, have been reduced to bones. Each man or woman in turn may contribute to the heritage of people to come, bones representing their living forms, and the form of their descendants. The ancestors, the living and the unborn are one people, the ancestors guiding the present generation and looking ahead to the wellbeing of those living in the future. Investigation into the title *the bone people* would discover that the words derive from the Māori proverb "E nga iwi o nga iwi" and that

---

[12] Stephen Greenblatt, "The Circulation of Social Energy," in Greenblatt, *Shakespearean Negotiations: The Circulation of Social Energy in Renaissance England* (Berkeley: U of California P, 1988): 6.

[13] Margaret Cezair–Thompson, "Beyond the Postcolonial Novel: Ben Okri's The Famished Road and its 'Abiku' Traveller," *Journal of Commonwealth Literature* 31.2 (1996): 35.

[14] Cezair–Thompson, "Beyond the Postcolonial Novel," 36.

[15] "Beyond the Postcolonial Novel," 40.

[16] Hulme, *the bone people*, 45.

[17] *the bone people*, 395.

proverbs are significant in Māori culture, providing practical guidance in appropriate values and influencing behaviour directly.

The New Historicism has been criticized for its application as an approach to books and articles "of a bewildering variety."[18] On the other hand, the very diversity of a cultural-historical reading can be regarded as an advantage, encouraging a delving into words and phrases carrying special energy, an appreciation of belief systems that have led to particular protocols, and the identification of symbols and myths intrinsic to a people's relationship to the natural world. Stephen Greenblatt describes his investigatory practice in the following way: "I have termed this general enterprise – study of the collective making of distinct cultural practices and inquiry into relations among these practices – a poetics of culture."[19]

A cultural-historical approach offers entry into contemporary indigenous works, opening up Witi Ihimaera's ideal perspective: "the view from the inside out."[20]

WORKS CITED

Allen, Paula Gunn. "The Sacred Hoop: A Contemporary Perspective," in *The Ecocriticism Reader: Landmarks in Literary Ecology* (Athens & London: U of Georgia P, 1996): 241–63.

Ashcroft, Bill, Gareth Griffiths & Helen Tiffin. *The Empire Writes Back* (London: Routledge, 1988): 78–137.

Banerjee, Jacqueline. "Mending the Butterfly: The New Historicism and Keats's 'Eve of St Agnes'," *College English* 57.5 (1995): 529–45.

Cezair-Thompson, Margaret. "Beyond the Postcolonial Novel: Ben Okri's *The Famished Road* and its 'Abiku' Traveller," *Journal of Commonwealth Literature* 31. 2 (1996): 33–45.

During, Simon. "New Historicism," *Text and Performance Quarterly* 2.3 (1991): 171–89.

Ellis, Juniper. "'The Singing Word': Witi Ihimaera interviewed by Juniper Ellis," *Journal of Commonwealth Literature* 34.1 (1999): 169–82.

Fee, Marjorie. "Why C K Stead didn't like Keri Hulme's "the bone people": Who can write as Other?" *Australian and New Zealand Studies in Canada* 1 (Spring 1989): 11–32.

Grace, Patricia. *Potiki* (Auckland: Penguin, 1986).

Greenblatt, Stephen. "The Circulation of Social Energy," *Shakespearean Negotiations: The Circulation of Social Energy in Renaissance England* (Berkeley: U of California P, 1988): 1–20.

Hulme, Keri. *the bone people* (1983; Auckland: Hodder & Stoughton, 1985).

Kawharu, I.H. *Waitangi: Maori and Pakeha Perspectives of the Treaty of Waitangi* (Auckland: Oxford UP, 1989): 316–21.

Love, Glen A. "Revaluing Nature: Toward an Ecological Criticism," in *Ecocriticism Reader: Landmarks in Literary Ecology* (Athens & London: U of Georgia P, 1996): 225–40.

Ngugi wa Thiong'o. "The Quest for Relevance," in Ngugi, *Decolonising the Mind: The Politics of Language in African Literature* (1981; Oxford, Nairobi & Portsmouth NJ: James Currey, E A E P & Heinemann, 1986): 87–95.

Okri, Ben. *The Famished Road* (1991; London: Vintage, 1992).

Roger, Warwick. "The Long Silence of Keri Hulme," *North and South* 149 (1998): 65–71.

---

[18] H. Amram Veeser, "The New Historicism," in *The New Historicism Reader*, ed. Veeser (New York: Routledge, 1994): 1.

[19] Greenblatt, *Shakespearean Negotiations*, 5.

[20] Ellis, "The Singing Word," 176.

Tompkins, Jane. "Introduction: The Cultural Work of American Fiction," in *Sensational Designs: The Cultural Work of American Fiction 1790–1860* (New York: Oxford UP, 1985): xi–xix.

Veeser, H. Aram. "The New Historicism," in *The New Historicism Reader*, ed. Veeser (New York: Routledge, 1994): 1–32.

《●》

MULTICULTURALISM AND ETHNICITY

"Fables of the Reconstruction of the Fables"
Multiculturalism, Postmodernism, and the Possibilities of Myth in Hiromi Goto's *Chorus of Mushrooms*

MARC COLAVINCENZO

H IROMI GOTO'S *Chorus of Mushrooms* (1994) tells the story of three generations of a Japanese-Canadian family living in Alberta, each generation represented mainly by one character in the novel. The youngest of these is Muriel, or Murasaki as she is called by her grandmother. She is first-generation Canadian, and it is she who narrates most of the novel – the reader is privy to the story of her family as she tells it to her lover. The second generation is represented by both of Murasaki's parents, but mainly by her mother Keiko, or Kay as she prefers to call herself. Finally, the third generation is represented by Murasaki's grandmother – or Obachan – Naoe. Large segments of the narrative are told from her perspective in a first-person voice, but it is questionable whether she really is the narrator at these points. Rather, the novel indicates that Murasaki is at the very least re-creating her grandmother's voice, unless it is Naoe who is speaking through Murasaki.

Each of these characters represents one particular possible attitude towards Canada, which is then reflected in their names. Kay, the mother, represents the possibility of assimilating Canadian culture as she tries to hide all traces of her Japanese heritage, which includes shortening her name from Keiko to Kay. By contrast Naoe, the grandmother, is antagonistic towards Canada and does not feel at home there at all, so that she rejects all the aspects of Canadian culture that she knows. She represents an isolationist attitude towards her new culture, since she encapsulates herself in memories of her Japanese roots, and therefore it is not surprising that she only has a Japanese name and no Anglo-Saxon one. Only when Naoe decides to leave the house, and her attitude towards Canada seems to become somewhat more positive, does she give herself an English 'name' – "Purple." Finally, Murasaki, the narrator, represents a position between these two, for in the course of her life as she narrates it she becomes more and more curious about her roots, which she feels more and more like acknowledging. This development is paralleled by her apparent feeling regarding her two names. Her mother has given her the name of Muriel, but she comes to favour the name by which the reader knows her, and which was given to her by her grandmother: Murasaki.

The novel thus sets up some clear polarities and tensions. At first glance, it presents a picture of the Canadian multicultural experience which seems both negative and clear. Murasaki relates various stories indicating that, behind the rhetoric of multicultural acceptance, Canadian culture is permeated by racism, intolerance, and homogenizing or assimilationist tendencies. She describes the racist jokes and exoticizing stereotypes about her Japanese heritage, to which she was subjected as a child. On Valentine's Day she gets the cards with the "press-out Oriental-type girl in some sort of pseudo kimono with wooden sandals on backwards and her [sic] with her hair cut straight across in bangs and a bun and chopsticks in her hair, her eyes all slanty slits."[1] Her words indicate that the image is inaccurate, based as it is on cultural stereotypes, and even as a child she knew, although she could not say why, that "there was something wrong about me getting these cards. What the picture was saying" (62). The image of Japan nourished by other children is further formed by the television show "Shogun," and her boyfriends expect her to be adept at "Oriental sex," whatever this might be. Confronted with the question, "You're Oriental aren'tchya?" she protests: "Not really [...]. I think I'm Canadian" (122). It is quite clear that, at this point in her life, Murasaki thinks of herself more as Canadian than as Japanese, or at the very least as Japanese-Canadian, whereas her boyfriend seems to view her primarily not even as Japanese, but as oriental. Murasaki is thus excluded from the Canadian mosaic and her exact heritage is blurred in the reference to a vaguely conceived orientalism. This lack of differentiation is confirmed elsewhere when a number of other children make fun of her because they think she is Chinese (52–53), or when she says that she did not talk to a certain Chinese-Canadian boy because "Oriental people in single doses were well enough, but any hint of a group and it was all over" (125). She says that she thought she was "proud of being Japanese-Canadian," but she now sees that she was "actually a coward" (125). Her reaction when she finds out that her house has a different smell because of her father's work with mushrooms is also telling: she is "horrified," the smell is found to be "insidious" and a "betrayal," to the point that she feels "contaminated" by the mushroom smell because it uncovers her "Oriental tracks" (62).

This goes on into her life as an adult. Murasaki continues to be confronted with what she perceives as ignorance and stereotypes. People ask her about things which they consider to be typically Japanese, such as feet binding – which was never practised in Japan – and *harakiri*. She also gets upset when people assume that she will be familiar with certain vegetables just because she looks oriental and is standing in the "ethnic ChinesericenoodleTofupattiesexotic vegetable section" of the supermarket (90). Again, she sees here evidence that oriental people are viewed as a large undifferentiated group by the rest of Canadian society. Therefore, she also includes in her story various views which other Canadians have of immigrants, their right to be in Canada, the question of language, and jokes about them (211–12). She is most scathing, however, with regard to the conferences held by postcolonial intellectuals:

---

[1] Hiromi Goto, *Chorus of Mushrooms* (Edmonton, Alberta: NeWest, 1994): 62. Further page references are in the main text.

You're invited somewhere to be a guest speaker. To give a keynote address. Whatever that is. Everybody in suits and ties and designer dresses. You're the only coloured person there who is not serving food. It's not about being bitter. You just notice. People talk race this ethnic that. It's easy to be theoretical if the words are coming from a face that has little or no pigmentation. (89–90)

Clearly, and quite justifiably in my opinion, Murasaki thinks that it is all too easy to seem clever in the postcolonial game, and to theorize about issues of multiculturalism and ethnicity, if one is not affected by this personally.

The novel is also quite damning with regard to the myth of multiculturalism in Canada. This is neatly summed up in the following statement, which appears twice: "An immigrant story with a happy ending. Nothing is impossible. Within reason, of course" (212). The suggestion that, though not strictly impossible, such a happy ending is nevertheless rather unlikely, is further supported by the third part of the novel, which is no more than one page in length, headed by the title: "An Immigrant Story With a Happy Ending." This brevity hints at the "amputations" or "erasures" of experience which the immigrant has to suffer in order to fit into the supposedly multicultural fabric of Canadian society. She refers to all these amputations as "Part three. The missing part" (159): namely, whatever the immigrant loses. There is, however, a second level of meaning here. The combination of the title "An Immigrant Story With a Happy Ending" with the statement that this is "The missing part" leads one to think that the part that is missing from her story is the happy ending. This is further strengthened later in the novel when she again questions the possibility of breaking the cycle of prejudice to achieve a happy ending (212).

All this fits in with the description of the novel's scathing attack on Canadian multiculturalism which I have given so far. The problem, therefore, is to assess the extent to which the book is itself "An Immigrant Story With a Happy Ending," since not all the main characters find it so easy to come to terms with their presence in Canada. Keiko, Murasaki's mother, is probably the most static character in this respect. She is 'introduced' to her Japanese heritage by way of the Japanese food which her daughter feeds her while she is sick, and it is indeed the loss of this same heritage, symbolically figured in her mother's disappearance, that had brought on Keiko's sickness in the first place. Her recovery, then, appears to depend on Murasaki's cooking. The novel thus clearly indicates the importance of cultural tradition, as Keiko accepts parts of it that she had tried to suppress. At the same time, this recognition remains superficial, since there is no radical change in her and she later reverts for the most part to her usual behaviour.

Naoe, however, seems to go through a deeper change from the moment when she leaves the house. The prairie wind, which she had always fought against and viewed as an enemy, suddenly becomes both "sister" (81) and "child" (82). Her encounter and friendship with the truck driver who picks her up is also a thoroughly good one. The end of her story is particularly positive, as it tips over into magic, the unlikely, and the legendary. She goes to the Calgary Stampede, a yearly rodeo, where she appears as "The Purple Mask," a mysterious bullrider who shows up each year and who can ride better than all others. There may be nothing more associated with Alberta than the

Stampede, but Naoe loves it: she is glad to be there and her bullride is ecstatically joyous. There is no doubt that she gives up her isolationist attitude and is therefore much happier by the end of the novel.

Murasaki is the character whose change we accompany most closely. Her childhood shame at being Japanese-Canadian is gradually replaced, as I have suggested, by an increasing interest in her cultural heritage. She develops a very close relationship with her grandmother, which even becomes a sort of magical psychic or soul connection as she talks with her absent grandmother in moments of need throughout the novel. By the end of the story she seems to have come to terms with her position in Canada and even with her parents' choice to deny their Japanese heritage. She is also preparing to leave in order to find that part of her which she is "missing" (209), whether this is something cultural or totally personal. In any case, she is quite positive, and in fact Murasaki herself tells us: "This is a happy story. Can't you tell? I've been smiling all along" (197). The moment sounds genuine and devoid of irony, as her further development in the course of the novel appears to confirm. Murasaki seems to have reconciled the Canadian culture she lives in with the Japanese culture that somehow continues to inform her.

Part of this reconciliation depends on the telling of the story itself. One point which she repeatedly makes – and which Naoe, her grandmother, also makes in the parts narrated in her voice – is that she is "making up the truth" (12) in the act of telling or that "these stories keep changing" (73). The mixture of fact and fiction is thematized all through the novel, and it is this mixture, together with the fact that the stories are constantly changing, that is so important for Murasaki's attempt to reconcile the two parts of herself. It is here that she negotiates the turn to myth to which I have alluded in my title, in an attempt to create the roots which she needs in order to 'come home' in Canada. Murasaki repeatedly includes in her narration Japanese folk tales or legends that she was told by her grandmother. In some cases the legend does not seem to have any particular connection to the story of her grandmother, while in others it does. But what is really interesting is the fact that, upon a close reading, one discovers that there are points of interchange between the legends and Murasaki's narration. Indeed, at times elements from Murasaki's story – or even from the narrative frame in which she tells the story to her lover – work their way into the legends; while at other times her own story is patterned after one of the legends included in the narration, which in turn influences and changes the legend.

The following example is one that combines the narrative frame, the core story, and one of the myths related by Murasaki. Early in the novel, there is a scene from the narrative frame in which Murasaki and her lover get their fingers and tongue respectively stuck to the garage door on an "icy [...] Alberta winter day" (27). When they finally free themselves, Murasaki's fingers and her lover's tongue sting and burn, of course, and by dint of distraction from the pain Murasaki goes on telling her story to her lover. A few pages later, the image of burning fingers and tongues recurs. Murasaki includes in her narration a legend told by her grandmother which deals, significantly enough, with a boy and girl who leave their old home in search of a new one. At the end of the story, the two sit around and tell each other stories while eating roasted gingko nuts. However, because the nuts are too hot to eat, the boy and girl also end up "burning their fingertips and tongues in their eagerness to eat them" (32). The image crops up once more later, as part of the actual story of Murasaki's family. Naoe is thinking about her brother Shige and how they both used to love gingko nuts: "And Shige and I peeled them when they were still too hot, cracking the thin shell between our teeth and burning our tongues and fingertips" (50). The recurrence of this image on all three narrative levels causes the borders between these to dissolve. The connections between the narrative frame, the family saga, and the surrounding myths multiply and ramify in various ways, until they coalesce into one and the same experience.

It is thus unclear whether the myths have influenced Murasaki's narrative or whether she altered the myths in the act of telling. In any case, the effect is such that the story of her grandmother moves beyond fact or history into the realm of myth – Murasaki becomes a myth-maker. She can do this because she is aware of the open, integrative, and dynamic nature of myth. Claude Lévi–Strauss makes this point in the introduction to *The Raw and the Cooked*: "Since it has no interest in definite beginnings or endings, mythological thought never develops any theme to completion: there is always something left unfinished. Myths, like rite, are 'in-terminable'."[2] He goes on to state explicitly that myth by nature absorbs and is "affected by external influences."[3] This idea, that myths are malleable and open to transformation, is of course echoed by many theorists.[4] This openness allows one to integrate aspects of the current Canadian reality into the Japanese myths. Thus Murasaki's myths are constantly changing in the telling: they integrate aspects of her current reality and tinge the current reality with myth, legend, and magic. It is, then, significant that her last words in the novel are the following: "*You know you can change the story*" (220). This myth-making must be regarded as a step in the not yet complete process of settling into the world of Canada, because myth, according to Marc Chénetier, "allows individuals to find their place in [the real]."[5] Murasaki's myths do just that: they place her in Canada by acknowledging and drawing upon the cultural heritage which she had lost.

---

[2] Claude Lévi–Strauss, *The Raw and the Cooked: Introduction to a Science of Mythology*, tr. John & Doreen Weightman (New York: Octagon, 1979): 6.

[3] Lévi–Strauss, *The Raw and the Cooked*, 13.

[4] See, for example, Franz Josef Wetz, *Hans Blumenberg zur Einführung* (Hamburg: Junius, 1993); Kees W. Bolle, "Myth," in *The Encyclopedia of Religion; Vol. 10*, ed. Mircea Eliade (New York: Macmillan, 1987): 263; K.K. Ruthven, *Myth* (London: Methuen, 1976): 47 and 57–58; Northrop Frye, *Fables of Identity: Studies in Poetic Mythology* (San Diego CA: Harcourt Brace Jovanovich, 1951): 32; and Richard Kearney, "Between Tradition and Utopia: The Hermeneutical Problem of Myth," in *On Paul Ricoeur: Narrative and Interpretation*, ed. David Wood (London: Routledge, 1991), where he discusses Ricoeur's view of tradition, which is applicable to myth also: "Ricoeur refuses the tendency to dismiss tradition as something complete in itself and impervious to change. On the contrary, he urges us to reopen the past so as to reanimate its still unaccomplished potentialities" (50).

[5] Marc Chénetier, *Beyond Suspicion: New American Fiction Since 1960*, tr. Elizabeth A. Houlding (Liverpool: Liverpool UP, 1996): 164. This point is echoed by various other writers. See Lévi–Strauss, *The Raw and the Cooked*, 17–18; Joseph Campbell & Bill Moyers, *The Power of Myth*, ed. Betty Sue Flowers (Garden City NY: Doubleday, 1988): 4; and Mircea Eliade, *Myth and Reality* (London: Allen & Unwin, 1963): 2.

It would seem, then, that the novel is very contradictory. On the one hand, it is pessimistic regarding the Canadian multicultural undertaking and states that "An Immigrant Story With a Happy Ending" is a pipe-dream. On the other hand, it does seem to have a happy ending, as Naoe comes to terms with Canada and Murasaki goes about establishing roots in Canada by fashioning myths which integrate both Japan and Canada, past and present. How can one reconcile this apparent contradiction? I would argue that the key to a reconciliation lies in the distinction between the public and the private. The novel distinguishes between two levels of the immigrant's experience of multiculturalism in Canada – the public experience of acceptance or non-acceptance in a society which is often regarded as being in the vanguard of multicultural policy, and the private experience of settling into one's own personal Canada, which entails attempting to reconcile and join the current Canadian reality with one's heritage and roots. This distinction makes it possible to explain the novel's apparently schizo-phrenic nature. Indeed, the novel is quite pessimistic with regard to the public experi-ence of multiculturalism, but it proves optimistic in the same degree about the possibi-lities of privately introducing oneself into a culture, if one is open to exchange and willing to make stories and legends in and about Canada – which, in turn, will improve the public experience. It is this distinction that makes the novel so interesting – without this, it would read like a simple diatribe against Canada and the ostensible failures of multiculturalism. The distinction is thus necessary, for, while the public and political levels are incredibly important, as the novel testifies, it also demonstrates that the per-sonal 'arrival' in Canada cannot be forgotten. It is on this level that one develops roots, truly connects, and really 'comes home', and Naoe's defiant words resonate: "I'll walk and sing and laugh and shout. I'll scrape my heel into the black ice on the highway and inscribe my name across this country" (108).

But Goto's turn to myth in this novel has a much wider significance. I would claim that her use of myth is a perfect example of what is following upon the cultural move-ment which frames postcolonialism: ie, postmodernism. There is no other way to say it: postmodernism as we knew it is dead. We have slowly come to realize that post-modernism is a dead-end with no prospects, and it is time for us to turn around and re-connect. The journey was necessary, for we have learned its important lessons, the most relevant of them being that, in Lyotard's words, we should exercise "incredulity towards metanarratives."[6] However, in our critical fervour, we ended up dismantling and rejecting not only the dangerous and outdated metanarratives, but also some of the productive, living myths which gave our world meaning and allowed us to "find our place in the real." At the moment there are numerous cultural manifestations which evidence a desperate desire for connection, all of which, however, are perversions of connection, or connection twisted into alienation and isolation. I am thinking of the Internet, online chat rooms, mobile phones, and the television show *Big Brother*.

Goto's text is an example of a postcolonial text which shatters postmodern sceptic-ism and succeeds in reconstructing and reconnecting, in this case through myth. In-deed, the rejection of myth as another of the metanarratives that needed to be dis-

---

[6] Jean–François Lyotard, *The Postmodern Condition: A Report on Knowledge*, tr. Brian Mas-sumi (Minneapolis: U of Minnesota P, 1984): xxiv.

mantled usually overlooks the dynamic, open, and integrative nature of myth, which rejects closure. As Paul Ricoeur points out, if myth reaches closure then it has become "perverted," which implies that true myth is open.[7] Clearly, the lessons of postmodernism are not to be forgotten, and *Chorus of Mushrooms* is full of postmodern notions and narrative techniques. However, these lessons must be given a more positive twist. The prevailing cynicism about the subject, and the focus on rupture and isolation, must give way to a renewed valuing of the individual but also of his/her connection to the public and global sphere. Myth is an ideal vehicle for transporting us out of the postmodern dead-end, because it creates a frame within which we can place ourselves, which "give[s] back to a real that has been scaled down within our culture perspectives that make it open out before our eyes."[8] As I have suggested, this frame is flexible, open, and non-totalizing, as the individual, the regional, or the local retain the power to, in Murasaki's words, "change the story" (220). As Chénetier says, "it remains possible to have recourse to [myth] even after suspicion and history have alerted us to its perils" (170). In truth, myth has always been there, hidden though it was in the shade of postmodern scepticism. From its coffin, however, postmodernism no longer casts a shadow, and myth has re-emerged as an important element of what can perhaps be called "reconstructionism."

WORKS CITED

Bolle, Kees W. "Myth," in *The Encyclopedia of Religion*, vol. 10, ed. Mircea Eliade (New York: Macmillan, 1987): 261–73.

Campbell, Joseph, & Bill Moyers. *The Power of Myth*, ed. Betty Sue Flowers (Garden City NY: Doubleday, 1988).

Chénetier, Marc. *Beyond Suspicion: New American Fiction Since 1960*, tr. Elizabeth A. Houlding (Liverpool: Liverpool UP, 1996).

Eliade, Mircea. *Myth and Reality* (London: Allen & Unwin, 1963).

Frye, Northrop. *Fables of Identity: Studies in Poetic Mythology* (San Diego CA: Harcourt Brace Jovanovich, 1951).

Goto, Hiromi. *Chorus of Mushrooms* (Edmonton, Alberta: NeWest, 1994).

Kearney, Richard. "Between Tradition and Utopia: The Hermeneutical Problem of Myth," in *On Paul Ricoeur: Narrative and Interpretation*, ed. David Wood (London: Routledge, 1991): 55–73.

Lévi–Strauss, Claude. *The Raw and the Cooked: Introduction to a Science of Mythology*, tr. John & Doreen Weightman (New York: Octagon, 1979).

Lyotard, Jean–François. *The Postmodern Condition: A Report on Knowledge*, tr. Brian Massumi (Minneapolis: U of Minnesota P, 1984).

---

[7] As Paul Ricoeur says, "To the extent that myth is seen as the foundation of a particular community to the absolute exclusion of all others, the possibilities of perversion [...] are already present. [...] Myths are not unchanging and unchanged antiques which are simply delivered out of the past in some naked, original state." See Ricoeur, "Myth as the Bearer of Possible Worlds," in *Dialogues with Contemporary Continental Thinkers*, ed. Richard Kearney (Manchester: Manchester UP, 1984): 40.

[8] Chénetier, *Beyond Suspicion*, 167.

MARC COLAVINCENZO

Ricoeur, Paul. "Myth as the Bearer of Possible Worlds," in *Dialogues with Contemporary Continental Thinkers*, ed. Richard Kearney (Manchester: Manchester UP, 1984): 36–45.
Ruthven, K.K. *Myth* (London: Methuen, 1976).
Wetz, Franz Josef. *Hans Blumenberg zur Einführung* (Hamburg: Junius, 1993).

《●》

Postcolonial Cities
Michael Ondaatje's Toronto
and Yvonne Vera's Bulawayo

ROBERT FRASER

A MONG THE ACHIEVEMENTS of the age of high imperialism – which was also the great railway age – was the creation of a new kind of city. Empires thrive on trade; trade feeds off industries; industries require centres of collection, transportation and distribution. The characteristic colonial town, then, if it possible to speak of such an entity, existed at a railhead, or at the nexus between different modes of conveyance: water, rail or road. Toronto was the mart of the Dominion of Canada, a terminus for railroad and waterway on the shore of Lake Ontario, that basin of rivers. In Central Africa in the 1890s, the adventurer and con man Cecil Rhodes persuaded the Ndebele to part with their land. He then moved Lobengula's *kraal* of Bulawayo, the "place of slaughter", three miles to the South, and set his stamp on it. It became a meeting place for trade, and the location of the Rhodesia Railway headquarters, conveniently close to the border with South Africa.

For the inhabitants of such settlements, the defining moment was that of arrival. Patrick Lewis, the protagonist of Michael Ondaatje's novel *In the Skin of a Lion* (1987), a study of urban friction in pre-Second World War Canada, has grown up among the timberlands and livestock farms of Western Ontario. Arriving in Toronto – Ondaatje's own city of adoption – he hesitates under the arches of Union Station: "Patrick sat on a bench and watched the tides of movement, felt the reverberations of trade. He spoke out his name and it struggled up in a hollow echo and was lost in the high air of Union Station. No one turned. They were in the belly of the whale."[1] The Zimbabwean novelist Yvonne Vera sets her fourth book, *Butterfly Burning*, a decade later in Makokoba township in Bulawayo.[2] Among its descriptive *tours de force* is an evocation of the central station, where Fourth Class ticket-holders with nowhere to go congregate and sleep.

---

[1] Michael Ondaatje, *In the Skin of A Lion* (London: Picador, 1988): 54.

[2] Vera was born and raised in Bulawayo. After a period spent in Toronto, she worked as the Director of the National Gallery in Zimbabwe. She died in early April 2005, aged forty.

"They are here," the narrator remarks, "to gather a story about the city."[3] They waylay the next wave of hopefuls with impossible tales: "the heels of black women clicking red shoes against the pavement and holding matching bags close to their bodies clad in tight slacks"[4] The neophytes practise unfamiliar vocabularies: "to describe a teacup, that is something else, it is necessary to creep up and peep through the windows or wander into the First Class waiting-rooms in order to say saucer with the right meaning." They hang around for the mere glamour of being here.

Such moments are colonial epiphanies observed with postcolonial hindsight. The anticipation and confusion of the newcomer are interpreted by a mind that has seen beyond them, foreseeing consequences. Ondaatje's Toronto and Vera's Bulawayo are bold imperial spaces that a resistant intellect has converted into traps. For Ondaatje, the mere existence of the *polis* is an act of fantasy or hubris. In an early passage he describes the civic impresario Commissioner Rowland Harris lying in bed in Neville Park, dreaming up an Augustinian "ideal city," to be achieved by bringing water from the lake though the Bloor Park Viaduct and St Clair Reservoir. Above the reservoir the Commissioner plans to erect a Byzantine-style municipal palace, gleaming with metalwork. The city in Harris's mind is both monumental and dynamic; it is late Romantic and decadent, a swarming hive. Alert to literary parallels, he confounds local opposition by quoting Baudelaire: "The form of a city changes faster than the human heart."[5]

The postcolonial novelist tends to distrusts such visions. For Ondaatje as for Vera, the novel does not so much express the structure of the city as posit an alternative art form. Both replace the symmetry of municipal organization with a disorder that they then arrange in a shape of their own, one less crushing, more alive to nuances of behaviour. As Ondaatje puts it, *"Only the best art can order the chaotic tumble of events. Only the best can realign chaos to suggest both the chaos and order it will become."*[6] Ondaatje's novel is initially impressed by Harris's urban dream but, like its principal character, it learns to dissent from it. Ultimately it excoriates the agendas of planner and civic official alike. In both of these books, the cities evoked are in effect deconstructed. In the process a corresponding overhaul is performed on the novel genre, turning it into a vehicle for a revolutionary, an anarchic urban consciousness.

Neither city, for example, is seen as the planners envisage it: as an integral community. Instead, each is glimpsed in miscellaneous snatches, polyglossic and precociously multicultural. Makokoba township, as Vera describes it, is a place of shifting allegiances and extravagant strangers, as daunting and challenging as the Harare of her third novel, *Without A Name*. It is a place of secrets, an environment that author and protagonist alike must constantly re-invent. Its emotional life, too, is improvised and precarious. In one passage, Phephelaphi, the ambitious and ardent young woman at the heart of the story, wonders what happened to the neighbourhood girls she grew up with. "Such girls had all but vanished. Instead, they had discovered a swinging slingbag love, a sunhat,

[3] Yvonne Vera, *Butterfly Burning* (Harare: Baobab, 1998): 45.
[4] Vera, *Butterfly Burning*, 47.
[5] Ondaatje, *In the Skin of a Lion*, 109.
[6] *In the Skin of a Lion*, 146 (italics in original).

sunglass, sunshine kind of love which burned out quicker than hope."[7] One of the few things that holds the township community together is music, the music of the street, the music of the *shebeens*. It draws the people like a magnet. Its lure sustains and destroys them.

Toronto, as Ondaatje realizes it, is a town without orthodoxies, full of surprises. When Patrick Lewis takes a job working alongside European migrants on Commissioner Harris's reservoir, he enters a world where every syllable of survival has to be learned anew: "The southeastern section of the city where he now lived was made up mostly of immigrants and he walked everywhere not hearing any language he knew, deliriously anonymous. The people of the street, the Macedonians and Bulgarians, were his only mirror. Her worked in the tunnels with them."[8] Harris's projects are constructed by such men, but he knows few of them, and few of them know him. Among these motley crowds Patrick drifts as an interloper, his only human contact being with the store where he buys food for his pet iguana. His anonymity is his freedom.

This creative anonymity extends to the reader, towards whom both novelists are merciless in their demands. Neither book possesses a consequential and consecutive plot. Instead, each writer assembles a collage, or a jigsaw puzzle with selected pieces missing. Patrick, for example, spends much of the first part of the book searching for a runaway plutocrat ironically named Ambrose Small. He proves as elusive as the city itself, or the mysterious protagonist of Ondaatje's second novel *The English Patient*, or as Sailor, the enigmatic murder victim in the recent *Anil's Ghost*. This is how Patrick's successive women appear to him as well, a shifting charade: "a series of masks or painted faces."[9] Ondaatje heightens this sense of fugitive reality by deliberately withholding clues. Half-way through the book, for example, Patrick's Marxist girlfiend Alice Gull dies. Although the circumstances change him forever, we are not told until much later how and why she perished. In the book's closing pages we find out that Alice has been the accidental victim of an anarchist's bomb. The information helps make sense of Patrick's vengefulness, his resentment against the city, which until then has seemed like a meaningless vendetta, a grudge without correlative motive. By such means Ondaatje makes extreme requirements of the reader, left for much of the narrative to wander like a migrant amidst turnings and side-turnings. After one such analepsis, he remarks: "The first sentence of every novel should be: 'Trust me, this will take time but there is order here, very faint, very human'."[10]

Vera delights in a very similar elusiveness. Phephelaphi has been raised by a woman called Gertrude, whom she believes to be her mother. In fact, her blood mother is Zandile, a local good-time girl. We do not learn these facts until six pages before the close of the book, and neither does Phephelaphi. She mildly despises Zandile, whom we belatedly learn has given up the chance to bring her up because lured by the multiple delusions of the city: "The city was beckoning and she had just knocked on its large waiting door. She was determined to find its flamboyant edges, its colour and light, and above

---

[7] Vera, *Butterfly Burning*, 79.
[8] Ondaatje, *In the Skin of a Lion*, 112.
[9] *In the Skin of a Lion*, 128.
[10] *In the Skin of a Lion*, 146.

all else if she could, then a man too to call her own. She needed lightness. That is what the city offered not the burden of becoming a mother."[11] Before she has learned these facts, Phephelaphi has induced an abortion on herself, in the certainty that her pregnancy will prevent her continuing to study to become Rhodesia's first black nurse. Like her mother before her, she has chosen freedom. The city exacts its revenge when she loses the respect and love of her middle-aged lover Fumbatha, himself tormented by memories of his father, brutally hanged after an act of collective protest in 1896, soon after the foundation of colonial Bulawayo.

Fumbatha has told Phephelaphi nothing of his history, and Zandile has been as silent about their relationship. The resulting enigmas produce throughout the book a peculiar transformative grammar of person and of gender.[12] When Phephelaphi is brusquely informed of her true identity by Fumbatha, the narrative, until then in the third person, swings abruptly into the first. The reader is again disorientated by a recognition that the syntax of recital has been a cover for an implied confessional monologue.[13]

By such means, both novels replace the official rhythms of the city with an informal music all its own. The "human" order that Ondaatje proposes, for example, is an alternative to the formal structures of Toronto, something etched against the economic infrastructure of the town. In both of these novels, the informal and shifting patterns of allegiance described are carefully defined against the economic life of the city. This is important because, for much of the time, they share a similar historical background: inter-war Depression and the New Deal in one case; post-war reconstruction in the other. The contrast between these political and economic initiatives and the lives of the characters is worked out stylistically. Both books in effect represent postmodern accounts of High Modernism. The vivid life of the streets is proposed as a series of *fin-de-siècle* reactions to the age of planning. Ondaatje's narrator, for example, seems preternaturally aware of some sort of gigantism creeping over the globe. In the year 1938, he observes, "The longest bridge in the world was being built over the lower Zambesi and the great water-works at the east end of Toronto neared completion."[14] In Ondaatje's book, such developments seem like a sinister proto-Fascist preamble to the unspoken threat of war. In both books, however, the economic life of the city is something against which its human reality is articulated and expressed.

In the prevailing economic dispensation, the working-class citizen has become a cipher in schemes of reconstruction that both novels consciously resist and transform. Both Ondaatje and Vera excel in evoking the drudgery of official work schemes, which they convert into a kind of subversive poetry. High above the Bloor Street Viaduct hangs Nicholas Temelcoff, a labourer from Macedonia. In the eyes of his employers, the Dominion Bridge Company, Temelcoff is a navvy: "a man is an extension of hammer,

---

[11] Vera, *Butterfly Burning,* 124.

[12] For a fuller investigation of such usages, see Robert Fraser, *Lifting the Sentence: A Poetics of Postcolonial Fiction* (Manchester & New York: Manchester UP, 2000), 65–98.

[13] The whole novel, in fact, represents an extended exercise in what I have called the "implied first person." See *Lifting the Sentence,* 87–93.

[14] Ondaatje, *In the Skin of a Lion,* 209.

drill, flame."[15] In Ondaatje's prose he becomes a dancer, the choreography of his skill exultant:

> Nicholas Temelcoff is famous on the bridge, a daredevil. He is given all the difficult jobs and he takes them. He descends into the air with no fear. He is a solitary. He assembles ropes, brushes the tackle and pulley at his waist, and falls off the bridge like a diver over the edge of a boat. The rope roars alongside him, slowing with the pressure of his half-gloved hands. He is burly on the ground and then falls with terrific speed, grace, using the wind to push himself into corners of abutments so he can check driven rivets, sheering valves, the drying of the concrete under bearing plates and padstones.[16]

In one episode, Nicholas Temelcoff is hanging suspended at his work when a nun, who has wandered by mistake across the incomplete viaduct, falls over the parapet towards him. He swings outwards and catches her with one outstretched arm. The piece of improvisation saves her life; it also changes him from operative to redeemer.

In the opening passage of her book, Vera describes the sweating labourers cutting the long grass in Makokoba Township with equivalent understanding. Their effort is bought, but it is also balletic:

> Their supple but unwilling arms turn, loop and merge with the shiny tassels of the golden grass whose stem is still green, like newborn things, and held firmly to the earth. The movement of their arms is like weaving, as their arms thread through each thicket, and withdraw. The careful motion is patterned like a dance spreading out, each sequence rises like hope enacted and set free. Freed, stroke after stroke, holding briskly, and then a final whisper of release. The grass falls.[17]

There is a parallel here with the celebrated "mowing" passage in *Anna Karenina*, but Vera's vision takes her well beyond Tolstoy's. She observes the way these men transform the alienation of production – neutral, degrading in itself – into a form of aesthetic expression by personalizing, even eroticizing it. This is labour not as compliance, or spiritual service as in Tolstoy, but as signalled protest, potential revolution.

The revolutionary reflex is faithfully reproduced by both authors. In each case it corresponds to a cycle of baffled desire and pointed destruction. Once again, there are nineteenth-century precedents: Elizabeth Gaskell's stories of Manchester life, for instance. For Ondaatje and Vera, however, there is no saving complicity with the *status quo*. Vera's perspective is caught in a passage half-way through her book in which she describes an accidental spill of grain from the Baloos neighbourhood store. It provokes a scuffle or riot as

> the crowd falls together and the bodies bend to the ground and finds between the ground and the wild vacancy in their hearts, the flour mixed with the soil, and with folded Fanta bottle tops, burnt matchsticks and a multitude of yellow cigarette stubs which say Peter Stuyvesant in pale white – and they gather this mess into the small metal bowls which they

[15] Ondaatje, *In the Skin of a Lion*, 26.
[16] *In the Skin of a Lion*, 34.
[17] Vera, *Butterfly Burning*, 2.

have brought, and examine it closely. Perhaps, between the grains of sand and the smoother grains of Red Seal Roller Meal, there was hope. They find none.[18]

Vera perfectly captures the flux of communal emotions: the limitless greed, the confusion, the grasping, final shame on recognizing that nothing has been gained.

The desire, disillusionment and anger are matched in Ondaatje's story by Alice Gull's account of the life of Toronto's bourgeoisie. In Gull's committed vision, it is counterpointed against the degradation and the stinking toil of Wickett and Craig's tannery, where Patrick is currently working:

> "I'll tell you about the rich," Alice would say, "the rich are always laughing. They keep on saying the same things on their boats and lawns: *Isn't this grand! We're having a good time!* And whenever the rich get drunk and maudlin about humanity you have to listen for hours. But they keep you in the tunnels and stockyards. They do not toil or spin. Remember that …"[19]

This is the very self-indulgence, and the sentimental philanthropy attending it, that Patrick, and through Patrick the novel, seeks to destroy.

The violence in both of these novels is therefore viewed as an expression both of anger and of thwarted desire Significantly, both books are obsessed with the *motif* of conflagration. In a brilliant concluding scene, Phephelaphi sets light to herself and her dreams, expiring as the butterfly burning of the title. The apotheosis is alarming; it is also beautiful. It is as if Phephelaphi has at last created from herself an aesthetic phenomenon worthy of her aspirations, the true expression of her colourful transience: "She is lightness, floating like flame, with flame. The flames wrap the human form, arms, knees that are herself, a woman holding her pain like a torn blanket."[20]

Alice Gull instructs Patrick to turn his violence against Commissioner Harris and all his works: "You name the enemy and destroy their power. Start with their luxuries – their select clubs, their summer mansions."[21] Accordingly, after Alice's death, Patrick torches the Muskoka Hotel, a haunt of the Ontario rich. He is jailed, and on his release makes an attempt to blow up Harris's now completed waterworks. Explosives strapped to his torso, he swims through the tunnel he once helped build, and confronts Harris amidst the tawdry splendours of his Art Deco palace. Two dreams face one another: the municipal Romantic and the postcolonial sceptical. "You forgot us," pleads Patrick, assuming the voice of the common man. Harris reacts with the standard New Deal justification: "I hired you." To which Patrick responds "Your goddam herringbone tiles in the toilets cost more than half our salaries put together."[22]

This closing scene has an immediacy that reminds the reader of the confrontational and irrational politics of Ondaatje's Sri Lanka. It anticipates the surreal and macabre world of *Anil's Ghost*. The affinity alerts us to the fact that Ondaatje, like Vera, has

---

[18] Vera, *Butterfly Burning*, 38.

[19] Ondaatje, *In the Skin of a Lion*, 132.

[20] Vera, *Butterfly Burning*, 128

[21] Ondaatje, *In the Skin of a Lion*, 124–25.

[22] *In the Skin of a Lion*, 235–36.

projected a complex postcolonial consciousness onto the screen of the historical novel. Although both books are set in periods when imperialism was apparently in full stride, the protagonists of each act as interpreters from a viewpoint that constantly shifts towards the reader's own. The city is a script written with a confident message that the novel re-inscribes and undermines. A process of defamiliarization is at work, as a result of which the common coin of colonial development – the fits and starts of progress, the oppression, the drift of events – is converted into a currency validated by freedom. Not the least of the advantages is a radical reassessment of the colonial enterprise itself. Vera has managed this feat several times before – in *Nehanda* with its recreation of the life and death of a female freedom fighter of the 1890s, in *Without A Name* with its angular perception of the private consequences of the civil war of the 1970s. In *Butterfly Burning* a colonial city of the 1940s and 1950s is radically redescribed by being mapped from its edges. In a sense, too, like Toronto in Ondaatje's book, it is evoked backwards, since episodes early in the story only make sense in the light of subsequent events. Among her most successful effects is Vera's word-painting of the public hanging of Fumbatha's father and his co-insurgents way back in the 1890s. Like Phephelaphi's self-incineration in the book's closing pages, it becomes a scene of aesthetic delight revitalized by language. The image used is that of drowning: "The voices of drowned men cannot be heard. They die in infinite solitude. The air leaves their bodies in a liquid breeze. [...] They touch the surface with their faces, not their arms, with their lips. Nothing will bring them back."[23]

   The fact is, that they have been brought back; their voices have been heard. It is Vera who has ventriloquized them, just as Ondaatje has given vent to the perceptions of the Toronto underclass. Both novels are achievements of an intelligent and unblinkered love for particular places. Ondaatje possesses a fierce but disenchanted attachment to Toronto, and Vera has a passionate and sad appreciation of Bulawayo. Each creates a world that is imaginatively prophetic of our own transcultural reality. The anachronism is part of their point. Ondaatje's Toronto and Vera's Bulawayo are postcolonial cities.

WORKS CITED

Fraser, Robert. *Lifting the Sentence: A Poetics of Postcolonial Fiction* (Manchester & New York: Manchester UP, 2000).
Ondaatje, Michael. *In the Skin of a Lion* (1987; London: Picador, 1988).
Vera, Yvonne. *Butterfly Burning* (Harare: Baobab, 1998).

《●》

---

[23] Vera, *Butterfly Burning*, 7.

"Hybridize or Disappear"
Exploring the Hyphen in Fred Wah's *Diamond Grill*

SUSANNE HILF

H OW TO DESCRIBE ONESELF not fitting into the commonly advertised norms of occidental and oriental 'culture'?"[1] This was one of the central issues raised by Asian-Canadian artists during an exhibition in Vancouver in 1990. Fred Wah's memoir *Diamond Grill*, published in 1996, can be considered as one of the literary answers to this question. Part (auto)biography, part fiction, Wah's "biotext," as he himself calls *Diamond Grill*,[2] is a poetic journey into his family's and thus, ultimately, his own past. Coming from a truly 'hybrid' family, Wah in this memoir explores his mixed-race heritage: his father, of Chinese and Scottish descent, was born in Canada but spent much of his youth in China before returning to North America as an adult; his Swedish mother immigrated to Canada when she was still a child.

Taking Wah's multifaceted hyphen as a starting-point and drawing on Homi K. Bhabha's ideas about the articulation of cultural difference(s),[3] this essay explores how Wah's prose text strategically blurs boundaries: textual and stylistic, temporal and spatial as well as cultural and ethnic boundaries. It will become clear that *Diamond Grill* is more than a very personal and idiosyncratic negotiation of a Eurasian identity. Wah in his memoir challenges simplistic models of ethnicity and explicitly criticizes Canada's concept of multiculturalism, which, favouring rigid and homogenous ethnic categories, does not provide room for 'mongrels' or 'half-breeds' like him.

Owing to his multicultural background, Wah does not fit into any well-defined categories; consequently, his text is marked by a prevailing sense of not belonging to a specific ethnic group. A recurring memory, for example, is his experience of how eth-

---

[1] Larissa Lai & Jean Lum, "Neither Guests nor Strangers," in *Yellow Peril Reconsidered: Photo, Film, Video*, ed. Paul Wong (Vancouver: On Edge, 1990): 20.

[2] "Acknowledgements," *Diamond Grill* (Edmonton, Alberta: NeWest, 1996): np. All further quotations are taken from this edition.

[3] Homi K. Bhabha, *The Location of Culture* (London & New York: Routledge, 1994).

nic minority groups are dealt with in a world which knows only 'pure', and ultimately abstract, racial categories:

> When I was in elementary school we had to fill out a form at the beginning of each year. The first couple of years I was really confused. The problem was the blank after racial origin. I thought, well, this is Canada, I'll put down Canadian. But the teacher said no Freddy, you're Chinese, your racial origin is Chinese, that's what your father is. Canadian isn't really a racial identity. That's turned out to be true. But I'm not really Chinese either. Nor were some of the other kids in my class *real* Italian, Doukhobor, or British. Quite a soup. Heinz 57 Varieties. There's a whole bunch of us who've grown up as resident aliens, living in the hyphen. (53, emphasis in the original)

The hyphen, "this flag of the many in the one yet 'less than one and double'," as Wah writes, becomes the focal point of his "poetics of opposition."[4] The hyphen is a silence made audible or a "negative transparency"[5] turned into a site for unearthing the ambivalence of hybridity. As Bhabha repeatedly stresses, hybridity must not be understood as a simple synthesis resolving the tension between two cultures.[6] Rather, it is "a persistent thorn in the side of colonial configurations,"[7] a disturbance of purist discourse, or, simply but provokingly put, "heresy."[8] And heresy, too, characterizes Wah's family chronicle, especially in terms of form and genre: *Diamond Grill* merges fiction and fact as well as reflection and description; it amalgamates first-person-narrative, dialogue and free indirect discourse, and thus transgresses all generic boundaries.

The book consists of 132 short prose texts of one to two pages each, some interspersed with a poem or documentary material such as newspaper clippings, some provided with annotations. As this unusual formal structure already implies, *Diamond Grill* – even though it can be called a memoir – differs widely from the conventions of (auto)biographical writing, such as chronology, causality, factuality and authenticity. In accordance with the book's fragmentary structure, the temporal pattern is neither linear nor chronological, mirroring the fact that a life can never be grasped in its entirety and completeness and that all a literary adaptation can provide is an erratic collection of impressions and glimpses of memory. *Diamond Grill* transcends the various time levels, jumping back and forth in history, oscillating between present and past. Logically, such a whirling chronicle cannot be teleological: there is no progress, no development, no culmination. Preparing the reader for the achronological journey through time, Wah on the very first page emphasizes that the beginning as well as the ending of his biotext are arbitrary. The opening words do not necessarily constitute the only possible point of entry into the narrative, and the ending is not a definite and

---

[4] "Half-Bred Poetics," in Fred Wah, *Faking It: Poetics and Hybridity; Critical Writing 1984–1999* (Edmonton, Alberta: NeWest, 2000): 73. Wah is here quoting the Indian theorist and critic Homi K. Bhabha's essay "Signs Taken for Wonders" in *Race, Writing & Difference,* ed. Henry Louis Gates, Jr. (Chicago: U of Chicago P, 1996): 177.

[5] Bhabha, *The Location of Culture,* 112.

[6] *The Location of Culture,* 113.

[7] Wah, "Half-Bred Poetics," 74.

[8] Bhabha, *The Location of Culture,* 225.

ultimate ending, either: "The journal journey tilts tight-fisted through the gutter of the book, avoiding a place to start – or end. Maps don't have beginnings, just edges. Some frayed and hazy margin of possibility, absence, gap" (1). With these words, which function as a *caveat lector*, the author/narrator clarifies that his version is only one of numerous imaginable variations of his family history – just as the ordering of different countries on a map is always only one possible way of depicting the globe.

The metaphors of maps and mapping, on the one hand, bring to mind the highly subjective representation of the world involved in life-writing (usually centred on one's own experiences and reality); on the other hand, they also touch upon the idea of spatiality, which plays a crucial role in *Diamond Grill*. The genealogy outlined by Wah has numerous ramifications. The family tree, a "dendrite map," as it says in the title of one of Wah's earlier poems,[9] spans the world; consequently, the chronicle is not restricted to the family's past in Canada but expands temporally and spatially. Intermingling the divergent experiences of the various family members, it links places as disparate and distant as Asia, Europe and North America. Although Wah primarily focuses on his half-Chinese father, his mother as well as other relatives are also granted a place in this extended family saga.

The multiplicity of nations and cultures referred to in *Diamond Grill* is paralleled by a multiplicity of voices. Wah's recollection of the past is no monologue; rather, it has a dialogic structure. He often addresses his parents and grandparents directly, asking them questions and imagining their answers, or he has them relate certain events of their lives themselves, thus allowing them their own voices. Such dialogism inevitably ruptures monologic discourse and calls into question the author's/narrator's position of power. Although it is Wah (as both author and as narrating I) who orchestrates and orders the polyphony, he never lays claim to the truth or to representational authority. On the contrary, as the brief disclaimer preceding the actual text further illustrates, he knows that the re-creation of his family history is always an unambiguously *imaginative* act: "These are not true stories, but, rather, poses or postures, necessitated as I hope is clear from the text, by faking it" (no page). Although it so obviously branches out into the fictitious realm, Wah's chronicle – by openly and uncompromisingly challenging the concepts of omniscience, authenticity and truthfulness – seems to be more honest than much forcefully 'factual' life-writing.

Whether fictitious or factual, the family story rendered by Wah counters homogeneity on more than just the level of genre. For instance, the family's particular linguistic code, too, refrains from being monolithic. As the author informs his readers, the idiolect of the Wah family, especially of the author's Chinese grandfather and father, is not only made up of English and Chinese phrases but turns out to be an intricate mixture of various languages. Being closely based on the so-called Chinook jargon, "the pidgin vocabulary of colonial interaction, the code switching talkee-talkee of the contact zone" (68), it also includes elements of the indigenous peoples' languages. By incorporating such a 'creole' form of communication, the collision and fusion of different languages, into his work, Wah articulates the intercultural encounter of the various

---

[9] "This Dendrite Map: Father/Mother Haibun," in Wah, *Waiting for Saskatchewan* (Winnipeg, Manitoba: Turnstone, 1985): 73–96.

peoples in North America and explicitly situates his family among the long and certainly not always harmonious tradition of colonial interaction:

> Whenever I hear grampa talk like that, high muckamuck, sitkum dollah, I think he's
> sliding Chinese words into English words just to have a little fun. He has fun alright,
> but I now realize he also enjoys mouthing the dissonance of encounter, the resonance
> of clashing tongues, his own membership in the diasporic and nomadic intersections
> that have occurred in northwest North America over the past one hundred and fifty
> years. (68)

In this passage Wah evokes a certain sense of uneasiness, of friction (with words such
as "dissonance" and "clashing"), which functions as a reminder, albeit subdued, of the
painful history of colonialism, migration and diaspora – quite in accordance with
Bhabha's claim that hybridity does not merely signify an unproblematic fusion or
synthesis.

The friction and discord involved in hybridity are further stressed by the polymorphous style of the chronicle: Wah switches between laconically sober passages and
poetic rhapsodies, between elliptic phrases and the stream-of-consciousness technique
or the listing of nouns in a catalogue-like manner. This colourful clash of styles and
tonalities serves Wah to express his various emotions, such as the love and affection
for his father and mother or the insecurity he feels when in Chinatown. Anger, in
particular, features largely in *Diamond Grill* and shines through many of the book's
paratactical passages:

> Just another tight lipped high muckamuck reception listening to the whining groans of an
> old-fart pink-faced investor worried about the Hong Kong real estate takeover, a wincing
> glance as he moans that UBC has become the University of a Billion Chinks, tense
> shoulder scrunch as I'm introduced, with emphasis on the Wah, to his built-and-fought-
> for-inheritor-of-the-country arrogant, raised-eyebrow, senior executive entrepreneur boss
> pig business associate. (165)

This passage nicely illustrates one of the sources of this anger – the reaction of
anglophone Canadians to the 'Other', to the immigrant or 'alien' of non-European
background.[10] Apart from such allusions to the at times subtle, at times explicit racism
and discrimination he has experienced, Wah furthermore evokes the history of the
Chinese in Canada, a history shaped by racist attitudes and legalized discrimination.
He refers to the Exclusion Act, which prohibited Chinese immigration to Canada from
1923 until 1947 (10, 85, 110, 113), as well as to other discriminating policies (55, 57),
to the Head Tax the Chinese immigrants had to pay (130–31) and to the construction of
the Canadian Pacific Railway (57, 79), which cost the lives of many Chinese labourers.
Reviving a forgotten or silenced history figures prominently in much minority writing:
as Wah himself states, all hybrid writers – be they mixed-bloods, immigrants or visible
minorities – seek to recuperate, to make palpable "what has been otherwise 'denied

---

[10] Wah himself called *Diamond Grill* "a work about racial anger". See [http://www.acs
.ucalgary.ca/~wah], visited May 25, 1998.

knowledges'."[11] Nevertheless, the evocation of Chinese-Canadian history does not form the basis of Wah's identity-formation (as it does in many other texts by ethnic minority writers). Rather, these historical events are further pieces in his mosaic-like family chronicle. For Wah, the "Diamond Grill," a family-owned restaurant in Nelson, B.C., is origin as well as pivot of his literary journey through present and past.

The café, described in meticulous and loving detail, lies at the heart of Wah's memoir (and memory). Consequently, his exploration of the past takes the form of a culinary journey: distinct smells and tastes are recurring elements of the book; rather than functioning as decorative embellishment, these sensory experiences trigger associations, inscribing an Asian past into a Canadian present. "Taste carries images" (168), Wah writes, and in a passage reminiscent of Marcel Proust's famous madeleine-episode he recalls how his grandfather seems to be lost in memories of his old life when eating rice soup: "A great distance dwells in his face. [...] I always think it's China, mysterious [...]. How taste remembers life. Sipping underneath that wet, burned rice [...] in his gaze is some long night far away on the other side of earth in other eyes and other pots" (74).

Although Wah here evokes the smells of Asian cuisine, he does not attempt to spur exoticism or to underline cultural contrast. Instead of elaborating on the different names or appearance of Chinese dishes, Wah centres on their smell and taste: ie, on very individual and subjective experiences. Besides, his memories are not restricted to Chinese food. The café where Wah spent most of his childhood is no purely oriental 'bastion' on the Canadian prairies. Milkshakes and Salisbury steak, Christmas turkey and apple pie are as much part of the Diamond Grill's menu as are "chicken or pork chow mein" and "egg foo young" (45). In accordance with the formal amalgamations, however, there are no rigid separations on the culinary level, either, in the same way as one mixes together the various ingredients when cooking. Going one step further, one could even read some of the dishes on offer in the café as metaphors of hybridity, such as the omnipresent "mixee grill" ("the typical improvised imitation of empire cuisine" (2)) or juk, which Wah himself describes as "a soup we always have after New Year's because it's made with left-over turkey. I think of it as the bridge between our white Christmas (presents and turkey stuffing) and our Chinese New Year (firecrackers and juk)" (167).

A similar metaphoric function is attributed to the café, which becomes the site of intercultural confrontation. At first glance, Wah seems to be working with a fixed dualism. The door which separates the dining room of the café from the kitchen signifies the cultural boundary between China and Canada: it is "the wooden slab that swings between the Occident and Orient" (16). The kitchen, the Orient, is the world of the Chinese cooks, "[there] echoes a jargon of curses, jokes, and cryptic orders. Stack a hots! Half a dozen fry! Hot beef san! Fingers and tongues all over the place jibe and swear You mucka high! [...]" (1). On the other side lies the Occident, "the white world out front" (63). However, just like the hyphen, "that marked (or unmarked) space that both binds and divides,"[12] the door, a swinging panel with windows, not only separates

---

[11] Wah, "Half-Bred Poetics," 74. Wah is here quoting Bhabha, *The Location of Cultures*, 181.

[12] Wah, "Half-Bred Poetics," 72.

SUSANNE HILF

but also connects the two worlds. The dualism is thus not kept up but soon blurs, especially since further doors and additional rooms (128, 164) as well as the basement (118) and the cold storage room (100) undermine the idea of a clearly divided locality.

Both the café and Wah's family can hence be read as microcosms of a truly hybrid rather than bicultural Canada: ie, of a nation whose citizens, due to mixing and inter-racial marriages, can no longer easily be 'classified' or 'dissected'. Furthermore, both the Wah family and the restaurant undermine the idea of a monolithic cultural strong-hold: "Chow, Freschi, Gee, Prysiaznuk, Yee, D'Andrea, Leier, Lyon, Wah. Never know they're all cousins" (84), Wah laconically lists the consequences of the numer-ous marriages across races and cultures that occurred among his parents and grand-parents. Nevertheless, despite these pluralistic family structures, Wah abstains from projecting a multicultural paradise; *Diamond Grill* does not gloss over the tensions and difficulties which arise even within the own family but instead exposes them, espe-cially the hostility towards his half-Asian father: "They wouldn't speak to me until after you were born, my mother explains when I ask her how [her Swedish family] reacted to her marrying a Chinaman" (13).

Wah's attitude towards his hyphenated identity is complex and complicated. He does not celebrate his cultural hybridity without reservations and repeatedly recalls the problems brought about by his liminality and the confusion he has been feeling ever since he was a child. For example, despite his rather Caucasian physiognomy (39), he is subject to derogatory remarks by other children: "I'm fairly blond in grade four and still she calls me a Chink. Out loud in the schoolyard at Central School, and with her eyes too, real daggers, a painful spike" (39). But the Chinese children do not accept him as one of them, either: "the Chinese kids who came over after 1949 couldn't take me into their confidence. I always ended up playing on the other team, against them, because I was white enough" (53). Since Wah's multi-ethnic origin eludes absolute norms and classifications, only the individual articulation of his unfixed 'Otherness' and its imaginative (re)construction in literature provides orientation. "We would rather be anywhere, as long as we are somewhere. We would rather be anyone, as long as we are someone" (139); Wah stresses the basic and necessary human need for home and for identity. For mongrels like him, whose search for identity cannot be solved simply by identification with some pre-existing sign system, the fulfilment of this basic need lies in establishing an idiosyncratic hybridity, both in life and in literature. "I don't want to be inducted into someone else's story, or project" (125), Wah angrily underlines his refusal to be appropriated or subsumed under a specific ethnic or cul-tural grouping. "Hybridize or disappear" (20) can thus be understood as his central poetological credo, which lies at the basis of his family biography and his own inter-cultural history.

And yet, despite its very personal nature, Wah's memoir is not restricted to the private realm but openly challenges the political conditions of the writer's home country, particularly the Canadian policy of multiculturalism. As Wah repeatedly em-phasizes, ethnic purity is rare in Canada: "there's a whole forest of us out here who don't like clear-cut, suspect the mechanical purity of righteous, clear, shining, Home-lite Americas" (125). The realities of those who have been, in Wah's words, "geneti-cally diluted" (125), are not recognized under the Multiculturalism Act. The Act's

major shortcoming, as has frequently been pointed out in recent decades, is the fact
that it is rooted in the assumption that cultures are natural and unchangeable givens:
"As a plan for managing cultural diversity, multicultural policy constructs communities in terms of an ethnic absolutism which results in separate and homogeneous
entities," observes Sneja Gunew, and Michael Thorpe, quite polemically, even speaks
of "the soft apartheid of multiculturalism."[13] The much contested Canadian mosaic
thus symbolizes little more than an ossified or frozen heterogeneity which reduces the
different cultures to a small number of seemingly idiosyncratic yet merely stereotypical characteristics – "Culture Disneyfied," as Neil Bissoondath aptly calls it.[14]

Such a fixed division, which leaves no room for those people who evade these categories and which ignores the permeability and fluidity of all cultural systems, also lies
at the heart of the criticism voiced by Homi K. Bhabha, who explains the promulgation
of cultural diversity as a political strategy of those in power to cement differences and
hierarchies: "Cultural diversity is [...] the representation of a radical rhetoric of the
separation of totalized cultures."[15] Against this controlled diversity Bhabha formulates
his concept of "cultural difference." "Cultural difference," he explains, "is the process
of the enunciation of culture as 'knowledge*able*', authoritative, adequate to the construction of systems of cultural identification."[16] In other words, he propagates a model
which, focusing on the articulation of difference, emphasizes the constructedness of all
cultures:

> The enunciative process introduces a split [...] between the traditional culturalist demand
> for a model, [...] a community, a stable system of reference, and the necessary negation
> of the certitude in the articulation of new cultural demands, meanings, [and] strategies
> [...]. It undermines our sense of the homogenizing effects of cultural symbols and icons,
> by questioning our sense of the authority of cultural synthesis in general. [...] *Cultures*
> *are never unitary in themselves, nor simply dualistic in the relation of Self to Other.*[17]

Works by authors like Wah ("Not the same anything if you're half Swede, quarter
Chinese and quarter Ontario wasp," 36) help to elucidate Bhabha's claim. Owing to
their hybrid background, these writers prove to be much more sensitive to the absurd-
ity of purist structures and systems and to the problem of cultural authority and domination implied in these systems. Wah's articulation of hybridity can thus be read as
cultural criticism according to Bhabha; his polymorphous and intercultural family

---

[13] Sneja Gunew, *Framing Marginality: Multicultural Literary Studies* (Carlton, Victoria: U of
Melbourne P, 1994): 22, and Michael Thorpe, "The Uses of Diversity: The Internationalization of
English-Canadian Literature," *ARIEL: A Review of International English Literature* 23.3 (1992):
123.

[14] Bissoondath, *Selling Illusions: The Cult of Multiculturalism in Canada* (Toronto: Penguin,
1994): 83.

[15] Bhabha, *The Location of Culture*, 34.

[16] *The Location of Culture*, 35–36 (my emphasis).

[17] *The Location of Culture*, 34 (emphasis in the original). The 'power-centre' as evoked by
Bhabha refers to the European colonial powers, while in the Canadian context it signifies the still
predominantly anglophone and francophone government.

chronicle "displays the necessary deformation and displacement of all sites of discrimination and domination."[18] The more general political message of *Diamond Grill*, an
ironic threat brought forward with the usual, only slightly suppressed rage, cannot be
overheard:

> Better watch out for the craw, better watch out for the goat. That's the mix, the breed, the
> half-breed, the metis, quarter breed, trace-of-a-breed true demi-semi-ethnic polluted
> rootless living technicolour snarl to complicate the underbelly panavision of racism and
> bigotry across this country. (53)

The anger, the political antagonism and the emphasis on ethnic hybridity place Wah's
Diamond Grill in the ranks of those literary texts which Bhabha – in a slightly different
context: ie, the discourse of the nation – has named "counter narratives." These
"counter-narratives [...] continually evoke and erase [...] totalizing boundaries – both
actual and conceptual – [and] disturb those ideological manœuvres through which
'imagined communities' are given essentialized identities."[19] Cultures, too, are "imagined communities"; just like nations they have for the most part been defined in terms
of coherence and unity. In the course of mass migration and of a growing world-wide
mobility, which lead to increasingly heterogeneous and permeable societies, Bhabha
rightly asks whether the concept of the public sphere, of the 'people', should not be reconsidered altogether: "The whole notion of the public sphere is changing so that we
need the notion of a politics which is based on unequal, uneven, multiple and potentially antagonistic, political identities."[20] Wah's *Diamond Grill*, bringing forward such
a contrasting and conflicting multitude of voices and exposing the deficiencies and
discriminatory undercurrents of purist structures, is a step towards such a redefinition –
and towards a truly *trans*cultural future.

WORKS CITED

Bhabha, Homi K. *The Location of Culture* (London & New York: Routledge, 1994).
Bissoondath, Neil. *Selling Illusions: The Cult of Multiculturalism in Canada* (Toronto: Penguin,
    1994).
Gunew, Sneja. *Framing Marginality: Multicultural Literary Studies* (Carlton, Victoria: U of Mel-
    bourne P, 1994).
Lai, Larissa, & Jean Lum. "Neither Guests nor Strangers" in *Yellow Peril Reconsidered: Photo,
    Film, Video*, ed. Paul Wong (Vancouver: On Edge, 1990): 20–24.
Rutherford, Jonathan. "The Third Space: Interview with Homi Bhabha," in *Identity: Community,
    Culture, Difference*, ed. Jonathan Rutherford (London: Lawrence & Wishart, 1990): 207–21.
Thorpe, Michael. "The Uses of Diversity: The Internationalization of English-Canadian Litera-
    ture," *ARIEL: A Review of International English Literature* 23.3 (1992): 109–25.

---

[18] Bhabha, *The Location of Culture*, 112.

[19] *The Location of Culture*, 149.

[20] Bhabha, in an interview with Jonathan Rutherford, "The Third Space: Interview with Homi
Bhabha," *Identity: Community, Culture, Difference*, ed. Rutherford (London: Lawrence & Wishart, 1990): 208.

Wah, Fred. *Diamond Grill* (Edmonton, Alberta: NeWest, 1996).
——. "Half-Bred Poetics" in *Faking It: Poetics and Hybridity; Critical Writing 1984–1999* (Edmonton, Alberta: NeWest, 2000): 71–96.
——. [http://www.acs.ucalgary.ca/~wah]. Visited May 25, 1998.
——. *Waiting for Saskatchewan* (Winnipeg, Manitoba: Turnstone, 1985).

⟨⟨•⟩⟩

Disillusionment With More Than India
Ruth Prawer Jhabvala's *Heat and Dust*

D.C.R.A. GOONETILLEKE

A POLISH-JEWISH ESCAPEE from Germany to England at the age of twelve, Ruth Prawer Jhabvala nourished a deep-rooted literary ambition (it inspired her as a child to write stories in German and pick "The Short Story in England 1700–1750" as the topic of her M.A. thesis) which burgeoned when she gained an entrée into Indian life as the wife of a Parsi architect. In her early novels, especially in *To Whom She Will* (1955) and *The Nature of Passion* (1956), she was critical of India like an outsider, yet she seemed an insider, in that she was inward with Indian realities and appreciative. *Heat and Dust* (1995) marks her disillusionment both with India and with more than India, intimating the new directions and emphases of her later novels (which travel through time as well as space and in which the Western psyche occupies more of her attention) and employing an innovative, radical departure in narrative technique.

Jhabvala has a woman's perspective, natural and inevitable, given that she is a female writer. It is obvious in *Heat and Dust*, because it focuses on two (English) women and because, given the fact that these two are fifty years apart, women are important, perhaps more important than men, as signifiers of change. The narrative is double-layered. The "I" of the narrative set in post-Independence India, in 1973, is Miss Rivers, though she does not carry her name as such in the novel, thereby widening its significance (in the film version of the novel, directed by James Ivory, and produced by Ismail Merchant in 1983, she is named Anne). She is also the narrator of the first story – of Olivia, who came to live in India in 1923, when it was a British colony, yet not in Victorian times and so not too distant from us. Olivia is the first wife of Douglas Rivers. Miss Rivers is the grand-daughter of his second wife, Tessie Crawford. Miss Rivers stays in India to unravel the mystery surrounding Olivia; the gothic element in the novel creeps in:

> I don't remember Douglas at all – he died when I was three – but I remember Grand-mother Tessie and Great-Aunt Beth very well. They were cheerful women with a sensible and modern outlook on life: but nevertheless, so my parents told me, for years they could

not be induced to talk about Olivia. They shied away from her memory as from something *dark and terrible.*[1] (my emphasis)

Miss Rivers' account of her story in India is revealed through a diary she kept at that time. We learn of Olivia through her letters written to her sister Marcia – as narrated by Miss Rivers. Olivia writes to Marcia "as if it was a relief to have someone to confide in" (47–48). Miss Rivers notes:

> Olivia's handwriting is clear and graceful, even though she seems to have written very fast just as the thoughts and feelings came to her. Her letters are all addressed to Marcia, but really they sound as if she is communing with herself, they are so intensely personal. (94)

Heat and Dust anticipates postmodernism though without fantasy. Its structure is that of an artefact. John Updike objected: "the alternation between plots drains both of momentum, or of the substance that lends momentum."[2] This alleged flaw, the cross-cutting, is really a postmodernist virtue: it prevents the reader from getting too absorbed in the worlds of the novel and thereby keeps him/her alert and critical, like the Brechtian alienation effect. The novel is written in an almost flat, bare style so as to focus the reader's attention on the content. There is no attempt to create character as in realist fiction. Comparisons to Jane Austen or Chekhov, usually made in regard to Jhabvala's novels, are inappropriate and inapplicable, given that *Heat and Dust* is very postmodern. The opening sentence states that "Olivia went away with the Nawab": Jhabvala is now capable of sacrificing the surprise and suspense this central fact could evoke.

Laurie Sucher remarks: "the words of the title, *Heat and Dust*, in addition to describing the climatic conditions in which Olivia's story is set, signify the largest literary themes: love and death, passion and the obscurity of the past."[3] "The climatic conditions" apply in both Olivia's and Miss Rivers' stories and function as real, not orientalist, ingredients. The symbolic significations of the title are generated as Sucher sees them. The "love" and "passion" of Olivia and Miss Rivers are central. Olivia's story is of the past and Miss Rivers tries to penetrate "the obscurity of the past." "Death" is not a symbolic pole of either narrative but graves are prominent in both. Yet these symbolic significations do not represent the themes of the novel as such. The theme is the quest for fulfilment – on the part of the individuals, projected through Olivia and Miss Rivers. Unlike *Get Ready for Battle*, this novel is not concerned with the country, India, as such.

At the beginning, Olivia is in love with her husband, Douglas. He was a personable, upright, capable, industrious administrator – manly yet unable to make her pregnant, though both he and Olivia feel that a child will end their respective dissatisfactions. He was a sahib but she thought that he was different from the Crawfords and the Minnies, whom she found boring. Olivia is placed in a situation typical of the memsahib: as Charles Allen notes,

[1] Ruth Prawer Jhabvala, *Heat and Dust* (1975; London: Futura, 1983): 1–2. Further page references are in the main text.

[2] John Updike, *Hugging the Shore: Essays and Criticism* (London: André Deutsch, 1983): 714.

[3] Laurie Sucher, *The Fiction of Ruth Prawer Jhabvala: The Politics of Passion* (London: Macmillan, 1989): 104.

Once her husband had left the bungalow in the morning She was alone, surrounded by servants with whom she could not communicate and by a complexity of Indian conventions – summed up in the word *dastur* – 'the stifling, enervating atmosphere of customs, against which energy beats itself unavailingly, as against a feather bed' – that far exceeded anything Anglo-India could come up with. She had precious little alternative but to turn to other memsahibs and adopt their standards.[4]

Olivia does not wish "to turn to other memsahibs and adopt their standards." In the hot season, she refuses to spend four months in Simla, the cool hill station, both because she dislikes the company of the memsahibs and their social round and because she does not want to be separated from Douglas, who will be toiling in the plains of Satipur. Olivia suffers from a sense of routine and boredom – while Douglas was at work, but her main dissatisfaction is sexual and with him. She wants to be the slave of his day and the queen of his night. Her romantic intensity finds no answering quality in Douglas. So she looks for it in the Nawab of the neighbouring princely state of Khatm. Indeed, given the male population in the area, he appears the only alternative.

The Nawab is, for Olivia, the exotic Other. He holds a Laurance Hope-ish attraction for her – as if he were The Sheik. E.M. Hull's novel of that name was published in 1921 and was as popular a success in book form as it was on the silent screen in the motion picture starring Rudolph Valentino. Jhabvala has an extraordinary sense of the period in which Olivia's narrative is set. Olivia is, certainly, naive, but this is understandable, perhaps inevitable, for one of her age, placed as she was, and not to be condemned for this – in Jhabvala's, and our, eyes. She does not seek the "real India" as Adela Quested did in Forster's *A Passage to India* but is attracted to an individual, a dark idol. The Nawab possesses a certain magnetism: when she visits him in his palace,

She followed him wherever he called her and did whatever he wanted. She too made no secret of anything. She remembered how Harry had once told her 'You don't say no to a person like him' and found it to be true. (152)

Harry the Englishman in the Palace is unable to leave the Nawab despite complaints of ill-health, being homesick and despite a desire to see his mother, alone in a little flat in South Kensington and not keeping too well. Olivia visits the Nawab regularly, though she is risking her marriage and reputation. She is so daring and independent as to break through the racial, social and gender restrictions of the colonial milieu. Even Fielding in *A Passage to India* does not sleep with India as she does. "Satipur" means "place/city of Sati"; the name is ironic. In the act of sati / suttee, the widow sacrifices herself on the pyre of her husband out of fidelity and loyalty, yet Olivia sacrifices herself in her liaison with the Nawab, but not for the sake of her husband, violating fidelity and loyalty. Ironically, the Nawab and Douglas are of the same height and almost the same build.

---

[4] Charles Allen, *Raj: A Scrapbook of British India 1877–1947* (Harmondsworth: Penguin, 1984): 18.

Yasmine Gooneratne observes of *Heat and Dust*: "the British Raj is seen to have been dishonest and deceitful, encouraging a similar dishonesty and deceit in its subjects."[5] When the local rich men come to pay their respects to Douglas the sahib, he speaks to them as if he "were playing a musical instrument of which he had entirely mastered the stops" (37). But, soon after they leave, he calls them a "pack of rogues" (37). Jhabvala's satire suggests that both parties are putting on an act. The same sort of thing happens when the sahibs and the Nawab meet or when the memsahibs meet Indian women: when Beth Crawford calls on the Nawab's mother, the Begum, at the Palace, "Everyone played their part well – the Palace ladies as well as Mrs Crawford – and gave evidence of having frequently played it before" (29).

To the British, the Indians are "lesser breeds without the Law" (to use Kipling's notorious phrase). The Indians are outside the pale of civilized order – even the Nawab and the Begum, though they enjoy positions to be reckoned with. The British are the norm of a people within the Law, uniquely endowed to carry out best the tasks of imperialism, a chosen race. Racism is in-built into their attitudes towards the Indians, and Jhabvala shows them up as desiccated, too. Jhabvala is particularly subversive of the British colonialists when she exposes what E.M. Forster noted in 1920, their "unconscious hypocrisy,"[6] and when she shows how the sahibs and memsahibs think the Indians are under their thumb but that this is not really the case, how the Indians (the Nawab included) use their humility, their powerlessness, to manipulate the British, to exercise a measure of power over them. In the latter instance, Jhabvala is dramatizing the trope of "sly civility" as explained by Homi K. Bhabha; this trope situates the slippages of colonial authority in a native appropriation of its signs, and points to both the excesses a discourse of presence cannot contain and to 'the native refusal to satisfy the colonizer's narrative demand'.[7] Jhabvala's larger image and the reality, however, are more complex, and in her depiction of Olivia and the Nawab she adds further dimensions. Olivia plays a double game with the other members of the English community in Satipur and with her husband. Amidst the subterfuges, including her own, the sincerity of her feelings for the Nawab stands out by contrast.

In presenting Khatm, Jhabvala does not consider the princely state in colonial India as such, but, rather, the personality of the ruler, the Nawab, though the political position of his state matters in that, under the British administration, his power has diminished. The emphasis is not so much on the smallness of the Nawab's state as on his powerlessness compared to his ancestors. He is chafing under, and complains about, the restrictions imposed on him by the British. He would love to be an autocrat like Amanullah Khan, whom he recalls, and who was the first to enjoy the title of the Nawab of Khatm, conceded by the British in 1817; he tells Olivia that he envies the kind of life Amanullah Khan led (135). The Nawab's Palace is grand, which thrills Olivia. But, ironically, the

[5] Yasmine Gooneratne, *Silence, Exile and Cunning: The Fiction of Ruth Prawer Jhabvala* (Hyderabad: Orient Longman, 1983): 213.

[6] E.M. Forster, "Notes on the English Character," in *Abinger Harvest* (1936; Harmondsworth: Penguin, 1967): 22.

[7] Homi K. Bhabha, "Sly Civility" (1985), in *The Location of Culture* (London & New York: Routledge, 1994): 99.

town in its shadow consisted of nothing but slummy lanes and ramshackle houses (165), its villages impoverished; the state without interesting ruins or hunting country (15); and, it is stressed, the Nawab is in want of money. "Khatm" means 'finished': the name is appropriate.

The Nawab has something in common with Charlotte Brontë's Rochester and Emily Brontë's Heathcliff, gloomy dominant gothic heroes who ultimately trace their ancestry to Byron's heroes. (The Nawab's mad wife is an echo of Rochester's.) The Nawab's character is invested with a gothic sense of mystery, which later disappears. Jhabvala shows many aspects to him, a complexity in him. The British criticize him for extorting money, encouraging communal friction which leads to an annual slaughter of Hindus by Muslims on Husband's Wedding Day, and allying himself with dacoits. The criticisms have substance, are admitted by Harry, and convince the reader, but Olivia refuses to believe these, and her view of the Nawab is ironically shown up as an idealization. But there is an added subtlety. What Jhabvala is, at bottom, projecting in the case of the Nawab is the different morality that belongs to a different kind of man, a morality alien to the British, to the West – a case of "East is East and West is West" (to quote Kipling's famous line). For such a man, a ruler to boot, the entertainment provided by *hijras* (male eunuchs) is perfectly normal and not a sign of a cad.

Ralph J. Crane's view that "the Nawab is bored by his routine and sees his days with Olivia as a pleasant diversion,"[8] is over-simple and indicates the least of his motives. Olivia does stimulate genuine emotional excitement in the Nawab; at the same time, he sees his affair with Olivia as a power ploy and a device to humiliate the British. Jhabvala is both understanding about and critical of the Nawab. His rotting pianos signify an empty attachment to Western symbols of class, leisure and culture. His unmusicality further indicates a lack of sensibility (for Jhabvala, musical sensitivity usually stands for emotional intensity and depth). By the same token, Olivia's playing the piano and musicality signify those virtues. The Nawab ill-treats Olivia at times. But they do share a certain togetherness, as when they dip their fingers in the little spring at Baba Firdaus' shrine while on a picnic (46) – a positive touch in the novel. Significantly, the water is shallow – like their feelings.

Jhabvala seems to have had E.M. Forster and his novel *A Passage to India* in mind when writing *Heat and Dust*, though *A Passage to India* is not an intertext of *Heat and Dust* as Conrad's *Heart of Darkness* is of V.S. Naipaul's *A Bend in the River*. (Jhabvala has stated that she read Forster's novel before she went to India.[9]) *A Passage to India* (first published in 1924) is about race and personal relations in colonial India in the first quarter of this century, and this is the basis for Jhabvala's 1923 narrative. The stirrings of nationalist consciousness in Forster's novel,[10] too, are reflected in *Heat and Dust* where Olivia expresses anxiety that 'things' may change with "Mr Gandhi and these

---

[8] Ralph J. Crane, *Inventing India: A History of India in English-Language Fiction* (London: Macmillan, 1993): 90.

[9] "Ruth Prawer Jhabvala," in *World Authors 1950–1970* (1975), quoted from *Current Biography*, ed. Maxine Block (New York: H.W. Wilson, 1977): 222.

[10] See D.C.R.A. Goonetilleke, *Developing Countries in British Fiction* (London: Macmillan & Totowa NJ: Rowman & Littlefield, 1977): 251.

people" (89) and the Nawab is unhappy with the diminution of his power under the
British and British control. Ralph J. Crane thinks that "there are obvious parallels to be
drawn between Olivia Rivers and Adela Quested, as well as between Douglas Rivers
and Ronny Heaslop."[11] To me, there seems to be no resemblance between frivolous,
feminine, fluttering Olivia and the unromantic, plain, earnest, flat-chested, politically
conscious Adela. It is arguable that there is a similarity between Douglas and Ronny,
since they are both Empire-builders, but it seems to me that they constitute a type and,
therefore, do not imply conscious intertextuality on Jhabvala's part.

Harry is a homosexual in the Nawab's court – as Forster was when he was Secretary
to the Maharaj of Dewas State Senior. Laurie Sucher rightly points out the parallel and
possible influence.[12] Moreover, the Nawab is using Harry to humiliate the British as
"H.H." did Forster. I think it is possible that Jhabvala is alluding to this aspect of Forster's experience, too, *pace* Sucher's view.[13] This aspect may have been current in oral
tradition in India before "Kanaya" was published in 1983, and Jhabvala may have had
access to the oral source when she wrote *Heat and Dust* (1975).

Olivia becomes pregnant and the Nawab is sure that he is the father. Olivia decides to
have an abortion and flees to the Palace after it:

> It isn't so very far from Satipur to Khatm – about 15 miles – and it was a journey that she
> had been doing daily by one of the Nawab's cars. But that time when she ran away from
> the hospital there was no car. Harry never knew how she came but presumed it was by
> what he called some native mode of transport. She was also in native dress – a servant's
> coarse sari – so that she reminded him of a print he had seen called *Mrs Secombe in Flight
> from the Mutineers*. Mrs Secombe was also in native dress and in a state of great agitation,
> with her hair awry and smears of dirt on her face: naturally, since she was flying for her
> life from the mutineers at Sikora to the safety of the British Residency at Lucknow. Olivia
> was also in flight – but, as Harry pointed out, in the opposite direction. (171–72)

The "Mutiny' of 1857 was a watershed in British–Indian relations: it marked the
estrangement of the races and undermined British confidence. It was invoked in times of
unrest, as reflected not only in *Heat and Dust* but in Rudyard Kipling's story "The Man
Who Would Be King," in E.M. Forster's *A Passage to India* and in Paul Scott's *The Raj
Quartet*. Harry points out the irony of Olivia's flight. She has ruined herself and cannot
stay either in British Satipur or in the Nawab's Khatm. She has to be put away, and the
Nawab shows his real consideration and attachment when he provides her with a cottage
and a piano in the Himalayas, and, though not affluent, even visits her. The coolness of
the Himalayas suits Olivia's Europeanness. Symbolically, she is away from the passion,
the heat, on the plains, and has access to the spirituality associated with heights, the
Himalayas, as Miss Rivers sees it. The image of Olivia in the mountains is of her playing the *same* music and doing the *same* embroidery. Her disappointment has shocked
her into stagnancy. Her window is befogged. Yet spiritual fulfilment cannot be completely ruled out.

---

[11] Ralph J. Crane, *Ruth Prawer Jhabvala* (New York: Twayne, 1999): 81.
[12] Laurie Sucher, *The Fiction of Ruth Prawer Jhabvala*, 136–39.
[13] Sucher, *The Fiction of Ruth Prawer Jhabvala*, 131.

The final impression of the Nawab in London is pathetic. He has lost his magnetism, naturally, with the years. There is no air or mystery about him. In fact, he seems prematurely aged – flabby, soft and mild. He has developed a sweet tooth and has got into the habit of devouring cream pastries. He is losing his memory and is begging for funds from the British authorities. Even in his heyday, the Nawab was chafing, because he was unable to cut a figure like his ancestor Amanullah Khan.

Olivia was beautiful and feminine. Miss Rivers typifies the gender blurring of recent times. She wears loose-fitting Indian clothes and men's sandals (women's do not fit her). She is much taller than Inder Lal, her landlord and partner, she walks with long strides, and keeps forgetting that this makes it difficult for him to keep up with her (49). Because she is not only tall but flat-chested (the gender difference is thus minimal), the Indians often call after her: *hijra*.

In colonial India, the English were the cynosure of all eyes – as in the 1923 narrative. Olivia's affair with the Nawab had political and social significance. In the modern narrative and modern India, the English are insignificant. Paul Scott's observation in Calcutta when he visited India few years earlier, in 1964, confirms this: "There was a [English] girl then, and an anglicized Indian. They were having an affair, as it was said. No one cares much these days, especially in Calcutta, about that sort of thing. It was simply part of the scene."[14] Therefore, Miss Rivers living among the Indians, her connection with Chid the British hippy (she allows him to sleep in her room and use her sexually with his monstrous erections) and her affair with Inder Lal, an Indian and married, are of no consequence. Indeed, there is a tendency to merge with the Indians – via clothes, food, love and spiritual experience; and this tendency is not confined to the narrator. She notes in her diary:

> [...] we must look strange to them, and what must also be strange is the way we are living among them – no longer apart, but eating their food and often wearing Indian clothes because they are cooler and cheaper. (9)

It is significant that she uses "we," not "I." From another perspective, the colonial restrictions have disappeared. Satipur itself is different from what it was fifty years earlier. The building that Olivia and Douglas occupied now houses the Water Board, the municipal Health Department, and a sub-post office. The bastions of privilege in colonial times have fallen and democratization has taken place

There are similarities and parallels between the narrative in the past and that in the present. Olivia has two sex partners, one British (her husband) and one Indian (her lover); so does the narrator (two lovers). Olivia visits the shrine of Baba Firdaus twice, the second time alone with the Nawab when he seduces her; the narrator also visits the shrine twice, the second time alone with Inder Lal when she seduces him. The contrast suggests how gender relations have changed between colonial and post-Independence times, and adds to the emphasis in the text on the gender blurring of recent times. The character of the Nawab's wife, "Sandy," is a parallel to that of Inder Lal's wife, Ritu.

---

[14] Paul Scott, "Method: The Mystery and the Mechanics" (1969), in Scott, *My Appointment with the Muse: Essays 1961–75*, ed. Shelley C. Reece (London: Heinemann, 1986): 59.

Both suffer from mental problems which negate their worth; they are put on the shelf by their husbands. Olivia's abortion is counterbalanced by the narrator's failed abortion – she changes her mind halfway through the process. Both ascend to the Himalayas. Olivia's discovery of herself, of India, parallels the narrator's discovery of Olivia, of India and herself.

These similarities, contrasts and parallels seem to me to constitute a (successful) post-modernist attempt to impose the writer's vision on the reader, and to exploit intratextuality which goes back to the ancient literary device of palimpsesting. When the Nawab's words to Olivia with reference to her pregnancy – "Really you will do this for me? You are not afraid? Oh how brave you are! " (152) – are used by Douglas too (154–55), the emphasis is, surely, non-realistic.

The final impression created by the novel is ambiguous. Olivia is a shadowy presence at the end. This is necessary. It is part of the poignancy and the sense of her failure. Her spiritual yearnings may have been a fact or merely imagined by Miss Rivers, reflecting her own. In any case, Olivia's success is doubtful. Ralph J. Crane's view that the narrator's quest is successfully fulfilled, that she "appears to merge with India successfully, probably because she has a purpose for being in India and is prepared to accept India as it is, to surrender herself to India without needing to throw off her own identity," that she "learns to swim in the flowing tide of India,"[15] is over-simple. So is Laurie Sucher's complementary view that when Miss Rivers "ascends to the Himalayas with a child within her: in the realm of the imagination and biology, her visit has borne fruit."[16] Miss Rivers is a representative figure as a seeker and she does fare better than numerous other seekers such as Chid and his two companions, who end up as derelicts. But pregnancy does not necessarily lead to a satisfactory issue; the ascent to the Himalayas is not necessarily going to result in spiritual fulfilment. The ultimate fate of Miss Rivers, too, is ambiguous.

Maji, however, is a positive figure. Her name in Hindi means 'mother' in a honorific sense, and, indeed, she measures up to her name. Her wide-ranging compassion is remarkable. It extends to the beggar woman, Leelavati, who dies in her arms. Maji recommends a pilgrimage as a solution to Ritu's mental problem. It seems positive, coming from her. But Chid has been left a nervous wreck as a consequence of his spiritual quest. Miss Rivers observes:

> The question as to whether Chid is holy may remain open, but as far as the town is concerned, he has made a promising first step in shaving his head and throwing away his clothes. For this they seem ready to give him the benefit of many doubts. I've seen them do the same with Indian holy men who often pass through the town with their ochre robes and beads and begging bowls. On the whole they look a sturdy set of rascals to me – some of them heavily drugged, others randy as can be, all it seems to me with shrewd and greedy faces. (63–64)

Even the swamis in the Himalayas raised doubts in the reader's mind as to their holiness: they "are cheerful men and they laugh and joke in booming voices with the people

---

[15] Ralph J. Crane, *Ruth Prawer Jhabvala*, 88–89.
[16] Laurie Sucher, *The Fiction of Ruth Prawer Jhabvala*, 134.

in the bazaar" (181). All this adds to the doubt as to whether Olivia succeeded in her quest and whether Miss Rivers will. The doubt is left unresolved; Jhabvala's novel is open-ended, a modernistic fictional innovation.

Heat and Dust is thus a disillusioned book – in regard to both the past and the present, in regard to India and more than India. Both its outlook and technique are in keeping with our postmodernist times. It is a considerable achievement – so much so, that its comparative brevity is hardly noticeable. It certainly deserved to win the Booker Prize.

WORKS CITED

Allen, Charles. *Raj: A Scrapbook of British India 1877–1947* (Harmondsworth: Penguin, 1984).

Bhabha, Homi K. *The Location of Culture* (London & New York: Routledge, 1994).

Block, Maxine ed., *Current Biography* (New York: H.W. Wilson, 1977).

Crane, Ralph J. *Inventing India: A History of India in English-Language Fiction* (London: Macmillan, 1993).

———. *Ruth Prawer Jhabvala* (New York: Twayne, 1999).

Forster, E.M. *Abinger Harvest* (1936; Harmondsworth: Penguin, 1967).

Gooneratne, Yasmine. *Silence, Exile and Cunning: The Fiction of Ruth Prawer Jhabvala* (Hyderabad: Orient Longman, 1983).

Goonetilleke, D.C.R.A. *Developing Countries in British Fiction* (London: Macmillan & Totowa NJ: Rowman & Littlefield, 1977).

Jhabvala, Ruth Prawer. *Heat and Dust* (London: Futura, 1983).

Scott, Paul. *My Appointment with the Muse: Essays 1961–75*, ed. Shelley C. Reece (London: Heinemann, 1986).

Sucher, Laurie. *The Fiction of Ruth Prawer Jhabvala: The Politics of Passion* (London: Macmillan, 1989).

Updike, John. *Hugging the Shore: Essays and Criticism* (London: André Deutsch, 1983).

《●》

Living on the Hyphen
Ayi Kwei Armah and the Paradox of the African-American Quest for a New Future and Identity in Postcolonial Africa

OBODODIMMA OHA

T O LIVE ON THE HYPHEN, or to live (as) a hyphenated identity, is to live between lives, cultures, languages, spaces, ideologies, etc. It already always suggests a destabilization and an ambivalence. Quite typical of postcolonial and transcultural circumstances, living on the hyphen is a condition which Ayi Kwei Armah, a Ghanaian novelist now resident in Popenguine, West Africa, significantly addresses in his *Osiris Rising: A Novel of Africa Past, Present and Future.* In this book he explores the African-American elites' intellectual and political attempts at recuperating their African philosophical values, and re-creating their futures from their pasts in postcolonial Africa. This essay analyses and discusses the attention Armah draws to the problems encountered by African Americans in relocating themselves in Africa, the place of their roots, especially in terms of personal and social tensions.

Armah's contrastive discourse in *Osiris Rising* is examined in relation to responses manifested by some African Americans who have relocated to some West African countries, particularly Ghana and the Republic of Benin. It turns out that, apart from being vulnerable to exploitation, African Americans who have returned to Africa face serious problems of alienation and marginalization as an emerging minority group in these African countries, and these problems tend to intensify the frustrations attendant on living on the hyphen, and which this return to the roots was meant to resolve in the first place.

My first task will be to provide a critical and theoretical background, especially with reference to Armah's literary concerns and practices, so as to locate the designs pursued in *Osiris Rising* within such literary concerns and practices. Ayi Kwei Armah, the author of *The Beautyful Ones Are Not Yet Born, Why Are We So Blest?, Fragments, Two Thousand Seasons,* and *The Healers,* has received much critical attention for his commitment to the exposure and interrogation of dismal conditions in postcolonial Africa, as well as of the racial problems faced by Africans both in the diaspora and on the continent. In fact, sometimes, Armah links the dismal conditions in Africa to racial tension and neocolonization. Colonization and racial exploitation are treated as two interactive weapons used in undermining and destroying community in Africa. The closeness of Armah's representations in his fiction to Frantz Fanon's philosophical arguments about the colonization of Africa has been noted by Kofi Anyidoho and Gareth Griffiths.[1] Anyidoho also draws our attention to the fact that "Armah's fiction is engaged in […] a continental, racial battle,"[2] in which the novelist clearly takes "sides with his people and assumes in his writing that he is addressing his side, and for the benefit of his side of the conflict, though others on the other side may listen if they are so disposed."[3]

In taking Africa (as a whole) as "his primary constituency"[4] in a racial political conflict, Armah operates within a vision which, as further noted by Anyidoho, has at its centre "the mythic reconstruction of a united Africa, a vision of all people of African descent as one people" – a vision which is pan-African and which is deemed "necessary as a force to oppose and neutralize the sense of fragmentation and of weakness in the face of 'world powers' which have reduced African peoples to scattered easy prey for much better united opponents."[5]

Some critics of Armah have queried his handling of race in his writings, especially in terms of his sentimental rhetoric and attempt at seducing his readers into racial hatred. Identifying *Why Are We So Blest?* as "an attempt to nail the novel down," as a "malignant fiction," James Booth, for instance, argues that the book "is not only an analysis of the psychological effects of racism, it is itself a racist book."[6] It is an interesting paradox that Armah's strategy of using racism against racism does seem to entrench his art in a form of pedestrian sentimentality. It is for this reason that Booth has further argued, with respect to *Why Are We So Blest?*, that "as a cry of resentment and suffering the book is unparalleled. As a universal myth of race relations it is deceptive,"[7] and that "Armah's work represents a peculiarly sophisticated version of the familiar dangers of theoretical commitment to 'black consciousness' or 'negritude': dangers which, ironically, he himself has clearly analysed, in their political manifestation, in his article on 'African Socialism: Utopian or Scientific?'."[8]

Armah, it seems, uses his promethean characters – for instance, Modin in *Why Are We So Blest?* – to play out the consequences of the African intellectual's attempt to belong to European and African worlds. Modin, the protagonist of the novel, "is pulled

---

[1] Kofi Anyidoho, "Literature and African Identity: The Example of Ayi Kwei Armah," in *Critical Perspectives on Ayi Kwei Armah*, ed. Derek Wright (Boulder CO: Three Continents, 1992): 42. Gareth Griffiths, "Structure and Image in Ayi Kwei Armah's *The Beautyful Ones Are Not Yet Born*," in *Critical Perspectives*, 84.

[2] Anyidoho, "Literature and African Identity," 42.

[3] "Literature and African Identity," 44–45.

[4] Chidi Amuta, "Portraits of the Contemporary African Artist in Armah's Novels," in *Critical Perspectives*, 13.

[5] Anyidoho, "Literature and African Identity," 42.

[6] James Booth, "*Why Are We So Blest?* and the Limits of Metaphor," in *Critical Perspectives*, 228.

[7] Booth, "The Limits of Metaphor," 240.

[8] "The Limits of Metaphor," 238.

in different directions by his intellectual involvement with Western civilization and his emotional involvement with his own people."[9] With Armah, we are trapped in a binary logic of either/or, and to cross to the other side is to become a casualty. His promethean figure in the case of Africa becomes "inevitably the vector of 'foreign culture'," and "although he makes a 'descent from Olympus', he cannot become part of the lives of the people whom he attempts to serve. Having voluntarily left the 'realm of the gods', the hero becomes trapped within *the gulf which lies between the two worlds.*"[10]

From a more critical perspective, crossing to another world to cross back later could be a process of education and reinforcement. The person who has crossed would be more familiar with the space of the (racial) Other, and by disturbing racial coordinates enables a rethinking of such boundaries as a dimension that is not necessarily natural, not necessarily permanent. Rosemary Colmer consolidates this perspective in arguing that, "however pessimistic Armah may be about the role of the intellectual in Africa, the man who has joined the blest but attempts to rejoin his people has a vision which is valuable, and which can never be attained by those who have never escaped their wretchedness."[11]

There seems, then, to be a lot of sense in Edward Said's argument in *Culture and Imperialism* that

> No one today is purely *one* thing. Labels like Indian, or woman, or Muslim, or American are no more than starting points, which if followed into actual experience for only a moment are quickly left behind. Imperialism consolidated the mixture of cultures and identities on a global scale. But its worst and most paradoxical gift was to allow people to believe that they were only, mainly, exclusively, white, or black, or Western, or Oriental. Yet just as human beings make their own history, they also make their cultures and ethnic identities.[12]

Indeed, for many African Americans, crossing back to their roots in Africa is more than just a ritual or an attempt at recognizing Africa and being recognized by Africa. Robert Fraser has rightly observed that "since the horror of the forced migration and the slave trade ceased at the beginning of the last century, a growing flow of visitors, first a trickle and now a steady stream, have crossed and recrossed the Atlantic in both directions seeking various sorts of experience."[13] Quite interestingly, just as many people in (West) African countries are trying to escape to America – either through the American visa lottery or through other means – and also to other parts of Europe and Asia, some of those who became African Americans through the experience of the slave trade would want to return 'home' to their 'roots' in Africa. This search for a

---

[9] Joyce Johnson, "The Promethean 'Factor' in Ayi Kwei Armah's *Fragments* and *Why Are We So Blest?*" in *Critical Perspectives*, 212.

[10] Johnson, "The Promethean 'Factor'," 215; my emphasis.

[11] Rosemary Colmer, "The Human and the Divine: *Fragments* and *Why Are We So Blest?*" in *Critical Perspectives*, 197.

[12] Edward W. Said, *Culture and Imperialism* (London: Chatto & Windus, 1993): 407–408.

[13] Robert Fraser, "The American Background in *Why Are We So Blest?*" in *Critical Perspectives*, 257.

future and identity in Africa is stimulated mainly by black-consciousness movements
in America. Also, the history of the slave trade has been repackaged as part of a tourist
attraction by some West African countries like Ghana and Benin, and African Americans visiting these countries are led through oral and visual narratives of their origins,
with a subtext about the need to 'return' to their African roots. It has been observed
elsewhere, in relation to the visualized drama of the 'return' on the slave trail at
Ouidah, Benin Republic, that "spiritual return to Africa is, in fact, the major idea com-
municated by the 'Tree of Return.'" Along this line of thought, the 'Tree of No-Return'
is a symbol of death"; and also that "walking round the 'Tree of Return' several times
– a ritual the returnees and visiting diasporic Africans are asked to perform [...] – is a
symbolic reversal and revocation of the journey to loss and death which the slaves
were forced to make round the 'Tree of No-Return' before being taken away finally."[14]
Further still,

> the climax of the evocation of anger and pity in the dramatic experience of the trail is the
> memorial on the mass grave of the slaves [...] with motifs of blood and tears shed by the
> slaves. The visualization of the slaves' blood and tears is a powerful means of sum-
> marizing the tragic experience of the slaves, and the grave itself generally returns and re-
> tains the presence of the dead ex-slave, a presence that accuses the enslaver, and reminds
> and recalls the descendants of the dead slave home.[15]

But apart from narratives of tours into the history of the trans-Atlantic slave trade,
festivals that involve the celebration of black heritage, such as PANAFEST (held in
Ghana), have done much to encourage African Americans to cross over to Africa. Of
course, some African Americans may have other reasons for wanting to return to
Africa. The crucial thing is that such return has its own important story, which is that
of the negotiation of identity and which must complement the stories of disaster Armah
has told about his promethean characters. Such questing for identity seems to be well
in line with Armah's vision and literary ideology, which he reveals when he says that

> at its best, Creative Writing engages the reader in a constant interactive process between
> the past, the present and the future, calculated to make educated persons not passive
> endurers of present conditions, but active protagonists aware of past causes, and willing
> to use their awareness to help shape future results.[16]

It will therefore be useful to discuss the paradox that attends the African-American
quest for identity and a future in Africa, focusing on Armah's *Osiris Rising*, which,
interestingly, he subtitled *A Novel of Africa Past, Present and Future* – in line with his
literary ideology and his sense of historicity. In his defence of Armah from criticisms
about his attitude to Africa's history, Anyidoho writes that "a historian with his eyes on

---

[14] Obododimma Oha, "The 'Tree of Return': Home, Exile, Memory, and the Visual Rhetoric
of Reunion," *Context: Journal of Social & Cultural Studies* 3.2 (1999): 72–73.

[15] Oha, "The 'Tree of Return'," 74.

[16] Ayi Kwei Armah, "Teaching Creative Writing," *West Africa* (20 May 1985): 994.

the future is under no obligation to merely reconstruct past events."[17] But the "futures" of the quest for identity in *Osiris Rising* are already full of fissures, the identities sometimes dented when their pasts are remembered. The problem of pessimism in Armah is still far from being settled.

Osiris Rising tells the story of Ast's return to and frustrating search for identity in Africa. Ast, an African-American lady professor, is made aware of her past by her grandmother, Nwt, who gives her some initial training on hieroglyphics and ancient Egyptian mysticism. Through her, Ast is able to reconnect to her African past:

> Conversations with Nwt turned into voyages. Crossing space and time, the growing Ast stayed up nights with ancestors thousands of years gone puzzling over the motion of stars, wind, flood. Connections. Wonder turned to knowledge of measurable time. She watched kindred priests divide the year into seasons departing and returning, the day into twelve hours going, night into twelve tirelessly coming. Her mind met ancestral priestesses, companions caring for green fields on Hapi's riverbanks, turning desire into myth, naming the myth Sekhet Iarw, perfect place, evergreen fields of the wandering soul returning home.[18]

Just like "typical Armah protagonists," who are "soul-searchers, caring for things of the mind and spirit rather than the heavy things of the flesh,"[19] Ast is determined "to follow her soul to a different outcome, a reversal of the crossing and its motivation, both" (11). Her decision to return to Africa was generated by the processes of her education in both the formal and the non-formal contexts, the latter stimulating and enhancing the choices she makes in the former. Armah tells us that

> She took World History for her first degree, then shifted closer home to Egyptology, for the second. Her doctorate focused on Kemt; she wrote her thesis on identity and social justice in the philosophy of Ancient Egypt. By graduation time her search for knowledge of self, of self within universe, had led her through a flow of changes, some so generous with knowledge they made pain worthwhile in the end. The search accelerated her decision: to return. (8)

On getting to the unnamed African country (obviously Ghana), Ast runs into trouble because of a document on an African philosophical revival which she carries and which the government of the host country associates with dissidence. This brings her into contact with Seth, a former ambitious classmate in the USA, who has rapidly risen to the position of head of security (referred to as Deputy Director or simply DD or SSS, to mystify him). Refusing to enter into a love affair with DD, Ast becomes a target for his vengeance on both a personal and a professional level. She locates Asar, another school friend – a typical Armah visionary and revolutionary – who is a member of the Companionship of the Ankh and a college teacher. Ast secures a teaching job at Asar's college after a long frustrating search and encounter with the decadent civil service system.

---

[17] Anyidoho, "Literature and African Identity," 41.
[18] Ayi Kwei Armah, *Osiris Rising: A Novel of Africa Past, Present and Future* (Popenguine: Per Ankh, 1995): 7. Further page references are in the main text.
[19] Anyidoho, "Literature and African Identity," 37.

Her rediscovery of her love relationship with Asar, and the attempt by members of the Companionship of the Ankh at the college to introduce cultural ideological direction in the curriculum, further intensify DD's bitterness and decision to destroy Asar and to make Ast rethink her inclinations. DD, ironically, uses some African Americans, Ras Jomo Cinque Equiano (formerly Sheldon Tubman) and Prince Wossen (formerly Earl Johnson, and later Rodney Jones) to betray Asar and Ast.

Cinque had been a student activist in America where he betrayed his fellow African Americans by joining a fraternity that promoted white exclusivity and supremacy. Cinque was admitted because he could be used by the group to undermine black consciousness and solidarity. He later emigrated to Africa after losing out in America and changed his name from Sheldon Tubman to Ras Jomo Cinque Equiano, establishing an ambivalent Africult that combines the doctrines of Islam, Christianity, Rastafarianism, Negritude, and African traditional religion. He desperately searches for means of legitimizing his claims about his having a royal ancestry, and about his ancestor having been sold into slavery through conspiracy. Cinque is able to brainwash members of his group, and to reduce his harem of wives to the position of slaves – in fact, zombies. While exploiting members of his group and constructing the identity of priest-king for himself, Cinque actually engages in dubious activities, running criminal errands for DD.

With the conflict between DD on one side and Ast and Asar on the other, Cinque, who has also been prevented by Ast from adding another helpless African-American lady to his harem of wife-slaves, comes in to play the dirty role of betraying Ast and Asar. His driver, Prince Wossen, another African American masquerading as an Ethiopian prince, is used by DD to plant incriminating items in Asar's apartment, to enable the execution of the latter under the pretence that he made an attempt to assassinate the Head of State and to undermine state security through espionage.

Obviously, while inviting a genuine spiritual and intellectual rediscovery of Africa by African Americans, Armah is critical of the roles played by some of these in their search for origin and identity, as well as of the criminality that attends their quest for power and survival. The authentic quest for a non-material African identity and commitment to Africa's redemption is presented in Ast's return and spiritual and intellectual quest in the ankh tradition. As she tells Asar, she is "trying to help create a future" (112). This commitment to the creation of "a future" in and for Africa is evident in Ast's role as Asar's companion, lover, and wife (analogizing the collaboration of god and goddess), in her involvement in the Companionship of the Ankh and in changing the colonial curricula at college, and finally in her interrogation and exposure of Cinque's and Wossen's criminal and disgraceful roles. In fact, the novel's story-line centres on Ast, so that it is against hers that other African Americans' quests for identity and futures in Africa are tested and judged.

It seems that Armah is not interested in the issue of the return of African Americans to Africa on a surface and emotional level. He appears to be more interested in motivations for return, and prefers a motivation that cannot be easily subdued – that, instead, subdues conspiracy as staged by (in)security agents, and subdues nostalgia and its symptoms, including the hunger for ketchup:

> "Ketchup?" Ast asked.
> "Hot dogs. Hamburger. Mayonnaise."
> "That what this grand ceremony was about?"
> "That, and nostalgia. He's one of a group of African-Americans come back into the black womb. Mother Africa. After a while they get homesick for America. Ketchup's just a symptom. (80)

What motivates the return to Africa of those like Cinque (Sink!) and Wossen (Worsen!) who insist on ketchup is more important to Armah than their big show about possessing royal African identities. Bailey and Ast are used as the authorial voices in exposing and interrogating the 'hidden' agenda:

> "What's Jomo really doing in this country?"
> Bailey sighed. "Razz Jomo Cinque Equiano has transposed his American Africult here. His line is he's offering the uprooted their lost roots. Turning Americans into Africans. Only his process has nothing to do with Africa. It's a funky mix of Christianity, Islam and Negritude. Take those three anti-African slave philosophies, mix them, and what d'you get? Something outasight weird. That's what he has to offer." (125)

Living between lives, cultures, spaces, and ideologies, Cinque has a destabilized and paradoxical identity. This is even signified in the multivoicedness of his name, "His Excellency Ras Jomo Cinque Equiano" – unlike Ast, who is simply "Ast," the name of an intelligent African divinity suggested by Nwt, her grandmother (7). Indeed, name-changing is one strategy used by some African Americans in negotiating their African identities, and is not necessarily wrong-headed. But in Cinque's case (just as in Wossen's) it is a way of putting on different masks, of cultivating ambiguity, which enables him to deceive and work out selfish objectives. His name-changes and additions may be seen as surface transformations of his identity, but his real dubious self remains constant. He uses these transformations or 'deaths' of surface identity for the sake of his duplicity. He prefers his dead selves or identities to be irrecoverable, as revealed in the following encounter he has with Ast:

> "Sheldon Tubman," she said, amazed her voice was so quiet. In the shock of recognition the man reacted as if Ast had shot him. The reaction lasted a sly moment, then yielded to something rigidly controlled. He shook his head in a slow, studied, dramatic movement meant to deny he was the one Ast had named.
> "Sheldon Tubman," Ast called him again.
> The man continued shaking his head. Then he said:
> "My sister, why keep calling up the dead?"
> Immediately the words were echoed by the three women:
> "Yes, sister, why keep calling up the dead… the dead… the dead?"
> "Who died?" Ast asked.
> "Sheldon Tubman," the man in gold said. "That's who died."
> "When?"
> "Long ago."
> Ast smiled. "But I can see you, Sheldon Tubman."
> The man shouted: "I am not Sheldon Tubman!"
> Under the anger Ast also heard the anguish of a soul in pain.

The explosion seemed to ease the anger. The golden man's tone grew calmer. "Hear me, sister, hear me well. This is not Sheldon Tubman." (85–86)

Indeed, quite ironically, apart from being morally dead, Cinque died a long time ago in the ancestor (Apo) whose history of enslavement he seeks to reconstruct to legitimize his claims to having royal blood, and whose life of duplicity he re-lives without knowing it. A traitor who had been subverting the efforts of members of the ankh cult fighting slave trade and oppression, Apo had submitted himself to white slave merchants to be taken to America, in order to escape being punished for his crime. He eventually found himself in slave chains and was shipped to America, becoming the victim of his own machinations.

Apo (in his second life as Cinque/Sheldon Tubman) continues to play this role of traitor, as shown in the diagram below:

First life	Second life
Apo	Ras Jomo Cinque Equiano
	Sheldon Tubman
1st betrayal:	2nd betrayal:
of the Ankh in the 'old' slave trade	of the blacks in America
Setting: (pre)colonial Africa	
	3rd betrayal:
	of African-Americans and of the
	Companionship
	Setting: (post)colonial Africa

The second and the third betrayals are actually a playback of the first. And while Cinque would not want his 'dead' identity to be called up, he still wants to use the history that goes along with Apo, to reinvent it, so as to create a grand but oppressive future for himself, only to abandon the project when the grand narrative turns out to be one of debasement and shame. Obviously, he is caught in the paradox of searching for an identity which he cannot accept when he eventually finds it.

Although Armah maintains the posture of anti-racist racism in his fiction generally, he nevertheless insists on our realizing that "the initiative for the slave trade came from Africans themselves," such a realization being very important for "a realistic appraisal of the African past and the future of Africa."[20] An archaeology of identity that cannot accept the facts when they are found is dubious indeed. The form of history and identity that Cinque is searching for is the one that gestures towards heroism, but at the same time cultivates what unmakes heroism. It is the kind of search for origin that Michel Foucault deplores, preferring a Nietzschean genealogy that recognizes the lower states of being and the fact that traditional history, as a means of recuperating an authentic past, is pretentious and is shot through with paradoxes – not high, but low; not sacred but profane.

In Cinque's driver, Wossen, the politics of name-changing and identity-construction is even more disturbingly demonstrated. First "Earl Johnson," then "Prince Wossen"

---

[20] D.S. Izevbaye, "Ayi Kwei Armah and the 'I' of the Beholder," in *Critical Perspectives*, 28.

("the Ethiopian," or simply "the Ethiopian Prince"), and much later "Rodney Jones," he wears several masks, reminding one of Michel Foucault's idea of the parodic mode of history, which "offers the modern European a number of masks or alternate identities, which serve to hide his own confusion and anonymity."[21] Wossen is more of a chameleon, each transformation corresponding to the deception and damage he could do as one manipulating his in-betweens. Such deceptive and harmful use of change of identity is seen in his role in the betrayal of Ast and Asar, whom he had deceived into allowing him to stay in the latter's apartment before travelling back to America:

> "So you didn't go back to America after all," Ast said.
> "Nat yet," Wossen answered. "Gat lotsa time."
> "What of the suitcase you planted in Asar's apartment, Prince Wossen?"
> "First place, Sis," Wossen said, "I aint no Wossen. Name's Jones. Rodney Jones. Good black American name. You c'see it on my new passport if you want, plain as life. Sister, you like digging up dead folks. Better stop. T'aint healthy.
> "What's the matter?" SSS asked.
> "Sister here calling me Wossen. Prince Wossen, no less." He laughed. "Sister's got imagination." He laughed louder. (95–96)

Names given to the characters, especially the African Americans, are particularly related to their conditions and roles in the novels, confirming Niyi Osundare's poetic assertion:

> names serve as the door to the house of experience, a guide to hidden meanings in the shadowy nooks of time and place. Names tell stories, liberate or imprison; they may also serve as self-fulfilling prophecies. Names commit; which is why the Yoruba say that it is only mad people who do not mind the names they are called, or who refuse to see the difference between the names they choose to bear and the ones the world prefers to call them by.[22]

But, indeed, some mad people do mind the names they are called, and would fight anybody who tries to joke with their names. For Armah, the stylistic–semiotic choice is to give characters like Cinque and Wossen names which seem, on their own, to hang the dog, as Osundare further puts it playfully. Anyidoho, who has done a proper cultural study of Armah's earlier works, also states that "with Armah's central characters, names begin to take on special significance beyond the expression of identity. They lead us into the very centre of the character's being, his fundamental conception of the self as a basis for action or inaction,"[23] which is what we find clearly expressed in Cinque's and Wossen's name-changing practices. Instability of their choices and uses of names relates to their unreliability and duplicity; the diversity of the stories told by them signifies the tension in the self of the bearer; whereas in the case of Ast, she is always the "African"

---

[21] Michal Payne, *Reading Knowledge: An Introduction to Barthes, Foucault and Althusser* (Oxford: Blackwell, 1997): 25.

[22] Niyi Osundare, *African Literature and the Crisis of Poststructuralist Theorising* (Ibadan: Option Book & Information Services, 1993): 3.

[23] Anyidoho, "Literature and African Identity," 37.

Ast, stable and reliable, with no need for name-changing, with no need to dig for her royal origin, because she already knows that she has it.

The tension in personal identity in the novel relates to that of social identity. The African-American characters indeed face a problem of integration within the African society they have relocated to. Only Ast barely manages to achieve this integration, and this is because of the assistance of Asar, coupled with her own personal decision to endure, which is based on her vision that she is returning to where she belongs, "to help create a future" (112), instead of helping to destroy such a future (like Cinque and Wossen). Probably because of the perception of the implications (for the future of the society) of the activities of people like Cinque and Wossen, the citizens who are committed to creating a liveable future, especially members of the Companionship of the Ankh, appear to hold returning African Americans in great suspicion. Even Asar at first is not very sure about Ast's motives for returning, and expresses his objection to the manner in which African Americans (like Cinque) search for origins. Also Tete, the female oral historian and sage, is initially suspicious of Ast's interest in her past as a commodity or treasure to be dug up and exported to America. Obviously, there is a silent hostility among these ordinary people in the society against African Americans who collaborate with internal and external forces of exploitation and oppression, and who do not see themselves as insiders or commit themselves, as Ast is doing, to the task of undermining oppression and the 'new' slavery. At a moment of deep spiritual insight and communion at Tete's house, Ast hands herself over completely:

> "I asked about the companionship of the ankh, the ancient, the new, the connection," Ast said. Still no answer. "Or is the choice of the symbol accidental?" She did not stop her gaze from wandering upward. Still that silence. "Whoever you are," she said, speaking neither to Asar nor to Tete but in the direction of the ankh, "I have sought you and found you. Here I am. I want to work with you. To live with you." (271)

Unlike Cinque, who is interested in discovering a past that would enable him to create a future in which the returning African American is betrayed to another slavery, Ast's commitment is to the revival of Africa's spiritual and intellectual traditions as means of liberating Africa, and so she easily negotiates and finds space in the underground group, the Companionship. In her, Armah idealizes the type of African-American group that deserves welcome. Conversely, Cinque represents the unwelcome and undesirable group, since his commitment is to restore slave-holding in another form in Africa, even paradoxically, using fellow African Americans as victims. In other words, Armah seems to be alerting us to the danger of a second enslavement of African Americans by fellow African Americans who, like Cinque, have always been agents of enslavement, even in their past lives.

Related to the views of some African Americans interviewed (orally and via e-mail), Armah's representations of the African-American quest for identity and new future in Africa appears to suffer from reductionism: it appears to reduce the problems of integration faced by the homecomers to mere perceptions of the misdemeanours of undesirable elements like Cinque and Wossen. Of course, there could be some saints still left among continental Africans who would want to act as guardians of Africa's philosophical and spiritual values, and who might be fighting or resisting the homecomers acting as agents of oppression. But my study shows that the increasing alienation and marginalization of the African Americans who have relocated to Africa is not based on the undesirable-element theory, nor on the roles played by them in the countries where they have settled. It should be clear, rather, that some continental West Africans, especially educated ones, feel that the African Americans are "difficult to handle," or "hard to please." (Those of us who have been nurtured in contexts of dictatorship will always be inclined to *handle* people, as if they were mules!) Some of them think that these African Americans still nurse grievances against Africans on the continent, and against Africa, for what their ancestors experienced in terms of slavery in America.

On the other hand, there is resistance to the possibility of the emergence of a powerful and rich immigrant group from among the African Americans, who would in time dominate and control the continental Africans. A professor of history at the Université Nationale du Bénin, who, from his comments during a conversation in Ghana recently, appeared to be opposed to the return or repatriation of African Americans to Africa, very strongly emphasized the aspect of economic competition and its power implications.

However, the 'voices' of African-American homecomers who either granted us interviews or responded to the questionnaire we designed and distributed through e-mail quite eloquently reveal that there is growing prejudice against African Americans who have relocated to Africa, and that this prejudice is not at all connected with the roles they play in the social or political system. They reveal that they are denied access to social services, refused employment, and, of course, denied access to positions of authority. One of our respondents, Abena Safiya Fosua, who, along with Kwasi Issa Kena, has been living in Ghana's Ashanti region capital, Kumasi, for the past four years, says:

> We are treated with contempt, regarded as strangers and heckled on the streets with the degrading epithets reserved for whites! We have not been accepted by the church that we work with here. In fact, they took several years to stop calling us by our previous names which someone dug up in a file. The whites among them receive far greater respect than we do.

In answer to the question, "How do you respond to the treatment you have been receiving?" she says: "We have finally begun to tell them how we feel about being misused. We have let them know it is a betrayal of our collective history." She also very frankly discloses that "We will be leaving in a few months and do not intend to attempt this again."

Another respondent, who wished to remain anonymous, reveals that she was also mistreated and that for a long time she "felt very hurt, angry and alienated," but that she has come to a better understanding now, particularly of the fact that African Americans and continental Africans do not inherently, by dint of colour or culture or history, share a bond – often an African-American misperception – but must work to build a relationship and to give it meaning."

Vanessa P. Williams (Togbo Si), who, like Ast in *Osiris Rising*, relocated to the Republic of Benin in search of spiritual and cultural self-fulfilment, to develop herself as a priestess of the water goddess in the area – she holds three Masters degrees from well-known American universities and is completing her PhD – also recounts her bitterness and frustration at not being offered any job, because, she says, "Getting a job here is based on either whom you know or whom you can bribe. Nepotism is the order of the day. As for me, I am an outsider and a foreigner... not to mention being a woman." In addition, the fact that she could speak neither French nor Fon, she says, makes matters worse, as if she could hear the society clearly telling her: "I cannot give you a job if my tonton does not have one. Your degrees mean nothing to me! You speak neither French nor Fon... you are not here!" Convinced that returning to Africa ought not be something based on theory or political motivations, she, like Armah's Ast, insists that her return is a call of the spirit:

> My ancestors dwelled in this place. Just recently their name was revealed to me. [...] The name is Agassou. I believe that I may be the first child, of Agassou, returning from the diaspora in over 400 years. So you see, Benin [...] I am not a foreigner [...] I belong here [...] for I am your child returning home. And for that Benin should rejoice.

Judging from these African-American voices, whose return has been fictionalized by Armah, I would argue that their marginalization tends to intensify the frustrations arising from living on the hyphen, which the 'return' to the 'roots' was attempting precisely to resolve. If African-American homecomers are denied jobs, mistreated, or alienated, then it is no wonder that some of them settle for dubious acts like those carried out by Cinque and Wossen. It is also when they are marginalized that they begin to think of ways of getting back at the society, and start working for themselves only, rather than for anybody else's fictional future.

It thus appears that Armah's fictional exploration of the African-American quest for identity and a new future in Africa fails to tally with the real-life evidence that we have gathered. For the novelist, the ideal return is portrayed as being motivated by the wish to rediscover and re-use African spiritual and intellectual traditions for the liberation of the continent. On the other hand, the undesirable return is that which is motivated by the desire to create self-importance and heroism, and to restore slavery in a different guise. This form of return, for the novelist, is full of paradoxes, because it restores what it is escaping from, or what it claims to eradicate. However, by relating Armah's narrative to the narratives offered by other African-American returnees, we have found that prejudice and discrimination against those who have returned is not based on a perception of the subversion of spiritual/intellectual systems of liberation. On the contrary: these returning Africans often make serious efforts to restore African values and to fight for meaningful liberation – but they are either resisted or alienated. I would therefore argue that Armah's vision of desirable return is shot through with paradox, because of its infection by pessimism – a typical inclination on Armah's part. The destruction of Asar and the frustration Ast is made to suffer tend to cancel out any meaning otherwise inscribed into the return to rebuild Africa or to create a future for this continent. Ast will bring forth Asar's baby probably; but the baby would be fatherless.

WORKS CITED

Amuta, Chidi. "Portraits of the Contemporary African Artist in Armah's Novels," in *Critical Perspectives on Ayi Kwei Armah*, ed. Wright, 13–21.

Anyidoho, Kofi. "Literature and African Identity: The Example of Ayi Kwei Armah," in *Critical Perspectives on Ayi Kwei Armah*, ed. Wright, 34–47.

Armah, Ayi Kwei. *Osiris Rising: A Novel of Africa Past, Present and Future* (Popenguine: Per Ankh, 1995).

——. "Teaching Creative Writing," *West Africa* (20 May 1985).

——. *Why Are We So Blest?* (London: Heinemann, 1974).

Booth, James. *"Why Are We So Blest?* and the Limits of Metaphor," in *Critical Perspectives on Ayi Kwei Armah*, ed. Wright, 227–41.

Colmer, Rosemary. "The Human and the Divine: *Fragments* and *Why Are We So Blest?*" in *Critical Perspectives on Ayi Kwei Armah*, ed. Wright, 191–203.

Foucault, Michel. "Nietzsche, Genealogy, History," in *Language, Counter-Memory, Practice: Selected Essays and Interviews*, ed. Donald F. Bouchard (Ithaca NY: Cornell UP, 1997): 204–17.

Fraser, Robert. "The American Background in *Why Are We So Blest?*" in *Critical Perspectives on Ayi Kwei Armah*, ed. Wright, 257–64.

Griffiths, Gareth. "Structure and Image in Ayi Kwei Armah's *The Beautyful Ones Are Not Yet Born*," in *Critical Perspectives on Ayi Kwei Armah*, ed. Wright, 75–91.

Izevbaye, D.S. "Ayi Kwei Armah and the 'I' of the Beholder," in *Critical Perspectives on Ayi Kwei Armah*, ed. Wright, 22–33.

Johnson, Joyce. "The Promethean 'Factor' in Ayi Kwei Armah's *Fragments* and *Why Are We So Blest?*" in *Critical Perspectives on Ayi Kwei Armah*, ed. Wright, 204–16.

Oha, Obododimma. "The 'Tree of Return': Home, Exile, Memory, and the Visual Rhetoric of Reunion," *CONTEXT: Journal of Social & Cultural Studies* 3.2 (1999): 61–87.

Osundare, Niyi. *African Literature and the Crisis of Poststructuralist Theorising* (Ibadan: Option Book & Information Services, 1993).

Payne, Michael. *Reading Knowledge: An Introduction to Barthes, Foucault and Althusser* (Oxford: Blackwell, 1997).

Said, Edward W. *Culture and Imperialism* (London: Chatto & Windus, 1993).

Wright, Derek, ed. *Critical Perspectives on Ayi Kwei Armah* (Boulder CO: Three Continents, 1992).

《•》

Multiculturalism and Ethnicity
in Alan Paton's Fiction

M.Z. MALABA

A LAN PATON'S FICTION foregrounds his ardent desire to promote cross-cultural understanding among South Africans. Nadine Gordimer's description of South African writing as the "literature of a fractured society" highlights the polarization that is the legacy of institutionalized racism in that country. Much of Paton's fiction attempts to address the nature and consequences of these divisions and tentatively suggests possible solutions to these tensions. One of his greatest achievements is his capacity to render credible and moving accounts of the plights of the major ethnic groups in South Africa, which demonstrates his quest for harmony. But this harmony will arise only if people are prepared to "love their neighbour."[1]

The fundamental basis for the establishment of a multicultural society in South Africa is mutual trust and the acknowledgement of the dignity of the 'Other'. One of the dilemmas that Paton grapples with is the deep-rooted antipathy between the major racial groups in his "beloved country": namely, the blacks and whites; but the hatred is also manifest between the English-speaking South Africans and the Afrikaners; the Afrikaners and the Jews. It is, therefore, not surprising that his fiction addresses these divisions and, given the fact that he was a devout Anglican, one could say that his central text was "A kingdom divided against itself cannot stand."

Cry, the Beloved Country is Paton's best-known book. Its publication in 1948, ironically, coincided with the coming to power of the National Party, which proceeded to institutionalize racial discrimination. At the heart of his message is his profound belief in tolerance and understanding, informed by a liberal, Christian humanism:

> By liberalism I don't mean the creed of any party or any century. I mean a generosity of spirit, a tolerance of others, an attempt to comprehend otherness, a commitment to the

---

[1] For a sophisticated analysis of the meaning of "love" in Paton's works, see Andrew Foley's "'Considered as a Social Record': A Reassessment of *Cry, the Beloved Country*," *English in Africa* 2.1 (1998): 81; and J.B. Thompson, "Poetic Truth in *Too Late the Phalarope*," *English Studies in Africa* 24.1 (1981): 44.

rule of law, a high ideal of the worth and dignity of man, a repugnance of authoritarianism and a love of freedom.[2]

The man who best exemplifies these traits in the novel is Arthur Jarvis, who, like
Paton, grew up in a sheltered environment and learned to transcend the limited horizons of his English-speaking community and come to terms with the larger reality of
the huge gulf between and within the races. This growth in consciousness is summa-
rized in Jarvis' "Private Essay on the Evolution of a South African".[3] Breaking out of
the cocoon of a sheltered childhood, Jarvis wrestles with the legacy of the ruthless
exploitation of the resources and black inhabitants of the land. His treatise challenges
white South Africa to face up to the fact that the endemic crime it fears is a result of its
failure to respect the 'Other'; its systematic denudation of the dignity and integrity of
black African culture; and its refusal to live up to the Christian ideals of loving one's
neighbour and upholding the principle of universal brotherhood:

> It is not permissible to add to one's possessions if these things can only be done at the
> cost of other men. Such development has only one true name, and that is exploitation. It
> might have been permissible in the early days of our country, before we became aware of
> its cost, in the disintegration of native community life, in the deterioration of native
> family life, in poverty slums, and crime. But now that the cost is known, it is no longer
> permissible. [...]
> It is true that we hoped to preserve the tribal system by a policy of segregation. That
> was permissible. But we never did it thoroughly or honestly. We set aside one-tenth of
> the land for four-fifths of the people. Thus we made it inevitable, and some say that we
> did it knowingly, that labour would come to the towns. We are caught in the toils of our
> own selfishness. No one wishes to make the problem seem smaller than it is. No one
> wishes to make its solution seem easy. No one wishes to make light of the fears that
> beset us. But whether we be fearful or no, we shall never, because we are a Christian
> people, be able to evade moral issues. It is time…. (126–27)

Ironically, the moral imperatives were ignored by successive South African govern-
ments and electorates for almost fifty years. The rational basis of Arthur Jarvis's analysis, which can safely be taken as mirroring Paton's views, was ignored in favour of
"self-interest." But the text argues, powerfully, that a heavy price has to be paid, not
only by the whites, but by the whole community.

Ironically, Arthur Jarvis is gunned down in cold blood by one of the delinquents
whose lot he wishes to ameliorate. Within the Christian framework of the author,
Arthur's sacrificial death paradoxically leads to good results. Arthur's father, James, is
deeply moved by his son's "mission" and charitably fulfils his son's vision of restoration – at a local level, at least.

James Jarvis's resolve to initiate the physical restoration of Ndotsheni is presented as
a sign of good triumphing over evil. His son's "Private Essay on the Evolution of a
South African" opens his eyes to the importance of extending "charity and generosity"

[2] Alan Paton, *Journey Continued: An Autobiography* (Oxford: Oxford UP, 1988): 294.
[3] Alan Paton, *Cry, the Beloved Country* (1948; Harmondsworth: Penguin, 1977): 150–51. Further page references are in the main text.

(150) beyond the narrow confines of his home, to all the people of South Africa. Arthur's son's intervention also enhances the quality of life of the children in Ndotsheni, as James sees to it that they are regularly supplied with milk. Paton's argument is that individuals can make a difference. Change comes when people are prepared to act on their beliefs.

Cry, the Beloved Country is a deeply moving book. Those with a knowledge of Zulu or Ndebele simultaneously translate many portions of it into either language, because the author, through the assistance rendered by his colleague at Diepkloof Reformatory, has captured the rhythms of Zulu idiomatic speech beautifully.[4] Nevertheless, the subtext of the book is also deeply disturbing. One of the criticisms levelled at white Southern African liberals is that of their "trusteeship mentality," their belief that redemption can only occur in Africa through the mediation of whites. James Jarvis very kindly funds the building of a dam in Ndotsheni and employs an agricultural demonstrator to teach the villagers environmentally friendly farming methods. Reverend Stephen Kumalo sees this as an answer to prayer, while the demonstrator's response borders on that of an "ungrateful native." That Paton juxtaposes the two responses highlights his sensitivity to such criticism:

> — I am impatient for the dam, said the demonstrator. When the dam is made, there will be water for the pastures. I tell you, umfundisi, he said excitedly, there will be milk in this valley. It will not be necessary to take the white man's milk.
> Kumalo looked at him. Where would we be without the white man's milk? he asked. Where would we be without all this white man has done for us? Where would you be also? Would you be working for him here?
> — It is true I am paid by him, said the young man stubbornly, I am not ungrateful.
> — Then you should not speak so, said Kumalo coldly.
> There fell a constraint between them, until the young demonstrator said quietly, Umfundisi, I work here with all my heart, is it not so?
> — That is true indeed.
> — I work so because I work for my country and my people. You must see that, umfundisi. I could not work so for any master.
> — If you had no master, you would not be here at all.
> — I understand you, said the young man. This man is a good man, and I respect him. But it is not the way it should be done, that is all.
> — And what way should be done?
> — Not this way, said the young man doggedly.
> — What way then?
> — Umfundisi, it was the white man who gave us so little land, it was the white man who took us away from the land to go to work. And we were ignorant also. It is all these things together that have made this valley desolate. Therefore, what this good white man does is only a repayment.
> — I do not like this talk. [...]
> He grew excited. We work for Africa, he said, not for this man or that man. Not for a white man or a black man, but for Africa. (227–28; 229)

---

[4] For a detailed discussion of this, see Peter F. Alexander, *Alan Paton: A Biography* (Oxford: Oxford UP, 1994): 220.

The demonstrator's last statement foregrounds the importance of dedication to a principle that transcends racial consciousness. What is important is not the superficial issue of pigment, but the devotion to the greatest good of the greatest number. Paton stresses the issue of mutual interdependence, which is the highest common factor between the conservative views of the priest and the more radical vision of the young man.

A far more sinister element is Paton's portrayal of black nationalist politicians, as exemplified by John Kumalo. An attraction–repulsion dynamic is evident in this portrait. Some of the most eloquent speeches in the novel are delivered by Kumalo. The logic of his critique of soulless capitalism is irrefutable (158–61) and his gifts as an orator are underlined:

> The crowd stirs as though a great wind were blowing through it. Here is the moment, John Kumalo, for the great voice to reach even to the gates of Heaven. Here is the moment for words of passion, for wild indiscriminate words that can waken and madden and unleash. But he knows. He knows the great power that he has, the power of which he is afraid. And the voice dies away, as thunder dies away over mountains , and echoes and re-echoes more and more faintly. (159)

Paton cunningly gives with the right hand and takes away with the left. John is simultaneously very powerful and very weak: he does not have the courage that should go with his convictions. He is afraid not merely of realizing his full potential – he is also petrified of the remorseless apparatus of the state. By presenting the budding nationalist leader as self-centred and cowardly, Paton tarnishes the cause he represents. Admittedly, the continent has been plagued by callous, self-seeking leaders, and statesmen of the calibre of Sir Seretse Khama and Nelson Mandela have been few and far between. It seems that Paton, as a liberal, feared the revolutionary potential of a nationalist uprising. He was inherently more comfortable with reform than with radical transformation. Hence his heroes are Christian pacifists like Stephen Kumalo and Theophilus Msimangu. Nevertheless, the novel ends with a resounding affirmation of the rightness of the Africans' quest for dignity and freedom, as revealed in Kumalo's meditation:

> And now for all the people of Africa, the beloved country. *Nkosi Sikelel' i Afrika*, God save Africa. But he would not see that salvation. It lay afar off, because men were afraid of it. Because to tell the truth, they were afraid of him, and his wife, and Msimangu, and the young demonstrator. And what was there evil in their desires, in their hunger? That men should walk upright in the land where they were born, and be free to use the fruits of the earth, what was there evil in it? Yet men were afarid, with a fear that was deep, deep in the heart, a fear so deep that they hid their kindness, or brought it out with fierceness and anger, and hid it behind fierce and frowning eyes. They were afraid because they were so few. And such fear could not be cast out, but by love. It was Msimangu who had said, Msimangu who had no hate for any man, I have one great fear in my heart, that one day when they turn to loving they will find we are turned to hating. Oh, the grave and the sombre words. (235)

Paton's anxiety stems from his understanding of the just nature of the Africans' modest aspirations. The pathos lies in the inordinate fear of decent, moderate and gentle people – a fear that undermines the liberal cause of promoting mutual understanding and cooperation between the races. The emphasis he places on "fear" is significant because, as a Christian, he is acutely aware that the opposite of faith is fear – not disbelief. From a Christian perspective, the love that casts out fear is that which approximates to divine love, an unconditional love that places the needs and welfare of the beloved before one's own. Needless to say, secular love can also share these qualities.

Paton's prophetic vision foresaw the centrality of trade-union pressure as a catalyst for change. His gloomy prognostication was largely echoed by most observers of the South African political scene. One can, however, argue that God did indeed "save Africa" by calling forth a leader of the calibre of Nelson Mandela, who, by virtue of his moral authority, his commitment to reconciliation regardless of the cost, made such a significant contribution to averting a bloodbath in South Africa.[5]

While the central focus of *Cry, the Beloved Country* is on the relationship between whites and blacks, it also points out the friction between the English and the Afrikaners. The chasm between blacks and whites is put into perspective by the gulf between whites. James Jarvis reminisces on this:

> Ixopo was full of Afrikaners now, whereas once there had been none of them. For all the police were Afrikaners, and the post office clerks, and the men at the railway station, and the village people got on well with them one way and the other. Indeed, many of them had married English-speaking girls, and that was happening all over the country. His own father had sworn that he would disinherit any child of his who married an Afrikaner, but times had changed. The war had put things back a bit, for some of the Afrikaners had joined the army, and some were for the war but didn't join the army, and some were just for neutrality and if they had any feelings they concealed them, and some were for Germany but it wasn't wise for them to say anything about it. (114–15)

The above quotation highlights the importance of understanding the 'Other', of respecting the other's humanity – and there is no greater testimony to that than marrying the other. The gulf between people can be bridged by a willingness to encounter them as individuals, rather than reducing them to stereotypes. Multiculturalism demands an openness to other cultures and external influences. Brian Worsfold has analyzed how the South African state used legislation to restrict marriages between members of different racial groups in order to short-circuit meaningful encounters across the colour bar:

> From the first moments of his election victory, [Dr. D.F.] Malan began the long, steady process of the apartheidisation of South African society. In 1949 he introduced the Prohibition of Mixed Marriages Act, which made marriages between Black and White individuals illegal, thereby extending the Immorality Act of 1927 to cover all Blacks, that is, all 'non-Whites'. In 1950 Malan introduced the Population Registration Act which entailed a system of classification of the peoples of South Africa on the basis of the compilation of a racial register and the issue of identity cards. In terms of the Act, the population of

[5] For a succinct assessment of Mandela's role, see Brian J. Worsfold, *South African Backdrop: An Historical Introduction for South African Literary and Cultural Studies* (Lleida: Edicions de la Universitat de Lleida, 1999): 114ff.

South Africa was divided into Cape Coloured, Cape Malay, Griqua, Indian, Chinese, 'other Asiatics' and 'other Coloured'.[6]

The colonial strategy of divide and rule is manifest here. The fragmentation of the society into several ethnic groups was designed to frustrate efforts to build a multi-racial state. It is deeply ironic that the Afrikaners, who are of hybrid stock, consisting of the original Dutch settlers, plus Huguenot refugees, Germans, English, Irish, Scottish and African ancestry, should have built a mythic identity based on racial purity. Much of Paton's subsequent writing challenged the inhumanity of apartheid legislation.

The white-supremacist basis of Afrikaner identity is predicated on a rejection of the egalitarian nature of Ordinance Number 50 of 1828, promulgated by the British Governor, which gave new rights to Khoikhoi, San and Coloured people, as noted in Paton's article "Afrikaners and the English," where he cites the objections expressed by Anna Steenkamp, Piet Retief's niece:

> And yet it is not so much their freedom which drove us to such lengths as their being placed on equal footing with Christians, contrary to the laws of God, and the natural distinction of race and colour, so that it was intolerable for any decent Christian to bow down beneath such a yoke, wherefore we withdrew in order to preserve our doctrines in purity.[7]

The "great trek" from abhorrent British legislation is the core of the Afrikaner identity, as noted in *Too Late the Phalarope*:

> The mist had gone, and the stars shone down on the grass country, on the farms of his nation and people, Buitenverwagting and Nooitgedacht, Weltevreden and Dankbaarheid, on the whole countryside that they had bought with years of blood and sacrifice; for they had trekked from the British Government with its officials and its missionaries and its laws that made a black man as good as his master, and had trekked into a continent, dangerous and trackless, where wild beasts and savage men, grim and waterless plains, had given way before their fierce will to be separate and survive. Then out of the harsh world of rock and stone they had come to the grass country, all green and smiling, and had given to it the names of peace and thankfulness. They had built their houses and their churches; and as God had chosen them for a people, so did they choose him for their God, cherishing their separateness that was now His Will. They set their conquered enemies apart, ruling them with unsmiling justice, declaring 'no equality in Church or State', and making the iron law that no white man might touch a black woman, nor might any white woman be touched by a black man. And to go against this law, of a people of rock and stone in a land of rock and stone, was to be broken and destroyed.[8]

---

[6] Worsfold, *South African Backdrop*, 67.

[7] Alan Paton, *Save the Beloved Country*, ed. Hans Strydom & David Jones (Melville: Hans Strydom, 1987): 116.

[8] Alan Paton, *Too Late the Phalarope* (1955; Harmondsworth: Penguin, 1986): 18. Further page references are in the main text.

The harshness of the landscape mirrors the harshness of the people and their God. The repetition of "rock" recalls, for the Southern African reader, the pejorative nickname given to Afrikaners: "rock spiders." The reference to "wild beasts and savage men" is reflected in Piet van der Merwe's attitude towards the indigenous inhabitants and animals of the Bokkeveld, in André Brink's powerful novel *A Chain of Voices*.[9] Both novels satirize the self-serving "New Israelite" myth cultivated by Afrikaner nationalists, since racial bigotry and fundamentalist zeal combined to entrench a viciously anti-Christian ideology.

Pieter van Vlaanderen, the anti-hero of *Too Late the Phalarope*, is struck down for committing an offence under Act 5 of the 1927 Immorality Act, which was supposed to guarantee the purity of the whites. Running through the book is the author's concern for the numerous lives that have been blighted by this unnatural Act, for love, passion, desire or lust are colour-blind. Besides Dick (20), there is the pathetic horror of the Smith case (33–34), and Pieter's own plight:

> For this is the greatest and holiest of all the laws, and if you [Stephanie] break it and are discovered, for you it is nothing but another breaking of the law. But if I break it and am discovered, the whole world will be broken. (94)

Paton judges the community by its own standards and shows how far it falls short of its professed Christian ideals. This is best exemplified by Pieter's father, Jakob, whose faith is essentially that of the Old Testament, of the relentless rigour of "an eye for an eye and a tooth for a tooth," rather than the new covenant of love, forgiveness and compassion that can be seen in his wife's gentle nature and that of Captain Massingham, who assumes the role of a father, in the end, when Jakob assumes that of a judge. Jakob's view is reinforced by Pieter's father-in-law:

> When we went into the house, Nella's father was waiting for us, the tall and fierce old man, with the face like that of an eagle, and the blue and piercing eyes. To him the captain told the story of all, and when he had finished, the fierce old man struck the arm of his chair and said, I would shoot him like a dog. Then because no one spoke, he said to the captain, wouldn't you? And the captain said, no.
> — You wouldn't?
> — No.
> — But he has offended against the race.
> The captain said trembling, *meneer*, as a policeman I know an offence against the law, and as a Christian I know an offence against God; but I do not know an offence against the race.
> So the old man turned to me and said, *mevrou* ....
> — *Mejuffrou*, I said
> Then he recognized me at last, for all his piercing eyes, and said, *mejuffrou*, I am sorry....
> — *Meneer*, said the captain, if man takes unto himself God's right to punish, then he must also take upon himself God's promise to restore. If we....

---

[9] André Brink, *A Chain of Voices* (London: Faber & Faber, 1982).

— You are an Englishman, said Nella's father, fiercely but without offence. You do
not understand these things.
— I am not an Englishman, I said, but I understand them.
The old man said, it will not help to stay any longer, and with a brief *goeie nag*, he
went. (195–96)

The human predicament is ignored in favour of racial solidarity. Group loyalty takes
precedence over compassion – Pieter's description of the Immorality Act as "*the
greatest and holiest of all the laws*" is proved correct. Yet, to those outside the laager,
the spiritual excellence of this law is by no means apparent.[10]

Pieter refers to his lust as a "mad sickness," but its pleasant aspects draw him repeatedly back to Stephanie. She is not fooled by the public perception of Pieter; she
realizes how much he desires her – she sees him as a man who sees her as a woman.
The attraction transcends man-made barriers and highlights the folly of legislating for
human emotions. The fact that Paton returned to this theme, in *Ah, But Your Land is
Beautiful*, which was first published in 1981, twenty-six years after *Too Late the
Phalarope*, shows how important it was to him. Pieter projects his lust onto Stephanie,
attempting to externalize his baser instincts.

Pieter, whose name means 'rock', is a colossus – with feet of clay. He epitomizes
the Afrikaner ideal – an outdoorsman, a great shot, a military hero (even though his
father never forgives him for fighting on the English side during the Second World
War), and a great rugby player. Yet he is more than just the stereotypical white Southern African "macho man." His gentler side bears eloquent testimony to the need for
white settler societies to transcend their limited horizons and seek to cultivate more
balanced personalities. His consciousness has been shaped, to some extent, by outside
influences, whereas his father's world is largely confined to a *dorp* like Venterspan.
Significantly, he has to emigrate, because "a people of rock and stone in a land of rock
and stone" will not forgive him for violating the colour bar. Furthermore, his closet
friend, Kappie, is Jewish. Some Afrikaners felt drawn to the Jews because of a shared
sense of suffering or persecution and because of the centrality of the doctrine of election in both faiths, while others, as noted earlier, sympathized with Nazism. The fact
that Pieter and Nella have to emigrate shows how the Afrikaner community refuses to
tolerate "deviants." The polarization of white South African society needs to be neutra-
lized, so that the crack shot and the lover of flowers can be appreciated for synthesiz-
ing the stereotypically male and female aspects of one's personality. Multiculturalism,
in its broadest sense, fosters wholeness, a balance between firmness and gentleness, the
spiritual and the material, the pure and the hybrid.

The difficulty of establishing meaningful connections between the races is brought
out powerfully in the story "A Drink in the Passage," where a young Afrikaner, Jannie
van Rensburg, tries to 'touch' the black narrator, Edward Simelane, by inviting him

---

[10] For incisive analyses of Paton's perceptions of the rule of law, see Michael Black, "Alan
Paton and the Rule of Law," *African Affairs* 91 (1992): 53–72, and David Medalie, "'A Corri-
dor Shut at Both Ends': Admonition and Impasse in Van der Post's *In a Province* and Paton's
Cry, the Beloved Country," *English in Africa* 25. 2 (1998): 103–104.

home for a drink. The tenuous nature of the gesture is captured in the manner in which they proceed to his flat:

> We didn't exactly walk abreast, but he didn't exactly walk in front of me. He didn't look constrained. He wasn't looking round to see if anyone might be watching.[11]

The burden of the past militates against meaningful contact – while van Rensburg appreciates Simelane's sculpture and his academic achievements, he is so imprisoned by his upbringing that he cannot invite Simelane into his flat to share the drink, which is consumed outside. Van Rensburg's family is very polite, but the uncle still patronizingly calls Simelane "boy" (23). The stressful encounter undermines the gesture, as Simelane is petrified that he could be arrested for trespassing and for consuming European liquor.

Segregation was designed to minimize social contact between members of different races, and in other stories in *Debbie Go Home* we see the harmful effects of this legacy. In "Ha'penny," Mrs Maarman is initially offended that a Mosuto orphan 'adopts' her, a coloured, as his mother, but she does respond to him as a person once he falls ill, after Paton's intervention, rather than dismissing him as a 'type'. Once she gets beyond the superficial aspect of ethnicity, her true humanity emerges.

The coloured community also suffered badly from the legal manoeuvres of the apartheid regime. "Debbie Go Home" highlights the devastating impact of the ironically named Industrial Conciliation Act on the de Villiers family. Job reservation policies were designed to protect the whites from competition and reinforce notions of white supremacy. The pathos is highlighted by the fissures in the de Villiers family, where we find the older generation leaning towards assimilationist attitudes, whereas Johnny actively challenges the status quo. The precarious position of coloureds under apartheid is also illustrated by the predicament of Mr Prinsloo in *Ah, But Your Land is Beautiful*, who has always 'passed' as white, but whose world falls apart when he is reclassified.[12]

Paton was particularly incensed by the use of the police to undermine law and order. In the profoundly moving story "Life for a Life," we see how the 'civilizing mission' of the settlers is undermined by their brutality. Paton builds up the tension beautifully:

> Guilt lay heavily upon them [Enoch and Sara Maarman] both, because they had hated Big Baas Flip, not with clenched fists and bared teeth, but, as befitted people in their station, with salutes and deference. (44)

Big Baas Flip's ruthlessness is mirrored by that of the sadistic detective, Robbertse:

> He knew that Robbertse was one, the big detective with the temper that got out of hand, so that the reddish foam would come out of his mouth, and he would hold a man by the throat till one of his colleagues would shout at him to let the man go. Sara's father, who

---

[11] Alan Paton, *Debbie Go Home* (1961; Harmondsworth, Penguin: 1965): 89. Further page references are in the main text.

[12] Alan Paton, *Ah, But Your Land is Beautiful* (London: Jonathan Cape, 1981): 241–46.

was one of the wisest men in all the district of Poort, said that he could never be sure whether Robbertse was mad or only pretending to be, but it didn't really matter, because whichever it was, it was dangerous. (44–45)

Robbertse toys with the humble shepherd and his wife, alternately treating them with mock politeness and unbridled scorn. Nevertheless, notwithstanding his great fear, Enoch insists on asserting his dignity as a man who deserves to be treated with respect in his own house and before his wife (48). As in Luis Bernardo Honwana's *We Killed Mangy-Dog*, the ritual humiliation of blacks by those in authority is meant to entrench the status quo.[13]

Cry, the Beloved Country foregrounds the tensions between blacks and whites, and *Too Late the Phalarope* focuses on the tensions between the white communities and among the Afrikaners. In *Debbie Go Home*, Paton highlights the plight of the coloureds in two of his stories. The role of the Indian community in the struggle for civil rights features prominently in *Ah, But Your Land is Beautiful*, where one of the protagonists in the first part of the book is the beautiful heroine of the Defiance Campaign, Prem Bodasingh. The text pays tribute to the discipline and industrious nature of many members of the community, who rose to great heights from humble origins as indentured labourers. The cooperation between the blacks and Indians in the Defiance Campaign irritated the Nationalist government, which felt threatened by the solidarity between the two major groups in Natal.[14]

One of the weaknesses of *Ah, But Your Land is Beautiful* is the fact that it is essentially a chronicle of the predicament of the Liberal Party, to which Paton devoted many years of his life. Characterization, which is one of his strengths as a writer, is subordinated to the philosophical issues the author wishes to discuss. The picaresque structure of the book and the plethora of historical figures disrupt the flow of the narrative. The characters tend to be one-dimensional – for example, the dispirited black liberal headmaster, Wilberforce Nhlapo, who is emotionally dependent on Robert Mansfield; and the ebullient, evangelical black liberal, Emmanuel Nene. Limitations such as these precipitated Robert J. Linneman's harsh critique of Paton's works:

> There can be no denying that Alan Paton is a master stylist who has produced numerous works of art. Unfortunately, however, his essential philosophy has not grown with the passage of time. He is the same man now as he was in 1948. Despite his literary merit, it would be impossible to regard him as a visionary. His ideas are at best Utopian and he lacks the understanding and the commitment to forge the world he says he wants. Optimally Paton can be regarded as an anachronism, a noble one perhaps in the eyes of some, but nevertheless a man whose artistic vision will do nothing to promote a South Africa based on the concept of multiracial equity.[15]

---

[13] Luis Bernardo Honwana, *We Killed Mangy-Dog*, tr. Dorothy Guedes (*Nós matámos o cão tinhoso*; 1969; London, Heinemann, 1986).

[14] Paton, *Ah, But Your Land is Beautiful*, 29.

[15] Robert J. Linneman, "Alan Paton: Anachronism or Visionary," *Commonwealth Novel in English* 3.1 (1984): 99.

Linneman's dismissal of Paton is excessive and based on philosophical differences. Paton's life-long devotion to liberal values is not a sign of a stunted personality, a refusal to face reality. As Tony Morphet has pointed out, the sources of Paton's public authority "lay in his refusal to temporize."[16] Furthermore, as Richard Rive notes, Paton is "one of South Africa's finest and most sincere writers."[17] Notwithstanding their electoral failure, white liberals in southern Africa exerted significant influence on the minds of many blacks, who realized that tarring all whites with the same brush was the equivalent of the racial stereotyping they themselves were subjected to by white supremacists.

By highlighting the position of the poor, powerless and oppressed, Alan Paton demonstrates the moral, philosophical and spiritual bankruptcy of Nationalist rule. Paton's endeavours to represent the majority of the people of his beloved country stressed the importance of a holistic approach to solving the ills of a "troubled land." And, despite his strategic shifts towards a federal rather than a unitary model for an independent nation, in later life,[18] his devotion to the liberal ideals of "a generosity of spirit, a tolerance of others, an attempt to comprehend otherness, a commitment to the rule of law, a high ideal of the worth and dignity of man, a repugnance for authoritarianism and a love of freedom" is indisputable.

WORKS CITED

Alexander, Peter F. *Alan Paton: A Biography* (Oxford: Oxford UP, 1994).

Black, Michael. "Alan Paton and the Rule of Law," *African Affairs* 91 (January 1992): 53–72.

Brink, André. *A Chain of Voices* (London: Faber & Faber, 1982).

Foley, Andrew. "'Considered as a Social Record': A Reassessment of *Cry, the Beloved Country*," *English in Africa* 25.2 (1998): 81.

Honwana, Luis Bernardo. *We Killed Mangy-Dog*, tr. Dorothy Guedes (*Nós matámos o cão tinhoso*; 1969; London: Heinemann, 1986).

Linneman, Robert J. "Alan Paton: Anachronism or Visionary," *Commonwealth Novel in English* 3.1 (Spring–Summer 1984): 88–100.

Medalie, David. "'A Corridor Shut at Both Ends': Admonition and Impasse in Van der Post's *In a Province* and Paton's *Cry, the Beloved Country*," *English in Africa* 25. 2 (1998): 93–110.

Morphet, Tony. "Courteous Confused: The Paton Biography," *Current Writing* 7.1 (1995): 117–24.

Paton, Alan. *Cry, the Beloved Country* (1948; Harmondsworth, Penguin, 1977).

——. *Debbie Go Home* (1961; Harmondsworth, Penguin: 1965).

——. *Journey Continued: An Autobiography* (Oxford: Oxford. UP, 1988).

——. *Save the Beloved Country*, ed. Hans Strydom & David Jones (Melville: Hans Strydom, 1987).

——. *Too Late the Phalarope* (1955; Harmondsworth: Penguin, 1986).

Rive, Richard. "The Liberal Tradition in South African Literature," *Contrast* 14.3 (1983): 19–31.

---

[16] Tony Morphet, "Courteous Confused: The Paton Biography," *Current Writing* 7.1 (1995): 123.

[17] Richard Rive, "The Liberal Tradition in South African Literature," *Contrast* 14.3 (1983): 31.

[18] For a detailed discussion of this issue, see Alexander, *Alan Paton: A Biography*, ch. 22.

Thompson, J.B. "Poetic Truth in *Too Late the Phalarope*," *English Studies in Africa* 24.1 (1981): 37–44.

Worsfold, Brian J. *South African Backdrop: An Historical Introduction for South African Literary and Cultural Studies* (Lleida: Edicions de la Universitat de Lleida, 1999).

⟨⟨●⟩⟩

Ridiculing Rainbow Rhetoric
Christopher Hope's *Me, the Moon and Elvis Presley*

JOCHEN PETZOLD

I
N *IMAGININGS OF SAND*, one of André Brink's more recent novels, the conservative Afrikaner Anna has difficulties in adapting to the political situation in
South Africa shortly before the first democratic elections in 1994. "There's a
whole new language developed in the country these last few years," she tells her
sister.[1] Obviously, this is a language which seems strange to her. In *The Devil's Chimney*, Anne Landsman does not have to tell her readers that the narrator Connie still
thinks in the racist categories of apartheid: words like 'hotnot', 'kaffir' or 'Bantu'
effectively expose Connie's views.[2] Both examples show that issues concerning language are highly charged in South Africa – not only on the level of choosing one of the
eleven official languages as a means of communication, but also on the level of the
lexicon within a given language. This may be especially valid where English and Afrikaans are concerned, the official languages of the former oppressive state-apparatus.

It is, of course, one of the basic insights of Foucauldian discourse analysis that language creates and stabilizes power-relations. As various critics have repeatedly shown,
discriminatory practices are manifest in the language used, and marginalized groups
are constituted through language. For example, this has been demonstrated convincingly in the analysis of colonial discourse, as becomes clear in Homi Bhabha's brief definition of the term:

> It [colonial discourse] is an apparatus that turns on the recognition and disavowal of ra-
> cial/cultural/historical differences. [...] It seeks authorisation for its strategies by the pro-
> duction of knowledges of coloniser and colonised which are stereotypical but antitheti-
> cally evaluated. The objective of colonial discourse is to construe the colonised as a
> population of degenerate types on the basis of racial origin, in order to justify conquest
> and to establish systems of administration and instruction.[3]

---

[1] André Brink, *Imaginings of Sand* (London: Secker & Warburg, 1996): 131.

[2] See Anne Landsman, *The Devil's Chimney* (Johannesburg: Jonathan Ball, 1998).

[3] Homi K. Bhabha, "Difference, Discrimination and the Discourse of Colonialism," in *The
Politics of Theory*, ed. Francis Baker (Colchester: U of Essex P, 1983): 198.

The strategies of 'othering' referred to by Bhabha all work on the level of language: differences are constituted, knowledge is established, and administration and instruction are effected through language. Of course, apartheid was legally different from colonialism – after all, South Africa had officially become independent with the creation of the South African Union in 1910. But oppression based on quasi-colonial categories is clearly not limited to 'official' colonies – and neither does it necessarily end after independence has been gained or granted.[4] Apartheid politics created a discourse that closely resembled that of colonialism: non-whites were excluded from political power by a classificatory system based on skin-colour, and the division was enforced by a white administration that claimed the right to define who was non-white, just as the colonizers had defined the colonized.[5] White apartheid-discourse had the same will to power, expressed in the strategies of 'othering' the non-white, that is at the heart of colonial discourse.

Consequently, South Africa is faced with the task of 'decolonizing'[6] its language-use, aiming at non-discriminatory representation of the various members of the "Rainbow nation." This situation is comparable to – if not identical with – the injustices addressed by the proponents of political correctness in the USA: Karol Janicki explains that "PC arose as a socio-political movement which was intended to combat social injustice in general and discrimination against minorities in particular."[7] Of course, the fact that language implies power and that reality is created through language (at least to some extent) does not mean that simple changes in the lexicon automatically alter sociopolitical realities or a person's system of values – despite the fact that many proponents and opponents of the political correctness debate seem to think differently.[8] When Anna's husband in Brink's *Imaginings of Sand* changes the offending words he

---

[4] This aspect of 'post-colonial' oppression has been treated more fully by Jorge Klor de Alva, "The Postcolonization of the (Latin) American Experience: A Reconsideration of 'Colonialism', 'Postcolonialism', and 'Mestizaje'," in *After Colonialism: Imperial Histories and Postcolonial Displacements*, ed. Gyan Prakash (Princeton NJ: Princeton UP, 1995).

[5] In fact, Section 5(1) of the Identification Act (No. 72 of 1986) "gives the Director-General: Home Affairs the expressed authority to classify every person whose name is in the population register as either white, coloured or black"; S. Girvin, "Race and Race Classification," in *Race and the Law in South Africa*, ed. A. Rycroft, L. Boulle, M. Robertson & P. Spiller (Cape Town: Juta, 1987): 5. Numerous laws, passed by the white legislature, gave definitions for 'racial' classification. Most importantly, the Population Registration Act (No. 30 of 1950) provided the first definition of three main groups: Whites, Natives and Coloureds.

[6] Salman Rushdie has coined this phrase in an article for the London *Times*, but his emphasis was on the creation of a distinctly Indian variaty of English; see Salman Rushdie, "The Empire Writes Back with a Vengeance," *The Times* (3 July 1982): 8. I am using it as an image for overcoming the lexical legacies of a racist system.

[7] Karol Janicki, "Political Correctness: Conflict-Ridden Language, Language-Ridden Conflict, or Both?" *Belgian Journal of Linguistics* 11 (1997): 301.

[8] This point is argued in more detail in Edna Andrews, "Cultural Sensitivity and Political Correctness: The Linguistic Problem of Naming," *American Speech* 71.4 (1996): 392–93.

frequently uses – for example, saying "blacks" instead of "kaffirs" – this switch is immaterial to his racist views and prejudices.[9]

This essay is not intended as an evaluation of the language-policies behind political correctness. The preliminary remarks were necessary to situate my discussion of Christopher Hope's satirical novel *Me, the Moon and Elvis Presley*, since Hope explores the humorous aspect of the discrepancy between a language deemed 'politically correct' and the preconceptions and evaluative categories still present in people's minds. Interestingly, the critique of double standards that is central to Hope's satire was the first use of the term 'political correctness': According to Kay Losey and Hermann Kurthen,

> [...] the term PC originated in Maoist and Stalinist literature. It came into use as a self-critical statement among Leftists in the 1960s when "guilt-tripping" or being "guilt-tripped" about their commitment to their beliefs. If they did something that was not consistent with their professed political belief, it would be called, either by themselves or by another member of their in-group, "not politically correct."[10]

The issue of naming – a central aspect of politically correct speech, as Edna Andrews has shown[11] – is emphasized repeatedly in Hope's novel. Even the setting highlights the political implications of naming: the novel is set in a small town in the Karoo, a town which had already changed names in the past to accommodate changing political realities. Starting out as Buckingham, it is renamed Lutherburg when Malan's National Party wins the elections in 1948. In 1994, the name is changed back to Buckingham. Streets that had names like Marlborough or George in the old Buckingham are renamed Voortrekker or Leibrandt in Lutherburg and are now called Democracy Drive or Freedom Street. However, as readers soon find out, little has changed in the minds of the town's inhabitants.

Hope chooses to explore the comical sides of this situation, particularly the hypocrisy at work when individuals try to find solutions for linguistic problems brought about by the "new South Africa." Inevitably, these solutions will leave prejudices untouched. For example, the white town's old doctor is embarrassed by the fact that his gardener, who is described as "plain simple Saul in his blue overall and his brown felt hat,"[12] is now the new health inspector. Facing the possibility that charges might be brought against him, Dr du Plessis needs to talk to Saul, but he is unsure of the proper form of address.

> But what the hell to call him? Saul always addressed the doctor as *meneer*. Now *that* was an idea! *Meneer...* So he tried. He put his heart into it. He practised in front of the mirror.

---

[9] Brink, *Imaginings*, 51.

[10] Kay Losey & Hermann Kurthen, "The Rhetoric of 'Political Correctness' in the U.S. Media," *Amerikastudien* 40.2 (1995): 228.

[11] Edna Andrews, "Cultural Sensitivity and Political Correctness: The Linguistic Problem of Naming," *American Speech* 71.4 (1996): 389–94.

[12] Christopher Hope, *Me, the Moon, and Elvis Presley* (London: Macmillan, 1997): 65. Further page references are in the main text.

And in the mirror, it worked; but the moment he tried a *meneer* anywhere near his gardener the word died on his tongue. [...] One day he couldn't stand it any longer so he downed a couple of brandies, waved to Saul [...] and pleasantly but firmly called: 'Oh – ah – *Mr* Saul ..'.[13] It should have been fine. A bloody good compromise. Exactly the right note. Respectful – but not obsequious. Formal but not fawning. But the stupid old fool pricked up his ears at the 'Mister' and goggled around the garden trying to work out who the boss was talking to. (66—67)

The act of politically correct re-naming misfires because the recipient of the message does not decode the new form of address as it was intended. While the gardener is not described as particularly intelligent, the joke is mainly at the expense of Dr du Plessis: His search for a proper form of address is revealed as hypocritical and self-centred, since he only thinks of a 'proper' title for his gardener when he becomes afraid of an inquiry into his professional record. In du Plessis's mind, his gardener remains "simple Saul" (66), but since he now occupies a position of power, du Plessis is torn between the fear of offending the new health inspector, thus jeopardizing his future, and the fear of overdoing it, of sounding "too servile" (66), and thus losing his standing among the white neighbours who might overhear him. Obviously, the real change has not yet taken place in Dr du Plessis's way of thinking – but nor has his gardener grasped the linguistic implications of the new situation.

Intention and perception of language-use are also central to the episode concerning a 'speaking' bird, the budgerigar Roy, who learns to categorize people according to ethnic background:

You only needed to hold the picture up to his cage bars, tell him who he was looking at, give him another glimpse and he knew it. He hopped up, fixed it with his bright, round eye and sang out: 'Four spear carriers' or 'Two Jewboys' or 'Six pansies', exactly as you'd told him, in your own voice. [...] Roy did ethnic groups; he did new categories, too. When the brown foreman who had replaced Bill Harding at the PO and five pole-planters marched past the window, he called out: 'Six affirmatives!' (118–19)

After the election in 1994, Roy's performances start to give offence. The new mayor leads a delegation to Roy's owner, which the bird duly describes as "Five affirmatives and one coolie" (121). The mayor now insists that Roy would have to change his language, since "words like 'coolie',' 'Jewboy', 'woodenhead', 'Hottentot' and 'Bushman' had no place in the new Buckingham" (121–22).

As both Karol Janicki and Günther Lampert emphasize, one of the problems behind politically correct naming is that an insult is not simply inherent in the lexical items used. Rather, it is intended by the speaker, and/or perceived by the receiver of an utterance.[14] In the case of the speaking bird Roy, Hope clearly satirizes an over-zealous

---

[13] Like the stereotypical white South African, Dr du Plessis does not of course know the family name of his domestic employee.

[14] See Günther Lampert, "*Political Correctness* und die sprachliche Konstruktion der Wirklichkeit: Eine Skizze," *Amerikastudien* 40.2 (1995): 252; Janicki, "Political Correctness," 304. This interactive aspect clearly poses problems for attempts of changing offensive language. Terms that are negatively marked for some speakers may be perfectly inoffensive for other speakers –

insistence on politically correct speech that remains on the lexical surface. Since the bird does not really understand what it says – its words are pure mimicry – it is unable to intend offence. Nonetheless, Roy's owner then tries to re-educate the bird by making him substitute new names for derogatory and racist terms. But since the bird does not understand the insulting quality of its words, Hope can use the new speech-code to ridicule language policies like those implemented by many universities in the USA. The futility of re-educating a bird who is unable to understand the level of con-notation is further emphasized by the list of methods used: solitary confinement, a rubber band around the beak, deprivation of sleep and food. These methods are cruel and mirror the practices of authoritarian systems – comparisons with South Africa's secret police (under apartheid rule) can easily be drawn. Interestingly, Hope's critique uses the same approach conservative opponents to language policies adopt towards political correctness in the USA: both equate PC with totalitarian methods or the Or-wellian 'thought police' in order to discredit speech codes.[15]

At the same time, Hope's text does not simply denounce the project of 'decoloniz-ing' the English language used in South Africa. This becomes obvious when we con-sider the fact that his critique goes deeper than the surface level of lexical items used. Since the bird simply repeats what it heard from humans, even copying the tone of their voices, Roy is clearly set up as a scapegoat on the level of the story. At the same time, the bird is a striking example of the fact that word-usage may be indicative of thought patterns but does not have to be. Unless we ascribe complex thought to the bird, its utterances are without intended meaning, and the true addressees of language policies would have to be its earlier teachers. But with them – i.e. the white inhabitants of Buckingham – change seldom goes deeper than the lexical surface. Thus, Dr du Plessis still thinks of his gardener as "simple Saul," and Hope insists that little has changed in the town except for the names: "In fact all that had changed were the tunes, the names, the codes, the words for not saying what you meant" (215).

Mindless insistence on politically correct re-naming is, of course, an easy target for satire. Günther Lampert insists that policies of language change are one possible aspect of addressing sociopolitical injustices, and I would agree.[16] While Hope's novel does point out that linguistic changes are not in themselves sufficient to change these reali-ties, Hope does not simply transplant anti-PC sentiments current in the USA (as de-scribed by Kay Losey and Hermann Kurthen) to the South African situation. Quite the contrary: Most opponents of political correctness in the USA today aim not at the sur-face level of appropriate speech; instead, they aim at the idea of emancipation and multiculturalism that is at the basis of such language policies. The term political cor-rectness has clearly shifted its meaning: As Lorna Weir argues convincingly, it was initially used, for example, to "criticize specific aspects of feminist practice," not in

---

even among the same minority group. Furthermore, previously neutral terms can acquire negative connotations, and virtually any name given to a group of humans can be used insultingly: i.e. can be intended or perceived as an insult.

[15] See Losey & Kurthen, "The Rhetoric of 'Political Correctness'," 243–44.

[16] See Lampert, "*Political Correctness* und die sprachliche Konstruktion der Wirklichkeit," 251.

order to "discredit feminism as a whole."[17] It was used from within leftist movements, not as fundamental opposition from outside the movement; use of the term PC "marked the sender as both hostile to dogmatism and aligned with the forces of social change."[18] The neoconservative use of the term 'politically correct', however, is an attack on the ideas behind language policies, and it "has succeeded in disseminating a new meaning potential for PC, one that unifies a diverse number of democratic struggles under the rubric of PC, and then associates PC with tyranny."[19]

Hope's satire is of a different nature: it takes up criticism of PC from within the social movements. While Hope clearly criticizes the danger of fetishizing politically correct re-naming into an empty gesture, he does not dismiss the political agenda behind it. His criticism is not aimed at sociopolitical changes. On the contrary: he satirizes the lack of change that hides behind a smokescreen of political correctness. This becomes obvious in the sympathetic characters Hope creates, characters who actually do change – without necessarily altering their lexicon to accommodate rainbow rhetoric.

One of the central characters in the novel is a woman from the "brown town," who is bought at an early age by an eccentric white woman, Aunt Betsy. She comes to be called "Me," and Aunt Betsy interprets this, in the vein of colonial discourse, to mean that Me belongs to her, is part of her – since she has bought her. When one of Me's friends is killed by a white farmer, Me alters her life. She leaves Aunt Betsy, moves into Golden Meadow, becomes the Clerk of Births and changes her name to Mimi, "because there's more of Me now," as she says (200). In fact, as the narrator remarks, she becomes "someone else" (206). People in Buckingham/Lutherburg are shocked by Mimi's behaviour, particularly her voluntary relocation: "Mayor Joost said what everyone thought: 'We're here and they're there. Isn't it? And you don't go there from here'" (199). Later, after the democratic elections, Mimi is again one of the few to change places – she moves back into the ancient cottage left to her by Aunt Betsy. With Mimi, these changes in name and address are merely external signs of inner changes. As deputy mayor she actually tries to help people – regardless of skin colour – and she is the only one to question the hypocrisy of the outward changes in the people around her.

Yet Hope's chief aim is clearly not the creation of role-models for the new South Africa. In this novel, he exposes the hypocrisy behind much rainbow rhetoric and, as Michael Morris remarks in his review, "probes the illusions and obsessions of the political renovation of the present."[20] That one of his main concerns is the deceptive relationship between language and reality is emphasized by the ending: Hope's novel closes with the fraudulent trick played by a con man – a man who can manipulate 'reality' through language. At the beginning of the novel, Pascal is ironically intro-

---

[17] Lorna Weir, "PC Then and Now: Resignifying Political Correctness," in *Beyond Political Correctness: Toward the Inclusive University*, ed. Stephen Richter & Lorna Weir (Toronto: Toronto UP, 1995): 58.

[18] Weir, "PC Then and Now," 55.

[19] "PC Then and Now," 81.

[20] Michael Morris, "Christopher Hope's Caustic Impulses," *Femina* (December 1997): 166.

duced as an ideal new South African, a man who has broken with his past to embrace the future:

> He completely forgot he had been an attorney who ran off with client's trust funds and fiddled shares and salted mines and watered Scotch and sold it to the shebeens [...]. Pascal took one look at the future and bought shares. [...] The rule was: anything would do as long as it did. And if in doubt, shout. (5–6)

Thus, Pascal installs himself as a shining example of new open-mindedness, but he always has his personal interests in mind. In a context where saying the right words is sufficient to be accepted as a 'new South African', he easily impresses most of the town, and he is able to rig the festivities in celebration of the political changes and run off with the prize money.

Clearly, issues of language policy *are* an important aspect of South Africa's transition from a country stratified by racial divisions to a multicultural society. However, Hope's novel points out that it is not enough to exchange labels. In many ways, *Me, the Moon and Elvis Presley* may itself not be politically correct. From the very beginning, even within leftist movements, the term 'politically correct' was associated with dogmatism and boredom. Thus, like the puritan Malvolio in Shakespeare's *Twelfth Night*, proponents of politically correct speech-codes are natural targets for comedy and satire. As a satire, Hope's text is open to misunderstandings, but it seems farfetched to read the novel as a right-wing attack on political change in South Africa. Hope's novel offers no easy solutions, but in exposing the emptiness behind much rainbow rhetoric it tries to expose the pitfalls of transition in a spirit of laughter.

WORKS CITED

Andrews, Edna. "Cultural Sensitivity and Political Correctness: The Linguistic Problem of Naming," *American Speech* 71.4 (1996): 389–94.

Bhabha, Homi K. "Difference, Discrimination and the Discourse of Colonialism," *The Politics of Theory*, ed. Francis Baker (Colchester: U of Essex P, 1983): 194–211.

Brink, André. *Imaginings of Sand* (London: Secker & Warburg, 1996).

de Alva, Jorge Klor. "The Postcolonization of the (Latin) American Experience: A Reconsideration of 'Colonialism', 'Postcolonialism', and 'Mestizaje'," in *After Colonialism: Imperial Histories and Postcolonial Displacements*, ed. Gyan Prakash (Princeton NJ: Princeton UP, 1995): 241–75.

Girvin, S. "Race and Race Classification," in *Race and the Law in South Africa*, ed. A. Rycroft, L. Boulle, M. Robertson, & P. Spiller (Cape Town: Juta, 1987): 1–10.

Hope, Christopher. *Me, the Moon, and Elvis Presley* (London: Macmillan, 1997).

Janicki, Karol. "Political Correctness: Conflict-Ridden Language, Language-Ridden Conflict, or Both?" *Belgian Journal of Linguistics* 11 (1997): 297–310.

Lampert, Günther. "*Political Correctness* und die sprachliche Konstruktion der Wirklichkeit: Eine Skizze," *Amerikastudien* 40.2 (1995): 247–57.

Landsman, Anne. *The Devil's Chimney* (Johannesburg: Jonathan Ball, 1998).

Losey, Kay, & Hermann Kurthen. "The Rhetoric of 'Political Correctness' in the U.S. Media," *Amerikastudien* 40.2 (1995): 227–45.

Morris, Michael. "Christopher Hope's Caustic Impulses," *Femina* (December 1997): 166–67.

Rushdie, Salman. "The Empire Wrties Back with a Vengeance," *The Times* (3 July 1982): 8.
Weir, Lorna. "PC Then and Now: Resignifying Political Correctness," in *Beyond Political Correctness: Toward the Inclusive University*, ed. Stephen Richter & Lorna Weir (Toronto: Toronto UP, 1995): 51–87.

《●》

The Birth-Pangs of Empowerment
Crime and the City of Johannesburg

ANNE FUCHS

I
N SEPTEMBER 1999 the alternative Nobel prizes (otherwise called "Ig-Nobel"
or ignoble prizes) were awarded at Harvard University; while the Physics award
went to Len Fisher and his team of Bristol University (UK) for the best way to
dunk a biscuit in tea or coffee, the most "ignoble" prize seems to have gone to South
Africa.[1] This was the "ignoble" peace prize given to two South Africans who in 1998
had commercialized their own version of the necklace: a car with a flame-thrower incorporated into the front doors; this option could vaporize liquid gas onto any potential
car-thief or aggressor, who would go up in flames on the application of the slightest
spark. This seems to have been the South Africans' response to the 13,000 attacks on
car-drivers recorded in 1997. One of the first clients to acquire the device was a Johannesburg police-chief. More will be said of Johannesburg police-chiefs in due course,
for the moment it suffices to point out the emblematic nature of this anecdote, particularly as homicides committed in self-defence are not punished in South Africa.

How did crime in the city of Johannesburg reach this point and what is its connection with South African literature? To attempt to answer these questions fully could fill
volumes, but it may be possible to isolate two or three salient features which would
indicate the links between crime and the empowerment of the black majority, and
show that this empowerment process, through and against crime, was both affected by,
and in turn itself influenced, different literary forms.

Before the Boer War and the formation of the Union, the path to political, social and
cultural empowerment for black South Africans was, to say the least, ambiguous. Because of superior technical achievement in the domains of war, transport and construction, the Europeans who took over parts of Africa were accepted at their own face-
value – as purveyors of Christian civilization, in every way a highly desirable state of
moral superiority which it was not sure a black man could ever attain.[2] It is certain that

---

[1] Pierre Barthélémy, "Une parodie de Nobel pour célébrer l'insolite ou l'ignoble," *Le Monde* (8
October 1999): 29.
[2] For a discussion of what Jeyifo calls the "civilizing process of capitalist modernity" in Europe

in the Boer States little hope was held out for the advancement of the inferior races, whereas in Cape Colony there was at first a timid step towards political integration with the enfranchisement of educated and propertied males. Social integration in general meant selling one's labour to the white man or, it may be said, participating in the new European economy as household slave, mineworker or tenant-farmer. The advance beyond subaltern participation depended, as did political integration, on the possibility of cultural integration. The attitude of Europeans towards black culture in the nineteenth century was at best based on curiosity; curiosity on the one hand about primitive man in general, the lowest of the low on the scale of human development, and curiosity about a human species whose racial characteristics seemed so exotic or 'other'. This 'otherness', accounted for by some as the result of a biblical curse and in consequence insurmountable by time or effort, was the reason why the black man's evolution would remain blocked. According to Lothrop Stoddard writing as late as 1920, some small progress might conveniently be hoped for thanks mainly to Christian missionaries:

> Degrading fetishism and demonology which sum up pagan religions will never survive, and all niggers will one day be either Christians or Muslims. In so far as he becomes a Christian, the savage instincts of the nigger will be restrained and he will be inclined to accept the tutorship of the white man.[3]

The missionaries themselves, once again, well into the twentieth century, would guilelessly proclaim (and this is Albert Schweitzer speaking): "The black is a child, and with children nothing can be achieved without the use of authority [...] for the Blacks, as a consequence, I have found the following formula: "I am your brother, it's true, but your elder brother'."[4]

Cultural integration into the European world-view, therefore, was first seen as the way to progress by the Christian blacks, guided by their older brothers. The despised oral forms of traditional dancing and music-making were not entirely abandoned but used as a basis for the writing and singing of choral hymns, entertaining Western visitors and, away from missionary influence, in customary pursuits. By the beginning of the twentieth century there were a considerable number of Western-style educated blacks leaving the mission schools and colleges. Among them was the author of *Mhudi*, Sol Plaatje, who at the same time as he was writing this first novel in English by a black South African, was, in another work, *Native Life in South Africa*, also denouncing the first major crime of the new Union of South Africa, which was the 1913 Natives' Land Act.[5] In fact, depriving the black majority of their land-rights was, over

---

and its 'civilizing mission' in the colonies, see Biodun Jeyifo, "In the Wake of Colonialism and Modernity," *Anglophonia* 7 (2000): 71–84.

[3] Lothrop Stoddard, *The Rising Tide of Colour* (New York: Scribner, 1920), quoted by John Coleman de Graft–Johnson in *African Glory: The Story of Vanished Negro Civilisations* (London: Watts, 1954): 50.

[4] See Charles Rhind Joy, *Albert Schweitzer: An Anthology* (Boston MA: Beacon, 1947): 85.

[5] Sol. T. Plaatje, *Native Life in South Africa, Before and Since the European War and the Boer Rebellion* (London: P.S. King, 1916). See also electronic text with introduction by Neil Parsons

the years, to drive them into the towns – more particularly, to Johannesburg – in search of work. But this growing population in Johannesburg, still confident in their ability to integrate, between 1920 and 1950 began to develop parallel cultures. An intellectual middle-class black population, inheritors of mission teaching, became more and more interested in combining African tradition and musical history with a sense of strict Christian morality. The power they sought was through concepts similar to those of the francophone Négritude movement. Sol Plaatje, Thomas Mofolo, the Dhlomo brothers and others were proclaiming to the world the dignity and human worth of the black African, and at the same time underscoring the possibility of his assimilation into European civilization. The emphasis in this 'middle-class' culture was to change, however, in the 1940s and 1950s with the adaptation of the novel form to describe the plight of the innocent black countryman suffering both from the crimes of apartheid and from the delinquency rife in the big cities where he was seeking work. The fictional locus became the city of Johannesburg, not only because it was the source of work for black South Africans and riches for the white, but also because it became a centre of education and culture.

Suffering and crime were not at first seen as the means of empowerment; the ur-hero of such novels, Robert Zulu in *An African Tragedy*, a novella written by R.R.R. Dhlomo as early as 1928, is, rather, a newcomer in a Johannesburg location corrupted by those Dhlomo calls the "slaves of vice." The drinking, gambling, fights and prostitution he describes as typical of the new black urban working class lead Dhlomo as a Christian moralist to exclaim: "No wonder Black Africa is cursed."[6] But, as Stephen Gray and Piniel Shava have both pointed out,[7] Dhlomo was writing for the missionary publishers of the Lovedale Press attempting to convert the sons of Ham. The first novels in which crime in Johannesburg is analysed in such a way that the reasons for the violence and degradation in the locations do not wholly reside in the private morality (or lack of it) of the black workers but at least equally in the living conditions created by the white oppressors are *Cry, The Beloved Country* by Alan Paton and *Mine Boy* by Peter Abrahams.[8] These novels, published at the end of the Second World War, have in common the fact that they were not published by a South African missionary press; they set the trend for the English-speaking protest novel which would be published in England over the next half-century and aimed at revealing to the world at large the plight of the black South African. In 1948 the English *Daily Herald* considered that *Cry, The Beloved Country* "should do for the native African what *Uncle Tom's Cabin* did for Negro slaves in America," although the *Church Times* still considered the real subject of this "account of a Zulu parson's search for his delinquent son in the maelstrom of Johannesburg" to be "the battle which Christianity is fighting

---

prepared by Alan R. Light (alight@vnet.net), July 1998: 1–53.

[6] R.R.R. Dhlomo, *An African Tragedy* (Johannesburg: Lovedale Institution Press, 1928): 5.

[7] See Stephen Gray, *Southern African Literature. An Introduction* (Cape Town: David Philip, 1979): 173, and Piniel Viriri, Shava, *A People's Voice: Black South African Writing in the Twentieth Century* (London: Zed & Athens: Ohio UP, 1989): 15–19.

[8] Alan Paton, *Cry, The Beloved Country* (1948; Harmondsworth: Penguin, 1958), and Peter Abrahams, *Mine Boy* (1946, London: Heinemann, 1963).

for the soul of Africa." In 1946 Peter Abrahams, a coloured writer, who had left South
Africa at the age of twenty and settled in England, had his first novel *Mine Boy* published by Faber. It was the story of a country boy, his arrival at the gold mines, and his
gradual transformation into boss-boy at the mine and into positive Marxist hero, leader
of a strike to save workers' lives. In *Mine Boy*, Christianity as such is irrelevant and
furthermore completely absent; the emphasis is on the construction of the subject
through trials of solidarity involving the black working class both in the mines and in
the black slum areas of the time, Malay Camp and Vrededorp, where Abrahams himself had grown up. For the first time, the hero, instead of being corrupted by his horrific living conditions for which the white man is responsible, transcends his crime-
ridden environment where black men and women have to fight among themselves and
get stupefied with drink in order to survive. Actual empowerment at the end of the
novel comes not through any specific action but from the fact that in the presence of
the 'Other' the subject has achieved the status of manhood and, in terms of Abrahams'
own metaphor, is no longer like the sheep frightened and confused by a barking dog
that the hero used to see "when he was at home on the farms" (41). The passage
"Xuma felt stronger than he had ever felt all his life. Strong enough to be a man without colour. And now, suddenly, he knew that it could be so. Man could be without
colour" (181) can be interpreted as a Marxist statement meaning that the hero has
passed beyond racial considerations, empowered as a worker to fight against all economic oppression.

   If these two works break new ground in providing fictional accounts of life in black
Johannesburg, they are still written from an assimilationist point of view, although for
different reasons. With the structural constraints of apartheid being imposed with increasing severity from the late 1940s onward (and incidentally constituting criminal
violence of such magnitude that location crime pales in comparison), it is not surprising that assimilation for the black artist loses all meaning. Finding a new voice not
dependent on European forms proved a gradual process stretching over the 1950s and
1960s. To begin with, the novel form, and theatre European-style, were more or less
abandoned, with writers turning to journalism and performers to music; African jazz-
men developed their music from a combination of black-American jazz and indigenous
urban music such as Marabi, originally played in the shebeens of Johannesburg. Their
attitudes and life-style self-consciously reflected those of Hollywood movie stars as
seen at the Bioscope in Johannesburg. Those who gravitated to this new urban culture
first played at, and then acted out in real life, the gang warfare of Chicago and the other
misdeeds of their American movie heroes. At the beginning of the 1950s, journalism
gave new impetus to black writers; in 1951 the new monthly magazine *African Drum*,
after four numbers published in Cape Town and devoted to music of the tribes, history
of the tribes, cartoons about Gulliver, and St. Paul, moved to Johannesburg. Later in
the year when Anthony Sampson replaced Bob Crisp as editor, he and Jim Bailey the
proprietor took the advice of prospective African readers they met through the black
journalist Henry Nxumalo:

   Ag, why do you dish out that stuff, man? said a man with golliwog hair in a floppy
   American suit, at the Bantu Men's Social Centre, "Tribal music! Tribal history! Chiefs!

We don't care about chiefs! Give us jazz and film stars, man! We want Duke Ellington, Satchmo, and hot dames! Yes, brother, anything American. You can cut out this junk about kraals and folk-tales and Basutos in blankets – forget it! You're just trying to keep us backward, that's what! Tell us what's happening right here, man, on the Reef![9]

The blossoming of the *Drum* journalists such as, among others, Todd Matshikiza, Arthur Maimane, Can Themba, Bloke Modisane and Lewis Nkosi is well-documented. I should like, however, to underline the importance of crime throughout this period. In 1956 Anthony Sampson writes of "Black Johannesburg [being] largely ruled by criminals" (96) and of survival depending on keeping on the right side of them. He continues: "The barrier of apartheid protected gangsters against the law: white police could never penetrate the black underworld, and were more concerned with passes and permits than with black men murdering each other" (97). This statement raises the whole complicated issue of the definition of crime in South Africa from the 1950s onwards. If the *Drum* journalists wrote reports, biographical pieces and short stories about the lives and petty crimes of the "tsotsis" as well as the more murderous crime "syndicates," it was with the same amount of indulgence as to be found in the enunciation of the American gangster movies those same tsotsis appreciated. Crime within the locations empowered those who committed it and those who wrote about it: both were indulging in a real-life fantasy world beyond the limits of apartheid; but, furthermore, it was equally a source of strength for the African reader. These empowering factors should not be exaggerated, but it must be remembered that the 1950s were also the years of the Defiance campaigns and the beginnings of solidarity between the African, Coloured and Indian Congress movements. Passes, labour, morality and censorship were more severely regulated under official apartheid at this time, and the *Drum* journalists began to report on the Janus-face of apartheid crime: the crimes of the African against apartheid law and the apartheid laws as crimes against humanity. They first investigated the horrific conditions of the Bethal farm workers, who, in fact, had been tricked into giving unpaid labour to white farmers, and then the conditions in African prisons. In 1963, Bloke Modisane, looking back in *Blame Me On History*, describes his part in the "Mr Drum goes to church" assignment when *Drum* journalists visited various white churches in Johannesburg and showed up the hypocrisy of even the Seventh-Day Adventist Christians. Modisane thinks of Christianity "as a snare intended to rivet upon [him] those chains which have reduced [him] into a chattel placed in South Africa for the convenience of the white man," and continues: "I will not be honeyed with snippets about the life in the Hereafter, other racialists have sermoned that even there white angels sleep late whilst the tan cherubs bring the morning tea."[10]

It has been important to analyse at some length black society and journalism in the 1950s, because, if one puts aside the more ideological work of Black-Consciousness artists, the forms and content of all black South African work right into the 1980s can be seen as a direct development of these 'birth pangs'. Indeed, at the end of the 1950s, many of the *Drum* journalists set off for self-imposed exile, where they subsequently

[9] Anthony Sampson, *Drum: A Venture into the New Africa* (London: William Collins, 1956): 20.
[10] Bloke Modisane, *Blame Me On History* (1963; Craighall, S.A.: Ad. Donker, 1986): 181.

explained their position as intellectuals, as the in-betweens of black and white society, popularly called at the time "the situations." Straight autobiographies, autobiographical novels and short stories, with the dual forms of apartheid crimes very much to the fore, were published overseas; this meant that, for Mphahlele, Nkosi, Modisane and others, their writing could not be considered as a way to black empowerment, as it was rapidly banned or even censored by the book distributors before even arriving in South Africa. But they were effective in making a major contribution to anti-apartheid movements world-wide and in inspiring other writers. These realist, backward-looking works also included to a greater or lesser degree passages describing the crime-ridden streets within Sophiatown or the locations of Johannesburg (in the case of Mphahlele, the streets of a Pretoria location),[11] but in each case the main desire was how to leave these streets. When they did leave, one might think it was personal empowerment, but this must be weighed against the heavy guilt-complex which pervades the work of the Drum authors.

The representation in the theatre of the seamier side of township life began in 1959 with King Kong, for which the Drum journalist Todd Matshikiza composed the music. This was the first of a whole series of white-funded black musicals, often produced in association with United Artists, whereby numerous black actors and musicians gained theatrical and show-business experience. After the events of Sharpeville, most fiction was published overseas and black–white collaboration split up, with writers such as Athol Fugard showing more interest in the universal truths of the South African situation and Gibson Kente, the new black dramatist, celebrating township life for a black township audience. It is significant that for the next two decades few common features emerge from the literary forms which might still be said to empower through crime: Kente, when dealing with crime in his commercial musicals, was depicting it largely as private sin, whereas the Black Consciousness Movement which influenced mainly poets and playwrights in the 1970s and 1980s tended to neglect township crime in favour of focusing on the overwhelming pressure of apartheid or public crime.[12] But how could these phenomena be considered as empowerment of the black majority? Kente certainly empowered within the community through the independent development of theatre skills and artistic form and what might almost be termed survival through entertainment, but whenever he crossed the line from private to public crime he was censored, banned and imprisoned. The Black Consciousness artists consciously started from the other side of this line: real empowerment as far as numbers were concerned was small: often banned before they took off, the protest plays of Maponya and Manaka attracted only small, frightened township audiences[13] and they, like the BCM poets, if they appeared in print, were published abroad for interested world audiences.

[11] Ezekiel Mphahlele, Down Second Avenue (1959; London: Faber & Faber, 1980).

[12] For play texts and details of Gibson Kente and 1970s Black Consciousness productions, see South African People's Plays, ed. Robert Kavanagh (Mshengu) (London: Heinemann, 1981), and Robert Kavanagh, Theatre and Cultural Struggle in South Africa (London: Zed, 1985).

[13] See Carola Luther & Maishe Maponya, "Problems and Possibilities: A discussion on the making of alternative theatre in South Africa," English Academy Review 2 (1984): 19–32.

After Soweto in the late 1970s, the theatre had a new burst of black-white collaboration with the opening of the non-racial Market Theatre, a venue which could protect anti-apartheid work more effectively than the severely controlled township venues.[14] Junction Avenue Theatre Company joined up with the black actors and devisers of Robert McLaren's pioneering Workshop '71 when this non-racial adventure ended in 1978. Junction Avenue is interesting because with such plays as *Marabi* and *Sophiatown* they looked back for inspiration to the 1950s *Drum* authors, and township crime was once again seen in relation to apartheid crime. In Johannesburg, Junction Avenue also contributed, with nearly all their productions, to the revelation of apartheid crime in its historical perspective. Where did it come from? Why did it come about? And (in *Tooth and Nail*) what was its effect in its cataclysmic end on the whole South African population?[15] In the collaborative work of Barney Simon with other black actors such as Ngema and Mtwa,[16] township crime is represented side-by-side with apartheid crime as in Junction Avenue work; in both cases, breaking the law in the form of violence towards whites or fellow-blacks is now bereft of moral judgments, is even 'glamorized' and excused, inasmuch as it is the direct consequence of the much greater crimes committed in the name of apartheid.

This collaborative theatre empowered, and was empowered by, the formation of the non-racial United Democratic Front and the non-racial stance of the ANC, who came more and more to the fore at home and overseas. Many white writers who had been considered as anti-apartheid – Brink, Gordimer, Coetzee – were writing of both aspects of apartheid crime but rarely treating 'ordinary' crime, black or white, as more than a distant background. In their eyes, writing novels that were read essentially by a foreign audience or by liberal-minded whites in South Africa was a way of bearing witness to the situation and incidentally advancing the cause. It might be thought that in the realm of empowerment (which in fact they never proposed to enter) the overall effect of *A Dry White Season*, *The Conservationist* or *Age of Iron*[17] was the disempowerment of white South Africans being slowly destroyed by their own ideology of violence. The same effect could be found in the realist theatre written by white South Africans dating from P.G. du Plessis' *Siener in die Suburbs* (Seer in the Suburbs)[18] in 1971, and plays by Fugard, Pieter–Dirk Uys and Paul Slabolepszy; this reached the abyss of self-de-

---

[14] See Anne Fuchs, *Playing the Market: The Market Theatre, Johannesburg* (Amsterdam & New York: Rodopi, 2002) Revised and updated edition.

[15] See Martin Orkin, *At the Junction: Four Plays by the Junction Avenue Theatre Company* (Johannesburg: Witwatersrand UP, 1995).

[16] Percy Mtwa, Mbogneni Ngema & Barney Simon, *Woza Albert!* (London: Methuen, 1983).

[17] André Brink, *A Dry White Season* (London: W.H. Allen, 1989); Nadine Gordimer, *The Conservationist* (London: Jonathan Cape, 1974); J.M. Coetzee, *Age of Iron* (London: Secker & Warburg, 1990).

[18] Pieter Georg Du Plessis, *Siener in die Suburbs; 'n spel in drie bedrywe* (Cape Town: Tafelberg, 1979).

struction with Anthony Akerman's *Somewhere on the Border* and Reza de Wet's *Diepe Grond*[19] in the mid-1980s.

The empowerment of the black South African did not come about through literature; apartheid crime in the 1980s assumed horrific proportions, with repression and the solidarity reactions of boycotts, strikes, demonstrations and bomb scares rapidly succeeding each other. Big business and other economic players demanded, and prepared for, change. Township crime as such no longer made the headlines but was replaced by what the regime cynically called "black-on-black violence." This could be in the form of necklacing or other attacks representing violent reactions to what was considered as collaboration of blacks with the regime. More often, it came, in the Johannesburg townships and in Natal, in the form of skirmishes between ANC supporters and Zulu impis, members of Inkatha, with the latter often being passively supported by the police. When empowerment of black South Africans actually materialized politically with the release of Mandela in 1990, the interim government with black participation, and the first democratic elections in 1994, other aspects of the power struggle had yet to be addressed – in particular, those concerning housing, education, employment and general economic conditions. "So What's New?" the playwright Fatima Dikewould ask in her eponymous play.[20] In fact, the 'birth pangs' over, during the 1990s the baby started to grow and develop in many expected and some unexpected ways. As far as literature, crime and Johannesburg were concerned, a white dramatist such as Paul Slabolepszy merely turned empowerment on its head; in the comedy *Mooi Street Moves*,[21] the empowered Johannesburg tsotsi now controls the poor white boy from the country. The reversal of fortune in this 1992 play was still very much a theme in J.M. Coetzee's 1999 novel *Disgrace*,[22] which is worth mentioning here because it deals with crime and empowerment, although set far from Johannesburg. It will, moreover, serve as a contrast with two of Gordimer's most recent novels. As always, it is the metaphoric aspect, however simplistic, that is important in Coetzee's work: the "Disgrace" of the title might be that of any white South African living under the new regime, although here it is that of a university professor, dismissed for not wanting to apologize for the sexual harassment of a student. The real reversal of power-roles, however, occurs when the professor's farmer-daughter, impregnated during multiple rape by black thieves, accepts her black neighbour's proposition to take over her farm and for herself to become part of his household in return for his protection; reversal of the way so many black women in the past had been part of the white master's establishment.

---

[19] Anthony Akerman, "Somewhere on the Border," in *South African Plays*, ed. Stephen Gray (London: Houghton & Stodder, Nick Hern & Heinemann–Centaur, 1993); Reza de Wet, *Diepe Grond* (Pretoria: H A U M, 1986). Both *Somewhere on the Border* and *Diepe Grond* were first staged in South Africa in 1986.

[20] Fatima Dike, "So What's New?" in *Four Plays*, ed. Zakes Mda (Florida Hills, S.A.: Vivlia, 1996).

[21] Paul Slabolepszy, *Mooi Street and other moves* (Johannesburg: Witwatersrand UP, 1994).

[22] J.M. Coetzee, *Disgrace* (London: Secker & Warburg, 1999).

In *None To Accompany Me*,[23] Nadine Gordimer had also talked of reversal, but of a different kind; in 1994 she defined it: "So it's some sort of historical process in reverse we're in. The future becomes undoing the past." And in the last section of the novel, entitled "Arrivals," Ms Vera Stark, the main protagonist, nominated to serve on a committee to draw up the Draft Constitution, suddenly asks: "Empowerment [...] what is this new thing? What happened to what we used to call justice?" To understand Gordimer's protagonist and even the setting-up of the Truth and Reconciliation Commission, it is perhaps necessary to go back to Black-Consciousness tenets: "Black culture above all implies freedom on our part to innovate without recourse to white values," said Steve Biko in 1973, envisaging for the future "a true humanity where power politics will have no place."[24] Several plays in the late 1990s were based on the Truth and Reconciliation proceedings, including Kentridge's *Ubu*.[25] Gordimer in 1998[26] chose to move on from this "undoing the past," showing how empowerment of the present could be seen almost as what Ndebele calls "ordinary."[27] Not playing down the reality of crime-ridden Johannesburg (as this is the reason for the "house gun" being on hand for the middle-class white boy to commit a crime of passion with), she nevertheless concentrates on the moral dilemmas of 'ordinary' white parents and their relationship with their son and the black lawyer, newly returned from exile, who defends him.

That crime is now endemic in Johannesburg is beyond all doubt, but the birth-pangs, which have lasted for almost a century, cannot be expected to subside in half a decade. The disappointments that are rife today had already been forecast in plays such as Zakes Mda's *We shall sing for the Fatherland*[28] and Nadine Gordimer's novel *July's People*.[29] If the majority of the population is still heavily embroiled in the problems which are a legacy of apartheid crime, whites are perhaps more concerned with private crime flooding out of the townships onto the streets of Central Johannesburg. Gradually, at least in the theatre, black dramatists are turning away from the high moral tone of 'protest' or apartheid-crime theatre to address issues of the relationships between men and women and even between black and white, as is to be found in the work of Aubrey Sekhabi and his followers.[30] Some white artists, however, tend to leave any aspect of

---

[23] Nadine Gordimer, *None to Accompany Me* (1994; Harmondsworth: Penguin, 1995): 261 & 285.

[24] Steve Biko, "Black Consciousness and the Quest for a True Humanity," in *Black Theology: The South African Voice*, ed. Basil Moore (London: Hurst, 1973), repr. in Biko, *I Write What I Like* (London: Heinemann, 1979): 96, 90.

[25] Jane Taylor, *Ubu and the Truth Commission* (Cape Town: U of Cape Town P, 1998).

[26] Nadine Gordimer, *The House Gun* (1998; Harmondsworth: Penguin, 1999).

[27] Njabulo Ndebele, *Rediscovery of the Ordinary: Essays on South African Literature and Culture* (Fordsburg: C O S A W, 1991).

[28] Zakes Mda, "We Shall Sing for the Fatherland," in *The Plays of Zakes Mda* (1972; Johannesburg: Ravan, 1990).

[29] Nadine Gordimer, *July's People* (New York: Viking, 1981).

[30] See Mark Fleishman, "Unspeaking the Centre: Emergent trends in South African Theatre in the 1990s," in *Culture in the New South Africa: After Apartheid*, vol. 2, ed. Robert Kriger & Abele Zegeye (Cape Town: Kwela & SA History Online): 91–115.

crime far below them while they indulge in postmodern poetic performance of universals.

May I conclude by saying that this essay was inspired by *Love, Crime and Johannesburg*,[31] a recent Junction Avenue Theatre Company play which faces head-on the situation I referred to at the beginning – Johannesburg today, the new democracy, and, within the play, a black woman police-chief, desperately underfunded and undermined on all sides. This musical play, in the tradition of *Marabi* and *Sophiatown*[32] and scripted by Malcolm Purkey and Carol Steinberg, leads to a comparison of the crime situation of the 1950s (very much idealized by Ramolao Makhene in the role of Bones, the former Sophiatown 'proper' gangster) with the present crime-scene in Johannesburg. This is populated by former comrades, returned liberation fighters, the new big-businessmen, corruption, and, according to Bones, once again "riff raff and violent little boys! [...] No school, no family, no God! [...] Burning, suffocating, raping, shooting!"[33] Surprisingly, this non-racial and realistic spectacular exudes optimism. As Malcolm Purkey himself is reported to have said, "Fortunately the world is mad, Johannesburg is crazy and South Africa has turned up some glorious new problems."[34] Perhaps we can forecast, with the last line of the play, "And all will be well in a hundred years time."[35]

WORKS CITED

Abrahams, Peter. *Mine Boy* (1946; London: Heinemann, 1963).

Akerman, Anthony. "Somewhere on the border," in *South African Plays*, ed. Stephen Gray (London: Houghton & Stodder, Nick Hern & Heinemann–Centaur, 1993).

Barthélémy, Pierre. "Une parodie de Nobel pour célébrer l'insolite ou l'ignoble," *Le Monde* (8 October 1999): 29.

Biko, Steve. "Black Consciousness and the Quest for a True Humanity," in *Black Theology: The South African Voice,* ed. Basil Moore (London: Hurst, 1973); repr. in Biko, *I Write What I Like* (London: Heinemann, 1979): 87–98.

Brink, André. *A Dry White Season* (London: W.H. Allen, 1989).

Coetzee, J.M. *Age of Iron* (London: Secker & Warburg, 1990).

——. *Disgrace* (London: Secker & Warburg, 1999).

de Graft–Johnson, John Coleman. *African Glory: The story of vanished negro civilisations* (London: Watts, 1954).

de Wet, Reza. *Diepe Grond* (Pretoria: HAUM, 1986).

Dhlomo, R.R.R. *An African Tragedy* (Johannesburg: Lovedale Institution Press, 1928).

Dike, Fatima. "So What's New?" in *Four Plays*, ed. Zakes Mda (Florida Hills, S.A.: Vivlia, 1996).

---

[31] Junction Avenue Theatre Company, *Love, Crime and Johannesburg* (Johannesburg: Witwatersrand UP, 2000).

[32] *Marabi* was first staged in 1983. *Sophiatown* is published in *At the Junction*.

[33] *Love, Crime and Johannesburg*, 28–29.

[34] Zaheda Mohamed, "Theatre noire [sic]," August 1999.

[35] *Love, Crime and Johannesburg,* 55.

Du Plessis, Pieter Georg. *Siener in die Suburbs; 'n spel in drie bedrywe* (Cape Town: Tafelberg, 1979).

Fleishman, Mark. "Unspeaking the Centre: Emergent trends in South African Theatre in the 1990s," in *Culture in the New South Africa: After Apartheid*, vol. 2, ed. Robert Kriger & Abele Zegeye (Cape Town: Kwela & SA History Online): 91–115.

Fuchs, Anne. *Playing the Market: The Market Theatre, Johannesburg* (Cross/Cultures 50; Amsterdam & New York: Rodopi, 2002). Revised and updated edition.

Gordimer, Nadine. *The Conservationist* (London: Jonathan Cape, 1974).

——. *The House Gun* (1998; Harmondsworth: Penguin, 1999).

——. *July's People* (New York: Viking, 1981).

——. *None to Accompany Me* (1994; Harmondsworth: Penguin, 1995).

Gray, Stephen. *Southern African Literature. An Introduction* (Cape Town: David Philip, 1979).

Jeyifo, Biodun. "In the Wake of Colonialism and Modernity," *Anglophonia* 7 (2000): 71–84.

Joy.,Charles Rhind. *Albert Schweitzer: An Anthology* (Boston MA: Beacon, 1947).

Junction Avenue Theatre Company. *Love, Crime and Johannesburg* (Johannesburg: Witwatersrand UP, 2000).

Kavanagh, R. (Mshengu), ed. *South African People's Plays* (London: Heinemann, 1981).

Kavanagh, R. *Theatre and Cultural Struggle in South Africa* (London: Zed, 1985).

Luther, Carola & Maishe Maponya, "Problems and Possibilities: A Discussion on the Making of Alternative Theatre in South Africa," *English Academy Review* 2 (1984): 19–32.

Mda, Zakes. "We Shall Sing for the Fatherland," in *The Plays of Zakes Mda* (1972; Johannesburg: Ravan, 1990).

Modisane, Bloke. *Blame Me On History* (1963, Craighall, S.A.: Ad. Donker, 1986).

Mphahlele, Ezekiel. *Down Second Avenue* (1959; London: Faber & Faber, 1980).

Mtwa, Percy, Mbogneni Ngema & Barney Simon. *Woza Albert!* (London: Methuen, 1983).

Ndebele, Njabulo. *Rediscovery of the Ordinary: Essays on South African Literature and Culture* (Fordsburg, S.A.: COSAW, 1991).

Orkin, Martin. *At the Junction: Four Plays by the Junction Avenue Theatre Company* (Johannesburg: Witwatersrand UP, 1995).

Paton, Alan. *Cry, The Beloved Country* (1948; Harmondsworth: Penguin, 1958).

Plaatje, Sol T. *Native Life in South Africa, Before and Since the European War and the Boer Rebellion* (London: P.S. King, 1916). See also electronic text with introduction by Neil Parsons prepared by Alan R. Light (alight@vnet.net), July 1998: 1–53.

Sampson, Anthony. *Drum: A Venture into the New Africa* (London: Collins, 1956).

Shava, Piniel Viriri, *A People's Voice: Black South African Writing in the Twentieth Century* (London: Zed & Athens: Ohio UP, 1989).

Slabolepszy, Paul. *Mooi Street and other moves* (Johannesburg: Witwatersrand UP, 1994).

Stoddard, Lothrop. *The Rising Tide of Colour* (New York: Charles Scribner's Sons, 1920).

Taylor, Jane. *Ubu and the Truth Commission* (Cape Town: U of Cape Town P, 1998).

〈〈•〉〉

Traps Seductive, Destructive and Productive
Theatre and the New South Africa[1]

MALCOLM PURKEY

L OVE, CRIME AND JOHANNESBURG is very likely to be Junction Avenue Theatre Company's last play. This is probably right, because the company conceived of itself very much as an anti-apartheid company, committed to using workshop to make new and subversive South African plays during the time of apartheid. Apartheid is now defeated.

Founded in 1976, the same year as the children's uprising in Soweto, Junction Avenue Theatre Company embraced a mission which involved a critical engagement with apartheid South Africa. The mantra we sounded time and again was that plays had to be made which critically reflected South African society. By this we meant plays which dealt with the truth of our times, engaged with the brutality of the apartheid regime, and provided a forum for what we called the revelation of hidden history. This did not mean that we wanted to make polemical and solemn plays without a delight in new form and a profound pleasure of reception. Rather, we knew that if our plays were to be effective in their mission they had better delight and engage and compel.

Junction Avenue Theatre Company came into being and flourished in that period of South Africa's history which saw a most significant development in South African theatre. 1976 was the year of the Market Theatre's establishment in Johannesburg. The Market Theatre brought together the genius of Mannie Manim and Barney Simon in a vision and a project that was to allow a most extraordinary flourishing of theatrical activity. Johannesburg had already seen the meteoric rise and fall of Workshop '71 under the direction of Robert McLaren, with plays such as *Uhlanga the Reed*, *Zipp*, *Survival* and *Smallboy*. Fugard, our most renowned playwright, had been working for a decade and a half establishing his particular voice and register; and the work of the Black-Consciousness playwrights such as Maishe Maponya and Matsemela Manaka was finding an audience of young aspirant revolutionaries.

---

[1] This article is in part based on the introductory article attached to the publication of *Love, Crime and Johannesburg* (Johannesburg: Witwatersrand UP, 2000), written by Carol Steinberg and Malcolm Purkey.

If you loved the theatre as I did, what a time to be alive! There was a string of productions, each more extraordinary than the last, each more challenging than the other, and each setting higher standards for aspirant South African theatre-makers. Each of these companies and individuals influenced our work in its own way, and we were eager to learn.

The struggle against apartheid gave an edge and an immediacy to this work that was electric. The passionate hunt for a style and a theatre language that was most revolutionary and engaged, most able to challenge the apartheid state, was everywhere creating the most intense debates. What kind of theatre should we make? Naturalist? Formalist? Expressionist? Carnivalesque? What was the role of Brecht in all this? Which theatre should we play in? Should we play in a theatre at all? Could we stage theatre at workers rallies? How would we cope when the scale of the gathering absolutely dwarfed the production? Was this an all-black affair, or could whites contribute meaningfully to the cultural struggle? In what way? Was Black-Consciousness theatre not just a romantic invocation of some mythical African ideal past, which had no root in historical reality? The questions and the debates abounded.

In Junction Avenue Theatre Company, we were in our own ongoing debate, a debate which almost always played out in a new production, for one of our implicit and hardly acknowledged principles was to take the debate into the workshop itself and give it a theatrical form. In its long and chequered career, Junction Avenue Theatre Company created a number of significant South African plays, including *The Fantastical History of a Useless Man*, *Randlords and Rotgut*, *Marabi*, *Dikitsheneng*, *Security*, *Sophiatown*, *Tooth and Nail* and its millennium post-apartheid play, *Love, Crime and Johannesburg*, which premiered at the Grahamstown Festival in July 1999, and then played a season at the Market Theatre in Johannesburg.

Apartheid South Africa threw up the most brutal and repressive conditions, and we had to manoeuvre through them with all the cunning we could muster. Yet, in a rather paradoxical way, we flourished in these dangerous waters. Like Letitia, the white-night-club singer in *Tooth and Nail* – created by Junction Avenue Theatre Company in 1989 (just months before the fall of apartheid and the release of Mandela) – we wanted the blood that ran in the streets to run in our veins. In spite of our commitment to making a theatre that conscientized and polemicized, or perhaps because of it, we never lost sight of Brecht's famous dictum, "A theatre that can't be laughed in, is a theatre to be laughed at." We wanted to make a political theatre that gave pleasure, a theatre that was challenging and subversive, a theatre that was engaging and compelling. We understood that we had to make a theatre that was so good that it couldn't easily be discounted. We knew that the white conservative community, and the Black-Consciousness movement, each in its own way, had an interest in our failure. We wanted to succeed. Song, dance, humour, wit, crudity, well-researched history and sociology, a well-worked narrative – these were some of our theatrical tools.

So how is it possible to imagine that such a creative flourish lasting over twenty-five years is now over?

South African anti-apartheid theatre was a most extraordinary and diverse theatre, created and driven in all its diversity by apartheid. And now, with the fall of apartheid, this theatre is finished. Surely this is the most difficult contradiction to swallow? Is it possible that this theatre, in all its wonder, existed only because of apartheid? That it got its intensity and its focus solely because of apartheid?

There is a nostalgia in some of us for that intensity, that gathering of like minds, that community of cultural revolutionaries, which is rather dangerous. During apartheid the ambitions were clear. The passions were focused – like a blinding sun setting fire to the touch-paper at the other end of a magnifying glass.

Now, as I write this in 2002, the South African theatre is in crisis, and has been in crisis for almost a decade. Audiences have radically diminished and such illustrious centres as the Market Theatre can hardly sustain a programme. Funding for culture in post-apartheid South Africa is in a political quagmire and the principles for funding, so progressive at first sight, are becoming highly contested. What little new production there is, is in my opinion of dubious quality.

There are of course exceptions. William Kentridge and the Handspring Puppet Company have sustained a brilliant series of projects, based on the reworking of European classics and European-festival funding – projects which, because of their European source, their formality and their reworked subjects, could probably only have been developed post-apartheid. These productions have had extensive world tours to great critical acclaim, while, paradoxically, hardly playing in South Africa at all. A failure of the imagination on the part of those South African theatres which do have money and, it must be acknowledged, a lack of local interest in such production (except in academe and among the intelligentsia) prevent these internationally acclaimed productions from being seen in their country of origin.

Out of Bounds, a one-person performance executed with great skill by the writer–director Rajesh Gopie, provides a vivid, comic and highly compelling portrayal of what it is like to be of Indian origin and growing up in KwaZulu–Natal. This production, so delightful in its own right, simultaneously suggests a model of theatrical exploration and subject-matter that, concentrating as it does on issues of ethnicity and cultural margins, could only have been developed post-apartheid. For apartheid was too deeply invested in a mode of brutal social control based on ethnicity and difference to allow such ethnicity and difference to be unproblematically a subject for progressive theatrical investigation. *Out of Bounds* offers a small hope for the South African theatre, otherwise floundering in its search for new, post-apartheid subject-matter.

The new Cape Town production, *Suip,* with its particular mix of old protest forms and Western Cape slang, style and song, provides a fresh glance at a theatre which is evocative of the old yet at the same time feels new. It feels old because of the invocation of tried and tested formulas. It draws on protest, *toi-toi,* direct address, song and a deeply felt political subject, performed with that wild intensity that only South African actors are able to muster. It feels new, I suppose, because of the imagined construction of the conditions of the Western Cape in post-apartheid South Africa – Table Mountain as myth, the elegant wine farms, and then, at the heart, alcoholism and the Bergies. There is no alcoholic like a Cape Town Bergie alcoholic; this the play make wildly and brilliantly clear.

It can be argued, therefore, that we still have some significant production potential, but very little, in my opinion, that can compare with those three decades of play-making that took us from the early 1960s to the late 1980s.

"Memory is a weapon, only a long rain can clear away these tears." These are the last lines of *Sophiatown*, one of Junction Avenue Theatre Company's most signal successes. Opening in 1986, the year of the first full state of emergency imposed by the apartheid regime, *Sophiatown* played season after season, both nationally and internationally. It is now published and set for study in post-apartheid high schools and universities like some old relic of an impossible and unimaginable past. A decade and a half later, we live in a new country, a new age, a new world, where forgetting, rather than memory, seems to be the key to the good life. Nobody wants to remember what it was like then: it is too painful. Memory gets in the way of advancement. History, once the most popular of subjects at university, is now in danger of atrophy: many university history departments are threatened with closure. History as a subject in the new school syllabus is not even taught. Who needs to know what happened in the days of the struggle? Just show us the way to the stairway to heaven, and let the *Four by Four* take us there.

I am not unsympathetic to this perspective. I think that certain forms of forgetting are most necessary – we need to forget that terrible state of *Ja Baas* psychology and oppression, which turned a whole nation into fearful and servile beings. Whites were not exempt, even in their great privilege. Oppression of the mind spread everywhere, and this oppression found its most painful expression in the twisted and distorted body. We need to forget that state of mind, which made us all so twisted, so committed to servility or *baaskap*, to white power or black subservience. But such forgetting comes at a terrible price. In this necessary forgetting, we forget also the fervour, the passion and the ideals for a new society that were so deeply embedded in the struggle days.

We in South Africa have abandoned all notions of equality and have embraced the economic policy entitled *Gear* (Growth, employment and redistribution.) We are deeply and, for the most part, willingly embedded in the global economy. Idealist notions of the African Renaissance have come to the centre of our language and discourse, but socialism is well and truly on the back burner. Our society is rapidly transforming and the conditions for theatre production are changed beyond all recognition. Should we mourn? Who says this change is a bad thing?

Well, some of us have a kind of nostalgia for that intense South African theatre-making of the 1980s, which I am sure is a seductive and monstrous trap. Come back apartheid, all is forgiven and let us have some passionate theatre again! Clearly this is a ridiculous position, even a destructive one, and yet we hear this thought, barely articulated, as a whispering in the wind.

Certainly, we often hear from many of the white theatre professionals a nostalgia for the old, properly funded apartheid theatres, with their proper standard of professional relationships and technical support, and well-funded acting companies. But these companies produced no new work of note, while the Market Theatre in Johannesburg and the Space Theatre in Capetown, with hardly a cent. generated new play after new play. The audiences came (for some of these plays) and these theatres flourished. Now the Space is closed and the Market Theatre is bereft of an audience, and can hardly sustain a significant programme.

How is it possible to imagine a new theatre in such conditions?

《●》

In the late 1990s, as the millennium approached, after some five years of African National Congress rule, first under Nelson Mandela and then under Thabo Mbeki, a series of extraordinary events made the headlines.

In 1997, Mzakhe Mbuli, the people's poet, was arrested and accused of robbing a bank. We, in Junction Avenue Theatre Company, were truly amazed. Mbuli was an icon of struggle, a hero of the young lions. He was a large, imposing figure of a man, whose booming voice spoke to a generation. In the 1980s, during the most bitter years of struggle, he would perform his poetry at mass rallies and funerals before tens of thousands of people. He had a power and hypnotic authority that everybody knew was quite remarkable, even if many were unsure of the ultimate value of his poetry. How was it that such a shining figure could find himself in such a perverse mess?

Our amazement was compounded when Robert McBride, a most controversial soldier in the struggle, a death-row prisoner, and then a Member of Parliament in South Africa's first democratic government, was arrested, accused of gun-running, and held in a Mozambican jail for six months without trial. How was this possible? What was going on? Had McBride joined the ranks of the criminals, running guns into Kwazulu–Natal, as some had claimed, or had he infiltrated these gun-running operations on behalf of the secret secret service? Is there a secret secret service in the 'new' South Africa? Does the new democratic government need a new secret service to spy on the old secret service? Is this what a new, fragile and democratic government needs to protect itself? Does one half of the secret service know what the other half of the secret service is doing? After McBride's arrest, the newspapers were full of these speculations.

When Colin Chauke, former *Umkhonto we Sizwe* commander, was arrested and accused of masterminding the bank heists that were plaguing Johannesburg, our amazement was complete. Were members of MK, the former guerrilla army, now putting their skills to work robbing banks?

Colin Chauke seemed extraordinary. This former guerrillero, while held in jail on suspicion of masterminding the heists, managed to retain his connection with senior government ministers, the then chief of police, and other senior members of the new government. Although he was the country's highest-profile prisoner, he still managed to escape from a closely guarded jail. While on the run from the law, he lived the glamorous high life, apparently partying with cabinet ministers, buying townhouses, exotic cars and fancy clothes, and moving with seeming ease in and out of the country. After he was finally re-arrested, his girlfriend, who shared his life-style, seemed unable to produce a small amount for bail or even the rent for her flat in Nelspruit. Where was all the money?

All these characters inflamed our imagination. Could the turns of their lives, so emblematic, so revelatory, be fictionalized? Could these extraordinary events, and their associated possible meanings, be made into theatre? What was it about these three figures that felt so compelling – so central to the tensions and contradictions of post-apartheid South Africa?

In attempting to answer these questions, after many years of silence and introspection of the kind described above, Junction Avenue Theatre Company set to work to make a post-apartheid play, *Love, Crime and Johannesburg*.

If we look back at our work, it is clear that at the very centre of much of it is this strange frontier city that we all live in – Johannesburg, notorious for its crime, brutality and corruption, yet full of creative and wondrous energy; a post-apartheid melting-pot of the African continent, one of the largest cities in the world not built on a river.

Johannesburg would provide the setting; Mbuli, McBride and Chauke would provide aspects of the central character.

"Why bother to rob a bank when you can own a bank?"

This is not an original thought, and in fact derives from Bertolt Brecht. It is one of the final speeches of Mac the Knife, the fictional hero of *The Threepenny Opera*.

As we have often acknowledged, Brecht's theories have played a very influential role in much of Junction Avenue Theatre Company's work, delivering not only an attitude to content but also a series of ideas about form and style which have always been provocative. *The Threepenny Opera*, the Brecht musical of 1928, provided a primary source of inspiration for *Love, Crime and Johannesburg*.

Many South Africans have asked us, with some trepidation, whether *Love, Crime and Johannesburg* is the story of Mzwakhe Mbuli. Our answer is resolutely "No." Jimmy "Longlegs" Mangane is a fictional character, a hybrid creation drawn from the historical events surrounding the lives of Mbuli, McBride and Chauke. Jimmy "Longlegs" Mangane's character and life-events are clearly a fictional amalgam of aspects of these colourful personalities. But of much more importance to Jimmy's life story is the narrative arc of Mac the Knife.

Mac the Knife is a gangster, a figure from the underworld who tangles with his old buddy the Chief of Police. He is love with two women, struggles with the protective father of his wife-to-be, spends too much time in the local whorehouse, and, when given the opportunity to escape from prison, gets re-arrested at the whorehouse and is taken to the gallows to be hanged. At the last moment, on the occasion of the queen's coronation, he is granted a pardon. A perfect model of almost mythic proportions for the narrative we were trying to create.

The basic story-line of *Love, Crime and Johannesburg* had almost written itself. Jimmy "Longlegs" Mangane, a poet of the struggle, would have intimate connections with the new Chief of Police, Queenie Dlamini, and the new Chairman of the Bank, Lewis Matome. They would be his former comrades. Jimmy would have two girlfriends – one black, Bibi Khuswayo; the other white, Lulu Levine. Bokkie Levine would be the protective father-in-law-to-be, full of anxiety and antagonism, and Bones Shibambo, the gangster from the Alex, the surrogate father and Jimmy's inspiration.

Jimmy would be arrested, would hold court in prison and, given the chance to escape and cross the border to Swaziland, would prefer to seek refuge in the arms of his lover, Bibi, in a Bruma Lake hotel. He would be re-arrested and taken back to C-Max and a life-sentence. At the last moment, on the occasion of the inauguration of the third president of the new democratic republic of South Africa, there would be a general amnesty, and Jimmy "Longlegs" Mangane would be granted a reprieve. In keeping with our previous work, much of the story would be conveyed in song designed to deliberately break into the action and provide distance.

In October 1998, we, the primary authors of the play (Carol Steinberg and Malcolm Purkey), meeting once a week, set to work to enrich the narrative we had sketched out. From the word go, the working processes and relationships were characterized by an ease, a lightness and a celebratory quality that were to find their way into the tone, content and style of the production.

In January 1999, phase one of the workshops began. A company of about ten people gathered in the new coffee shop at the University of the Witwatersrand Theatre. In this phase, we were inviting the members of the company to test the viability of the narrative, the resonance of the themes, and the verisimilitude of the characters. To our delight, we discovered that the work we were proposing seemed to resonate at a deep level. The personal, political and social issues we wished to engage with seemed to be on the minds of everyone in the company. In the best sense of the word, the work seemed popular: the company's political antennae were vibrating and their creative energies were ticking.

After each workshop we would retire to write and rewrite. We were struck by two things. One, the degree to which our friends and colleagues were still so politicized and highly articulate about the city and country in which we live. They constantly fed us with new ways of thinking about crime, corruption, democracy, personal relationships, Johannesburg and the 'new' South Africa. The constant debate that takes place between the highly opinionated characters in the play is, in some way, in honour of those endless coffee- and dinner-table conversations. Two, no matter how outrageous and absurd the story we were creating seemed to be, the daily tale of woe and delight from the newspapers proved yet again the cliché that reality is stranger than fiction. Nothing that the imagination could invent had not already been invented by Johannesburg.

Parallel to this process was the creation of the music. We were writing lyrics and taking them, in raw form, to the irrepressible Ed Jordan. He would scrutinize them for lack of scansion, rhyme and rhythm, transform them, and from his magic fingers popular and haunting music emerged. Junction Avenue Theatre Company's more traditional methods of making music were also being used. The company would improvise endless rhythms and musical lines in African jazz workshops that would evolve into snatches of songs. Later these bits would be refined into a completed work.

In phase two of the workshop, we took a well-developed narrative and set of characters to the company, who worked with us to transform the material into scenes. Each company member was instructed to inhabit a character for the course of a given exercise and to role-play a given encounter. Sometimes the actor/creators would write scenes together; sometimes they would improvise the scenes directly into a tape recorder. These scenarios were transformed into finished dialogue and playable action, and the dialogue was enriched to capture the diverse registers of Johannesburg's languages and culture. There was an intense and creative flow between the study and the workshop, and particular emphasis was placed on developing a poetic and rigorous script. We had ambitions to make a highly polished and finished work.

We have been influenced by many playwrights and theatre theorists on the question of the relationship between language, politics and power. The name "Brecht" has been invoked many times. In the context of the making of *Love, Crime and Johannesburg*, one other in particular is worth mentioning. David Mamet, the American playwright, screenwriter and film director, can teach us much about the way in which language hides what the speaker wants to reveal and reveals what the speaker wants to hide. The way people talk, and their silences, implicates them in moral and political questions and transgressions. We wanted to capture some of these qualities in Jo'burg-speak. A great deal of the writers' work was hunting for this heightened and purified language, without sacrificing the particular cadences and registers of South African speech, as given to us by the members of our multicultural workshop. In every beat and every pause, to quote the ageing gangster in the play, Bones Shibambo, we wanted something to mean something.

By April 1999 we had a first draft, which was given to Sarah Roberts, the designer, who began working on a visual environment for the production. In late May, rehearsal began for our premiere at the Standard Bank National Festival of the Arts in Grahamstown in June and the follow-on season at the Market Theatre in Johannesburg.

We were delighted when the play received a wealth of warm critical response. Our real delight, though, was that the audiences were young, diverse and clearly engaged. We were also puzzled: we were experiencing the 'death of the author' at first hand. The play that we had so carefully crafted, word by word, became something other, something alien, as the season developed. It became the property of the audience, who received it in the most unexpected ways.

Was it really this funny? Had we set out to write a comedy? Could we have predicted that Bones Shibambo's passionate outburst against contemporary crime – a gangster's condemnation of gangsterism – would provide the moral touchstone? What was it exactly about Lulu Levine's confession, "I know you'll think I'm mad, but I love Johannesburg," that touched audiences? How is it that a diverse South African audience knows that the concept of a secret secret service is at once absurd and feasible? We knew that the cell-phone scene between the Chief of Police and Lewis Matome captured aspects of contemporary mis-communications. How could we have known that it would also come to represent the powerlessness of the supposedly powerful in face of the complex machinations of the post-apartheid state and the criminal underworld?

When we reflect on the workshop, the production process and the play's receptions with over a year's hindsight, one thing seems particularly striking. The entire process was infused with a sense of celebration despite the dark subjects the play was tackling. We were celebrating Johannesburg. Johannesburg is a hard city, but it is also a wonderful and creative city for those who know how to look. Further, we were celebrating the achievements of South Africa's new democracy and, most importantly, we were also celebrating a release from the intense moral burden that playmaking in apartheid South Africa imposed. In the context of the extraordinary achievement of the 'new' South Africa, we are granted a wonderful freedom to be critical, to be dissident, to be irreverent, to be playful.

What I have written implies a profound contradiction for me. I believe that Junction Avenue Theatre Company's work is over, yet *Love, Crime and Johannesburg* suggests that the world of theatre work is not so bleak as I implied at the beginning of this article. That the times are different is undeniable. We cannot make work in exactly the same way we used to, and certainly the subject-matter has to change. No doubt the new South Africa will throw up endless contradictions which are worthy of theatrical examination. The politics will be different, but politics and cultural representation will remain.

《•》

THE BLACK EXPERIENCE IN BRITAIN

In the Eyes of the Outsider
Buchi Emecheta's Been-To Novels

ELEONORA CHIAVETTA

I N THE EXTENSIVE LITERARY PRODUCTION of Buchi Emecheta, four of
her novels have a Western background. Her first novel, *In the Ditch* (1972), is set
entirely in London, while her second one, *Second-Class Citizen* (1974), as highly
autobiographical as the first, is initially based in Nigeria but mostly set in London. The
same dual setting can be found in the novel *Kehinde* (1994), while *Gwendolen* (1989),
whose American title is *The Family* (1990), has a double setting again, Jamaica and
the British capital. To these four London novels, Emecheta's autobiography, *Head
Above Water* (1986), may be added, and this again has both a Nigerian and an English
background, as it follows the life of the writer herself, who moved to England in 1962.
The Nigerian and the West Indian scenarios are usually rural ones, while the British
setting is an urban environment. As regards time, the first two novels are set in the
1960s and the other two in the 1970s.

All these works deal with the theme of migration. C.L. Innes has observed that "the
generations of writers who came from the Caribbean, or Africa or Asia in the 1950s
and 1960s were typically male, typically single and, so they believed, typically transient."[1] They would propose the point of view of single, male characters often living in
hotel rooms and always aspiring to return to their native countries as soon as possible.
With Emecheta, there is the point of view of married educated women, who are
mothers of many children and who seem determined to make London their home base.
The first two novels have the same main character, Adah, a Nigerian Igbo woman,
who is abandoned by her husband and has to bring up five children by herself. She is a
cultured immigrant who reads books, becomes a university student, and whose aspiration is to become a writer. Gwendolen, a girl from the West Indies, is the main character of the eponymous novel; she arrives in England when she is twelve to rejoin her
family, and is uneducated. Kehinde, an Igbo Nigerian woman, works in a bank and has
been living in London for eighteen years with her husband and her two children.

---

[1] C.L. Innes, "Wintering: Making a Home in Britain," in *Other Britain, Other British: Contemporary Multicultural Fiction*, ed. A. Robert Lee (London & East Haven CT: Pluto, 1995): 21.

The experiences and difficulties these black women face while adjusting to a different culture concern the women themselves as immigrants in an English context and involve their families as well, with problems ranging from housing and job-hunting to children's illnesses, the choice of child-minders, and schooling and education in a Western world. Emecheta's realistic documentary novels usually record the daily lives of black women in North London and are based on the writer's personal experience and on the experiences of the women she has known. As a matter of fact, in a much-quoted interview the writer affirms that "being a woman, and African born," she sees "things through an African woman's eyes. I chronicle the little happenings in the lives of African women I know."[2] In describing her writing experience, Emecheta stresses the autobiographical element of her literary work: when she began writing fiction she knew that "if only I could stick to the subjects I knew best, and write about them truthfully, about the way I felt or saw them, in the type of language I could manage best, then I would not go wrong." [3] Her experience as an emigrant becomes, then, at least in the first two novels, her main source of inspiration. As Katherine Fishburn emphasizes, the marginality of her situation ("She thus found herself in the unexpected position of living on the margins of British life, far from home and estranged from many of her own people"[4]) turned out to be useful for the artist, "allowing her the distance necessary for what Herbert Marcuse calls the 'Great Refusal – the protest against that which is'."[5] As an emigrant writer, Emecheta is certainly in "a liminal situation, because from the perspective of England she sees problems for women within patriarchal Nigerian culture but from the perspective of her homeland she sees the problems for blacks within racist British culture."[6]

The other two less obviously autobiographical novels are still based on Emecheta's double cultural setting. Even if her true first novel, *The Bride Price*, a romance later burnt by the writer's husband, was set in Nigeria, her first published work, *In the Ditch*, is set in London, and her whole career shows her need to partake of both worlds, her continuous exigency to go back and forth from Africa to England. It is interesting to notice that the writer openly admits that she feels torn between her two countries – Nigeria and England – and that she uses her books as the deposit of her "grievances" and also "to cope with [her] anger in Britain."[7] This is what happens to Adah in *In the Ditch* and *Second-Class Citizen* and seems to confirm Katherine Frank's opinion on Adah/Emecheta's need to gain power over her own experiences through her writing.

---

[2] Buchi Emecheta, "Feminism with a small 'f'!" in *Criticism and Ideology*, ed. Kirsten Holst Petersen (Uppsala: Scandinavian Institute of African Studies, 1988): 175.

[3] Buchi Emecheta, " A Nigerian Writer Living in London," *Kunapipi* 4.1 (1982): 114.

[4] Katherine Fishburn, *Reading Buchi Emecheta: Cross-Cultural Conversation* (Westport CT & London: Greenwood, 1995): 52.

[5] Fishburn, *Reading Buchi Emecheta*, 52.

[6] Christine W. Sizemore, "The London Novels of Buchi Emecheta," in *Emerging Perspectives on Buchi Emecheta*, ed. Marie Umeh (Trenton NJ: Africa World Press, 1996): 368.

[7] Emecheta, "The Dilemma of Being in between Two Cultures," in *African Voices: Interviews with Thirteen African Writers*, ed. Raoul Granqvist & John Stotesbury (Mundelstrup & Sydney: Dangaroo, 1989): 17.

According to Frank, "this literary impulse towards imaginatively restructuring and gaining control over one's life has always been particularly strong among those women writers most liable to repressive social constraints,"[8] which is the case of Emecheta both in Nigeria and London.

In the first two novels, there are no hints about the main characters meeting other ethnic groups; there are no West Indians and no Asians and, therefore, there is a restricted view of multicultural London. However, things change in the other two novels, where other Africans, Pakistanis, and West Indians are introduced, and the scope of the immigrants' world becomes wider. In *In the Ditch*, the English urban world is seen mainly through the eyes of Adah, but also through the eyes of white women belonging to the same underworld where Adah lives. In this novel Adah is marginalized on three accounts, as she is black, poor, and a woman. She discovers that two of these three reasons for being marginalized also apply to white women, as they all "share the degrading experience of poverty and dependence on welfare."[9] Even if she does not idealize it, Emecheta portrays female solidarity[10] in this novel where a possible sisterhood between black and white women is suggested.

All four novels show that the author is interested in women's everyday life, and her fiction can be considered as a true sociological report of the feminine perspective on immigrant reality. Adeola James stresses how "all her writings benefit from her sociological training in that they focus attention on sociological issues such as black oppression in a white society, man–woman relationships in traditional society, and tradition versus modernity."[11] It is significant that *In the Ditch* was first published as a series of articles on life in London. Entitled "Observations of the London Poor" in *The New Statesman*,[12] which Emecheta describes as "well respected in English sociological discipline,"[13] only afterwards was it published as a book. This novel manages to weave together "the different strands of Emecheta's social-scientific international background," as has been pointed out by Chikwenje Ogunyemi, fictionalizing "the teaching of Karl Marx's *Das Kapital*, Simone de Beauvoir's *The Second Sex*, Frantz Fanon's *The Wretched of the Earth*, and Richard Wright's *Native Son*" while focusing on the impact of class, gender and race on "the black woman as *femme seule*."[14]

---

[8] Katherine Frank, "The Death of a Slave Girl: African Womanhood in the Novels of Buchi Emecheta," in *World Literature Written in English* 21.3 (1982): 494.

[9] Dagmar Schmidt–Grözinger, "Problems of the Immigrant in Commonwealth Literature: Kamala Markandaya, *The Nowhere Man* and Buchi Emecheta, *Adah's Story*," in *Tensions Between North and South: Studies in Modern Commonwealth Literature and Culture*, ed. Edith Mettke (Würzburg: Königshausen & Neumann, 1990): 116.

[10] Schmidt–Grözinger, "Problems of the Immigrant in Commonwealth Literature," 116.

[11] Adeola James, *In Their Own Voices, African Women Writers Talk*, ed. James (London: James Currey, 1991): 34.

[12] Emecheta, *Head Above Water* (London: Flamingo, 1986): 69.

[13] *Head Above Water*, 71.

[14] Chikwenje Okonjo Ogunyemi, *African Wo/Man Palava: The Nigerian Novel by Women* (Chicago: U of Chicago P, 1996): 234.

As Olga Kenyon points out, Emecheta "believes, like Toni Morrison, that fiction has a vital social responsibility now that oral tradition is less strong. Fiction keeps racial memories alive – and helps to make sense of the community threatened by alien groups and values."[15] Emecheta is, then, a modern storyteller, who types her stories in her room, instead of telling them to a circle of children under a tree. Her stories have a moral, too, and aim above all at teaching how to maintain important and basic values of one's culture intact (the importance of family relationships, of human dignity), without betraying them in a disruptive alien world. Yet they also reveal how to acquire other, equally important values from the Western culture by integrating them. Moreover, even if the author calls herself a feminist with a small 'f',[16] she describes the process through which her female characters take advantage of their immigration to find a space of their own which allows them more inner freedom. In this context, London may be considered as a gendered space that offers the possibility of seeing a different pattern in women's lives, and where the conditions for change are possible.

Emecheta's London novels explore, then, the transformations which occur in the lives of her immigrant characters and the way in which the immigrant experience shapes their identity. Speaking about the relationship between migration and identity-shifts, Paul White points out that it is possible to "conceptualise a number of overlapping multiple identities which are the subject of constant renegotiation in the face of the conflicts and compromises of everyday life."[17] The search for identity can be mainly considered in gender terms, as it often coincides with a significant change in the heroine's self awareness, gendered behaviour and role within her family and society in general. However, it also involves an economic identity (as poverty and the importance of a decent job are recurrent themes in both the novels and the autobiography), a religious identity (quite ambiguous, as it is balanced between the traditional Igbo beliefs and the only superficially accepted Christian faith), a linguistic one (as the novels often show a shift between standard British English and pidgin, with the introduction of Igbo and Yoruba words), and, finally, a cultural one.

With respect to identity-shifts, a distinction between the female characters and their male counterparts has to be made. Female characters have a more dynamic attitude to the host cultural system and undergo a variety of changes. They often do not fit into their original culture even before leaving their mother countries and show a critical attitude towards both their native culture and English culture. Their attitude towards

---

[15] Olga Kenyon, "Buchi Emecheta and the Black Immigrant Experience in Britain," in Kenyon, *Writing Women: Contemporary Women Novelists* (London: Pluto, 1991): 113.

[16] Emecheta, "Feminism with a small 'f'!" 175. Emecheta strongly refuses to be called a feminist, as this is a European definition. This comes out, for example, in statements such as: "if you look at everything I do, it is what the feminists do, too; but it is just that it comes from Europe, or European women, and I don't like being defined by them. [...] I do believe in the African kind of feminism"; *African Voices: Interviews with Thirteen African Writers*, ed. Granqvist & Stotesbury, 19; and "I still feel very African and I don't think feminists have the right to tell me what to do"; in Olga Kenyon, *The Writer's Imagination: Interview with Major International Women Novelists*, 51.

[17] Paul White, "Geography, Literature and Migration" in *Writing Across Worlds: Literature and Migration*, ed. Russell King, John Connell & Paul White (London: Routledge, 1995): 2.

Nigeria, for example, is quite ambivalent. Nigeria is at the same time the place of sacred memory, the origin of Adah's storytelling, the source of her creative powers through the example of the big mothers of her family, and is also the place of unchanged, oppressive traditions. England, however, has a multifaceted image, too, as it can be seen in turn as a dreamland, a sacred place to be reached, the land of opportunities, but also as the land of discrimination, of cultural stereotypes and prejudices, of poverty and loneliness. It is also the land where only the toughest survive and weaker immigrants can easily lose their own inherited values or renounce their dreams. Emecheta's novels revolve around the theme of the journey from Nigeria to England (or from Jamaica to England) and, in the case of *Kehinde*, from England to Nigeria and back. Such a journey is far from being simply geographical and becomes the symbol of a quest for a better life and of the evolution of the heroine's self. Both places and cultural worlds are necessary for the writer's and her heroines' development. The clash between the two places and the two cultures forces her characters (and the writer herself) to form a fresh, personal pattern of life, and a new, unique, identity. Thus, the characters end up by creating their own personal cultural identity, partaking of elements from both their native and host cultures. All the novels show an upward movement which sees the heroines climb the social ladder – getting better and better jobs, for example, or better and better housing. Above all, we see them adjusting to the outer world, negotiating a relationship where one's own black culture is not considered inferior but is respected, where one's own dignity is not trampled on. The blows from the outside world, but also from one's own immigrant companions, help the female characters build a stronger, self-conscious personality that maintains a deeper integrity, which is mainly spiritual – as can be seen in the continuous presence of a *chi* in the lives of the Igbo Adah and Kehinde. The self-assertion of the 'London' heroines is consistent with the thematic message of Emecheta's novels in general, as, it has been observed, her female characters show how "passivity is acquiescence to the *status quo* and so a perpetuation of it" and "an aggrieved female [...] must work out a strategy for survival and recognition."[18]

It seems that deep changes are more easily looked for, and accepted, by women than men immigrants, as all the novels indicate an increased awareness of the heroine's aspirations and needs, with a consequent renunciation of already acquired solid advantages (a husband, a settled role in society) for a more fluid possibility of life, often conquered with great pain and suffering. Male characters, on the contrary, are more static and passive, as in the case of Francis, Adah's husband. He does not alter his cultural identity and maintains his male-centred Igbo cosmogony, within a cultural frame where such a pattern is continuously challenged. At the same time, he keeps his distance from the host cultural system. He is only superficially touched by the host culture, which has taught him to kiss his wife in public (the same happens in *Kehinde*), but not to accept a relationship on equal terms. His attitude towards English life is still reverential and he does not even try to come to grips with it, often showing an inferior-

---

[18] Helen Chukwuma, "Positivism and the Female Crisis : The Novels of Buchi Emecheta," in *Nigerian Female Writers: A Critical Perspective*, ed. Henrietta C. Otukunefor & Obiageli Nwodo (Ikeja, Lagos: Malthouse, 1989): 5.

ity complex towards British culture and English as a language. This attitude is overtly expressed in the bitter lesson he teaches his newly arrived wife about their place on the social English ladder:

> "You must know, my dear young *lady*, that in Lagos you may be a million publicity officers for the Americans; you may be earning a million pounds a day; you may have hundreds of servants; you may be living like an élite, but the day you land in England, you are a second-class citizen. So you can't discriminate against your own people, because we are all second-class."[19]

This explains why he prefers to live in a Nigerian ghetto rather than confront the whites. According to Oladele Taiwo, "Francis works with the blacks for reasons of self-preservation. He is anxious to cultivate a sense of belonging and therefore stays close to the black community whose members share with him the common burden of being black," and he suffers mainly "because he is unable to relate the past to the present."[20] According to this view, Adah succeeds only because she is tougher than her husband and better equipped to balance the old and new cultural factors. The fact must be underlined that men usually get humbler and lower-paid jobs than their wives in these novels and that, consequently, wives maintain their traditional role of bread-winners in their families.

The first two novels analyse the life-style of newly arrived immigrants who try to integrate successfully, while the other two novels refer to families who have already lived in the country for some time (eighteen years in the case of *Kehinde*) and have succeeded. In *Gwendolen*, however, the inferiority complex of Winston, Gwendolen's father, is still explicit in the way he approaches the teacher on his daughter's first day at school. His stammering and his rough English reveal his inability to communicate with the establishment in a successful way. Albert in *Kehinde*, on the other hand, who works as a storekeeper with white people, has no apparent problems; he plays "to per-fection the role of the Igbo family man in London," but is "far from satisfied with its restrictions" and still wishes to go 'home' to Nigeria, as he wants

> to go back to the way of life my father had, a life of comparative ease for men, where men were men and women were women, and one was respected as somebody. Here, I am nobody, just a storekeeper.[...]No, to be at home is better. There I can have my drink on the verandah, and people will pay attention to me, including my wife.[21]

From his London experience Albert acquires only the material advantages it can offer him (money, a nice house, a Jaguar); they do not compensate for the loss of his identity as a man, a chief, the first son of his family. He exploits the cultural system only when it is useful for him: for example, when he forces his wife to have an abortion. This practice would be unthinkable at home, where children are more valuable than money,

---

[19] Emecheta, *Second-Class Citizen* (1974; London: Flamingo, 1987): 43. Further page refer-ences are in the main text.

[20] Oladele Taiwo, *Female Novelists of Modern Africa* (London: Macmillan, 1984): 105–106.

[21] Emecheta, *Kehinde* (Oxford: Heinemann, 1994): 35.

but is so convenient for him at this stage of his life. What neither Francis nor Albert can accept is the strengthening of a woman's role in the English cultural system, with what they perceive as the consequent loss of their own strength, power and gendered identity. This is also felt by other immigrants such as Prahbu, a Pakistani friend of Albert's in *Kehinde*, who stresses how his and Albert's traditional roles are challenged in a country "where a woman is Queen and where it's beginning to look as if we're soon going to have a woman Prime Minister" (with an obvious reference to Margaret Thatcher).[22]

For all the characters, then, the act of migration involves "a challenge to earlier self-perceptions and self-images" whatever their attitude is and causes a revision of "projects, dreams and ultimate goals."[23] Such a challenge, with a consequent development or refusal to move from one's position, needs time to take place, and Emecheta gives the reader the opportunity to observe the various stages of the entire immigrant experience and to follow her characters' evolution and identity-shifts. First, the author describes what England means before one actually touches its shores, when English life is mainly imagined through the filter of been-to people's words or of the teachers at the mission schools or of books. In *Second-Class Citizen*, Adah says that going to England has been like a dream for her since her childhood. This is due to her father's attitude: she says, with a strong sense of irony, that the title United Kingdom "was so deep, so mysterious, that Adah's father always voiced it in hushed tones, wearing such a respectful expression as if he were speaking of God's Holiest of Holies" (8). From such a reverential attitude derive the assumptions of the child Adah that "going to the United Kingdom must surely be like paying God a visit. The United Kingdom, then, must be like heaven" (8). These assumptions, seen now from the adult Adah's point of view, assume an explicitly ironical twist. In like manner, the arrival from the United Kingdom of a been-to lawyer is welcomed with a similar religious zeal: women dye their hair, buy new outfits, compose songs for him, with a sense of pride, as "to them it meant the arrival of their very own Messiah. A Messiah specially created for the Ibuza people. A Messiah who would go into politics and fight for the rights of the people of Ibuza" (8). Further on in the novel, the lawyer becomes a Minister in Northern Nigeria and the narrator adds that he "just stayed put in the North making barrels and barrels of money" (27). As a young woman, a bride and already a mother of two children, Adah nourishes her dream of going to England and finally manages to join her husband, who has gone there as a student. She obtains her husband's family's permission by stressing all the advantages of going to the land of her dreams: work and money are easy there. The main reason to go is to provide money from abroad for the extended family and to play the role of the rich been-to people once they can come back. The big cars that they will certainly be driving become the symbols of their success. So determined to go and so sure of her rosy future is Adah that she even gives her mother-in-law her golden necklaces as a deposit before leaving, as she will not need them in England and she will be possibly wearing something even more precious when she returns. She lies to her husband's family, telling them she is only going for a year and six months, even

---

[22] Emecheta, *Kehinde*, 35, 36.
[23] Paul White, "Geography, Literature and Migration," 3.

though she is planning to complete her education there. She is sure, though, that she will come back. At this stage England is seen as a basket full of riches waiting to be picked up by willing hands; it is merely considered as a country to be taken advantage of, reversing the traditional colonial image of Africa as a land to be exploited.

A similarly unrealistic and dangerous attitude towards England is introduced in *Head Above Water*, when the writer describes the young black people (African and West Indian) that hang about the youth club she works for. She underscores, with the tone of a sociologist, the fact that most of these young people

> had been brainwashed into thinking that England was their mother country, that England belonged to them. At the time when the myth of the 'mother country' was being perpetuated, it was beyond the imaginings of the white colonials that one day the blacks would turn round and say to them, 'Fulfil your promise'. (147)

She describes what happens when educated blacks "spill into London in search of middle-class jobs" with "nothing but their dreams" (146). The contrast is mainly between the world of fantasy in which the black boys live and the real world they face once they arrive. Behind the boys are all the expectations of their families and of all those who contributed towards their journey, hoping to be repaid one day; behind the boys are also all the stereotyped images of English life, according to which, for example, all English schools are equally good and formative (because of the presence of white teachers). The reality is that not all the schools are good and that not all the teachers care. If the boys find school rather hard going, they may play truant and be allowed to do so, "except for the occasional reports to [...] parents" (147). Despite the difficulties they encounter as students (Emecheta herself admits to having failed some university exams), it is difficult for them to renounce their ambitions of becoming a lawyer or a doctor, professions that "even middle class English boys [...] would not dream of mentioning " (147). Any suggestion of a lesser job, or a manual job, would be considered as the end of their dreams, as a hint that

> he is no better off than his poor parents or the people who helped him to come to England. He has to be in an elitist position to rub shoulders with the whites he sees around him, the whites who tell him on the one hand that this is his mother country and on the other, that he cannot reap any benefits from her. He will soon learn also that the darker his skin, the meaner his job. These are not salubrious experiences for a young person. But these young people will carry this hurt and humiliation in their hearts. (147)

The failure that most black young people face is, therefore, the result of a wrong initial attitude, created by white-induced myths The problem of education is also stressed in *Gwendolen,* where the adolescent who cannot even pronounce her name properly is so ashamed of her limited knowledge, her bad pronunciation of English, and above all of her illiteracy that she prefers not to ask her teachers anything, to behave rudely, despite her sweet character, and finally to play truant. The English schoolteachers are unable to understand any of the dramas that are taking place in the girl's mind and prefer to consider her as a slow, dumb, good-for-nothing student. By stressing the fact that English schools do not meet the expectations of young immigrants and fail to help them,

Emecheta is bringing a charge against the English educational system, and the charge is particularly severe, given Emecheta's consideration of the enormous importance of education for people's (especially women's) fulfilment and emancipation.

We enter the second stage of the immigrant experience upon arrival in England. According to Ned Seelye, "conflict is present whenever two cultures come into contact. This may be because of a clash of values – a cultural difference in the perception of the appropriate way to satisfy basic physical and psychological needs."[24] Emecheta's characters face a series of culture shocks as soon as they land and in the long months of their adjustment to the English cultural context. Their first impressions generally concern the weather[25] and the environment. Despite the excitement Adah in *Second-Class Citizen* feels at the thought of having finally made it by arriving in the United Kingdom, England gives her "a cold welcome" (39). With her ironical use of figurative language, where religious elements from her white formal education are mixed in, the narrator adds that "if Adah had been Jesus, she would have passed England by. Liverpool was grey, smoky and looked uninhabited by humans" (39). The criticism is fundamentally directed at the bleak surroundings. In *Head Above Water* the author recalls her first impressions and explains that "it felt like walking into the inside of a grave. I could see nothing but masses of grey, filth, and more grey [...] So I said quietly, 'Pa, England is not the Kingdom of God you thought it was'" (29). Of course, nothing much can be done at this stage, as the immigrant experience has already started and no chances are left but to "make it here or perish" even if the "cold was beginning to touch [her] African bones" (29). The land of dreams quickly turns into a "God-forsaken country."[26] Remarks about the weather and how it helps to make the immigrant's life difficult are present in all four London novels. Little Gwendolen is caught by snow going back home on her first day at school. The only snow she has ever seen is on Christmas cards, and only on them can she appreciate its beauty. What she feels under the snowflakes is that "the cold that was biting her fingers seemed determined to meet the one that was creeping into her body from her near-frozen feet. She suppressed a sob. For the first time since she'd arrived in England, she longed for Jamaica."[27]

Still within the range of first impressions, remarks about places can be found: namely, the houses where people live, and the churches they attend. The new places are observed and contrasted with the familiar ones. Here, for example, is the description of English terraced houses in *Second-Class Citizen*:

---

[24] H. Ned Seelye, *Teaching Culture* (Skokie IL: National Textbook Company, 1976): 84

[25] An observation on the English weather can be also found in the first paragraph of *A Kind of Marriage* where it is said. " England is one of those countries where you can live for many years and still not get used to the cold weather. One might have thought that for an African like myself, who had lived two decades in London, the biting wind of autumn would have been no problem, but I have never got used to it" (1).

[26] Emecheta, *Second-Class Citizen*, 42.

[27] Emecheta, *Gwendolen* (Oxford: Heinemann, 1989): 64.

she could not tell where the house began and where it ended, because it was joined to
other houses in the street. She had never seen houses like that before, joined together like
that. In Lagos houses were completely detached with the yards on both sides, the compound at the back and verandas in front. These ones had none of those things. [...] We
may never be as bad as this. Jammed against each other. (40–41)

Adah will be lodged in much worse conditions, but Kehinde, at the end of the cycle,
will eventually end up living comfortably in a "typical East London mid-terraced
house." An equally desolate impression is produced by English churches. The narrator
admits that

it took her years to erase the image of the Nigerian church which usually had a festive
air. In England, especially in London, 'church' was a big grey building with stained-glass
windows, high ornamental ceilings, very cold, full of rows and rows of empty chairs,
with the voice of the vicar droning from the distant pulpit, crying like the voice of John
the Baptist lost in the wilderness. In London, churches were cheerless. (2)

In both cases, a negative impression develops as the new world is seen through eyes
which are still filled with images from one's own country. The new cultural system is
approached and evaluated in comparison, or in contrast, with the well-known one. The
main character in *In the Ditch* lives in a block of flats, whose outside looks "like a
prison"[28] and which is ironically called Pussy Cat Mansions. Adah applies what she
knows to what she sees, even if it is so different from her culture. Therefore, she calls
the inner courtyard of the Mansions "a compound" (20), as it has the same shape or
function as the area with the chief's hut at the centre and the wives' huts all around. In
this case, "it was an open space into which all the front doors opened out. In the centre
of the compound were some ill-looking buildings. Adah's African friends called these
little houses "Juju man's house" (20). She re-creates the village life she has left behind
and the social assistant's room plays the role of the market place where women exchange goods along with gossip and laughter, thus meeting the need for a communal
atmosphere where no woman is isolated and all problems are shared. This comforting
reality disappears in other works such a *Kehinde* and *Gwendolen*, where the pattern of
life follows a British model, where there is less sharing. Even if friendship is still possible, the communal atmosphere of the compound is lost.

   From remarks on the weather and on places, the character shifts her attention to
people and their habits. With her usual irony, Emecheta affirms in her autobiography
Head Above Water that her idea of English people was based on the books she had
read at school and that she thought that "people in England lived like they did in Jane
Austen's novels and that the typical Englishman was like Mr Darcy, and the women
like Mrs Bennett and her daughters" (28–29). Her characters underline a mismatch between expectations and reality, especially as they have been brought up to respect the
whites so much. In *Second-Class Citizen*, Adah's surprise in finding out that Trudy,
her white child-minder, steals her children's milk and toys and does not look after
them properly, explodes in the words "she listened to Trudy destroying forever one of

---

[28] Emecheta, *In the Ditch* (1972; London: Allison & Busby, 1979): 18.

her myths she had been brought up to believe: that the white man never lied" (57). This leads Adah to the discovery "that the whites were just as fallible as everyone else. There were bad whites and good whites, just as there were bad blacks and good blacks! Why, then, did they claim to be superior?" (58). Adah's judgments on the whites get sterner and harsher: they are seen as "remote, happy in an aloof way, but determined to keep their distance" (39). The more she lives in the English environment, the more she realizes that "this was a society where nobody is interested in the problems of others" (39). The contrast is once again with one's own cultural system. The indifference she feels around her is very different from the communal life she has left behind:

> [...] And whose attention do you attract ? The attention of paid listeners. Listeners who make you feel that you are an object to be studied, diagnosed, charted and tabulated. Listeners who refer to you as 'a case'. You don't have the old woman next door who, on hearing an argument going on between a wife and husband, would come in to slap the husband, telling him off and all that, knowing that her words would be respected because she was old and experienced. (72)

Later on she adds that

> England is a silent country; people are taught to bottle up their feelings and screw them up tight, like the illicit gin her parents drank at home. If you made a mistake and un-corked the bottle, the gin would bubble out. She had seen English men and women be-have like humans once or twice, but why was it that they only behaved like humans when they were straggling out of the pubs on Saturday nights? (106)

Culture shocks or culture clashes, then, transform the dreamland into a harsh reality: the land of opportunities, chosen for the material advantages it can offer, becomes a land of problems, poverty, and failures. The initial images of *In the Ditch* show the bedroom where the protagonist Adah is to sleep. Consistent with her style as a novelist, and her intention to be a chronicler of everyday events, Emecheta carefully describes Adah's mattress and the sounds caused by her room-mate, The Great Rat. The main antagonist in this opening scene is a rat with "sharp piercing eyes, long mouth and his big brown body" (7), and what the author describes is a silent fight between Adah and the rat, won by Adah when she throws a book at the animal. The room is also inhabited by a "group of sleeping cockroaches" (7). The scene exudes poverty, filth, and fright. To make things worse, Adah's Nigerian landlord makes her life miserable and is shown at the beginning of the novel draped in colourful African material, "just like juju masqueraders in Lagos" (9) in an attempt to scare her. Adah is not afraid, how-ever, perhaps because "in England one's mind was always taken up with worrying about the things that really matter" (9) or perhaps because Nigerian customs in London have lost their weight and their meaning. She repeats to herself "I am tough and free," where "free" is a keyword:

> In England she was free to keep her job, keep her kids, do her studies; she felt safe to ignore the juju man and his pranks. No, the juju trick would not work in England, it was out of place, on alien ground. God dammit, juju, in England, where you're surrounded by walls of unbelief! (9)

According to Fishburn, the episode might show how Adah has "chosen the language of Western rationality" and how "the authoritative discourse of Western rationality has supplanted the traditional authoritative discourse of her African upbringing. That is, Western rationality has become internally persuasive to her."[29] Two aspects of life in London are thus emphasized in this novel's opening: on the one hand, England is the land of poverty; on the other, it is also the land of freedom. It is at the same time a land of opportunity and of difficulties, where the difficulties, rats, cockroaches, are accepted in the name of freedom. It is also clear that one's culture cannot survive in such a context. England becomes a land where the same beliefs that would have frightened Adah no longer have the same value, and can be laughed at.

Together with culture shock, however, the characters have to face more serious problems, above all that of discrimination. In *Second-Class Citizen*, discrimination by whites is stressed when Adah and Francis try to find a house – "Sorry, no coloureds" is the notice board they find outside many doors of the houses for rent. Once again the contrast is between expectations and reality. White people did not seem to care about the colour of one's skin when living in Nigeria, but it obviously matters in their own country. Adah learns that

> her colour was something she was supposed to be ashamed of. She was never aware of this at home in Nigeria, even when in the midst of whites. Those whites must have had a few lessons about colour before coming out to the tropics, because they never let drop from their mouths the fact that, in their countries, black was inferior. (76–77)

Even social workers, despite their good intentions, may become disruptive elements, offending or humiliating the people they are trying to help, considering them only as 'cases'. The psychological effect of the unexpected discovery of being considered inferior because of her skin colour makes Adah look for discarded items every time she goes into a clothing store, even if she has enough money to buy the best. This means that she behaves in the way she is expected to behave. The difference between her and her husband or her husband's men friends is that Adah only initially behaves according to the expected role, as she wants to work her way up ("was going to regard herself as the equal of any white," 77), while Francis and the other men will always adhere to such conformist behaviour.

In the novels where there are immigrants from other countries, Emecheta points up how sharing the immigrant situation does not automatically mean there are no prejudices among the various ethnic groups.[30] In the first two novels, where only Africans are introduced, a kind of contrast between Igbo and Yoruba cultures is shown, and in *Gwendolen* there are constant references to misunderstandings between Africans and West Indians. The turning-point in the novel, Sonia's temporary return to Jamaica to look after her sick mother, is a result of a cultural mismatch between herself and her African landlord. The African landlord acts according to his culture, where news of a death cannot be given as such, but has to be softened by saying that the person is only

[29] Fishburn, *Reading Buchi Emecheta*, 54.
[30] Emecheta, *Second-Class Citizen*, 77.

ill. This is the reason why Sonia leaves for Jamaica, with boxes of medicines, only to find out that her mother has already died. This novel also reveals prejudices against Gwendolen's Greek boyfriend. Greeks are white, but only a second-class type of whites. Again in this novel we find the derogatory term "yellow nigger" used to define half-castes, while West Indians consider all the people coming from Africa uncivilized. In *Kehinde*, Albert does not share with his good friend Prahbu from Pakistan his wish to go back to Nigeria and be the head of his family, as he is sure that "their images of African chiefs were gathered from old Tarzan films and *Sanders of the River*, and that trying to give his colleagues an up-to-date picture of Nigeria would be a waste of time."[31] All these references stress the fact that the immigrants' world does not produce mutual understanding, even if its inhabitants share the same problems and even though multicultural London may be a lonely place to live.

Moreover, the author stresses that there is a gap, or at least a difference between parents and children, between the first and the second generations. Such a gap is visible in *Kehinde*, where, for example, children eat beans on toast, while their parents still eat ground rice and *egusi* soup, or in the fact that Joshua, Kehinde's son, considers English as his mother tongue (3). Stereotyped images also arise about one's own culture among the second generation. They have been born and brought up in a Western environment and know nothing about their place of origin. Emecheta's children, for example, born in London, imagine Nigeria as a jungle[32] full of lions and tigers, while Kehinde's children refuse to learn the Igbo language, as their own native language is English. The second generation, educated in English schools and fed on baked beans and fish and chips, feels distant from the parents' original culture and can aspire to a complete integration within the host system. The author, however, mainly stresses the distance of these children from their own culture rather than their integration with the host culture. Moreover, this integration appears to be rather superficial. The children born in London are already excluded from the use of their ancestral tongue, as they have been exposed to English rather than to the Igbo language. This is perhaps inevitable, but indicates an important identity-shift and is the sign of a loss. The dialogue between Kehinde and her son stresses the contrast between a language which no longer belongs to the children, as they refuse to use it. A language belongs only to those who use it to express their feelings.

The saddest aspect, however, is the fact that the immigrant experience does not bring people belonging to the same ethnic group together, and if they remain united against the outside world, they are so with a strong sense of envy towards any member of the group who successfully integrates. Along with discrimination on the part of the white people there is thus an inner discriminating ghetto where black people confine themselves, lowering their standards of living and somehow performing as expected by prejudiced whites. The inner ghetto, built mainly as a protection against external difficulties, becomes a prison of ethnocentrism where no changes are allowed, no differences

---

[31] This is also stated in Jussawalla's "Interview with Buchi Emecheta," in *Interviews with Writers of the Post-Colonial World*, ed. Feroza Jussawalla & Reed Way Dasenbrock (Jackson & London: U of Mississippi P, 1992): 82–91.

[32] Emecheta, *Head Above Water*, 85.

are permitted, and any hypothesis of improvement in one's standard of living is seen only as a way to highlight failure on the part of others. Adah, for example, is different from the Nigerians her husband befriends, as she does not want to lower the standards she attained in Nigeria before leaving for England. England was meant as a place where economic, educational, social and personal improvement could be guaranteed, and certainly not as a place of failure. Francis's reaction to his difficulties and to the discrimination around him is simply to lower his standards, not to challenge his culturally established role. He becomes trapped within his traditions, his ethnocentric views, and his anger towards, and refusal of, the outside culture. Adah, even if a prey to culture shock and still able to evaluate what she perceives as different, strange or wrong in the host culture, strives to conquer a space where her dreams may be fulfilled and to maintain her aspirations and standards. Hence her refusal to give her children up for adoption, and to accept a job as a cleaner, as she considers the qualifications she obtained at home too good for the menial jobs her husband would like her to accept. Adah's innate self-esteem, even when it receives blows from the outside world, helps her fight back against the two worlds of discrimination: that of the whites and that of her own people, where the latter is more difficult to fight. She also appears willing to change, to adopt other ways of living when she considers them useful or better than those she has inherited and brought with her from home.

Novels such as *Gwendolen* and *Kehinde* give readers the opportunity to observe immigrants after they have somehow settled into the new country. The problems of finding a job and a decent place to live, of providing children with schools, are over. Social life is established; all the characters have friends: Sonia and Winston (Gwendolen's mother and father) have befriended African people, while Albert is on friendly terms with his Pakistani colleague and Kehinde has her Moriammo. No white friends are mentioned, even if Albert works with whites. Winston and Sonia have not taken advantage of the school system and still cannot read or write. They do not think of going back to Jamaica, and even if Sonia has to go there, she eventually returns to England. Immigrants seem to have grown accustomed to the whites' strange customs, even if they have not been entirely accepted, and seem finally integrated.

England has definitively lost its sacred aura, and a reversal of the initial situation can be seen in *Kehinde:* after so many years of life in London, Nigeria now assumes the role of a dreamland. This is explicit in Albert's wish to go back 'home' and in his explanation to Prabhu: "he pined for sunshine, freedom, easy friendship, warmth" (6). It is Nigeria now which is seen as the land of the easy life, as "the standard of living is not as high as it is here" (37), and Albert has no doubts that "we'll make it in Nigeria. It's our country, isn't it?" (38). After exploiting England for so many years as the land of opportunity (and the sale of the house in London may be considered as the final act of exploitation), Albert dreams of a triumphant return to Nigeria and a satisfactory life as a been-to. Kehinde is satisfied with her English life, but has no power to make decisions, and, reluctantly, she becomes involved in such a dream, fancying herself in the role of the been-to madam. She even prepares herself for the role –

she was going to buy more Western luxuries she knew she would need to establish herself as the been-to madam of the house – essentials like a washing machine, a fridge, a television and a video recorder. As for a music centre, she would buy the biggest and loudest she could afford. (38)

– while her friend Moriammo depicts the life she is going to enjoy once she goes back: "go home, go relax. Be a been-to Madam. Put your feet up. Be a white woman. Make you enjoy the sunshine. There go plenty of servants too" (52). Only some doubts arise in Kehinde's mind about the possibility of Albert being chased by women: as Moriammo says, "Those young overeducated women dey thirst for been-to men as small baby dey thirst for suck" (102), but this scenario is refused by Kehinde: "which Nigerian girlfriend would be able to stand the presence of a rich, been-to madam? They wouldn't dare compete with her!" (47). Ironically, this is exactly what happens to Albert.

Nigeria is the place of memory for Albert, who fancies himself performing the rituals of palm-wine drinking and kola-nut eating performed by his father when he was a child. Nigeria is also the place where traditions have been kept, mainly those traditions that are so comforting for his male ego (polygamy, for example, and the respect due to him as the first son of the family). The contrast is now between England, as the land where changes and identity-shifts are inevitable, and Nigeria, as the place where no dangerous identity-shifts take place. He has not been able to maintain the values of his original Yoruba culture while living in London (as his decision about his wife's abortion shows) and needs the support of a suitable environment. He will go back and remain in Nigeria, perhaps happily ever after. Kehinde is different. She has preserved her original cultural identity, as is underlined by her continuously talking to her *chi* and by the way she behaves at the farewell party, where she changes attire five times and gives presents to everybody, in accordance with the true Nigerian tradition. She has, however, also been deeply changed by eighteen years of Western life. She will no longer be able to cope with the traditional role imposed upon women by Nigerian patriarchal culture; she will not accept polygamy and her role as senior wife; she will not accept the loss of her intimacy and relationship as an equal with Albert; she will not accept the loss of her family, her children easily forgetting what they have learnt in London and adapting to the Yoruba way. Kehinde finds she is relegated to the margins in Nigeria, while England had given her the possibility of living a full, respectable life. This is why she will go back to London on her own, leaving behind both husband and children, her past and her disappointing present, ready to start from scratch again.

Strangely enough, the English weather, that element of distress for all the immigrants in Emecheta's stories, is suddenly considered nostalgically:

this was October, autumn in England. The wind would be blowing, leaves browning and falling. In a few weeks, the cherry tree in her back garden would be naked of leaves, its dark branches twisted like old bones. On a day like this, after the Friday shopping, her feet would be stretched in front of her gas fire, while she watched her favourite serials on television until she was tired and until her eyes ached. Autumn in England. (96)

This is a turning-point in the story, when the heroine realizes she may feel more at home under a grey sky than under the sun she had pined for so much.

Kehinde, then, depicts a final stage in the life of an immigrant woman and shows how London can become a synonym for independence and can finally be considered a home. It is with a different, realistic attitude that Kehinde, the black immigrant woman, returns to England. She now has the awareness that her identity has changed. She is an example of a woman who, despite the displacement implicit in her role as an immigrant, manages to find a place of her own. She is aware that, even if major culture shocks have been overcome, she will always "be made to feel unwelcome" (96) in England. There is no more dreaming now in her views of England, as there are no longer dreams about Africa, either. The dichotomy between her two worlds is still at work when she opens the door of her London house. The voice inside her that sings "Home, sweet home" fights the other inner voice that affirms that *Nigeria* is her home. The open-ended novel portrays a woman fully aware of being distant from both her Nigerian heritage and her European ambience, but who has also learned not to be ashamed of her difference. As no country is a fairyland, Kehinde pragmatically chooses the place where she can realistically enjoy the greater freedom the Western world offers her as a woman.

If the four London novels are seen as a sequence, the house appears to be a central thematic element: from the one-room apartment where Adah's family lives in cramped conditions, to the council house inhabited by rats and cockroaches, to the Pussy Cat Mansions where Adah discovers that poverty and womanhood are stronger links than race, to Gwendolen's house, which is clean and overfurnished, but which cannot protect Gwendolen from her father's assaults and the failures at school, to Kehinde's house. The house that the English laws guarantee her becomes the base from which Kehinde can start all over again. The final step she takes, of not selling the house and instead considering it her own property, establishes not only her distance from the oppressive patriarchal Nigerian family system, but also her belonging to a country which gives her the chance to proclaim her newly re-gendered role. Thus, the house may become a home and England a place where she belongs, because 'home' is the place where you can cut out a space for yourself, wherever that is.

WORKS CITED

Chukwuma, Helen. "Positivism and the Female Crisis: The Novels of Buchi Emecheta," in *Nigerian Female Writers: A Critical Perspective*, ed. Henrietta C. Otukunefor & Obiageli Nwodo (Ikeja, Lagos: Malthouse Press, 1989): 2–18.
Emecheta, Buchi. "The Dilemma of Being in between Two Cultures," in *African Voices: Interviews with Thirteen African Writers*, ed. Raoul Granqvist & John Stotesbury (Sydney: Dangaroo, 1989): 16–20.
——. "Feminism with a small 'f'!" in *Criticism and Ideology*, ed. Kirsten Holst Petersen (Uppsala: Scandinavian Institute of African Studies, 1988): 173–85.
——. *Gwendolen* (Oxford: Heinemann, 1989).
——. *Head Above Water* (London: Flamingo, 1986).
——. *In the Ditch* (London: Allison & Busby, 1979).
——. *Kehinde* (Oxford: Heinemann, 1994).
——. *A Kind of Marriage* (London: Macmillan, 1986).
——. "A Nigerian Writer Living in London," *Kunapipi* 4.1 (1982): 114–23.

——. *Second-Class Citizen* (London: Flamingo, 1987).

Fishburn, Katherine. *Reading Buchi Emecheta: Cross-Cultural Conversations* (Westport CT & London: Greenwood, 1995): 51–73.

Frank, Katherine, "The Death of a Slave Girl: African Womanhood in the Novels of Buchi Emecheta," *World Literature Written in English* 21.3 (Autumn 1982): 476–97.

Innes, C.L. "Wintering: Making a Home in Britain," in *Other Britain, Other British Contemporary Multicultural Fiction,* ed. A. Robert Lee (London & East Haven CT: Pluto, 1995): 21–32.

James, Adeola, ed. *In Their Own Voices: African Women Writers Talk* (London: James Currey, 1991): 34–45.

Jussawalla, Feroza. "Interview with Buchi Emecheta," in *Interviews with Writers of the Post-Colonial World,* ed. Feroza Jussawalla & Reed Way Dasenbrock (Jackson & London: U of Mississippi P, 1992): 83–99.

Kenyon, Olga. *The Writer's Imagination: Interviews with Major International Women Novelists* (Bradford: U of Bradford Print Unit, 1992): 45–54.

King, Russell, John Connell & Paul White, ed. *Writing across Worlds. Literature and Migration* (London: Routledge, 1995.)

Ogunyemi, Chikwenje Okonjo. *African Wo/Man Palava. The Nigerian Novel by Women* (Chicago: U of Chicago P, 1996): 220–83.

Schmidt–Grözinger, Dagmar. "Problems of the Immigrant in Commonwealth Literature: Kamala Markandaya, *The Nowhere Man* and Buchi Emecheta, *Adah's Story,*" in *Tensions Between North and South: Studies in Modern Commonwealth Literature and Culture,* ed. Edith Mettke (Würzburg: Königshausen & Neumann, 1990): 112–17.

Seelye, H. Ned. *Teaching Culture* (Skokie IL.: National Textbook Company, 1976.)

Sizemore, Christine W. "The London Novels of Buchi Emecheta," in *Emerging Perspectives on Buchi Emecheta,* ed. Marie Umeh (Trenton NJ: Africa World Press, 1996): 367–85.

Oladele, Taiwo. *Female Novelists of Modern Africa* (London: Macmillan, 1984): 100–27.

《●》

The Other Women's Guide to English Cultures
Tsitsi Dangarembga and Buchi Emecheta

MICHAEL MEYER

T HOSE ENGLISHMEN who think about the multicultural metropolis in terms of English culture *versus* black culture presuppose that both these cultures are coherent and mutually exclusive. Conservative Englishmen tend to regard nations as "cultural homogeneous 'communities of sentiment'"[1] and multiculturalism as a threat to English culture. Liberal Englishmen consider other cultures as basically equal under the premise of a universal humanity, which subordinates the difference of the other to anthropological sameness. If liberal Englishmen accept the coexistence of diverse cultures within their country, they may merely indulge in a "semblance of pluralism,"[2] which reduces minority cultures to exotic commodities and ignores any challenge on the part of the dominant culture. In response to the English denigration and assimilation of others, some ethnic minority groups assert their different homogeneous cultures.[3] Because of their marginalization, black women seem to be privileged to meet Paul Gilroy's demand: "What must be challenged is the way that these apparently unique customs and practices are understood as expressions of a pure and homogeneous nationality."[4]

Not only Englishmen, but also Africans, West Indians, and even some white feminists conceive of black women as sites of racial and sexual difference but not as subjects who make a difference.[5] Carol Boyce Davies suggests that the African diaspora turned

---

[1] Paul Gilroy, "'The Whisper Wakes, the Shudder Plays': 'Race', Nation and Ethnic Absolutism," in *Contemporary Postcolonial Theory: A Reader*, ed. Padmini Mongia (1991; London: Arnold, 1996): 262.

[2] Abdul JanMohamed & David Lloyd, "Toward a Theory of Minority Discourse: What is to be Done?" in *Postcolonial Criticism*, ed. Bart Moore–Gilbert, Gareth Stanton & Willy Maley (1990; London & New York: Longman, 1997): 241.

[3] Gilroy, "'The Whisper Wakes, the Shudder Plays'," 266–68.

[4] "'The Whisper Wakes, the Shudder Plays'," 270.

[5] According to Chandra Talpade Mohanty, Western feminists may succumb to the "hegemonic humanistic problematic"; "Under Western Eyes: Feminist Scholarship and Colonial Discourses," in *Contemporary Postcolonial Theory: A Reader*, ed. Padmini Mongia (1991; London: Arnold,

black women into migratory subjects with complex identities, which transgress cultural norms and boundaries.[6] The writers Buchi Emecheta and Tsitsi Dangarembga as well as their female protagonists could be described as migratory subjects (of more or less their own choice). These women deconstruct the view of English culture and of black culture as being homogeneous. Their realization of heterogeneity within cultures and potential compatibilities between cultures challenges cultural puritans.[7]

For Emecheta and Dangarembga, multiculturalism means a great deal more than the juxtaposition of antagonistic cultures or the erasure of the other culture through assimilation. These writers are intermediaries, who provide not only Africans with insights into English culture, and English readers with views on African cultures. Multiculturalism provides "us" (Europeans) with other views of ourselves. Katherine Fishburn writes: "Africans know more of us than we do of them,"[8] and I would to add: they may even know more of us than we know or like to know. Buchi Emecheta and Tsitsi Dangarembga represent *different English cultures* in England and in African countries. I will discuss, first, the immigrants' encounter with English cultures in the "moder kontry," and second, the importing of English cultures by "been-to's" into their mother countries.

"Moder kontry" England

The alienating "moder kontry" England is an important topic in Buchi Emecheta's works, such as her novels *Second-Class Citizen* and *In the Ditch*, published as *Adah's Story*, *Gwendolen*, *Kehinde*, and in her autobiography *Head Above Water*. The outsider's preconception of the "moder kontry Englan'" is very different from the English mother country. Emecheta destroys the immigrants' and the Englishmen's illusions about England as a tolerant land of opportunity with a model culture. To the immi-

---

1996): 191, as they reduce Third-World cultures to patriarchal domination and female victimization on the basis of an assumed universal cross-cultural gender difference. If they regard other women as victims and treat them as objects of their analyses, they neglect that these women also take part in interactions that form relationships; Mohanty, "Under Western Eyes," 174–79.

[6] Carole Boyce Davies, *Black Women Writing and Identity: Migrations of the Subject* (London & New York: Routledge, 1994): 36–37.

[7] Frantz Fanon already proposes a complex model of heterogeneous black cultures. He closely associates culture with nation, but he also maintains that national culture does not mean nationalism. Fanon stresses the interrelationship between African Negro culture and different national cultures in Africa, which share the burden of and the fight against colonialism (*The Wretched of the Earth*, tr. Constance Farrington [1963; New York: Grove, 1968]: 247). He defines national culture as a heterogeneous and dynamic unity: "culture is first the expression of a nation, the expression of its preferences, of its taboos, and of its patterns [...] A national culture is the sum total of all these appraisals; it is the result of internal and external tensions exerted over society as a whole and also at every level of that society" (Fanon, *The Wretched of the Earth*, 244). However, Fanon only implies gender conflicts, whereas Emecheta and Dangarembga stress the important but difficult position of women in patriarchal African cultures.

[8] Katherine Fishburn, *Reading Buchi Emecheta: Cross-Cultural Conversations* (Westport CT & London: Greenwood, 1995): 10.

grants from Africa and the Caribbean, England appears, rather, to be a stepmother country,[9] in which they are less the lost and found children than unwelcome aliens. The discrepancy between the colonial image of England as the Kingdom of God and the sobering reality is most distressing to the immigrants and probably embarrassing for English readers.[10]

Unofficial segregation pervades external and internal spaces. Buchi Emecheta questions the myth of mutual enrichment in the multicultural metropolis: London is neither a melting-pot nor a salad bowl but, rather, an Indonesian dinner with a separate dish for each ingredient. The multicultural residential areas of the "black English" are small islands within the metropolis.[11] With a few exceptions of showing mild interest in others out of curiosity (*HW* 106–108), the English attitude towards African and Caribbean residents ranges from indifference to xenophobia. The English, paradoxically, seem to expect others to assimilate but pursue a strategy of exclusion that prevents integration.

Far from idealizing the non-white multicultural communities, Emecheta shows that they, too, are pervaded by discrimination according to gender, class, and ethnicity (*AS* 60–61). Emecheta does not exclude her well-educated Ibo heroine Adah from active discrimination against others, such as illiterate Yoruba, who in turn belittle the Ibo (*AS* 34–36). Thus, she contests the homogenizing English label "black" for all non-white residents.

However, apart from their differences, Africans and West Indians may discover mutual traditions in their encounter within the "moder kontry." African immigrants, who are themselves dislocated in England, inform black West Indians about the cultures of their African mother countries which the West Indians lost in the diaspora caused by the English slave trade. On the one hand, the loss of the African heritage leads to serious misunderstandings between the West Indian Winston Brillianton and his Yoruba landlord, on the other hand, Winston's friend Mr. Ilochina informs him about the Ibo appreciation of virginity and the bride-price.[12] Winston's daughter Gwendolen gives her baby the Yoruba name Iyamide, establishing a positive African bond between mother and daughter to erase the biological conception through the rape by her alienated father (*G* 178). Emecheta suggests that the female inscription of an African name covers the biological evidence of her father in her baby's face: the shame of incest is reversed in the power of independent motherhood in *Gwendolen*.[13] Thus,

---

[9] Fanon, *The Wretched of the Earth*, 145.

[10] Emecheta, *Head Above Water* (1986; Oxford: Heinemann, 1994): 104, 137–39. In the main text as *HW*.

[11] Emecheta, *Adah's Story* (London: Allison & Busby, 1983): 34. In the main text as *AS*.

[12] Emecheta, *Gwendolen* (Oxford: Heinemann, 1989): 99–100, 120–21. In the main text as *G*.

[13] The ending is rather too optmistic for an incest victim, Christine W. Sizemore remarks; "The London Novels of Buchi Emecheta," in *Emerging Perspectives on Buchi Emecheta*, ed. Marie Umeh (Trenton NJ: Africa World Press, 1996): 377. Emecheta seems to opt for a symbolic denouement of her novel rather than a realistic one. It is hardly credible for me as a European that Gwendolen completely 'effaced' the rape by her father, who is present in the face of her baby. Gwendolen's mother, the betrayed wife, is far more enraged at the rape than the victim herself. - It

England does not ease integration into the "moder kontry" but provides Caribbean immigrants with insight into the loss of the cultures of their native mother countries and the opportunity for a partial recovery of lost traditions.

Emecheta reverses the widely held notion of ethnic outsiders as the cause of English problems (*HW* 109). Rather, ethnic minorities are turned into problematic cases by the English. In Emecheta's texts, the English avoid private contacts and institutionalize the encounter with non-white citizens: the immigration authorities, schools, social security, and the police submit ethnic minorities to official and unofficial rules designed to construct and contain the Other as a problematic subject.

In England, Africans and West Indians look for education and work, which creates as many opportunities as problems for ethnic individuals and their relationships to their families and their communities.

English schools are seen as important institutions for socializing others in the sense of assimilating them.[14] Emecheta presents the reverse effect, because Gwendolen, from the Caribbean, is clearly socialized as the Other: her problems with British English are interpreted as stupidity, a misreading of her as a "slow" English child, which triggers her resistance and truancy (*G* 61, 76, 82). Instead of promoting assimilation, her English school generates alienation.

Gwendolen's problems at school are compounded because she has to help her working mother with the household chores and child-care. Her mother, still adhering to the traditions of the Caribbean, does not consider the education of girls as important, and the domestic work does not give Gwendolen enough time to catch up with her peers. Emecheta's representation reflects not only the economic difference between underpaid black working parents and white employees, but also a cultural difference concerning the role of the mother, which the English limited to the domestic sphere. In contrast to this, the Nigerian Kehinde in Emecheta's eponymous novel looks down on dependent English wives: "For an Igbo woman, her capacity for work is her greatest asset."[15] The African mother's desire to study and to work goes beyond the restricted concepts for and of English mothers in the 1960s, according to Emecheta's autobiography (*HW* 52). In these respects, the 'backward' African women seem to have preceded the expansion of the 'modern' mother's roles in England, be it for better or for worse.[16]

---

would be inadequate to attribute, as Sizemore does, Winston's rape to the loss of Ibo culture, which places a great value on the daughter's virginity ("The London Novels of Buchi Emecheta," 376), because incest is also an important taboo in Christian cultures, as the preacher Winston must know.

[14] Gilroy, "'The Whisper Wakes, the Shudder Plays'," 263.

[15] Emecheta, *Kehinde* (Oxford: Heinemann, 1994): 52. In the main text as *K*.

[16] Whereas Emecheta's African women expand their potential in combining traditional African and modern English cultures, her male African characters use cultures to enhance their own position at the cost of their wives. In *Kehinde*, 'modern' culture conflicts with both Roman Catholic and Nigerian norms as the Nigerian husband Albert makes his wife abort their baby for economic reasons (*Kehinde*, 15; Sizemore, "The London Novels of Buchi Emecheta," 379). Paradoxically, her 'modern' sacrifice is meant to pay for his return to traditional Nigeria, where he has more children with a younger wife.

Even if blacks succeed in higher education and hold university degrees, they will not necessarily find adequate jobs in England; due to ethnic discrimination, prestigious and well-paid jobs would go to English applicants only. "But if the job is degrading, with marginal reward, your colour becomes an asset," Emecheta ironically remarks (*HW* 125). The English impede the "social and economic mobility" of minorities (*HW* 125). The English expect members of ethnic minorities to work far below their level of qualification. Towards the close of Emecheta's novel *Kehinde*, the academically qualified heroine is working as a cleaner in a hotel (*K* 122, 125). If the black English do white-collar work, they do not become middle-class black but, rather, black middle-class (*HW* 133): Apparently, racism leads to the establishment of a class system among ethnic minorities, which runs both parallel and subordinate to the English one. To be a second-class citizen means to be second in any of the English classes which members of ethnic minorities might lay claim to because of their professional and economic status.

Coloured applicants may be 'privileged' in the case of badly paid jobs as social workers, who might be used to mediate between ethnic cultures. However, working in the social services on behalf of ethnic minorities does not serve mediation, as Emecheta, who holds a doctorate in sociology, knows from experience. She discovered that a centre for African teenagers did them no good; it merely wasted their time. Emecheta realized that she had become complicit in the attempt to contain possible unrest and to prevent the black teenagers' participation in the British economy and society. Instead of bridging the social and cultural gap between ethnic groups, social work serves, rather, as a means to reinforce the segregation and the surveillance of the "hated and scapegoatable group" (*HW* 125). The social services are likely to reassert English superiority over minorities, because they keep them dependent on condescending welfare instead of helping them to act on their own.

Both failure and success in education and at work may disrupt relationships between ethnic husbands and wives, parents and children. Emecheta writes how the discrepancy between men's poor and women's good economic performance and academic proficiency creates conflicts because it undermines the traditional hierarchy of gender. She describes how English attitudes towards individual freedom and the legal equality between the sexes support ethnic women's resistance to abusive husbands. The welfare system enables women who separated from husbands to survive – at the cost of their dignity. Adah's fall from the middle class into the working class and finally to the bottom of English society provides readers with a fresh insight into diverse English cultures.

Social and spatial segregation go hand in hand. In extreme cases, council houses form a ghetto that becomes a "problem place" (*AS* 157), which seems to create rather than solve social problems. Segregation rules the ghetto itself, as the working class discriminates against the very poor, such as old-age pensioners and single mothers (*AS* 159, 181). Adah, who is separated from her husband, learns that her polite middle-class behaviour fails with the lower classes. Polished manners, excuses, even pretending to be stupid, which evoked middle-class condescension, are met with foul language and aggression on the part of prejudiced members of the working class (*AS* 158–59; *HW* 54). When Adah has to give up her job in order to take care of her children, she lacks the "code for daily living" of the working class (*AS* 167) and is reduced to helpless dependency by and on the welfare system. Adah regrets the loss of pride occasioned by her being regarded as a lazy parasite by society (*AS* 167). The virtual prohibition of beneficiary's work tends to perpetuate unemployment and dependency (*HW* 53–54).

The social system fosters segregation of the sexes among the poor. Single mothers are better off if they receive unemployment benefit than if they are married to poor working men (*AS* 176–77, 227). Single mothers are made to shun men because possible support by male friends is deducted from unemployment benefit (*AS* 185–86). To the surprise of Adah and the reader, however, the female pariahs form a subculture that is superior to the established class cultures in terms of cooperation, solidarity, and humanity. The community the black single mother finds among her white equals recalls women's communal life in Africa: Emecheta reveals the compatibility and the superiority of the 'primitive' cultures in Africa and in England.[17] "Differences in culture, colour, background and God knows what else had all been submerged in the face of greater enemies – poverty and helplessness" (*AS* 193). The marginalized single mothers transcend cultural boundaries, forming a community that would literally merit the name of a multicultural 'mother country': a promise England holds but does not fulfil.

Emecheta's representation of her "moder kontry" England and the immigrants alike is bound to disillusion both her African and her English readers, because she subverts clichés of gender and national cultures. Emecheta clearly portraits the "moder kontry" as a place of alienation pervaded by racial and social discrimination and bound to frustrate hopeful immigrants, who desire to improve their lot by education and work. If ethnic minorities succeed, it is as much in spite of as because of English circumstances. Emecheta stresses the ambivalent function of the welfare system, which alleviates but also perpetuates economic and social problems because it helps people to survive but not to regain work, a decent living, and social esteem. The welfare system provides needy single mothers with rooms of their own and freedom from male domination and sexual harassment in their families (*AS* 156), but at a certain cost. Despite the inadequate support welfare gives to single mothers and the restrictions imposed upon them, Emecheta's coloured female protagonists are able to prepare for a professional career. Cross-cultural solidarity seems to be limited to female outsiders who neglect ethnic differences. In spite of the positive communal life experienced among the down-and-out Londoners in the ghetto, Emecheta's class-conscious female protagonists aspire to independent lives. In London, Emecheta's Caribbean and African women Gwendolen and Kehinde are able to combine their need for personal and economic independence with a network of multicultural friends, their desire for Western education, and links to African cultures.[18]

---

[17] Sizemore, "The London Novels of Buchi Emecheta," 373.

[18] Sizemore, "The London Novels of Buchi Emecheta," 382; Jana Gohrisch, "Crossing the Boundaries of Cultures: Buchi Emecheta's Novels," in *(Sub)Versions of Realism: Recent Women's Fiction in Britain,* ed. Irmgard Maassen & Anna Maria Stuby (Heidelberg: Carl Winter, 1997): 138–139.

Return to the mother countries

Emecheta and Dangarembga depict the return of African families from England to their mother countries in *Kehinde* and in *Nervous Conditions*.[19] Their repatriation inevitably produces transcultural conflicts within the families between the been-to's and the stay-homes, husbands and wives, parents and children. In *Kehinde*, the husband's return to Nigerian polygamy antagonizes his wife, who had to give up her job in England and is now sandwiched between her husband's sister and his new young bride. Back in his mother country, he retrieves the traditionally respected position, which he felt was impaired by his wife's "white" middle-class woman's role and her superior income in England (35). In Nigeria, the husband seems to have reduced his use of English culture to driving an old Jaguar. For the wife, the situation is reversed. Disappointed by her "homecoming" (96) to Nigeria, where she is not respected but marginalized, she feels nostalgia for England in spite of the fact that she does not feel welcome there. Being westernized, she prefers her independence to integration in the Nigerian extended family, which does not respect her personal needs. The frustrated and unemployed wife emigrates again to England in order to start a new life with a home of her own, a new job and a new lover.[20] Whereas the Nigerian husband returns to African traditions in Emecheta's *Kehinde*, the patriarch Sigauke heralds English culture in Dangarembga's *Nervous Conditions*. However, the return to Zimbabwe results in serious setbacks for his wife and his daughter.

Tsitsi Dangarembga unravels the complex transcultural conflicts in a remarkable way by the clever choice of the female teenage character and narrator Tambudzai, who is torn between her affiliation to her traditional Shona family and the anglicized beento's, who are themselves riven by conflicts between English cultures and their lost Shona heritage. Dangarembga's book inverts the unofficial segregation between ethnic groups in the multicultural metropolis in England: English 'minority' culture thrives in isolated missionary compounds between rural villages in Zimbabwe.[21] In opposition to

---

[19] Tsitsi Dangarembga, *Nervous Conditions* (London: The Women's Press, 1988; Harare: Zimbabwe Publishing House, 1988; Seattle WA: Seal, 1988). The page references are the same in all three editions.

[20] In *Gwendolen*, the mother Sonia returns to Jamaica in order to take care of her grandmother, who, however, has died in the meantime. At first, Sonia is tempted to lead an independent and convenient life on the money she saved in England, free from responsibilities towards her family, but soon she finds that her "Home is where the people she loved lived" (118), which is in London.

[21] Dangarembga selects the countryside in order to mark the impact of English cultures on rural traditions. In the capital Harare, international modern influences may already have diminished both the positions of conservative English and traditional African cultures. Biman Basu correctly maintains that modern culture encroaches upon rural places, as the government builds Council houses for administration and a beer-hall, which sells American soft-drinks;"Trapped and Troping: Allegories of the Transnational Intellectual in Tsitsi Dangarembga's 'Nervous Conditions',"\
A R I E L : A Review of International English Literature 28.3 (1997): 16. Maybe it is irony that English culture is largely restricted to educating the (un)happy few at the mission and the Sacred Heart convent, whereas American culture seems to serve immediate economic interests and appeals to every consumer.

the English indifference towards other cultures, the been-to's and the other members of the family vividly negotiate the value and the use of English cultures. The husband and headmaster Babamukuru Sigauke tries to disseminate with missionary zeal his version of puritan English culture in his nuclear and his extended family in Zimbabwe. He clearly disparages Shona culture, proposing as he does "full immersion" to educate selected children among the family not only at school but also on the mission compound: "A child must also be provided with the correct atmosphere which will encourage his mind to develop even when he is not in the classroom" (46).

In the beginning, Tambudzai is strongly attracted to Babamukuru's conservative and Christian English culture. His submission to English culture leads to greater power, "as an early educated African, as headmaster, as husband and father, as provider to many – in positions that enabled him to organize his immediated world and its contents as he wished" (87). Against the resistance of her Shona parents, who believe that a Western education is too expensive and unnecessary for their daughter, the teenage girl Tambudzai opts for an education at her uncle's mission school. The uncle maintains that her mental emancipation will lead to her material emancipation, which is to serve her family. He stresses that Tambudzai should become an educated *but* good woman her parents could be proud of (88). Babamukuru implies that the girl's English education should not lead to her *personal* emancipation from patriarchal ethics.

In opposition to her brother, who dislikes speaking Shona and coming back to the village, Tambudzai initially seems to be able to combine her loyalty to Shona and to English culture, which is expressed by her voluntary alternating stays with her parents in the homestead and her uncle's family at the mission.[22] But later it shows that Tambudzai also takes to her brother's English attitude, which prefers hygiene, the colonization of the body, and the cultivation of reason to native dirt and smelly bodily labour (1–2, 92–93).[23] In the end, Elleke Boehmer maintains, Tambudzai inhabits "borderlines"[24] between the cultures.

Tsitsi Dangarembga uses the perspective of the traditional country girl who enters her uncle's English middle-class home at the mission in order to convey the striking difference between the rural Shona culture and the 'refined' English culture. The first-person narrator Tambudzai depicts, not without irony, her initial amazement at "the heavy gold curtains flowing voluptuously to the floor, the four-piece lounge suite upholstered in glowing brown velvet, the lamps with their tasselled shades, the sleek

---

[22] Basu calls the mission a hybridized space ("Trapped and Troping: Allegories of the Transnational Intellectual in Tsitsi Dangarembga's 'Nervous Conditions'," 15), but, except for Babamukuru's claim to eat before the rest of the family, hardly anything at the mission recalls Shona culture; see Derek Wright, "'More than Just a Plateful of Food': Regurgitating Colonialism in Tsitsi Dangarembga's *Nervous Conditions*," in *Commonwealth: Essays and Studies* 17.2 (1995): 17–18.

[23] Flora Veit–Wild, "Borderlines of the Body in African Women's Writing," in *Borderlands. Negotiating Boundaries in Post-Colonial Writing*, ed. Monika Reif–Hülser (Cross/Cultures 40 & ASNEL Papers 4; Amsterdam & Atlanta GA: Rodopi, 1999): 131.

[24] Elleke Boehmer, *Colonial and Postcolonial Literature* (Oxford & New York: Oxford UP, 1995): 228.

bookcases full of leather-bound and hard-covered volumes of erudition" (68), the ritual of taking tea in delicate china cups with biscuits, and the bland English food served for dinner by her aunt Maiguru. The literally and metaphorically 'white' home, which ostentatiously conveys luxury and class, compares favourably with the miserable, dirty hut Tambudzai used to live in. But the introduction into the anglicized family life has consequences the patriarchal uncle has not anticipated.

Tambudzai's trust in the usefulness of English education is qualified by her growing insight into her aunt Maiguru's and her cousin Nyasha's positions. At first, Tambudzai seems to share her uncle's attitude that requires women to be educated *but* good. She admires her submissive aunt and despises her obstinate cousin. Then she learns that her aunt does not profit from her English education and her work. Maiguru has a higher degree than her husband and works as a teacher, but as an obedient Shona wife hands over all of her earnings to her husband. Tambudzai realizes that her uncle's admirable generosity is based on his wife's unacknowledged work (101). She plays the perfect wife and mother, albeit with a grudge that surfaces only intermittently. Her English education seems to be of use only for her husband.

Nyasha becomes Tambu's other guide to English culture. Nyasha suffers from the clash between her two different English educations, in addition to her loss of Shona culture.[25] In England, Nyasha received her official and unofficial education in the Swinging Sixties. The mission school inculcates conservative Christian values and an obsolete colonial ideology that might have been current from the Victorian age until the 1950s. Nyasha's modern English ways meet with resistance from her African peers, including Tambudzai, and from her conservative parents, who consider her to be "too Anglicized" (74). Since it does not seem to bother the couple that the uncle and his son are almost completely anglicized, the parents' problem is the girl's appropriation of another English culture which undermines their authority. At this point, the gendered question is less whether to identify with English culture or African culture but who is entitled to which English culture.[26]

First, Nyasha's progressive English views make her claim the right to develop, to control, and to enjoy her body and her mind on her own terms (96, 119).[27] In opposition to her parents and to her peers, Nyasha uses Englishness for personal emancipation. Her Shona peers resent that she speaks English with an English accent and accuse her of thinking that she is white (94). The teenager smokes cigarettes, uses tampons

[25] If Pauline Ada Uwakweh focuses on the conflict between two cultures – meaning the Shona and the English one – she reduces Nyasha's problem; "Debunking Patriarchy: The Liberational Quality of Voicing in Tsitsi Dangarembga's *Nervous Conditions*," *Research in African Literatures* 26.1 (1995): 82.

[26] Derek Wright accurately perceives that the conflict between father and daughter results from "rival modes and manners of Englishness"; "'More than Just a Plateful of Food': Regurgitating Colonialism in Tsitsi Dangarembga's *Nervous Conditions*," 18.

[27] Johannes Lorentzen, "Black Teenage Girls in Search for [*sic*] Identity: A Cross-Cultural Comparison of Toni Morrison's *The Bluest Eye*, Tsitsi Dangarembga's *Nervous Conditions*, and Buchi Emecheta's *Gwendolen*" (M.A. thesis, Bamberg University, 1999): 33.

(96), wears mini-skirts (109), and even flirts with white boys (94). She claims the right
to stay at home by herself and to read whatever she likes (83, 121).

Secondly, Nyasha's education in England makes her criticize the colonization of her
native country and its minds.[28] She applies her knowledge about oppression and discrimination (63) to colonial history and present rule in Rhodesia, which she compares
to South Africa, to the dismay of her mother (93). Nyasha criticizes the distinction between masters and servants in her own home – an import of the English class system.[29]
She rebels against her patriarchal father and the conservative English culture he represents. She defies her father's authority in intellectual and physical ways: she criticizes
his colonized mind, refuses food and text books, and finally strikes back.

Her bulimia expresses her cultural (in)digestion as she devours but then vomits
British food and knowledge.[30] Rosemary Gray defines her illness as of Western
origin.[31] I would stress that this female individual embodies Fanon's metaphoric description of decolonization under her father's (neo)colonial rule:

> In the colonial context the settler only ends his work of breaking in the native when the
> latter admits loudly and intelligibly the supremacy of the white man's values. In the
> period of decolonization, the colonized masses mock at these very values, insult them,
> and vomit them up.[32]

Fanon advocates violence as a liberating force,[33] but Dangarembga links decolonizing
violence with gender, which is largely absent in Fanon's *Wretched of the Earth*.[34]
When Nyasha hits back, her father accuses her of fighting like a man, and reduces
Nyasha's problem to her debunking his authority as a man and a father (115). But
Nyasha correctly perceives the link between patriarchal and neocolonial rule, because
her father's power is based on the dissemination of his paternalist version of English
culture. Nyasha sees that Babamukuru is a product of colonization, a "historical arti-
fact" (160). But so is Nyasha, who faces the problem that there is hardly an escape

---

[28] Keith M. Booker, *The African Novel in English: An Introduction* (Portsmouth NH: Heinemann, 1998): 194

[29] Booker, *The African Novel in English*, 194.

[30] Veit–Wild is right when she interprets Nyasha's self-destructive illness as a claim to autonomy. But her thesis that Nyasha's use of a tampon and her wearing her mini-skirt evades norms
imposed upon the female body ("Borderlines of the Body in African Women's Writing," 131)
seems too general because here Nyasha follows an English model of woman.

[31] Rosemary Gray, "'Unnatural Daughters': Postmodernism and Tsitsi Dangarembga's *Nervous Conditions*," *Commonwealth: Essays and Studies* 17.2 (1995): 6.

[32] Fanon, *The Wretched of the Earth*, 43.

[33] Fanon, *The Wretched of the Earth*, 94.

[34] Michelle Vizzard, "'Of Mimicry and Woman': Hysteria and Anticolonial Feminism in Tsitsi
Dangarembga's *Nervous Conditions*," *SPAN* 36 (1993): 205; Supriya Nair, "Melancholic Women: The Intellectual Hysteric(s) in *Nervous Conditions*," *Research in African Literatures* 26.2
(1995): 133; Keith M. Booker, *The African Novel in English: An Introduction*, 191; Veit–Wild,
"Borderlines of the Body in African Women's Writing," 130.

from English culture, since both her colonizing and her emancipatory education are English (63, 93, 147).

She cannot and would not go back to Shona culture, either. Her dabbling in traditional pottery does not really involve her in Shona culture, which confines women more than she could bear. Her violent rage, in the end, is directed against the English and, what is often ignored, the Shona culture as much as against herself, as she shreds a history book, smashes her clay pots, and jabs the fragments into her flesh (201). Does she succumb to the colonial manichaean dichotomy and punish herself for being "evil" (200)[35] and for resisting Englishness? She seems to use and refuse English and Shona cultural paradigms, living inside and outside patriarchal cultures. Instead of combatting her father, who is a victim of colonial history himself, she wants to retreat to a mental asylum (200–201), a space on the margins of her patriarchal mother country, which does not offer her a positive alternative to Englishness. Her psychosomatic, physical, and intellectual resistance to her neocolonial father and her subsequent retreat mark her "self-imposed 'otherness',"[36] which may be based on English culture but finally refuses any submission to it.[37]

Tambudzai's aunt, who tries to combine her English education with Shona submissiveness, and her cousin, who tries to escape any cultural restrictions, serve as negative rather than positive models to Tambu. Nyasha and Tambudzai's uneducated but critical mother warn her of the alienating assimilation to English culture as she wins a scholarship to the Sacred Heart convent school (179, 184). But Tambudzai decides on attending the school, which promises to make a "lady" out of her. The expected status and esteem are as attractive to Tambudzai as the linen costume with gloves she is to wear on Sundays (178). The convent school, which segregates black and white girls, promotes an even more obsolete form of English middle-class culture than the mission school, because it promises to elevate middle-class girls to cultural nobility. After years of English education, earlier warnings of assimilation surface and Tambudzai becomes aware of an unease with English culture: "something began to assert itself, to question things and refuse to be brainwashed" (*NC* 204). Biman Basu argues convincingly that Tambudzai's desired escape from repression by a new critical awareness results from her subjection to Western intellectual discipline, an insight prefigured by Nyasha.[38] Even if Tambudzai begins to realize the submission effected by her education, it is questionable whether she would or could retrieve her Shona cultural heritage.

---

[35] Sally McWilliams, "Tsitsi Dangarembga's *Nervous Conditions*: At the Crossroads of Feminism and Post-Colonialism," *World Literature Written in English* 31.1 (1991): 108.

[36] Rosemary Gray, "'Unnatural Daughters': Postmodernism and Tsitsi Dangarembga's *Nervous Conditions*," 6.

[37] The ambiguity of Nyasha's position between rebellion, submission, and her assertion of her independence beyond categories imposed upon her by others is enhanced by her statement: "'Look what they've done to us', she said softly. 'I'm not one of them [i.e. the English] but I'm not one of you" (*Nervous Conditions*, 201).

[38] Biman Basu, "Trapped and Troping: Allegories of the Transnational Intellectual in Tsitsi Dangarembga's *Nervous Conditions*," 21–22. I fail to see why Lindsay Pentolfe Aegerter correctly argues that these young women are alienated from themselves and their culture but then

Emecheta and Dangarembga deal with the gendered use of diverse English cultures within an African context. Their novels do not deny that English education in Africa leads to material improvement. However, they maintain that neither education nor work is meant to lead to women's individual emancipation. Educated women are expected to work for their husband's and their family's immediate benefit. The women who have first-hand experience of English cultures and who return to their African mother country face particular difficulties resulting from the patriarchal English or native culture in Africa. These women lose the singular position they held in their nuclear families in England, and have to submit to their relative positions in their extended families. They are subject to more restrictive rules concerning their behaviour. Emecheta and Dangarembga provide alternative solutions to these women's problems: Maiguru grudgingly submits to Christian patriarchal rule, Nyasha retreats into an exile of her own within the country after her futile rebellion against her neocolonial father, and Kehinde escapes from her husband's traditional polygamy by returning to England.

Whereas Emecheta stresses the positive aspects of an English education as a means to advancement, Dangarembga focuses on the alienating neocolonial effects of English education in Africa. The African representatives of English cultures in *Nervous Conditions* seem to have lost almost all trace of their traditional Shona culture. Vicious neocolonial circles sustain the power of the anglicized patriarch. The poor Shona pay school fees to the English mission schools, which alienate their children from their traditional culture. Their fees contribute to the wealth of the anglicized headmaster, who uses his capital to support his poor Shona relatives. The African patriarch also uses his power in order to control his family and to impose Christian English culture on them. Babamukuru interprets economic and gender conflicts within his extended Shona family as consequences of sin because his brother had no church wedding. The enforced Christian marriage encroaches upon Shona culture and solves neither material nor social problems, leaving them dependent on economic support by their anglicized patriarch.

Emecheta's and Dangarembga's narratives perform what they show: black women, being marginalized by Africans and Englishmen alike, do better to rely on other black women as guides to their particular intercultural encounter with the English.[39] These African writers demythologize the glorifying illusion of the mother country England without denying that English culture offers other women in particular (limited) oppor-

---

goes on to say that they "together symbolize the 'wholeness' and 'healing' of African womanist identity"; "A Dialectic of Autonomy and Community: Tsitsi Dangarembga's *Nervous Conditions*," *Tulsa Studies in Women's Literature* 15.2 (1996): 238. Whereas Tambudzai testifies to her doubt about English education after her mother's and Nyasha's warnings, she nevertheless overcomes her unease and returns to "the more concentrated 'Englishness' at Sacred Heart" (203), leaving Nyasha to the care of her aunts.

[39] Olga Kenyon, "Buchi Emecheta and the Black Immigrant Experience in Britain," in *Writing Women: Contemporary Women Novelists* (London: Pluto, 1991): 132.

tunities to gain independence.[40] The two authors also address white women, as Eme-cheta maintains, in order to invite cross-cultural co-operation against male domination (*HW* 1). The writers negotiate English culture and point out comparable if different intercultural patterns of patriarchal repression and women's resistance.

Emecheta's and Dangarembga's books serve as a supplement to the English versions of English culture in Homi Bhabha's sense: they add to the English constructions of their culture but they do not add up. The other women's texts do not merely present different perspectives on English culture, but point out the difference between the discursive construction of a homogeneous English culture and the contending forces of heterogeneous English cultures.[41] The other women's guides to English cultures contest the construction of a homogeneous English culture intended to fortify the boundaries between cultures, an act that turns the promise of a multicultural mother country into a farce. Their representations of heterogeneous English cultures in England and in Africa complement each other: They represent different kinds and changes of English cultures. Emecheta and Dangarembga tend to reveal the *synchronic diversity* of contemporary English cultures within England, and the *diachronic diversity* of coexisting historical forms of English middle-class cultures abroad. According to the novels discussed, the conservative English cultures taught in Africa tend to prolong (neo)colonial patriarchal rule at the cost of local traditions, whereas the English cultures encountered in London offer African women opportunities for emancipation from patriarchal domination – which, however, they cannot transfer to their African motherland.

WORKS CITED

Aegerter, Lindsay Pentolfe. "A Dialectic of Autonomy and Community: Tsitsi Dangarembga's *Nervous Conditions,*" *Tulsa Studies in Women's Literature* 15.2 (1996): 231–40.

Basu, Biman. "Trapped and Troping: Allegories of the Transnational Intellectual in Tsitsi Dangarembga's 'Nervous Conditions'," *ARIEL: A Review of International English Literature* 28.3 (1997): 7–24.

Bhabha, Homi. "DissemiNation: Time, Narrative, and the Margins of the Modern Nation," in *Narration and Nation*, ed. Bhabha (London & New York: Routledge, 1994): 139–70.

Boehmer, Elleke. *Colonial and Postcolonial Literature* (Oxford & New York: Oxford UP, 1995).

Booker, M. Keith. *The African Novel in English: An Introduction* (Portsmouth NH: Heinemann, 1998).

Dangarembga, Tsitsi. *Nervous Conditions* (London: The Women's Press, 1988; Harare: Zimbabwe Publishing House, 1988; Seattle WA: Seal, 1988).

---

[40] Lisa H. Iyer, "The Second Sex Three Times Oppressed: Cultural Colonization and Coll(i)(u)sion in Buchi Emecheta's *Women*," in *Critical Studies: Writing the Nation*, ed. John C. Hawley (Self and Country in Post-Colonial Imagination 7; Amsterdam & Atlanta GA: Rodopi, 1996): 131. Susheila Nasta denotes the same quality of disillusionment about the mother country in and by Caribbean women writers' literature; *Motherlands: Black Women's Writing from Africa, the Caribbean and South Asia* (1991; London: The Women's Press, 1992): 30.

[41] Homi Bhabha, "DissemiNation: Time, Narrative, and the Margins of the Modern Nation," in *Narration and Nation*, ed. Bhabha (London & New York: Routledge, 1994): 148.

Boyce Davies, Carole. *Black Women Writing and Identity. Migrations of the Subject* (London & New York: Routledge, 1994).

Emecheta, Buchi. *Adah's Story* (London: Allison & Busby, 1983).

——. *Gwendolen* (Oxford: Heinemann, 1989).

——. *Head Above Water* (1986; Oxford: Heinemann, 1994).

——. *Kehinde* (Oxford: Heinemann, 1994).

Fanon, Frantz. *The Wretched of the Earth*, tr. Constance Farrington (1963; New York: Grove, 1968).

Fishburn, Katherine. *Reading Buchi Emecheta. Cross-Cultural Conversations* (Westport CT & London: Greenwood, 1995).

Gilroy, Paul. "'The Whisper Wakes, the Shudder Plays': 'Race', Nation and Ethnic Absolutism," in *Contemporary Postcolonial Theory. A Reader*, ed. Padmini Mongia (1991; London: Arnold, 1996): 248–75.

Gohrisch, Jana. "Crossing the Boundaries of Cultures: Buchi Emecheta's Novels," in *(Sub)Versions of Realism – Recent Women's Fiction in Britain*, ed. Irmgard Maassen & Anna Maria Stuby (Heidelberg: Carl Winter, 1997): 129–42.

Gray, Rosemary. "'Unnatural Daughters': Postmodernism and Tsitsi Dangarembga's *Nervous Conditions*," *Commonwealth: Essays and Studies* 17.2 (1995): 1–7.

Härting, Heike. "The Profusion of Meanings and the Female Experience of Colonization. Inscriptions of the Body as Site of Difference in Tsitsi Dangarembga's *Nervous Conditions* and Margaret Atwood's *The Edible Woman*," in *Fusion of Cultures?*, ed. Peter Stummer & Christopher Balme (Amsterdam & Atlanta GA: Rodopi, 1996): 237–46.

Iyer, Lisa H. "The Second Sex Three Times Oppressed: Cultural Colonization and Coll(i)(u)sion in Buchi Emecheta's Women," in *Critical Studies: Writing the Nation: Self and Country in Post-Colonial Imagination* 7, ed. John C. Hawley (Amsterdam & Atlanta GA: Rodopi, 1996): 123–37.

JanMohamed, Abdul, & David Lloyd. "Toward a Theory of Minority Discourse: What is to be Done?" in *Postcolonial Criticism*, ed. Bart Moore-Gilbert, Gareth Stanton & Willy Maley (1990; London & New York: Longman, 1997): 234–47.

Kenyon, Olga. "Buchi Emecheta and the Black Immigrant Experience in Britain," in *Writing Women: Contemporary Women Novelists* (London: Pluto, 1991): 113–33.

Lorentzen, Johannes. "Black Teenage Girls in Search for Identity. A Cross-Cultural Comparison of Toni Morrison's *The Bluest Eye*, Tsitsi Dangarembga's *Nervous Conditions*, and Buchi Emecheta's *Gwendolen*" (unpublished MA thesis, Bamberg University, 1999).

McWilliams, Sally. "Tsitsi Dangarembga's Nervous Conditions: At the Crossroads of Feminism and Post-Colonialism," *World Literature Written in English* 31.1 (1991): 103–12.

Mohanty, Chandra Talpade. "Under Western Eyes: Feminist Scholarship and Colonial Discourses," in *Contemporary Postcolonial Theory. A Reader*, ed. Padmini Mongia (1991; London: Arnold, 1996): 172-97.

Nair, Supriya. "Melancholic Women: The Intellectual Hysteric(s) in *Nervous Conditions*," *Research in African Literatures* 26.2 (1995): 130–39.

Nasta, Susheila, ed. *Motherlands: Black Women's Writing from Africa, the Caribbean and South Asia* (1991; London: The Women's Press, 2nd ed. 1992).

Sizemore, Christine W. "The London Novels of Buchi Emecheta," in *Emerging Perspectives on Buchi Emecheta*, ed. Marie Umeh (Trenton NJ: Africa World Press, 1996): 367–85.

Uwakweh, Pauline Ada. "Debunking Patriarchy: The Liberational Quality of Voicing in Tsitsi Dangarembga's *Nervous Conditions*," *Research in African Literatures* 26.1 (1995): 75–84.

Veit–Wild, Flora. "Borderlines of the Body in African Women's Writing," in *Borderlands: Negotiating Boundaries in Post-Colonial Writing*, ed. Monika Reif-Hülser (Cross/Cultures 40, ASNEL Papers 4; Amsterdam & Atlanta GA: Rodopi, 1999): 123–34.

Vizzard, Michelle. "'Of Mimicry and Woman': Hysteria and Anticolonial Feminism in Tsitsi Dangarembga's *Nervous Conditions*," *Journal of the South Pacific Association for Commonwealth Literature and Language Studies* 36 (1993): 202–10.

Wright, Derek. "'More than Just a Plateful of Food': Regurgitating Colonialism in Tsitsi Dangarembga's *Nervous Conditions*," *Commonwealth: Essays and Studies* 17.2 (1995): 8–18.

《•》》

"Searching for a Sense of Self"

Postmodernist Theories of Identity and the Novels of Salman Rushdie

MICHAEL HENSEN AND MIKE PETRY

A LTHOUGH JEAN–FRANÇOIS LYOTARD claims, in one of the founding texts of postmodern cultural criticism, that a key constituent of postmodernism is an incredulity towards all master-narratives,[1] postmodernism continues to tell itself grand narratives as a matter of course. We may even say that tolerance of or, rather, indifference towards the plurality of metanarratives is postmodernism's paradoxical ideology – the most significant of these grand tales being that of the existence of postmodernism itself.

A somewhat more credible instance of these great narratives concerns the history of self-identity in the West. Postmodernist histories of personal identity usually develop along these lines: in archaic cultures, as Douglas Kellner writes: "the self was basically fixed, solid and stable. Identity was a function of predefined social roles and a traditional system of myths which provided orientation and religious sanctions to one's place in the world."[2] A conscious form of self-reflexiveness was, as Kellner has it, non-existent in traditional societies: "Individuals did not undergo identity crises, or radically modify their identity. One was a hunter and a member of the tribe and that was that."[3] However, besides Kellner's postmodernist creed, there is also the poststructuralist position, holding that it is precisely this notion of an earlier, less problematic, stable identity that has always been a myth – a cultural, linguistic construct of Western metaphysics.

Most critics writing about self-identity (including those not subscribing to the poststructuralist notion) believe that what we today understand as *self* has its origins in modernity, there being, however, a significant difference between the subject of mod-

---

[1] Jean–François Lyotard, *The Postmodern Condition: A Report on Knowledge*, tr. Geoff Bennington & Brian Massumi (Minneapolis: U of Minnesota P, 1984): passim.

[2] Douglas Kellner, "Popular Culture and the Construction of Postmodern Identities," in *Modernity and Identity*, ed. Scott Lash & Jonathan Friedman (Oxford: Blackwell, 1992): 141.

[3] Kellner, "Popular Culture," 141.

ernity and that of postmodernity. While the subject of modernity is generally referred to as relatively stable but 'alienated', the postmodern subject is imagined as highly unstable and 'fragmented'.[4] So while, in modernity, "identity still comes from a circumscribed set of roles and norms,"[5] there is in postmodernity, as Terry Eagleton polemically says, "no longer [even] any subject to be alienated and nothing to be alienated from, 'authenticity' having been less rejected than merely forgotten."[6]

But the contemporary subject is, of course, never only stable, or alienated, or fragmented; rather, it is a mixture of all such aspects. Still, we may say that late-capitalist economics, new ways of communication and information, and postmodern sociocultural processes undermine the subject's psychological and emotional unity and foster its fragmentation.

Now that we have very briefly presented some key issues concerning postmodernist theories of self, the question arises of the viability of a postmodern approach to conceptions of identity in Salman Rushdie's novels. In the very special case of Rushdie, the supposed gap between postmodernism and postcolonialism is quite easily bridged: as Christoph Reinfandt has pointed out, Rushdie enjoys the status of being "one of the cosmopolitan champions of Western postmodernism on the one hand" and, conflictually perhaps, "a non-Western, post-colonial writer on the other hand."[7]

This is certainly not the place for an in-depth analysis of the compatibility of postmodernist and postcolonial theory.[8] In general, however, we can say that the discourses of postcolonialism and postmodernism need not necessarily be read as strictly opposed to each other. Bernd–Peter Lange is quite right to identify major mutual concerns in the two approaches: "Both deconstruct the great narratives of modern cultures in the West. While postmodern theory dismantles universalist models of signification, postcolonial theory rejects Eurocentric discourse."[9] Or, as Linda Hutcheon remarks with direct reference to Rushdie,

> Postmodernism does not move the marginal to the center. It does not invert the valuing of centers into that of peripheries and borders, as much as *use* that paradoxical doubled

---

[4] See also Fredric Jameson, "Postmodernism and Consumer Society," in *The Anti-Aesthetic: Essays on Postmodern Culture*, ed. Hal Foster (Seattle WA: Bay Press, 1983): 111–25.

[5] Kellner, "Popular Culture," 141.

[6] Terry Eagleton, "Capitalism, Modernism and Postmodernism," in *Modern Criticism and Theory: A Reader*, ed. David Lodge (London: Longman, 1988): 386.

[7] Christoph Reinfandt, "What's the Use of Stories that Aren't Even True: Salman Rushdie as a Test Case for Literature and Literary Studies Today," *Literatur in Wissenschaft und Unterricht* 31.1 (1998): 76.

[8] A concise discussion of this kind, with direct reference to Rushdie and numerous suggestions for further reading, can be found in M.D. Fletcher, "Introduction: The Politics of Salman Rushdie's Fiction," in *Reading Rushdie: Perspectives on the Fiction of Salman Rushdie*, ed. Fletcher (Cross/Cultures 16; Amsterdam & Atlanta GA: Rodopi, 1994): 1–22. See also Stephen Connor, *Postmodernist Culture: An Introduction to Theories of the Contemporary* (Oxford: Blackwell, 1989): 231–37.

[9] Bernd–Peter Lange, "Post-Colonial Gothic: Salman Rushdie's *The Moor's Last Sigh*," *Literatur in Wissenschaft und Unterricht* 31.4 (1998): 369.

positioning to critique the inside from both the outside and the inside. Just as Padma, the listening, textualized female narratee of Rushdie's *Midnight's Children*, pushes the narration in directions its male narrator had no intention of taking, so the ex-centric have not only overlapped in some concerns with postmodernism, but also pushed it in new directions. Though I would insist that the ex-centrics' agendas only *partially overlap* and do not coincide with that of the postmodern, it still seems to me that the perspective of these inside-outsiders has added race, ethnicity, sexual orientation and gender to the class analysis of ideology of Althusserian Marxists.[10]

About the fiction that concerns us in this essay, we may generally say that the 'location' of Rushdie is pretty much the same as that of Homi K. Bhabha: ie, at the intersection of theories of the postmodern and the postcolonial. Actually, both the writer of fiction – Rushdie – and the foremost theoretician of *hybridity* – Bhabha – have successfully blended typical issues concerning migrant-identities and cultural diversity with poststructuralist and postmodernist theory. In their respective works, both have pointed to a concept beyond the postmodern and its fragmentation of the personal and the social. This is a concept of fruitful 'in-betweenness' – a powerful "third space" between one's own and an Other's culture, a space that acknowledges a certain incommensurability between cultures. It is, furthermore, a concept that at least tries to use the paradigms of poststructuralist and postmodernist discourses for more satisfactory ends. Thus Bhabha says, for instance, that "the fragmentation of identity is often celebrated as a kind of pure anarchic liberalism or voluntarism, but I prefer to see it as a recognition of *the importance of the alienation of the self in the construction of forms of solidarity*."[11] With particular respect to Rushdie, Reinfandt further argues that "the emergence of a *positive concept of cultural hybridity* is one of the most prominent features" of his work.[12] Bhabha, again, has said: "I try to place myself in that position of liminality, in *that productive space of the construction of culture as difference*, in the spirit of alterity or otherness."[13]

It is, in fact, precisely this kind of *productive difference* that links thinkers such as Bhabha, Derrida, Charles Jencks and Paolo Porthoghesi (and thus postcolonial, poststructuralist and postmodernist discourses). Productive difference, however, is also what energizes the writings of Salman Rushdie – and what informs his portrayals of our searching for a sense of self.

---

[10] Linda Hutcheon, *A Poetics of Postmodernism: History, Theory, Fiction* (London & New York: Routledge, 1988): 69; our emphasis.

[11] Homi K. Bhabha, "The Third Space (an Interview)," in *Identity: Community, Culture, Difference*, ed. Jonathan Rutherford (London: Lawrence & Wishart, 1990): 213; our emphasis.

[12] Reinfandt, "What's the Use of Stories that Aren't Even True," 85; our emphasis. This being said, Rushdie's opinions on hybridity are anything but naive. As Reinfandt also says in the same article: "There are certainly many passages in *The Moor's Last Sigh* which point to the pitfalls of pluralism or hybridity. Even 'India's deep rooted secularism' appears to have mutated into an 'inter-community league of cynical self-interest'" (Reinfandt, "What's the Use of Stories that Aren't Even True," 87).

[13] Bhabha, "The Third Space (an Interview)," 209; our emphasis.

The question is therefore to what extent postmodern theories of subjectivity are relevant to Rushdie's novels. We shall try to answer this question with the help of three separate though interconnected categories: *fragmentation*, *mutability* and *identity vs alterity*. These three aspects of personal identity-formation were, in fact, already alluded to in this central passage from Rushdie's oeuvre: "O eternal opposition of inside and outside! Because, a human being, inside himself, is anything but a whole, anything but homogenous; all kinds of everywhichthing are jumbled up inside him, and he is one person one minute and another the next."[14]

Fragmentation of personal selves is a recurring theme in Rushdie's novels. Physical fragmentation, for example, is particularly significant as a central metaphor for psychic fragmentation in *Midnight's Children*. Quite apart from Aadam Sinai's 'fragmented' views of his future bride through the perforated sheet at the outset of the novel and the 'symbolic hole' inside of him (expressing Aadam's religious disbelief), there is further textual evidence regarding Saleem Sinai's bodily mutilation. For example, Saleem's hair is torn out by a teacher, a part of his middle finger is cut off in a struggle with other pupils about a girl, he is sterilized, and, of course, all through the narrative he discovers "cracks in his body."[15]

The physical mutilations thus point towards Saleem's split identity – his schizophrenia[16] – an aspect underscored by the frequent mistakes which Rushdie's narrator deliberately plants in his tale.[17] Saleem's psychic split is formally emphasized by the fact that he is continually speaking of himself in the first *and* third person.[18] Thus he is presented, interestingly, as having (and providing the reader with) a double perspective which makes him a seemingly omniscient *and* limited first-person narrator at the same time.[19]

Furthermore, Saleem's psychological fragmentation is symbolized by the famous pickling of his life in jars, each jar of pickles "containing one year of his life."[20] A similar metaphor for the preservation of identity is employed in *The Moor's Last Sigh* (where Moraes has to write down his story in order to prolong his life), and in *The Ground Beneath Her Feet* (where Rai takes photos in order to structure and understand a chaotic world). Rushdie seems to be saying that life becomes understandable only

---

[14] Salman Rushdie, *Midnight's Children* (London: Vintage, 1995): 236–37.

[15] *Midnight's Children*, 232, 234–35, 439, 179.

[16] See V.V. Subba Rao, "Salman Rushdie's *Midnight's Children*: A Study," *Indian Journal of English Studies* 32 (1993/94): 92, and Ron Shepherd, "*Midnight's Children* as Fantasy," *Commonwealth Review* 1.2 (1990): 35.

[17] Salman Rushdie, *Imaginary Homelands: Essays and Criticism 1981–1991* (London: Granta, 1990): 22–25.

[18] Rushdie, *Midnight's Children*, 167; 309; 419.

[19] See Erhard Reckwitz, "Der Roman als Metaroman: Salman Rushdie, *Midnight's Children*; Kazuo Ishiguro, *A Pale View of Hills*; John Fowles, *Mantissa*," *Poetica: Zeitschrift für Sprach- und Literaturwissenschaft* 18.1–2 (1986): 151, and Barbara O. Rajkowska, "The Reality of the Alien: An Exploration of Salman Rushdie's Novels," *Revista Canaria de Estudios Ingleses* 13–14 (1987): 17.

[20] Rushdie, *Midnight's Children*, 460–61.

retrospectively, by putting together the various pieces of the 'puzzle of life' as an attempt to find coherence. But the protagonists of Rushdie's novels most often cannot actively build up a coherent identity by themselves. Accordingly, some characters (for example, Saleem in *Midnight's Children*) admit that others will more easily determine "who he really is,"[21] especially since he feels like a "person to whom things *have been done*."[22]

The Moor's Last Sigh and The Ground Beneath Her Feet share yet another feature of identity-fragmentation – a feature that is symbolized, in both novels, by a broken mirror. After Moor is thrown out of his parental home he laments:

> I stumbled through [the gates], giddy, disoriented, lost. I was nobody, nothing. Nothing I had ever known was of use, nor could I any longer say that I knew it. I had been emptied, invalidated; I was, to use a hoary but suddenly fitting epithet, ruined. I had fallen from grace, and the horror of it shattered the universe, like a mirror. I felt as though I, too, had shattered; as if I were falling to earth, not as myself, but as a thousand and one fragmented images of myself, trapped in shards of glass.[23]

The mirror image is also to be found in a passage where Rai, the photographer and narrator of *The Ground Beneath Her Feet*, describes the rock-star Vina Apsara:

> To her last day, I could always see in her the skittish, disintegrated creature she'd been when she first came to us, looking as if she might run away again at any moment. What a piece of jetsam she was then, what a casualty! Literally selfless, her personality smashed, like a mirror, by the fist of her life. Her name, her mother and family, her sense of place and home and safety and belonging and being loved, her belief in the future, all these things had been pulled out from under her, like a rug. She was floating in a void, denatured, dehistoried, clawing at the shapelessness, trying to make some sort of mark. [...] She was a rag-bag of selves, torn fragments of people she might have become.[24]

This last passage also introduces the second aspect of our analysis: identity's *mutability*. In most of Rushdie's novels, the main characters are set off against strong alter egos. In *Midnight's Children*, for example, Saleem Sinai's antagonist is Shiva who in fact is the very child Saleem believes to be. Shortly after their birth, the nurse Mary Pereira had swapped the two babies so that Saleem is in reality Shiva and Shiva is Saleem. In the context of the novel this means that Saleem is neither the "inspirational force" nor the "mirror-image to India" that the Prime Minister saw in him.[25] Instead, he becomes the destroyer which the antagonist's and arch-rival's name "Major Shiva," as well as his mostly evil actions, so aptly depict. However, although Saleem knows about the swapping, he rather continues to believe that Ahmed and Amina Sinai (and

---

[21] Rushdie, *Midnight's Children*, 192.

[22] *Midnight's Children*, 237.

[23] Salman Rushdie, *The Moor's Last Sigh* (London: Jonathan Cape, 1995): 278–79.

[24] *The Ground Beneath Her Feet* (New York: Henry Holt, 1999): 121–22.

[25] Rushdie, *Midnight's Children*, 122. Thus Saleem is clearly a 'self-subverting' narrator, an aspect of narrative strategy that supports the (typically postmodern) concept of unstable identity.

not Vanita and William Methwold) are his real parents.[26] This might be read as yet another indication that he is subject to a process of oscillation between different parts of his self.

Saleem also has various names that stand for the different roles he has to act out in life: "I, Saleem Sinai, later variously called Snotnose, Stainface, Baldy, Sniffer, Buddha and even Piece-of-the Moon."[27] While, for example, "Snotnose" refers to Saleem's telepathic abilities and the "Midnight Children's Conference" he organizes, "Sniffer" stands for his degradation to the subhuman soldier called "man-dog" in the Sundarbans episode. Mutability of identity is thus reflected in Saleem's different names and his various roles in life,[28] a multiplication that is wonderfully captured in Mary Pereira's singing: "Anything you want to be, you kin [sic] be, / You kin [sic] be just what-all you want."[29]

The most overt protagonist–antagonist dualism can be detected in *The Moor's Last Sigh* as well, although here it is not as powerful and complex as in *Midnight's Children*. Moraes Zogoiby's alter ego is his girlfriend Uma, who also functions as a more active counterpart opposed to Moraes' generally passive nature. Uma says: "*I will be your mirror, your self's other self, your equal, your empress and your slave.*"[30] Their relationship ends when Uma commits suicide; in dying she passes through various changes, "as if the pages of a book were turning, as if she were giving up, one by one, all her numberless selves."[31] Interestingly, Moraes' father[32] – in true Jekyll-and-Hyde manner – also constructs various selves by letting his identity oscillate between an official business personality and his sly underworld self:

---

[26] What is more, he almost randomly designates further people as his parents; see Rushdie, *Midnight's Children*, passim but especially 127, 148–49). This seemingly nonsensical multiplication of parentage also points to Saleem as being in a state of orphanhood and displacement, or as lacking a symbolic centre. It is also a commentary upon the arbitrariness of identity-building, or, in the words of Jean–Pierre Durix, "that any identity is purely accidental and often made up"; Durix, "Salman Rushdie's Declaration of Kaleidoscopic Identity," in *Declarations of Cultural Independence in the English-Speaking World: A Symposium*, ed. Luigi Sampietro (Milan: D'Imperio Editore Novara, 1989): 173–84.

[27] Rushdie, *Midnight's Children*, 9.

[28] This is confirmed in *The Ground Beneath Her Feet* when the first-person narrator Umeed Merchant comments on his nickname, Rai: "Pseudonyms, stage names, work-names: for writers, for actors, for spies, these are useful masks, hiding or altering one's true identity" (18). The use of the phrase "true identity" reveals that Umeed dreams of what might be called a core identity, which, however, is never fixed in the novel.

[29] Rushdie, *Midnight's Children*, 383.

[30] *The Moor's Last Sigh*, 248.

[31] *The Moor's Last Sigh*, 281.

[32] In this novel, the question of (non-)authentic parentage is again put forward. It is by no means clear whether Abraham Zogoiby really is Moor's father – this might as well be Pandit Nehru (see Rushdie, *The Moor's Last Sigh*, 175). Like Saleem in *Midnight's Children*, Moraes consciously opts for one possibility: ie, in this case, Moraes chooses to believe that Abraham is his father, which may be read as an additional comment upon the fragmentation and the constructedness of identity; see Rushdie, *The Moor's Last Sigh*, 177.

The truth about Abraham Zogoiby was that he had put on a disguise; had created a mild-mannered secret identity to mask his covert super-nature. He had deliberately painted the dullest possible picture of himself [...] over the thrilling but unacceptable reality. The deferential, complaisant surface was what Vasco would have called his "overneath"; underneath it, he ruled a Mogambo-ish underworld.[33]

The Ground Beneath Her Feet similarly exploits mirror-images and alter egos. Ormus, the leader of a band called "VTO," is heavily in love with Vina, the singer. In their passionate relationship, one cannot live without the other, but, to make matters worse, they cannot really live with each other either: their selves are simultaneously drawn to each other and continuously forced apart. Furthermore, Umeed/Rai can be read as the antagonist to Ormus, for both are fighting for the love of Vina. Then again, Ormus's brothers take up various shades of self from the respective brothers: "Punishment caused Cyrus, too, to conceal himself beneath a falsehood, a self he had borrowed from his sweet-natured twin, which was not truly his,"[34] so that their identities have to be seen in relation to each other. This may, then, be interpreted as a metaphor for identity in relation to mutability as well as alterity.

This leads us to the last point we want to discuss: ie, the question of *identity* in relation to *alterity*. Identity, of course, cannot be scrutinized in isolation: the Other (rather, the self's relation to Others) has to be taken into consideration as well. This aspect has already been observed in the previous discussion, but what we are looking into now is the formation of the self in a larger context. This concerns the question of how a migrant who is moving between different nations and cultures is able to form his or her personal identity. This also refers to Bhabha's theory of hybridity and alterity, which conceptualizes a "third space" that is used to "deconstruct the boundaries between the self and other."[35] It is this sort of migrant identity that most of Rushdie's novels elaborate, particularly because *travelling* constitutes a most central metaphor in his texts.

In *Midnight's Children* the leitmotif of the nose bridges the gap between the inside and the outside world.[36] Saleem recurrently states: "To understand just one life, you have to swallow the world,"[37] a remark which is taken up again in *The Moor's Last Sigh*: "We inhale the world and breathe out meaning."[38] In a later passage of *Midnight's Children*, Saleem tries to answer the question

Who what am I? My answer: I am the sum total of everything that went before me, of all I have been seen done, of everything done-to-me. I am everyone everything whose being-in-the-world affected was affected by mine. I am anything that happens after I've

---

[33] Rushdie, *The Moor's Last Sigh*, 179–80.

[34] Rushdie, *The Ground Beneath Her Feet*, 138.

[35] Monika Fludernik, "The Constitution of Hybridity: Postcolonial Interventions," in *Hybridity and Postcolonialism: Twentieth-Century Indian Literature*, ed. Monika Fludernik (Tübingen: Stauffenburg, 1998): 51; see also Paul Goetsch, "Funktionen von Hybridität in der postkolonialen Theorie," in *Literatur in Wissenschaft und Unterricht* 30.2 (1997): 135–45.

[36] Rushdie, *Midnight's Children*, 10; 307.

[37] *Midnight's Children*, 109.

[38] Rushdie, *The Moor's Last Sigh*, 54.

gone which would not have happened if I had not come. Nor am I particularly exceptional in this matter; each "I," every one of the now-six-hundred-million-plus of us, contains a similar multitude.[39]

Here the interaction between personal and collective identity is alluded to already.
More or less the same approach to identity/alterity can be found in *The Moor's Last
Sigh* when Moraes speaks of "boundaries of your self [which] began to dissolve […] in
crowds or in love."[40] This aspect of identity-building is taken up yet again in *The
Satanic Verses*, where Saladin Chamcha and Gibreel Farishta are the two opposing
figures. Whereas Saladin tries to adapt to English manners as much as possible, finally
becoming "more English than the English,"[41] Gibreel wants to stick to his 'Indianness'. In the course of the novel, Gibreel is seemingly rewarded, because he obtains a
"halo"[42] and passes his bad breath on to Saladin, who, in contrast, is being punished
for having selected adaptation: Saladin grows horns and finally also a hoof. The narrator comments on the migrant status of Gibreel and Saladin:

> Should we even say that these are two fundamentally different types of self? Might we
> not agree that Gibreel […] has wished to remain, to a large degree, *continuous* – that is,
> joined to and arising from his past […] so that his is still a self which, for our present
> purposes, we may describe as true … whereas Saladin Chamcha is a creature of *selected*
> discontinuities, a *willing* re-invention; his *preferred* revolt against history being what
> makes him, in our chosen idiom, "false"? […] While Gibreel, to follow the logic of our
> established terminology, is to be considered "good" by virtue of *wishing to remain*, for
> all his vicissitudes, at bottom an untranslated man.
> – But, and again but: this sounds, does it not, dangerously like an intentionalist
> fallacy? – Such distinctions, resting as they must on an idea of the self as being (ideally)
> homogeneous, non-hybrid, "pure," – an utterly fantastic notion! – cannot, must not,
> suffice.[43]

The differentiation between good and evil with regard to the migrant's position towards adaptability is not only verbally deconstructed by the narrator. Later, back in
India, Gibreel's problem of "sulphurous halitosis" returns with a vengeance, and he
loses his girlfriend as well as his job before finally committing suicide. Saladin, on the
other hand, is finally reconciled with his father, inherits his wealth and even re-unites
with his girlfriend Zeeny Vakil. Thus, in the end, it is Saladin rather than Gibreel who
comes up with a successful concept of a person's *self*-positioning *as migrant* in both a
foreign *and* a familiar culture.

D.C.R.A. Goonetilleke argues that the end of *The Satanic Verses* suggests the failure
of hybridity as process. He gives three reasons for this: Saladin's return to his ancestral
home; his resuming his original name; and his mother tongue Urdu coming back to

[39] Rushdie, *Midnight's Children*, 383.
[40] Rushdie, *The Moor's Last Sigh*, 193.
[41] Salman Rushdie, *The Satanic Verses* (Dover DE: The Consortium, 1992): 56.
[42] Rushdie, *The Satanic Verses*, 142.
[43] *The Satanic Verses*, 427.

him.[44] We contend, however, that this argument is not necessarily valid, because Gibreel also comes back to India but fails to 'survive'.

Furthermore, Saladin's re-uniting with Zeeny Vakil, who favours "an ethic of historically validated eclecticism, for was not the entire national culture based on the principle of borrowing whatever clothes seemed to fit, Aryan, Mughal, British, take-the-best-and-leave-the-rest,"[45] clearly shows that he has decided to live in a culture of hybridity. And, most significantly, Saladin does not go back to his "one and only former self," but, rather, "feels closer to many old rejected selves, many alternative Saladins."[46] Thus even individual cultures are in themselves always already hybrid constructs. The migrant travelling between two or more cultures will eventually have to develop a sense of a 'third space' or hybrid identity.[47] This is confirmed towards the end of *The Satanic Verses*:

> We are here to change things. I concede at once that we shall ourselves be changed; African, Caribbean, Indian, Pakistani, Bangladeshi, Cypriot, Chinese, we are other than what we would have been if we had not crossed the oceans, if our mothers and fathers had not crossed the skies [...]. We have been made again: but I say that we shall also be the ones to remake this society, to shape it from bottom to top.[48]

In Rushdie's novels, the third space is often alluded to when the respective protagonists fly from one to another country. Thus the aeroplane becomes a powerful symbol for Bhabha's third space of in-betweenness. In *The Satanic Verses*, for example, Saladin and Gibreel fall out of an exploding aircraft towards England and some of their transformations in terms of personality already start then, because the exploded plane ejects not only the passengers but also "the debris of the soul, broken memories, sloughed-off selves, severed mother-tongues, violated privacies, untranslatable jokes, extinguished futures, lost loves, the forgotten meaning of hollow, booming words, *land, belonging, home.*"[49]

When, towards the end of *The Moor's Last Sigh*, Moraes Zogoiby has to fly to Granada, he talks about leaving behind the "place, language, people and customs [he] knew [...]; and these, for most of us, are the four anchors of the soul."[50] Accordingly, after his arrival he feels that he "was a nobody from nowhere, like no-one, belonging

---

[44] D.C.R.A. Goonetilleke, *Salman Rushdie* (London: Macmillan, 1998): 90–91.

[45] Rushdie, *The Satanic Verses*, 52.

[46] *The Satanic Verses*, 523.

[47] What the narrator of *The Satanic Verses* also displays is the pressure that the chosen country can apply to the individual immigrant self. The brutal arrest of the immigration officers and the resulting changes of Saladin as a response (Rushdie, *The Satanic Verses*, 157–64) are a first clue to this, but there is further evidence in the novel. Saladin has to develop masks in school in order to socialize with the other pupils (43); and other immigrants in a hospital mutate into animals because "they have the power of description, and we succumb to the pictures they construct" (168).

[48] Rushdie, *The Satanic Verses*, 413–14.

[49] *The Satanic Verses*, 4.

[50] Rushdie, *The Moor's Last Sigh*, 383.

to nothing," but this is something he has to convince himself of: "That sounded better. That felt true. All my ties had loosened."[51] Later Moraes will no longer be sure of anything, except of finding comfort and strength in the Japanese painter he has met. She, the painter, celebrates rootlessness and the autonomy of the self; yet she eventually dies and Moraes has to find another way of claiming his personal identity: after having undergone the change from the (over-)celebrated hybridity of his parental home to the somewhat simplistic concept of a 'mono-identity' à la Raman Fielding, he arrives at the final conclusion: "The need for flowing together, for putting an end to frontiers, for the dropping of the boundaries of the self."[52]

Yet another example of an aeroplane serving as a symbol for an inter-cultural 'third space' can be found in *The Ground Beneath Her Feet*. Ormus, the lover and future husband of Vina Apsara, "sheds his old skin [...] like a snake"[53] when flying from India to Britain. Strikingly, the whole chapter dedicated to the flight is termed "Membrane," which suggests that all migrant travellers, by having to penetrate this filter of the membrane, can only save some parts of their identity and thus have to leave behind some other parts:

> Detached from the indifferent earth, he feels a certain resistance in the air. Something fighting back against the aircraft's forward movement. As if there's a stretchy translucent membrane across the sky, an ectoplasmic barrier, a Wall [...]. But it's so springy, this invisible restriction, it keeps pushing the airplane back, boeing!, boeing!, until at last the Mayflower breaks through, it's through! Sunlight bounces off the wing into his bleary eye. And as he passes that unseen frontier he sees the tear in the sky [...]. He intuits that every bone in his body is being irradiated by something pouring through the sky-rip, a mutation is occurring at the level of the cell, of the gene, of the particle. The person who arrives won't be the one who left, or not quite.[54]

This, finally, is interesting with regard to the migrants' 'cultural translation'. The term 'translation', as Rushdie himself has pointed out, derives etymologically from the Latin word *translatio*, which originally designates a neutral 'bearing across'. As Rushdie says, "Having been borne across the world, we [migrants] are translated men. It is normally supposed that something always gets lost in translation; I cling, obstinately, to the notion that something can also be gained."[55] Consequently, Rushdie's novels depict identity not as being stable or monolithic but, rather, as various, continuously changing, oscillating between disparate elements.[56] Identity cannot be pinned down easily, for it is always – and this has to do with its very nature and is thus wholly independent of whether we talk of a migrant's or a native's identity – process-bound rather than fixed. Saladin's statement about his identity in *The Satanic Verses* can therefore be seen as representative for the concept of self that emerges in the whole of

---

[51] *The Moor's Last Sigh*, 388.
[52] *The Moor's Last Sigh*, 433.
[53] Rushdie, *The Ground Beneath Her Feet*, 250.
[54] *The Ground Beneath Her Feet*, 253.
[55] Rushdie, *Imaginary Homelands*, 17.
[56] See also *Imaginary Homelands*, 394.

Rushdie's work: "*I'm not myself today*, he thought. The heart flutters. Life damages the living. None of us are ourselves. None of us are *like this.*"[57]

WORKS CITED

Bhabha, Homi K. "The Third Space (an Interview)," in *Identity: Community, Culture, Difference*, ed. Jonathan Rutherford (London: Lawrence & Wishart, 1990): 207–21.

Connor, Steven. *Postmodernist Culture: An Introduction to Theories of the Contemporary* (Oxford: Blackwell, 1989).

Durix, Jean–Pierre. "Salman Rushdie's Declaration of Kaleidoscopic Identity," in *Declarations of Cultural Independence in the English-Speaking World: A Symposium*, ed. Luigi Sampietro (Milan: D'Imperio Editore Novara, 1989): 173–84.

Eagleton, Terry. "Capitalism, Modernism and Postmodernism," in *Modern Criticism and Theory: A Reader*, ed. David Lodge (London: Longman, 1988): 385–98.

Fletcher, M.D. "Introduction: the Politics of Salman Rushdie's Fiction," in *Reading Rushdie: Perspectives on the Fiction of Salman Rushdie*, ed. M.D. Fletcher (Cross/Cultures 16; Amsterdam & Atlanta GA: Rodopi, 1994): 1–22.

Fludernik, Monika. "The Constitution of Hybridity: Postcolonial Interventions," in *Hybridity and Postcolonialism: Twentieth-Century Indian Literature*, ed. Monika Fludernik (Tübingen: Staufenburg, 1998): 19–53.

Goetsch, Paul. "Funktionen von Hybridität in der postkolonialen Theorie," *Literatur in Wissenschaft und Unterricht* 30.2 (1997): 135–45.

Goonetilleke, D.C.R.A. *Salman Rushdie* (London: Macmillan, 1998).

Hutcheon, Linda. *A Poetics of Postmodernism: History, Theory, Fiction* (London & New York: Routledge, 1988).

Jameson, Fredric. "Postmodernism and Consumer Society," in *The Anti-Aesthetic: Essays on Postmodern Culture*, ed. Hal Foster (Seattle WA: Bay Press, 1983): 111–25.

Kellner, Douglas. "Popular Culture and the Construction of Postmodern Identities," in *Modernity and Identity*, ed. Scott Lash & Jonathan Friedman (Oxford: Blackwell, 1992): 141–77.

Lange, Bernd–Peter. "Postcolonial Gothic: Salman Rushdie's *The Moor's Last Sigh*," *Literatur in Wissenschaft und Unterricht* 31.4 (1998): 365–75.

Lyotard, Jean–François. *The Postmodern Condition: A Report on Knowledge*, tr. Geoff Bennington & Brian Massumi (Minneapolis: U of Minnesota P, 1984).

Rajkowska, Barbara O. "The Reality of the Alien: An Exploration of Salman Rushdie's Novels," *Revista Canaria de Estudios Ingleses* 13–14 (1987): 9–27.

Reckwitz, Erhard. "Der Roman als Metaroman: Salman Rushdie, *Midnight's Children*; Kazuo Ishiguro, *A Pale View of Hills*; John Fowles, *Mantissa*," *Poetica: Zeitschrift für Sprach- und Literaturwissenschaft* 18.1–2 (1986): 140–64.

Reinfandt, Christoph. "What's the Use of Stories that Aren't Even True: Salman Rushdie as a Test Case for Literature and Literary Studies Today," *Literatur in Wissenschaft und Unterricht* 31.1 (1998): 75–92.

Rushdie, Salman. *The Ground Beneath Her Feet* (New York: Henry Holt, 1999).

——. *Imaginary Homelands: Essays and Criticism 1981–1991* (London: Granta, 1991).

——. *Midnight's Children* (1981; London: Vintage, 1995).

——. *The Moor's Last Sigh* (London: Jonathan Cape, 1995).

——. *The Satanic Verses* (1988; Dover DE: Consortium, 1992).

---

[57] Rushdie, *The Satanic Verses*, 65.

Shepherd, Ron. "*Midnight's Children* as Fantasy," *Commonwealth Review* 1.2 (1990): 33–43.
Subba Rao, V.V. "Salman Rushdie's *Midnight's Children*: A Study," *Indian Journal of English Studies* 32 (1993–94): 87–93.

《●》

An Introduction to
Salman Rushdie's Hybrid Aesthetic

The Satanic Verses

STÉPHANIE RAVILLON

> *The Satanic Verses* celebrates hybridity, impurity, intermingling, the
> transformation that comes of new and unexpected combinations of
> human beings, cultures, ideas, politics, movies, songs. It rejoices in
> mongrelization and fears the absolutism of the Pure. *Mélange*, hotch-
> potch, a bit of this and a bit of that is *how newness enters the world*. It
> is the great possibility that mass migration gives the world, and I have
> tried to embrace it. *The Satanic Verses* is for change-by-fusion,
> change-by-conjoining. It is a love-song to our mongrel selves.[1]

B
EING A MAN OF EAST AND OF WEST, Salman Rushdie occupies a
unique position as theorist and practitioner of hybridity. His claim to represent a new hybrid identity and literary style is therefore fully justified. For
this reason, his writing can be regarded as a good example of mixing, and matching,
linguistic, cultural, literary, religious and political influences. *The Satanic Verses* is no
exception to the rule. It celebrates hybridity, and strives to demonstrate that it is a complete fallacy to suppose that purity exists. Like most of Rushdie's novels, it embodies
the hope that out of the collapse of colonialism, a better and more hybrid world may be
created. To help his characters fight against the apostles of purity, Rushdie has developed a new aesthetic theory and has turned hybridity into a dynamic. As a consequence, *The Satanic Verses* is both a variation on the vocal theme (the characters, who
hover somewhere in the limbo between different cultures and languages, are tormented
by unceasing mutations of identity, and suffer from the effects of the mutability of their
voices) and a literary experiment (different genres are leaking into each other, giving
birth to new forms of literature). It is also a plea for justice and tolerance and, as such,

---

[1] Salman Rushdie, *Imaginary Homelands: Essays and Criticism 1981–1991* (London: Granta,
1991): 394.

it exposes the failings of British society, as well as the tendency British people have to look down upon migrants and to regard them as monstrous hybrids.

The term 'hybridity' is itself a hybrid: it can be derived both from the Latin *hybrida* 'of mixed blood' and from the Greek *ubris* 'excess'. It implicitly refers to the coming together of unrelated and often contradictory elements, and carries within itself the seeds of an art, which is usually, and rightly, said to be an art of excess. It designates the transformation that comes of new and unexpected combinations (of cultures, languages, ideas, etc), and is used by Rushdie as a byword for regeneration, novelty, and richness. As Jean–Pierre Durix remarks,

> the term 'hybridity' has been questioned by some critics who feel that it contains definitely negative connotations and smacks too much of the half-caste or mongrel syndrome. It need not be so, however, if one uses 'hybrid' in the dynamic sense of a representation which goes beyond the initial polarity of its component elements. While one may understand the reservations of intellectuals originating in countries where people 'of mixed blood' were traditionally sneered at by both the native and the white population, the term 'hybrid' still contains enough positive potential to be used as description of a major post-colonial characteristic.[2]

The Satanic Verses is an exploration of the potentialities of 'hybridity'. The term, which is used by Rushdie as an explicit term of praise, refers to the creation of new transcultural identities and forms. It stresses the mutuality of cultures, and insists on the advantages of cross-fertilization. It unsettles the supremacy of 'authenticity', and suggests that it is dangerous to replace the reality of the mixed tradition by the fantasy of purity. "Authenticity," Rushdie says,

> demands that sources, forms, style, language and symbol all derive from a supposedly homogeneous and unbroken tradition [...] [but] it is completely fallacious to suppose that there is such a thing as a pure, unalloyed tradition from which to draw. The only people who seriously believe this are religious extremists. The rest of us understand that the very essence of Indian culture is that we possess a mixed tradition, a *mélange* of elements as disparate as ancient Mughal and contemporary Coca-Cola American. To say nothing of Muslim, Buddhist, Jain, Christian, Jewish, British, French, Portuguese, Marxist, Maoist, Trotskyist, Vietnamese, capitalist, and of course Hindu elements.[3]

If anything, *The Satanic Verses* is an attempt to face up to the bogy of authenticity and resist the call for unicity and homogeneity. It criticizes the apostles of purity and strives to demonstrate that "human beings understand themselves and shape their futures by arguing and challenging and questioning and saying the unsayable; not by bowing the knee, whether to gods or to men."[4] It reasserts the importance of dialogue and dissents from the view that the world is one thing and not the other, thereby testifying to Rushdie's desire to celebrate hybridity and extol the merits of plurality. It

---

[2] Jean–Pierre Durix, *Mimesis, Genres and Post Colonial Discourse: Deconstructing Magic Realism* (Basingstoke: Macmillan, 1998): 148.

[3] Salman Rushdie, *Imaginary Homelands*, 67.

[4] *Imaginary Homelands*, 395.

evidences Rushdie's attachment to the notion of multiplicity and points to the fact that he is, like Saleem Sinai in *Midnight's Children*, a "swallower" of lives and cultures, who draws his inspiration from many distinct traditions and borrows from a whole host of writers (Rabelais, Carroll, Joyce, Dante, Boccaccio, Dickens and Nabokov, to name but a few).

Rushdie's attachment to the notions of hybridity and multiplicity is further indicated by the fact that he weaves together many plots and subplots. Indeed, *The Satanic Verses* resembles a jigsaw puzzle: cut into irregular shapes, it has to be fitted together again by the reader. It can therefore be considered Rushdie's most successful and extreme experiment with fragmented narration. The main narrative, which exemplifies the plight of immigrants to Britain, contains two recurrent embedded stories, which appear in the form of dreams. The first dream depicts the birth and growth of the Islamic religion, and the advent of Mahound, Prophet of Jahilia. In the second dream, a young girl dressed in butterflies, Ayesha, persuades the people in her village to embark on a pilgrimage to Mecca. These narratives, which also contain several tales of love, faith and betrayal, are made to reflect the profusion of life, which explains why the novel seems to be teeming with stories.

The device that Rushdie uses to hint at the multiplicity of lives and at the infinite possibilities of the world is reminiscent of the French *mise-en-abyme*. The term *mise-en-abyme* was adapted from the language of heraldry by André Gide, who commented on it in an entry in his journals. A true *mise-en-abyme*, Brian McHale remarks,

> is determined by three criteria: first, it is a nested or embedded representation, occupying a narrative level inferior to that of the primary, diegetic narrative world; secondly, this nested representation *resembles* [...] something at the level of the primary, diegetic world; and thirdly, this 'something' that it resembles must constitute some salient and continuous aspect of the primary world, salient and continuous enough that we are willing to say the nested representation *reproduces* or *duplicates* the primary representation as a whole.[5]

The episode of the "satanic verses" qualifies as a true *mise-en-abyme*: it is an icon of the text as a whole, and is present on the three levels of the novel. Its effect is clearly to disrupt the logic of the narrative and to undermine its unity.

The layering of stories, which is one of the most disconcerting aspects of the novel, also confirms Rushdie's indebtedness to the art of storytelling. As a boy, Rushdie was fascinated by the storytellers who recounted the great epics orally and could bring together hundreds, if not thousands, of people. *The Satanic Verses* borrows freely from the art of the storyteller. The shape of its narrative – non-linear, bizarre, and pyrotechnical – makes it an obvious tribute to the oral tradition.[6] It revolves around the idea of

[5] Brian McHale, *Postmodernist Fiction* (London & New York: Routledge, 1987): 124.

[6] Salman Rushdie, "*Midnight's Children* and *Shame*," *Kunapipi* 7.1 (1985): 7–8: "An oral narrative does not go from the beginning to the middle to the end of the story. It goes in great swoops, it goes in spirals and in loops, it every so often reiterates something that happened earlier to remind you, and then takes you off again, sometimes summarizes itself, it frequently digresses off into something that the story-teller appears just to have thought of, then it comes back to the

literature as performance, and testifies to Rushdie's determination to create a literary form which might correspond to the form of the oral narrative and which might succeed in holding readers in the same way that the oral narrative holds audiences. It reassesses the value of the oral by bringing to the fore the interrelationship between orality and literacy, and shows that it is possible to render oral forms into written ones. It therefore betokens Rushdie's desire to turn the novel into a privileged arena, a place where traditions and influences can meet and mingle, and where "*voices* [can talk] *about everything in every possible way.*"[7]

The Satanic Verses is a vast arena of discourse resonant with the sound of many voices. As will presently appear, these voices are all but reliable; they are all designed to reflect the mutability of the self and the instability of the world. They first seem to suggest that there is a close relationship between "voice" and "identity," but, as the story unfolds, one cannot fail to realize that the characters of the novel are, more often than not, betrayed by their own voices. Salahuddin Chamchawala, aged thirteen, grows increasingly impatient of Bombay, and spends his time gabbling out, like a mantra, the six letters of his dream-city, ellowen deeowen. When his father offers him, out of the blue, an English education, Saladin reckons that such an opportunity occurs only once in a lifetime. Once in England, Saladin decides to turn his artistic gifts to good account by becoming "The Man of a Thousand Voices and a Voice." What with his fair skin and his gift for vocal impersonations, Saladin finds it easy to trick people into believing he is an Englishman born and bred ... or almost. With his female equivalent, Mimi Mamoulian, he rules the airwaves of Britain, but the benefit they get is double-edged: "the gravitational field of their abilities draws work towards them, but they remain invisible, shedding bodies to put on voices."[8] Deprived of their own voices and, along with them, of their identity, Saladin and Mimi realize that it is completely fallacious to suppose that there is such a thing as a stable, immutable self.

The characters of the novel learn to their cost that voices are unreliable and cannot be trusted to reveal the true nature of the self. Pamela's voice, to give but one example, is "composed of tweeds, headscarves, summer pudding, hockey-sticks, thatched houses, saddle-soap, house-parties, nuns, family pews, large dogs and philistinism."[9] Saladin, who is in love with this voice, and all that it stands for, first refuses to acknowledge the

---

main thrust of the narrative. Sometimes it steps sideways and tells you about another, related story which is like the story that he's been telling you, and then it goes back to the main story. Sometimes there are Chinese boxes where there is a story inside a story, then they all come back, you see. So it's a very bizarre and pyrotechnical shape. And it has the appearance of being random and chaotic, it has the appearance that what is happening is anything the story-teller happens to be thinking, he just proceeds in that contingent way. It seemed to me in fact that it was very far from being random and chaotic, and that the oral narrative had developed this shape over a very long period, not because story-tellers were lacking in organization, but because this shape conformed very exactly to the shape in which people liked to listen, that in fact the first and the only rule of the story-teller is to hold his audience: if you don't hold them, they will get up and walk away. So everything that the story-teller does is designed to keep the people listening more intensely."

[7] Salman Rushdie, *Imaginary Homelands*, 429.
[8] Salman Rushdie, *The Satanic Verses* (New York: Viking, 1988): 61.
[9] *The Satanic Verses*, 180.

fact that Pamela actually feels more comfortable with greenies and peace marchers than with gentlemen farmers. But he finally understands that that voice "stinking of Yorkshire pudding and hearts of oak, that hearty, rubicund voice of ye olde dream-England which he so desperately [wants] to inhabit"[10] is essentially misleading.

The episode of the "satanic verses," which is probably the most crucial in the book, is illustrative of Rushdie's desire to reflect on "the subject of mistakes with voices."[11] The incident of the "satanic verses" – which is defined in *Imaginary Homelands* as "the quasi-historical tale of how Muhammad's revelation seemed briefly to flirt with the possibility of admitting three pagan and female deities into the pantheon, at the semi-divine, intercessory level of the archangels, and of how he then repudiated these verses as being satanically inspire"[12] – clearly indicates that Rushdie disapproves of certainties. It centres on the question of inspiration – "is inspiration good or evil, to be trusted or dismissed, or examined in the sceptical light of reason?"[13] – and explores both the nature of revelation and the power of faith. More importantly, it testifies to Rushdie's desire to translate into words the multiple nature of all things, and to render "the essential plurality of the inspiration, of the voices."[14]

Rushdie's fondness for the notions of multiplicity and plurality can also be felt in his use of English. According to Rushdie,

> it is [not] always necessary to take up the anti-colonial [...] cudgels against English. What seems [...] to be happening is that those peoples who were once colonized by the language are now rapidly remaking it, domesticating it, becoming more and more relaxed about the way they use it – assisted by the English language's enormous flexibility and size, they are carving out large territories for themselves within its frontiers.[15]

What Rushdie is implying is that emigrants cannot simply use English the way the English do: they have to conquer English, and to remake it for their own purposes. Having managed his own mix of cultures and languages, Rushdie coins new words and sentences, and uses a language that combines English, Hindi, Urdu, etc. As a consequence, *The Satanic Verses* seems to be constructed on concrete social speech diversity. It arises out of a welter of conflicting but dynamic voices and opinions which produce the effect of heteroglossia; and it is this concrete heteroglossia that serves as the vehicle for the confrontation of ideas in the novel and brings out its orchestrated polyphony of voices.

The idea of a polyphony of voices, so central to the novel, implies that it is possible to articulate the conflicts and contradictions at work in the world. It points to the multiple nature of reality and embodies man's whole range of attitudes and responses

---

[10] Salman Rushdie, *The Satanic Verses*, 180.

[11] *The Satanic Verses*, 179.

[12] Salman Rushdie, *Imaginary Homelands*, 399.

[13] Jacqueline Bardolph, "Language is Courage: *The Satanic Verses*," *Commonwealth: Essays and Studies* 12.1 (Autumn 1989): 3.

[14] Jacqueline Bardolph, "Language is Courage: *The Satanic Verses*," 6.

[15] Salman Rushdie, *Imaginary Homelands*, 64.

to the world. It also suggests that, no matter how exuberant and eccentric a work of art may be, there is always a shape to it. With its many distinct shapes and meanings, *The Satanic Verses* rises up against the absolutism of the Pure ; it celebrates hybridity and struggles to knit together contradictory patterns of thinking. It shows that opposites attract and have a surprising tendency to pass into each other, "like flavours when you cook."[16] Unsurprisingly, then, *The Satanic Verses* is a vivid account of the intimate but sometimes flawed encounter between East and West, the sacred and the profane, the fictitious and the real. The city of London, which is the scene of this encounter, appears to be quite deceptive: it refuses to submit to the dominion of cartographers, and changes shape at will. The fact that London does not lend itself to being mapped does not really come as a surprise. A map is an authoritarian representation, designed to divide, enclose and exclude, and rules out the possibility of change. The impossible task facing the cartographers underscores the point that only when borders are abolished can transformation take place. It also implies that London is an essentially hybrid city, whose nature cannot be easily pinned down. Tropicalized by Gibreel, London becomes the symbol of the encounter between East and West. It also becomes the scene of the eternal struggle between Good and Evil.

When their jumbo jet blows apart above the English Channel, Gibreel and Saladin miraculously survive and are washed up on a beach. However, it appears that strange changes have come over them: Gibreel is turned into his namesake, the Archangel Gabriel, and Saladin finds himself transformed into a goatish devil. And yet it would be rather simplistic to assess Gibreel as the incarnation of good and Saladin as the embodiment of evil. Indeed, the 'satanic' Saladin generally acts more 'humanely' than the 'angelic' Gibreel. The two characters are neither entirely good nor wholly wicked. They simply embody the intertwining of Good and Evil, of sacred and profane, that lies both in the hearts of men and in the world. Baal, the poet who appears in the Jahilian sections of the book, is emblematic of the opposition between the sacred and the profane. He is the most feared satirist in all Jahilia, but his cutting tongue is no match for Mahound. Fearing for his life, the poet takes refuge in Jahilia's most popular brothel, "The Curtain." There he realizes that there are several ways of refusing to submit. To take his revenge on the Prophet, he urges the whores of The Curtain to take the names of Mahound's wives. The men of Jahilia, obviously aroused by this trick, flock to The Curtain, which reports a threefold upturn in business. But Baal's triumph is short-lived and, finally, the pure eradicates the impure. Against all expectations, the death of the poet does not spell the end of the profane. It simply suggests that there might be subtler ways of refusing to submit, for, as Salman the Persian demonstrates, it is possible to pollute the word of God and get away with it.

Interestingly, the 'brothel sequence' occurs in one of Gibreel's dreams. As Rushdie observes in *Imaginary Homelands*, these dreams

> are *agonizingly painful to the dreamer*. They are a 'nocturnal retribution, a punishment'
> for his loss of faith. This man, desperate to regain belief, is haunted, possessed, by
> visions of doubt, visions of scepticism and questions and faith-shaking allegations that

---

[16] Salman Rushdie, *Imaginary Homelands*, 394.

grow more and more extreme as they go on. He tries in vain to escape them, fighting against sleep; but then the visions cross over the boundary between his waking and sleeping self.[17]

Gibreel, who is out of his mind with grief and torment, gradually loses the ability to distinguish between dream and reality. Longing for a moment of respite, he seeks refuge in the artificial, fabricated world of the cinema, but the films he makes (*Gibreel in Jahilia, Gibreel Meets the Imam, Gibreel with the Butterfly Girl*) only add to his confusion. Infected with dream-visions and cinematic revelations, his life becomes unbearable, and he finally kills himself.

The coming together of dream, reality and the cinema highlights Rushdie's concern with hybridity, and illustrates his attempt at crossing over boundaries. It brings out the existence of 'in-between' modes of being, and points to the impossibility of drawing exclusive lines between identities and genres. It also epitomizes Rushdie's ideas concerning the art of writing novels. The novels he cares most about, he says, "are those which attempt radical reformulations of language, form and ideas, those that attempt to do what the word *novel* seems to insist upon: to see the world anew."[18] *The Satanic Verses* is wholly in keeping with Rushdie's expectations of what novels have to offer. It laments the absence of a third way between to the polarity of right and wrong, and advocates the reconciliation of the Old and the New. It obviously springs from Rushdie's desire to turn the transgression of genre-boundaries into an art, and expresses his belief in the necessity of creating new synthetic forms.

The form that Rushdie uses in *The Satanic Verses* has much in common with Menippean satire. The genre of Menippean satire, which developed out of verse through the practice of adding prose interludes, is generally associated with carnival. The interesting thing about the Menippean mode is that it "has been reconstituted at intervals throughout the course of literary history as the dialectical response to the consolidation of 'official', monological literary genres."[19] As Brian McHale remarks,

> where the traditional genres of official literature are stylistically homogeneous, carnivalized literature is heterogeneous and flagrantly 'indecorous', interweaving disparate styles and registers. Where the official genres are typically unitary, both generically and ontologically, projecting a single fictional world, carnivalized literature interrupts the text's ontological 'horizon' with a multiplicity of inserted genres.[20]

The Satanic Verses is indisputably a modern Menippean satire: it contains most of the Menippean elements that Bakhtin enumerates in *Problems of Dostoevsky's Poetics*, and is made up of heterogeneous fragments.

Magical realism is generally said to have affinities with the carnivalesque tradition and Menippean satire. As a consequence, it is only natural that *The Satanic Verses* should be labelled as magical-realist. To label *The Satanic Verses* as magical-realist is

---

[17] Salman Rushdie, *Imaginary Homelands*, 398.

[18] *Imaginary Homelands*, 393.

[19] Brian McHale, *Postmodernist Fiction*, 172.

[20] McHale, *Postmodernist Fiction*, 172.

to acknowledge the fact that Rushdie's attempts at breaking down the boundaries which stand between the Real and the Magical have been successful. To label *The Satanic Verses* as magical-realist is also to acknowledge the fact that only by letting magic and fantasy take over from reality can one arrive at a definition of the world which feels true. According to Jean–Pierre Durix,

> what many 'magic realistic' works have in common is this mixture of fantasy and a clear concern with reference, historical allegory and social protest. Such novels often evokes the process of liberation of oppressed communities. The scope of these books largely transcends the individual fate of a few characters in order to constitute an imaginary re-telling of a whole nation through several decades.[21]

Magical realism, therefore, points to the fact that politics and literature are inextricably mixed, and that that mixture has repercussions. For this very reason, *The Satanic Verses* can be considered the result of Rushdie's determination

> to create a literary language and literary forms in which the experience of formerly colo-nized, still-disadvantaged peoples might find full expression. If *The Satanic Verses* is anything, it is a migrant's eye-view of the world. It is written from the very experience of uprooting, disjuncture and metamorphosis (slow or rapid, painful or pleasurable) that is the migrant condition, and from which [...] can be derived a metaphor for all humanity.[22]

The characters at the centre of *The Satanic Verses* all share a status as exiles, emi-grants or expatriates. They are mostly of Indian descent, and struggle to clear a space for themselves in another, and not always welcoming, country. They are obsessed with the question of the mutability of the essence of the self but do not know whether to pledge allegiance to Lucretius or to Ovid, whether to stand up for the mutability or the immutability of the self. They live, as Homi Bhabha remarks in *The Location of Cul-ture*, "in the interstices of Lucretius and Ovid [and are] caught in-between a 'nativist', even nationalist, atavism and a postcolonial metropolitan assimilation,"[23] and their experience is no less a transitional phenomenon than a translational one. What the book actually reveals, Homi Bhabha adds,

> is a life lived precariously on the cultural and political margins of modern society. Where once we could believe in the comforts and continuities of Tradition, today we must face the responsibility of cultural Translation. In the attempt to mediate between different cul-tures, languages and societies, there is always the threat of mistranslation, confusion and fear. [...] *The Satanic Verses* is a postcolonial work that attempts the onerous duty of un-ravelling this cultural translation. The book is written in a spirit of questioning, doubt, interrogation and puzzlement which articulates the dilemma of the migrant, the émigré, the minority.[24]

---

[21] Jean–Pierre Durix, *Mimesis, Genres and Post Colonial Discourse*, 116.
[22] Salman Rushdie, *Imaginary Homelands*, 394.
[23] Homi Bhabha, *The Location of Culture* (London: Routledge, 1994): 223.
[24] Homi Bhabha, *New Statesman* (3 March 1989); also in *The Rushdie File*, ed. Lisa Appi-gnanesi & Sara Maitland (Syracuse NY: Syracuse UP, 1990): 114.

Saladin, to take but one example, is torn between Bombay and London, East and West. He longs to belong but dithers over which road to take: he wavers between the meekness of imitation and the ambivalence of mimicry. He is unsure whether to submit or subvert. When Saladin finds himself transformed into a supernatural imp, he realizes that, for all his fair skin and English education, he will never be considered an Englishman. He understands that racism is a topical and sensitive issue, and that stereotyping will always be the rule. He realizes that London is the locus of incompatible realities, of irreconcilable elements, but he still longs to be part of that dream-city of poise and moderation that had come, in his childhood, to obsess him. But after spending some time in a bizarre sanatorium full of monstrous hybrids, Saladin finally yields to the evidence: England is not the land of welcome he had hoped for. Locked up in this sanatorium, he realizes to his dismay that the hardships that are the lot of the migrants are nothing but the result of the host culture's attitude to them.

Cast in the role of the exotic and threatening Other, Saladin learns to his cost that the world is the product of the difference, as well as of the interaction, between the West and the East, the colonizers and the colonized, the Self and the Other. This, of course, can create a sense of alienation from the real world – Gibreel, who is a schizophrenic, meets with a tragic end – but, according to Rushdie, this hybridity does not necessarily result in confusion or fragmentation. He believes, like Homi Bhabha, that hybridity

> is the sign of the productivity of colonial power, its shifting forces and fixities; it is the name for the strategic reversal of the process of domination through disavowal (that is, the production of discriminatory identities that secure the 'pure' and original identity of authority). Hybridity is the revaluation of the assumption of colonial identity through the repetition of discriminatory identity effects. It displays the necessary deformation and displacement of all sites of discrimination and domination. It unsettles the mimetic or narcissistic demands of colonial power but reimplicates its identifications in strategies of subversion that turn the gaze of the discriminated back upon the eye of power.[25]

Saladin, who is the very embodiment of these strategies of subversion, is turned into a symbol by his fellow citizens and becomes the prime mover in the revolt against the government. He participates, albeit unwillingly, in a scheme for reclaiming language and points to the purpose of the novel, which is "to attempt the sort of act of affirmation that, in the United States, transformed the word *black* from the standard term of racist abuse into a 'beautiful' expression of cultural pride."[26]

With a little help from his djinn, Zeeny Vakil – she also functions as a spokesperson for Rushdie – Saladin finally succeeds in mending his divided self, in stepping out of his skin of glass. Stung back into life, he understands that 'hybridity' is both something to reckon with and something worth striving to attain, and finally realizes the necessity of replacing the confining myth of authenticity with an ethic of historically validated eclecticism based, as Zeeny makes a point of saying, "on the principle of borrowing whatever clothes [seem] to fit, Aryan, Mughal, British, take-the-best-and-leave-the-rest."[27]

---

[25] Homi Bhabha, *The Location of Culture*, 112.
[26] Salman Rushdie, *Imaginary Homelands*, 403.
[27] Salman Rushdie, *The Satanic Verses*, 52.

WORKS CITED

Appignanesi, Lisa, & Sara Maitland, ed. *The Rushdie File* (Syracuse NY: Syracuse UP, 1990).

Bardolph, Jacqueline. "Language is Courage: *The Satanic Verses,*" *Commonwealth: Essays and Studies* 12.1 (1989): 1–10.

Bhabha, Homi. *The Location of Culture* (London & New York: Routledge, 1994).

Durix, Jean–Pierre. *Mimesis, Genres and Post-Colonial Discourse. Deconstructing Magic Realism* (Basingstoke: Macmillan, 1998).

McHale, Brian. *Postmodernist Fiction* (London & New York: Routledge, 1987).

Rushdie, Salman. *Imaginary Homelands: Essays and Criticism 1981–1991* (London: Granta, 1991).

——. "*Midnight's Children* and *Shame,*" *Kunapipi* 7.1 (1985): 1–19.

——. *The Satanic Verses* (London & New York: Viking, 1988).

《●》

East is West
Hanif Kureishi's Urban Hybrids
and Atima Srivastava's Metropolitan Yuppies

CECILE SANDTEN

> I believe in Hindu philosophy
> I am not religious
> I am a pacifist
> I am a British Asian
>
> My identity and my history are
> defined only by myself – beyond
> politics, beyond nationality,
> beyond religion and beyond skin.
>
> Nitin Sawhney

T HE NEED TO CHARACTERIZE authors' writings with a view to interpretation, analysis, comparison and contrast always goes hand in hand with the
danger of pigeonholing them into fixed categories by applying certain labels
to their works or, worse, to the authors themselves. In the case of Hanif Kureishi, this
has been done quite frequently, whereas Atima Srivastava is relatively new in the
'ethnic/urban/postcolonial/hybrid/storyteller' section – all terms which can be applied
to both authors interchangeably.
    This essay sets out to discuss issues such as the immigrant dreamer, the urban hybrid
and the metropolitan yuppie, as well as these writers' respective attempts to redefine
nationalism. I am not greatly interested in engaging in a terminological debate about
ethnicity or race, as I would rather opt for an even greater commitment to nuances in
terms of racial taxonomy. My interest lies in a discussion of the above-mentioned
issues, and in contrast to my analysis of some of Kureishi's works I will focus on and
highlight Srivastava as a writer of the younger Asian-British generation, "further
down"[1] than Kureishi.

---

[1] Adnan Ashraf, "Into the Unknown: An Interview with Hanif Kureishi," *A Gathering of the
Tribes* 7 (1996): 3.

Hanif Kureishi has emerged as a leading voice among immigrant cultures, particularly Pakistani and Indian, in Britain. Kureishi's main interest lies in immigrant experience and ethnic conflict, though, in his recent works, such as *Intimacy* (1998) or
Midnight All Day (1998), he downplays these topics for a more personal or general
engagement with love and human relationships – indeed, as if he was suffering from a
feeling of loss or of having missed the life and spirit of the 60s altogether. India or the
introduction of Indian characters only function as signifiers of the writer's former political engagement with racism in Britain. Nonetheless, he is conceiving the immigrant
experience not as an isolated and self-contained issue but, more importantly, as an
issue pertaining to England as a multicultural society, in which acculturation processes,
diasporic situations and second-generation immigrants' fanaticism go hand in hand
with the search for a British national and cultural identity, and in that sense for hybridity. Becoming aware of this perspective, Kureishi wrote: "I realise that the issues of
race, immigration, integration and the colonial legacy are closely connected to other
issues and attitudes, they are like cracks in a wall through which you can view landscapes."[2] This leads me to the thesis that Kureishi is more and more negotiating, and
thereby erasing, that which lies between "East" and "West," unlike Salman Rushdie,
who, in his book of short stories *East, West* (1994), sees the comma as "precisely the
place where history has thrust itself."[3] Kureishi considers himself primarily British:
"People think I'm caught between two cultures, but I'm not. I'm British; I can make it
in England. It's my father who's caught."[4] Confronted with prejudices, stereotypes and
racism because of his Indian origins, Kureishi investigates a postcolonial dimension to
national identity: "It is the British, the white British, who have to learn that being British isn't what it was. Now it is a more complex thing, involving new elements. So
there must be a fresh way of seeing Britain."[5]

Atima Srivastava, who was born in Mumbai, India, and has been living in England
(in North London) since her eighth birthday, has written two novels, *Transmission*
(1992) and *Looking For Maya* (1999), as well as several short stories and film scripts
for Channel 4. The two novels basically represent young Indian women who are *not*
looking for their roots, or trying to live something down. They just want more – life,
love, success – without working too hard for it. Both of her novels are about Asian-
British culture, Indian diaspora and hybridity, while they also gesture towards a 'brave
new world' of inter-racial harmony.

Anthony Smith has listed several features of the traditional definition of national
identity: an historic territory, common myths and historic memories, a mass culture, a
common economy and common legal rights as well as duties for all members.[6] Such

---

[2] Alpana Sharma Knippling, "Hanif Kureishi," in *Writers of the Indian Diaspora: A Bio-Bibliographical Critical Sourcebook*, ed. Emmanuel S. Nelson (Westport CT: Greenwood, 1993): 161.

[3] Tobias Döring, "A Battle Between Opposing Forces and a Plea for Pluralization," review of
The Black Album, *Hard Times* 56 (1996): 20.

[4] Knippling, "Hanif Kureishi," 159.

[5] Hanif Kureishi, *My Beautiful Laundrette and Other Writings* (London: Faber & Faber, 1996):
101–102.

[6] See Anthony Smith, *National Identity* (Harmondsworth: Penguin, 1991): 11.

commonality inevitably supposes discontinuity with other groups who do not share the same features. Considering aspects such as the social and historical context of colonization, decolonization and the postcolonial situation (including immigration to Britain and the ensuing racism and multiculturalism), Kureishi therefore asks for a new delineation of national identity in the multicultural England of today. In the twenty-first century, the formerly strict limitations of nationalism and national identity can no longer be applied to a 'nation' that is continuously and thoroughly mixed. Still, there is the difficulty of integration into the former imperialistic culture and society. Kureishi's characters are in search of cultural or personal identity as a recurrent, even central, motive, though what they find is not restricted to one perspective only. Srivastava even goes a step further by presenting characters that are not only in search of cultural identity but also in search of economic possibilities and success, though not in an assimilationist, Thatcherite way as was the case for Nasser in *My Beautiful Laundrette* (1986): "Bring us champagne. And we'll drink to Thatcher and your beautiful laundrette";[7] or: "But we're professional businessmen. Not professional Pakistanis. There's no race question in the new enterprise culture."[8] In contrast, Srivastava presents her characters as Indians in Britain who seek equal opportunities regarding work and everyday life. In her first novel, *Transmission*, the protagonist Angie thinks her brother Rax is a gangster and businessman because he is making money without getting his hands dirty. Their conversation reveals how young Indians take their opportunities or search for niches and have gradually ascended the social ladder towards further equality and sameness. Mimicking his mother's accent, Rax is of the opinion that "Indian people get too much humbleness. What them people need is a good hiding."[9] DJing and organizing warehouse parties, he reflects on his problems and the motive for organizing his own business, illegally: "We never got paid. And these pasty white boys who organise them parties were just too untogether anyway. Even if we never got busted you'd have to hassle them for the money and they'd be out of it on their heroin or ecstasy or something."[10] Therefore, his politics, which are characteristic of the metropolitan yuppie generation, go as follows: "You're nobody unless you're somebody. And you're somebody if you got money. [...] If you can control you got everything. Simple really."[11]

Whether writing of school, work or home, aspects of life which have always been divided into the binary structure of modernity and tradition when it comes to the stereotypes of the Asian immigrant or diasporic community, Srivastava seems to avoid the culture-clash of first- and second-generation immigrants. The relationship between parents and children is, rather, one of mutual understanding. Even in public, this seems to prevail: in Soho, London, "the Pakistani newsagent [...] sold European papers."[12] And the next generation, like the narrator of *Looking for Maya* (an Indian girl called Mira who

---

[7] Kureishi, *My Beautiful Laundrette*, 37.

[8] *My Beautiful Laundrette*, 41.

[9] Atima Srivastava, *Transmission* (London: Serpent's Tail, 1992): 146.

[10] Srivastava, *Transmission*, 147.

[11] *Transmission*, 149.

[12] Atima Srivastava, *Looking for Maya* (London: Quartet, 1999): 1. Further page references are in the main text.

goes out with an English boyfriend, Luke) are all out for "interracial harmony" as they make "a creature which was IndianEnglish," a phrase that Mira "had stolen [...] from Indian cinema magazines which had gossip columns in that strange hybrid language full of Indian words written in English italics" (3–4). Language, as the most important site of cultural and national identity, is presented as a terrain of hybridity that is characterized by the notion of "East is West" or "EastWest." Mira coins the term "IndianEnglish" for herself in order to define her relationship, though unconsciously she subverts the concept of hybridity when she refers to the Indian cinema magazines: they are about the unreal, the illusory world of cinema and gossip, and do not have to be taken seriously. Another example of subverting hybridity is when Luke and Mira are asked by a woman from *Pinned* magazine if she could take a photo of them, as she is "doing a photo spread of Londoners. Interesting looking people" (4). Here, no national, racial or ethnic differentiation is made – both black and white are integrated into the category of urban metropolitans. The term "interesting looking people" already suggests what Srivastava is aiming at: even hybridity is no longer an issue.

Looking for Maya is a novel about a young Indian woman who is about to become a writer. Her "fake cosmopolitan experience" (3) in London is admired by her white boy-friend, Luke. Mira defines this relationship which is IndianEnglish as "white boyfriend and his dusky damsel" (4). By using the term "dusky" about herself – some people would consider this offensive – Mira mocks racist stereotypes. Further, by using the term "damsel" she defines herself as a girl or woman of high rank, indicating that she thinks of herself as somehow special and is possibly quite ambitious. Soon, Luke goes on a scholarship to India for six months, and Mira becomes the lover of Amrit, an enigmatic 47-year-old decrepit Indian man who already has several children by two different white women. But, strangely enough, Mira is drawn to him, if not obsessed with him or, rather, by the idea of love, of being loved, or by the illusion of love. This becomes clear when Mira's friend Tash warns her: "Maybe he isn't what you think. Maybe he's not the fictional person you've made him out to be" (181). This strong feeling is also expressed by the title of the book, which refers to Maya, a Hindi word for illusion. But Maya is also the name of an Indian girl – Amrit's unfulfilled love. The novel is therefore clearly about loving illusions. Both novels by Srivastava celebrate a youth and a metropolitan yuppie culture, as young people – whether British, Jewish or British Asian – like to own flashy cars and motorbikes, exorbitant CD-ROMs, and designer leathers. They drink Calvados, eat luxury chocolates or drink organic soya milk; they smoke, take drugs and have parties in posh Soho media circles (39).

Both Kureishi and Srivastava write about London with a strong sense of place: Srivastava's favourite places are North London and Soho, where her characters try to climb the social ladder and to cross all the boundaries and walls of the city. They use the city as a stage for self-representation and demonstrative consumerism. Kureishi's favourite places are the suburbs, such as Bromley, and the city. As his characters change over time, so do their surroundings – and vice versa. London, the metropolitan centre, is by nature an ethnically diverse place encapsulating a diversity of realities, which Kureishi also acknowledges in the portrayal of his characters. He uses place and time as literary devices. Pop music, sex, drugs and politics are described against the background of urban Pakistani diasporic life in Britain. In a way, Kureishi always tells his own life-story, as elements of his own youth, adolescence, and adult life are integrated into his writings. *The Buddha of Suburbia* (1990) and, even more clearly, *Intimacy* have a discernible autobiographical source.[13] Yet it is Kureishi's productive creativity that distinguishes the novel from the memoir as a conscious literary (autobiographical) construction. In general, the novel functions as a portrayal of the decade (the 1970s) in such a way as to bring it to literary, not documentary, life.[14] In his constructed autobiographical novel, most characters gain from the freedom of the postcolonial situation. Kureishi questions the concept of national identity and problematizes patronizing trends which reinforce stereotypes. Already in the first few sentences of *Buddha*, Kureishi directs the reader's attention to the questionable nature of national identity. In the first paragraph he states his idea of a postcolonial approach to identity, making fun of the 'two worlds' concept:

> My name is Karim Amir, and I am an Englishman born and bred, almost. I am often considered to be a funny kind of Englishman, a new breed as it were, having emerged from two old histories. But I don't care – Englishman I am (though not proud of it), from the South London suburbs and going somewhere. Perhaps it is the odd mixture of continents and blood, of here and there, of belonging and not, that makes me restless and easily bored.[15]

Not only are Karim's mixed identity and race presented, but it is also clearly stated that his cultural mixture is characterized by pride and resentment. At the same time, the novel's main themes are introduced: initiation, identity conflict, the outsider looking in and out of racial conflict. Further, Kureishi investigates different immigrant attitudes, points out problems, and shows different ways of coping in the country of migration. He portrays the dreams and aspirations of a pair of immigrants, Haroon and Anwar, as well as those of their children. Both Haroon and Anwar might wish to be accepted and assimilated in their new 'home' country (since a return to India would not be possible) but they are facing a constant conflict of identity, for it is very difficult to consolidate old and new traditions:

> Too many immigrants have never attained their dreams after moving to the new promised lands. Even among those who do realise their dream, many immigrants question the price paid for having done so. They refuse to forsake their identities; they struggle both with old conflicts and with revisionism within their traditions. They dream of assimilation, and they demand acceptance.[16]

As Kaleta further says, "The new immigrants are sometimes in line with the cultural crosscurrents of the twentieth century, at other times embraced by them, and at still

---

[13] Like Kureishi, Karim Amir in *The Buddha of Suburbia* is the son of an Indian immigrant father and an English mother, grew up in the suburbs of London, and in the 1970s became involved in London's theatrical scene.

[14] Kenneth C. Kaleta, *Hanif Kureishi: Postcolonial Storyteller* (Austin: U of Texas P, 1998): 74.

[15] Hanif Kureishi, *The Buddha of Suburbia* (London: Faber & Faber, 1990): 3.

[16] Kaleta, *Hanif Kureishi*, 14.

other times haunted by them."[17] Thus London-born Jamila defends her Indian origins and combats racism, oppression and prejudices against minority groups. She has assimilated by taking over parts of British culture but at the same time demands for herself and for all members of ethnic minorities equal rights in British society.

Kureishi shows that identity is always fluid, never stable. Every character, whether of mixed descent or of 'pure' British or Asian descent, constructs his or her own identity out of the various fragments of today's multicultural society. Kureishi turns to a notion of identity that is characterized by self-definition and, ultimately, by hybridity in urban England. The second-generation immigrants, Karim and Jamila, are constantly changing, fighting various battles and breaking down the barriers of fixed identities, like the traditional Indian relationship between man and woman or heterosexuality. After facing some difficulties and problems when growing up, they are now able to draw strength from their lack of fixed identity and integrate Indian and English features into their personalities, which enables them to become strong-willed and independent. In overcoming the old binary systems and thus embracing hybridity, they see a possibility of enrichment. In Kureishi's case, the term 'postcolonial' thus comes to signify a certain mode of labelling: urban, metropolitan, Asian, hybrid, are words which can all be used interchangeably.[18]

Whether or not the terms 'hybrid' or 'postcolonial' can be applied to Kureishi (we shall see that the case of Atima Srivastava is even more difficult) is a question that should also be addressed from his own perspective, through an analysis of both his fictional writings and his critical output in essays and interviews. In a 1995 interview Kureishi makes it quite clear that the terms and labels which are commonly used to characterize his writings are not his own. Asked whether he detects "any particular direction being taken by the new cultural fusions and hybridities," Kureishi answers as follows:

> There are new hybridities and fusions as you say which are springing up all the time. As long as people from different worlds or different aspects of the same world mix together, there will be new fusions and new hybrids. It's impossible to say what they will be.[19]

His disapproval of being seen in terms of these categories and fashionable labels becomes very clear in the following statement from the same interview:

> Our specific cultural inheritance, as you put it, is often used by the owners of the media only in very specific ways and [...] we are seen as presenting the so-called ethnic point of view and that's what we do. When the BBC or Channel 4 need an Asian they get us in and we do whatever we do. I'm sure people like us or the next generation to us, further

---

[17] Kaleta, *Hanif Kureishi*, 199.

[18] Emmanuel S. Nelson included Hanif Kureishi in his *Writers of the Indian Diaspora: A Bio-Bibliographical Critical Sourcebook* (1993), without even questioning his mixed parentage or his upbringing as an Asian–British subject in England. Kenneth C. Kaleta, in his *Hanif Kureishi: Postcolonial Storyteller*, does the same with regard to the term 'post-colonial', since the term is here systematically used as a generic label considered from a metropolitan perspective.

[19] Kureishi, "Into the Unknown," 3.

down, is going to become rather impatient with those kinds of categories because, as you say, we are all such mixtures and there are so many possibilities within us, and I hope there will come a time when we are seen beyond the fact that we have some kind of cultural background that the owners of the media wish to use, sometimes for the best of reasons, sometimes for the worst, and sometimes for a mixture, but often we're confined by what's special about us as artists, and that limitation can be rather tiresome.[20]

Kureishi considers labels like 'ethnic' and 'hybrid' and the generic usage of the term 'Asian' to be confining. However difficult the question of how to 'categorize' works by Kureishi or Srivastava, I would prefer phrases like black or Asian-British writing: indeed, Kureishi's consciousness of being 'black' and of wanting to fight racism has been strongly influenced by the Black Power movement in the USA during the 1960s,[21] whereas Srivastava clearly considers herself as an Asian-British, rather than a postcolonial, writer.[22] Her protagonist Mira says in *Looking for Maya*: "I had taken a Literature option in my final year called Post Colonial Literature and studied Naipaul and Rushdie and Desai, been given lots of A3 photocopied articles on Race Deconstruction, which I'd used to line my underwear drawers with" (21), thereby mocking the postcolonial nomenclature and its ideological contexts. As I suggested, this sort of stance is vindicated by critics like Kaleta, whose evasion of the questions of neo-colonialism and power relations is symptomatic of much 'postcolonial' discourse today.

However, from an interview with Atima Srivastava as well as from her novels, one learns that the next generation, as Kureishi prophesied, is rather impatient with those categories and labels. Srivastava has her protagonist ask herself if she, too, is inauthentic, a "hybrid out of place, with a cockney accent and a yen for decadence, contradicting the deep-seated austerity of a country [India] which had changed beyond contradiction" (88). And the protagonist's parents snigger at those who they thought were hybrids: people, like the British soldiers who looked red and puffy and could not even speak English properly, or those sahib men, those Indians who spoke English like English gentlemen and used a fork to eat dahl and rice (87–88). Though racism against Asian and black British people is also mentioned in her novels, especially in a retrospective account of the protagonist's school life in *Transmission*, nevertheless Srivastava, while acknowledging severe changes in India itself, constantly subverts the notion of hybridity in favour of an even more open concept of national and cultural identity. Typically, this accommodates job opportunities and a certain self-confident behaviour which can be ascribed to the metropolitan yuppie generation: "I was a successful television researcher on the way up and I was earning more money than all of them... and damn goodlooking to boot."[23] Her young pubbing and clubbing protagonists decide for themselves to which class or organization they want to belong and they even adopt different life-styles simultaneously: "If the kind of people I worked with ever came to a place like this they would probably have a heart attack. It was full of old black men

---

[20] Kureishi, "Into the Unknown," 3.
[21] See Kureishi, *My Beautiful Laundrette*, 76–77.
[22] She said this at a reading in Bremen, 12 November 1999.
[23] Srivastava, *Transmission*, 9.

swaying at the bar, young dudes in knitted tams wrapped around their thick dreadlocks, dirty looking white punks wearing torn leather jackets..."[24] By contrast, Angie, who works as a freelance television researcher, describes her new boss, Madelaine, as follows: "A woman with a broad New York accent and expensive diamante earrings extended her hand. She was wearing a suit with padded shoulders and too much Poison."[25] To have a broad New York accent signifies metropolitan life, experience, and ultimately success.

Kaleta is not wrong in proposing his "outsider-turned-insider" theory,[26] when he presents Kureishi as someone who grew up as a "racial misfit" but then became, through his storytelling, "an integral part of that world on the other side of the glass." Postcolonial writers are often seen as "hybrid in the sense that they juxtapose and fuse objects, languages and signifying practices from different and normally separated domains and [...] challenge an official, puritanical public order."[27] Kaleta uses the term "hybridity" to describe everything about Kureishi himself, from his "hybrid, cinematic dream" to his "hybridity of the urban condition."[28] The critic also has a biological notion of hybridity in mind, since he refers to Kureishi as a "racial misfit" or a "racial mix."[29] He describes Kureishi's characters as "often racially hyphenated [...] hybrid immigrants [that] are usually culturally hyphenated as well."[30]

Homi Bhabha refers to Salman Rushdie as a "hybridizing" writer.[31] This would be a useful terminological clarification for Kureishi, too. Rather than *being* essentially hybrid, which would carry unsavoury implications, to the effect that he may be leading a "bastardized life"[32] also, Kureishi employs a literary technique or a method of composition that results in the 'hybridization' of culture through the depiction of its heterogeneity and diversity. This accords with his literary technique of actively constructing reality as fiction in which both are juxtaposed. The "outsider-turned-insider" theory that Kaleta proposes can, then, also be applied to Srivastava since she, even more clearly than Kureishi, uses an assimilationist style when looking at issues like language, setting or characters. Both her novels are classic rite-of-passage novels[33] written as first-person

---

[24] Srivastava, *Transmission*, 11.

[25] *Transmission*, 32.

[26] Kaleta, *Hanif Kureishi*, 4–5.

[27] Pnina Werbner, "Introduction: The Dialectics of Cultural Hybridity," in *Debating Cultural Hybridity: Multi-Cultural Identities and the Politics of Anti-Racism*, ed. Pnina Werbner & Tariq Modood (London: Zed, 1997): 1.

[28] Kaleta, *Hanif Kureishi*, 22.

[29] *Hanif Kureishi*, 20.

[30] *Hanif Kureishi*, 205.

[31] Homi K. Bhabha, "Introduction" to *Nation and Narration*, ed. Bhabha (London: Routledge, 1990): 6.

[32] Sabine Broeck, "White Fatigue, Or: Supplementary Notes on Hybridity," unpublished MS (2000): 5.

[33] See Mark Stein, "The Black British *Bildungsroman* and the Transformation of Britain: Connectedness across Difference," in *Unity in Diversity Revisited? British Literature and Culture in the 1990s*, ed. Barbara Korte & Klaus Peter Müller (Tübingen: Gunter Narr, 1998): 92.

narration. In *Looking for Maya*, the protagonist's Indian parents, "RaviKavi" (who are poets themselves), have returned to India. They seem to serve as a constant reminder of Mira's past and they represent the fundamental difference in values between East and West. However, because they are a world away from the Cambridge-educated Amrit and from Mira herself, it becomes obvious that they no longer have a strong influence on their daughter's life. As a consequence, Mira, who was brought up in Britain, does not experience "the phenomenon of migration, displacement, life in a minority group" (as Salman Rushdie put it)[34] but has, like her creator, become an insider.

Neither Kureishi nor Srivastava presents homogeneous Asian communities. Srivastava does not even include many Indian characters in her novels, to show that it is their relationships with whites, blacks, Jews and their 'assimilationist', and in this sense metropolitan, perspective that counts – though it might be 'faked'. But neither do her characters fit a stereotypical representation of immigrated and assimilated Indians. Though there might be one exception to this rule (in a minor character like Maama ji, Angie's uncle in *Transmission*), Srivastava subverts the stereotype of the first-generation immigrants and the diasporic situation: on the one hand, Maama ji is all for Indian food, Indian magazines, and Indian videos;on the other, he is obsessed with the idea of buying in secondhand shops like Oxfam. "He had come to England in 1969 for further study, his head full of Wordsworth and Shakespeare,"[35] and thus embodies the Indian stereotype *par excellence*. He thinks that English "television is rubbish" and only finds it good when he sees Angie's name on it – in a programme on *Cooking around the British Isles*.[36] In all, Maama ji reconstructs his own Indian reality out of what is offered to him as an immigrant in England, but he reconstructs his memories of India without being stereotypically obsessed with the past, traditions and values and belief systems.

Kureishi also uses stereotypical characters that at the same time subvert the stereotype. His characters adopt one position or the other but constantly construct and reconstruct their own identities against any stereotypical invention. The 'ethnic' characters in *The Buddha of Suburbia* are so diverse that ethnicity has to be seen as a synonym not for homogeneity but, rather, for diversity. Identity, as Kobena Mercer put it, "only becomes an issue when it is in crisis, when something assumed to be fixed, coherent and stable is displaced by the experience of doubt and uncertainty."[37] Kureishi depicts the doubt and uncertainty surrounding British identity by replacing this supposedly fixed category with a notion of identity as fluid and multiple. In Srivastava's protagonists, doubt and uncertainty are replaced by a search for personal and professional opportunities of the kind also pursued by the Asian-British musician, composer and philosopher Nitin Sawhney, whom I quoted in my epigraph. By contrast, Shahid in *The Black*

---

[34] Salman Rushdie, *Imaginary Homelands. Essays amd Criticism 1981–1991* (London: Granta, 1991): 20.

[35] Srivastava, *Transmission*, 22.

[36] See Srivastava, *Transmission*, 22.

[37] Kobena Mercer, "Welcome to the Jungle: Identity and Diversity in Postmodern Politics," in *Identity: Community, Culture, Difference*, ed. Jonathan Rutherford (London: Lawrence & Wishart, 1990): 43.

Album feels the pressures that come with social and racial expectations and the "politics of identity":

These days everyone was insisting on their identity, coming out as a man, woman, gay, black, Jew – brandishing whichever features they could claim, as if without a tag they wouldn't be human. Shahid, too, wanted to belong to his people. But first he had to know them, their past and what they hoped for.[38]

Identity is both constructed and assigned in Kureishi's novels, especially in *The Black Album*. Shahid learns to see beyond these 'tags' and, after affiliating himself with different groups and searching for his "real, natural self," tries to reconcile the "many warring selves" within him.[39] This is a development with no final conclusion, for "there [is] no fixed self" as "surely our several selves melted and mutated daily" and consequently there have to be "innumerable ways of being in the world."[40]

Transmission is about Ungelliee, called Angie, a young Indian woman who is eager to establish herself as a serious researcher in the media in London's trendy Soho. The novel's title has three meanings. First, it stands for sexually transmitted diseases, here Aids (HIV). Second, it stands for the transmission of stories that were "transported, transmitted from the Indian village to town and from town to a [European] metropolis."[41] Indeed, Angie's father is a writer and, through a picture that forms in her mind like a collage of old photographs, stories, as well as her own memories, programmes about India she had seen on TV, or trashy films, she gets to know India.[42] Interestingly, the picture which she conjures up "was probably unreal, a mish mash for sure."[43] And third, the title stands for broadcasting: the novel is about a documentary movie about a young girl who is HIV-positive – though Angie, who first established contact with this girl and who directs the film, has moral scruples and finally destroys it before it can be broadcast by Channel 4.

In *Looking for Maya*, Mira and Luke also draw on memories, and Mira puts forward the idea of "Race memory," which she defines as follows: "You might not have been born in India or Africa for instance, but the memory of your ancestors lingers in your blood [...] engraved in deep memory" (41). But immediately she qualifies this by adopting a more realistic definition of memory: "You can only remember what happened for real. All the rest is suggestion and fantasy" (41). Yet, when she thinks about Amrit, she has the feeling that she had known him once, an impression to be placed somewhere between fact and fiction or myth (41). So memory is relative and can be constructed or re-constructed according to one's own state of mind, feeling and position. To invoke hybridity in this case, just because it is an Indian writer who is responbile for inventing identities, does not seem particularly necessary or relevant.

---

[38] Hanif Kureishi, *The Black Album* (London: Faber & Faber, 1995): 92.
[39] Kureishi, *The Black Album*, 147.
[40] *The Black Album*, 274.
[41] Srivastava, *Transmission*, 109.
[42] See *Transmission*, 111.
[43] *Transmission*, 112.

The same is true of India as an idea: the India that Angie gets to know is, like Karim's, a secondhand India, imagined and transmitted, so that authenticity or originality get lost. But unlike Karim, Angie and Srivastava's other characters accept being Indian – or, to be more precise, their Asian-British identity. They accept their Indian past and history, their skin colour, their identities as individuals among individuals. They do not regret anything, but make choices without being positioned from the outside because of their race, class or gender, as opposed to Karim and Shahid, who are still struggling with their hybrid identities. In *Looking for Maya*, India becomes a place that everybody can use according to one's individual needs: as a site for cultural adventure or as just place to go for a holiday – as the Indian protagonist herself frequently does. India is then no longer privileged in the search for cultural and national identity, nor is it a signifier of cultural difference. Even Mira's strange love-relationship with Amrit does not imply any search for national or cultural identity; rather, it shows different perspectives on life and on love, as well as the different options, mythologies and fates available in a multicultural and multiracial England.

Kureishi characterizes himself as a "cultural translator" and as someone who belongs to a "multi-cultural society."[44] Mediating and interpreting, Kureishi links the changes in British society to "the psychological loosening of the idea of Empire."[45] He manages to embrace difference and to stretch the boundaries of otherwise limiting categories. Hybridity, for him, means literary "non-fixity," as he points out when describing *The Black Album*:

> The book was an attempt to just present a young man's journey through a number of worlds. It wasn't as if I had any kind of final point of view. I think the good thing about writing is that you don't have to have a final point of view, that you can try out different ways of seeing, or different selves.[46]

He presents characters that are British and Asian at the same time. Therefore, one could say that his works present a fusion and a 'transculturation', in the sense that they delineate, in the words of Mary Louise Pratt, a "contact zone" or a social space where "disparate cultures meet, clash, grapple with each other, often in highly asymmetrical relations of domination and subordination." Consequently, hybridity is presented as a "process of inter-cultural negotiation."[47]

Kureishi does not redefine national identity, but presents social reality within national boundaries which no longer fit the traditional concept of the nation-state but are characterized instead by multiculturalism and cosmopolitanism. His depiction of social realities is an ambivalent narration of the nation; or, to use Bhabha's words, "The ambivalent, antagonistic perspective of nation and narration will establish the cultural boundaries of the nation so that they may be acknowledged as 'containing' thresholds of

[44] Hanif Kureishi, *Plays One* (London: Faber & Faber, 1999): x.
[45] Kureishi, *Plays One*, x.
[46] Ashraf, "Into the Unknown" 2.
[47] Quoted in Ania Loomba, *Colonialism/Postcolonialism* (London: Routledge, 1998): 68.

meaning that must be crossed, erased, and translated in the process of cultural production."[48]

For her part, Srivastava depicts characters that are beyond hybridity, beyond the need to bridge binarisms. Both writers are English writers who draw from the English literary tradition with which they grew up. Kureishi is not a spokesperson for a given community but an explorer of social reality in an inceasingly hybrid, multicultural society. He has written about immigrant experiences and racism, but cannot be confined to this topic alone. As to Srivastava, she leaves aside the immigrant experience and racism and engages with the social and cultural as well as the personal struggle of her characters – whatever their nationality – as they strive to achieve personal success or to enhance their careers. The depiction of "bastardized life"[49] in Kureishi's urban hybrids has often been identified, but this is an aspect which seems less relevant in the light of his more recent work. Srivastava circumvents hybridity altogether. Both of these authors can, then, be seen to represent stages in the process of arriving at some sort of 'centre' position: Kureishi is a post-immigration writer who has hybridized the diaspora situation; and Srivastava goes even further than this.

WORKS CITED

Ashraf, Adnan. "Into the Unknown: An Interview with Hanif Kureishi," *A Gathering of the Tribes* 7 (1996): 1–8.

Bhabha, Homi K. "Introduction" to *Nation and Narration*, ed. Bhabha (London: Routledge, 1990).

Broeck, Sabine. "White Fatigue, Or: Supplementary Notes on Hybridity," unpublished MS (2000): 1–12.

Döring, Tobias. "A Battle Between Opposing Forces and a Plea for Pluralization," rev. of *The Black Album*, *Hard Times* 56 (1996): 18–20.

Kaleta, Kenneth C. *Hanif Kureishi: Postcolonial Storyteller* (Austin: U of Texas P, 1998).

Knippling, Alpana Sharma. "Hanif Kureishi," in *Writers of the Indian Diaspora: A Bio-Bibliographical Critical Sourcebook*, ed. Emmanuel S. Nelson (Westport CT: Greenwood, 1993): 159–68.

Kureishi, Hanif. *The Black Album* (London: Faber & Faber, 1995).

——. *The Buddha of Suburbia* (London: Faber & Faber, 1990).

——. *Intimacy* (London: Faber & Faber, 1998).

——. *Midnight All Day* (London: Faber & Faber, 1998).

——. *My Beautiful Laundrette and Other Writings* (London: Faber & Faber, 1996).

——. *Plays One* (London: Faber & Faber, 1999).

Loomba, Ania. *Colonialism/Postcolonialism* (London: Routledge, 1998).

Mercer, Kobena. "Welcome to the Jungle: Identity and Diversity in Postmodern Politics," in *Identity: Community, Culture, Difference*, ed. Jonathan Rutherford (London: Lawrence & Wishart, 1990): 43–71.

Rushdie, Salman. *Imaginary Homelands: Essays and Criticism 1981–1991* (London: Granta, 1991).

Smith, Anthony. *National Identity* (Harmondsworth: Penguin, 1991).

Srivastava, Atima. *Looking for Maya* (London: Quartet, 1999).

——. *Transmission* (London: Serpent's Tail, 1992).

---

[48] Bhabha, "Introduction," 4.
[49] Broeck, "White Fatigue," 5.

Stein, Mark. "The Black British *Bildungsroman* and the Transformation of Britain: Connectedness across Difference," in *Unity in Diversity Revisited? British Literature and Culture in the 1990s*, ed. Barbara Korte & Klaus Peter Müller (Tübingen: Gunter Narr, 1998): 89–105.

Werbner, Pnina. "Introduction: The Dialectics of Cultural Hybridity," in *Debating Cultural Hybridity: Multi-Cultural Identities and the Politics of Anti-Racism*, ed. Pnina Werbner & Tariq Modood (London: Zed, 1997): 1–26.

《•》

Rescue Me? No, Thanks!
A Wicked Old Woman and *Anita and Me*

CHRISTINE VOGT–WILLIAM

> Rescue me!
> Oh take me in your arms!
> Rescue me!
> I want your tender charms
> Coz' I'm lonely and I'm blue
> I need you and your love too
> Come on and rescue me
>
> Come on, baby and rescue me!
> Coz' I need you by my side
> Can't you see that I'm lonely?
>
> Come on and take my heart
> Take your love and conquer every part
> Coz' I'm lonely and I'm blue
>
> Come on and take my hand
> Come on, baby, and be my man
> Coz' I love you
> Coz' I want you
>
> Take me, baby
> Love me, baby
> Need me, baby
> Can't you see that I'm lonely
> Come on and rescue me![1]

ONE OF THE MOST COMMON SITUATIONS depicted in postcolonial literature is that of the migrant in Western societies, who finds herself, more often than not, in conflict with her 'home' culture as well as that of the 'new' country. The present migrant experience is typified by rootlessness, displacement and intercultural uneasiness. Symptoms of intercultural uneasiness are racism and ideological discrimination. While dealing with these external maladies, the migrant also has to confront the conflicts generated within herself by the influences and demands of both

---

[1] Fontella Bass©EMI Music.

the cultures she is part of. Hybridity, a term introduced into postcolonial discourse by Homi Bhabha, is the label given this phenomenon.

Putting aside Homi Bhabha's claim that hybridity is the basis where a "subversive political effect of migrant discourse on the dominant Western episteme"[2] is practised, a more exact form of migrant hybridity remains to be defined – its colonial forerunners and postcolonial origins are not necessarily the determining factors in hybridization. In contrast, the postcolonial basis of globalized hybrid communities comes to light as the result of a political intervention by the migrants themselves, especially when they realize that their marginal status is politically significant within a postcolonial criticism of hegemonic Western discourse.

The migrant hybrid identity generally develops on the territory of a Western state which might be, to all intents and purposes, a former colonial power. For my purposes in this essay, I will be concentrating on migrant writing by Indian writers in Britain, more specifically that of Indian women writers. The works of these writers often, and sometimes exclusively, illustrate their own situations of migrancy, displacement and alienation from the mother country.

Until recent years Asian British literature itself had excited relatively little scholarly interest. The academic and media spotlights had been trained on the actual lived situations of Asians in Britain, especially those of Indian women and young Indians, whereby the general assumption was that the Indian women and youngsters had difficulties in culling their identities from the existing bicultural social framework.[3] Their lives and experiences are reduced to a seemingly unending series of psychological conflicts, whereby they appear to the British mainstream to have fractured and rootless concepts of their selves. They allegedly yearn for the 'progressive' liberties of Western society while simultaneously being forced to comply with the rules and regulations of their supposedly 'non-liberated' families, who are at pains to keep the 'old', 'home' cultural traditions and customs alive in an alien atmosphere.

Although to a certain extent this is no doubt true and it is in itself a very real problem, other important aspects like racism and socio-economic status are often disregarded. Another way of treating the difficulties of Indian British migrants and their children reductively is to adopt an ethnicist perspective; Avtar Brah defines this as follows:

> Ethnicism, I would suggest, defines the experience of racialized groups primarily in "culturalist" terms: that is, it posits "ethnic difference" as the primary modality around which social life is constituted and experienced. [...] a group identified as culturally different is assumed to be internally homogeneous, when this is patently not the case. [...] ethnicist discourses seek to impose stereotypic notions of "common cultural need" upon heterogeneous groups with diverse social aspirations and interests. They often fail to address the relationship between "difference" and the social relations of power in which it may be inscribed."[4]

---

[2] See Monika Fludernik, "Colonial vs. Cosmopolitan Hybridity," in *Hybridity and Postcolonialism: Twentieth Century Indian Literature* (Tübingen: Stauffenburg, 1998): 261–90.

[3] See Martina Michel, "Under Cover: Ravinder Randhawa's *A Wicked Old Woman*," *anglistik & englischunterricht* 60 (1997):143–57.

[4] Avtar Brah, "Difference, Diversity and Differentiation" in *"Race," Culture & Difference*, ed. James Donald & Ali Rattansi (London: Sage, 1992): 129 .

Thus, their essential difference is exoticized from that of the British while being independent of other significant social experiences; thus, culturalist views on the modes of living of Indian migrants and their children presuppose a homogeneity among Indians which does not leave room for class, caste and gender relations within the community. In the novels to be discussed here, I have found that the novelists have taken the trouble to depict the diversified experiences of their protagonists and their Indian contemporaries, with respect to the various constellations of their familial, socio-economic and dialectal situations.

In most Indian-British novels, the host culture is often conceived of as being antagonistic to the migrant minority (whereby the latter could be considered a threat, since it might usurp the power of the previous colonial apparatus). This is a frequently encountered situation, since immigrants of working–class status often experience social discrimination based on racist attitudes, which tend to treat Indians and other migrant groups as racially inferior. Bhabha maintains that the host culture (in this case, the former colonial power, England) is both fascinated and threatened by the difference of the migrant. The common thread running through most migrant novels is the fascination for the Other – an ambivalent sensation which invokes attraction and anxiety in equal measure – a rather 'unheimlich' sensation, if one were to consider Homi Bhabha's term in the more popular use of the German word.

Bhabha believes that the fundamental process of identifying the Other, on the side of the host, is based on the fact that he experiences anxiety because the 'foreign body' has already successfully infiltrated the host's sanctum, as it were, his space of identity articulation – where he could safely say "I'm British." However, the migrant is here to stay, no matter how often she says to herself "I'll go home some day. I'm just renting the country!" More often than not, the migrant concludes by setting up a more permanent abode in the new mother country. The host is anxious about, yet fascinated by, this strange new entity, while the Other is just as fascinated by the host herself. Hence the *Unheimlichkeit*, the ambivalence of the 'unhomeliness'of it all, since the host can no longer claim his home, his turf as his own. The stranger Other has come, thinking to call this new country her new 'home'. These are the theoretical considerations I will apply to my reading of two novels, written by two Indian-British women writers of Punjabi origin.

I take issue, however, with the fact that Homi Bhabha's theories of hybridity seem to propound a singular purpose lodged at the heart of migrant writing: that the native's sole aim in writing herself back into the mainstream is to undermine the hegemony of the dominant colonialist discourse. According to Bhabha, the native or, rather, the hybrid native, transplanted from her indigenous society into a new one, is perceived as living to fulfil this one subversive function.

But what of those natives, synonymous with those hybrid identities in today's postmodern societies, leading postcolonial lives? Are their existences for the sole purpose of setting up an alternative discourse to topple the master's building blocks? What of those women who are at pains, in Shashi Deshpande's words, to "make life possible" for themselves, to go about the business of day-to-day living in the new host culture? Have they accepted that 'freedom' as bestowed on them, without questioning whether or not it suits their purposes, their histories, their present multicultural social contexts? These are some of the questions which occurred to me while writing this essay. I will thus try to illustrate my criticism of Bhabha's notion of hybridity through my reading of these fictional texts.

I will be looking at the conflicts inherent in the Indian-British immigrant experience – more specifically, at the way in which the Indian female protagonists negotiate the demands of the two cultures which go into their cultural make-up. The novels I will be looking are Meera Syal's *Anita and Me* (1997) and Ravinder Randhawa's *A Wicked Old Woman* (1987). Both novels can be read as *Bildungsromane*, which trace the developments of the protagonists while exploring in varying degrees of complexity the issue of taking freedom on one's own terms and not giving in to the condescension of the dominant culture, which is more often that not based on the racist stereotypes rampant even today. I would like to note at this point that the particular novels I have chosen to elaborate my ideas are by no means representative of the gamut of Indian British writing.

Anita and Me

Syal's narrative explores a particular year in her protagonist's life where she hovers on the brink of adolescence. The protagonist, Meena, narrates her childhood experiences of growing up in the only Indian family in a typical working-class mining village in the heart of the Black Country in the early 1970s. It becomes quite apparent that the young girl's struggle for independence while growing up is augmented by her increasing awareness of her difference from the mainstream of English life, which she yearns to be a part of.

Meena is fascinated by Anita Rutter, the bad girl of Tollington village, and yearns to be accepted by her as her best friend, for Anita is everything Meena is not: beautiful, popular, irreverent, grown-up for her age and, of course, white. Moreover, being Anita's best friend brings the added bonus of not being different and of being accepted; this, of course, blends in with Meena's growing awareness of her brown skin in a white society; a marker of her difference, her otherness.

Besides being under Anita's spell, Meena is secretly in love with Sam Lowbridge, the leader of the village skinhead gang. He instigates attacks on foreigners, notably Indians, and openly articulates his racist sentiments at a public festival, jolting Meena into a realization of the palpable undercurrent of racist feeling among many of the villagers, whom she had largely considered her friends. Though these attacks were not levelled consciously at Meena and her family, she suddenly becomes aware of her difference and realizes that, despite all her efforts to be assimilated, she will have to live with her Otherness. However, Sam seems to have a liking for Meena and is kind to her on several occasions. At the end of the novel, when Meena finally comes to terms with her double heritage, she sees Sam for what he really is and does not idolize him further. When Meena finally confronts him about his brutish behaviour at the village fest; he claims to have always considered her as different from the others – the other foreigners of the community as well as the other Tollington girls:

> "Those things you said at the spring fete, what were you trying to do?"
> Sam shrugged.[...] "I wanted to make people listen," he said finally.

"You wanted to hurt people you mean!" I yelled at him. "How could you say it, in front of me? My dad? To anyone? How can you believe that shit?"
Sam grabbed me by the wrists. [...] "When I said them," he rasped, "I never meant yow, Meena! It was all the others, not yow!
"I am the others, Sam. You did mean me."[5]

Meena sees through Sam's tempting offer to free her from the racist stereotypes; it's as if he were accepting her as an 'honorary member' of white Tollington society. She vehemently turns down his attempt to treat her differently, taking her stand as one of the others, refusing to deny that other half of her multicultural heritage just to belong to the mainstream. At this, Sam realizes that Meena has taken freedom on her own terms, to stand up for herself and others like her; she is not going to deny herself, to please the likes of Sam Lowbridge by accepting the definition he has been pleased to confer on her. Sam is powerless against Meena's new-found confidence and her ability to defend herself:

> Sam gripped my wrists tighter for support. "You've always been the best wench in Tollington. Anywhere. Dead funny! [...] But yow was never gonna look at me, yow won't be staying will ya? You can move on. How come? How come I can't?" And then he kissed me [...] and I let him, feeling mighty and huge, knowing I had won and that everytime he saw another Meena on the street corner he would remember this and feel totally powerless. (314)

On one level, one has to note, Sam is right: Meena is not really the 'others'; she is a hybrid – born of Indian immigrant parents, in Britain. Unlike her English friends and her Indian parents, Meena does not have the role-models she needs thaa could help her to come to terms with her hybrid status. She does finally find potential surrogate parents, who lead hybrid lives like hers – Harinder Singh and his French wife Mireille, the mysterious couple who live in the Big House and who had

> "lived, you know, through all of you, so fascinating [...] we felt proud like parents. There are not many places left like this now [...] And in here we only needed each other. 'Oo else would have understood us, strange creatures like us?" (319)

Ah, but Meena understood them and was fascinated by them in turn, and disappointed by the fact that they

> had kept them hidden for all these years, wasting their gifts and zest for life instead of sharing them with people whom they could have inspired and entertained, for whom they could have been living proof that the exotic and the different can add to and enrich even the sleepiest backwater. (319

They show her that it is possible to reconcile the differences between her two cultures and to form a composite identity for herself. Meena is conscious of who she is – an Indian-British girl who has found her own space and is able to move between both her worlds without wanting to discard either one.

---

[5] Meera Syal, *Anita and Me* (London: Flamingo, 1997): 313. Further page references are in the main text.

There is an additional dimension to this new-found acceptance: Meena has the freedom to 'move on' to new and better things because she has an increasing number of options, thanks to the love, support and acceptance of her parents as well as her own diligence at school and her personal ambition to make something more of her life. Sam, Anita and many others of Meena's contemporaries lack these mainstays. Indeed, Meena has managed to establish a firm basis for her fledgling identity, by finally recognizing her superiority over Sam; she turns Sam's stereotypical racial prejudices against himself; since he does not seem to have any scope for development, he is forced to see himself as the 'Other'.[6] Meena has won a significant victory over Sam and over herself:

> "I [...] hated Anita for speaking to me all those years ago [...] hated Sam for not being cruel to me so that I could have dismissed him long ago, and mainly hated myself for having forgotten all about it [...] all that potential, all that hope all gone because I made friends once with Anita Rutter." (321–22)

This hate and anger enables her to free herself finally in a twofold sense – both from the stereotypical framework set up for people like her by Sam and those of his ilk and from the yearning to be like and be accepted by Anita and Sam.

Considering that Meena is still young, the end of the novel evokes the promise of more to come: Meena's journey into young adulthood has just begun. Thus, the encounter with Sam and the final split from Anita are just the beginning of a long list of successes and failures on her way to her self.

A Wicked Old Woman

Randhawa's story is about an Indian woman, Kulwant, who grew up in an unnamed English city and at a certain point in her adult life starts taking stock of her life. Lonely and disillusioned, her marriage wrecked, her children estranged, Kulwant creates a new persona for herself, that of a wandering, homeless, helpless old woman, who needs a stick to move about. Dressed in her Oxfam castoffs and sporting NHS spectacles, she goes through life confronting the spectres of the past and the present, taking life as it comes. The story is narrated in the third-person, incorporating flashbacks to the past from Kulwant's perspective interpersed with other mini-narratives of the other female characters who all stand in some connection to Kulwant.

As she ventures from one tryst to another, trying to make peace with her children and coming to terms with the consequences of her decisions of long ago, Kulwant encounters others of her kind, women who have been cast off, who have not been able to find a place for themselves, who have not found their voices and who refuse to open their eyes. Another key figure in the novel whose fate is intertwined with that of the older Kulwant is Rani, a young Indian- British woman who, in contrast to Kulwant, chooses to ignore her Indian heritage and embrace the British aspect of her life instead. One symptom of this is her adoption of the name Rosalind, instead of Rani, the name given

[6] Mark Stein, "The Black British Bildungsroman and the Transformation of Britain: Connectedness Across Difference," in *Unity in Diversity Revisited? British Literature and Culture in the 1990s*, ed. Barbara Korte & Klaus Peter Müller (Tübingen: Gunter Narr, 1998): 89–105.

her by her mother, Shanti. Rosalind leaves home and wanders around town aimlessly, shunning all contact with the Indian community as fiercely as Kuli embraced it. As the novel progresses, she moves in with a squatter group, where her obvious exoticized difference from the white drug-addicts living there serves to get her into rather unpleasant situations. In her confused way she makes her own choices to prevent herself being allocated some predefined role among the other Indian-British women of her acquaintance and to find her own niche in life, however uncomfortable it may be. After escaping an attempted rape and killing her would-be assailant, she ends up in a coma in hospital. In the latter part of the novel, the women in the story, including Kulwant, come together in their efforts to wake her out of her coma and to heal her. In the process they find companionship and healing themselves.

As interesting as Rani/Rosalind's story is, my purpose here is to examine the main protagonist's progress in the novel; hence I will turn back to Kulwant and her adventures. Kulwant's family consider her "a wicked old woman" because she does not do what is expected of a good Indian wife and mother; nor does she conform to the ideas of her English friends and acquaintances. The pivotal scene in the narrative is a flashback Kulwant has of herself as a teenager, which appears at the beginning of the novel. It is an account of her first and disastrous love-affair with a young Englishman, Michael. He appears to be madly in love with her and attempts to force a marriage proposal on her, supposedly in order to liberate her from the restrictive traditions and customs of the Punjabi community. He wants to save her from an arranged Indian marriage, where she apparently has no say in the matter of choosing her husband.

Kulwant, who is seventeen at the time, is astute enough to realize that Michael does not really love her; in fact, he patronizes her and tries to force her into marriage (which he has arranged for her!) without even consulting her or considering the consequences of such a decision. He was going to save her from the 'heathen' depravity of her Indian culture and at the same time enlighten her about good, solid, English values. This sense of missionary purpose is reflected in the nickname given to Michael by Kulwant and her English friend Caroline: he is known as the Archangel. This rather ironic label puts Michael into the customary stereotype of the colonial, Christian, English gentleman in all his arrogance, who is convinced of his own missionary munificence towards the 'heathen' colonial subjects, the Indians, who were made to believe in their own inferiority. As C.L. Innes observes, Michael's behaviour can be read as

> a shadowing of the larger history of England's relationship with India, from its status as 'jewel in the crown' of the empire and the laboratory for turning Indians into British subjects through education (as well as other and blunter means), to India's assertion of independence and emphasis on cultural nationalism.[7]

Michael vindictively accuses her of exoticizing himself and the English; indeed he seems to be turning the tables on her while simultaneously defining her Otherness in rather uncomplimentary terms, when she tries to defend her right to decide what she wants for herself:

---

[7] C.L. Innes, "Wintering: Making a Home in Britain," in *Other Britain, Other British: Contemporary Multicultural Fiction,* ed. A. Robert Lee (London: Pluto, 1995): 21–34

> "But I didn't go out with you to marry you. I didn't think that […]"
> "What did you think? You thought you'd find out about the weird customs of the English […] We're not animals in a zoo. And I thought you were the shy and innocent one. You were just holding back […] watching me. You never took us seriously […] unfair […] that's another English idea for you […]
>   "But not everybody marries their boyfriend […]
>   "But they might […] for those who play fair […] I forget, you wouldn't know about playing fair, would you? […] you had me feeling sorry for you, wanting to help you, rescue you […]" [8]

Kulwant reacts quite violently to Michael's presumption: "Rescue me! How dare you! You are the dream come true aren't you? Galahad on his white horse!" (25–26).

On receiving her vehement and indignant response to his rather insulting manner of courting her, Michael rebukes her with some of the typical prejudices the English have towards the Indian immigrant:

> "[…] you are living in a dream. Come the time, you'll get arranged off to some village boy from India , who'll only marry you to get into England. And you people like to marry young. Start early and get in lots of practice. That must be the motto […] They should realise they haven't transported a bit of their village here you know […] 'a corner of England that shall forever be India' […] If they're going to stay here they'll have to change…" (25)

At this, she throws the comment back at him:

> "You lot didn't when you came to our country."
> "That was different. We ruled it."
> "Just like you want to rule me." (25)

Here Kulwant uses colonial history to try and make Michael see the parallels of the said history to his own current strategy to get what he wants: to possess Kulwant, the Indian 'princess' of his dream, while she resists a freedom she is not necessarily looking for. Here in his tirade and Kulwant's growing awareness of the differences she has tried to ignore (while trying to explore a terrain new to her, that of romance and freedom, which is normally not allowed to a young Indian woman), the ambivalence of desire and anxiety addressed by Homi Bhabha in the relations between the former colonial masters and the Indian native is emphasized: the fascination with and the desire to possess the migrant 'native' in her 'exoticism', while simultaneously fearing and deriding her as inferior to him. Yet this ambivalence is also apparent on the side of the migrant native herself: she too is fascinated by the white Archangel, she wants to be accepted by him and his kind and she wants to be integrated into a society which is now supposed to be her 'home', never having known another.

Kulwant tears herself free of her fascination for Michael and rebuffs the offer of freedom he sees fit to bestow on her. She sees his insistence on their future together as a threat to her sense of self as well as her own dreams for her future: pursuing tertiary education and a career. She is determined to take charge of her own fate and decides to

---

[8] Ravinder Randhawa, *A Wicked Old Woman* (London: The Women's Press, 1987): 25. Further page references are in the main text.

wrest freedom for herself; as she says quite explicitly elsewhere later on in the novel, "Freedom is taken, not given" (114).

After this explosive encounter, Kulwant turns to the institution of arranged marriage in her desperation to secure a measure of Indianness for herself; a rather extreme choice, which unfortunately reaffirms the stereotypes commonly held by her English friends. Yet in this she is again able to wrench a measure of freedom for herself, the freedom of choice, without having to give in to her parents' expectations of finishing school, going to college and finally arranging her marriage on their terms. Instead of openly rebelling against Indian traditions, Kulwant seeks a modicum of rootedness in the community which seems to want her, while trying to block out the other half of her migrant heritage:

> She felt as if she had been turned inside out and forced to choose. No more trying to walk in the middle. There were too many potholes and she was like a blind woman without a stick. Safer to stay in territory she knew. If she had stuck to her Indian way Michael wouldn't have been so hurt [...] she would have been free of the pain she lugged around like a cross. She'd messed it all up because she had wanted everything, wanted to be Indian and English, wanted to choose for herself what she wanted out of both. Couldn't be done. Thinking of all that, she rubbed the colour on her skin, which wasn't ever going to rub off, and made her decision. (29)

Kulwant's mother is most affected by her daughter's running into the arms of Indian tradition in her mistaken belief that she would finally belong somewhere. She silently reproaches her daughter on the eve of the wedding feast, wanting for "you to know all that I can never know, to see in all the ways in which I am blind, wished you to go beyond the confines of my living, give life to your dreams for life to change" (52). The mother is more than aware of her daughter's confusion and wishes that she had never been party to it in the first place; yet she knows herself and wishes that type of certainty for her daughter, by freeing herself of the chains of tradition, by broadening her own horizons. Her mother gives vent to her own disappointed hopes for her daughter and expresses her doubts about the wisdom of Kulwant's decision,

> "I have known what I am, that has guided me to what I should be. I have never lost my anchor of certainty, this country has put you in one of its mixers and whirled you around till you can't tell your inside from your outside, your duty from your rights, your needs from your responsibilities." (54)

Kulwant's mother wanted her daughter to come into her own, to be independent and have a different life from hers; she regrets having migrated to England in the first place and yet she justifies the parents' past decision, when Kulwant levels an accusation at her commonly voiced by migrant children against their parents:

> "You brought me here."
> "We were tired of bartering with hunger."
> "A few more years and I could have ended up marrying an Englishman."
> "A few more years and you could have been the equal of any man." (54)

Kulwant finally reminds her mother that she has lived her own life as she saw fit and that she, Kulwant, would in her turn make her own decisions and live with the consequences: "Can't live your life for you mother – this is mine and it'll be me who'll live it" (54).

Despite this rather drastic decision in her life, Kulwant cannot completely root out the English facet of her identity; it keeps impinging on her later life, on the bringing up of her sons as well as on her relationship with her husband. It is rather ironical that it is Kulwant's desire to become a good Indian wife and mother, a role defined for and expected of her by others of the community, that leads to the failure of her marriage and the blame finally being laid on her. Kulwant has experienced various endings and beginnings; her journey to herself has not quite ended yet.

To conclude: Bhabha's rather undifferentiated and singular definition of migrant hybrid writing as having a mainly subversive function within the dominant discourse does not hold, as my analysis has illustrated. I believe that it is just one of numerous functions. Migrant literature addresses multi-directional purposes which are more complicated and intricately interwoven than the singular function attributed to it by Bhabha. Different life-styles, different socio-economic situations and familial constellations and the different reasons for migration have all to be taken into consideration. Thus the development of migrant agency is an active dynamic process which is significant in today's postmodern context, where all cultural identities, not just that of the migrant, seem to be amorphous, shifting entities anyway, as pointed out by Stuart Hall (1987):

> in the post-modern age, you all feel dispersed, I become centred. What I've thought of as dispersed and fragmented comes, paradoxically, to be the representative modern experience! This is "coming home" with a vengeance.[9]

I believe that the migrant Indian woman is engaged in turning in on herself and searching out new potential within her dual cultural heritage to articulate her own identity. It is not just a question of denying being 'you people' with vehemence or being the potentially subversive Other. It is a matter of looking for a new self-definition, a new sum total of her experience, her multifarious backgrounds, her sense of herself and of finding the next step in the process of moving on.

The migrant woman writer writes herself into the centre in order to create an effective agency for herself, to articulate her need to claim and carve out a space for herself which will facilitate her identity-formation. As mentioned earlier, the political intervention by the migrants themselves, in this case by Indian-British women writers like Syal and Randhawa, is activated by their realization of their doubly-marginalized status. Hence, the very act of writing is a conscious effort to remember, reclaim and redefine one's identity in the new host culture. The Indian-British women in these novels claim their space on their own terms, taking the freedom to do so. Thus, contrary to the lyrics of the song quoted at the beginning of this essay, they have decided *not* to be rescued by their respective 'lovers'; they have to make life possible for themselves, and they will do this on their own terms. They accept their Englishness and their Indianness, they celebrate their Otherness, turning it into an empowering source of new identity for themselves. This basically confirms what Chilla Bulbeck observes: "Ultimately [...] women of

---

[9] Stuart Hall, "Minimal Selves," in *Identity: The Real Me* (ICA Documents 7; London: Institute of Contemporary Arts, 1987): 44–46.

colour retain their right to a moral and political claim to their history and their own betterment in their own terms."[10] The migrant is indeed here to stay; she has come home 'with a vengeance' and she is not about to remain gratefully and pliantly satisfied with the leavings from the master's table that he has deigned to let fall.

WORKS CITED

Brah, Avtar. "Difference, Diversity and Differentiation," in *"Race," Culture & Difference*, ed. James Donald & Ali Rattansi (London: Sage, 1992): 126–45.

Bulbeck, Chilla. "Third World Women: Dialogues with Western Feminism," *Meanjin* 51.2 (Winter 1992): 319–32.

Fludernik, Monika. "Colonial vs. Cosmopolitan Hybridity," in *Hybridity and Postcolonialism: Twentieth Century Indian Literature* (Tübingen: Stauffenburg, 1998): 261–90.

Hall, Stuart. "Minimal Selves," in *Identity: The Real Me* (ICA Documents 7; London: Institute of Contemporary Arts, 1987): 44–46.

Innes, C.L. "Wintering: Making a Home in Britain," in *Other Britain, Other British: Contemporary Multicultural Fiction*, ed. A. Robert Lee (London: Pluto: 1995): 21–34.

Michel, Martina. "Under Cover: Ravinder Randhawa's A Wicked Old Woman," *anglistik & englischunterricht* 60 (1997): 143–57.

Randhawa, Ravinder. *A Wicked Old Woman* (London: The Women's Press: 1987).

Stein, Mark. "The Black British Bildungsroman and the Transformation of Britain: Connectedness Across Difference," in *Unity in Diversity Revisited? British Literature and Culture in the 1990s*, ed. Barbara Korte & Klaus Peter Müller (Tübingen: Gunter Narr, 1998): 89–105.

Syal, Meera. *Anita and Me* (London: Flamingo: 1997).

《•》

---

[10] Chilla Bulbeck, "Third World Women: Dialogues with Western Feminism," *Meanjin* 51.2 (Winter 1992): 323.

Notes on Contributors

KEN ARVIDSON, formerly an associate professor of English at the University of Waikato, has retired from teaching and is now a research associate of that university. He has taught at Auckland, Flinders, and the University of the South Pacific. Among his publications are *Riding the Pendulum* (poems; 1973) and a new edition (2001) of John Eldon Gorst's *The Maori King* (first published in 1864). He is a Research Associate of CRNLE, Flinders, 1979—, a Professional Associate of the East–West Centre, Honolulu 1980—, and has been an Associate Member of Darwin College, Cambridge 1986–87. Since 2001 he has edited the *Journal of New Zealand Literature*.

THOMAS BRÜCKNER took his postdoctoral degree in African Studies at Leipzig University. He has held teaching positions at the Universities of Essen and Mainz. He now works as a freelance translator, especially in African literature, and as a performer. He recently initiated a major project on "Africa Writing Europe." He is currently based at the University of Växjö.

DAVID CALLAHAN, after studies in Auckland and London, teaches American and postcolonial issues at the University of Aveiro in Portugal. Recent publications include the edited volume *Contemporary Issues in Australian Literature* (2002), and articles on Janette Turner Hospital, James Baldwin and Sindiwe Magona. He is at present writing a monograph on Janette Turner Hospital.

ELEONORA CHIAVETTA teaches English in the Facoltà di Lettere e Filosofia of Palermo University. She has published various essays and articles on Modernist women's fiction (Virginia Woolf, Jean Rhys, Vita Sackville–West, Katherine Mansfield) and on postcolonial women writers (Buchi Emecheta, Flora Nwapa, Anita Desai, Ruth Prawer Jhabvala, among others).

MARC COLAVINCENZO, after teaching Canadian literature at the University of Giessen, is now a wine merchant. His areas of interest have included fiction and history, poetry and landscape, Canadian identity, and notions of the self and the individual, and he continues to cultivate a special interest in the work of Michael Ondaatje. His book *"Trading Magic for Fact," Fact for Magic: Myth and mythologizing in postmodern Canadian historical fiction* was published in the Rodopi Cross/Cultures series.

GORDON COLLIER teaches postcolonial literature, film and culture at the University of Giessen. He is the author of a narratological study of Patrick White (1992) and is the editor of *US/THEM: Translation, Transcription and Identity in Postcolonial Literary Cultures* (1992); he has also co-edited *Shuttling Through Cultures Towards Identity* (1996), *Postcolonial Theory and the Emergence of a Global Society* (1998), *Crabtracks: Progress and Process in Teaching the New Literatures in English* (2002), and *A Pepper-Pot of Cultures: Aspects of Creolization in the Caribbean* (2003). He is currently editing the earlier journalism of Derek Walcott and compiling a comprehensive biblio- and filmography of the African Diaspora. He co-edits the journal *Matatu* and the postcolonial book series Cross/Cultures, and is a founder-member of ASNEL.

JOHN DOUTHWAITE teaches English and linguistics at the University of Turin. His most recent books are *Towards a Linguistic Theory of Foregrounding* (2000) and *Migrating the Texts: Hybridity as a Postcolonial Literary Construct* (2003; co-ed. with Alessandro Monti).

DOROTHY DRIVER is a professor in the English Department at the University of Cape Town, and is currently visiting professor at Stanford University. She has published numerous essays and edited various books on South African literature. Her most recent book is the co-edited 600-page anthology *Women Writing Africa*, vol. 1: *The Southern Region* (2003).

CLAUDIA DUPPÉ, presently a freelance academic, recently completed a doctorate on New Zealand women's poetry at Trier University, Germany, her research being supported by a grant from Cusanuswerk Germany. She was educated at Saarbrücken, Leeds, and Freiburg, where she finished her MA in 1999, on the concept of home in Lauris Edmond's poetry. The concept of home and its sociocultural dimension in New Zealand poetry over the past century has been the focus of her research in recent years.

ROBERT FRASER is a biographer and critic, dramatist and historian of ideas. He has taught at the Universities of Cambridge, Leeds and London, and is currently Senior Research Fellow in the Literature Department of the Open University. His publications on postcolonial literature include monographs on Ayi Kwei Armah (1980) and Ben Okri (2002), a history of West African poetry (1986), and "The Death of Theory: A Report from the Web," *Wasafiri* (1999). His report on the ASNEL conference in Aachen / Liège appeared in the *Times Literary Supplement* (2000).

ANNE FUCHS taught comparative literature and theatre studies at the University of Nice for nearly thirty years. The author of numerous articles on anglophone and francophone theatre, she has edited or co-edited *Écritures d'ailleurs et autres écritures* (1994), *Theatre and Change in South Africa* (1996) and *New Theatre in Francophone and Anglophone Africa* (1999). During the 1980s she worked with French anti-apartheid groups to bring several South African theatre companies to France, including the Junction Avenue Theatre Company, the Vusisizwe Players and Matsemela Manaka's Soyikwa Theatre.

KATHERINE GALLAGHER worked as a laboratory assistant and secretary before graduating from the University of Melbourne. After a period of high-school teaching in that city, she moved to Europe, spending most of the 1970s in Paris before settling in England, where she has remained ever since, while maintaining strong connections with her native Australia. She has published several volumes of verse, including *The Eye's Circle* (1974/1978), *Passengers to the City* (1985), *Fish-Rings on Water* (1989), *Finding the Prince* (1993), and *Tigers on the Silk Road* (2000).

JOHN GAMGEE was awarded a BA Hons degree in French by the University of Wales, an MA in French by the University of London, and a *maîtrise* in English literature by the University of Lyon 2, where he also obtained the *agrégation*. Having taught English at Lyon 2 and French at the University of London, he now works at the University of Clermont 1 and is completing a doctorate on J.M. Coetzee at the University of Burgundy in Dijon. A recent monograph publication is *Une Lettre d'adieu, douce-amère: «Age of Iron», de J.M. Coetzee* (2001).

PETER GOLDSWORTHY grew up in various towns in South Australia and in Darwin. After graduating in medicine from the University of Adelaide some thirty years ago, he has combined the practice of medicine with a busy writing career. He has published four books of short fiction, collected in *The List of All Answers: Collected Stories* (2004); several books of poetry, including *This Goes with This* (1988), *This Goes with That* (1991), *if, then* (1996), and *New Selected Poems* (2001); and a number of novels, including *Maestro* (1989), *Honk If You Are Jesus* (1992), *Wish* (1995), and his latest, *Three Dog Night* (2004), winner of the Christina Stead Award.

D.C.R.A. GOONETILLEKE is a professor and Head of the Department of English at the University of Kelaniya, Sri Lanka. He obtained his doctorate on a Commonwealth Scholarship at the University of Lancaster and has been a visiting scholar in the Faculty of English at the University of Cambridge as well as a Fellow Commoner of Churchill College, Cambridge. He is the author of *Developing Countries in British Fiction*.

KONRAD GROSS, since 1978 a professor of American and Canadian Literature at Christian-Albrechts-University at Kiel, Germany, studied English, political science and cultural anthropology at the Universities of Marburg and Cologne, where he took his doctorate in English. After spending the academic year 1972/73 at the University of British Columbia, he obtained his postdoctoral qualification at the University of Freiburg in 1977. He has published on Victorian, American, Canadian and Irish literature and the New English Literatures.

SYD HARREX is a critic and poet, Reader in English and Director of the Centre for Research in the New Literatures in English (CRNLE) at Flinders University, Adelaide. He has published widely on NLE, and in 1999 two new collections of his poems appeared, entitled *Dedication* and *No Worries, No Illusions, No Mercy*.

BERND HERZOGENRATH is currently teaching American Studies at the University of Cologne. He studied English and German at the RWTH Aachen, where he also earned his doctorate. His fields of interest are nineteenth- and twentieth-century American literature, literary theory, and cultural and media studies. He is the author of *An Art of Desire: Reading Paul Auster* (1999), and the editor of *From Virgin Land to Disney World: Nature and its Discontents in the USA of Yesterday and Today* (2001). His current project deals with the image and metaphor of the fragmented body in American literature, history, art, and cinema.

SUSANNE HILF studied English and American literature, comparative literature and art history at the Universities of Bonn (MA) and British Columbia, Vancouver. Her chief research interests include Asian-American writing and contemporary Canadian literature. She currently works as a journalist in Frankfurt am Main. Publication: *Writing the Hyphen: The Articulation of Interculturalism in Contemporary Chinese-Canadian Literature* (2001).

CLARA A.B. JOSEPH is an assistant professor in the Department of English at the University of Calgary, Alberta, Canada. Her research and teaching are in the areas of South Asian literatures and literary theory. She has published on the relationship of literature to ethics, nationalism, feminism and religion.

JAROSLAV KUŠNÍR graduated from P.J. Šafárik University, Prešov, Slovakia in 1987 and obtained his doctorate at the Institute of World Literature of the Slovak Academy of Sciences, Bratislava, Slovakia, in 2000. He has been a lecturer in American, English and Australian literature at the Prešov University, Slovakia, since 1990. His publications include *Poetika americkej postmodernej prózy (Richard Brautigan a Donald Barthelme)* [Poetics of American postmodern fiction – Richard Brautigan and Donald Barthelme] (2001), *Austrálska literatúra po roku 1945* [*Australian Literature after 1945*] (1997), *Recepcia austrálskej literatúry na Slovensku v rokoch 1990–1996* [The reception of Australian literature in Slovakia between 1900 and 1996] (2002).

CHANTAL KWAST-GREFF currently holds a lecturership at the Université de Nîmes, France. She has a doctorate from James Cook University and a Doctorat d'Université from Toulouse-le-Mirail. Her research interests are Australian and postcolonial literatures and gender studies. She has published on body and image, distorted bodies and suffering souls, and female madness. Her recent publications include *Narcissus, or the Writer as a Madwoman* (2002), *Spectacular Sacrifice: Not to Be or Not to Eat* (2001), *Anger, Madness, and Suffering in Australian Fiction* (2000), and *Fat vs. Fate, or Why a Woman of Destiny Needs to Be Fat* (2000). Current areas of research centre on body marking, suffering, and mysticism.

M.Z. MALABA teaches at the University of Zimbabwe in Mount Pleasant, Harare. He has worked on the literature of Southern Africa for many years and wrote his doctoral dissertation on literature representations of Shaka. He recently co-organized a major conference on contemporary Zimbabwean writing.

SIGRUN MEINIG holds an interdisciplinary degree in English philology and business from the University of Mannheim and an MA in modern literature from the University of Kent at Canterbury. The subject of her doctoral dissertation is the representation of history in Australian historical novels by Henry Handel Richardson, Patrick White, Peter Carey and Rodney Hall. She has taught postcolonial literatures at the University of Mannheim, and is now at the University of Bielefeld.

MICHAEL MEYER graduated from the University of Freiburg; after teaching at the University of Bamberg, he is now in the English Department, University of Koblenz–Landau. He is the author of *Struktur, Funktion und Vermittlung der Wahrnehmung in Charles Tomlinsons Lyrik* (1990) and *Gibson, Mill und Ruskin: Autobiographie und*

Intertextualität (1998). In 1994 he edited *Vom Hörsaal zum Tatort: Neue Spuren vom Hochschulunterricht?* He has published articles on the teaching of literature, autobiography, Romantic poetry, the Gothic novel, the dandy, and colonial and postcolonial literature.

MIKE NICOL was born in Cape Town, lives in South Africa, and is a poet, novelist and essayist who also works as a freelance journalist. He has published numerous books, most recently *The Invisible Line* (photos and text, with Ken Osterbroek, 2000) and *Sea-Mountain, Fire City: Living in Cape Town* (2001). He was recently poet in residence at the University of Essen.

OBODODIMMA OHA is a lecturer in stylistics at the Department of English, University of Ibadan. His publications include *Culture and Gender Semantics in Flora Nwapa's Poetry* (1997), "L.S. Senghor's Feminization of Africa and the Africanization of Feminist Aesthetics" (1999) and "Pursuing the Night Hawk: The Political Thought of Chukwuemeka Odumegwu Ojukwu" (2000). He recently edited *The Visual Rhetoric of the Ambivalent City in Nigerian Video Films* (2001) for Blackwell.

VINCENT O'SULLIVAN, who was educated at Auckland and Oxford Universities, recently retired from his position as a professor of English at Victoria University, Wellington. He is widely published as a poet, fiction writer, and critic, and has edited several volumes of Katherine Mansfield's correspondence. He was recently appointed a Distinguished Companion of the New Zealand Order of Merit. His latest volumes of poetry are *Seeing You Asked* (1998) and *Lucky Table* (2001).

JUDITH DELL PANNY, Honorary Research Associate, Massey University, obtained her BA at Victoria University of Wellington, and her MA and doctorate at Massey University. She has taught New Zealand literature at the University of Trier and has been a guest professor at Christian Albrecht University, Kiel. Her current research concerns history, culture and Māori literature, and her chief publications are *I Have What I Gave: The Fiction of Janet Frame* (1992, 1993 and revised edition 2002) and *Turning the Eye: Patricia Grace and the Short Story* (1997). Two publications are pending: a volume of poetry, and a book about the paintings of the Māori artist John Bevan Ford.

MIKE PETRY studied English and American literature, linguistics, and political science at Aachen University. He wrote his doctoral dissertation on the novels of Kazuo Ishiguro (published as *Narratives of Memory and Identity*, 1999). His major research interests include the nineteenth- and twentieth-century English novel, narrative theory, and cultural criticism.

JOCHEN PETZOLD studied English and German in Freiburg and Eugene, Oregon. In 2001 he completed his doctoral dissertation on contemporary South African fiction entitled *Re-Imagining White Identity by Exploring the Past: History in South African Novels of the 1990s* (2002). He has published on South African writers (André Brink, Christopher Hope, Robert Kirby), on nineteenth-century adventure fiction (H. Rider Haggard, R.M. Ballantyne), and on Joseph Conrad. He is now working as an assistant professor in the English Department of Freiburg University.

NORBERT H. PLATZ recently retired from his professorship in English literature at Trier University, but is currently continuing to teach there as a senior professor. He studied at the universities of Heidelberg and Munich and received his doctorate and postdoctoral qualifications from Mannheim University. Among his main teaching and research interests were the New Literatures in English (with a special focus on Australia and New Zealand) and the relationship between literature and the environment. 1993–1997: President of the Association for the Study of the New Literatures in English. 1999–2002: President of the Association for Australian Studies. Since 1999: Treasurer of the European Association for the Study of Australia (EASA).

MALCOLM PURKEY is a professor of drama at the University of the Witwatersrand. Well-known for his work with the Junction Theatre Company both as co-director and co-author of such plays as *Marabi*, Sophiatown, *Tooth and Nail*, and *Love, Crime and Johannesburg*, he has also directed plays at the Market Theatre and Wits Theatre.

STÉPHANIE RAVILLON, who recently completed her doctorate on the subject of hybridity in the novels of Salman Rushdie at the University of Burgundy, teaches at Brown University, Rhode Island, USA.

ANNE HOLDEN RØNNING is an associate professor of British literature at the University of Bergen, Norway. She is the author of *Hidden and Visible Suffrage* (1995) and has edited several books including *Feminismens Klassikere* (1994), *Women and the University Curriculum* (1996), *Dialoguing on Genres* (2001) and *Identities and Masks: Colonial and Postcolonial Studies* (2001; co-ed. with Jakob Lothe and Peter Young). Her research interests, on which she has written several articles, are in women's studies and postcolonial writing, especially from New Zealand and Australia. She is currently President of the European Association for the Study of Australia (EASA).

RICHARD SAMIN is a professor of English at the University of Nancy 2. His research interests are in South African literature and culture. His doctorate (1985) was on the fiction of Alex la Guma and Es'kia Mphahele. He has been engaged on several research projects with the French Institute of South Africa (Johannesburg). His most recent articles include: "'Burdens of Rage and Grief': Reconciliation in Post-Apartheid Fiction" (2000) and "Marginality and History in Zakes Mda's Ways of Dying" (2000). He is presently working on the literary and critical writings of the South African writer Es'kia Mphahlele.

CECILE SANDTEN studied English and American literature and cultural studies at the Universities of Bremen and Coleraine. She has been a visiting scholar at the University of Aalborg, where she was involved in a research programme on interculturalism and transnationality. Her research interests also include Shakespeare within the context of postcolonial literatures, and the poetry of the Indo-American writer Sujata Bhatt, on whom she also wrote her doctorate.

NICOLE SCHRÖDER studied at the Free University of Berlin as well as at Stanford and Duke Universities. She works in the American Studies Department of Düsseldorf University, where she is writing her doctoral dissertation on "Moving Places: Spatial concepts in contemporary American literature." Her publications include "'Travelling' as Metaphor for Emerging Cultural Identities: Wendy Rose's 'Excavation at Santa Barbara Mission'" (2001), *Kulturelle Selbstentwürfe in zeitgenössischer indianischer Literatur: N. Scott Momaday, Sherman Alexie, Wendy Rose* (2003), and "Locating the Other/Self: Memory and Place in Michelle Cliff's Works" (2003).

JOSEPH SWANN studied philosophy and German in Rome, Canterbury, and London, and has taught at the University of Wuppertal for many years. He has published extensively on African, Indian, Australian, and New Zealand literature, with a special focus on poetry.

ANDRÉ VIOLA is a professor of English and postcolonial literatures at the University of Nice. He has published a collection of short stories in French (*Latitudes/Solitudes*, 1997) and numerous articles on British writers (Kipling, Woolf, Conrad, Greene) and on South African literature. He has co-authored a survey of *New Fiction in English from Africa: West, East and South* (1998) and his *J.M. Coetzee: romancier sud-africain* appeared in 1999.

CHRISTINE VOGT–WILLIAM is a Singaporean who has lived and worked in Germany for a number of years now. She is currently employed as an assistant in the Department of the New English Literatures and Cultures (NELK) at the University of Frankfurt, where she is completing her doctorate.

BERNARD WILSON is an Australian academic on secondment to the Centre for American Education, Singapore. His contribution to the present volume is part of an ongoing research project conducted jointly with Syd Harrex.

JANET WILSON is a reader in English at University College, Northampton. She studied at Victoria University of Wellington, the University of Sydney and St Catherine's College, Oxford (DPhil). She has taught at the University of Auckland, Trinity College Dublin and the University of Otago. Her research interests are in postcolonial writing and New Zealand literature. Publications include *Preaching in the Reformation* (1993) and *Intimate Stranger* (2000), reminiscences of the New Zealand writer Dan Davin. She is currently editor of the *Journal of Postcolonial Writing* (previously known as *World Literature Written in English*) and secretary of the New Zealand Studies Association in the UK.

BRIAN WORSFOLD is a member of the Department of English and Linguistics at the University of Lleida in Catalonia. He is the author of *South African Backdrop: An Historical Introduction for South African Literary and Cultural Studies* (1999) and has published articles on various aspects of South African literature. he is also the editor of *Multi-Cultural Voices* (1998), a collection of interviews with well-known writers and academics.

《•》